September 26-29, 2010
São Carlos, São Paulo, Brazil

Association for
Computing Machinery

Advancing Computing as a Science & Profession

SIGDOC'10

Proceedings of the 28th ACM International Conference on
Design of Communication

Sponsored by:
ACM SIGDOC

Supported by:
*Federal University of São Carlos,
University of São Paulo, SBC, FAPESP, CAPES*

Edited by:
*Junia C. Anacleto, Renata Pontin M. Fortes,
and Carlos J. Costa*

**Association for
Computing Machinery**

Advancing Computing as a Science & Profession

The Association for Computing Machinery
2 Penn Plaza, Suite 701
New York, New York 10121-0701

Notice to Past Authors of ACM-Published Articles

ISBN: 978-1-4503-0403-0

Additional copies may be ordered prepaid from:

ACM Order Department
PO Box 11405
New York, NY 10286-1405

Phone: 1-800-342-6626 (USA and Canada)
        +1-212-626-0500 (all other countries)
Fax: +1-212-944-1318
E-mail: acmhelp@acm.org

ACM Order Number: 613100

Printed in the USA

Foreword

We warmly welcome you to SIGDOC 2010 – the 28th ACM International Conference on Design of Communication, which is held in the city of São Carlos, State of São Paulo, Brazil. The purpose of ACM SIGDOC 2010 is to bring together academic and industry researchers, as well as computer engineers and practitioners, to address the advance of research and development in the field of design of communication, focusing this year on sustainable communication.

ACM SIGDOC provides a leading international forum to bring together researchers and practitioners from diverse fields, such as Computer Science, Information Technology, Documentation, Human Computer Interaction, Multimedia, Graphic Design, Education, Human Factors, among others. The objectives of SIGDOC are: firstly, examine the design principles and performance characteristics of various approaches in Information Technology, and secondly, increase the cross-fertilization of ideas on the development of new ways of communicating information, taking into consideration local and global characteristics. ACM SIGDOC 2010 will foster the development of novel paradigms and advanced solutions in design of sustainable communication, by encouraging idea-sharing and discussions on the underlying logical, cognitive, and experimental foundations as well as the enabling technologies of communication.

SIGDOC 2010 could count with the hard work of everyone who volunteered numerous hours of their time. For that, we are deeply indebted to many people. We hope that besides the SIGDOC 2010 technical program, the breaks, reception, and the banquet are part of the SIGDOC 2010 experience that participants could bring back with them. We also appreciate for Prof Margaret Burnett, Dr. Claudio Pinhanez and Robert Pierce for giving invited talks. We are honored to have their participation. Our thanks to the SIGDOC Steering Committee Chair Brad Mehlembacher and Vice-chair Robert Pierce, for their continuous support, suggestions and guidance in part lead to the success of the SIGDOC 2010.

We thank to ACM for their continued sponsorship of SIGDOC, to the Universidade de São Paulo (USP) and Universidade Federal de São Carlos (UFSCar) for hosting the conference. We would like to express our thanks, to the authors of technical papers presented at the conference, whose work made possible to put together a high quality program and to all attendees, who have traveled from all over the world to participate to SIGDOC. Our thanks also go to the PC members for reviewing papers, and many volunteers who make the conference a comfortable environment. Special thanks go to Ashley Williams for managing the online registrations, and to Eduardo Pezutti and Roberto Fagá, for the design work of the website and helping on compiling the proceedings. The ACM SIGDOC conference takes place for the second time in a non-English speaking country. Brazil has the honor to host the SIGDOC Conference.

The Program Committee of the conference lists an impressive 43 members – twenty seven (27) from the USA and Canada, nine (9) from Brazil, six (6) from Europe, one (1) from Africa. The topics of ACM SIGDOC 2010 will cover the following: (a) Games and Design of Communications, (b) Learning and Design of Communication, (c) Social Media, (d) Design of Communication in Organizational Context, (e) New frontiers in the Documentation, (f) Accessibility, and (g) Culture and Design of Communication.

Continuing its strong presence among similar events, ACM SIGDOC 2010 managed to attract 88 submissions to the research and industry tracks. The submissions include full-length papers, technical reports and posters. The submitted full-length papers, technical reports, and posters went through a rigorous reviewing process: each of the 88 submissions was reviewed by at least two program committee members, and the borderline cases were re-reviewed by additional program committee members and by chair(s). Twenty eight (28) research papers, along with five (5) technical papers, three (3) posters and one workshop represent the wide range of perspectives which inform our multidisciplinary field in SIGDOC 2010.

We hope that everyone enjoys this exciting conference that occurs at the edge of Broa´s lake and has a good time in São Carlos, São Paulo, Brazil. We hope we will join again at the next edition of the SIGDOC in 2011.

Junia C. Anacleto
General Co-Chair
LIA–DC/UFSCar
São Carlos, Brazil

Renata Fortes
General Co-Chair
ICMC / USP
São Carlos, Brazil

Carlos J. Costa
Program Chair
ISCTE - IUL
Lisboa, Portugal

Table of Contents

SIGDOC 2010 Conference Organization..ix

Session 1. Games and Design of Communications

- Experiencing a process to create a multimedia game and validating results
  application in a socio-cultural environment...1

  Junia Anacleto, Diego Desani da Silva (Federal University of São Carlos),
  Victor Hugo Boqui Rodrigues dos Santos (Federal University of São Carlos),
  Johana Rosas, Marcos Alexandre Rose Silva, João Porto (Federal University of São Carlos)

- Is Agility out there? Agile Practices in Game Development...9

  Fábio Petrillo, Marcelo Pimenta (Federal University of Rio Grande do Sul)

- Design of Multilingual Participatory Gaming Simulations with a
  Communication Support Agent...17

  Keisuke Tsunoda (Waseda University Graduate School of Creative Science and Engineering),
  Reiko Hishiyama (Waseda University Graduate School of Creative Science and Engineering)

- Solar Scramble: an Educational Children's Game for
  Collaborative Multi-touch Digital Tabletops....*(Experience Report)*...27

  Ashley Kelly, James Wallace, Katie Cerar, Neil Randall (University of Waterloo),
  Phillip McClelland, Amanda Mindy Seto (University of Waterloo)

Session 2. Design of Communication in Organizational Context

- Organizational Wiki as a Knowledge Management Tool..33

  Fernando Sousa, Manuela Aparicio, Carlos J. Costa (Instituto Universitário de Lisboa)

- RESOLVE DISSATISFACTORY COMMUNICATIONS:
  A Measurement-Method for Satisfied Communication in Business Organizations.................41

  Eldar Sultanow, Edzard Weber, Robert Lembcke (University Potsdam)

- Accessible organizational elements in wikis with model-driven development.........................49

  Thiago Bittar, Luanna Lopes Lobato, Renata Fortes, David Neto (University of São Paulo)

- Cultural Probes in the Design of Communication...57

  Zoe McDougall, Sidney Fels (University of British Columbia)

Session 3. Social Media (I)

- Social media for sustainable engineering communication..65

  Brad Mehlenbacher, Sarah McKone, Christine Grant, (North Carolina State University)
  Tuere Bowles, Steve Peretti, Pamela Martin (North Carolina State University)

- DREAMER: a Design Rationale Environment for Argumentation, Modeling and Engineering Requirements......73

    Célia Martinie, Philippe Palanque, Marco Winckler, Stéphane Conversy (University Paul Sabatier)

- Advertising Network Formation based on Stochastic Diffusion Search and Market Equilibria......81

    Nikos Salamanos, Stavros Lopatazidis (Athens University of Economics and Business),

    Michalis Vazirgiannis, Antonis Thomas (Athens University of Economics and Business)

- Kolline: a task-oriented system for collaborative information seeking......89

    Fernando Figueira Filho, Paulo de Geus (University of Campinas),

    Gary Olson (University of California)

- Best Practices for Designing Third Party Applications for Contextually-Aware Tools......95

    Dave Jones, Liza Potts (Old Dominion University)

Session 4. Social Media (II)

- Exploring a Sustainable and Public Information Ecology......103

    Brian McNely (Ball State University)

- Digital Humanities and digital repositories: sustainable technology for sustainable communications....*(Experience Report)*......109

    Paolo Battino Viterbo (Royal Irish Academy), *Donald Gourley* (Digital Initiatives Consultant)

- A Method for Measuring Helpfulness in Online Peer Review......115

    William Hart-Davidson, Michael McLeod (Michigan State University),

    Christopher Klerkx, Michael Wojcik (Michigan State University)

- Toward an Ontology of Rhetorical Figures......123

    Ashley Kelly, Nike Abbott, Randy Allen Harris, Chrysanne DiMarco (University of Waterloo)

Session 5. New frontiers in the Documentation

- Modularizing in Glossaries - an Experience Report....*(Experience Report)*......131

    Kathy Haramundanis (Hewlett-Packard Company)

- Globally Distributed Content Creation: Developing Consumable Content for International Markets....*(Experience Report)*......135

    Robert Pierce, Kevin Minerley (IBM Corporation), *Kirk St.Amant* (East Carolina University)

- The importance of Documentation, Design and Reuse in Risk Management for SPL......143

    Luanna Lopes Lobato, Silvio Meira (Federal University of Pernambuco),

    Pádraig O'Leary, Eduardo Almeida (Federal University of Bahia)

- Improving multimodal interaction design with the MMWA
  authoring environment..151
  Americo Talarico Neto, Renata Fortes (University of São Paulo)

Session 6. Accessibility

- Design, Development and Performance Evaluation of Reconfigured Mobile
  Android Phone for People Who are Blind or Visually Impaired.....................159
  Akbar Shaik, Gahangir Hossain, Mohammed Yeasin (University of Memphis)
- WCAG Conformance approach based on Model-Driven Development and WebML................167
  Willian Watanabe, David Neto, Thiago Bittar, Renata Fortes (University of São Paulo)
- Improving WCAG for Elderly Web Accessibility..175
  Silvana M. A. de Lara, Willian Watanabe, Eduardo dos Santos, Renata Fortes (University of São Paulo)
- Using cultural knowledge to assist communication between people
  with different cultural background..183
  Bruno Sugiyama, Junia Anacleto, Sidney Fels, Helena Caseli (University of British Columbia)

Session 7. User Interface and Design of Communication

- An Approach Based on Multiple Text Input Modes
  for Interactive Digital TV Applications...191
  Didier Vega Oliveros, Diogo Pedrosa, Renata Fortes, Maria Graça C. Pimentel (University of São Paulo)
- Musical Interaction Patterns: Communicating Computer
  Music Knowledge in a Multidisciplinary Project...199
  Luciano Flores, Evandro Manara Miletto, Marcelo Pimenta (Federal University of Rio Grande do Sul),
  Eduardo Miranda (University of Plymouth), *Damián Keller* (Federal University of Acre)
- Model Driven RichUbi - A Model Driven Process for Building
  Rich Interfaces of Context-Sensitive Ubiquitous Applications.........................207
  Carlos Eduardo Cirilo, Antonio Francisco Prado (Federal University of São Carlos),
  Wanderley Lopes de Souza, Luciana Zaina (Federal University of São Carlos)
- A Flexible Model for Improving the Reuse of User Interface Design Patterns...........215
  Jordan Janeiro, Thomas Springer, Alexander Schill (Technische Universität Dresden),
  Simone DJ Barbosa (Pontifical Catholic University of Rio de Janeiro),

Session 8. Learning and Design of Communication

- An Approach to Design the Student Interaction Based on
  the Recommendation of e-Learning Objects..223
    Luciana Zaina (Federal University of São Carlos),
    Jose Fernando Rodrigues Jr, Graça Bressan (University of São Paulo)
- Combining Ontologies and Scenarios for Context-Aware
  e-Learning Environments 229
    Isabela Gasparini, Marcelo Pimenta, José Palazzo M. de Oliveira (Federal University of Rio Grande do Sul),
    Amel Bouzeghoub (TELECOM & Management SudParis)
- Reviewing the research on distance education and e-learning...................................237
    Brad Mehlenbacher, Krista Holstein, Brett Gordon, Khalil Khammar (North Carolina State University)
- Designing the user experience in iTV-based interactive learning objects 243
    Diogo Martins, Lilian Simão, Maria da Graça Campos Pimentel (University of São Paulo)

Invited Talks

- Gender HCI: What About the Software?...251
    Margaret M. Burnett (Oregon State University)
- Designing the Interaction with Service Systems..253
    Claudio Pinhanez (IBM Research Brasil)
- SIGDOC – Reviewing the History from a Company Perspective................................255
    Robert Pierce (IBM Corporation)

Posters

- An Interactive Dialogue Modelling Editor for Designing Multimodal Applications...................257
    Sebastian Feuerstack (Federal University of São Carlos)
- Designing Interactive Presentation Systems for Classrooms.......................................259
    Rahul Budhiraja, Shekhar Verma, Arunanshu Pandey (Indian Institute of Information Technology Allahabad)
- Improving users communication to promote the organicity
  of online social networks...261
    Fernando Balbino, Junia Anacleto (Federal University of São Carlos)

Author Index..263

SIGDOC 2010 Conference Organization

General Chairs: Junia Anacleto (*Federal University of São Carlos, Brazil*)
Renata Pontin Fortes (*University of São Paulo, Brazil*)

Program Chair: Carlos J. Costa (*DCTI/ISCTE, Portugal*)

Local Arrangements Chairs: Renata Pontin Fortes (*University of São Paulo, Brazil*)
Junia C. Anacleto (*Federal University of São Carlos, Brazil*)

Program Committee: Antonio Ceroni (*IIST/ United Nations University, USA*)
Aristidis Protopsaltis (*SGI - Coventry University, UK*)
Ashley Wlliams (*User Experience Design Consultant, USA*)
Bill Hart-Davidson (*Michigan State University, USA*)
Brad Mehlenbacher (*North Carolina State University, USA*)
Carlos J. Costa (*DCTI/ISCTE, Portugal*)
Cesar Camilo Teixeira (*Federal University of São Carlos*)
Clay Spinuzzi (*University of Texas at Austin, USA*)
Dave Clark (*University of Wisconsin-Milwaukee, USA*)
David G. Novick (*The University of Texas, USA*)
David K. Farkas (*University of Washington, USA*)
Douglas Eyman (*George Mason University, USA*)
Eduardo B. Fernandez (*Florida Atlantic Univ, USA*)
Henry Lieberman (*MediaLab-MIT, USA*)
Ivan Ricarte (*FEE/UNICAMP, Brazil*)
Jason Swarts (*North Carolina State University, USA*)
John Stamey, Jr. (*Coastal Carolina University, USA*)
Johndan Johnson-Eilola (*Clarkson University, USA*)
José Leopoldo Nhampossa (*Universidade Eduardo Mondlane, Mozambique*)
Junia C. Anacleto (*Federal University of São Carlos, Brazil*)
Kathy Haramundanis (*HP, USA*)
Liza Potts (*Old Dominion University, USA*)
Lucia Filgueiras (*University of São Paulo, Brazil*)
Manuela Aparicio (*Adetti / ISCTE*)
Marcelo Pimenta (*DI/UFRGS, Brazil*)
Marco Winkler (*IRIT/University of Toulouse, France*)
Maria da Graça Pimentel (*University of São Paulo, Brazil*)
Mark Zachry (*University of Washington, USA*)
Patti Wojahn (*New Mexico State University, USA*)
Philippe Palanque (*IRIT/University of Toulouse, France*)
Renata Pontin Fortes (*University of São Paulo, Brazil*)

Program Committee:
(continued)

Robert Pierce (*IBM Corporation, USA*)

Rudinei Goularte (*University of São Paulo, Brazil*)

Ryan M. Moeller (*Uutah State University, USA*)

Sean Zdenek (*Texas Tech University, USA*)

Sebastian Feuerstack (*TU Berlin, Germany*)

Shihong Huang (*Florida Atlantic University, USA*)

Sidney Fels (*University of British Columbia, Canada*)

Simone Barbosa (*DI/PUC-Rio, Brazil*)

Steve Murphy (*IBM Canada Ltd., USA*)

Stewart Whittemore (*Auburn University, USA*)

Stuart Selber (*Penn State, USA*)

Susan B. Smullin Jones (*Usability Consultant, USA*)

William Hart-Davidson (*Michigan State University, USA*)

Reviewers:

Americo Talarico, Neto (*University of São Paulo, Brazil*)

Clara Fernandez (*MIT, USA*)

Dave Jones (*Old Dominion University, USA*)

Evandro Manara Miletto (*Federal Institute of Rio Grande do Sul, Brazil*)

Fatima Penedo (*ITML Network, Portugal*)

Fernando Sousa (*ISCTE, Portugal*)

Gerianne Bartocci (*Design Science, USA*)

Hélio Guardia (*Federal University of São Carlos, Brazil*)

Isabela Gasparini (*UDESC and UFRGS, Brazil*)

João Paulo Preti (*Federal University of Mato Grosso, Brazil*)

Luciana Borges (*Federal University of Mato Grosso, Brazil*)

Luciana Nedel (*Federal University of Rio Grande do Sul, Brazil*)

Luís Filipe Costa (*ISCTE Lisboa, Portugal*)

Richard Faust (*Federal University of Santa Catarina, Brazil*)

Sebastian Feuerstack (*Technische Universitaet Berlin, Germany*)

Soraia Prietch (*Federal University of Mato Grosso, Brazil*)

Sponsor:

S I G D O C

Special Interest Group on
Design of Communication

Supporters:

Experiencing a process to create a multimedia game and validating results application in a socio-cultural environment

Junia Coutinho Anacleto, Diego Desani da Silva, Victor Hugo B.R Santos, Johana M. Rosas Villena, Marcos Alexandre R. Silva, João Carlos Porto

Advanced Interaction Laboratory – LIA
Federal University of São Carlos – UFSCar
Rod. Washigton Luis KM 235 – São Carlos – SP – Brazil
{junia, johana_villena, marcos_silva}@dc.ufscar.br, {diego_desani, visanto, joao_porto}@comp.ufscar.br

ABSTRACT
This paper aims to show the experience on adopting a certain process model to guide the task of designing a project with a multidisciplinary team, involving two different institutions - the LIA laboratory and a social community center called SESC, to develop a 'scientific' and 'fun' computer application, to serve the community center's main public that should be a cultural context-sensitive software considering the center's interests (fun and related to a certain theme they have interest in working on with their public) and the academic interests (scientific - collecting statements from users related to their common sense for the OMCS-BR project), showing the software process model based on user centered design, collaborative and iterative, pointing out the achieved results during and at the end of this process of development, when the software was used at the center by that users. It will be presented here the adopted process model, interactive, iterative, User-centered with some 'drops' of participatory design.

Categories and Subject Descriptors
H5.m. Information interfaces and presentation (e.g., HCI): Miscellaneous.

General Terms
Documentation, Design, Experimentation, Human Factors, Standardization, Verification

Keywords
user centered design, participatory design, collaborative design, multimedia game for cultural and social expression.

1. INTRODUCTION
In the context of the OMCS project [2], cultural knowledge is defined as the set of facts known by most people who live in a culture, "covering a large part of human experience, knowledge about the spatial aspects, physical, social, temporal and psychological of day-to-day of the human beings "[2]. This definition is also adopted in the OMCS-Br project, context of this work, where the knowledge is given by ordinary web visitors, also considered as a type of cultural knowledge. The project Open Mind Common Sense in Brazil (OMCS-Br) aims to collect as much facts as possible among Brazilians through the participation of volunteers who, visiting the project website, give statements about their common sense that are then inserted into the project's knowledge base. Currently such base is around 1,500,000 concepts [6]. Liu and Singh mention an estimation made by Minsky that suggests the number of facts that constitute the common sense of an adult would be between 30 and 60 million [2]. Compared to the OMCS project with the optimal number of events suggested by Minsky, it can see that the knowledge base is a small base of common sense. So, the ultimate goal of the project OMCS-Br is the development of culturally contextualized interactive applications that besides using the common sense knowledge for the application context, can also collect information from the users while they are interacting with the application to speed up the process of collecting such kind of knowledge. Also, the applications are developed adopting the principle of fail-soft application, considering the nature of such knowledge, uncertain, composed of myths, misunderstandings, among other beliefs, and the size of the knowledge base of the project, which is not enough to map all the Brazilian cultural knowledge. But it is assumed that some cultural knowledge is better than none, so culturally contextualized applications can be developed.

Thus, the OMCS-Br project aims at new ways of collecting cultural knowledge and mechanisms for the confirmation, by peers, of existing facts. This last factor is the motivation for the work presented here. The researchers looked up for environments and partnerships during the year-end 2009 to be in contact with a growing number of people of different genders, ages, and especially ideas. This provoked a listing of possible cultural centers where a significant number of people can be gathered for the possibility of interaction with the activities of the project OMCS-BR. After some time, SESC São Carlos was contacted, and during 3 months of conversation it was possible to work with the institution and develop the application presented here.

To start working with that team, it was adopted the User Centered Design Process Model defined by Anacleto in [12], as a LIA research result. The ideas' evolution took 3 months with the active participation of SESC team of professionals from humanities area, when they proposed to develop an application considering their 2010 summer program theme: Corporeity.

The constant focus during in all discussions was the need for providing users a fun environment to easily attract more people where the result was a massive use of images with real-time broadcast for HDTVs scattered in the institution, arousing the curiosity of those who transited through the area. This experience is presented here as well as the evolution of participatory development process between the institution and the laboratory in creating the game "Finders of Myths." This article is divided in 8 sections: section 2 describes the social educational motivation, section 3 and 4 show Prototype and Game's development process, section 5 brings the performed tests, section 6 shows the game application, section 7 describes the Process Model instatiation, and section 8 states some results and conclusions.

2. PARTNERSHIP PROCESS

Common Sense is a subset of the cultural knowledge and can be defined as the knowledge of every-day things based in life experience or beliefs of a group considering the time, space and social aspects Examples of common sense knowledge are "a lemon is sour", "when you receive a gift you may be happy" or "A pineapple is a kind of fruit". In Figure 1 is shown the architecture of the OMCS-Br Project that aims at collecting this kind of knowledge from people through the web. In the Brazilian website (Figure 1 - I), this knowledge is collected by a fill-the-gap mechanism: semi-structured sentences (templates) with gaps to be completed by people. For example:

A **breezy** is also known as _____.

A **milkshake** is made of _____.

Soccer is a kind of _____.

The templates are made of three parts: a dynamic part, a static part and a blank part. The dynamic part, represented by the bold words, is filled automatically by the computer; the static part is a fixed query structure; the blank part is where the user writes what he/she thinks.

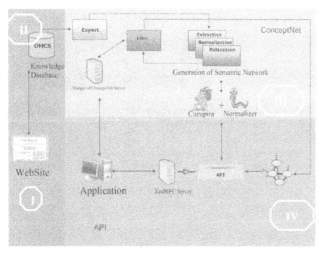

Figure 1. Architecture of OMCS-Br.

The full sentence is stored in a database (Figure 1 - II) and, then, is processed by some Natural Language Processing (NLP) mechanisms (a lemmatizer, a PoS tagger, etc.) that break it in interconnected concepts (Figure 1 - III). The link between two concepts is tagged by a Minsky's Relation. Minsky [11] defined that the human knowledge can be mapped through 20 relations

such as defined-as, is-a, part-of, made-of, property-of and others. These relations give more semantic in the link between two concepts. The set of concepts and relation forms a semantic network of concepts called ConceptNet (Figure 1 - IV). Some examples of facts in ConceptNet are presented below:

defined-as(breezy, girlfriend)

made-of(milkshake, ice cream)

is-a(soccer, sport)

The computer applications work with the ConceptNet through an Application Program Interface (API) that provides some function to manipulate its data. The OMCS-Br project has more than 1,500,000 concepts, 280,000 sentences stored in its database and just over 1,800 contributors.

In order to provide another source to collect common sense statements, LIA researchers decided to look for partnerships with other institutions that were closer to people in general and could help us to speed up the knowledgebase increasing.

The Advanced Interaction Laboratory (LIA) felt the need to have a partnership with a national institution to promote the collect and validation of sentences from Open Mind Common Sense in Brazil project, beyond the conventional collection at the project website (www.sensocomum.ufscar.br), developed in partnership with MediaLab-MIT.

There were iterations in order to experience the process model [12], as show in Table 1, these iterations are described during the paper. Two centers were considered in which LIA researchers make a communication through emails. The first institution was *Estação Ciência (EC)*, which is an interactive science center in São Paulo, which goal is to popularize science and promote science education in a playful and pleasurable way [1] as show in Table 1 - row 1 The conversation with EC generated a project that is being written jointly with another institution of higher education, POLI-USP - *Escola Politécnica da Universidade de São Paulo*. The second institution was SESC (Social Service of Commerce) that is an organization maintained by business of trade in goods and services, which operates in the areas of education, health, leisure, culture and care. As an example of the actions of SESC, projects and activities with young people are held in various areas, providing experiences of participation and citizenship. Free internet, dental care, social and environmental education are also offered to the population. The partnership process with the SESC will be described.

The LIA coordinator came into contact with a person responsible for administration of the cultural center, which indicated the event coordinator of the community center, Vilma, to discuss the partnership. This process of conversation lasted three months.

At that first meeting, it was discussed the possibility of LIA setting up a kiosk at SESC to disseminate the laboratory projects, as well as its site, and explain the coordinator about OMCS-Br project, the laboratory researches and what aims with this partnership. The meeting was very productive, many ideas and possibilities were discussed, giving way to a partnership that resulted in the project described in this article.

Vilma made a suggestion to hold this event during the program Summer SESC 2010, between the months of January and February, which theme was Corporeity, which according

Professor Dr. Wagner Way Moreira, "it is not a concept, but a change of attitude that we should have in relation to our bodily experience. " [4]. Thus, it was decided to do a game project related to the theme of the program, using moving objects, live colors, and encourage the user to do some kind of motion, like a simple face or something more abrupt, as show in Table 1 - row 2. In this way, the prototyping of the project began, which will be explained in the next items. Once games are kinds of applications that the Lab usually develops [7], [8], [9], [10], the researcher team was very comfortable with that decision.

3. PROTOTYPE DEVELOPMENT PROCESS

Once obtained the partnership with SESC, the next stage has began with a discussion of what would be the project that LIA would lead to the Summer SESC, a project that involves objectives from LIA and SESC. An initial idea of the members of the laboratory was to show the laboratory site and some applications. But Vilma thought the project should be related to corporeality, the event theme. Thus, it was discussed what the site should have and what kind of interaction with the user should have. The first thing defined is that the game should be entertaining, providing fun for users, because if it would be an activity without any attraction, there would be little contribution.

To attract people's attention, it was decided to put some movement on the site with animations, videos, pictures of people who have been playing, that would be taken by the webcam. There would also be a possibility to do a wireless broadcast with the images of people playing on HDTVs throughout the center. Thus ended the first meeting and the next one was scheduled for the following few weeks later. Vilma sent to the LIA's researchers some articles about corporeality by Michel Foucault and Wagner Wey Moreira to understand the theme, as show in Table 1 - row 3.

In the following days, there were internal meetings in the laboratory to decide which game would be ideal for this event, something simple and playful. There were two ideas, one of them was to use templates on the project site. The other one was to make a quiz with answers "yes" or "no." The first idea was discarded because the site would not be something attractive for this event, and create these templates would be something that would take some time. So it was decided that would be a game of questions and answers.

It has been developed a paper prototype of the interface and it was taken at the next meeting to show to the event coordinator. At that meeting was also informed that it could not take pictures of people and put them on the site because of their privacy, as show in Table 1 - row 4. Videos would not be possible for the same reason. So it was decided that the site would have included some pictures of SESC itself, which would automatically switching. The broadcast images to the HDTVs should be live, without any type of storage to avoid legal problems. With the feedback from the center staff, some changes were made, generating a new paper prototype of the interface, as show in Table 1 - row 9. Once introduced to Vilma, it has had some more changes in the layout. These changes were presented in a web prototype that is medium fidelity, where you could see the face that the game was taking.

4. GAME DEVELOPMENT PROCESS

The development of this game has involved a evaluation process separated into 4 phases.

The first phase begins when LIA team develops the first paper prototype of the game (Figure 2). Based on this first prototype, the teams of SESC and LIA worked together to define the goals of the game. SESC team reports that the game should have some kind of movement and the interface design should be lively and motivating. LIA's team worked on the first model of the interface for the web environment (Figure 3), having as main feature some animate parts related to the theme corporeity.

Considering the paper prototype and the interface modeling, the SESC team actively participated in the creation of a second paper prototype, giving hints, suggestions and setting the location of elements in the interface. LIA's team suggests using images from the public to be displayed in the game interface and recorded films about the events. The team of SESC, worried about infringing the copyright of images and movies of the public, so they decided not to use this type of interface elements, but suggested using televisions scattered throughout SESC environments as a way to publish in real time what happened during the game.

Figure 2. First paper prototype.

Both teams set a way to hit the people around, in a way to invite them to play and move, there could be an activity during some moments of the game that calls the player to appear on distributed televisions in real time in the main SESC environment.

Figure 3. Web environment prototype.

The player would appear with gestures, movements or imitations of funny figures shown at the interface of the game, during the game other people can see the player in the environment of SESC through HDTV's, which is the fun or the challenge. With these considerations, by completing this second phase, it has been generated a medium fidelity prototype shown in Figure 4.

The dynamic of the game was decided in this phase. Many original sentences related to the theme of the game were selected, taking into consideration the corporeity theme with some subjects, such as: swimming, sports, race, etc., through a filter in the ConceptNet of the OMCS-Br project, as show in Table 1 – row 5. These original sentences were shown to the participants and they confirm if the sentence make sense for them (Figure 5). During the game the user is logged in real time by computer's webcam to televisions around the SESC. Below the sentence, it was placed two buttons for making this response, which would pass to the next step and then sequentially. The last point, which was the motivation for this partnership and the invitation to move to the public, was the presentation of images of people and animals with funny faces and positions in an interval of 3 sentences for the user to replicate the movement in real time in front of the camera, as show in Table 1 - row 8.

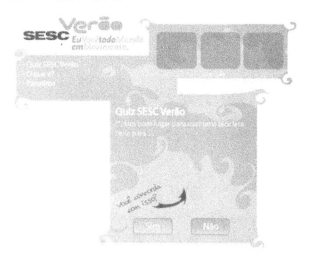

Figure 4. Medium fidelity prototype.

Figure 5. Original sentences.

This "imitation" would step up the funniest moment since such a move would be seen by all the public who walked or stood near the television. At the end of this imitation, which had a free time by the user, the application made an evaluation of the compatibility between the three responses and the current knowledge base provided by the various contributions of the project, thereby deciding four levels of compliance in accordance with the model SAM satisfaction with demonstrated in Figure 6. This iteration is described in Table 1 - row 6. SAM is a nonverbal questionnaire used to collect users' emotional reactions, moreover, is known as Self Assessment Model, developed by Lang (1985). This questionnaire measures a set of three emotions: satisfaction, motivation and sense of control. Each emotion is portrayed by facial expressions and there are nine values along each of three dimensions, on a continuous scale. Users can report their answers by selecting the animations that match the emotions they felt [5].

Figure 6. SAM Questionnaire [adapted from 5].

In an agreement among those involved in the project, it was decided that the user would be free to practice motion as much as to proceed in the responses of sentences or even discontinue their participation at any time. It was necessary to obtain a base of sentences that were necessarily related to the theme corporeity. This database was originated on the set of more than 275,000 sentences from OMCS-Br project, where the use of all this content was not particularly justified by our goals to keep the theme corporeity as main subject. To resolve this situation, LIA's team has implemented a series of filters that fit the theme proposed, resulting in a total of 5343 sentences that would be available to our application. The final interfaces of the game are shown in Figure 7 and Figure 8.

Figure 7. Home page.

Figure 8. Interface of the game.

In order to observe the players interacting with this game, it was necessary to verify the environmental infrastructure and to test the connection between the computers that would run the application, the camera of each notebook and televisions as shown in Figure 9. This iteration is described in Table 1 - row 10.

Figure 9. Infrastructure of the Community Center.

5. TESTING AT THE ENVIRONMENT

After all the meetings and email exchanges, was stipulated a time before the presentation so that the ideas were placed in practice to test the environment. LIA's team attended the SESC and met with officials responsible for implementing the project in that environment. Ideas was discussed for interesting places where the movement of people was more consistent with parallel events that occur within two days of the weekend that the game would be open to the public. For private institution reason's, was granted only one television and testing of connection and transmission of images were performed. The images from the webcam on laptops, to be shown on TV in Figure 10, were clearly presented in the television. An interesting fact was that at that moment, the attention of some people how was walking around has addressed to the equipment and some curious ventured stopped wondering about what would be broadcast on television.

The site for develop the activity was settled, and television was in the main hall of the environment where the movement of people was greater. With all cables connected, broadcast tested and game running, we turn to the presentation that lasted for the next two days.

Figure 10. The TV environment to display images from webcams.

6. GAME APPLICATION

The game Myths Finders had its presentation throughout the weekend and was attended by 78 people during those two days. People were invited and invitations were distributed (Figure 11). It was a very interesting experience through direct contact between those who participated in the process of game creation and the public that circulated in SESC, as show in Table 1 - row 11. This contact resulted in several memories presented here, reported data that were not possible to be registered by other ways instead the memory itself. Moments like two children (A and B) interacting with the game and the child A saying to her friend: "Make a funny face so I can see you on the TV." Even moments where the play overcame the shame in front of the webcam: "Oh what a shame." - a woman trying to imitate an image. The selected images involve faces (Figure 12) and animals in funny positions, where some users portrayed, "Oh. It's so cute" – a girl speaking about the faces of the game.

Figure 11. Invitation for the Community Center users to play the game.

There was a higher participation of children in the event, those who could read to those who lacked this domain, it was common to help the reading the sentences for some children. Sometimes they were helped without notice if they could or not read: "(undergraduate) - Oh, Can you read? (child playing) - Yes, but I feel better when you read."

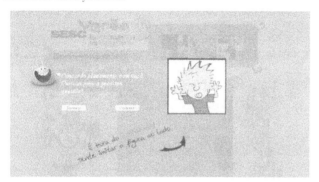

Figure 12. Interface of the game for invitation to the movement.

Some users weren't attracted to participate, demonstrating a degree of shame for being in front of the webcam, while others have enjoyed for a while, as in the case of a 10 year old girl that spent much of Sunday in our company. This girl played several times and was helping some other kids to play. She made all funny faces, just like the one represented in Figure 12, and has shown certain affection for the presence of researchers from LIA in the environment, including hugging some of the researchers, and asking for sitting with her (Figure 13 and 14).

Figure 13. Participants engaged into the activity.

Some tried to guess how the game knew that the participant really made the funny face and asked if the time they spent making the move was enough to keep up with the sentences: "(child) - How did it know I made a grimace "(undergraduate) - Ah, he does not know. But it's the funny moment. You can do it faster if you like and will be fine."

Many images do succeed, like a penguin in a position of fight. A boy who had played before and was watching his friend playing, saw the picture and said, "Why did not this penguin come to me? I wanted to imitate it."

Figure 14. Participant asking for company during the activity.

7. EXPERIENCING THE PROCESS MODEL

We perceived a certain progress during the development of the project. This progress we describe using a user-centered design (UCD) process with some techniques of participatory design. Four user-centered design process phases are presented, each phase include some stages. For each stage, which based in UCD, include: design strategies (What strategy we followed in the stage in question), followed by the design questions to be addressed in that stage, then a resource or prototype, that incorporate the strategies to answer the question, analysis and evaluation, artifact or decision to be took based in the analysis, and the stakeholders involved in each stage to help on answering the questions. The process has been successful for the conception, creation, development, application and evaluation of the project. We are formalized this process in the Table 1. The color blue means the development of the first paper prototype. Green means the development of the second one. Yellow means the validation of the game and the infrastructure. Finally, red shows the event day.

8. RESULT ANALYSIS - CONCLUSIONS

Adopting the UCD process model proposed in [12], it was realized that the game allowed researcher to reach the goal that was to design new forms of using and collecting cultural knowledge while the participants use the developed application. The community center participants played over a thousand phrases, which is a significant amount during the period of time we stay at SESC. Confirming the sentences showed to participants it could be increased or decreased the frequency of sentences on the cultural knowledge base, allowing that sentences to be more representative and related what most people think. The numbers related to the sentences confirmed or rejected during the game point out satisfactory results on collecting this kind of knowledge through the game. According to some statements and behaviors, it is possible to observe that participants were really enjoying to play the 'Myths Finders' game. We can conclude that games are an option to increase the collection of cultural knowledge in socio-educational centers, in which the target group was most closely involved, was children under 12 and youths between 13 to 17 years. The multimedia interaction was a factor that had a strong influence on the game because most of the participants enjoyed interacting with others through the webcam and television. Others were attracted by the faces that the participants did the game on television, sparking their interest in the game.

Table 1. Experiencing a Process Model

Design Strategies	Questions	Resource/Prototype	Evaluation / Analysis	Stakeholders	Artifact/Decision Making
Create a new source of common sense collection	Where collect?	Options: - Estação Ciência - SESC - Emails between SESC and LIA - Emails between Estação Ciência and LIA	1- The project 'Estação Ciência' is being writing and involves money and another educational institution 2- SESC: near and cheaper.	- Diego - Victor - Junia - Marcos	- SESC was chosen by proximity, cost and the disposal of the institution's event coordinator to make a real partnership.
Collect common sense at SESC	How?	1- Use the OMCS-Br website at SESC	1- Vilma said that there was something more attractive. 2- Something playful. 3- Junia, LIA's coordinator, said that can be a game 4- Possibility of being at Summer SESC 2010	- Diego - Victor - Junia - Vilma - SESC employees	- A game that envolves Corporeity.
Create an activity where the common sense collection has playful touch	- Can we work with games? - Which games?	1- We can work with games 2- Quiz game 3- Template games 4- Vilma sent to LIA's researchers documents about corporiety (Michel Foucault, Wagner Wey Moreira).	- The quiz game was chosen because it's easier to develop in a short time. - It's funnier than a template game.	- Diego - Victor - Junia - Vilma - SESC employees	Game with filtered sentences from OMCS-Br related with body and movement.
Design of the game elements	- Which elements are interesting to the game?	1- Animations, Images, People faces 2-Movement 3- Paper Prototype 4- Mock-up web	- Pictures of the people face have been denied, so they were canceled.	- Diego - Victor - Junia - Vilma - SESC employees	- Second paper prototype - Elements of the interface and game definide
Selection of common sense sentences related to corporeity	- Which sentences?	1'- A table of sentences of OMCS-Br project	- A filtering was done with a theme related to corporeality, such as swimming, sports, race	- Diego - Victor - Junia	- Table with 5434 sentences about corporeity.
Choice of the Feedback	- What early percentage to start sentences?	- SAM	- SESC didn't support the SAM's images, so we used smiles with the sentences.	- Diego - Victor - Junia	- 4 motivate feedback sentences to the user continues to play the game
Choose the storage mode	- How to interacting with OMCS-BR project basis?	Use ConceptNet to storage the answers	- A table was created where the sentences are storaged, another one where the answers "yes" and another for the "no"	- Diego - Victor - Junia	Separeted tables to help to add the new sentences in the basis of OMCS-Br.
Relate the game with motion	- How to make people move?	1 - Inviting people to move through images 2 - Search images.	- Some movements/grimacing images where searched for people imitate	- Diego - Victor - Junia	- Fun imagens about people and animals grimacing
Make the game attractive	- How to promote the curiosity of people to participate in the game?	1- Use of live images of people's movements	- Was investigated the possibility of broadcasting live images to HDTVs throughout SESC	- Diego - Victor - Junia	- We used webcams to broadcast live images to televisions around SESC
Test the environment	- Is the game working? - Structure of SESC working?	1 - The game works! 2 - We make a local network so the game could run in some notebooks. 3 - Images are broadcast to the HDTV. 4 - Only an HDTV was used by institutional issues	- The equipment was tested at SESC, everything worked	- Diego - Victor - Junia - Vilma - SESC employees	- Validation of the game and infrastructure.
Event Day	- How was it? - Did the people like? - Does everything work just like was planned?	Game	- It was a very nice experience. The interaction with users, to see what they thought of the game. - User interaction with the game. - Some liked, others not. - We had some technical problems that were solved in time.	- Diego - Victor - Junia - Vilma - Game Users - SESC employees	- Statistics - Sentences validated

9. ACKNOWLEDGMENTS

The authors thank CAPES, Fapesp (proc. nº 05/60799-6) and CNPQ for partially financial support and all the volunteer users that participate in this research. We also thank all the collaborators of the OMCS-Br project who have been building the common sense knowledge base considered in this research.

10. BIBLIOGRAPHY

[1] Estação Ciência - http://www.eciencia.usp.br/ec/index.html Available in April, 2010

[2] Open Mind Common Sense project from Brazil (OMCS-Br). Available in: <http://www.sensocomum.ufscar.br>. Access in: June/2009.

[3] SINGH, P. (2002A) The OpenMind Commonsense project. 2002. Avaliable at: http://web.media.mit.edu/~push/OMCSProject.pdf Access:dez. 2009.

[4] MOREIRA, W. W. (2010). Corporeidade

[5] LANG, P. J.; BRADLEY, M. M.; CUTHBERT, B. N. Digitized photographs, instruction manual and affective ratings. In: INTERNATIONAL AFFECTIVE PICTURE SYSTEM (IAPS), 1999. Technical Report... University of Florida, Gainesville

[6] OMCS_Br, www.sensocomu.dc.ufscar.br. Acessed June 2010.

[7] SILVA, M. A. R. ; DIAS, A. L. ; ANACLETO, J. C.(2010) . Using Contextualized Narrative Game to Improve Students and Teachers Communication. In: International Conference on Computer Supported Education (CSEDU 2010), Valencia, Spain. Proceedings International Conference on Computer Supported Education.

[8] VILLENA, J. M. R. ; SILVA, M. A. R. ; ANACLETO, J. C. (2010) Using Culture to Help People Communication Throught Computer Games in Educational and Therapeutic Environment. In: IEEE International Conference on Systems, Man, and Cybernetics (SMC 2010), 2010, Istanbul. Anais SMC 2010, 2010. p. 1-8.

[9] FERREIRA, A. M. ; PEREIRA, E. N. ; CARELLI, I. M. ; ANACLETO, J. C. ; SILVA, M. A. R. ; DIAS, A. L.(2009) . A Culturally Contextualized Web based Game Environment to Support Meaningful Learning. In: International Conference on Computer Supported Education (CSEDU 2009), 2009, Lisbon, Portugal.

[10] PEREIRA, E. N. ; FERREIRA, A. M. ; ANACLETO, J. C. ; CARVALHO, A. F. P. DE ; FABRO, J. A.(2008) . What is it? : A Culture Sensitive Educational Games. In: The 20th International World Computer Congress (WCC 2008), 2008, Milan. Learning to Live in the Knowledge Society, KENDALL, M.; SAMWAYS, B. (Eds.). Berlin : Springer, 2008.

[11] MINSKY, M. 1986. "The Society of Mind". New York: Simon and Schuster. 339 p.

[12] ANACLETO, J. C. ; FELS, S. ; VILLENA, J. M. R. . Design of a web-based therapist tool to promote emotional closeness. In: ACM Conference on Human Factors in Computing Systems (CHI 2010), 2010. Atlanta. Conference Proceedings & Extended Abstracts (CHI 2010). New York, NY : Sheridan Printing, 2010. v. 1. p. 3565-3570.

Is Agility out there? Agile Practices in Game Development

Fabio Petrillo
Institute of Informatics - Federal University of Rio
Grande do Sul (UFRGS)
9500 Bento Gonçalves Avenue
Porto Alegre, Brazil
fabio@petrillo.com

Marcelo Pimenta
Institute of Informatics - Federal University of Rio
Grande do Sul (UFRGS)
9500 Bento Gonçalves Avenue
Porto Alegre, Brazil
mpimenta@inf.ufrgs.br

ABSTRACT

Game development is a very complex and multidisciplinary activity and surely the success of games as one of most profitable areas in entertainment domain could not be incidentally. The goal of this paper is to investigate if (and how) principles and practices from Agile Methods have been adopted in game development, mainly gathering evidences through Postmortem Analysis (PMA).

Then we describe how we have conducted PMA in order to identify the good practices adopted in several game development projects. The results are discussed, comparing similarities and differences on how these practices are taken in account in (traditional) software development and game development.

1. INTRODUCTION

The creation of electronic games is nowadays an incredibly complex task [12], much harder than someone might initially imagine [6].

The increased complexity, combined with the multidisciplinary nature of the process of game development (art, sound, gameplay, control systems, artificial intelligence, human factors, among many others) interacting with the traditional software development, creates a scenario which also increases this complexity. Some authors (for example [7]) recommend a methodology for taking in account software engineering expertise in the field of digital games.

However, despite these difficulties, the gaming industry is currently one of the most powerful in the entertainment industry, with billions of dollars in profit and creating trillions of hours of fun. Major game projects have cross-functional teams formed by highly skilled individuals, including software developers, designers, musicians, script writers and many others. Thus, the game developer career is currently one of the most dynamic, creative, challenging and potentially profitable that someone can choose [12]. This scenario

suggests that the strength and profitability do not happen by chance. From the analysis of real projects' reports, it seems that to achieve these results, a common set of good practices were adopted in these projects.

The games industry can benefit tremendously by acquiring knowledge of software engineering, allowing developers to use good and proven practices. In fact, according to [11], a clear understanding of the tools available and how to apply them can enhance the results in game development.

In the traditional software industry, many papers and books have been published about good practices in software engineering [23, 30, 32]. However, are these practices also found in game development? Which practices are most prominent? How often these practices are found in game projects? What practices are found in both industries? Are there good practices found only in game development? Our intention in this paper is to discuss these issues.

The game development community has a vast literature, especially when it comes to technology issues. However, few works of software engineering dedicated to the electronic game industry, standing out above all the works [4] and [11]. It is interesting to note that these two are eminently philosophical view of the propagators of the waterfall development process (more details in section 2). In particular, the work of [4], one of the most quoted by the gaming community, demonstrating a rooted culture processes prescriptive and non-iterative. In this paper, [4] explicitly advocates the adoption of a "comfortable" subset of the Unified Process (UP - Unified Software Development Process) as a process of development of electronic games, for the simple fact of being a standard in he software industry.

The aim of this paper is to investigate whether (and how) some agile principles and practices [15, 18] have been applied in game development. This research can help demystify the impression that the adoption of agile practices by game developers is a difficult process. Indeed, if many of the agile practices are already being (even partially) taken, we believe that many developers may try to better understand the fundamentals of agile software development, and more easily find ways to put it into action in their daily work.

The paper is structured as follows: after this introduction, section 2 presents a summary of the games development process. Section 3 discusses the best practices of software engineering found in process of game development, from analysis of the literature on game development and mainly through the analysis of postmortems. Section 4 discusses the results of these analysis. Finally, the conclusions are presented in section 5.

2. THE TRADITIONAL GAME DEVELOPMENT

The game development community has a vast specialized literature, especially about technical issues. The industry also has a series of titles that describe how to teach and work in a games company, such as Gershenfeld et al. [12].

However, not many software engineering works are dedicated to the gaming industry: two remarkable exceptions are Bethke [4] and Schofield [11]. It is interesting to emphasize that these two works are related to a *waterfall* philosophical viewpoint, in particular the work of Bethke [4], one of the most cited by the games community, demonstrating the existing culture of prescriptive and non-iterative procedures. Bethke [4] explicitly advocates the adoption of a subset of the *Unified Software Development Process* as the development process for electronic games, for the simple fact that this is a "standard" in the software industry.

According to [10], it is possible to identify a common cycle of development in different teams: basically, the waterfall model [23] adapted to produce games. In particular, two stages of this model may be highlighted: a) defining the game rules and b) the production of **Document Set** or **Project Document**.

The rules of a game determine the behavior and interaction among the characters and their environment, and can be viewed as requirements. In fact, game designing is nothing more than creating a set of rules [9], usually defined in an informal process, involving all members of the development team [26].

The Project Document ((Design Document)) is the main, often the only, documentation of a game. Your goal is to describe and detail the mechanics of the game, in other words, what the player is able to do within the environment of the game, as he is able to do it and how it can lead to a satisfactory experience. It also usually includes the main components of the story and describes the scenarios in which the game is set, supporting the description of the player's actions. Many developers refer to it as a functional specification, using it as a basis for the architectural design [24].

The creation of a solid project document is considered, traditionally, as the most important step in the game development. The difficulties in creating this document are caused, mainly, by the nature of the task and the tools used in their conception, it is not possible, for example, document the "fun" [19]. The development team could use his experience and intuition in defining the mechanics of the game, but the quality of entertainment provided by the game in general can only be assessed in stages of testing.

The game modeling is not changed in recent years and continues based on narrative techniques, like scripts and storyboards, borrowed from other entertainment media, such as cinema [17]. The conception of a game can also count on a higher abstraction level, organized in the Concept or Proposal Document. This document can analyze aspects such as market, budget, schedule, technology, art style, profile of the development group and some high level description of the gameplay. However, the preparation of the Concept Document is not common to all projects [24].

The development process used in the production of most games is based on the waterfall model [25]. This process consists of phases that are executed sequentially, in which each one generates a product and is independent from the others. The features inherent in producing games require some adjustments to the classic process, which can be showed in figure 1.

Some authors argue that the waterfall model, while serving as a common denominator between the cycles exist, **not to be fully implemented**. Typical features of a game, as dynamics of design or difficulties in planning the gameplay, make it difficult - or impossible - to specify completely a game without writing any code, that is, without a version of the system in which the project can be tested. This results in development cycles that involve links between the stages of specification of the game and test procedures. [25] quotes a cycle of incremental development, the Staged Delivery Model, as an alternative to the waterfall model.

3. PMA TO IDENTIFY GOOD PRACTICES

In this section, we describe how we have gathered evidences of adoption of good practices in game industry. The Postmortems Analysis (PMA) is a technique borrowed from Empirical Software Engineering. Empirical Software Engineering aims to investigate and collect relevant data to generalize the results, learning from mistakes and successes, providing a future reuse of this knowledge.

Controlled experiments, case studies and surveys approaches are most commonly used and better known than the PMA [29, 33, 28]. The main reason for the PMA not be adopted in software projects in different fields of application is not their difficulty of operationalizing, neither the resources involved or much less cost, but rather the absence of postmortems.

The term *postmortem* designates a document which summarizes the project development experiences, with a strong emphasis on positive and negative aspects of the development cycle [14]. It is commonly done right after the project finishes, by managers or senior project participants [7]. In a software engineering viewpoint, postmortems are important tools for knowledge management [5], from which the group can learn from its own experiences and plan future projects. In fact, the postmortem analysis can be so revealing that some authors [5] argue that any project should be finished without it's own postmortem.

Traditionally, IT teams have no habit of creating postmortems, although there are obviously exceptions (see for example [31]) and strong recommendations to do it [5]. Fortunately, a rare exception is the domain of games.

Postmortems are much used in the game industry. Many game websites devote entire sections to present these doc-

Figure 1: Waterfall process applied to game development

uments, such as *Gamasutra* (http://www.gamasutra.com) and *Gamedev* (http://www.gamedev.net). It is also very interesting to note the variety of development teams profiles and projects behind these documents, varying from few developers in small projects to dozens of developers in five-year-long projects.

The postmortems published by *Gamasutra* mainly follow the structure proposed by the *Open Letter Template* [20], which is composed by three sections. The first section summarizes the project and presents some important aspects of the development. The next two sections, however, discuss the most interesting aspects to the game developers:

- **What went right:** it discusses the *best practices* adopted by developers, solutions, improvements, and project management decisions that have improved the efficiency of the team. All these aspects are critical elements to be used in planning future projects.

- **What went wrong:** it discusses difficulties, pitfalls, and mistakes experienced by the development team in the project, in both technical and management aspects.

The postmortem is closed with a final message from the author, commonly followed by a project technical brief, which includes the number of full- and partial-time developers,

length of development, release date, target platforms, and the hardware and software used in the development.

The information contained in the postmortems constitute knowledge base that can be reused by any development team, which includes examples and real life development experiences. They can help in knowledge sharing, and can be very useful for planning future projects.

Thus, the 20 *postmortems* were examined to find good practices. The process of recognizing the good practices took place in 3 phases. At first, each *postmortem* has been read and the quotes that were deemed relevant were highlighted. In the second stage, based on traditional and agile software engineering knowledge [1, 23, 3], the practices to be tabulated were selected. In the third stage, each report was read again, with special attention to highlighted passages, and each citation was tabulated according to the classification previously made.

To perform the postmortems analysis and the organization of good practices, we need to select some postmortems, analyze them and compile the results, forming a set of practices that are approved or disapproved by these developers. We performed the same procedure (analysis of literature and analysis focused on the postmortems) to carry out a diagnosis of the major problems and difficulties encountered in the development of games (see [21]).

Among the various existing postmortems, we selected 20 postmortems posted on Gamasutra, listed in tables 1 and 3. The 20 postmortems analyzed were selected randomly, having one important criterion for the selection: we selected postmortems of projects that resulted in a complete game and delivered to market, not been analyzed reports of projects failed, canceled or terminated without a product.

In preparation stage, we studied the main agile practices [8, 1, 3, 22] and good practices in the gaming industry [27, 13]. In this study, 12 good practices were listed for analysis.

The 20 postmortems were read and sentences quoting practices were highlighted. During this stage, another practice was found ("Belief in the success of the project"), which was added to the analyzed set, totaling 13 practices, which are listed in Tables 1 and 2 and also in Figure 2. Finally, a table for data collection was organized (table 1), with projects arranged in rows and practices in columns.

4. DISCUSSION

In order to somehow quantify the practices found in the postmortems, the number of "Yes" occurrences was recorded both in terms of lines as of columns. This way, the quantity of "Yes" found in the lines represents how many different types of practices were presented in a certain game. As for the number recorded in columns, it represent the number of occurrences of this practice in a set of analyzed games. The count of columns, which can be seen in the penultimate line, made possible to organize them in order of occurrence. The last line contains the percentage of occurrences in relation to the number of projects studied.

When we look more carefully to these results, we can see that the most common practices were a **qualified, motivated or cohesive team** or the **belief in the project's success** with 90% (18 out of 20) of the projects reporting these 2 practices. Then, the **stimulus to creativity** and **focus on the product** were highlighted, with 80% of the project citing them (16 out of 20). Even in that context, the next most common 2 practices were **source version control**, with 65% (13 out of 20) and the **utilization of simple or productive tools**, with 60%. Figure 2 shows the good practices occurrence histogram in descending order, where a graphic comparison of these results can be made.

Despite these results being not be surprising, they show the importance of the team for the project success, confirming the statements made by Bach [2] that processes are useful, but not the central elements for the success of software projects. The central point is the man - the hero who solves ambiguous problems, which distinguishes between an expressed need and the one which will actually make the client fully satisfied [2]. Moreover, it is clear the persistence and belief in the success of teams who intensely focused on the software product.

Another interesting point is that management practices are a clear problem in the games industry. It does not reach 50% the number of projects in which a **defined process** is adopted and only 25% (5 of 20) of the projects adopted **good management practices**. Moreover, only 40% of the projects used practices of quality control and was 10% (2 to

20) the occurrence of **continuous integration** found the analyzed projects.

If we calculate the average number of good practices adopted in the analyzed projects, we will see that it is 7.2 practices, with standard deviation of 2.6. This means that most projects employed between 5 and 11 practices, and that the average is about **half** of the examined practices (7 to 13). This result shows that the game industry adopts a considerable number of good practices in their projects, undoing a little pessimistic view of some authors, as [4] and Flood [10].

If we analyze these results, we can see that in general, **good practices adopted in the traditional software industry are also found in the games industry**. In both studies, the quality of the team was dominant for the success of the project, as well as the concern with the adoption of good practices for programming.

The game industry, informally, has employed best practices in software development, as presented in section 3. We can combine the agile practices analyzed in accordance with the agile practices of Scrum, XP and Agile Modeling (AM), forming the Table 2.

Good practice already adopted	It adheres to the method...
Qualified team	AM, Scrum, XP
Belief in the success of the project	Scrum, XP
Creativity stimulus	Scrum, AM
Focus on the product	XP, Scrum
Version control	XP
Using simple tools	AM, XP
Programming good practices	XP
Agile modeling	XP, AM
Defined process	Scrum, XP
Quality control	XP
Feedback quickly	XP, Scrum
Good practices of management	XP, Scrum
Continuous integration	XP

Table 2: Adherence of best practices already adopted in games to agile methods

Game development teams are adopting agile practices instinctively. This scenario - the deployment of agile methods like Scrum and XP - can occur naturally, since the teams already use several principles of agility in their routines. Thus, the table 2 can point to the adoption of agile methods related to good practices analyzed in this work.

A new analysis can be offered to collate the results presented by [21], which outlines the problems encountered with the analysis results of the section 3, which contains good practice raised in postmortems. In evaluating, for example, the project *Cel Damage*, who took **85%** of good practice, we observed a lower incidence of problems, with only **20%** of reported problems. Are there a linear correlation between the number of problems encountered and good practices adopted in game projects?

For this analysis, was prepared to table 3, which is made up of the game projects analyzed, the percentage of problems found and the percentage of good practices adopted.

The management practices are a clear deficiency in the game industry. Not reach 50% the number of projects in which we identified the adoption of a **defined process of work**

Table 1: Occurrence of good practices in projects

Game	Qualified team	Belief in the success of the project	Creativity stimulus	Focus on the product	Version control	Using Vesple tools	Programming good practices	Agile modeling	Defined process	Quality control	Feedback quickly	Good practices of management	Continuous integration	Total	% good practices found
Beam Runner Hyper Cross	Yes	Yes	Yes	Yes	Yes	Yes	Yes	Yes	Yes	No	No	No	No	9	69%
Gabriel Knights	Yes	No	No	No	Yes	No	No	No	Yes	Yes	No	No	No	3	23%
Black & White	Yes	Yes	Yes	Yes	No	No	No	Yes	No	Yes	No	No	No	6	46%
Rangers Lead the Way	No	No	No	No	No	Yes	Yes	No	No	No	No	No	No	2	15%
Wild 9	Yes	Yes	Yes	Yes	Yes	Yes	No	Yes	No	No	No	No	No	7	54%
Trade Empires	Yes	Yes	Yes	Yes	Yes	Yes	Yes	Yes	Yes	Yes	Yes	Yes	No	12	92%
Rainbow Six	Yes	Yes	Yes	Yes	Yes	No	No	No	No	No	No	No	No	5	38%
The X-Files	Yes	Yes	Yes	Yes	Yes	No	No	No	No	No	No	No	No	5	38%
Draconus	Yes	Yes	Yes	No	No	No	Yes	No	No	No	No	No	No	4	31%
Cel Damage	Yes	Yes	No	Yes	Yes	Yes	Yes	No	Yes	Yes	Yes	Yes	Yes	11	85%
Command and Conquer: Tiberian Sun	Yes	Yes	Yes	Yes	No	Yes	Yes	No	Yes	No	No	No	No	8	62%
Asheron's Call	No	Yes	Yes	Yes	Yes	Yes	Yes	No	Yes	Yes	No	No	Yes	9	69%
Age of Empires II: The Age of Kings	Yes	Yes	Yes	No	Yes	No	No	No	No	Yes	No	Yes	No	7	54%
Diablo II	Yes	Yes	Yes	Yes	Yes	Yes	Yes	No	Yes	Yes	Yes	No	No	9	69%
Operation Flashpoint	Yes	Yes	Yes	Yes	Yes	Yes	Yes	Yes	Yes	No	Yes	No	No	10	77%
Hidden Evil	Yes	Yes	Yes	Yes	Yes	No	No	No	No	Yes	No	No	No	6	46%
Resident Evil 2	Yes	Yes	No	Yes	No	Yes	No	Yes	Yes	No	Yes	Yes	No	8	62%
Vampire: The Masquerade	Yes	Yes	Yes	Yes	No	Yes	Yes	Yes	Yes	No	No	No	No	8	62%
Unreal Tournament	Yes	Yes	Yes	Yes	No	No	Yes	Yes	No	No	Yes	Yes	No	8	62%
Tropico	Yes	Yes	Yes	Yes	Yes	Yes	No	No	No	No	No	No	No	6	46%
Occurrences	18	18	16	16	13	12	11	9	9	8	6	5	2	143	7.2
%	90%	90%	80%	80%	65%	60%	55%	45%	45%	40%	30%	25%	10%	0,55	55%

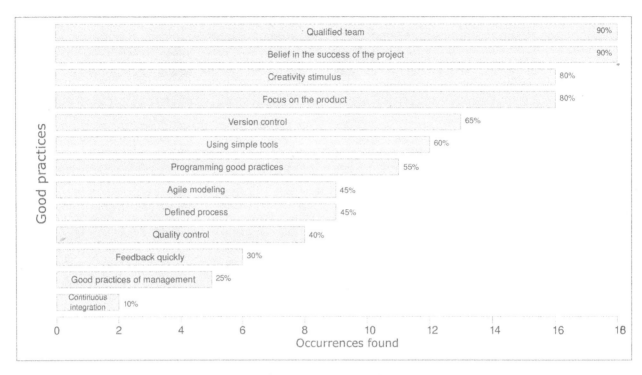

Figure 2: Occurrence of good practices

Project	% of problems found in project	% of good practices found in project
Cel Damage	20.0%	84.6%
Trade Empires	26.7%	92.3%
Diablo II	33.3%	69.2%
Command and Conquer	33.3%	61.5%
Tropico	26.7%	46.2%
Age of Empires II	33.3%	53.8%
Resident Evil 2	40.0%	61.5%
Beam Runner	46.7%	69.2%
Asheron's Call	46.7%	69.2%
Hidden Evil	33.3%	46.2%
Vampire	46.7%	61.5%
Unreal	46.7%	61.5%
Wild 9	53.3%	53.8%
The X-Files	40.0%	38.5%
Operation Flashpoint	80.0%	76.9%
Black & White	60.0%	46.2%
Rainbow Six	73.3%	38.5%
Draconus	80.0%	30.8%
Rangers Lead the Way	46.7%	15.4%
Gabriel Knights	86.7%	23.1%

Table 3: Comparison between the good practices and problems found by projects

and only 25% (5 of 20) of projects adopted **good management practices**. In addition, only 40% of projects used quality control practices and was 10% (2 of 20) recorded the occurrence of the **continuous integration**.

5. CONCLUSION

The major contribution of this work was helping to organize the universe of agile practices for the domain of games, from the analysis of problems and good practices found, being a point of departure for the use of agile methods in the process development of electronic games.

If we think that all major problems of the traditional software industry are also found in the games industry (see [21], we can note that they are correlated and the solutions adopted in the traditional software industry also should be investigated for the gaming industry.

Even informally, the game development teams are adopting a set of agile practices . In this scenario, the deployment of agile methods like Scrum and XP, can occur naturally, since the teams already adopt in their activities several principles of agility.

Our discussion of the results described in this article lead us to believe that game developers often **not** adopted **deliberately** these good practices because are **Agile Practices**. Perhaps, like many software developers, they think - because they are informal - do not correspond to the notions of rigor and systematization usually associated with software engineering.

However, these practices are studied and applied increasingly by the community of software engineering, although not always recognized and disclosed as disciplined ways of solving the chronic problems of development. As we have seen, many of the agile practices are already being adopted (even partially), and we believe that developers - if they are willing to better understand the fundamentals of agile software development - can easily incorporate them into their activities.

Since there are few academic studies on the use of agile methods in game development, this work opens perspectives for further research. We believe for example that modeling (preferably agile) of complex elements such as fun gameplay and fun deserves more investigation.

Based on studies done by [34], [16] and [13] we believe that the adoption of agile practices in development of games can achieve promising results. The agile practices seem to include the best features of the game industry, as multidisciplinarity and the difficulties in modeling aspects like user experience, the fun and enjoyment, whereas empirical methods are more adaptive and react better to changes during project implementation. We hope that this paper is a contribution to increasing adoption of agile practices in the process of game development.

6. REFERENCES

[1] S. W. Ambler. *Modelagem Ágil*. Bookman, São Paulo, 2004.

[2] J. Bach. Enough about process: what we need are heroes. *IEEE Software*, 12(2):96–98, março 1995.

[3] K. Beck. *Extreme Programming Explained: Embrace Change*. Addison-Wesley Professional, Reading, MA, 1st edition, 1999.

[4] E. Bethke. *Game Development and Production*. Wordware Publishing, Plano, 2003.

[5] A. Birk, T. Dingsoyr, and T. Stalhane. Postmortem: never leave a project without it. *IEEE Software*, 19, maio/junho 2002.

[6] J. Blow. Game development: Harder than you think. *ACM Press Queue*, 1(10):28–37, February 2004.

[7] D. Callele, E. Neufeld, and K. Schneider. Requirements engineering and the creative process in the video game industry. In *13th IEEE International Conference on Requirements Engineering*, August 2005.

[8] A. Cockburn. *Agile Software Development*. Addison Wesley Longman, Reading, MA, 1st edition, 2000.

[9] D. Cook. Evolutionary design - a practical process for creating great game designs. *GameDev.net*, janeiro 2001.

[10] K. Flood. Game unified process. *GameDev.net*, Maio 2003.

[11] J. P. Flynt and O. Salem. *Software Engineering for Game Developers*. Software Engineering Series. Course Technology PTR, 1st edition, November 2004.

[12] A. Gershenfeld, M. Loparco, and C. Barajas. *Game Plan: the insider's guide to breaking in and succeeding in the computer and vieo game business*. St. Martin's Griffin Press, New York, 2003.

[13] A. Gibson. Agile game development and fun. Technical report, University of Colorado Department of Computer Science, 2007.

[14] W. Hamann. Goodbye postmortems, hello critical stage analysis. *Gamasutra - The Art & Business of Making Games*, julho 2003.

[15] J. Highsmith and A. Cockburn. Agile software development: The business of innovation. *IEEE Computer*, 34:120–122, 2001.

[16] L. C. C. Kasperavicius, L. N. M. Bezerra, L. Silva, and I. F. Silveira. Ensino de desenvolvimento de jogos digitais baseado em metodologias Ágeis: o projeto primeira habilitação. In *Anais do XXVIII Congresso da SBC - Workshop sobre Educação em Computação*, pages 89 – 98, Belém do Pará, Julho 2008.

[17] B. Kreimeier. The case for game design patterns. Gamasutra - The Art & Business of Making Games, http://www.gamasutra.com/features/20020313/kreimeier_01.htm. March 2002.

[18] M. Marchesi, G. Succi, D. Wells, and L. Williams. *Extreme Programming Perspectives*. Addison Wesley, 2002.

[19] M. McShaffry. *Game Coding Complete*. Paraglyph Press, Scottsdale, 2003.

[20] M. Myllyaho, O. Salo, J. Kääriäinen, J. Hyysalo, and J. Koskela. A review of small and large post-mortem analysis methods. In *IEEE France*, Paris, November 2004. 17th International Conference Software & Systems Engineering and their Applications.

[21] F. Petrillo, M. Pimenta, F. Trindade, and C. Dietrich. What went wrong? a survey of problems in game development. *ACM Computer in Entertainment*, CIE: 7(1), 2009.

[22] M. Poppendieck and T. Poppendieck. Principles of lean thinking. 2003.

[23] R. S. Pressman. *Engenharia de Software*. McGraw-Hill, São Paulo, 6th edition, 2006.

[24] R. Rouse. *Game Design: theory & practice*. Wordware Publishing, Inc, 2001.

[25] R. Rucker. *Software Engineering and Computer Games*. Addison Wesley, December 2002.

[26] E. Schaefer. Postmortem: Diablo ii. *Gamasutra - The Art & Business of Making Games*, outubro 2000.

[27] B. Schofield. Embracing fun: Why extreme programming is great for game development. Gamasutra: The Art & Business of Making Games, March 2007.

[28] F. Shull, M. Mendonça, V. Basili, J. Carver, J. C. Maldonado, S. Fabbri, G. H. Travassos, and M. C. Ferreira. Knowledge-sharing issues in experimental software engineering. *Empirical Software Engineering*, 9(1-2):111–137, 2004.

[29] F. Shull, J. Singer, and D. I. Sjoberg. *Guide to Advanced Empirical Software Engineering*. Springer-Verlag, London, 2008.

[30] I. Sommerville. *Software Engineering*. International computer science series. Addison-Wesley, London, 6th edition, 2001.

[31] T. Stalhane, T. Dingsoyr, G. K. Hanssen, and N. B. Moe. *Post Mortem? An Assessment of Two Approaches*, chapter Empirical Methods and Studies in Software Engineering, pages 129–141. Springer Berlin / Heidelberg, 2003.

[32] F. Tsui and O. Karam. *Essentials of software engineering*. Jones and Barlett Publishers, São Paulo, 6th ed edition, 2007.

[33] C. Wohlin, M. Höst, and K. Henningsson. *Empirical Methods and Studies in Software Engineering*, chapter Empirical Research Methods in Software Engineering, pages 7–23. Springer Berlin / Heidelberg, 2003.

[34] S. Xu and V. Rajlich. Empirical validation of test-driven pair programming in game development. *Computer and Information Science, 5th IEEE/ACIS International Conference on*, 0:500–505, 2006.

Design of Multilingual Participatory Gaming Simulations with a Communication Support Agent

Keisuke Tsunoda
Waseda University Graduate School of Creative
Science and Engineering,
3-4-1 Okubo, Shinjuku-Ku, Tokyo, Japan.
k-tsunoda@cs.mgmt.waseda.ac.jp

Reiko Hishiyama
Waseda University Graduate School of Creative
Science and Engineering,
3-4-1 Okubo, Shinjuku-Ku, Tokyo, Japan.
reiko@waseda.ac.jp

ABSTRACT

People communicating through machine translators cannot tell what the purpose of their communication is or what other people are thinking because of the poor quality of translation services. If they are able to share their understanding within a "common ground" like a communicative or behavioral protocol, they can overcome their difficulties in communication, and we can improve information systems to help them improve mutual understanding. We designed a multilingual participatory gaming simulation, and conducted multilingual gaming experiments with Japanese and Korean participants. We extracted the protocol for conversation with mistranslations from the game logs and designed an agent to support conversation. Then, Japanese and Chinese played it and we observed and analyzed the behaviors of agents and the interaction between players and agents. Consequently, we obtained two main sets of results: (1) an agent function that notified players of the time that had elapsed since the conversation had broken down effectively speeded up their negotiations and achieved more active communications. (2) Tagging by participants was difficult and ineffective in leading to specific protocols and conversations when mistranslations occurred.

Categories and Subject Descriptors

H.5.3 [**Group and Organization Interfaces**]: *Computer-supported cooperative work. Synchronous interaction,*

General Terms

Design, Experimentation, Human Factors.

Keywords

Intercultural collaboration, participatory approach, gaming simulation, language-grid, common ground, communication support.

1. INTRODUCTION

There are numerous intercultural and multilingual collaborations in global businesses, nonprofit organizations (NPOs), and other activities. However, as these involve too many language barriers, many people use machine-translation systems. These people cannot tell what the purpose of communication is or what other people are thinking due to the poor quality of translation services. Nevertheless, if communication is supported through shared knowledge and understanding, participants can overcome mistranslations and continue to communicate with one another. We designed a participatory gaming simulation called "Langrid Gaming" with which we conducted multilingual gaming experiments and extracted conversation protocols. Using these results, we designed an agent to support communication in multilingual collaborations and conducted multilingual gaming experiments with this agent. We analyzed communication logs and interactions between participants and the agent. We also discuss the possibility of multilingual communication and multilingual participatory gaming simulation by minimizing the number of "breakdowns" and disruptions due to mistranslations using the support agent.

2. Related Work

2.1 Coordinator [1]

Winograd and Flores [1] aimed at finding the structures of task-oriented conversations. According to their research, there were communication gaps or disruptions to communication (they called these "breakdowns"). They proposed software called the "Coordinator", which expected "breakdowns", created and prompted conversations, and managed time lags in communication.

Noticeable "breakdowns" are expected to occur in multilingual communication due to mistranslations caused by using machine translators. If "breakdowns" caused by mistranslations occur, another form of communication is needed to rectify these "breakdowns" and guides are useful for more effective communication.

2.2 Studies on multilingual collaboration

Nomura et al. [2] researched the development of collaborative software in an experiment using machine translation with a *Bulletin Board System* (BBS) and a document sharing system. The quality of translations was poor according to their results and assessments, but if systems have functions to confirm translation results, provide re-translations, or give feedback, participants can continue to communicate effectively with one another. It is important for multilingual communication tools to have translation-support systems that repair source statements and tagging systems that enable participants to tag statements by their level of importance or by topic.

Yamashita et al. aimed at finding the differences in conversational efficiency and content, and at shortening referring expressions in a figure-matching experiment using a machine translator [3][4]. The process of shortening referring expressions was disrupted according to their experimental results and conclusions, and participants merely confirmed the meanings of statements.

These previous studies were aimed at the quality of translations or translated statements. However, we consider multilingual communication using a translator to be a conversation chain (protocol) and an aggregate of the communicative process in this paper. Therefore, we analyzed multilingual communication with a macro-view approach. This is because it is likely that analysis of conversations in multilingual collaborations not only needs to take into account mistranslations or categorize statements, but also to consider a "common ground" [5], i.e., the processes of communication and interaction, or speculation about the meaning of mistranslated statements so that multilingual communication support functions can be designed.

2.3 Gaming Simulation [6]

Gaming simulation is a kind of participatory approach where participants play a given role to understand meanings, share real problems, or create and discuss new approaches to solving problems in a shared environment. Many researchers have used gaming simulation for solving global or complex problems such as those with the environment [7][8]. We think that gaming simulation is useful for communication and collaboration in problem-solving, innovation, or design.

In addition, we believe that gaming simulations are useful as the basis of multilingual collaborations because they have designed tasks, rules, and environments that motivate participants toward solving problems and sharing a communicative environment through mutual understanding in gaming simulations.

3. Proposal and Hypothesis

We propose the following hypothesis referring to related work.

Participants can still communicate with one another and participate in gaming simulations when mistranslations due to poor-quality translators if they use communication support.

Figure 1 outlines the environment for the proposed communication model.

Figure 1 Model of proposed communication environment

The process in our hypothesis involved five steps.

Step 1.   We designed the multilingual participatory gaming simulation using the Language-Grid.

Step 2.   Participants, none of whom had the same first language, participated in the gaming simulation. We then extracted the logged data on communication, negotiation, and behavior.

Step 3.   We extracted the protocol that was needed for overcoming mistranslations by analyzing the process of interpreting mistranslations.

Step 4.   Using the results of analysis, we designed an agent to support communication that had the needed functions and could guide a participant's conversation toward an efficient protocol.

Step 5.   We conducted a multilingual collaboration experiment using our gaming simulation with the support agent we designed. We evaluated the agent by using the results obtained by analyzing its behavior and the interaction between participants and the agent.

4. System for experiment

4.1 Language-Grid [9]

We used "Language-Grid" as the basis of machine-translation services. "Language-Grid" is the infrastructure for language services on the Web. Users can wrap an original service using a normalized interface, and use atomic and composite services.

We designed a dictionary service for gaming that contained proper nouns used in the game and designed the composite service using a dictionary and the Kodensha J-server machine translator[1] to maintain the minimum translation quality necessary for gaming. We also connected it to a participatory gaming simulation (Langrid-Gaming).

4.2 Langrid-Gaming

We designed the multilingual participatory gaming simulation using the Language-Grid (Langrid-Gaming) as the basis of multilingual collaboration.

Langrid-Gaming makes it possible to design a multilingual environment for collaboration in which participants use their mother tongue to communicate and interact with one another. We think that the gaming Langrid-Gaming provides is suitable for solving global problems like those concerning the environment and economic gaps. Participants can also understand problems by using their mother tongue through role playing. Researchers can control a participant's target status, rules, resources, and behaviors in the game. Therefore, it is suitable as the basis of multilingual collaboration experiments to enable multilingual communicative interactions to be understood.

[1] http://www.j-server.com/index.shtml

Table 1 Status of countries

Table 1 Status of countries

Country	Money	Taxable income	Land	Extendable land	Increasing demand for food
A	Much	Much	Much	A little	No
B	Much	Much	A little	None	No
C	A little	Medium	Medium	Much	Yes
D	A little	A little	A little	Much	Yes

4.3 Food Education Game

We designed Langrid-Gaming, which participants can participate in on the Web. Figure 2 shows the gaming architecture.

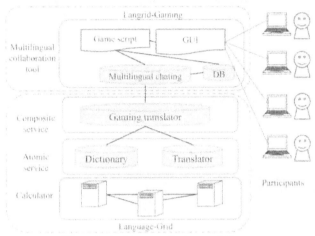

Figure 2 Architecture for Langrid-Game

The theme of the game is the "food problem". Four participants role play countries we called A, B, C, and D. A and B were advanced nations, while C and D were developing countries. They all need food such as crops and meat. They have different prices and quantities for crops, and different environments in which to cultivate them. Table 1 lists details on the default status of these countries.

Participants in the game engage in "raise and support", "food products", "exchange and trade", and "consume food" in turn. If the requirements for winning are completed or the seventh turn ended, the game will be over. Figure 3 shows the flow for this game. One turn contains two phases.

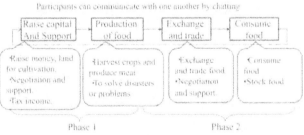

Figure 3 Flow of game

First, each country gets a taxable income in phase 1. Then, participants can extend their land, support others, be supported by others, or decide when to sow seeds to grow crops. They grow two kinds of crops, "wheat" and "corn".

An event may occur at the beginning of phase 2, i.e., a "good harvest", a "bad harvest", "increasing taxable income", "decreasing taxable income", "emergency food aid", or "emergency monetary aid". If any of these happen, they must solve it collaboratively. They must pay monetarily or send food to continue the game especially in "emergencies". If this is impossible, the game is over.

In phase 2, participants produce "meat" to consume "corn". They can also communicate, negotiate, exchange, and trade with one another for food and money. They consume the food at the end of phase 2.

There are three parameters in this game, i.e., the "hunger level", "trust", and "stability" to determine who will win or lose. They are the participants' targets in this game.

The "hunger level" indicates the hunger status in that country. If a country does not have enough food, it gets one "hunger level" point. As the total "hunger level" increases, the number of "emergencies" increases.

"Trust" indicates the trust level for that country. If all countries have enough food, each country gets one "trust" point. If the "trust" points amount to five, advanced countries (A and B) would win. Therefore, it is important for advanced countries to not only get enough food, but also to support other countries and prevent a lack of food.

"Stability", which only developing countries have, indicates wealth from food. If a country has enough food, it gets one "stability" point but if not, it gets none. Therefore, it is important for developing countries to obtain sufficient food.

The main feature of this game is the difference in the resources or environments of the countries [10]. Therefore, they need to communicate with one another to trade or give support to solve problems and hunger through multilingual chatting. The user interface for Langrid-Gaming is Web-based, as seen in Figure 4. It can be divided into three basic components: a frame that displays chatting, a frame that displays user conditions, and a frame that enables the participant's decisions to be to input.

5. Experiment 1

5.1 Settings

We conducted Experiment 1 with this game system. The participants were two Japanese native speakers and two Korean native speakers (not bilingual). Because Japanese-Korean translators have better quality translations, we thought that the game would be more successful by using one of these. Figure 5 has a photograph of the setting used for the experiment. The roles of the participants in the game were randomly determined and they did not know which role they would play or for which country. In the all experiments in this study, participants play Langrid Gaming using laptop computers in the same room, and we asked them not to communicate each other without chatting. Before the experiment, we briefly instructed them on negotiations using hints. We started from "proposal" or "request" and finally ended with "agree" or "disagree". The roles they were randomly assigned in Experiment 1.

In this paper, we conducted gaming experiments twice in each experiment, Experiment 1 and 2. Because in a game, a lot of communications and negotiation processes occur, therefore we think that a pair of experiments is enough to give us the log data and we can analyze communications and negotiations in Langrid-Gaming.

Figure 4 Langrid-Gaming interface

Figure 5 Participants in Experiment 1

After the experiment, a Japanese native speaker and a Korean native speaker, who also understood Japanese, together created a "source thread" and a "translated thread" for each statement. To compare these threads, we determined whether a statement contained a mistranslation. A "source thread" means the speaker could tell the original meaning of the statement, and a "translated thread" means the translated meaning that would be read by speakers of different languages.

5.2 Tagging with "DAMSL" [11]

We referred to the Dialog Act Markup in Several Layers (DAMSL) framework to tag and classify statements. DAMSL is a framework for tagging human task-oriented statements. DAMSL has a hierarchal structure and has four broad categories.

- Communicative-status: Clarification of meaning and completion.
- Information Level: Relations between task and statement.
- Forward-communicative Function: Influence of participant's behavior before this statement.
- Backward-communicative Function: Influence of participant's behavior after this statement.

In this paper, we focused on the "forward-communicative-function" and the "backward-communicative-function" because we focused on mistranslations and the protocol that overcomes mistranslations in the flow of communication. We selected seven tags for tagging and analysis.

- Forward-communicative Function
  - Info-Request (IR)
  - Action Directive (AD)
  - Offer
- Backward-communicative Function
  - Accept
  - Reject
  - Signal non-understanding (SNU)
  - Answer: Other response.

5.3 Results of Experiment 1

5.3.1 Mistranslations

There were 438 statements in the two experiments in which the four participants (two Japanese and two Koreans) participated. There were 49 mistranslated statements in these results, which represented about 10 percent of the total of 438 statements. Table 2 lists details on the statements and mistranslated statements.

Table 2 Statements in Experiment 1

	1st	2nd	Total
Number of statements	146	292	438
Number of mistranslated statements	29	20	49

To determine whether a statement contained a mistranslation, we created a "source thread" and a "translated thread". Figure 6 shows examples of a "source thread" and a "translated thread" in Japanese and English, which have been analyzed in English.

First, we created two threads and prepared two statements in them for each statement. If the two threads had different meanings, we discussed whether the receiver could understand the meaning of the source thread by reading the translated thread, and determined whether a mistranslation had occurred.

The results from tagging indicated that there were many "AD" statements in monolingual and multilingual statements.

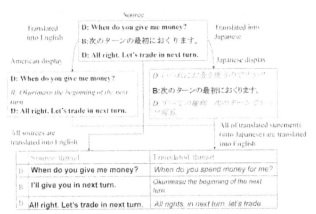

Figure 6 Source thread and translated thread*

*The *italics* font means translated statements. The **bold** font means source statements.

5.3.2 Tagging with DAMSL

To obtain these results, we tagged the following DAMSL-based tags. Table 3 lists the results from tagging. A statement may have more than two tags.

The table shows there are more statements tagged "AD" and "Offer" than the others. It was important in this game to demand support and negotiation to play it. Statements in multilingual communication contained "SNU" caused by mistranslation.

Table 3 Results of tagging

Tag	Statements in monolingual communication	Statements in multilingual communication
AD	94	152
Offer	50	112
IR	21	35
Accept	29	71
Reject	11	9
Answer	64	109
SNU	0	4

6. Analysis and discussion

6.1 Negotiation protocols

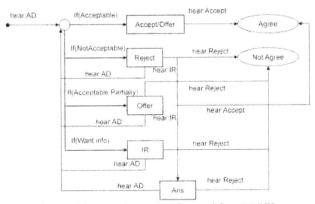

Figure 7 Negotiation protocol started from "AD"*

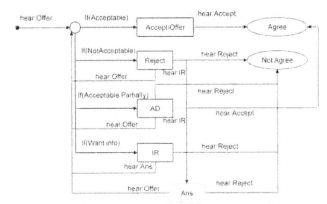

Figure 8. Negotiation protocol started from "offer"*

* The ellipses mean goals, the rectangles mean receiver's behaviors. "hear: XXX" means the receiver heard the speaker say XXX.

The results obtained from tagged statements indicated that the negotiation process tended to start from "AD" or "offer", and negotiation continued as outlined in Figures. 7 and 8, which show the flow for the negotiation protocol viewed by a receiver. They indicate that after "AD" or "Offer", if the receiver wanted to "accept" or "reject", he/she would say so. If he/she wanted to partially accept, partially reject, wanted more information ("IR") or "Offer", he/she would state "IR", "offer", or "AD".

6.2 Patterns of responses to mistranslations

According to the debriefing we had with the participants after the experiment, some said that, if mistranslations occurred, they tried to reflect the meaning of the speaker or guessed his/her meaning to continue to play the game. Therefore, we analyzed situations when mistranslations occurred and what receivers did. Table 5 lists the results obtained from analysis, where "if (not understandable)" was determined by communications before and after the misunderstanding occurred. Therefore, if there seemed to be contradiction in the meaning of the communications or the receiver tried to reflect the meaning the speaker, the statement was tagged "if (not understandable)". In contrast, if statements were not tagged "if (not understandable)", there were no discrepancies in the communications. Also, "if (re-heard: AD)" meant that the receiver heard the same meaning "AD" again. "If (have done xxx)" meant that the receiver had done "xxx" before he/she heard the statements.

If we focus on the receiver's response to mistranslations, SNU only occurred four times. If a receiver heard a mistranslation, they responded with "accept", "reject", or "IR" to successfully communicate and negotiate by guessing. Participants said that they guessed the meaning of mistranslation in the debriefing. Table 4 shows that many mistranslations have "if (understandable)" because it seemed the receiver has guessed or understood the meaning.

Focusing on the response to mistranslated "AD", if a receiver had heard mistranslated "AD", he/she repeatedly heard the same or a similar meaning of "AD" after that. Therefore, they overcame mistranslation in repetitious communications and negotiations. Figure 9 shows the protocol for negotiation started from "AD" with mistranslations.

Table 4 Patterns of responses to mistranslations

Input	Conditional	Response	Frequency	Response time (sec)
Heard: AD	If (have made offer)	Offer	1	71
	If (have heard: AD) And (do not need IR)	Offer	1	65
	If (have heard: AD) And (do not need IR) And (partially acceptable)	Accept	2	25, 58
	If (Acceptable)	Accept	4	35, 47, 43, 91
	If (Re-heard: AD) And (Acceptable)	Accept	4	77, 73, 93, 70
	If (Re-heard: AD) And (not understandable)	SNU	1	61
	If (have done Ac)	Offer	1	27
	If (not acceptable) And (understandable)	Reject	1	14
Heard: IR		Ans	3	41, 106, 68
	If (not understandable)	SNU	1	36
Heard :offer	If (not understandable)	No res	1	
	If (not understandable) And (want IR)	IR	1	243
	If (want AD)	AD	1	8
	If (Acceptable)	Accept	1	175
Heard: SNU	If (have made offer)	Offer	1	33
		Ans	1	27
	(Have not accepted former AD)	Reject	1	70

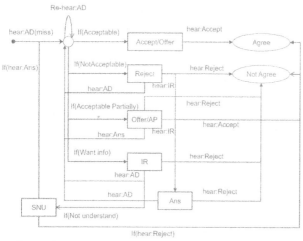

Figure 9 Protocol for negotiation started from "AD" with mistranslations

It shows where there was "no response" (No res) for mistranslations. It seemed that the receiver could not guess the meaning and neither the receiver nor speaker made any effort to overcome the mistranslation.

The response time was distributed from 14 to 243 sec but most of this was distributed from 30 to 90 sec. If participants overcame mistranslation in negotiation, the response-time distribution was about 60 sec. Therefore, if there were supporting functions for participants to rapidly overcome mistranslations in negotiation and communication, they could communicate effectively and the response time could be shortened.

It seemed possible for participants to guess and overcome mistranslations in repetitious negotiations and communications if they had a shared understanding and environment. Therefore, it seemed possible to overcome lapses in communication and long response times by using supporting functions that speeded negotiation and notified them about responses.

7. Design of agent to support communication

The previous results suggested two necessary items for support.

● Management to speed up communication and negotiation even if mistranslations occurred.

● Support for participants to guess the meaning of mistranslations to be able to communicate and negotiate effectively.

We propose four functions that will satisfy these two items to realize smoother Langrid Gaming.

Time management

To prevent breakdowns or lapses in communication, we need to shorten the time it took participants to succeed in negotiation and communication. Therefore, a useful function for smoothing communication and ensuring that it continued was to manage the response time of the receiver, display the time, and notify participants that breakdowns and lapses in communication would occur when there were no responses given to the receiver.

Speed up communication

The results and discussion below suggested that participants can overcome mistranslations if they actively communicate and negotiate with one another. Therefore, to accomplish successful communication, it is useful to propose and recommend the next receiver's behavior such as "reflect" and "re-propose" if there is no communication over a defined period of time since the last communication occurred.

Tagging statements

It is useful to use meaning tags to support the meanings of mistranslations being guessed at. We propose a function where participants tag self-statements in communication if it is impossible to tag these automatically.

7.1 Support agent

From the results and discussion of Experiment 1, we designed a communication support agent that had four functions.

- Observe the time that has passed since the last communication spoken by each participant.

- Offer participants the opportunity to tag self-statements, which contain the meaning and for whom, when they input a statement.

- Display a message that urges participants to communicate and negotiate if there has been no communication for more than 60 sec.

- If there have been no responses for more than 20 sec to statements where the meaning was tagged for a particular participant, display and recommend the next participant's behavior.

Figure 10 shows the flow for the behavior of the agent. Table 5 lists the behaviors to recommend.

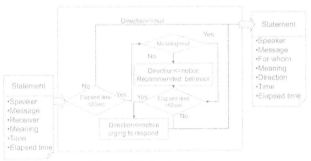

Figure 10 Behavior of agent

Table 5 Behaviors to recommend

Meaning tag	Recommended behavior
Action directive	Accept or reject.
Offer	Accept or reject
Info request	Answer.
Accept	Accept, reject, or act
Answer	Continue negotiation
Reject	Other action directive
Signal non-understandable	Explain meanings

8. Experiment 2 (with agent)

Two Japanese native speakers and two Chinese native speakers participated in the same game in Experiment 2 because it is generally believed that the quality of Japanese-Chinese translators is worse than that of Japanese-Korean translators. It was therefore more useful to research and experiment on the agent using a Japanese-Chinese translator. Before the experiment, we instructed the participants on rules and how to tag meaning tags, and asked them to tag self-statements.

After the experiment, we and a Chinese native speaker created the "source thread" and "translated thread" together and analyzed mistranslations with the same rules as in Experiment 1. We also analyzed the responses to mistranslated statements, the response times, and the influence of the support agent on the experiment.

9. Results of Experiment 2
9.1 Mistranslations

We conducted two experiments and obtained the logs for 394 statements from them.

Table 6 Statements and mistranslated statements in Experiment 2

	1st	2nd	Total
Number of statements	91	303	394
Number of mistranslated statements	14	34	48

Table 6 lists the number of statements and mistranslated statements. 48 of the statements contain mistranslations.

9.2 Tagged by participants and tagging with DAMSL

We and the Chinese native speaker (who also spoke Japanese) tagged the statements in Experiment 2 following the same rules as in Experiment 1 if speakers had not tagged self-statements. Tables 7 and 8 list the results obtained from tagging. They indicate that statements tagged by participants accounted for only 6.7 % of all statements. Therefore, in real-time collaboration like that in this game, participants merely tag statements.

Table 7 Results of tagging in Experiment 2 (monolingual communication)

	Self tagging	Our tagging	Total
AD	1	42	439
Offer	7	22	29
Accept	0	18	187
Reject	0	6	6
IR	2	16	18
SNU	0	1	1
Answer	6	51	57
Total	16	156	172

Table 8 Results of tagging in Experiment 2 (multilingual communication)

	Self tagging	Our tagging	Total
AD	1	88	89
Offer	5	42	47
Accept	0	17	17
Reject	0	14	14
IR	2	33	35
SNU	1	8	9
Answer	6	77	83
Total	15	279	294

Table 9 Responses to mistranslated statements in Experiment 2

Input	Response	Passed time(sec)	Frequency	Matching response and recommended behavior
AD	Of	7	1	
	IR	3	1	1
	Accept	104	1	
	AD	73, 152, 89, 22, 44	5	
	No response	-	1	
	Re AD	58, 215, 54, 153, 95	5	5
	Answer	100	1	
Of	Reject	100	1	
	SNU	84, 51, 41, 37, 7	5	5
	No response	-	1	
IR	Answer	57	1	
	Re AD	250	1	
Accept	SNU	71	1	1
	Answer	36	1	
	Answer	39	1	
Reject	AD	90	1	
	SNU	13, 527	2	2
Answer	Offer	314	1	
SNU	Answer	42	1	1
	Reject	35	1	
	No response	-	1	
	Re AD	95	1	1
Total			35	16

Table 10 Distribution of response times

	Lighting up rate(%)	Response rates after lighting up(%)
With mistranslation	45.71	62.5
Without mistranslation	27.43	58.33
Total	30.48	59.38

10. Discussion

10.1 Responses to mistranslations and urging of behaviors

The agent urged the receiver to undertake recommended behaviors. Table 9 lists pairs of response behaviors for mistranslations and recommended behaviors. In the table, "Re" means that a speaker has spoken again unless the receiver has responded.

Table 9 shows that 16 responses to mistranslations coincided with recommended response behaviors. However, the agent merely urged the participants to respond with the recommended behavior because participants merely had tagged self-statements. Therefore, auto-tagging is required to urge participant's to undertake behaviors.

10.2 Response times and urging participants to communicate

The agent urged participants to communicate or negotiate if 60 sec has passed. Therefore, we classified response times into three categories.

- Less than 60 sec: The agent did not light up.
- From 61 to 120 sec: Participants started to communicate or negotiate again within 60 sec after the agent had lit up.
- More than 121 sec: The agent lit up and participants did not communicate.

Figure 11 shows the distribution of response times and that about 90 % of statements were responded to in less than 120 sec.

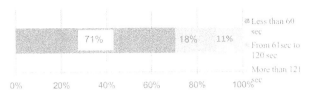

Figure 11 Distribution of response times

Table 10 lists the agent's lighting up rate for the function urging participants to communicate after 90 sec has passed and the participants' response rates after the agent lit up.

The table shows the lighting up rate is about 30% and the response rate is 60%. According to Miyabe[12], people will wait for a message during translated text-based chats less than 120 seconds. Therefore, this suggested that the agent is useful for urging participants to communicate and negotiate actively on various levels. The rates are relatively high especially when mistranslations occurred.

11. Conclusion

We obtained two main results. First, the agent function that notified participants of the time that had elapsed since communication and negotiation had broken down and discontinued was useful for encouraging active communication and negotiation. Second, tagging by participants was difficult, and it was ineffective in leading them to specific protocols or behaviors when mistranslations occurred.

We need more effective support for communication when mistranslations occur in future work, for example, when multi-facilitation agents communicate with one another and in managing the behaviors and communications of participants.

12. REFERENCES

1. T. Winograd and F. Flores: Understanding Computers and Cognition: A New Foundation for Design, Addison-Wesley Professional, U.S, 1987.

2. S. Nomura, T. Ishida, N. Yamashita, M. Yasuoka, and K. Funakoshi. Open Source Software Development with Your Mother Language: Intercultural Collaboration Experiment. *International Conference on Human-Computer Interaction (HCI-03)*, Vol. 4, pp. 1163–1167, 2002.

3. N. Yamashita and T. Ishida: "Effects of Machine Translation on Collaborative Work," *Proceedings of ACM Conference on Computer Supported Collaborative Work (CSCW'06)*, pp. 515–524, 2006.

4. N. Yamashita, R. Inaba, H. Kuzuoka, and T. Ishida "Difficulties in Establishing Common Ground in Multiparty Groups Using Machine Translation," *Proceedings of ACM Conference on Human Factors in Computing Systems (CHI'09)*, pp. 679–688, 2009.

5. H. H. Clark: "Arenas of Language Use", The University of Chicago Press, U.S, 1992.

6. R, D. Duke: GAMING: THE FUTURE'S LANGUAGE, New York: Sage Publications, U.S, 1974.

7. M. E. Camargo, P. R, Jacobi and R. Ducrot, Role-playing games for capacity building in water and land management: Some Brazilian experiences, *Journal of Simulation and Gaming*, Vol. 38, No.4, pp472-493, 2007.

8. K. Günter and L. Johannes, Validation of Simulation: Patterns in the Social and Natural Sciences, *Journal of artificial societies and social simulation*, Vol. 8, No.4, *http://jasss.soc.surrey.ac.uk/8/4/3.html* , 2005.

9. T. Ishida, "Language Grid: An Infrastructure for Intercultural Collaboration", *IEEE/IPSJ Symposium on Applications and the Internet (SAINT-06)*, pp. 96--100, 2006.

10. M. Nestle, E. Millstone and T. Lang: "The Atlas of Food: Who eat what, Where and Why", Earthscan Publications Ltd., U.K, 2005.

11. M. Core and J. Allen: Coding Dialogs with the DAMSL Annotation Scheme, *Working Notes in AAAI Fall Symposium on Communicative Action in Humans and Machines 1997*, pp. 28-35, 1997.

12. Mai Miyabe and Takashi Yoshino: How long will people wait for a message during text-based chats?. *The Fifth International Conference on Collaboration Techonologies*, pp.48–55, 2009.

Solar Scramble: an Educational Children's Game for Collaborative Multi-touch Digital Tabletops

Ashley R. Kelly*
Department of English
Language & Literature
arkelly@uwaterloo.ca

James R. Wallace
Department of Systems
Design Engineering
jrwallac@uwaterloo.ca

Katie Cerar
Department of Systems
Design Engineering
kcerar@uwaterloo.ca

Neil Randall†
Department of English
Language & Literature
nrandall@uwaterloo.ca

Phillip McClelland
Department of Systems
Design Engineering
pjmcclel@uwaterloo.ca

Amanda Mindy Seto
Department of Systems
Design Engineering
amkseto@uwaterloo.ca

ABSTRACT

Our experience report describes the design and development of an educational game for interactive, multi-touch tabletop displays. The game has been designed for children aged 5-10 on the SMART Tabletop platform. This experience report describes the process, design and development of our application and the implications we have drawn from this work in the design of educational technologies for interactive multi-touch tabletops. To investigate the effectiveness of our design, and to identify potential issues in deploying our software, we conducted participant interviews. Based on our design and development process, as well as our participant feedback, we have identified several key issues regarding the development of educational software for K-5 aged (5-10 years old) children on digital tabletops. This research was conducted at the University of Waterloo jointly by the Collaborative Systems Laboratory and the Critical Media Lab.

Categories and Subject Descriptors

H.5.2 [**Information Systems**]: Information Interfaces and Presentation— *User Interfaces*

General Terms

Design, Human Factors, Theory

---

*All authors are from the University of Waterloo, 200 University Avenue, Waterloo, Ontario, Canada N2L 3G1.

†Dr. Neil Randall is the Acting Director of the Critical Media Lab.

Keywords

Tabletop displays, digital tabletops, interactive surfaces, educational games

1. INTRODUCTION

The software application, a game, that we present in this paper, was created as an educational tool to assist in teaching the order of planets in the Solar System to K-5 students. Our game, which we titled "Solar Scramble," has been designed as a collaborative, interactive game on a multi-touch digital tabletop system produced by SMART Technologies, Inc., and was originally created as a submission for the SMART Table Application Design Contest at the 2009 *ACM International Conference On Interactive Tabletops And Surfaces*.

Our application was designed and implemented through a cross-disciplinary venture between the Collaborative Systems Laboratory (CSL), part of the Faculty of Engineering, and the Critical Media Lab (CML), part of the Faculty of Arts, at the University of Waterloo. Throughout the project, our teams came together to design and evaluate Solar Scramble by integrating our disciplinary knowledge of collaborative tabletop design and interaction, game studies, and pedagogy.

The interface and interactions were designed using an iterative design method that moved from initial requirements gathering stages to the final game implementation. The final game was then evaluated through feedback from the 2009 ITS SMART Tabletop Competition, and through an ethics-approved group interview with children's education experts. The feedback elicited from these evaluations provides a better understanding of how Solar Scramble might prove valuable in different educational contexts, and in which ways it could be improved or enhanced. This information, in turn, provides a better understanding of how educational games for the interactive digital tabletops should be designed to maximize their educational value. Finally, this understanding allowed us to propose a number of design guidelines that should provide assistance to designers of future interactive digital tabletop systems for educational use.

2. SOLAR SCRAMBLE

As noted, Solar Scramble was initially developed for the 2009 ITS SMART Tabletop Competition, where it won the interest of SMART Technologies, Inc. Subsequently the software was demonstrated at BETT 2010 (an educational technology exhibition), held in London, UK. The game was designed to explore the relationship between the tabletop platform and educational games. SMART tables provided a suitable development platform as they are designed specifically for children. Indeed, the tables are designed for children, standing only 65.4 cm with a length of 91.5 cm and a width of 74 cm. Additionally, the exterior is made of resilient plastics that are both water and scratch resistant. SMART Technologies Inc.'s products, including the table and digital whiteboards, are marketed to Canadian elementary schools as learning aids.

While the classroom is the typical learning space for SMART tables, we saw a new context for the interactive tabletops in science centres and museums. With the assistance of the Waterloo Regional Children's Museum we were able to better understand the design requirements of educational software on digital tabletops for use in museums or science centres. It is important to note that the Children's Museum exhibits are complementary to the elementary school curriculum in Ontario, Canada. By exploring both the classroom context, through the Ontario Ministry of Education's curriculum, and the museum or science centre context, through the Waterloo Regional Children's Museum, we were able to approach the design and pedagogical concerns of educational games from multiple perspectives.

2.1 Game Play

Solar Scramble, as the name would suggest, is related to the ordering of planets in the Solar System. The narrative begins when an alien ship enters the Solar System, enticing children to "Catch me if you can!" The ship, when pressed, hurdles towards the planets and crashes in to them, subsequently knocking the planets from their respective orbits. With the planets disorderedly floating about the screen, the alien then prompts the children to "Put the planets back in order" (see: Figure 1).

Instructions are displayed on all four sides of the table to ensure visibility and promote collaboration. Children can interact with the game by dragging and dropping the planets to their respective orbits by touch interaction. Each planet is labeled with its name around its circumference to help children identify each planet. Because the SMART table supports multi-touch, multiple children can play the game at the same time, hence the multiple orientations.

When a planet is placed on its correct orbit, the orbit lights up momentarily and the planet becomes fixed to its orbit; it can no longer be interacted with or moved. If a planet is placed on an incorrect orbit, the planet shakes on the spot, a message is displayed around the planet indicating that it is "Incorrect," and the planet flies around the screen. These multiple reactions were implemented to provide redundant, yet playful, feedback. To help reduce frustration in the case of multiple errors, after four incorrect matches, a mnemonic is momentarily displayed on the screen - "Martha Visits Every Monday and Just Stays Until Noon." The purpose of the mnemonic is to provide a hint to the children about the order of the planets. Similar to how the instructions were displayed, the mnemonic is also

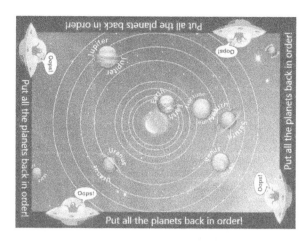

Figure 1: Screen shot of initial game state.

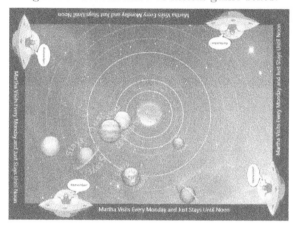

Figure 2: Game with mnemonic, provided after four errors.

displayed on all four sides of the display. As the mnemonic is displayed, the labels of each planet momentarily change to match its respective word in the mnemonic (i.e., Mercury changes to "Martha"). When all of the planets have been placed on their correct orbit, each orbit consecutively lights up and the planets start to orbit around the sun. This animation was implemented to provide positive feedback to the children and to promote a feeling of accomplishment.

The game features two levels: in the first level, children are only presented with the four inner planets (i.e., Mercury, Venus, Earth and Mars) and in the second level, children are presented with all eight planets; both levels are played using the same rules and interactions. Levels were designed to help children learn in stages, allowing them to master part of the content first. Level two can only be played after successfully completing level one.

3. METHODS

3.1 Design Methods

The design team is a multidisciplinary group composed of systems design engineers and rhetoricians. Our engineers are all members of CSL and have experience in both tabletop design and interaction. Our rhetoricians, from the CML, include Dr. Neil Randall, who is an expert in design of communication as well as game studies. Combining our efforts, with both groups coming from already interdisciplinary fields, was fairly seamless, even in the integration of methods of analysis, which blended semi-structured and group interviews.

Drawing inspiration from an upcoming exhibit about space exploration from the Canadian Space Agency at the Waterloo Regional Children's Museum, the team decided on the theme of the Solar System. The topic of space also fit with the Ontario Ministry of Education Elementary school curriculum for grades 5 and 6. The game, Solar Scramble, was designed to make the learning of the planet ordering in the Solar System more interactive and attractive to children.

Solar Scramble was written using SMART's Table Software Development Kit (SDK) in the C# programming language. The SMART SDK supports multi-touch interaction functionality through a provided set of widgets, allowing software developers to focus more closely on game mechanics and the look-and-feel of their application. Using the SDK, we rapidly developed a high-fidelity prototype of the game, and iterated on its design by adding features and fine-tuning interaction within the application. During this iterative design phase we conducted evaluations to identify as many interaction design issues as possible, which were then addressed through revisions to the game's interface.

Using an iterative approach, an initial prototype that simply demonstrated the concept and functionality of the game was developed and presented to the University of Waterloo Human Factors group for feedback. Responses from this focus group influenced the second iteration of design and development. In the second prototype, the graphics and design were refined and the full functionality of the game was implemented. Finally, the fully-functioning prototype was presented to a number of University of Waterloo students; participants provided informal feedback regarding the overall usability and look-and-feel. These suggestions were taken in to account for the final iteration of the game.

3.2 Evaluation Methods

Initial feedback regarding Solar Scramble was provided by a panel of three judges, with rather disparate backgrounds, including: an elementary school teacher, a user experience designer, and a member of the digital tabletop academic community. The judges were asked to evaluate the game with respect to three dimensions: creativity, educational value, and technical excellence. Following this competition, we gathered additional feedback from children's education experts. Using a semi-structured group interview format, these experts were given an opportunity to freely explore a small collection of simple educational tabletop games, including Solar Scramble, using the SMART table and encouraged to speak aloud any comments or criticisms deemed relevant to the design of such educational activities. Immediately after this session, the experts were asked follow-up questions, examining such topics as children's interaction styles, ways in which an activity can hold a child's interest, and how the rapid evolution of consumer electronics influences children's perceptions of technology.

3.3 Limitations

Our study was designed as a pilot study to begin exploring the difficulties in creating educational games on interactive multi-touch tabletops. As we expected, there are a multitude of issues to consider in the development of such technologies, from the level of interaction to the match with age and provincial curriculum. It was difficult to evaluate the usefulness of the game in a broader educational context as it was tailored to Ontario curriculum, which may be too specific for profitable or, even, sustainable software development.

Furthermore, our participants, while having a variety of educational backgrounds and expertise, were quite limited in number. We would hope to run more extensive and comprehensive studies of the software in the classroom to attempt to account for regional or economic variation in ability and adoption.

Conducting our interviews with groups may also provide different data than individual interviews would yield. Indeed, this is substantial evidence [6] [7] that group-based interviews are markedly different than individual interviews, and, as Mag notes, it should be rather evident that one's thoughts and responses are altered and dependent upon social context [6].

4. PARTICIPANT DISCUSSION

4.1 Group Interview

Of the five participants who were experts in children's education there was considerable consensus in their assessment of Solar Scramble. However, these experts were unable to completely delineate between the software application, Solar Scramble, and the platform that executes the software, the SMART table. Though our interest was primarily in an assessment of the software application itself, the discussion of the relationship between software and hardware is crucial to understanding the context in which Solar Scramble, or its counterparts, will be used. Accordingly we treat some of the issues created by the hardware that will, unsurprisingly, affect the interaction with the software.

Beginning with the hardware, the platform on which the software runs, our children's education experts noted that there was colour variation on the screen, dependent upon the angle at which the screen was viewed. The ideal viewing orientation was from a 90 degree angle, approximately three feet above the table. While the angle at which the table was being view was comfortable for adults, this would certainly become problematic for small children, children well within the age rage for which the application was developed. While there are several games developed for, and included with, the SMART table that do rely on colour for task-completion our application does not–regardless, a noteworthy design consideration.

Another issue related to the platform is the sheer force with which children often interact with technology and, in the case of science centres and museums, exhibits more broadly. One participant noted that "children like to touch things, bash them." (D)[1] but more importantly, another participant noted, "kids think that everything is a touch screen. They've grown up with this technology and will try to interact with all screens as if they're touch-technologies; they even try to interact with plain old TVs this way" (B). Bashing the hardware is, thankfully, a concern addressed by SMART and allows us to focus instead on the children's understanding of touch-technologies as interactive media. It is an advantage that children have come to expect touch-based technol-

---

[1] Group interview participants are labeled A through E.

Figure 3: CSL members with the SMART table, playing Solar Scramble

ogy as they will be willing to, as one participant exclaimed, "touch everything" (C) and test how the technology functions. With that response our question became, "how long would a child interact with this kind of table if left to their own devices?" and the answer moves us into the domain of the software itself.

For our target age range of 5-10, it is expected that children under 8 would be likely engage the software for "some time," according to one of the children's education experts, but it would ultimately "depend on the software itself" (B). In the case of a classroom, explicit instruction and guidance could be provided, but if moved to a science centre or museum the mode of interaction changes: it becomes more exploratory. Some support may be offered, a participant notes, saying that "many exhibits need to be explained, and that influences how long someone will spend there, because if they don't understand how to interact with the exhibit they'll leave" (B). But our users are not limited to children in this case, another participant notes, because "instructions are really for the parents; if the parents don't understand the exhibit they'll feel stupid and leave" (D). As noted in Wallace & Scott (2008) [9], the tabletop presents a highly visible context for errors to occur in, making them more socially significant than errors or confusion with a tradition personal computing device. Explicit instruction, such as our mnemonic, then, may be a useful method for assisting users in progression through the game by providing positive feedback. That is, by providing assistance we help the user correct their error without marking it as a significant failure, as flashing the word "incorrect!" or "Wrong!" might. Additionally, while in a classroom an instructor may be present to assist children, a table presented in an exhibit is significantly more self-contained, isolated, and accordingly requires a more intuitive or explicitly instructional approach than may otherwise be necessary.

It is more than the explicit instruction or intuitive nature of an exhibit that makes it popular; rather, it is what is what can be manipulated that is popular because "children like to touch things and make things happen" (C). Further, competitive or other multi-user games and exhibits are popular with children (D), according our participants, and increased engagement with technology in a multi-user interaction scenario has been noted in previous studies [8]. While this analysis helps us understand how to create popular and well-

used applications it does not fully engage the collaborative or learning aspects of the software. Indeed, one participant admitted that when it comes to games "educational quality is really game-dependent; some are valuable and others are not" (C).

How does Solar Scramble hold up with our education experts? According to one expert, our application is "the best on the table" (E) and that is specifically because it is married to the Ontario Ministry of Education's curriculum. One downside of having the application corresponding to the curriculum is, of course, that the children are very familiar with the subject matter; for example, in the case of Solar Scramble, "grades 4-5 [ages 9-10] can do space in their sleep: they know more about space than anyone" (B.) Perhaps, then, the educational value of such an application comes more easily if targeted to a smaller subset of children who are only beginning their studies in the subject matter; alternatively, more sophisticated, adaptive systems might be developed that increase the level of difficulty based on the user's interaction with it. At present the processing power required for such efforts are severely limited on the SMART table–another concession we must make to the platform itself.

User's interactions will necessarily be shaped by other users as well as the application itself, given the SMART table's collaborative nature, which allows for multiple points of interaction; this design, however, is not always evident to adult users in a museum context. Often parents will assume that an exhibit is for an individual child to interact with, as many are, and for this reason the collaborative nature of the technology must be made explicit (A). However, the children's behaviour being managed by parents, as noted by our participants, means that some children will be left unattended. In some cases children will take a less participatory role and dominate the game play, "take things over" (B). Fleck et al. have drawn out important implications for children's use of collaborative, interactive digital tabletops, arguing that the behaviour one might see as negative is actually much more complex and physical (gestural) behaviour such as blocking can be supplementary to verbal negotiations [2]. Children also exhibit different gestural behaviour than adults, and gender appears to be a factor as well [5]. A detailed treatment of behaviour-related design considerations can be found in Hourcade (2008) and more fully treats the considerations outlined above [3]. It is evident that the mode of interaction for children must be considered in its own right, but so too must the technology.

Perhaps the most interesting of all notes from the children's education experts undermined both the functioning of the hardware and software itself. It was argued that the SMART table, and subsequently, Solar Scramble offered an outmoded experience: "It's difficult," they said, "to find *new* digital exhibits that are actually *new* technology, cutting edge. Kids want to interact with the technologies on a level we're not seeing. For example, with the tables they'd want to be able to paint a picture in the paint program and then print that off and take it with them. The table can't do that level of interaction" (emphasis added, A). What this argument underscores is the profound impact that the platform has on the user's experience with the software, with the educational experience provided by the system as a whole. There is no tangible, physical, take-away for the child who, as has been noted multiple times, loves to touch and to physically interact with objects.

4.2 SMART Competition Feedback

However, the dramatic overhaul of our platform, at this time, is quite beyond our abilities. Judges from the ITS 2009/SMART table application design competition provided us with feedback on the game. Rather than focusing on the platform, attention was given to the software applications themselves. Our application was well-received by the judges who very much liked our design of interaction and implementation of the game in software. The interaction was described as "immediately usable," which, after conducting our group interview where the immediate usability or discovery of usability was noted as highly important, was reassuring indeed. It was in the context of the game that the judges provided some insightful comments, which we would come to see as crucial insight into the development of similar games in this genre.

One note made by a judge was short, but incredibly insightful: "mostly memorization" (*Judge 2*). Other concerns included the fact our planets do not follow an elliptical orbit, or the limited range of the game's application, but the issue of memorization seemed the most damning in our evaluation. While memorization is an important part of learning, this platform is highly collaborative and interactive. Creative play is a highly valuable learning tool and one which the group interviews would suggest is popular with children. Our application failed to use the strengths of the platform, in its current incarnation, by not allowing creative expression in the game. [2]. Indeed, it is not essential that all games provide this kind of creative space, but we feel that to fully explore the context of the digital tabletop in children's educational contexts it is utterly necessary to include elements of creative play.

5. DESIGN CONSIDERATIONS

The following considerations are limited to the discussions elucidated by our pilot study and are necessary at an early stage in their development. However, we believe that the following design considerations begin important discussions in the design, development and deployment of educational games on interactive collaborative surfaces, including multi-touch tabletop displays:

- **Context** is an important consideration in the design of educational games. As identified by Wallace & Scott, and confirmed by our evaluations of Solar Scramble, there are several aspects of context that may influence the appropriateness of a particular design, including the software interface and physical form of the table on which the game will run, the physical space where the game will be located (i.e., ecological considerations), and the educational space the game must act within (i.e., social and cultural considerations).

- **Pedagogical design**, related to the educational space, is a key element for educational games. Designing for young children creates at least two distinct trajectories for educational games: curriculum-bound games and more broadly applicable games designed to develop children's cognitive skills and abilities. Specific pedagogical design will be highly context-dependent,

but the take away from our study is that it is largely overlooked, according to our participants, in game design and must be a more significant element in any design considerations.

- **Educational Instructions**, as noted during our evaluation with the children's education experts, are often included for both parents' and childrens' benefit. The existence of these instructions indicates that designers may focus on providing a simplified, engaging interface that encourages interaction with the software, and that the educational value can be more subtly incorporated into the game mechanics. (e.g., participant *B* argued that games are effective learning tools because "kids will see something fun and flashing and not realize that they're learning").

- **Multi-User Interaction** with collaborative surfaces like the SMART table requires a number of considerations: how many children will be using the table, and how does this impact classroom learning or field trips where tables are not available for all children; what are the norms under which children are socialized for group play (i.e., a classroom vs a public space, or different cultures); are the levels of interaction sufficient (e.g., should the platform be modified to support application development more fully by allowing the creative products of children to be printed or emailed to them); and what is the ideal level of engagement with the application (i.e., is there a clear goal or is the application an open-ended exploratory tool).

- **Re-playability** concerns whether or not the game can be played multiple times. As suggested by our participants, a system adaptive to users' abilities would be ideal. Certain limitations, such as a child mastering the subject, are unavoidable, but there is a necessity in creating games that can progress with the child, in particular when designing curriculum-based games.

6. FINAL REMARKS

Solar Scramble is a singular artefact constructed to explore the genre of educational games on interactive, multi-touch tabletop computers. Standing alone the game offers little exploration of the various pedagogical strategies that might be explored on this developing platform. However, as an artefact, Solar Scramble has offered some important insights into the relationship between the platform, software and educational context. Indeed, our findings underscore the importance of the questions that we asked when approaching this study: 1. How do we craft an educational experience that is tied to a curriculum, yet independently playable? 2. How does the mode of interaction create and constrain the educational content? 3. With multiple contexts (e.g., the classroom, the science centre, etc.) and a significant range in users' age and abilities (e.g., five to ten years old), how can we create an adaptive system that is capable of enriching multiple environments?

While many of the children's educational experts claimed that they saw greater "educational value" in Solar Scramble than some of the other games on the table, we believe this to be due to the relationship of our game to the curriculum that the participants are working with. It became evident in the group interview that creativity is deemed to be a more

---

[2]For an example of creative, collaborative play on shared interfaces please see: Benford et al. (2000) [1] and Hourcade et al. (2004) [4].

valuable product of digital technologies and games that allow for more creative play are not only more fun for children, but offer a better use of the technologies than wrought memorization, which our application is largely based upon.

Lesson we have taken away, lessons that will indeed shape our future work, include: a better blending of creative play and curriculum-based lessons in the applications; greater effort in creative adaptive systems, which are capable of responding to a user's age, skills, and understanding; better integration of the software with the platform and vice versa; finally, a more comprehensive understanding of the pedagogical considerations that must be made for games on collaborative surfaces.

7. ACKNOWLEDGMENTS

We would like to thank everyone in the Critical Media Lab and the Collaborative Systems Lab for their support. Additionally, we would like to thank the Waterloo Regional Children's Museum for their time and feedback. Finally, we would like to thank SMART Technologies for their interest, support, and the hardware that they provided us with for future research. This research is funded in part by the Natural Science and Engineering Council of Canada (NSERC).

8. ADDITIONAL AUTHORS

Stacey D. Scott (Dr. Scott is the Director of the Collaborative Systems Laboratory, Department of Systems Design Engineering, University of Waterloo: s9scott@uwaterloo.ca).

9. REFERENCES

[1] S. Benford, B. B. Bederson, K.-P. Åkesson, V. Bayon, A. Druin, P. Hansson, J. P. Hourcade, R. Ingram, H. Neale1, C. O'Malley, K. T. Simsarian, D. Stanton, Y. Sundblad, and G. Taxén. Designing storytelling technologies to encourage collaboration between young children. The Hague, April 2000. Conference on Human Factors in Computing Systems.

[2] R. Fleck, Y. Rogers, N. Yuill, P. Marshall, A. Carr, J. Rick, and V. Bonnett. Actions speak loudly with words: Unpacking collaboration around the table. Banff, November 2009. In Proceedings of the ACM International Conference On Interactive Tabletops and Surfaces.

[3] J. P. Hourcade. Interaction Design and Children. Now Publishers Inc., Delft, 2008.

[4] J. P. Hourcade, B. B. Bederson, and A. Druin. Building kidpad: an application for children's collaborative storytelling. Software: Practice and Experience, 34(9):895–914, July 2004.

[5] K. Inkpen, K. Booth, M. Klawe, and R. Upitis. Playing together beats playing apart, especially for girls. Bloomington, 1995. In Proceedings of Computer-Supported Collaborative Learning (CSCL'95).

[6] T. May. Social Research: Issues, Methods and Process. Open University Press, Buckingham, 2001.

[7] D. Reilly and K. Inkpen. White rooms and morphing don't mix: setting and the evaluation of visualization techniques. San Jose, April 2007. In Proceedings of the SIGCHI Conference on Human Factors in Computing Systems (CHI '07).

[8] S. Scott, R. Mandryk, and K. Inkpen. Understanding children's collaborative interactions in shared environments. Journal of Computer-Aided Learning, 19(2):220–228, 2003.

[9] J. R. Wallace and S. D. Scott. Contextual design considerations for co-located, collaborative tables. Amsterdam, The Netherlands, October 2008. Proceedings of IEEE Workshop on Tabletop and Interactive Surfaces.

Organizational Wiki as a Knowledge Management Tool

Fernando Sousa
ISCTE
Lisboa - Portugal
fplsa@iscte.pt

Manuela Aparicio
Adetti/ISCTE
Lisboa - Portugal
manuela.aparicio@iscte.pt

Carlos J. Costa
DCTI/ISCTE and Adetti/ISCTE
Lisboa - Portugal
carlos.costa@iscte.pt

ABSTRACT

Knowledge management has an increasing importance in organizations. Not only as a way to capture knowledge, but also to allow the incorporation of knowledge in products and services provided. Wikis are finding their way into organizational departments serving as collaborative tools for knowledge creation. In this paper, we study how an organizational wiki can be used as a knowledge management (KM) tool from the point of view of two KM models.

A survey was conducted in a corporate IT department. It was used to identify the processes of the SECI model and the contexts of the four competencies of a learning organization in which wikis can be used.

Categories and Subject Descriptors

H. Information Systems; H.3 Information Storage and Retrieval, H 3.5 On-Line Information Systems

General Terms

Documentation, Human Factors, Management, Measurement.

Keywords

Knowledge Management, Wiki, SECI, Learning Organization.

1. INTRODUCTION

Knowledge is seen as one of the most important assets in any organization [1]. Although more and more companies have knowledge management (KM) initiatives, they are usually focused in technological solutions, considering only the existence of explicit knowledge and placing it in enterprise portals, disregarding the full benefits of KM [2]. Companies are changing their focus to a more relational, inter-dependent and collaborative approach, using strategies that promote tacit knowledge sharing among employees [3], [4].

KM has focused on knowledge as a process, recognizing that it may be easier and more cost effective to find simple ways to help individuals and groups quickly locate others with relevant knowledge, rather than attempting to codify and catalog

knowledge that may not be needed [5].

Wikis are widely accepted to be valuable tools for successful collaborative knowledge building [6] and are increasingly finding their way into organizational environments, supporting both collaborative knowledge creation and sharing [7], [8], [26]. In this paper, we study how the usage of a wiki in an organizational environment may work as a knowledge management (KM) tool, identifying the processes of the SECI model [9] in which the use of wikis can bring benefits to a business organization, and understanding the extent to which wikis could be used in the contexts of the four competencies of a learning organization [10], [11].

We begin with a theoretical approach to KM, presenting two KM models and how wikis – usage and features – fit these models. Based on these findings, three research hypotheses were defined:

H1: Wikis are irrelevant in the socialization process;

H2: Wikis are predominantly used for internalization;

H3: Wikis are mostly used to diffuse knowledge within the organization.

To test these hypotheses, a survey was carried out amongst wiki users in an IT corporate department. Results on this research are presented and discussed at the end of this paper.

2. KNOWLEDGE MANAGEMENT

In this study we applied two distinct KM models: the SECI model [9] and the four competencies of a learning organization model [11].

2.1 Knowledge Conversion

All organizational knowledge is rooted in tacit knowledge. Yet, as long as tacit knowledge remains the private property of individuals or select groups, the organization cannot multiply its value [12][27].

Nonaka, et al. [9] identifies four different processes in which knowledge is created and transferred, the tacit/ explicit model (SECI).

The SECI model [9] proposes that knowledge is created through the interaction between tacit and explicit knowledge and presents four modes of knowledge conversion: socialization, externalization, combination and internalization.

This model was later extended by [13], giving it a context or shared space where knowledge is created, and then by [1], considering knowledge assets.

Organizations should decide whether their primary KM objective is to capture explicit knowledge, or map tacit knowledge. The first option allows the development of materials that can easily be reused or customized for different purposes; this requires a larger investment for infrastructure, creating, and disseminating, but once materials are developed they can be reused very efficiently. The latter option makes it easy to identify and connect with experts [5].

2.1.1 Socialization

Socialization is the process that people transfer tacit knowledge to tacit knowledge [14].

Transitive memory, the combination of a group's knowledge and awareness of individual's knowledge and skills can help teams to coordinate and apply individual expertise to problems [15].

Many organizations are using electrönic knowledge repositories for improving information reuse and identifying experts within the organization [16]. Wikis can help to create maps or directories of tacit knowledge [5]. Features like recent changes listings, revision history and last version authorship can be accessed by users in order to identify potential experts on specific subjects [16].

An alternative to this process is to access user profile pages where wiki users keep their contacts and specialties, as well as their projects portfolio they were involved in [15], [17].

Therefore, two different angles can be used in order to understand how wikis can be used in the socialization process. From the producer point of view, it is relevant to know if users place their contacts, portfolio and specialties on their profile page. From the consumer standpoint, users can identify specialists and access their contacts through:

- The page last version author [16];

- The page revision history [16];

- The page content, when people involved in that project are referred to [15];

- User profile pages [15].

2.1.2 Externalization

The externalization process converts tacit to explicit knowledge [13].

As organizations seek innovative ways to capture and distribute knowledge, particularly tacit knowledge, many corporate intranets now include wikis to encourage sharing [18]. Wikis are convenient tools for collaborative writing and, consequently, for collaborative production of knowledge [6]. The informal and unstructured nature of wikis makes it ideal to capture tacit knowledge, fact that is corroborated by a case study [16], [5] where 58% and 23% of the company wiki content was in unstructured or semi-structured formats, respectively. This means that wikis are well suited to documenting rapidly changing and growing subjects or sets of information [19].

Previous research mentions that the wiki was used as a repository to exchange ideas, document decisions and rationales, and coordinate project tasks and collaboration [16]. Bring together knowledge from distributed individuals to form a repository of organizational knowledge and to retain information that would

otherwise be lost due to the loss of experience staff is also a concern [17].

With the purpose of understanding how wikis are used in the process of converting tacit to explicit knowledge, the following tasks can be analyzed:

- Adding content to existing pages [8];

- Adding content to new pages [8];

- Making comments on existing pages [8];

- Making small corrections in factual inaccuracies [19];

Concerning the nature of externalized information, here are some examples referred to by [8], [16], [17]:

- Writing information that is not available anywhere else [17];

- Writing information that has no place in organization's formal documents [17];

- Storing meeting minutes [16];

- Storing decisions and their rationale [16];

- Keeping wish lists and ideas to take into account in future projects [8];

- Propose ideas to new products or services [8], [16].

2.1.3 Combination

This knowledge conversion process involves combining different forms and sources of explicit knowledge [1], like documents and computerized data. Reconfiguration of existing information through sorting, adding, combining and categorizing of explicit knowledge can lead to the generation of new and more complex knowledge [9].

Previous research allowed the identification of two main groups of wiki contributors: adders and synthesizers [8]. While the first group had more focus in adding new content, the latter group has more concerns with rearranging existing knowledge executing tasks like:

- Integrating ideas that have been posted onto existing pages [8];

- Reorganizing a set of pages [8];

- Rewriting whole paragraphs [8];

- Generate reports and listings on existing information [1], [20].

2.1.4 Internalization

Internalization is the process that converts explicit to tacit Knowledge [9].

In order for internalization to take place, knowledge has to be assimilated by users [9]. Being wikis essentially used to promote knowledge sharing and reuse [18], it is most likely that it will be primarily used to access externalized knowledge.

As individuals perceive the discrepancy between their own (internalized) knowledge and the information that is available in the wiki (externalized), an advancement of knowledge will take place. Dealing with the wiki's content, adding new information and acquire new knowledge at the same time, a co-evolution of individual and collective knowledge will occur [6].

With the purpose of understanding what drives wiki users to search for information and how they take advantage of available knowledge for internalization, the following scenarios are suggested in the literature:

- To solve the immediate problem they have in hands [16];
- To know how to perform a procedure [16];
- To learn about a procedure [16];
- To know more about a specific subject [19];
- To understand the reasons that lead to a decision being made [16];
- To look for solutions to similar problems they have in hands [19], [21];
- In order to update themselves on a specific subject [19], [21];
- To access information, in general [17], [19], [21].

In the sense of information sources, it might be relevant to understand how the wiki is used:

- As a primary source of information [17];
- As an alternative to formal documents [17];
- In addition to other informal information sources [15], [21].

2.2 Four Competencies of a Learning Organization

Focused in an organizational level, rather than a people perspective of the previous model, the model presented by [10], proposes four competencies that organizations should master in order to manage the knowledge flow: absorption, diffusion, generation and exploitation.

Rather than knowledge itself, it is the combined ability of an organization to handle these competencies that secures true competitive advantage [22].

This model was later extended by [11], where these competencies are regarded as phases in the introduction of KM in an organization, and priority should be given to the first two phases.

2.2.1 Absorption
Absorption is considered to be the process of obtaining new knowledge from outside of the organization [10]. This could be accomplished by having external entities interacting with the organization, such as:

- Customer contacts and feedback [22];
- Supplier co-operation [22];
- Training and workshops [11].

2.2.2 Diffusion
Distributing knowledge among the members of the organization is called diffusion [11]. This seems to include – but is not limited to

– the internalization process of the SECI model presented earlier. Consequently, besides those same items pointed out earlier, we could extend the analysis to consider some additional items:

- Storing meeting minutes [16];
- Sharing knowledge with their team [11], [22];
- Sharing knowledge with the whole organization [11], [22].

2.2.3 Generation
The development of new knowledge and the process of making explicit existing tacit knowledge are considered to be the generation process [11]. This definition suggests that this process is somewhat similar to the externalization and combination processes of the SECI model. As such, in addition to the items presented in the combination process, we consider the following items, included in the externalization process, as contributing to generate new knowledge:

- Writing information that is not available anywhere else [17];
- Writing information that have no place in organization's formal documents [17], [22];
- Storing decisions and their rationale [11].

2.2.4 Exploitation
Exploitation is regarded as the commercialization of knowledge [11], that is, applying knowledge in products and services [10]. Although previous research focused on how to give direction to knowledge strategies [11], we suggest a simpler and direct approach on:

- Keeping wish lists and ideas to take into account in future projects [8];
- Propose ideas to new products or services [8].

3. EMPIRICAL STUDY
This research was made in an IT corporate department where a wiki is in use for about 7 years. As in most cases of wiki adoption in organizations [23], it began by serving only one team of that department and, over the years, its usage spread to other teams of the department.

Only a few teams try to incorporate in their work procedures processes of using the organizational wiki, as the wiki is not yet perceived as a formal corporate tool to support everyday's work activities; as such, most teams still regard wiki usage as optional, although they recognize its advantages and benefits. This wiki currently supports work activities like:

- Software development, including technical documentation, issues tracking, reference information, setup information, configurations, application maintenance and operations;
- Project management, including meeting agendas, status reports, ideas saved for later, standards and practices;
- Technical support, including best practices, customer support information-sharing, software download;
- Ad-hoc collaboration, like hashing out ideas;

- Posting of general information and knowledge management, including vacation schedules, how-tos, best practices, corporate procedures).

There are essentially two sets of wiki users: company's internal resources, like project managers and team leaders, and external resources (outsourcers) that work with the organization on a long-term basis, like software developers, testers and technical support team elements. Both these groups of users are considered to be internal users. Other outsourcers that are only working for the organization for a short period of time. like developers on a small project, do not usually have access to the wiki. This wiki is considered to be for internal use only, which means that neither customers nor suppliers have access to it.

In this paper we try to understand how employees use the wiki in their work processes and to assess whether the wiki may, in fact, be regarded as a valid contribute to KM, identifying the processes of the SECI model in which the use of wikis can bring benefits to a business organization. and understanding the extent to which wikis could be used in the contexts of the four competencies of a learning organization.

Since wikis are not a socialization tools per se (like instant messaging) and given that the studied organization has other alternative and more effective ways of getting all coworkers contacts (not just only wiki users), we propose the following hypothesis:

H1: Wikis are irrelevant in the socialization process.

According to [24], the majority of online communities follow the 90-9-1 rule: 90% of users are lurkers (read but never contribute), 9% contribute occasionally, and 1% of participants contribute most of the content. Although our research is confined to an organizational environment where users may share the same goals, this participation inequity is probably present. As such, it is hypothesized that:

H2: Wikis are predominantly used for internalization.

As referred by [11], the four competencies of a learning organization may be regarded as phases in the introduction of KM in the organization, where the absorption of knowledge and the diffusion among members should precede and have priority over remaining phases.

In our organization, only internal users have access to the wiki. For that reason, the absorption competency is disregarded in this research, and the following hypothesis is defined:

H3: Wikis are mostly used to diffuse knowledge within the organization.

This paper's research process started with literature review on knowledge management and wiki usage as knowledge management tools. This review allowed the creation of a questionnaire to help to understand how an organizational wiki can be used in a knowledge management context, considering two KM models: the SECI [9] model and the four competencies of a learning organization [10], [11] model. This questionnaire was first pre-tested by five former employees. Collected data and feedback allowed for the refinement of the initial questionnaire. A survey was then conducted amongst wiki users in an IT corporate department.

The survey consists of 33 questions, addressing 7 components of the research models (4 for the SECI model, and 3 for the four competencies model). Components from different models may overlap each other.

We asked inquired people to report on the frequency with which they used the wiki for different tasks and scenarios. With the exception of the questions presented in Table 1, all questions used a 1-to-7 Likert scale, 1 being "never" and 7 being "all the time".

The survey was advertised by email to wiki users and through a link placed on top of every wiki page. The 70 respondents from the 5th to the 21st of May of the current year represent about 75% of active wiki users (considering users that accessed the wiki) in that period, with an average of 3 years contributing to the company wiki and an average of 4 years in the current team.

4. RESULTS AND DISCUSSION

As is observable in Table 1, the majority of the respondents has a wiki user profile page where they keep their contacts (65.7%) as well as their specialties and project portfolio (51.4%). Since there is no formalized procedure to ensure that wiki users create and maintain their profile page, these results are satisfactory.

Table 1. Contents available in wiki user profile pages

	Yes	No
Contacts	65.714%	34.286%
Specialties and/or project portfolio	51.429%	48.571%

Table 2 generally illustrates how employees use the organizational wiki in the knowledge conversion processes. These 4 indexes were built with the mean of responses to the questions related to each conversion mode. Cronbach's alpha represents the internal consistency estimate and indicates the degree to which a set of items measures a single unidimensional latent construct, being 0.7 the cutoff value for being acceptable [25].

Table 2. Wikis and knowledge conversion (based in Nonaka, et al. [9])

Socialization	Externalization
Mean: 3.375	Mean: 3.760
Std. Deviation: 1.305	Std. Deviation: 1.132
Cronbach's Alpha: 0.831	Cronbach's Alpha: 0.877
Internalization	**Combination**
Mean: 4.620	Mean: 2.855
Std. Deviation: 0.879	Std. Deviation: 1.307
Cronbach's Alpha: 0.833	Cronbach's Alpha: 0.798

Although only occasionally, results suggest that the wiki is occasionally used for socialization (3 out of 7), which counters the proposed hypothesis H1, where wikis were believed to be irrelevant to this process.

Perhaps in line with findings by [15], despite the ability to freely change wiki content, workers prefer contacting the authors in order to suggest changes rather than altering contents themselves, thus suggesting that wikis can serve as a starting point for socialization, since workers will use them to get in touch with other coworkers, sharing ideas, experiences and suggestions.

Nevertheless, this result could possibly be increased by encouraging users to use profile pages as a knowledge map and thus using the wiki to identify specialists [21]. According to [15], a collection of linked project, process and user pages increases group and individual reputation management and raises awareness of group members expertise.

Somewhat surprising is that externalization processes are not much more frequent than socialization ones. In fact, a paired sample t-test confirms that statistically there is no significant difference between both processes (t(69)=-2.621; p=0.011) [25].

The relatively low externalization results indicate that only a few people contribute knowledge, and there may be a considerable amount of lurkers [24]. This could also be justified by only a few teams of the studied organization have incorporated the process of adding content to the wiki as their day-to-day procedures, seeking content quality enhancement and retaining knowledge that would otherwise be lost or hard to find.

According to [5], if only a few people contribute knowledge, then the system may not be useful, or those few people may become overwhelmed and lose their will to share. On the other hand, a KM system run by a handful of knowledgeable or well-connected brokers might function quite well in some organizations [24].

Unlike users from [8] where two contributing groups stand out – adders (externalization) and synthesizers (combination) – findings suggest that rearranging and reorganizing contents is not a focal point to respondents. However, it is interesting to notice the correlation between these two knowledge conversion processes (Table 3).

Table 3. Knowledge conversion correlations

	Socialization	Externalization	Combination	Internalization
Socialization	-	0.500** sg	0.522** sg	0.484** sg
Externalization	-	-	0.775** sg	0.487** sg
Combination	-	-	-	0.509** sg
Internalization	-	-	-	-

**Correlation is significant at the 0.01 level (2-tailed). sg indicates a statistically significant.

The low frequency of the combination process could indicate that there is no structured or semi-structured contents on the wiki, or may confirm that users avoid changing contents they perceive and being owned by others, and therefore are reluctant in reorganizing it.

Confirming hypothesis H2, wikis seem to be predominantly used for internalization, which means that employees use the organization wiki primarily to access information available.

These results seem to point towards the capturing of explicit knowledge – and consequently its reuse in internalization processes – being the company's primary objective in KM [5].

Figure 1 reflects how this organization's wiki is being used from the four competencies model approach. Once again, these indexes were built with the mean of responses to the questions related to each competency. However, as stated earlier, the absorption process does not apply to the usage that this organization makes of its wiki system. Therefore, only 3 indexes are presented.

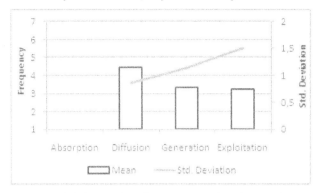

Figure 1. Wikis and the four competencies of a learning organization (based in Sprenger [10])

The internal consistency estimate given by Cronbach's alpha is 0.842, 0.822 and 0.703, for diffusion, generation and exploitation, respectively, thus it is considerable acceptable that the variables in each group are measuring the same underlying attribute [25].

Following phase prioritization referred by [11], the organizational wiki is contributing primarily to knowledge diffusion, as this is the most developed competency (Mean; 4.454; Std. Deviation: 0.858), thus corroborating hypothesis H3.

This phase forms the basis for the generation of new knowledge and the externalization of implicit knowledge [11].

The low frequency of using the wiki in the process of generating new knowledge (Mean: 3.306; Std. Deviation: 1.141) suggest that tacit knowledge is not being externalized as desirable so that it can be subsequently transferred and reused. This may occur since the organizational wiki is not a formal corporate tool, and only a few teams incorporated wiki usage in their work procedures.

This points towards a lot of knowledge remaining implicit in the heads of the coworkers rather than being made explicit which can lead to knowledge of inferior quality or even being wrong, poor problem solving abilities or reinventing the wheel. Thus, it is important that all members be committed to and participate in KM activities.

Considering that this wiki is only used by the IT department of the studied organization, which means that departments like Marketing and Sales are excluded, and that there are other formal channels to propose ideas to new products and services, the exploitation indicator (Mean: 3.228; Std. Deviation: 1.517) does not seem to be a bad result.

In a different scenario, these results could indicate that the wiki was failing on the innovation processes, since existing know-how was not being used for new products or services.

A paired sample t-test confirms that statistically there is no significant difference between generation and exploitation competencies ($t(67)=0.635$; $p=0.528$) [25].

5. FUTURE WORK

As to further develop the work presented in this paper, some sort of refinement or polishing the questionnaire could be done, as later research could be performed in different contexts and organizations where wikis are being used.

Comparing results based on this survey against wiki system logs, which hold information on content creation, editing and viewing, could give a deeper and a more solid perspective on how exactly is the wiki used by organization members, and perhaps help to understand potential differences between system data and users perceived reality.

Additionally, new statistical indicators could be made available in wiki implementations, allowing to distinguish, for example, between externalization and combination processes, as now they represent the same system operation.

Integrating and formalizing wiki utilization in corporate procedures could help to increase wiki usage and adoption to the entire organization, as well as enhance knowledge sharing and reuse.

In this research, we noticed that wikis are used primarily to getting information and not so much to writing it. This suggests that wiki users are still facing some obstacles that are preventing them to take advantage of wikis full potential. Perhaps the wiki markup is too hard to use, or the WYSIWYG editor is not user friendly enough. Other features may be missing and may possibly be developed as plug-ins.

6. CONCLUSION

This study shows how a wiki is being used in an organizational environment and how it is contributing to the knowledge management processes.

We noticed that the internalization process is the prevalent knowledge conversion process as most users access the wiki seeking information.

The wiki also makes it easy to identify specialists through the information available in the system, as the majority of the respondents tend to maintain their contacts and portfolio updated in their profile pages. This tool enables the socialization process as users can easily exchange ideas, experiences and suggestions.

The combination process is regarded as the least relevant for members of this organization. This means that externalized knowledge is rarely rearranged and combined with other sources of externalized knowledge and there may be the need to structure some knowledge available in the wiki.

As for the competencies of a learning organization, diffusion of knowledge within the organization is the most developed one, and efforts must be made in order to promote generation of new knowledge through the conversion from tacit to explicit knowledge.

7. ACKNOWLEDGMENTS

Partially financed by The Fundação para a Ciência e a Tecnologia (FCT), Portuguese Ministry of Science, Technology & Higher Education.

8. REFERENCES

[1] Nonaka, I., Toyama, R., & Konno, N. (2000). SECI, Ba and Leadership: a Unified Model of Dynamic Knowledge Creation. *Long Range Planning, 33*(1), 5-34. doi:10.1016/S0024-6301(99)00115-6

[2] Chen, M., & Chen, A. (2006). Knowledge management performance evaluation: a decade review from 1995 to 2004. *J. Inf. Sci., 32*(1), 17-38.

[3] Chou, T., Chang, P., Tsai, C., & Cheng, Y. (2005). Internal learning climate, knowledge management process and perceived knowledge management satisfaction. *Journal of Information Science, 31*(4), 283-296. doi:10.1177/0165551505054171

[4] Parise, S. (2007). Knowledge Management and Human Resource Development: An Application in Social Network Analysis Methods. *Advances in Developing Human Resources, 9*(3), 359-383. doi:10.1177/1523422307304106

[5] Kussmaul, C., & Jack, R. (2009). Wikis for Knowledge Management: Business Cases, Best Practices, Promises, & Pitfalls. In *Web 2.0* (pp. 1-19). Retrieved from http://dx.doi.org/10.1007/978-0-387-85895-1_9

[6] Harrer, A., Moskaliuk, J., Kimmerle, J., & Cress, U. (2008). Visualizing wiki-supported knowledge building: Co-evolution of individual and collective knowledge. In *Proceedings of WikiSym'08 - International Symposium on Wikis 2008*. New York: ACM Press.

[7] Müller, C., Meuthrath, B., & Baumgraß, A. (2008). Analyzing Wiki-based Networks to Improve Knowledge Processes in Organizations. *Journal of Universal Computer Science, 14*(4), 526-545.

[8] Majchrzak, A., Wagner, C., & Yates, D. (2006). Corporate wiki users: results of a survey. In *Proceedings of the 2006 international symposium on Wikis* (pp. 99-104). Odense, Denmark: ACM. doi:10.1145/1149453.1149472

[9] Nonaka, I., & Takeuchi, H. (1995). The Knowledge-Creating Company: How Japanese Companies Create the Dynamics of Innovation. Oxford University Press, USA.

[10] Sprenger, C. (1995). *Four Competencies of the Learning Organisation.* 's-Gravenhage: Delwel.

[11] Kerkhof, C., Ende, J. V. D., & Bogenrieder, I. (2003). Knowledge management in the professional organization: a model with application to CMG software testing. *Knowledge and Process Management, 10*(2), 77-84. doi:10.1002/kpm.167

[12] Choo, C. W., & Bontis, N. (2002). *The Strategic Management of Intellectual Capital and Organizational Knowledge* (1st ed.). Oxford University Press, USA.

[13] Nonaka, I., & Konno, N. (1998). The Concept of "Ba": Building a Foundation for Knowledge Creation. *California Management Review, 40*(3), 1-15.

[14] Nonaka, I. (1994). A Dynamic Theory of Organizational Knowledge Creation. *ORGANIZATION SCIENCE, 5*(1), 14-37. doi:10.1287/orsc.5.1.14

[15] Munson, S. A. (2008). Motivating and Enabling Organizational Memory with a Workgroup Wiki. In *WikiSym'08*. Presented at the WikiSym'08, Porto: ACM.

[16] Chau, T., & Maurer, F. (2005). A case study of wiki-based experience repository at a medium-sized software company. In *Proceedings of the 3rd international conference on Knowledge capture* (pp. 185-186). Banff, Alberta, Canada: ACM. doi:10.1145/1088622.1088660

[17] Chau, T., Maurer, F., & Melnik, G. (2003). Knowledge Sharing: Agile Methods vs. Tayloristic Methods. In *Proceedings of the Twelfth International Workshop on Enabling Technologies: Infrastructure for Collaborative Enterprises* (p. 302). IEEE Computer Society. Retrieved from http://portal.acm.org/citation.cfm?id=939783

[18] Dave, B., & Koskela, L. (2009). Collaborative knowledge management—A construction case study. *Automation in Construction*, *18*(7), 894-902. doi:10.1016/j.autcon.2009.03.015

[19] West, J. A., & West, M. L. (2008). Using Wikis for Online Collaboration: The Power of the Read-Write Web. Jossey-Bass.

[20] Hasan, H., & Pfaff, C. C. (2006). The Wiki: an environment to revolutionise employees' interaction with corporate knowledge. In *Proceedings of the 18th Australia conference on Computer-Human Interaction: Design: Activities, Artefacts and Environments* (pp. 377-380). Sydney, Australia: ACM. doi:10.1145/1228175.1228250

[21] Davenport, T. H. (2005). Thinking for a Living: How to Get Better Performances And Results from Knowledge Workers. Harvard Business Press.

[22] Sprenger, C., & ten Have, S. (1996). Knowledge as the engine of the learning organization. *Holland Management Review*, (51), 69-78.

[23] Woods, D., & Thoeny, P. (2007). *Wikis For Dummies*. For Dummies.

[24] Nielsen, J. (2006, October 9). Participation Inequality: Encouraging More Users to Contribute. Retrieved June 27, 2010, from http://www.useit.com/alertbox/participation_inequality.html

[25] Pallant, J. (2004). *SPSS Survival Manual* (2nd ed.). Open University Press.

[26] Costa, C. J., Nhampossa, J. L., and Aparício, M. 2008. Wiki content evaluation framework. In *Proceedings of the 26th Annual ACM international Conference on Design of Communication* (Lisbon, Portugal, September 22 - 24, 2008). SIGDOC '08. ACM, New York, NY, 169-174.

[27] Tavares, M. & Costa, C. J. 2007. Knowledge management process in the local government. In *Proceedings of the 25th Annual ACM international Conference on Design of Communication* (El Paso, Texas, USA, October 22 - 24, 2007). SIGDOC '07. ACM, New York, NY, 182-188. DOI= http://doi.acm.org/10.1145/1297144.1297183

RESOLVE DISSATISFACTORY COMMUNICATIONS

A Measurement-Method for Satisfied Communication in Business Organizations

Eldar Sultanow
University Potsdam
August-Bebel-Str. 89
14482 Potsdam
+49 177 7982193

eldar.sultanow@wi.uni-potsdam.de

Edzard Weber
University Potsdam
August-Bebel-Str. 89
14482 Potsdam
+49 331 9774472

edzard.weber@wi.uni-potsdam.de

Robert Lembcke
University Potsdam
August-Bebel-Str. 89
14482 Potsdam
+49 331 9773406

robert.lembcke@wi.uni-potsdam.de

ABSTRACT

Communication in widely distributed organizations is in many cases unsatisfactory. This contribution presents a method, which enables scalability for satisfied communication in business organizations. This method has been applied in practice and further evaluated by two IT-companies, which operate globally in the field of Web Engineering, E-Commerce and Usability. In the course of the evaluation for a one-month period, personnel were introduced to a checklist, which is specially designed for capturing communication dissatisfaction. The findings within these two companies are alarming in several respects. Many communication channels, which personnel choose by default, are inadequate and thus unacceptable for them and for the respective communication partners.

Categories and Subject Descriptors

H.1.1 [**Models and Principles**]: Systems and Information Theory – *General systems theory, Information theory, Value of information.*

General Terms

Algorithms, Management, Measurement, Design, Experimentation, Human Factors.

Keywords

Communication Management, Global Business Organizations, Measurement-Method, Satisfied Communication, Explorative Research, Empirical Investigation, Communication Channels, Social Network Analysis (SNA).

1. INTRODUCTION

Experts often clash, not because of technical or domain specific reasons, but because of the way they communicate with each other, which may often end in a dispute. A retrospective is a method [1] for reflecting what happened during the last project period and allows for ideas and suggestions to improve project steps and processes that have been passed. If discords and conflicts arise in this period the project members talk these out and may repair their relationships with each other [2].

On one hand, not every company is in the habit of conducting retrospectives. On the other hand, in optimal circumstances, a retrospective should not even be necessary because many of these conflicts would not arise.

This contribution aims to give companies a practical tool that identifies and solves the aforementioned conflicts and communication problems by way of prevention. A comprehensive number of exemplary conflicts have been discovered and classified in an empirical study, see [3], [4].

Our research project to develop a Measurement-Method for Satisfied Communication in Business Organizations is an exploration in reference analysis: we aim to empirically collect data in one company for a one-month period and to compare the results with data collected in a comparable company for the same period. The results thus far are promising; in both companies we identified the use of improper and deficient communication channels.

Figure 1 shows the general approach of this paper, including the initial methodology, the empirical inquiry, data analysis, and the concluding résumé.

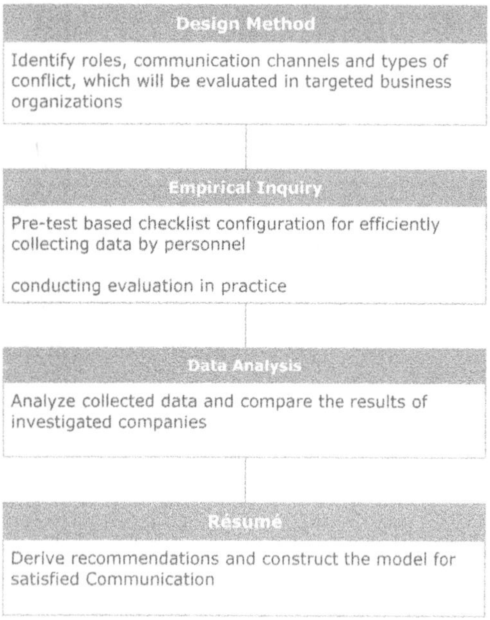
Design Method
Identify roles, communication channels and types of conflict, which will be evaluated in targeted business organizations
Empirical Inquiry
Pre-test based checklist configuration for efficiently collecting data by personnel
conducting evaluation in practice
Data Analysis
Analyze collected data and compare the results of investigated companies
Résumé
Derive recommendations and construct the model for satisfied Communication

Figure 1. Four steps in this paper to build the measurement method for satisfied communication.

2. MEASUREMENT METHOD DESIGN

In order to perform a measurement of communication satisfaction within the given period of one month, the roles are to be identified and the checklist is to be designed with as much user-friendliness as possible in order to ensure peak efficiency.

2.1 Identifying Roles and Channels

Both IT companies, which have been investigated, are distributed nationwide and both contain staff in the following common roles: developer, marketing, project manager. These delegates communicate through well-established channels such as e-mail, phone, face-2-face talk and chat. Other forms of communication, such as videoconferencing, are not currently being implemented.

The above mentioned roles and channels have been identified by means of an interview with the business executives taken in advance. The identified roles and channels are relevant for designing the checklist, where a contact maker contacts a contact taker. If the contact maker's attempt to get in touch with the contact taker fails or the communication between them is unsatisfactory from the view of the contact maker, he makes a short annotation into his checklist by checking his chosen communication channel, the appropriate role of the person he contacted and the reason of dissatisfaction. If the contact taker perceives an attempt of a contact maker's contact as inconvenient/inadequate or the contact taker is dissatisfied by the communication initiated by the contact maker, the contact taker annotates this in the checklist as same as done by the contact maker as described above.

2.2 Design checklists

As introduced in the previous section, a communication requires at least two members, a contact maker and a contact taker. Analogously, two checklist types are designed, one for the contact maker and another one for the contact taker.

Figure 5 shows the checklist, which is designed for the contact maker. The structure of both checklists must allow personnel to input quickly without spending a disproportionate amount of time for understanding what is meant and where to check correctly. For that reason, pre-tests were performed to improve the checklist's efficiency.

Each checklist is self-explanatory. For an unsatisfied communication case, the contact maker indicates who he tried to contact, which channel he used, the reason for dissatisfaction, the range to be improved and the new attempt of contact including its rating. The checklist for the contact taker is similarly designed, as depicted in Figure 6.

In checklist for contact takers, in the case of an unsatisfied communication a contact taker indicates on which channel who tried to contact him, why and how he counteracted including a rating for his counteraction.

3. EMPIRICAL INQUIRY

The empirical inquiry is performed in two mid-sized IT companies each with approximately fifty employees. The business profile of both companies investigated can be summarized as follows:

- Company A develops and maintains an E-Commerce web portal, which provides products, offers and consumer information.
- Company B provides consulting in the manner of Design Led Innovation (DLI) and elevates the market and user demands for developing a user feedback driven solution.

Personnel situated in key roles, such as developers, marketing professionals and project managers, are introduced into the inquiry and trained for the usage of the checklists, which have been designed for this inquiry.

Before starting the inquiry, both checklists – the one for contact makers and the other one for contact takers have been evaluated during a pre-test. During this pre-test staff members are requested to annotate exemplary hypothetical situations within the checklist. For example a marketing employee was given following imaginary situation:

"You tried to contact a developer by phone in order to ask for an estimated development time for a new module planned for sale. The developer didn't pick up the phone and you went into his office for giving your question in a face-2-face talk".

For a month period the staff member filled out the checklist, during the first week at each end of the day feedback dialogs where performed in order to ensure that the checklist was accurately used and not forgotten in moments when they are to be used.

After this period, Company A collected from their personnel 79 checklists from contact makers and 62 from contact takers. Company B collected 145 checklists from contact makers and 142 from contact takers.

This data collected forms the basis for the analysis given by the next section.

4. DATA ANALYSIS

The data analysis consists of three parts. First there is a descriptive analysis of each company separately. Another part is the network analysis of each company. And finally there is the comparison of a company with another particular company or a set of companies.

4.1 Descriptive SPSS Report

The descriptive analysis was done with the statistic application SPSS. Due to the fact that the collected data is collected anonymously it is not possible to join/merge the two databases based on different checklists. The checklists only ask for the role of the communication partner but not for his identity. But each database still enables a various kind of analysis.

The checklist "Somebody tried to contact me" gives an insight into the view of receivers on dissatisfying communication (see Table 1).

Table 1. "Somebody tried to contact me."

	Addressed problem
1	How often and which communication channels are subject to a dissatisfying communication (overall; per role)?
2	What are the reasons for counter action (overall; per role)?
3	What is the frequency of different kinds of counter actions?
4	Which counter action is preferred to react on dissatisfying communication using which channel?
5	What is the frequency of dissatisfying communication between the different roles of contact maker and contact taker?
6	Which communication channel causes the most trouble for a particular role of the contact taker?
7	How is the applied counter action rated?
8	How often and which communication channels are subject to a dissatisfying communication (overall; per role)?

The other point of view is the one of the contact maker. An excerpt of possible subjects to an analysis is shown in Table 2.

Table 2. "I tried to contact somebody."

	Addressed problem
1	What is the frequency of dissatisfying communication between the different roles of contact maker and contact taker?
2	How often and which communication channels are subject to a dissatisfying communication (overall; per role)?
3	What are the reasons for counter action (overall; per role)?
4	What is the cause of counter actions (overall; per role)?
5	Which communication channel is prone to which reason for counter action?
6	Which communication channel is prone to which cause of counter action?

7	Which communication channel is followed by another channel used for the new communication trial?
8	Who prefers which role for the new communication trial?
9	How is the new communication channel rated?

Figure 2 shows the results of the question "Which counter action is preferred to react on dissatisfying communication using which channel?" As you can see, in both companies the employees documented dissatisfying communication by phone, e-mail, chat or face-to-face-talk. But the reaction and the executed counter actions are completely different. The members of Company A (Figure 2a) prefer to ignore untimely or inconvenient communication requests or place them on hold. Members of Company B (Figure 2b) choose more intensive the alternative of forwarding communication requests to a project manager. In this case the project manager is able to recognize the occurring communication overflow of its project members and he is able to satisfy the communication resp. information request without delay. After having a deeper view on company B we observed that the company made some organizational rule: In the past the developer had been contacted by other departments frequently and the work rhythm was interrupted each time. Therefore the project manager has acquired the responsibility to be the first contact point for technical request of non-developers. The descriptive analysis (Figure 2b) shows that the learning process is still in progress. Not all employees are ready to contact the project manager first, but the developer already makes use of that service. They forward the technical request to the project manager and he will answer or preselect the requests without disturbing the development. A future snapshot in this company will show if this service has been accepted by the non-development departments.

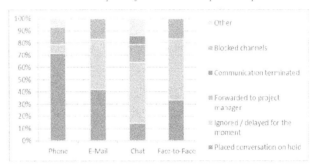

Figure 2a. *"Somebody tried to contact me"*: Communication channel crossed by counter action (Company A).

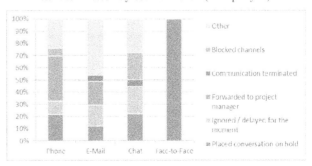

Figure 2b. *"Somebody tried to contact me"*: Communication channel crossed by counter action (Company B).

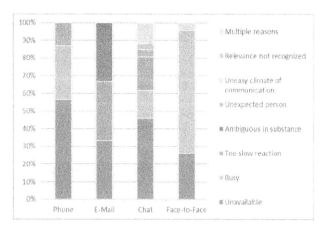

Figure 3a. *"I tried to contact somebody"*: **Communication channel crossed by reason for dissatisfying communication (Company A).**

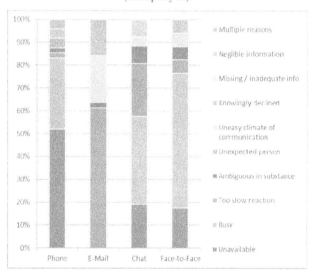

Figure 3b. *"I tried to contact somebody"*: **Communication channel crossed by reason for dissatisfying communication (Company B).**

The results, however, cannot speak for themselves. They have to be interpreted by someone who knows the enterprise. Maybe the organizational behavior differs from other organizations because of very special institutions, e.g. workflow organization vs. self-organization. Based on the primary result it is possible to see that something in the organization is different, but without an expert view it is not clear whether it is a symptom of something good or bad.

4.2 Social Network Analysis (SNA) Report

The different SNA values for the investigated example are listed in Table 3. In this example indegree, outdegree, degree centrality, closeness centrality and prestige are analyzed.

The density of a network shows how many connections exist between the different nodes in the network in comparison to all potential connections in the network [5, pp. 105]. In this case the density of the network has the score D = 0.3214. The density of a network awards information about the connectivity in the

network. In dense networks the social control is higher than in sparse networks.

The in- and outdegree of the network are shown in Table 3, row 2 and 3. The indegree counts all inbound connections of a node and the outdegree counts all outbound connections of a node. The degree centrality of a node in a network describes the attendance of a node in a network. In a directed network it is calculated with the help of the outdegree. To get the degree centrality the outdegree is divided by the maximum of the possible outdegree (n-1). In a non-directed network the degree centrality is right the degree of a node. The degree of a node is calculated by adding every edge of a node [5, pp. 125-127]. Row 4 in Table 3 shows the degree centrality for this network.

Opposite to the degree centrality, the closeness centrality considers not only direct connections between network nodes, but also indirect connections. Closeness centrality accrues how near a node is by all other nodes, even with the help of its indirect connections. Indirect connections are weaker than direct connection. The closeness centrality is used to get to know about the star of a network.

If the closeness centrality of a node is high, it can be assumed that this node has a high potential of social control in the network. Row 5 in Table 3 shows, that the closeness centrality of marketing has the highest score, this indicates that marketing is nearest by all other persons in the network. The closeness centrality is calculated by adding all distances from the node together and afterwards calculating the reciprocal value of it. If there is a node without any connections all nodes have an endless distance. To get used with it and to assure comparison of the closeness centrality of different networks, the closeness centrality is calculated by dividing the maximum distance between nodes (n – 1) by the reciprocal value of adding all distances of a node [5, pp. 127-128].

Prestige is a value, which is based on the asymmetry in correlations of nodes in networks. Indegree based prestige is a network value which gives the value of connections directed onto the node. To get the indegree based prestige of a node the indegree of the node is divided by the maximum possible value of

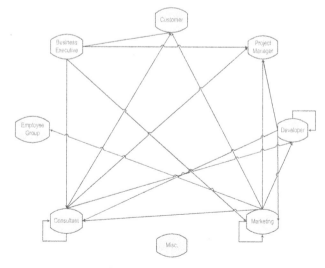

Figure 4. SNA Graph of investigated roles.

indegree based prestige (n-1). The result is between 1 and 0. 1 is the value for the highest measurement of indegree based prestige [5, pp. 136-137].

Column 6 in Table 3 shows that in this case the prestige for the consultant and the project manager is at a high level in comparison to the other nodes. High Prestige indicates important nodes in a network, even if these nodes are no stars in the network. The project manager in this example isn't a network star, if only the value of his degree centrality is considered. His high prestige Value indicates, that he nevertheless is important for the organization whose social network is represented by the values in Table 3.

Table 3. SNA values for the investigated example.

Role	In Degree	Out Degree	Degree Centrality	Closeness Centrality	Prestige
Consultant	4	4	0.5714	0.77	0.5714
Marketing	3	6	0.8571	1.4	0.4286
Developer	3	4	0.5714	1	0.4286
Project Manager	4	0	0	0	0.5714
Customer	3	0	0	0	0.4286
Employee Group	1	0	0	0	0.1429
Misc.	0	0	0	0	0
Business Executive	0	4	0.5714	0.875	0

5. RÉSUMÉ
In the case of the first company, which has been investigated, the results can be interpreted as a performance of success: namely, the communication between IT and other departments including marketing etc. has been mediated by introducing a special role. So it is not to be negatively interpreted, that contact makers are delivered to a dedicated person, which communicates between them. It shows a kind of organizational learning: the use of a mediator between different departments. A direct communication was previously overloaded.

6. FUTURE WORK
The results of the comparative analysis becomes better the bigger the database is. As databases expand it will be possible to make much more specific comparisons, e.g. organizations of the same size, business branch, and communication structure or role distribution. It will be possible to make an analysis for particular roles independently from their organizational affiliation.

The biggest challenge is to make the data collecting efficient. At the moment every dissatisfied communication event has to be reported manually by paper and pen. Data is collected manually and therefore the proposed method does not scale. But this offline tool has been chosen because of its independence of PC accessibility. Even a mobile device would be too inconvenient. The perfect solution would offer different ways for reporting but must still guarantee anonymity.

Whenever possible, the analysis has to take advantage of automatic data collection, for example by analyzing log files, always guaranteeing the privacy of the employees. Only then will it become possible to create reports in time and to offer individual communication profiles. These individual reports will only be posted to the specific user. This might be a personal outer distant signal. The user has an empirical indication that his communication behavior is "very special" and might be the cause for some communication problems in the past.

7. REFERENCES
[1] Kerth, N. L., 2001. Project Retrospectives: A Handbook for Team Reviews. Dorset House Publishing Co., Inc. (February 2001)

[2] Rupp, C., Steiner, A. N., 2009. Projektretrospektiven, Part 1: Nutzen und Vorbereitung. Projekt Magazin, Vol. 2009-19.

[3] Sultanow, E., Weber, E., 2009. Klassifikation und Identifikation von Kommunikationsbarrieren in Unternehmen. In Lecture Notes in Informatics – Proceedings of the 5th Conference of Professional Knowledge Management. Gesellschaft für Informatik e.V. (GI).

[4] Sultanow, E., Vladova, G., Weber, E., 2009. Overcoming Communication Barriers for CMC in Enterprises. In Proceedings of 15th Americas Conference on Information Systems.

[5] Jansen, D. 1999. Einführung in die Netzwerkanalyse: Grundlagen Methoden, Anwendungen. Leske und Budrich, Opladen Germany.

8. APPENDIX
Figure 5 shows the checklist designed for contact makers in an unsatisfied communication situation. The analogous form for contact takers is shown in Figure 6.

| Role: | | Company / Code: | | Date: | | Number: |

I tried to contact somebody

Who?	How?	Unsatisfied – Why?		

Partner	Channel	Reason for dissatisfactory communication?	Which part is to be enhanced?	New attempt to contact:		
				Same Partner ☐	Same Channel ☐	Mark
☐ Customer ☐ Consultant ☐ Marketing ☐ Sales Partner ☐ Developer (intern) ☐ Developer (extern) ☐ Project Manager (intern) ☐ Project Manager (extern) ☐ Group of Employees	☐ Phone ☐ SMS ☐ E-Mail ☐ Letter Mail ☐ Chat ☐ Face-to-Face Talk ☐ Fax ☐ Wiki / Forum	☐ Not Available ☐ Being Engaged / Busy ☐ Ambiguous in Substance ☐ Knowingly Declined ☐ Uneasy Climate of Communication ☐ Too Slow Reaction ☐ Missing / Inadequate Info ☐ Wrong Info ☐ Information Overload ☐ Negligible Information ☐ Relevance not recognized ☐ Unexpected Partner	☐ Information Technology ☐ Corporate Culture / Social Interaction ☐ Company Policy ☐ Release of Funds / Financing ☐ Organization of Procedure and structure ☐ Legal basic conditions ☐ Linking data / information / knowledge	**Same Partner** ☐ Customer ☐ Consultant ☐ Marketing ☐ Sales Partner ☐ Developer (intern) ☐ Developer (extern) ☐ Project Manager (intern) ☐ Project Manager (extern) ☐ Group of Employees	**Same Channel** ☐ Phone ☐ SMS ☐ E-Mail ☐ Letter Mail ☐ Chat ☐ Face-to-Face Talk ☐ Fax ☐ Wiki / Forum	☐ A ☐ B ☐ C ☐ D ☐ E ☐ F
☐ Others:	☐ Other:	☐ Other:		☐ Others:	☐ Other:	

Perfect, I will do so directly in future time	Good, I will do so in problem case again	Acceptable, got relevant Information	Sufficient, did not get all information	Poor, relevant information was wrong	Failed, because nothing worked
A - Perfect	B - Good	C - Acceptable	D - Sufficient	E - Poor	F - Fail

Figure 5. Checklist for contact makers.

Role:	Company / Code:	Date:	Number:

Somebody tried to contact me

Who?   How?   Unsatisfied – Why?

Partner	Channel	Reason for counter action	Counter action	Mark
☐ Customer	☐ Phone	☐ Being under deadline pressure	☐ Forwarded to project manager	☐ A
☐ Consultant	☐ SMS	☐ Irrelevant Small talk	☐ Ignored / delayed for the moment	
☐ Marketing	☐ E-Mail	☐ Communication difficulties	☐ Communication terminated	☐ B
☐ Sales Partner	☐ Letter Mail	☐ Inefficient / ineffective communication	☐ Blocked channels (e.g. deactivated chat)	☐ C
☐ Developer (intern)	☐ Chat	☐ Content not / poorly imparted	☐ Placed conversation on hold	
☐ Developer (extern)	☐ Face-to-Face Talk			☐ D
☐ Project Manager (intern)	☐ Fax			☐ E
☐ Project Manager (extern)	☐ Wiki / Forum			☐ F
☐ Group of Employees				
☐ Others:	☐ Other:	☐ Other:	☐ Other:	

Perfect, I will do so directly in future time	Good, I will do so in problem case again	Acceptable, got relevant Information	Sufficient, did not get all information	Poor, relevant information was wrong	Failed, because nothing worked
A - Perfect	B - Good	C - Acceptable	D - Sufficient	E - Poor	F - Fail

Figure 6. Checklist for contact takers.

Accessible organizational elements in wikis with model-driven development

Thiago Jabur Bittar
UFG - Catalão - GO, Brazil
Tel: +55 64 3441-1510

USP - ICMC
São Carlos, SP, Brazil

jabur@icmc.usp.br

Luanna Lopes Lobato
UFG - Catalão - GO, Brazil
Tel: +55 64 3441-1510

UFPE - Recife - PE, Brazil
Tel: +55 81 2126-8430

lll@cin.ufpe.br

Renata P. M. Fortes
USP - São Carlos – SP
ICMC
Caixa Postal 668
São Carlos, SP, Brazil

renata@icmc.usp.br

David Fernandes Neto
USP – São Carlos – SP
ICMC
Caixa Postal 668
São Carlos, SP, Brazil

david@icmc.usp.br

ABSTRACT
Wiki is a web collaborative tool for promoting rapid publication of information, by allowing users to edit, add or revise content through a web browser. Despite various benefits offered by the use of wikis, there is no guarantee of a good structure of its content. This occurs, especially, because of the flexibility and easiness on creating and referencing pages and also for the reason that difficulty to graphically visualize the information architecture. In this paper it is proposed a Model-Driven Development (MDD) approach that supports creating graphical models of namespaces to generate structured wikis code. In addition, this approach also aims to include accessibility features on models from official W3C guidelines such as WCAG and ATAG, allowing access by a wider range of users.

Categories and Subject Descriptors
D.2.2 [**Design Tools and Techniques**]: User Interfaces;
H.5.4 [**Hypertext/Hypermedia**]: User issues;

General Terms
Management, Design, Human Factors

Keywords
Information Architecture, Wiki, Accessibility, Model-Driven Development (MDD)

1. INTRODUCTION
Wiki is a web collaborative tool for promoting rapid publication of information, by means of allowing users to edit, add or revise content via a web browser [10]. Despite various benefits offered by the use of wikis, there is no guarantee that a good structure of its content. This occurs principally because of flexibility and easiness to create and referencing pages, and also because of the difficult to visualize its information architecture graphically.

On most wikis, its structure is accomplished by links created by users with the textual definition of categories. Haake, Lukosch and Schummer (2005) identified the need to structure wikis and

argue that inexperienced users have difficulty to create structured content, even they want [7]. Graphical viewers are not usually available for better understanding and planning of the wiki structure, which are very important in web information architecture.

Information architecture aims to organize the content in an intelligible and organized way, improving the search and understanding of information by users in a given context. According to Nielsen (2009), a poor information architecture results in the majority of the users failures, increasing the rate of usability and accessibility problems on the web [16]. Thus, a challenge faced in this context is to organize wiki content in a structured and accessibly way, which is important to the user for understanding the information and having a good interaction with it.

Therefore, in this research we propose a way to structure the content graphically. For this, information structures in models, named as namespaces, were used. This makes possible the organization of the content with namespaces, similar to use of folders concept in Operational Systems. In addition, these models can be graphically edited and viewed, providing easiness for the user in a better planning on the content that will be inserted.

To provide a correct use of the models and to support the generation of structured wikis, with good accessibility features, we used concepts related to Model-Driven Development (MDD). MDD proposes the use of high-level abstract models and successive transformations to increase the details in each ones.

These transformations are done until the models become specific enough to be executed in a specific platform [17]. In MDD, conceptual diagrams are not only a reference that developers use to build executable code; models become "live" artifacts, serving as input to code generation tools, reducing the developer's effort [13]. The transformations from one model to another create a chain which enables the automated implementation of a system starting from requirements [5]. The MDD has been shown as a promising approach and the research in this area has evolved over the past decades consequently, have been achieved significant productivity gains in software development [14][1].

Therefore, this work proposes that the information architecture is developed from the namespaces creation, which are models that allows that the wikis code can be generated automatically, characterizing the use of MDD principles. Furthermore, with this automated transformation process it is possible the inclusion of accessibility and usability practices in the software development [3].

Using these features, it is possible to structure wikis more efficiently and effectively, providing a friendly environment to the user, since it becomes possible to model graphically the concepts using the transformations to generate the pages structure and menus in an organized and agile way.

The concept proposed here does not attempt to undermine the flexibility of the wiki, or to propose a general model, it is only an aid in defining useful models in the context, in this case to creation of namespaces as scaffolding. The use of namespaces is recommended and supported by most wikis, but many users do not use because of difficulty in coding and organizing them.

The MDD can help the user to define these namespaces without syntax and path errors. And, once generated the architecture (skeleton of pages), he can see how it was done and learn from it.

The choice of MDD was made considering the complications of proposing a single general purpose model, because the user to develop his own specific purpose meta-model according to his needs and adapting to his problems. This is especially important in large teams in which some information architects can define models to assist writers, for example. And these authors will not be limited by this model, which is only a guide that can be extended and improved.

This paper is divided as follows: in Section 2 are explored wiki concepts and the issue of its structure. Section 3 presents MDD concepts, which are essential to a better understanding of this research. In Section 4 some guidelines for accessibility are described. In Section 5 we present the case study and its results and, finally, in Sections 6 and 7 the related work and conclusions are presented, respectively.

2. WIKI

The wikis have been a significant support tool to organize and disseminate information, which are open to the general public or, at least, to all the people who have access to its server. This is supported by its increasing use since its creation in 1995.

One of the essential characteristics to wikis popularization is how easy its pages can be created and edited, providing mechanisms that allow flexibility for collaborative editing of content. Thus, the wiki supports editing documents collaboratively with a simple markup language using a web browser. This enables different types of users, including non-specialists, to become familiar with its syntax more easily.

This easiness in editing is different compared to conventional methods of web development. It is usually required knowledge of HTML and file transfer tools such as FTP (File Transfer Protocol). The conventional development is often more complex and susceptible to developer errors; resulting, for example, in a bad structure or existence of broken links. In wikis, on the other hand, a link to a nonexistent page is not broken and is accessible: it is simply a new page waiting for its creation by a user with appropriate permission.

Additionally, with the content into wiki pages, several features are supported, like: access control by user (viewing, editing), version management, uploading of different media types (PDF, DOC, and others), textual search, inserting plug-ins to extend its functionalities and availability of RSS (Really Simple Syndication) feeds, among others.

Thus, wikis allow the creation of agile hypertext source of non-linear structures of navigation and communication. In this way, the authoring process is motivated by the users interacting at different templates and using tools to edit the online content through the creation of new pages and its links.

The biggest and well known example of using a wiki is Wikipedia, a free multilingual encyclopedia. It was created in 2001 and, currently, has over three million articles in English. However, Buzzi and Leporini (2008) [4] in a study of this encyclopedia, point out various accessibility barriers that hinder access to its content by individuals with visual disabilities. Even for those people using assistive technologies such as screen readers, the access has been limited.

2.1 Structure

A good web structure refers to the sense of having website elements in order to compose the information architecture. It is important to provide some appropriate navigation elements, as supports the user's location in relation to the structure, which takes the users to more easily find what they are looking. In addition, a good web structure of information, with links visible and identifiable, helps the users to move on the pages without errors or unfulfilled expectations, reinforcing their sense of location within the information architecture.

To provide these facilities some points must be considered, which are used to support the signaling of information structure [15]:

- **Easy understanding of the titles:** the texts should be succinct, clear and have good legibility, including understandable and predictable organization;

- **Have adequate feedback:** messages must be clear and contextualized;

- **Economy of action and time:** the fewer steps are necessary to go a better way;

- **Shortcuts to more experienced users:** they like and it should be possible to go directly to the sections that interest them most.

As method to display structural elements, breadcrumbs can be used, whose function is to show the page location in the website hierarchy [15][20].

Nielsen (2007) points out reasons to use breadcrumbs:

- They show people their current location relative to higher-level concepts, helping them to understand where they are in relation to the site entirely;

- They afford one-click access to higher site levels and, thus, rescue users who arrive in very specific but inappropriate destinations through search or deep links;

- They rarely cause problems in user testing: people might overlook this small design element, but they almost never have trouble operating them.

Breadcrumbs are almost always implemented in the same way, with a horizontal line that: i) progresses from the highest level to the lowest, one step at a time; ii) starts with the homepage and ends with the current page; iii) has a simple text link for each level (except for the current page), and iv) has a simple and one-character separator between the levels (usually ">"). [15].

2.2 The structure issue in wikis

Despite various benefits offered by the use of wikis, there is no guarantee about a good structure of its content. This occurs mainly because of flexibility and easiness to create and referencing pages and also because of difficult to visualize the architecture graphically of the information.

The wiki structure is normally generated from the created pages and, mainly in the educational context, it can facilitate the learning. Due to freedom to edit, by the users, its structure can be made in an unsystematic way [7].

It is important to highlight that its collaboration feature is not a factor of disorganization, however as the users have distinct thoughts and actions, there is a greater chance of getting disorganized content, since these do not provide an initial mechanism for structuring. This lack of structure can be presented in several phases of the wiki development, for example whether user does not correctly use the title hierarchical tags, as h1, h2, h3 and others.

Other common points are related to user placing the different semantically content on the same page, with this the issues are mixing and, consequently, the tree navigation branch can be expanding in a demised way. This can occur due to users that do not have a initial knowledge or not enough training made in order to make them understand.

Thus, the wikis provide resources for organizing content, but many users do not know how to use [7]. In most of the wikis that organization is done via links topology in the source code with assigning of categories and labels to the link texts, making it complex of writing this code correctly by inexperienced users.

2.3 Namespace

Namespaces are textual expressions used to categorize pages and other media files (PDF documents, MP3 music, videos, data in XML, among others). Thus, a namespace is the key to access the resources [21], the concept involved in its use is similar to using folders and pages are similar to the use of files [6].

Many default installations of wikis come with an initial pre-defined namespace: the "wiki". Usually, to create new namespaces it is necessary simply to enter a desired name in the link followed by a colon character. The name after the last two points will be the name of the page itself, while other names are the namespaces.

In Table 1, as follows, examples about the syntax of the namespace use are presented. The syntax for relative and absolute internal links is non-unique and complex relative to directory and filename conventions. Absolute paths are started with "/". Links are absolute whether they have a ":" prefix. Links relative to the current namespace may also begin with either "." or ".:" (".." or "..:" for parent namespace).

Table 1. Syntax examples of paths for wiki structure [6]

Path	Description
.:example	Refers to the page "example" in the **current** namespace.
:example	Refers to the page "example" in the **root** namespace.
..:example	Refers to the page "example" in the **parent** namespace.
wiki:example	Refers to the page "example" in **wiki** namespace.
ns1:ns2:example :ns1:ns2:example	Refers to the page "example" in the namespace ns2. The namespace ns2 is located beneath of the namespace ns1; The namespace ns1 is located **beneath of the root namespace.**
.ns1:ns2:example ..ns1:ns2:example	Refers to the page "example" in the namespace ns2. The namespace ns2 is located **beneath of the namespace ns1**; The namespace ns1 is located **beneath of the current namespace.**
..ns1:ns2:example ..:ns1:ns2:example	Refers to the page "example" in the namespace ns2. The namespace ns2 is located **beneath of the namespace ns1**; The namespace ns1 is located **next to the current namespace.**
.ns1:ns2:start	Refers to the page "start" in the namespace ns2. The namespace ns2 is located **beneath of the namespace ns1**, which is located **beneath of the current namespace.**

Every namespace has a default page that is accessed whether in the link it is informed only the namespace.

3. MODEL-DRIVEN DEVELOPMENT

In Model-Driven Development, known as MDD, conceptual diagrams are not only a reference that developers use to build executable code; models become "live" artifacts, serving as input to code generation tools, reducing the developers' efforts [13].

The idea behind MDD is that modeling and transforming are a better base to system development and maintenance than coding [13].

MDD encompasses the concepts of CIM (Computation Independent Model), PIM (Platform Independent Model) and PSM (Platform Specific Model). These concepts are based on transformations that aim raising the abstraction level during software development.

In Figure 1, it illustrates the software development cycle with an MDD process as opposed to a traditional.

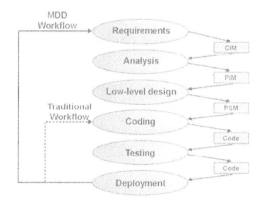

Figure 1. Adapted from [13] – illustrates a MDD development cycle in comparison with the traditional cycle.

As presented in Figure 1, the process begins with the requirements identification, producing the CIM, which describes the system utilization. This model is independent of how the system will be implemented. The next step is the requirements analysis, producing the PIM, which is a representation of how the requirements will be achieved, but without detailing platform-specific characteristics.

In the low level design, the PIM is transformed into a PSM, taking the platform into consideration. The concept is that one PIM could originate several PSM. From the PSM, the development workflow follows as usual, with coding, in which model and processors originate executable code, the basis for testing and deployment.

In a first analysis, this development workflow does not differ much from the traditional software development workflow. However, in MDD, a model is a formal description that can be understood by computers. In traditional workflow, transformations between models are done manually. As a result, whenever changes are necessary, developers do it directly in the code, because returning to the initial requirements and analysis steps would take too much time.

The primary goals of MDD are portability, interoperability, maintainability and reusability. A model-driven approach requires languages for specifying models, defining transformations and describing meta-models.

There are still problems with appropriate tool support and exchange formats that are necessary for a coherent implementation of this workflow. But recent years have witnessed a great effort from the academia and industry, which is producing reliable standards and solutions to support a complete MDD workflow.

There is the conceptual basis with three patterns created by OMG (Object Management Group): UML (Unified Modeling Language)[1], MOF (Meta Object Facility)[2] and CWM (Common Warehouse Metamodel)[3].

For language specification MOF can be used, which presents in its terminology some common elements:

- **Model**: an abstraction of a physical system with a certain purpose. A model is often presented as a combination of draws and text;

- **Meta-model**: a model that defines the language for expressing a model. It includes the precise definition of the constructs and rules;

- **Meta-data:** data describing other data;

- **Meta-object:** a generic term for all meta-entities in a meta-modeling language. For example, meta-types, meta-classes, meta-attributes, and meta-associations.

---

[1] http://www.uml.org/

[2] http://www.omg.org/mof/

[3] http://www.omg.org/cwm/

Using models, software engineers and stakeholders can discuss conceptually about a problem without caring about specific platform issues.

In MDD the idea is to automate the transformations using tools, encouraging developers to return to the initial requirement and analysis steps, because the automatic transformations will take them faster to the coding and testing activities.

4. ACCESSIBILITY

Accessibility can be interpreted as the possibility of using any resource universally, without barriers or with alternative ways to access and use of them. In the web context, the websites contents are this resource; the concept is being related to any user, using any agent (software or hardware that retrieves web content) can understand and interact with the content provided [19].

According to Kelly *et al.* (2005) [12], the pre-eminent reference when addressing web accessibility is the WCAG (Web Content Accessibility Guidelines), prepared by WAI (Web Accessibility Initiative)[4].

The WCAG document establishes a set of guidelines that discuss accessibility issues and provides accessibility design solutions, explain how to make web content accessible to disabled individuals, from several user agents types that are being used (desktop browsers, voice browsers, cell phones, among others) and operations restrictions (noisy environments, low light, among others). The first WCAG (1.0) version was presented in 1999 when each guideline was described as checkpoints, which define projects parts that can show barriers for users with some limitation (i.e., with visual disabilities, deaf, cognition problems). In each checkpoint it is determined a priority value, 1-3, according to their impact on accessibility and conformance with the document. The value 1 is equivalent of the most important checkpoint follow the second and third priorities.

Currently WCAG is in version 2.0 and technological conditions to satisfy the accessibility requirement are not described, although it provides information about the known methods to develop application in accordance with the guidelines [18]. This document is complemented by a non-normative section, which describes specific details of how the technology should be used [11].

The WCAG 2.0 sections that emphasize the organization and navigation in an accessibly way are found in the Principle 3, called Understandable, focusing on how to make the content comprehensible. This principle has two relevant success criteria to the context of the structure: **i) consistent navigation (3.2.3)** - the navigation mechanisms should be repeated on different pages in a logical order and **ii) consistent identification (3.2.4)** - components with the same functionality and similar semantically should be organized logically.

Other document that must be verified is the ATAG 1.0. This is necessary since the wiki is too named as authority tools. Consequently, the *checkpoint* 3.2 should be analyzed, which mention that these tools should help to create structured content [2].

Thus, through the Model Driven Development and conformity of models over the accessibility guidelines, we hope to assist

---

[4] http://www.w3.org/WAI/

graphically the wiki's author during the organization and editing accessible content.

5. CASE STUDY AND RESULTS OF MDD TO STRUCTURE WIKIS

We conducted a case study to verify the approach presented and then we made the development of a wiki, modeling its namespaces structure graphically. For this purpose we selected a free wiki software, called Dokuwiki.

The choice of wiki software was made by Dokuwiki tool for its easiness of use, simple syntax and its structure was made via the file system. This allows that data files are readable outside the wiki, so no database manage system is required [6].

To modeling the wiki we used the Graphical Modeling Project (GMP)[5] available in Eclipse and to code generation processors it were used JET (Java Emitter Templates) transformers. To structure the navigation we adopted to model a hierarchical menu, which will conform to the namespaces.

The initial step of this approach is called as conceptual analysis, in that is verified how the content will be integrate the information architecture. The second step is to model, graphically, the architecture, with elements and characteristics them. And finally, the third step is focused on selecting a wiki and develops transformers for them, or to use ready transformers for code generation.

For code automated generation it is made a reading and parsing in the model, which is persisted in XMI, and based on transformations rules, it are created structured new files in folders. These files are pages with only title, which will be used as initial labels for each menu item.

In follow, to generating menus and breadcrumb we utilized a search resource in the files system returned an items hierarchical array. This will ensure an updated menu and the real representation of the stored pages. Thus, whether a page is deleted, it will not exist in file system and, consequently, in menu and breadcrumbs.

The idea behind this approach and case study does not propose a single model to be used in general purpose. The proposed concept is that developers know how to use an extra tool for modeling them needs. Each new meta-model must represent the user needs to help them.

An interesting point is that the MDD is quite flexible in the construction of meta-models with their own rules to adapt to the problems of content organization. Suppose that the difficulty is not in the menus, but in the definition of forms, so it is possible create a meta-model to assist in building forms, if this is the difficulty.

We admit it's not easy to build meta-models that generalize problems, even for wikis being used for multiple purposes. So, the recommendation given is that each organization to make it's meta-model with the rules and attributes specific to your problem and this initial cost of development tends to fade with the reuse of models.

---

[5] http://www.eclipse.org/modeling/gmp/

5.1 Deployment and Results

From studies of different structuring and navigation standards, we checked the importance of the namespaces hierarchy and consistent navigation on the web for better organization and information retrieval [7] [20].

In Figure 2 it is presented a meta-model to the conceptual and structural organization of the wiki. The elements hierarchy can be seen based in a menu element and its items.

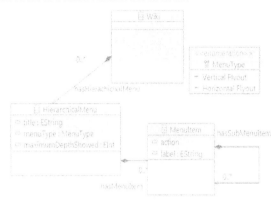

Figure 2. Meta-model of a menu developed in Eclipse GMP platform

According to the diagram in Figure 2, a wiki can have 0 or more hierarchical menus which must contain: title attributes (also important for the accessibility of the element), menu type (which can be extended) and maximum depth shown, to store up what level the user wishes to display in the menu.

We can also see that each menu item can have zero or more recursively sub menu items. From the definition of a meta-model, it can be created different designs for each application (wikis in this case) bringing flexibility to the destination application. As an example, was created in this work, a hierarchical menu shown in Figure 3, which includes five items on its initial level.

It can be seen that the persistence of the model was done in the file system in a XMI format, in the file "Wiki.xmi", which will be parsed to generate the desired wiki structure.

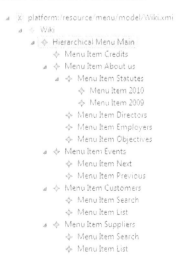

Figure 3. Model with data from a sample menu

For each new menu item created in the model the user must inform the content of attributes, it can be done on the tab "Properties", as seen in Figure 4.

Figure 4. Item propriety of the model

Finally, with all the conceptual planning of the wiki organization stored in a XMI model, we made the automatic transformation to HTML (wiki pages) that can be seen below, in Figures 5 and 6.

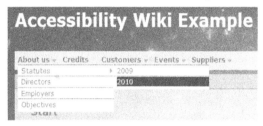

Figure 5. Hierarchical flyout menu generated for the wiki

Figure 6. View of generated wiki according to the planned structure

The main advantages of this generation include: i) easier and fast creation of efficient navigational structures graphically by people not necessarily experts in HTML; ii) the menu reflects consistently the available content on the wiki (including its namespaces); iii) better planning via graphical interface, allowing validation by the final customer and iv) the typography styles and color styles can be easily changed by Cascading Style Sheets (CSS).

Some numbers may show the worked scenario: 17 options were modeled in 3 hierarchies, namely: Root Level (1) with 5 options; Level 2 with 10 options and Level 3 with 2 options. These menu options topology, which are relatively simple compared to real cases, results in 6 folders and 18 files.

We do not change any code from the wiki engine, because it already supports and recommends the use of namespaces, we just added a template that contains the styles and code generation of the menu.

Through manual or automatic generation, this files structure must be developed. Thus, using automated tools, this can be guarantee in a correct and quickly way. In addition, after files generation, the user could test the deployment and whether some conceptual problem is found the changes will be managed, changing the start model and re-generating the wiki files.

What is noticeable in a practice is that many developers make a structuring of content manually and talk about this with stakeholders in the project. This is usually done on paper or in conventional text editors and the documents generated in this process are a kind of guide for the implementation, which is not always followed faithfully.

We also identify an advantage for the novice user, who can plan graphically the structure of the desired information and quickly view his wiki running, simply he will fill the content of pages created.

6. RELATED WORKS

Holtzblatt, Damianos and Weiss (2010) research on the use of wikis in knowledge sharing in business environment. Their research found that although wikis have gotten wide acceptance and was widely used, especially in the business environment wikis are not widely used for information sharing. There are two possible reasons for this: i) a reluctance to share specific information or ii) a greater reliance on other methods (non-wiki) to share information [9].

In general, there are no defined conventions, guidelines or moderators in business wikis. There is no formal hierarchy for contribution and the content does not go through an official approval. The study attested that the disagreement of opinions is often the reason for new instances of wikis and as a consequence, there are various wikis. The object of study of the article is to find a way to achieve success, through wikis, facilitate the information search, while minimizing duplication of information in various wikis.

Thus, it is believed that the use of wikis better structured, using graphical models, as proposed in this work, can help to reduce the difficulty of information searching as well as duplication of content, contributing to more use of wikis in the environment business. It was seen that some users prefer a hint of pages skeleton to being become familiar with wiki syntax and what content their bosses expect it to be placed. This will be done without limiting their creativity, enabling them to extend or alter this initial suggestion; it was seen that the MDD allowing it.

Leporini and Buzzi (2008) presented a study of usability and accessibility of wikis for users with visual disabilities. They argue that interact with wikis is more complicated for a user with visual deficiency, since it needs assistive technology, which adds a level of complexity in the interaction. This paper analyzes the Wikipedia in order to try to understand how blind users interact with wikis via screen readers, noting some usability and accessibility issues and finally present some possible solutions [4].

These authors suggest some elements that should be taken into consideration when designing the interface of a wiki. Each area of the wiki should be clearly identifiable both visually and by a screen reader, to after are used structuring mechanisms.

Still, in some cases (such as content pages), a summary with links to the main content can make it easier to identify the content and navigate through them. Thus, we believe that the use of organized wikis, can facilitate the interaction of people with visual disabilities.

Already Haake, Lukosch and Schummer (2005) identified the need to structure wikis and requirements that must be met for such. They argue that inexperienced users have difficulty to create structured content, even they want. To solve this problem, these authors suggest the use of templates on wikis to achieve these requirements, since the use of templates separates editing the content of editing structure, making this edition more concise and standardized [7].

This work is what is closest to our proposal, however, one of the main advantages of our work is the process of automating the code generation with the use of MDD.

7. CONCLUSIONS

The wikis, although widely accepted by users, may require a difficult start planning, especially for individuals with disabilities, which impairs the information design and retrieval. This work presented the use of meta-models, developed on Eclipse Modeling Framework (EMF) to generate wiki codes. And, unlike what occurs in the normal process, using this approach, the wiki namespaces are created visually and then pages and menus are generated.

It is important to emphasize that the approach mentioned here does not affect the flexibility and freedom of users, and they can usually create new pages and structure. The idea here is to support them in the difficult task of structuring the content and use navigational elements in a consistent and effective way.

Another advantage of this approach is the use of graphical models, helping the user to have a better view, navigation and consistent identification.

Using MDD, we found that structuring elements can be created for different wikis platforms, allowing data exchange via XMI files, since one of its principles is focused on the use of models to provide interoperability between platforms.

We emphasize that it is not easy to build meta-models that generalize problems. So, we recommend that each organization has its own meta-model and efficient code generation structures.

As future work, we intend to model user permissions graphically and integrate the CSS editing with high-level, allowing a non-HTML specialist to choose custom colors and layouts. Another idea is to use tools for natural language processing to find unusual expressions and abbreviations, indicating some suggestions to the developer.

8. ACKNOWLEDGMENTS

Our acknowledgments to the Institute of Mathematics and Computer Sciences - University of São Paulo (USP) and also to the FAPESP, project number 2010/05626-7.

9. REFERENCES

[1] Aho, P., Merilinna, J., and Ovaska, E. 2009. Model-Driven Open Source Software Development - The Open Models Approach. In *Proceedings of the 2009 Fourth international Conference on Software Engineering Advances* (September 20 - 25, 2009). ICSEA. IEEE Computer Society. Washington, DC, pp. 185--190. DOI: http://dx.doi.org/10.1109/ICSEA.2009.37

[2] ATAG 1.0. Authoring Tool Accessibility Guidelines 1.0 - *W3C Recommendation* February 3 2000

[3] Bittar, T. J., Fortes, R. P. M., Lobato, L. L. and Watanabe, W. M. 2009. Web communication and interaction modeling using model-driven development. In *Proceedings of the 27th ACM international Conference on Design of Communication* (Bloomington, IN, USA, October 05 - 07, 2009). SIGDOC '09. ACM, New York, NY, pp. 193--198. DOI: http://doi.acm.org/10.1145/1621995.1622033

[4] Buzzi, M. and Leporini, B. 2008. Is Wikipedia usable for the blind?. In *Proceedings of the 2008 international Cross-Disciplinary Conference on Web Accessibility* (W4a) (Beijing, China, April 21 - 22, 2008). W4A '08, vol. 317. ACM, New York, NY, 15-22. DOI: 10.1145/1368044.1368049

[5] Distante, D., Pedone, P., Rossi, G., and Canfora G.. Model-driven development of web applications with UWA, MVC and JavaServer faces. In *Proceedings of the 7th international conference on Web engineering*, pp 457--472, Como, Italy, 2007. Springer-Verlag.

[6] DokuWiki. 2010. http://www.dokuwiki.org/

[7] Haake, A., Lukosch, S. and Schümmer, T. 2005. wiki-templates: adding structure support to wikis on demand. In *Proceedings of the 2005 international Symposium on wikis* (San Diego, California, October 16 - 18, 2005). wikiSym '05. ACM, New York, NY, 41-51. DOI= http://doi.acm.org/10.1145/1104973.1104978

[8] Hailpern, B. and Tarr, P. 2006. Model-driven development: the good, the bad, and the ugly. *IBM Syst. J. 45, 3* (Jul. 2006), 451-461. DOI: http://dx.doi.org/10.1147/sj.453.0451

[9] Holtzblatt, L. J., Damianos, L. E. and Weiss, D. 2010. Factors impeding Wiki use in the enterprise: a case study. In *Proceedings of the 28th of the international Conference Extended Abstracts on Human Factors in Computing Systems* (Atlanta, Georgia, USA, April 10 - 15, 2010). CHI EA '10. ACM, New York, NY, pp. 4661--4676. DOI= http://doi.acm.org/10.1145/1753846.1754208

[10] Jang, S.; Green, T. M. Best practices on delivering a wiki collaborative solution for enterprise applications. In *Collaborative Computing: Networking, Applications and Worksharing*, 2006. CollaborateCom 2006. pp.1--9, 17-20 Nov. 2006. DOI:10.1109/COLCOM.2006.361852

[11] Kelly, B.; Sloan, D.; Brown, S.; Seale, J.; Petrie, H.; Lauke, P. and Ball, S. Accessibility 2.0: people, policies and processes. *Proceedings of the 2007 international cross-disciplinary conference on Web accessibility (W4A)*. Banff, Canada: ACM. 2007. pp. 138--147. ISBN 1-59593-590-X. DOI: 10.1145/1243441.1243471.

[12] Kelly, B.; Sloan, D.; Phipps, L.; Petrie, H.; Hamilton, F. 2005 Forcing standardization or accommodating diversity?: a framework for applying the WCAG in the real world. *Proceedings of the 2005 International Cross-Disciplinary Workshop on Web Accessibility (W4A)*. Chiba, Japan: ACM. 2005. pp. 46--54. ISBN 1-59593-219-4. DOI: 10.1145/1061811.1061820.

[13] Kleppe, A.; Warmer, J. and Bast, W. 2003. *MDA Explained – The Model Driven Architecture: Practice and Promise.* Addison-Wesley (Object Technology Series). 192 p.

[14] Liggesmeyer, P. and Trapp, M. 2009. Trends in Embedded Software Engineering. *IEEE Softw. 26, 3* (May. 2009), 19-25. DOI: http://dx.doi.org/10.1109/MS.2009.80

[15] Nielsen, J. 2007. Breadcrumb Navigation Increasingly Useful. *Jakob Nielsen's Alertbox*, April 10, 2007.

[16] Nielsen, J. 2009. Top 10 Information Architecture Mistakes. *Jakob Nielsen's Alertbox*, May 11, 2009: ISSN 1548-5552.

[17] Nunes, D. A. and Schwabe, D. 2006. Rapid prototyping of web applications combining domain specific languages and model driven design. In *Proceedings of the 6th international conference on Web engineering ICWE '06*, pp 153--160, New York, NY, USA, 2006. ACM.

[18] Reid, L. G.; Snow-Weaver, A. WCAG 2.0: a web accessibility standard for the evolving web. *Proceedings of the 2008 international cross-disciplinary conference on Web accessibility (W4A)*. Beijing, China: ACM. 2008. pp. 109--115. ISBN 978-1-60558-153-8. DOI: 10.1145/1368044.1368069.

[19] Thatcher, J.; Cynthia, W.; Henry, S.; Swierenga, S.; Urban, M.; Burks, M. and Bohman, P. 2002. *Constructing Accessible Web Sites*. 1a. ed. [S.l.]: Glasshaus. 415 p. ISBN 1904151000.

[20] van Welie, M. and van deer Veer, G. C. 2003. Pattern Languages in Interaction Design: Structure and Organization. *INTERACT 2003* – September 1 to 5. Zürich, Switzerland: [s.n.]. 2003. p. 8.

[21] Wilde, E. 2006. Structuring namespace descriptions. In *Proceedings of the 15th international Conference on World Wide Web* (Edinburgh, Scotland, May 23 - 26, 2006). WWW '06. ACM, New York, NY. 881-882. DOI: http://doi.acm.org/10.1145/1135777.1135925

Cultural Probes in the Design of Communication

Zoe McDougall
University of British Columbia
FSC 3640 – 2424 Main Mall
Vancouver BC V6T 1Z4
1.604.329.9093

zedoe@interchange.ubc.ca

Sidney Fels
University of British Columbia
2356 Main Mall
Vancouver BC V6T 1Z4
1.604.822.5338

ssfels@ece.ubc.ca

ABSTRACT
In this paper, we discuss cultural probes and how they can be used to benefit the design of communication community. A cultural probe is an experimental research method that provides "inspirational data" [9] for design. Through a cultural probe study that we undertook we were able to gain new insights into approaches toward a research project regarding collaboration between artists and scientists. Cultural probes offer the possibility for sustainable communication between designers and those being designed for. It does so by allowing a mental shift in the designer to be able to think from the target demographic's perspective so that designs can reflect that population's desires and concerns.

Categories and Subject Descriptors
A.0 [**General**]: Conference proceedings.

General Terms
Design, Experimentation, Human Factors.

Keywords
Cultural Probes, William Gaver, Communication.

1. INTRODUCTION
Cultural probes, developed in 1999 by William Gaver et al., are a design-led approach that facilitates design of artifacts when the designer generally has little personal knowledge or experience with the target user group. They are meant to challenge thoughts and assumptions about people and situations being designed for. Cultural probes are not designed to communicate anything specific nor be scientifically analyzed, they are designed to stimulate ideas [9]. Not being able to predict the outcome of a cultural probe is the point of undertaking it. This paper will: a) discuss what cultural probes are, how they have been used and how they may help create insights about a group of people being studied with an argument as to why they are appropriate for the design of communication where cultural differences between the target group and the designer can be large; b) discuss our cultural probe study conducted with a group of artists and scientists involved in a collaborative project and what insights were gained; c) identify characteristics of cultural probes and how design of

communication projects may benefit by the implementation of a cultural probe using some examples from existing literature.

2. RELATED WORK
Gaver introduced Cultural Probes as a means to explore new technologies through an artist–designers approach [9]. A cultural probe consists of a number of individual probe tasks contained in a larger cultural probe package. Probes are instruments that are metaphorically based on the concept of sending probes into the complete unknown of outerspace and then waiting for data that may or may not come back to try to make sense of it without assuming what it might be or where it comes from. Each person participating in a cultural probe study is given an identical package with probes inside, called a Probe kit, to be returned anonymously, ideally, within an allotted period of time. Probe kits often include a disposable camera, journal or sketchbook and various cards, postcards and/or basic craft materials. It is important to the probe process that probe materials are custom designed for the specific project, people and environment they are exploring. They represent a personal communication from the researcher that invites a personally communicative response [9]. Probes should be aesthetically pleasing and ambiguous. They should not lead the participants to any particular conclusion or response. Why probe for what researchers already know or think they know? Cultural probes offer the possibility of discovering something new.

Cultural probes are a non–traditional ethnographic method used to study new environments. As a method "they suggest the use of multiple, easy–to–use tasks to make the job of collecting data more engaging" and "as an approach, they advocate the use of open, ambiguous, and even surreal tasks as a way of undermining the assumptions of both volunteers and researchers" [7]. Probes present the possibility to get to know research subjects in their private/domestic settings where direct observation can be intrusive or impossible and while direct observation can show you what people do, cultural probes can reveal what people feel [4]. Such insights present the possibility of being able to make design decisions for target populations that reflect what people feel is important so that designs do not come off as arrogant or irrelevant. In general terms, cultural probes are a way for researchers to get to know their research subjects better, and vice versa. Gaver likens them to astronomic or surgical probes, which are left behind to return fragmentary data over time [9].

Cultural Probes have been used successfully in the "Presence Project" [9] to uncover insights about elderly community members from three sites in Europe. Eighteen to twenty probes were given to ten elderly members of each community. The process worked because the probes revealed a different flavour from each community. Insights came in the form of "strong and differentiated views of the three sites" [9]. One community was revealed to be a "paradox of a strong community in a dangerous area," one was affluent, educated and enthusiastic, and one was a community that enjoyed a relaxed social lifestyle in a beautiful setting [9]. It was this differentiation of characteristics discovered through the probes that lead to the development of three different design scenarios that would increase the presence of the elderly in each community while addressing each community's unique needs.

Other Probes have been used for a large variety of purposes. Examples include cultural probes being used for the collection of data from the everyday context of chronic disease [11], for studying and designing in a hostel and associated semi–independent living accommodation for former psychiatric patients [5], for dependability research of technology [3], and for exploring mediated intimacy in domestic life [13].

Gaver finds it heartening as well as troubling that the cultural probe approach has been adopted by several research and design groups around the world as there is often a tendency to adapt probes to other social science research methods and rationalize the probes, which betrays the original values of uncertainty, play, exploration, and subjective interpretation that embraces the notion that knowledge has its limits [10].

2.1 How Cultural Probes Create Insights

Cultural probes create insights by going beyond more traditional user study techniques that rely on what people say and do (questionnaires, interviews and observation studies). [10]. Probes combine interpretation, ambiguity and fun, inspiring and stimulating probe users who in turn stimulate the designers to tell a stories about what they get back from the places probed. These stories provide insights. The probes themselves do not create insights but stimulate designers to have insights about their target group/design space or problem. Probes are not meant to reflect objective needs but a more impressionistic account that could include beliefs and desires. Probes embrace the subjectivity avoided by most research techniques.

Probes can overcome distance between researchers and research subjects, whether that distance is generational, cultural, geographic or simply an "expert" vs. subject dichotomy. Using functional aesthetics with pleasure as a criterion for design [9], probes are aesthetically pleasing but not commercial looking. Thereby probes personalize or bridge the gap between researchers and research subjects through their design and open communication. Probe returns "reverberate with mutual influence," making it "impossible to arrive at comfortable conclusions about volunteers' lives or to stand back and regard them dispassionately" [10].

Something can be learned at every step in the probe process:

1. Creating probes can inform researchers about their own biases, special concerns, and assumptions or reveal further questions.

2. Personally distributing and introducing the probes can spark personal dialogue between researchers and participants that could be mutually beneficial to the probe process as each group is better able to get to know the intentions of the other.

3. Completing the probes can reveal to participants, the energy researchers are putting towards their designs,

researcher interests and tastes and hint at eventual designs.

4. Rate of returns and number of returns in total can indicate participant interest in the probe topic and/or distraction by their daily lives, i.e., lack of time to complete the probes.

5. Interpreting probe returns/creating stories about them can further reveal biases, assumptions, questions and concerns of researchers and can generate new ideas for designs and/or research.

Cultural probes help designers get insights as much through the process of creating and administering them as by actually getting them back and looking at them.

3. ART/SCIENCE 1(AS1) CULTURAL PROBE STUDY

To understand the usefulness of this technique, we conducted a cultural probe study with fourteen participants from a collaborative, highly multi and interdisciplinary research project betweens scientists, artists and engineers called the Visual Voice project [8] being done at the University of British Columbia, Vancouver, Canada. In this project, the team is creating new technologies and approaches to map hand gestures, measured by instrumenting the singer's movements, to control parameters of a digital, artificial vocal tract so that a user can sing and speak with her hands in the same way a person uses their vocal tract to speak and sing. A user speaking/singing with the device is called a **DI**gital **V**entriloquized **A**ctor (DIVA). See Figure 1. Collaborators include a composer, singers and instrumentalists, linguists, cognitive scientists, electrical and computer engineers, software programmers, a fashion designer, a lighting designer, a director, and a librettist. Once trained, a performer onstage can create a chorus of her own vocal tract based voice and her hand generated voice. The project also plans to include three–dimensional digitally projected talking heads whose facial movement will be controlled by the same hand gestures to add additional visual elements to the performance.

We chose this group for our study as our ongoing research is to understand and develop models of collaboration between artists and scientists involved in larger interdisciplinary collaborative projects.

Figure 1: A DIVA

Cultural probes were chosen as one of our techniques to help us recognize, articulate and expose our own biases going into this complex topic, as well as to generate new insights within the mixed disciplinary cultures involved in the visual voice project.

Step 1: Identifying Biases

Typical in a cultural probe study is to identify biases explicitly before creating the probes. It is quite typical that biases manifest themselves in the cultural probes, which can make them ineffective. However, when they do, it allows the researcher/designer to see them, redo the cultural probe design and then articulate the bias, which can be very helpful when doing the actual design later. In our study, expectations from the first author's artistic tradition going into the probe had to be mediated because they were antithetical to the probe process. Likewise, her bias about this being a research project that needs data leads to probes that are more like data logging than for gaining insights, which is common when first using cultural probes. From our experience, it is important for a research/designer to have faith that something may be learned by undertaking a cultural probe since it is intended to go in opposite directions of their existing knowledge and patterns. Cultural probes involve many hours of preparation and even more time exploring the possibilities in probe returns, not to mention participant time demands. However, creating individual probes based on specific expectations can result in the creation of closed and leading probes resulting in the possibility of learning nothing beyond what was already assumed. For this project, mediation came in the form of recruiting outside help from peers with and without previous cultural probe experience. These peers did however share expertise and experience with some of the future probe participants as computer scientists. The process of questioning ourselves, articulating our biases for determining whether the probes are going to provide information we already know was ongoing throughout the creation process but forms a good starting point.

One of the main benefits cultural probes offer to the design of communication process is their potential to reveal bias and obviate the need to continually mediate it.

Step 2: Creating the Probes

Probe creation involved several brainstorming sessions and a few visits to 'dollar stores' to spark ideas about how probes could be physically manifested. Having delightful, stimulating raw materials is very helpful for the creative process of making interesting, ambiguous and provocative probes. The Probe kits were packaged in clear vellum envelopes and contained eighteen probes in total including one group probe. Creating probes often leads to insights as well.

Some of the probes contained in the kits were packaged as sub–kits providing all the materials necessary to complete a given probe task; however, it was never stated that participants could not supplement with their own outside materials, some of whom did. Participants were originally given two weeks to complete the probes, which they could return individually or as a kit to a drop box adjacent to the lab where most of them worked. The deadline was extended to three weeks due to delays getting kits to some of the participants. We also welcomed returns after the deadline had passed and were pleased to receive a few more returns over the course of about a month while we were pouring through previously received probes.

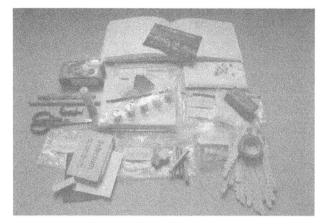

Figure 2. Probe Kit Contents

3.1.1 The Probes

A USB flashdrive was one of the items in the Probe kit that housed a contents list, basic instructions (that also appeared as labels on each probe task), deadlines and ten labeled folders that constituted one of the probe tasks: "Put one or more items of your choice into the appropriately labeled folders". The folders were:

1. Digital Beauty, 2. Efficient Truth, 3. Hypothetical Graph, 4. Linear Concession, 5. Phenomenological Diagram, 6. Random Compound, 7. Relational Fiction, 8. Religious Formula, 9. Synthetic Fact, 10. Triadic Segment.

Because the group to be probed was working with several digital tools, we felt it apt to include a digital task. Folder labels were created that juxtaposed words that were somewhat antithetical to each other.

Ten probes were fastened or tucked into a plain white sketchbook. These included:

- a thank–you card; "Write a thank–you note to someone who has inspired you."

- A small plastic envelope; "Put something(s) in the envelope that inspire(s) your daily research." This envelope was very small – about 1 inch square.

- A postcard that depicted a night view of downtown Vancouver; "Write a postcard to your best friend telling him or her something you have discovered about yourself or someone else."

- Surprise birthday party invitation; "You are planning a surprise birthday party for whomever you deem "the biggest liar in history". Complete the surprise party invitation card."

- A Picasso print of Les Demoiselles d'Avignon, 1907 (scissors and a glue stick were also provided for this task); "Cut apart the Picasso print and re-compose the pieces to represent *truth* (glue your creation into the sketchbook)."

- An envelope containing seven pages of various types of paper (handmade rag paper, Bristol board, canvas, watercolour paper, data paper, graph paper, illustration paper); "Construct a narrative about *aggravation with the colour green* on one or more pages — begin with the paper you like best, then second best, third, etc."

- An envelope containing one page; "Write a haiku about *concrete fact* on one side of the page and write a haiku about *aesthetic love* on the other side." The form for haikus was provided as well as a website link for more information on haikus.

- An Escher print of Relativity, 1953; "Who in the image would you most trust to give you a tour of this space? Why?"

- A Mondrian print, Composition 10, 1939-42; "Add one line to the image."

- "Use pencil, graphite or pastels/wax provided to take rubbings of "stuff you use every day" in the sketchbook."

Participants were invited to journal any thoughts/ideas they may have throughout the probe on unused pages of the sketchbook and document what order they took pictures on the disposable camera if they deviated from the listed order. We put several probes in the sketchbook for the purpose of portability. The book was quite thin and small (5x7 inches) and our hopes were that participants would carry it with them encouraging a higher rate of probe returns and maybe receiving some personal written comments as well.

Other probes included:

- A disposable camera with flash and indoor/outdoor film; "take a picture of: 1. Your favorite space, 2. Something beautiful, 3. Where you go to be alone, 4. Something desirable, 5. Something that you think is true, 6. Take a self–portrait, 7. Somewhere secret, 8. Something you hate, 9. Something boring, 10. Something exciting, 11. Anything you want."

- A 4x5 inch canvas, paint set with paintbrush and a Monet print 2x2.5 inches of Haystacks 1890–91. "Attach the Monet print to the canvas and add to the image."

- Plasticene and plaster of paris. "Use plasticene to shape a mold for the plaster of paris: "mold the shape of creativity." Instructions were included for how to mix and cure the plaster of paris.

- A lino square, razor blades and a stamp pad; "Carve a stamp that represents you. Stamp into the sketchbook."

- Popsicle sticks and tape; "Build a monument to Athena, goddess wisdom, arts and war."

- White paper envelope containing letter beads, string and a small plastic envelope; "String a secret word with the beads and put it in the small plastic envelope."

- Post-it Notes strips. This was a group activity called the "Beauty Board," which was located adjacent to the lab where most participants worked beside the drop point for the rest of the probes. Participants were asked to "create a storyline on the "theme of beauty." "When you feel inspired, write a word on one of the provided sticky notes. Use your words to create/add to the ongoing storyline." No deletions or re-arrangement of words already placed on the board were allowed.

Probe tasks were chosen and worded to explore the ideas of art and science without actually using those words. We wanted the probes to appeal to the artists and scientists in the group aesthetically and contextually and we wanted tasks to be provoking, fun and interesting.

3.1.2 Probe Returns

An online questionnaire (Survey Monkey) was distributed electronically through email after the probe deadline had passed. Twelve of fourteen participants filled it in. It revealed that ten people had completed at least some if not all of the probes and two people had completed none, both citing they were too "busy/not enough time". Favourite probe tasks based on number of returns (10 each) were the Escher print, the Mondrian print, collage truth with the Picasso print and the secret word in beads. Other probes with a high incidence of return were the canvas/Monet painting, an item that inspires daily research, rubbings, the thank–you note, build an Athena monument and the camera with eight returns each and the postcard with nine returns. Many of these probe tasks were fairly time–consuming and it was re-assuring to us that time–to–complete was not a determining factor in return rate but that the probes must have genuinely inspired participants to complete them. We may have included too many probes in the kit itself but because we wanted as many items as possible to be returned and inspire new ideas in us, we reasoned that a larger variety of tasks means more possibility that at least some of the probes would inspire each participant. Overall we were very pleased with the incidence of returns. Of a possible 252 returned tasks we received 141 completed or partially completed tasks. Interestingly one of the two least participated in probes at 5/14 was the group probe, the "Beauty Board," and three of those five people reported in the survey that they "completed but did not enjoy" the task. Despite all these participants being involved in a collaborative project together they were not very interested in participating in a group probe together even though it was located where the probes were to be dropped off and was adjacent to the lab where many of the participants worked. However, it may have been the probe task itself rather than the fact that it was a group task that was unappealing to participants.

Figure 3. Some Returned Probes

Step 3: Interpreting the Probe Returns

We spent time with probe returns as they trickled in after the deadline passed. We distributed the online survey a week after the probe return deadline. The survey helped us to organize our thoughts about the probes in a general sense and confirmed the rate of participation as well as level of enjoyment. As we suspected Probes reported as "completed and enjoyed" fairly closely matched the number of returns for that probe. Seven people reported that they did not complete all of the probes because they were "at a creative loss," four reported that some of the probes "did not appeal to them." General comments included that it was "fun" and participants "enjoyed being creative."

Because not all returns came in as kits but were returned piecemeal, returns were looked at by task rather than participant. We returned to the probes over time so that we could explore them with a fresh eye. Initially it was interesting to try to discern if a given return came from and artist or a scientist/engineer but that quickly became an obvious hindrance to gaining insight through the returns. Stories about why something was done a certain way or even what some objects were evolved. If we could understand our participants on a more personal and abstract level through the probes maybe we could be better able understand how they could relate to each other in a collaboration.

3.1.3 Insights Gained

We had three main insights that came from this study:

1. Similarities: Similarities are more important than differences in looking at art/science collaborations. Looking for differences is a non–constructive way to understand artists and scientists working in collaboration. Similarities and mutual creative needs inform why such collaborations are sought out and increasing in proliferation and how any given one can come to fruition. Interviews or questionnaires will allow us to generate background and experience profiles of our participants to see what similarities there are. Are participants more interdisciplinary than either 'artist' or 'scientist'?

This insight came from creating stories about similarities and differences that we saw in probe returns, whether similarities or differences were actually present and whether they were important or not. What was the role of similarity and difference in our larger project and how significant was it? The probes were designed to provoke creative responses that could illuminate something about artists and scientists so that we could see any differences more clearly. Expectations that there *would be* any differences were ultimately challenged by the probe process. Returns were indiscernible as to whether they came from either culturally specific group. One of the strengths of the probes was illuminated in that they revealed that as an artist, the first author had strong biases that impacted her ability to understand the target population; specifically the scientists but also the artist/scientist relationship in a larger contemporary context. One of the stories that contributed to stimulating this thought process evolved around a conversation about two Monet/Canvas probe returns that initially appeared as similar. See Figure 4. In both cases the Monet print was attached to the canvas dead centre and the sky, haystack and earth were extended out into the blank canvas. Both also used the paint like a watercolour wash. If the orientation of the second example were inverted however, which the participant *could* have intended, there appears to be a root vegetable like a beet growing in stratified soil, which would make it markedly different from the first example.

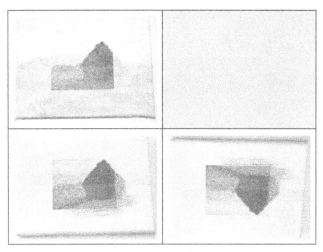

Figure 4. Monet Print

2. History: It is important to place our research within an art historical context. Everyone has a different historical context. How our participant's (art) historical context manifests and impacts their views will play a role in our thesis. Questionnaires or interviews will have to frame this historical context.

This insight came out of stories about probes that referenced art history in some way. Examples from the Monet probe and Picasso probe follow:

Two other Monet canvases seemed to have been done by someone familiar with art history. One plays on a classic allegory of painting: including the artist or the artist's hand in the painting (a painting of the painter painting). The other is also somewhat allegorical in that the Monet print is almost obliterated by making it a part of a painting that looks like a different Monet painting: not haystacks but waterlilies or one of his garden paintings. See Figure 5.

Figure 5. Allegorical Probes

Assuming that an artist had rendered these probes would be biased. The hand painting the painting could be the technical work of someone from a science background unfamiliar with art historical references and the Monet–like revision could be simply a pointillist style. It is also possible that a participant with a science background could have knowledge of these allegorical art historical references and reasoned that the painting should reference this.

The Picasso chosen for the truth collage lends itself to being sectioned up because the original already depicts a fractured cubist style. But this is a highly subjective statement not true for all people because art historical tastes, knowledge and contexts are individual. Two returned collages actually incorporated the word "truth" in the collage. The other eight returns were all abstract in nature, one of which depicted a school of fish all swimming to the left except one, which pointed up. See figure 6 for the returns.

Figure 6. Picasso Collages

3. Technology: Technology helps the convergence of the group. Their common language is "Google." It is a common access point to knowledge and that knowledge is the same. This also goes back to history — everyone can access the same historical perspective. A renaissance where delineation becomes less important because everyone accesses the same information reflects on the delineation of artists and scientists themselves. Our structure of knowledge changes the larger context; it binds people in an historical and cultural context. Interviews/questionnaires will gather information about the level of technical expertise of participants as well as the role technology plays in their lives. How their relationship to technology arose is also important.

This insight came out of a curiosity about how two different probe participants had managed to return an identical image in the "Phenomenological Diagram" folder of two different USB keys. See Figure 7.

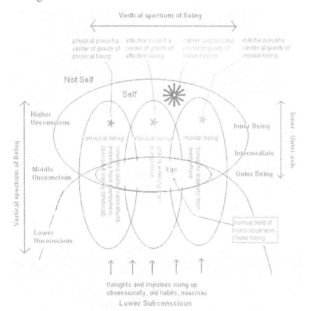

Figure 7. Phenomenological Diagram [12]

Six out of fourteen participants completed all or part of the USB task (54 of a possible total of 140 files were returned) and no other images were duplicated amongst participants. The two images were of different physical sizes and bit depths but the duplication could still be the result of a search engine query rather than any similarity between these two participants. Other digital artifacts returned on the USB keys were both humourously literal and highly abstract. In the folder entitled "Linear Concession" there were images of street vendor concession stands as well as a line graph on an X, Y axis. These again could be the result of search queries but no other images were duplicates.

There was definitely not a one–to–one relationship between probes returned to insights gained but we look forward to being able to come back to the probes for inspiration as our larger project evolves. The probes challenged us as designers of communication as well as acted as a vehicle for us to better understand what particular issues are important to address to improve our communication outcomes.

One observation gained by repeatedly going through probe returns was just how creative *everyone* in the group was, which could lead to insights about how the study as a whole could address *individual* creativity. Other insights included that 'facts' about artists and scientists are irrelevant to our research as such 'facts' cannot be fully discerned; both cultures defy strict definition and are constantly evolving.

Because of the insights we were able to gain we are convinced that the cultural probe process worked for our purposes.

4. APPLICATION TO DESIGN OF COMMUNICATION

Cultural probes present an opportunity to the design of communication community. Touted by some as 'laughable' simply because of the name "Cultural Probe" or because they invite *play* into the research process while abandoning strict analysis; cultural probes can reveal very tangible issues and generate real possibilities.

Design of communication often involves researchers designing for people outside of their own culture, gender or age group and as demonstrated by AS1 having an 'insider' perspective can also lead to bias. This is not to say that designers should seek to design for those outside of their expertise, but it is often the case that there is potential for some bias even due to excessive experience in a given area leading to the formation of patterns overlooking differences that can make a difference. Cultural probes offer the potential for researchers to step aside of the design process and let those being designed for offer a new objectivity and subjectivity. By allowing a possible mental shift in the designer to be able to think from the target demographic's perspective cultural probes lead to a sustained connection to the group for ongoing design strategies and outcomes. Cultural probes can illuminate unpredictable or overlooked possibilities beyond interviews and ethnographic research challenging expectations about a research group and these insights can evolve as well as be revisited over time simply by returning to the probes. Communication is thus sustained reciprocally as a sort of feedback loop between designer's reasoning and subject's desires mediated by probe objects.

We have selected some publications from the design of communication community and present some ideas about how a cultural probe could serve to augment the research. See Table 1.

Table 1. Summary Table

Examples	Type of probe	Insight Areas
"Providing Culturally Contextualized Metadata to Promote Sharing and Reuse of Learning Objects" [2]. This research discusses learning object (LO) development in the context of the Brazilian culture.	• Camera — take pictures of things you learn from, favourite LO, etc. • Physical LO — what did you learn/what would you add • Common–sense maps • Use multiple locations like the "Presence Project" [10]	• LO use scenarios • Meta–metadata tags • Cultural specificity/transferability • LO interface design • Role of physical object in mental model
"The collaborative structure of "fact" on Wikipedia" [14]. This research looks at how collective intelligence through mass collaboration can result in the creation of stable facts on Wikipedia.	• Personal fact diary • Story circle online — one-person starts, next continues, etc. • Camera — photos of "facts" • Collective intelligence map	• Collaboration manifestation • Fact creation/persistence • Fact corruption • Fact formation tools
The macro-structure of use help [1]. This research discusses problem-solving strategies of people using computer applications and how help systems might be better designed to support users.	• Help diary • Help tolerance — reactions to Help scenarios • Support map • Camera — document help	• Acquisition of help • Deterrents to help • Physical vs. intellectual help • Help use scenarios

5. CONCLUSION

We have found the use of probes to be beneficial to our research process; however the effective design and implementation of a cultural probe is not a simple process and insights are not guaranteed. In the Equator project [6], which Gaver took part in, "Domestic Probes" were designed to "reveal details of people's home lives" [7] but probe results were "impossible to analyze or even interpret clearly because they reflect[ed] too many layers of influence and constraint" [10]. Instead of generating insights the probes only served to provide "a kind of intimate distance" fruitful for new design ideas [10].

Based on our experience however, we can recommend the use of cultural probes as a means to facilitate the design of communication. As a type of metacommunication, probes return possible communication about the communication that created them. Thus Probes have the potential to contribute to more sustainable design of communication.

6. ACKNOWLEDGEMENTS

Thanks to Roberto Calderon and Tony Tang for their assistance with probe creation for AS1.
This work was supported in part by the Faculty of Graduate Studies, the Interdisciplinary Studies Graduate Program (ISGP) and the Institute for Computing, Information and Cognitive Systems (ICICS) at UBC.

7. REFERENCES

[1] Andrade, O. D., Bean, N., and Novick D.G. 2009. The macro-structure of use help. In *Proceedings of the 27th ACM international SIGDOC conference on Design of communication* (Bloomington, Indiana, USA, October 5-7, 2009). DOI= http://doi.acm.org/10.1145/1621995.1622022.

[2] Buzatto D., Anacleto J.C. and Dias A.L. 2009. Providing Culturally Contextualized Metadata to Promote Sharing and Reuse of Learning Objects. In *Proceedings of the 27th ACM international SIGDOC conference on Design of communication* (Bloomington, Indiana, USA, October 5-7, 2009). DOI= http://doi.acm.org/10.1145/1621995.1622026.

[3] Crabtree, A., Hemmings, T. and Rodden, T. 2002. Presented at the 1st DIRC Conference on Dependable Computing systems, November 20-21, London :The Royal Statistical Society. www.mrl.nott.ac.uk/~axc/documents/papers/DIRC02.pdf.

[4] Dix, A. , Finlay, J., Adowd, G. D. and Beale, R. 2004. *Case Study: cultural probes – methods to study new environments*. In Human-Computer Interaction (3rd Ed.). England: Pearson/Prentice Hall. http://www.hcibook.com/e3/casestudy/cultural-probes/.

[5] Dix, A. , Finlay, J., Adowd, G. D. and Beale, R. 2004. *Case Study: SPAM — coordination in residential care using SMS*. In Human-Computer Interaction (3rd Ed.). England: Pearson/Prentice Hall. http://www.hcibook.com/e3/casestudy/spam/.

[6] Engineering and Physical Sciences Research Council. Equator Website. Accessed Jun. 21st, 2010 at http://www.equator.ac.uk/.

[7] Engineering and Physical Sciences Research Council. Equator Website Domestic Probes. Accessed Jun. 27th, 2010 at http://www.equator.ac.uk/index.php/articles/629.

[8] Fels, S., Pritchard, B., Lloyd, J. and Vatikiotis-Bateson, E. 2010. DIVAs. Visual Voice: Gestural Control of DIgital Ventriloquized Actors. Accessed June 26th, 2010 at http://www.magic.ubc.ca/artisynth/pmwiki.php?n=VisualVoice.HomePage.

[9] Gaver, W. 1999. Design: Cultural Probes. Interactions. Vol. 6, Issue 1 (Jan./Feb. 1999) Pages: 21-29. http://portal.acm.org/citation.cfm?id=291235.

[10] Gaver, W. W., Boucher, A., Pennington, S., and Walker, B. 2004. Cultural probes and the value of uncertainty. Interactions 11, 5 (Sep. 2004), 53-56. DOI= http://doi.acm.org/10.1145/1015530.1015555.

[11] Hassling, L., Nordfeldt, S., Eriksson, H. and Timpka, T. 2005. Use of cultural probes for representation of chronic disease experience: Exploration of an innovative method for design of supportive technologies. Technology and Health Care. Vol. 13 (Number 2/2005) Pages 78-95. http://iospress.metapress.com/content/md8cf8jdv9g9a7l4/.

[12] Kazlev, M. A. 2005. A New Integral Paradigm – Psychology. "Map of consciousness using an Aurobindonian-Assagiolian paradigm". Accessed Aug. 9th, 2010 at http://www.kheper.net/integral/psychology.html.

[13] Kjeldskov, J., Gibbs, M., Vetere, F., Howard, S., Pedell, S., Mecoles, K. and Bunyan, M. 2004. Using Cultural Probes to Explore Mediated Intimacy. Australasian Journal of Information Systems, Vol. 11, No 2. http://dl.acs.org.au/index.php/ajis/article/view/128.

[14] Swarts, J. 2009. The collaborative construction of "fact" on Wikipedia. In *Proceedings of the 27th ACM international SIGDOC conference on Design of communication* (Bloomington, Indiana, USA, October 5-7, 2009). DOI= http://doi.acm.org/10.1145/1621995.1622051.

Social media for sustainable engineering communication

Brad Mehlenbacher[1], Sarah McKone[3], Christine Grant[2],
Tuere Bowles[1], Steve Peretti[2], Pamela Martin[3]
[1]College of Education / [2]College of Engineering /
[3]College of Humanities and Social Sciences
North Carolina State University
Raleigh, NC 27695-7801
1.919.515.6242
brad_m@unity.ncsu.edu

ABSTRACT

This paper provides an overview of current research on social media applications, including user demographics and how social media websites define themselves. The paper also describes user activities using social media and suggests known strengths and weaknesses of social media, and concludes by outlining several recommendations for developing strong online communities.

Categories and Subject Descriptors

K. [Computing Milieux], K.3. [Computers and Education], K.3.1. [Computer Uses in Education].

General Terms

Design, Documentation, Human Factors, Theory.

Keywords

Collaboration, Community, Social media, Social networking applications, User demographics.

INTRODUCTION

Social media have emerged as a significant element of what we mean when we describe the Web 2.0 learning revolution [18]. Although discussions about the social nature and purpose of the Web date back to the 1960s, the first commercial web application, SixDegrees.com, was launched in 1997 [12]. Since that time hundreds of social networking applications have been created (see Alexa/TechCrunch's boom of social sites graphic at http://www.focus.com/fyi/other/boom-social-sites/, Wikipedia's growing list of social media networks and applications at http://en.wikipedia.org/wiki/List_of_social_networking_websites, and ethority's comprehensive social media graphic at http://www.ethority.de/weblog/social-media-prisma/).

Today, when researchers refer to social networking media, they are usually including self-publishing media such as podcasts, wiki, blogs, RSS/XML feeds, mashups, bookmarking applications, and so on. Increasingly, social media applications support various common tasks, such as establishing public and private groups, maintaining profiles, tagging, note-taking, summary presentations, commenting, email, real-time posting, instant messaging, and the integration and display of data from other common social media applications [7].

As part of a preliminary research investigation of community formation related to chemical engineering research and practice on sustainability, energy, and the environment, we have become increasingly interested in the interactive potential of numerous Web 2.0 applications with a special emphasis on social media. Our initial work focused on a single blended graduate course, Advances in Pollution Prevention, offered to on-campus and off-campus engineering students simultaneously, but efforts have been extended to include other chemical engineering courses and, ultimately, the project aim is to design social learning spaces to facilitate communication between on-campus students, alumni, and practicing engineers.

This paper reviews some initial demographic findings related to social networking media, examines how social media websites currently define themselves, provides a brief overview of emerging research on social media including describing the numerous activities engaged in by users, and presents several research-based suggestions for facilitating online community via social media. Our ultimate motivation is to document how social media augments or challenges group work related to collaborative document, spreadsheet, database, and presentation activities (via applications such as Google Docs™ or Zoho™ or online social networking spaces such as Bebo™, Delicious™, Facebook™, Flickr™, LinkedIn™, MySpace™, Ning™, Photobucket™, Plaxo™, Twitter™, and YouTube™). Because social media research is burgeoning and spread across disciplines and journals, our goal is also to bring together research on the subject in one place. Data amassed over the last several years suggests that social media applications are attracting (exponentially) growing numbers of users and this has drawn the attention of commercial and educational leaders alike.

SOCIAL MEDIA DEMOGRAPHICS

Rainie [41] phone interviewed 2054 Internet using adults living in the U.S. in 2007 and found that a 48 percent had visited video-sharing applications such as YouTube, double the number reported the year before. Video-sharing sites appear to appeal most to younger adult males who are college educated. Madden [30] found that 57 percent of Internet users not only watched videos online (19 percent on a typical day) but also shared what they found with others. Indeed, social network websites—although still most popular with American teens (65 percent use them)—are increasingly attracting older users: 75 percent of online adults 18-24 have a social network profile, 57 percent of online adults 25-34 have a profile, 30 percent of online adults 35-44 have a profile, and so on [28]. Not surprisingly, user behaviors are changing to reflect the affordances of social media. Madden and Smith [31], for instance, note that approximately half the adult Internet users search for themselves online, create and revise their profiles, and edit or remove digital footprints (e.g., privacy settings, unwanted comments, etc.). Hargittai [24] notes that, while differences exist between the demographics of social media users and non-users (e.g., age), it is important to also note that differences also exist between different users of different social media sites (e.g., gender, race, education). Researchers need to keep this in mind when reflecting on social media behaviors in general.

HOW SOCIAL MEDIA DEFINES ITSELF

As new social networking tools enter our web space, it is becoming increasingly difficult to strictly categorize new tools as the social networking "type" of Internet technology. According to Boyd and Ellison [12], social networks can be defined as sites that "allow individuals to (1) construct a public or semi-public profile within a bounded system, (2) articulate a list of other users with whom they share a connection, and (3) view and traverse their list of connections and those made by others within the system." However, many sites are now completing these three tasks among a multitude of others; some sites seem to offer the networking capabilities only because they feel as if they are supposed to do so, and not because the networking purpose is one of the site's objectives.

As these emerging social networks develop networking capabilities as optional features rather than site design focal points, it is useful to ask if they are still social networks. Some blog sites may function as networking sites, but might focus on the delivery of podcasts. What are the inherent or definitive characteristics of a blog? And when does a blog space become a file sharing space? Photo-sharing tools are integrating geo-tagging features that increase their networking capabilities and social aspects. Again, at what point—in terms of features and use—does an application designed to support photo-sharing communities become a social network?

We observe that numerous practitioners and researchers have begun to creatively categorize emerging social media as a way to meaningfully describe the online phenomenon. Baird and Fisher [7], drawing on Gardner [21], distinguish between social media that support thinking (logical-linguistic and logical-mathematical), sensational (visual-spatial, body-kinesthetic, auditory-musical), communicational (interpersonal-communications, intrapersonal-communication), and naturalist (pp. 26-30). Go2Web20 (http://www.go2web20.net) distinguishes social media according to popularity and a mix of activities (collaboration, fun, search) and topics (travel, business, communication). As we work to define the network spaces and the influence they are having on the way we create and consume information, we need to first take a look at the way these tools are defining themselves.

Boyd and Ellison [12] note that, "The nature and nomenclature of these connections may vary from site to site" (p. 211). The varying nomenclature has been increasingly noticeable as networks begin integrating other social media and Web 2.0 tools into their functionality. Interestingly, the most popular social

networks have begun adapting their own perceptions of themselves to the interactions they offer. The following Wordle™ provides a visual summary of how the world's top social networks currently *describe themselves* (ultimately, we hope to extend this analysis to the sites' constructs and related activities for a much richer analysis). To create this Wordle™ graphic, the descriptions from the world's top social networking communities were combined, counted, and then arranged to illustrate which words were most common within the descriptions.[1]

Figure 1: Wordle™ representation of the most common words within site self-descriptions of the world's top 50 social networks (See Appendix A)

Interestingly, "people" and "social" rank highly as orienting principles for social media websites, along with various activities frequently associated with the (e.g., sharing, creating, discovering, allowing, searching, finding, etc.). Content words (e.g., photos, videos, links, etc.) are de-emphasized and, although "platform" and "tools" rank representation, they are not a focus any more than the particular forms that the websites take (e.g., blogs, wiki, etc.).

CHALLENGES FOR SOCIAL MEDIA

Before one gets too excited about the potentials of social media for communication design, it is useful to proceed with caution whenever a technology or set of technologies emerge that promise, as Ajjan and Hartshorne [2] posit, to all users to "access and create collective knowledge through social interactions" (p. 71). Alexander [3] thankfully qualifies our tendency to rally around attractive (but potentially misleading) terms such as "Web 2.0," writing

> Many people—including, or perhaps especially, supporters—critique the "Web 2.0" moniker for definitional reasons. Few can agree on even the general outlines of Web 2.0. It is about no single new development. Moreover, the term is often applied to a heterogeneous mix of relatively familiar and also very emergent technologies. The former may appear as very much "Web 1.0," and the latter may be seen as

---

[1] Common words such as "a," "an," "the," and "or" were removed, in addition to the names of networks. For example, if Facebook claims "Facebook helps you…" then the entry for Wordle™ is "helps you…." References to other networks within descriptions such as TwitPic™'s reference to Twitter™ have not been altered.

too evanescent to be relied on for serious informatic work (p. 33).

Simonson [47], in his call for research on social networking, suggests that we need to define and trace their history, that we need to understand design for "profiling, blogging, wiki-ing, and friending" (p. vii), to study ethical, support, and policy issues related to social networks, and that we need to better understand how to better understand how to teach, learn, research, and build theory within these spaces. Many researchers currently spend considerable time introducing us to the developing definition and short history Web 2.0 applications.

Most discussions about social media applications inevitably begin by distinguishing between Web 1.0 and Web 2.0 applications. Web 2.0 represents a significant advance over Web 1.0 because it allows users to create and upload content to the Internet [51]. This is not to suggest that users did not generate considerable content for the Web prior to the development of Web 2.0 and social media applications, but that the ease with which they can construct, revise, share, comment, and repost has certainly become easier with the advent of blogs, wikis, and shared spaces such as Flikr™, Facebook™, del.icio.us™, and so on. As Purdy [40] argues, "People have, of course, written and researched together in pre-Web 2.0 spaces, but they have not done so in a space that integrates these activities as fully" (p. 49). These spaces encourage creative application both commercially [18] and educationally [11, 49]. The interactions between these two audiences are obvious and so, although Parker and Chao [37] are describing for wikis for instructional audiences, they recommend that ideal uses include project planning, requirements management, test case management, defect tracking, client notes and user documentation (pp. 9-10).

Soon after this distinction is made, educators are reminded that today's Net Generation learner is a "digital native" [39] and that they differ significantly from older users or "digital immigrants" — digital natives "… are able to deal with the huge amounts of information coming at them" [38], they grew up on "twitch speed" (p. 3), and expect "future" content (e.g., robotics, nanotechnology, genomics, etc.) in addition to "legacy" content (e.g., reading, writing, arithmetic, etc.) (p. 4). Certainly the preference of younger users for social networking sites would suggest that differences exist demographically, but Stoerger [50] cites research that suggests that "melting pot" is a more productive metaphor for how different users "… speak with different technology tongues" and bring ranges of experience to the hardware and software they use.

To this research conversation, a discussion over the short- and long-term implications of multitasking on social media users has begun to surface [20, 23, 36, 43, 53]. At one end of the continuum are proponents who argue that Net Gen learners are becoming proficient multitaskers [54] and, at the other end, are those who believe users are becoming "stupid" and shallow [14]. This comes as no surprise to communication designers familiar with the challenges of getting users to read manuals [42] or to toggle between what they are doing and what they need to learn to do it [15]. The ultimate truth may be somewhere in-between as research on situational awareness (how humans focus strategically on more than one thing at a time) and split-attention and cognitive workload suggest [6, 13, 34].

Finally, some researchers note developing issues with social media use, including illegal file sharing [45], copyright infringement, and plagiarism [48]. Schweitzer [44] warns that some social media applications can operate as "online minefields" inviting users to engage in personal expression and sharing (e.g., recreational drug use or controversial political rants) when their audiences might well include professional, administrative, or commercial representatives [1]. Table 1 outlines the strengths and weaknesses of social media as currently described in the research.

Table 1: Strengths and weaknesses of social media

Issue	Opportunities	Challenges
Aggregation	Links web applications and content	Diffuses one's identity across fractured spaces, marketing profiles
Openness	Shares objects with numerous audiences across platforms [27]	Allows peer surveillance and undermines privacy [10]
Personal	Serves as excellent repository for personal and professional data	Increases flow of personal information across networks [57]
Productive	Generates solutions through large group collaboration	Exploits free labor for commercial gain
Shared Responsibility	All groups to own, share, and manipulate single objects	Undermines traditional authorship model and raises specter of copyright infringement
Pleasurable	Compels users to share, compare, create, play [22]	Highlights certain creator attributes and interests at the expense of others
Identity Formation	Allows users to represent themselves strategically, over time, and across applications [33]	Challenges individual control over reputation and personal data by spreading profiling information across social networks [8]
Engagement	Creates new opportunities for civic engagement, especially among disenfranchised and the young	Introduces new concerns about Internet addiction in all settings [56]
Rich Site Summary	Supports design by providing host of automated templates, widgets, apps, syndication mechanisms	Undermines creative design by emphasizing content summary and providing propriety posts or defaults [5]
Critical Interaction	Allows information consumers to evaluate producer contributions [29]	Encourages non-reflective feedback, including ad hominem, flaming, errors in argumentation (unless carefully monitored)

SOCIAL MEDIA ACTIVITIES

In our preliminary review of the research on social media, the ultimate goal has been to outline research-based instructional strategies for effectively connecting learners with instructors, learners with learners, learners with content, learners with interface features, and content with content [4]. Understanding how social media websites have developed historically and how they define themselves currently is a productive part of that process. Moreover, research on the activities that make social media so attractive to so many users is currently emerging. Table 2 presents one such description of new media literacies that have been associated with social media [26].

Table 2: New media literacies associated with social media [26]

Skills	Definition
Play	The capacity to experiment with one's surroundings as a form of problem-solving
Performance	The ability to adopt alternative identities for the purpose of improvisation and discovery
Simulation	The ability to interpret and construct dynamic models of real-world processes
Appropriation	The ability to meaningfully sample and remix media content
Multitasking	The ability to scan one's environment and shift focus as needed to salient details
Distributed Cognition	The ability to interact meaningfully with tools that expand mental capacities
Collective Intelligence	The ability to pool knowledge and compare notes with others toward a common goal
Judgment	The ability to evaluate the reliability and credibility of different information sources
Transmedia Navigation	The ability to follow the flow of stories and information across multiple modalities
Networking	The ability to search for, synthesize, and disseminate information
Negotiation	The ability to travel across diverse communities, discerning and respecting multiple perspectives, and grasping and following alternative norms
Visualization	The ability to interpret and create data representations for the purposes of expressing ideas, finding patterns, and identifying trends

Many of the activities described by Jenkins, Purushotma, Clinton, Weigel, and Robinson [26] are inherently social in nature. Researchers who emphasize social learning have begun to develop work models that capitalize on this orientation. For example, research suggests that successful community-based online environments support various cognitive activities performed by participants (e.g., questioning, negotiating, discussing), various forms of argumentation and exchange, the sharing of useful resources for the exploration of new meanings, and evidence of changes in understanding or the creation of new objects for learning and interaction [19, 52, 55]. Derven [18] argues that these activities can reinforce and sustain learning by archiving team communications and artifacts, setting schedules, linking to shared resources, producing summarizing documents, presentations, or videos, and communicating quickly and efficiently using real-time applications (p. 61).

Web environments that effectively support community development should also support, as Lévy (2001) describes it, "Multilogues", including multiparticipant interaction, community-developed hyperdocuments, artifact creation, and community debate and exchange (p. 65). Mallan and Giardina [32], in their study of teen MySpace use, suggest that contemporary teenagers are actively engaged in "collaborative identity work," or "wikidentities" whenever they manipulate their "profile content and design, the profile image, the Friends list, and the comments section" Coppola, Hiltz, and Rotter [16] suggest that faculty need to "change ... their teaching persona, toward more precision in their presentation of materials and instructions, combined with a shift to a more Socratic pedagogy, emphasizing multilogues with students" (p. 169). Changing teaching persona may not be a minor reorientation, either, given that Mazer, Murphy, and Simonds [35] found that "teacher self-disclosure has a positive influence on important variables such as teacher clarity...., student participation..., and affective learning... (pp. 12-13). Thus, the managers of social media spaces can influence community members and their engagement.

Bonk and Dennen [9] suggest that online community interactions should "widen one's views on the range of online participants, the forms of online instruction, the degree and type of interactions online, and the online environments that may soon be common (p. 336). Dawley [17] suggests that "social networking knowledge construction" can be facilitated by first identifying networks, then lurking, contributing, creating and, finally, leading. Organizing community around shared contributions and topics that leverage partnerships among various group members builds online sustainability (p. 118). And Howard [25] maintains that successful online communities support renumeration (positive return on investment), influence (allowing individual member contribution), belonging (encouraging member identification and group formation), and significance (articulating community goals and achievements).

CONCLUSIONS

We have only touched on the issue of developing strategies for sustaining community using social media. Howard [25] provides a four-step process for encouraging the development of successful online communities. These include *renumeration* (e.g., by collecting user data, seeding the discussion, ranking contributions and member value, streamlining rules for participation, etc.), *influence* (e.g., by setting up an advisory, encouraging profiles and avatars, addressing problems quickly, establishing policies, etc.), *belonging* (e.g., by building on shared stories, creating rituals and routines, building on shared goals and identities, etc.), and *significance* (e.g., by interacting with other communities, building your own community, making connections, etc.). Howard's [25] principles for developing and supporting online communities are similar to Shneiderman's [46] four stages of human activities, that is, collecting, relating, creating, and donating (or disseminating) ideas, products, or processes (pp. 84-86). Principles for facilitating the development of online communities are still in the early stages. Still, it is clear that community development is not a technical challenge but, rather, a human-communication challenge where issues of investment, reward, identification, trust, expression, and creativity are central to the enterprise.

Exploring technologies that facilitate interactions between instructors, learners, and practitioner-experts is an exciting area for research that continues to grow in popularity. Ultimately, our goal will be to catalog existing and emerging technologies, to develop instruments for evaluating their various purposes, usability, and effectiveness for facilitating the maintenance of community exchange, and to employ what we learn to reach out to the growing number of communities interested in sustainable engineering communication, research, and practice.

ACKNOWLEDGEMENTS

This research was sponsored by the National Science Foundation (NSF), Award # 0935161. The views and conclusions contained herein are those of the authors and should not be interpreted as necessarily representing the official policies or endorsements, either expressed or implied, of the NSF or any other organization. In addition, the authors wish to thank the anonymous reviewers who helped us focus this manuscript.

REFERENCES

[1] Abel, M. (2005). Find me on Facebook … as long as you are not a faculty member or administrator. *ESource, December*. Available online: http://citeseerx.ist.psu.edu/viewdoc/download?doi=10.1.1.1 34.2431&rep=rep1&type=pdf

[2] Ajjan, H., & Hartshorne, R. (2008). Investigating faculty decisions to adopt Web 2.0 technologies: Theory and empirical tests, *Internet and Higher Education, 11* (1), 71-80.

[3] Alexander, B. (2006). Web 2.0: A new wave of innovation for teaching and learning? *EDUCAUSE Review, March/April*.

[4] Anderson, T. (2003). Modes of interaction in distance education: Recent developments and research questions. In M. G. Moore and W. G. Anderson (eds.), *Handbook of Distance Education* (pp. 129–144). Mahwah, NJ: Lawrence Erlbaum.

[5] Arola, K. L. (2010). The design of Web 2.0: The rise of the template, the fall of design. *Computers and Composition, 27* (1), 4-14.

[6] Ayres, P., & Sweller, J. (2005). The split-attention principle in multimedia learning. In R. E. Mayer (ed.), *The Cambridge Handbook of Multimedia Learning* (pp. 135–146). Cambridge: Cambridge UP.

[7] Baird, D. E., & Fisher, M. (2005). Neomillennial user experience design strategies: Utilizing social networking media to support "always on" learning styles. *Journal of Educational Technology Systems, 34* (1), 5-32.

[8] Bilton, N. (2010). Price of Facebook privacy? Start clicking. *New York Times, May 12*. Available online: http://www.nytimes.com/2010/05/13/technology/personalte ch/13basics.html?pagewanted=print

[9] Bonk, C. J., & Dennen, V. (2003). Frameworks for research, design, benchmarks, training, and pedagogy in Web-based distance education. In M. G. Moore and W. G. Anderson (eds.), *Handbook of Distance Education* (pp. 331–348). Mahwah, NJ: Lawrence Erlbaum.

[10] Boston, I. (2009). Racing towards academic social networks. *On the Horizon, 17* (3), 218-225.

[11] Boyd, D. (2007). Viewing American class divisions through Facebook and MySpace. *Apophenia Blog Essay*. Available online: http://www.danah.org/papers/essays/ClassDivisions.html

[12] Boyd, D. M., & Ellison, N. B. (2008). Social network sites: Definition, history, and scholarship. *Journal of Computer-Mediated Communication, 13* (1), 210-230. Available online: http://jcmc.indiana.edu/vol13/issue1/boyd.ellison.html

[13] Burns, C. M., and Hajdukiewicz, J. R. (2004). *Ecological Interface Design*. Boca Raton, FL: CRC P.

[14] Carr, N. (2008). Is Google making us stupid? *The Atlantic, July/August*. Available online: http://www.theatlantic.com/magazine/archive/2008/07/is-google-making-us-stupid/6868/

[15] Carroll, J. M. (ed.) (1990). *The Nurnberg Funnel: Designing Minimalist Instruction for Practical Computer Skill*. Cambridge, MA: MIT P.

[16] Coppola, N. W., Hiltz, S. R., & Rotter, N. G. (2002) Becoming a virtual professor: Pedagogical roles and asynchronous learning networks, *Journal of Management Information Systems*, 18 (4) 169–189.

[17] Dawley, L. (2009). Social networking knowledge construction: Emerging virtual world pedagogy. *On the Horizon, 17* (2), 109-121.

[18] Derven, M. (2009). Social networking: A force for development? *T&D, July*, 58-63.

[19] Ellis, A. P. J., Bell, B. S., Ployhart, R. E., Hollenbeck, J. R., & Ilgen, D. R. (2005). An evaluation of generic teamwork skills training with action teams: Effects on cognitive and skill-based outcomes. *Personnel Psychology, 58* (3), 641–672.

[20] Foehr, U. G. (2006). *Media Multitasking among American Youth: Prevalence, Predictors, and Pairings*. Report of the Program for the Study of Entertainment Media and Health. Menlo Park, CA: Kaiser Family Foundation. Available online: http://www.kff.org/entmedia/entmedia121206pkg.cfm.

[21] Gardner, H. (1983). *Frames of Mind: The Theory of Multiple Intelligences*. NY, NY: Basic Books.

[22] Griffiths, M., & Light, B. (2008). Social networking and digital gaming media convergence: Classification and its consequences for appropriation. *Information Systems Frontier, 10* (4), 447-459.

[23] Hafner, K. (2005). You there, at the computer: Pay attention. *New York Times, February 10*. Available online: http://www.nytimes.com/2005/02/10/technology/circuits/10 info.html?r=1andex=1156132800anden=2549daec886676c 2andei=5070

[24] Hargittai, E. (2008). Whose space? Differences among users and non-users of social network sites. *Journal of Computer-Mediated Communication, 13* (1), 351-380.

[25] Howard, T. W. (2010). *Design to Thrive: Creating Social Networks and Online Communities that Last*. Burlington, MA: Morgan Kaufmann Publishers.

[26] Jenkins, H., Purushotma, R., Clinton, K., Weigel, M., & Robinson, A. J. (2006). Confronting the challenges of participatory culture: Media education for the 21st century.

An Occasional paper for digital media and learning. MacArthur Foundation. Available online: http://digitallearning.macfound.org/atf/cf/{7E45C7E0-A3E0-4B89-AC9C-E807E1B0AE4E}/JENKINS_WHITE_PAPER.PDF

[27] Lange, P. G. (2008). Publicly private and privately public: Social networking on YouTube. *Journal of Computer-Mediated Communication, 13* (1), 351-380.

[28] Lenhart, A. (2009). *Adults and social network websites.* Project Data Memo of the PEW Internet and American Life Project. Available online: http://www.pewinternet.org/~/media//Files/Reports/2009/PIP_Adult_social_networking_data_memo_FINAL.pdf.pdf

[29] Lundin, R. W. (2008). Teaching with wikis: Toward a networked pedagogy. *Computers and Composition, 25* (4), 432-448.

[30] Madden, M. (2007). *Online video.* Report of the PEW Internet and American Life Project. Available online: http://www.pewinternet.org/~/media//Files/Reports/2007/PIP_Online_Video_2007.pdf.pdf

[31] Madden, M., & Smith, A. (2010). *Reputation management and social media: How people monitor their identity and search for others online.* Report of the PEW Internet and American Life Project. Available online: http://www.pewinternet.org/~/media//Files/Reports/2010/PIP_Reputation_Management.pdf

[32] Mallan, K., & Giardina, N. (2009). Wikidentities: Young people collaborating on virtual identities in social networking sites. *First Monday, 14* (6). Available online: http://www.uic.edu/htbin/cgiwrap/bin/ojs/index.php/fm/article/view/2445/2213

[33] Maranto, G., & Barton, M. (2010). Paradox and promise: MySpace, Facebook, and the sociopolitics of social networking in the writing classroom. *Computers and Composition, 27* (1), 36-47.

[34] Mayer, R. E., & Moreno, R. (2003). Nine ways to reduce cognitive load in multimedia learning. *Educational Psychologist, 38* (1), 43–52.

[35] Mazer, J. P., Murphy, R. E., & Simonds, C. J. (2007). I'll see you on "Facebook": The effects of computer-mediated teacher self-disclosure on student motivation, affective learning, and classroom climate. *Communication Education, 56* (1), 1-17.

[36] Mulder, I., de Poot, H., Verwijs, C., Janssen, R., & Bijlsma, M. (2006). An information overload study: Using design methods for understanding. In T. Robertson, J. Kjeldskov, and J. Paay (eds.), *OzCHI'06: Proceedings of the 18th Australia Conference on Computer-Human Interaction: Design: Activities, Artefacts and Environments* (pp. 245–252). NY, NY: ACM P.

[37] Parker, K. R., & Chao, J. T. (2007). Wiki as a teaching tool. *Interdisciplinary Journal of Knowledge and Learning Objects,* 3, 57-72. Available online: http://www.ijello.org/Volume3/IJKLOv3p057-072Parker284.pdf

[38] PBS. (2010). Digital_nation: Life on the virtual frontier. *Frontline, February 2.* Available online: http://www.pbs.org/wgbh/pages/frontline/digitalnation/view/

[39] Prensky, M. (2001). Digital natives, digital immigrants. *On the Horizon, 9* (5), 1-6.

[40] Purdy, J. P. (2010). The changing space of research: Web 2.0 and the integration of research and writing environments. *Computers and Composition, 27* (1), 48-58.

[41] Rainie, L. (2008). *Video sharing websites.* Project Data Memo of the PEW Internet and American Life Project. Available online: http://www.pewinternet.org/~/media/Files/Reports/2008/Pew_Videosharing_memo_Jan08.pdf.pdf

[42] Rettig, M. (1991). Nobody reads documentation. *Communications of the ACM, 34* (7), 19–24.

[43] Richtel, M. (2010). Hooked on gadgets, and paying a mental price. *New York Times, June 6.* Available online: http://www.nytimes.com/2010/06/07/technology/07brain.html?emc=eta1

[44] Schweitzer, S. (2005). When students open up—a little too much: Colleges cite risks of frank online talk. *The Boston Globe, September 26.* Available online: http://www.boston.com/news/local/articles/2005/09/26/when_students_open_up____a_little_too_much/

[45] Sheir, M. T. (2005). The way technology changes how we do what we do. *New Directions for Student Services, 112,* 77-87.

[46] Shneiderman, B. (2003). *Leonardo's Laptop: Human Needs and the New Computing Technologies.* Cambridge, MA: MIT P.

[47] Simonson, M. (2007). Social networking for distance education: Where is the research? *Quarterly Review of Distance Education, 9* (2), vii.

[48] Sterngold, A. Confronting plagiarism. *Change, May/Jun,* 16-27.

[49] Stewart, P. (2009). Facebook and virtual literature circle partnership in building a community of readers. *Knowledge Quest, 37* (4), 28-33.

[50] Stoerger, S. (2009). The digital melting pot: Bridging the digital native-immigrant divide. *First Monday, 14* (7). Available online: http://www.uic.edu/htbin/cgiwrap/bin/ojs/index.php/fm/article/view/2474/2243

[51] Thompson, J. (2007). Is education 1.0 ready for Web 2.0 students? *Innovate, 3* (4). Available online: http://www.innovateonline.info/pdf/vol3_issue4/Is_Education_1.0_Ready_for_Web_2.0_Students_.pdf

[52] Tolmie, A., and Boyle, J. (2000). Factors influencing the success of computer mediated communication (CMC) environments in university teaching: A review and case study. *Computers and Education, 34* (2), 119–140.

[53] Turner, J. W., and Reinsch, N. L., Jr. (2007). The business communicator as presence allocator: Multicommunicating, equivocality, and status at work. *Journal of Business Communication, 44* (1), 36–58.

[54] Wallis, C. (2006). The multitasking generation. *Time, March 19.* Available online: http://www.time.com/time/magazine/article/0,9171,1174696,00.html

[55] Walther, J. B., and Bunz, U. (2005). The rules of virtual groups: Trust, liking, and performance in computer-mediated communication. *Journal of Communication, 55* (4), 828–846.

[56] Young, K. S. (2004). Internet addiction: A new clinical phenomenon and its consequences. *American Behavioral Scientist, 48* (4), 402-415.

[57] Zimmer, M. (2008). Preface: Critical perspectives on Web 2.0. *First Monday, 13* (3). Available online: http://www.uic.edu/htbin/cgiwrap/bin/ojs/index.php/fm/article/view/2445/2213

APPENDIX A: WORDLE™ GRAPHIC CONSTRUCTION

The world's top 50 social network communities that were included[2] in the development of this Wordle™ graphic are listed below.[3] The following descriptions have been pulled directly those site's About, Terms, or Home pages. All the networking sites listed below average at least [-] hits a day.[4] Importantly, these 50 social networks are within the ranks of the top 375 sites currently used globally, meaning that social networking sites account for over 13 percent of the 375 most visited websites in the world.

1. facebook.com [2]: Facebook helps you connect and share with the people in your life / [Facebook:] Giving people the power to share and make the world more open and connected.
2. youtube.com [3]: YouTube is the world's most popular online video community, allowing millions of people to discover, watch and share originally-created videos. YouTube provides a forum for people to connect, inform, and inspire others across the globe and acts as a distribution platform for original content creators and advertisers large and small.
3. blogger.com [8]: Blogger is a free blog publishing tool from Google for easily sharing your thoughts with the world.
4. twitter.com [11]: Twitter is a real-time information network powered by people all around the world that lets you share and discover what's happening now.
5. wordpress.com [18]: WordPress.com lets you easily create your own blog, and write about the things that interest you. It is a blogging community managed by makers of the open source WordPress software. WordPress.com blogs are free with the option of adding upgrades such as personalized domain names, custom CSS, video storage, and more.
6. myspace.com [25]: MySpace.com... is a social networking platform that allows Members to create unique personal profiles online in order to find and communicate with old and new friends.
7. LinkedIn [29]: LinkedIn is the world's largest professional network, helping people share and find opportunities every day.
8. flickr.com [32]: Flickr is almost certainly the best online photo management and sharing application in the world. / Flickr is a way to get your photos and videos to the people who matter to you.
9. vkontakte.ru [37]: (The following text has been translated from Russian. This site is also available under vk.com, which is ranked 160th) VK is an all-purpose tool for finding friends, both old and new. Our goal is to keep old friends, ex-classmates, neighbours and co-workers in touch.
10. photobucket.com [61]: Photobucket is the premier destination for uploading, sharing, linking and finding photos, videos and graphics.
11. orkut.com [67]: orkut is an online community designed to make your social life more active and stimulating. orkut's social network can help you maintain existing relationships with pictures and messages, and establish new ones by reaching out to people you've never met before.
12. tudou.com [70]: (The following text has been translated from Chinese) Tudou is the largest online video sharing platform in China, where users can upload, view and share video clips.
13. hi5.com [85]: hi5 is a global destination where young people meet and play. As the world's largest social entertainment destination, our focus is on delivering a fun, interactive, and immersive social experience online to our users around the world.
14. livejournal.com [80]: Rooted in a tradition of global participation, LiveJournal is on the forefront of personal publishing, community involvement, and individual expression. Already one of the world's most respected blogging platforms, look for LiveJournal to continue to deliver improved technologies and services to its members in the coming months and years.
15. kaixin001.com [101]: (The following text has been translated from Japanese) Happy Network is a social network, through which you can with friends, classmates, colleagues and family members to keep more closely in time to understand their dynamics; share with them your life and happiness.
16. digg.com [114]: Digg is a place for people to discover and share content from anywhere on the web. From the biggest online destinations to the most obscure blog, Digg surfaces the best stuff as voted on by our users. You won't find editors at Digg — we're here to provide a place where people can collectively determine the value of content and we're changing the way people consume information online.
17. deviantart.com [115]: As a community destination, deviantART is a platform that allows emerging and established artists to exhibit, promote, and share their works within a peer community dedicated to the arts. The site's vibrant social network environment receives over 100,000 daily uploads of original art works ranging from traditional media, such as painting and sculpture, to digital art, pixel art, films and anime.
18. twitpic.com [124]: TwitPic lets you share photos on Twitter.
19. tumblr.com [124]: Tumblr lets you effortlessly share anything. Post text, photos, quotes, links, music, and videos, from your browser, phone, desktop, email, or wherever you happen to be. You can customize everything, from colors, to your theme's HTML.
20. ning.com [137]: Ning is the leading online platform for the world's organizers, activists and influencers to create their own social network. Design a custom social experience in under 30 seconds giving you the power to mobilize, organize and inspire.
21. tinypic.com [144]: TinyPic is a photo and video sharing service that lets you easily upload, link, and share your images and videos on MySpace, eBay, Orkut, scrapbooks, blogs, and message boards.
22. badoo.com [150]: Badoo is a worldwide socializing system that provides its members with the ability to meet new girls and guys in and around their local area. It includes many great social network fundamentals, but really focuses on giving users the games and tools to gain attention and expand their social circles.

---

[2] Data were collected during June, 2010. Site rankings and hits were tracked through Alexa.com.

[3] Sites chosen from this list were listed on Alexa's Top 500 Websites, Wikipedia™'s List of Social Networking Websites, or sites similar to them were listed. For example, there was no listing for Blogger™ on Wikipedia™'s list but since LiveJournal™ was listed, Blogger was included.) Due to translation issues, mixi.jp™, odnoklassniki.ru™, and kaskus.us™ were not included in this study. Social dating and gaming sites were also not included in this list.

[4] The information that was pulled from the website includes a 1-3 sentence site-identified description. These descriptions were pulled from the social network's website and not from another site describing the network. The information was found on the network's homepage, About Us/About Me/About page, Terms/Terms and Condition, FAQ, or another page that included descriptive information about the site, depending upon the layout and content of the network's website. Statements about features and pricing were avoided.

23. bit.ly [153]: bit.ly allows users to shorten, share, and track links (URLs).

24. tagged.com [171]: Tagged is all about social discovery. We are the social network for meeting new people. Every day, all around the world, people make millions of new social conections on Tagged.

25. nasza-klasa.pl [174]: (The following text has been translated from Polish) Teenagers, students, centenarians - one hundred percent will find your friends!

26. typepad.com [181]: TypePad blogs make it simple for you to share your interests and get noticed. Easily design and customize your own blog, and use our SEO (Search Engine Optimization) and SMO (Social Media Optimization) tools to promote your blog and attract an audience and following.

27. blogfa.com [185]: (The following text has been translated from Persian) Blogs and blogging phenomenon with well received among the Persian-speaking diplomats, and site blogfa the same subject with the aim of creating the context and tools for creating and managing blogs has been established. The ultimate goal of long-term blogfa site hosting thousands of blogs and blogger is obviously to achieve this goal accuracy and requires many efforts. Blogfa in the beginning and what it will interest and we are sure to provide confident Persian-language bloggers and users blogfa also hope to achieve this goal we can help.

28. stumbleupon.com [191]: StumbleUpon helps you discover and share great websites. As you click   Stumble!, we deliver high-quality pages matched to your personal preferences. These pages have been explicitly recommended by your friends or one of 8 million+ other websurfers with interests similar to you. Rating these sites you like automatically shares them with like-minded people – and helps you discover great sites your friends recommend.

29. vimeo.com [195]: Vimeo is a respectful community of creative people who are passionate about sharing the videos they make. We provide the best tools and highest quality video in the universe.

30. wikia.com [202]: Wikia, is a collaborative publishing platform that enables communities to create, share and discover content on any topic in any language.

31. hubpages.com [205]: HubPages is the most rewarding place to publish, discover and interact with people who share your interests.

32. douban.com [219]: (The following text has been translated from Chinese) Random 12 recommendations, not only passed their own true feelings, but also includes the taste of your judgments and followed the line of the screen.

33. xing.com [231]: Around the world every day, over 9 million business professionals use XING – the global business network – in 16 languages to do business and promote their career. XING makes networking and professional contact management simple, with made-to-measure networking functions and services. Even more, XING allows you to see how people are connected, which is an excellent tool in generating new contacts of your own.

34. 51.com [234]: (The following text has been translated from Chinese) 51.com was founded in August 2005, is China's largest social networking site. 51.com committed to providing stability and security of data storage space and convenient platform. Registered as 51.com users can not only facilitate the release of photographs, diaries, music, etc., can easily share these data with friends.

35. netlog.com [235]: Netlog is a social portal for more than 65 million young people in Europe. Your own profile with a guestbook, blog,friends, pictures and videos. Search forfriends, cool events and music. All on Netlog!

36. scribd.com [247]: Scribd is the largest social publishing and reading site in the world. We've made it incredibly simple for anyone to share and discover informative, entertaining and original written content on the web and mobile devices.

37. hatena.ne.jp [248]: (The following text has been translated from Chinese) Founded in 2001, with human Hatena service that we turned out the update check services (Hatena Antenna,Hatena Diary and Hatena Bookmarks for social bookmarking service such as was previously we have been continuously creating services.

38. squidoo.com [249]: Squidoo is the popular publishing platform and community that makes it easy for you to create "lenses" online.

Lenses are pages, kind of like flyers or signposts or overview articles, that gather everything you know about your topic of interest--and snap it all into focus. Like the lens of a camera, your perspective on something.

39. narod.ru [257]: Yandex service to create and free hosting sites, storage and file sharing. Tools for creating and editing site can create a website, set up its appearance or to customize a design and fill its content. It does not require special skills. Service provides users with an infinite space to store any number of files. You can share a link to their friends, keep backups of the file you want, quickly navigate to them from any computer.

40. yelp.com [274]: Yelp is an online urban city guide that helps people find cool places to eat, shop, drink, relax and play, based on the informed opinions of a vibrant and active community of locals in the know. Yelp is the fun and easy way to find, review and talk about what's great — and not so great — in your world.

41. formspring.me [297]: With approximately 100 million questions answered every month, Formspring is giving people across the globe a new way to connect and express themselves. Just like a good conversation in person, Formspring helps our over 12 million users do what comes naturally: ask questions and give answers, about anything and everything.

42. reddit.com [300]: Reddit is a source for what's new and popular on the web.
Users like you provide all of the content and decide, through voting, what's good and what's junk. Links that receive community approval bubble up towards #1, so the front page is constantly in motion and (hopefully) filled with fresh, interesting links.

43. justin.tv [312]: Justin.tv is the easiest way to create live video and show anyone in the world what's happening right now.

44. tweetphoto.com [320]: With over 50 million API requests a day, the TweetPhoto platform offers developers the most expansive and robust real-time media sharing API across the social web.

45. multiply.com [315]: Multiply combines the fun of social networking with the usefulness of photo printing and photo-management software, making it the ideal home for your most cherished memories.

46. studivz.net [319]: (The following text has been translated from German) studiVZ.net is the largest online network for students in Germany. On studiVZ exchange students stay with their friends and fellow students in contact with each other off. About six million registered members * studiVZ are already an integral part of their daily campus life and reduce the anonymity of active network culture in European universities.

47. slideshare.net [342]: SlideShare is a business media site for sharing presentations, documents and pdfs. SlideShare features a vibrant professional community that regularly comments, favorites and downloads content.

48. delicious.com [349]: Delicious is a Social Bookmarking service, which means you can save all your bookmarks online, share them with other people, and see what other people are bookmarking. It also means that we can show you the most popular bookmarks being saved right now across many areas of interest. In addition, our search and tagging tools help you keep track of your entire bookmark collection and find tasty new bookmarks from people like you.

49. etsy.com [351]: The Etsy community spans the globe with buyers and sellers coming from more than 150 countries. Etsy sellers number in the hundreds of thousands.

50. over-blog.com [375]: (The following has been translated from French) The portal of all blogs. JFG Networks offers, as part of its website www.ova-blog.com a tool that allows anyone with the wish to create and edit a blog.

DREAMER: a Design Rationale Environment for Argumentation, Modeling and Engineering Requirements

Célia Martinie, Philippe Palanque,
Marco Winckler
IRIT – University Paul Sabatier
118, route de Narbonne
31062 Toulouse Cedex 9, France
(+33) 561 556 359
{martinie, palanque, winckler}@irit.fr

Stéphane Conversy
ENAC & IRIT – University Paul Sabatier
7, avenue Edouard Belin
31055 TOULOUSE Cedex
(+33) 562 174 019
stephane.conversy@enac.fr

ABSTRACT
Requirements engineering for interactive systems remains a cumbersome task still under-supported by notations, development processes and tools. Indeed, in the field of HCI, the most common practice is to perform user testing to assess the compatibility between the designed system and its intended user. Other approaches such as scenario-based design promote a design process based on the analysis of the actual use of a technology in order to design new technologies better supporting users' tasks and activities. Some of them also support a critical element in the development of interactive systems: creativity. However, these approaches do not provide any support for a) the definition of a set of requirements that have to be fulfilled by the system under design and b) as a consequence for assessing which of these requirements are actually embedded in the system and which ones have been discarded (traceability and coverage aspects). This paper proposes a tool-supported notation for addressing these problems of traceability and coverage of both requirements and design options during the development process of interactive systems. These elements are additionally integrated within a more global approach aiming at providing notations and tools for supporting a rationalized design of interactive systems following a model-based approach. Our approach combines and extends previous work on rational design and requirements engineering. The current contribution, DREAMER, makes possible to relate design options with both functional and non functional requirements. The approach is illustrated by real size case study from large civil aircraft cockpit applications.

Categories and Subject Descriptors
D.2.1 [**Software Engineering**]: Requirements/Specifications.

General Terms
Documentation, Design, Human Factors.

Keywords
Design rationale, requirementss traceability, user interface design.

Permission to make digital or hard copies of all or part of this work for personal or classroom use is granted without fee provided that copies are not made or distributed for profit or commercial advantage and that copies bear this notice and the full citation on the first page. To copy otherwise, or republish, to post on servers or to redistribute to lists, requires prior specific permission and/or a fee.
SIGDOC 2010, September 27-29, 2010, S.Carlos, SP, Brazil.
Copyright 2010 ACM 978-1-4503-0403-0...$5.00.

1. INTRODUCTION
Traceability of choices and systematic exploration of options is a critical aspect of the development processes in the field of safety critical systems. Some software standards such as DO 178 B [23] (which is widely used in the aeronautical domain) require the use of methods and techniques for systematically exploring design options and for supporting the traceability of design decisions. Similarly, ESARR (Eurocontrol Safety Regulatory Requirement) on Software in Air Traffic Management Systems [8] explicitly requires traceability to be addressed in respect of all software requirements (p. 11 edition 0.2). However, such standards only define what *must* be done in terms of traceability but provide no information on *how* such goals can be reached by analysts and developers. Approaches such as scenario-based design [9][22][24] promote a design process based on the analysis of the actual use of a technology in order to design new technologies better supporting users' tasks. Work such as [15][14] address the aspect of creativity that is 'of high relevance as far as interactive systems are concerned. However, these approaches provide few support for (a) defining the requirements in a way they can be directly associated to every component of the system under design and (b) as a consequence, for assessing which of these requirements are embedded in the system and which ones have been discarded during the development process (maybe due to resources constraints, conflicting requirements, …).

Recent work in the field of software engineering has been trying to provide solutions to that problem. One of the remaining problems pointed out by many contributions presented in [7], such as chapters 1, 19 and 20, is that requirements are poorly or even not addressed. As discussed in [25], this is critical as Requirements Engineering provides input to all the subsequent phases in the development process. This paper addresses the problem of traceability and coverage of requirements in a model-based development process. It addresses the problem by providing an extension to a notation TEAM and its associated tool DREAM which have previously been presented in [12]. The current contribution, DREAMER, makes it possible to relate design options with both functional and non functional requirements. While the approach could address any kind of requirements, we put the emphasis on requirement expressed in standards such as SRS's ARINC [1] and ISO 9126 Software Quality [11].

This paper starts by presenting the basic principles of the TEAM notation and the extensions that have been made to include information related to requirements. Section 3 introduces a case study describing alternative design options for implementing ARINC user interface components. This case study exemplifies how the DREAMER approach supports the design process with respect to requirements providing ways of answering two fundamental questions: 1) Which current design (among the many ones available) satisfies a given requirement and 2) What is the exhaustive list of requirements fulfilled by a particular design. Section 4 illustrates all the functions provided by our tool-supported notation for supporting traceability, versioning and collaborative edition of TEAM diagrams. Lastly, section 5 summarizes the finding, conclusion and perspectives to this work.

2. THE TEAM NOTATION in a NUTSHELL

TEAM notation (Traceability, Exploration and Analysis Method) and its CASE tool DREAM (Design Rationale Environment for Argumentation and Modeling) have been originally proposed in [18] to support the systematic exploration of options during the development process of interactive safety critical systems [12]. Hereafter we describe the main concepts of the TEAM notation and the extensions made for tracing requirements.

2.1 The original TEAM notation

TEAM notation is based on Question Option Criteria (QOC) which is design rationale notation introduced by MacLean and al. [13]. QOC notation allows the description of available options for a design question and the selection of an option according to a list of criteria. The TEAM notation is an extension of QOC that enables the structuring and the recording of information produced during design meetings. TEAM diagrams cover:

- The questions that have been raised;
- The design options that have been investigated and the ones that have been selected;
- The evaluation performed for the different options;
- The collection of criteria that have been used for evaluating the options considered;
- The collection of factors that have been taken into account and how they relate to criteria;
- The task models corresponding to options;
- The scenarios extracted from the task models that are used to compute, for each option the value of the criteria.

TEAM notation and its associated tool DREAM can leverage the design rationale process for interactive applications by helping engineers in deciding to reuse or not design choices when facing an already experienced issue. Indeed, TEAM diagrams can be considered as very specific design patterns and, as such, can be reused in another design context. Besides this structuring and recording of information, an important feature of TEAM is to record design decisions and relate them to desired quality factors.

Figure 1 illustrates a simple TEAM model aiming at structuring argumentation around the design of the navigation in a list of candidates for a voting system. Supposed that not all the candidates can be displayed in a single window the model represents two options (i.e. circles): the upper one provides scrolling facilities to the users while the lower one proposes a vocal display with navigation commands (previous and next) in that sequence. The triangles on the right hand side of the figure represent a subset of the usability criteria (time to learn, retention over time, error rate ... see [11] for a full list) and their connection to the usability factor. The different types of lines between the criteria and options represent the fact that a given option can support (favor) a criterion (bold line) or do not support (hinder) it (dotted line). For instance, a bold line is used to represent that the

option "provide-scrolling" strongly supports time-to-learn. On the other side, a dotted line is used represent that the option "vocal presentation" does not support time-to-learn criterion. TEAM supports more precise connection between elements (including absolute and comparative values) but this is not presented here due to space constraints.

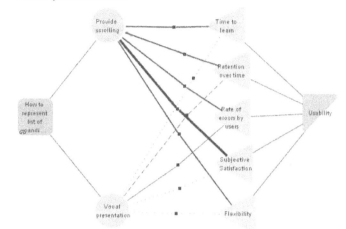

Figure 1. Using TEAM notation to represent relations between criteria and factors in usability

2.2 Adding requirements to notation

Figure 2 provides an exhaustive list of elements in the TEAM notation which also includes all the extensions for supporting requirements. Requirements are depicted as rectangles, questions as rectangles with rounded corners, options as circles, criteria as horizontal triangles and factors as upper part of half a square. Scenarios used to describe a detailed usage of a design option are depicted as squares while arguments (resp. tasks) are depicted as vertical upwards triangles (resp. downwards triangles). The occurrence of any other artifacts used to describe a particular design option (e.g. documents or models specifying the implementation, videos, low-fidelity prototypes, etc) are depicted as paper clip icon and can be attached to any TEAM element.

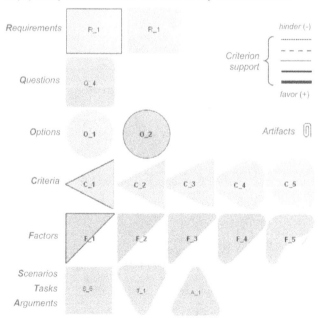

Figure 2. Graphical representation of TEAM notation.

Outlined graphical elements (e.g. the top-left rectangle in Figure 2) represent the fact that, that element has a higher priority than other elements in the design (e.g. top-right rectangle in Figure 2). It is noteworthy that in the case of criteria and factors the graphical representation might also change according to several levels of importance from statured colors and straight shape (very important) to faded colors and irregular shapes (less important). Outlined options (e.g. O_2 in Figure 2) indicate choices made by designers and developers amongst the set of available options.

In its original version, the notation TEAM did not have a representation for requirements. The need for including requirements in rational design diagrams emerged from actual designers whilst trying to determine if the selected options in TEAM diagrams meet functional and non-functional requirements. Indeed, the lack of relationship between design options and requirements prevents designers from exploiting requirements for the generation of options and/or to take into account identified requirements when designing an option. Whilst the integration of requirements represents a small extension to the TEAM notation it has a huge impact on the decision making process based on TEAM diagrams. Indeed, whatever is quality with respect to criteria and factors, a design option might be chosen only on its merit with respect to the coverage of a given critical requirement (such aspect will be detailed in next sections).

3. CASE STUDY

The case study presented in this section is extracted from an industrial cooperation project funded by the DGAC (French civil aviation authority). In this project, one of the main goals was to specify and implement interactive applications in the new generation of interactive cockpits available in small jets but also in large civil aircrafts such as Airbus A380 or Boeing 787.

This project had two main goals:

a) To develop a formal description technique for describing widgets in user applications for cockpit display system; This issue has been addressed by extending the ICO notation [17];
b) To specify user applications compliant with ARINC 661 standard [1], which is an aeronautical international standard.

Due to space reasons, hereafter we only provide the overall context for the use of rational design approach using a single component from the set of ARINC 661 widgets. In our case study, design options are associated to models describing the actual behavior of user interface widgets used in the Cockpit Display System by means of ICOs.

In this section we start by presenting the standard ARINC 661 specification. We then present the context of the case study i.e. the specification of a widget to be used in interactive applications. Section 3.3 presents the formal model of the widget while section 3.4 provides a list of requirements for it. Lastly, section 3.5 presents the design rationale for that widget and its relationship with respect to the identified requirements.

3.1 The standard ARINC 661

The Airlines Electronic Engineering Committee (AEEC) (an international body of airline representatives leading the development of avionics architectures) formed the ARINC 661 Working Group to define the software interfaces to the Cockpit Display System (CDS) used in all types of aircraft installations. The standard is called ARINC 661 - Cockpit Display System Interfaces to User Systems [1].

The CDS (the software system embedded in an aircraft) provides graphical and interactive services to user applications within the flight deck environment. When combined with data from user applications, it displays graphical images and interactive components to the flight deck crew. It also manages user-system interactions by integrating input devices for entering text (via keyboard) and for interacting with these interactive components (via mouse-like input devices). The CDS provides graphical and interactive services to user applications (UA) within the flight deck environment. The communication between the CDS and UAs is based on the identification of user interface components hereafter called widgets. Figure 3 provides a view at glance of the ARINC 661 specification for the widget RadioBox2 (p. 100 and 101). As can be seen on Figure 3, ARINC 661 does not specify the "look and feel" but only the parameters and events.

The next section describes review in the detail all the requirements embedded into the specification of RadioButton2. As the ARINC specification does not impose a particular implementation of user interface widgets that should be embedded into Cockpit Display System (CDS), we have employed DREAMER to document and argument the decisions made on alternative design options.

Figure 3. Complete description of RadioBox2 in ARINC 611

75

3.2 Description of the context

The case study is focused on the design of the ARINC widget RadioBox2 that is used for selecting one button out of several exclusive ones. Even though ARINC 661 specification does not define the look and feel of widgets, examples of such widget are presented in Figure 4.

Figure 4. RadioBox2 alternatives for 'look and feel"

The widget RadioBox2 (circled on Figure 5) is used in several applications embedded into aircraft cockpits such as the Multi Purpose Interactive Application (MPIA) user application (UA). MPIA is a real User Application (UA) aimed at handling several flight parameters. It is made up of 3 pages (called WXR, GCAS and AIRCOND) between which a crew member is allowed to navigate using 3 buttons (as presented at the bottom of each window of Figure 5). WXR page is for managing weather radar information; GCAS is for Ground Anti Collision System parameters while AIRCOND deals with air conditioning settings. Further details about this application can be found in [2].

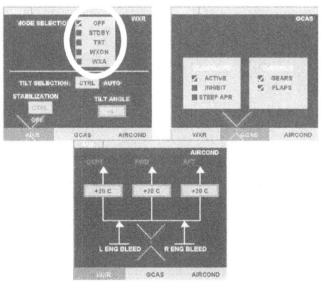

Figure 5. The 3 windows of the user application MPIA

3.3 Formal modeling of ARINC RadioBox2

The use of formal models for describing the behavior is an important requirement to build complex systems such as cockpit display systems. For this reason, the RadioBox2 widget, as well as other widgets contained in the MPIA UA, has been specified using the ICO notation and PetShop tool [20]. Figure 6 provides a view at a glance of the entire ICO models designed to describe the behavior of the ARINC 611 widget RadioBox2.

ICO notation is based on Petri nets. ICO models consist of a set of connected places and transitions; the distribution of tokens among places indicates the availability of actions in the application. Figure 7 shows part of the model of ARINC 661 RadioBox 2, it highlights how to set on/off the visibility of items in the group box widget.

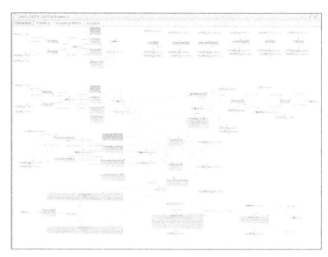

Figure 6. ICO model describing the behavior for the widget ARINC 661 RadioBox2

The details about how to model the behavior of ARINC widgets using ICO is out of the scope of this paper and the interested reader should refer to [16][19] for further information. The main question hereafter is: assuming we need models (ICO models in the present case study) to build complex systems [25]; how we can justify that a given model comply with the requirements (such as ARINC 611)? Other critical and more detailed ones can be derived: Does it comply with all the requirements? Does it comply with only part of them? If so which ones and why some are not taken into account?

Figure 7. Zoom in ICO model of ARINC 661 RadioBox2 (upper left part of the entire model in Figure 6)

3.4 Requirements for RadioBox2 widget

It is noteworthy that the formal specification of widgets cannot be handled at once and some aspects of the specification are located at different levels of priority according to the phase of the development process (of the project) or to resources availability (such as time, budget and man power for instance).

From the A661 RadioBox2 Domain System Requirement Specification (SRS) the requirements are:

- SRS_SGTK_RB2_DOMAIN_REQ001: RadioBox2 shall be of the Widget library categories: Container.
- SRS_SGTK_RB2_DOMAIN_REQ002: A RadioBox2 shall have only children types: ToggleButton2, PictureToggleButton2, and CheckButton2. Only one type shall be used in a given RadioBox2 at a time. The CDS shall assure that internal state of the children is consistent (one and only one is selected) at all times, including when the user changes the state of the children (the change of child state

shall generate two events: one for deselect and one for select).

- SRS_SGTK_RB2_DOMAIN_REQ003: RadioBox2 shall be defined with the parameters as described in the following table:

Parameters	Change	Description
Commonly used parameters		
WidgetType	D	A661_RADIO_BOX2
WidgetIdent	D	Unique identifier of the widget.
ParentIdent	D	Identifier of the immediate container of the widget.
Visible	DR	Visibility of the widget
Enable	DR	Ability of the widget to be activated

- SRS_SGTK_RB2_DOMAIN_REQ004: RadioBox2 shall be created using the parameters defined in the following table:

CreateParameterBuffer	Type	Size (bits)	Value/Range when necessary
WidgetType	ushort	16	A661_RADIO_BOX2
WidgetIdent	ushort	16	
ParentIdent	ushort	16	
Enable	uchar	8	A661_FALSE A661_TRUE
Visible	uchar	8	A661_FALSE A661_TRUE

- SRS_SGTK_RB2_DOMAIN_REQ005: Available SET_PARAMETER identifiers and associated data structure shall be as described in the following table:

Name of the parameter to set	Type	ParameterIdent used in the ParameterStructure	Type of Structure Used
Enable	uchar	A661_ENABLE	A661_ParameterStructure_1Byte
Visible	uchar	A661_VISIBLE	A661_ParameterStructure_1Byte

- SRS_SGTK_RB2_DOMAIN_REQ006: The creation of the RadioBox2 shall be refused if one of the conditions defined in the table below is raised:

Creation error cases	ErrorId
Visible ∉ [A661_TRUE ; A661_FALSE]	CREATE_ABORTED
Enable ∉ [A661_TRUE ; A661_FALSE]	CREATE_ABORTED
Widget hierarchy constraints are not respected	CREATE_ABORTED

- SRS_SGTK_RB2_DOMAIN_REQ007: The RadioBox2 shall send a A661_SET_ABORTED error message with the following identifier ErrorId to UA on SetParameter command if one of the condition defined in the table below is raised:

Run-time error cases	ErrorId
Enable ∉ [A661_TRUE ; A661_FALSE]	A661_OUT_OF_RANGE_ERROR
Visible ∉ [A661_TRUE ; A661_FALSE]	A661_OUT_OF_RANGE_ERROR

- SRS_SGTK_RB2_DOMAIN_REQ008: The RadioBox2 shall be able to change its feel upon reception of an A661 parameter modification command or CDS internal message. For space constraints, we do not present the behavioral requirements in this article.

3.5 Rationalizing the Design of the ARINC RadioBox2

This section describes how we have used DREAMER to support a rationalized and argued design for the complete and unambiguous specification of the widget ARINC 661 RadioBox2. The final DREAMER diagram that is presented in Figure 8 was built according to the following steps:

- First of all, known requirements were added to the diagram. We started with requirement of highest priority for the project that is to have a *Formal description of widgets (using ICO notation)*. Then we added all ARINC 661 requirements for the RadioBox 2 (they have been listed in section 3.4);
- Questions raised by designers during brainstorming meetings were included in the diagram; These questions are explained latter in this section;
- For each question raised, several design options were explored and the relationships between them are depicted by edges in the diagram;
- Any artifacts (i.e. ICO models in the case of the project) related to a particular element were connected to the corresponding design option. The presence of artifacts (if available) is indicated by a paper clip symbol next to the element;
- Prior the selection of design options, criteria and factors influencing the choice were added to the diagram; The selection of criteria and factors has been guided by the ISO 9126 standard on Software Quality [11] as one of the main goals of this project was to address reliability issues for interactive applications in cockpits. For the specification and development of the RadioBox2 widget, three factors have been carefully considered: Reliability, Learnability and Operability (the last two ones being sub-factors of usability in ISO 9126)[1].
- Edges were added for connecting options and criteria. In addition they hold the measures representing the level of compliancy between criteria and options. Lately, edges were connected between requirements and options thus making sure that all requirements were taken into account.

Three main questions have arisen while trying to make unambiguous the behavior of the widget. These questions were driven by two main requirements (i.e. REQ002 and REQ008).

The first question is issued from REQ002 (i.e. *should an option be selected by default?*) and it aimed at deciding the detailed behavior related to the selection of items in the group box. Indeed, the text of SRS specification states that *"The CDS shall assure that internal state of the children is consistent (one and only one is selected) at all times"* but the snapshots given as examples show a state in which no child is selected (see Figure 4b) and another where there at least one child selected (see Figure 4.c). Indeed, this question might lead to two design options: (i) to allow that none can be selected, or (ii) to always have one selected, thus requiring a default selection when none has been selected by the crew.

---

[1] It is interesting to note that ISO standard 9241 proposes another set of sub-factors for usability namely: Effectiveness, Efficiency and satisfaction. According to that standard, it would have been necessary to identify other criteria for assessing the options.

Three criteria might influence the decision making process on design options: the learning effort, the possibility to manage to use it and the last one concerns the frequency of failure of this widget. The links between options and criteria are given a weight between strongly denied, denied, neutral, supported and strongly supported. For this first question, we can see from Figure 8 that option "0 or 1 selected" is ranked as the best option for the "Learning effort" criterion. In the designers' point of view, it allows a better understanding of the usage of the widget. Then the learnability factor (sub-factor of Usability) that is linked to this criterion could be better supported by this option. The same notation has been performed concerning the operability factor. We can see from the black circle around the second option that it is the one which has been selected. The requirements are filled or not by none or several options. In our case, the second option "0 or 1 selected" is filled in by all the requirements except the second one. The SRS document was presenting a contradiction (that raised this first design question) and the designers have decided rather to select the second option because it should have higher levels of learnability and operability.

In Figure 8 the requirement number 008 is connected to the last two questions which are "How to handle the Focus Management System" and "How to oversee the method call *setParameter*?" Indeed, these questions are directly issued from the definition of the requirement REQ008 concerning the behavior of the widget RadioBox2.

The first question refers to the management of the focus i.e. are the designers going to include the management of focus it in their behavioral description or not? At that time in the project they have chosen not to implement it because they evaluated that the time required to do so was not fitting within the project timeline. Developing the Focus Management using the ICO formalism was not possible in the time frame, even if this solution would have best suited to learnability and operability factors. In this case the reliability factor and formal modeling requirement were considered as more important than the other factors and requirements and this has been captured in the DREAMER model.

The second question is related to the handling of a procedure call that is named *setParameter* and that takes as input parameters the identification of the widget and the state it has to be set to. The SRS document does not indicate how this procedure should handle the *setParamter* when the widget is already in the state that corresponds to the one required by the *setParameter* method call. For instance, this would be the case if the receives a setParamter call to set the selection to the first element of the RadioBox2 widget while it is already selected. The designers chose the second option which only impacts the Reliability factor and that was the more appropriate according to it.

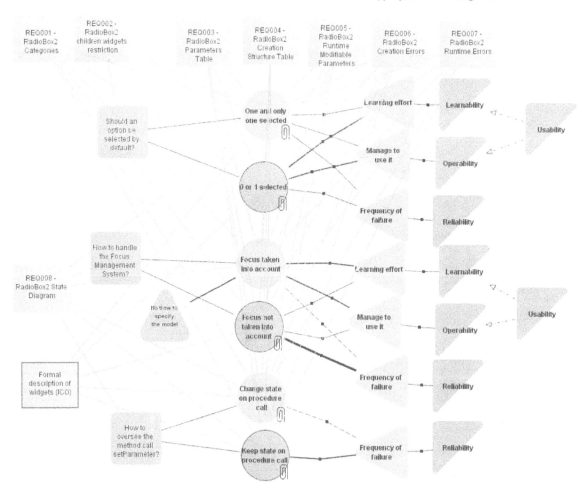

Figure 8. Snapshot of the DREAM diagram for the design of the behavior of the ARINC 661 RadioBox2 widget

4. Tool Support for DREAMER

The diagram presented in Figure 8 was set by the designers using of the DREAMER CASE tool. This CASE tool, which is an extension of DREAM [12], is a software environment supporting edition, storage and analysis of TEAM diagrams. The tool is publicly available on the Internet [6] and free of charges. A couple of hours of training is required for users starting to build their own diagrams. The first version of the tool, DREAM allows performing the following actions:

- Edit (add, modify and delete) any item from the TEAM notation.
- Connect questions to options elements.
- Connect options to criterion and set a weight to link, depending on how much the option is fulfilling a criterion.
- Connect criterion to factors.
- Connect models to options as an option can be described by a model (formal or not).
- Connect scenarios to criteria as scenario can be used to evaluate how an option is fulfilling a requirement.
- Attach various types of documents to the different types of TEAM artifacts. They can be related to the design itself or to the project as a whole.

In addition to the functions described above, team work can also be recorded using the two following features:

- Diagram versioning according to the design sessions that took place.
- User roles of the people involved in the design (for instance who decided to select a given option and who was involved in that meeting).

Sometimes diagrams are crowded with a large number of artifacts, and then there is a need to support designers in managing and analyzing the diagram. To this end, a set of visualization tool have been added. For instance, a bifocal view of the diagram has been added to allow focusing on a particular item to explore the various connections it has with the other items in a diagram. Further details about the capabilities of the tool can be found at [12].

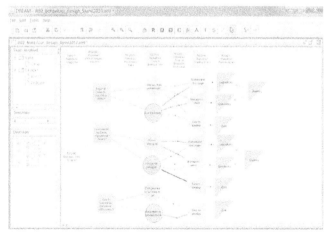

Figure 9. DREAM Software environment

The new version of the tool (see Figure 9) now supports the edition and traceability of requirements within the existing DREAM environment. DREAMER features four main improvements:

- Support for requirements representation;

- Support for relating requirements to design option;
- Visualization of coverage of requirements, options and criteria.

One of the major improvements introduced is the use of visualization techniques for analyzing the coverage of requirements by design options. These visualization techniques, largely inspired from the previous work of Bertin [3] and Henry & Fekete [10], are shown in Figure 10 and Figure 11.

As described in the section 3, REQ001 and REQ003 to REQ007 are fulfilled by all of the design options and then the connecting edges between them and the options make the diagram crowded with edges. To focus on the relationship between design options and requirement they support, Figure 10 shows at a glance which requirements are supported by which options (red color for unsupported requirements and green color for supported requirement). The same kind of view can be used to display the evaluation of an option with regards to criteria (Figure 11). In this colored matrix, the red color corresponds to the strongly denied value and the green color corresponds to the strongly supported value. Between them, a mix of red and green is used to represent the denied, neutral and supported evaluation weights.

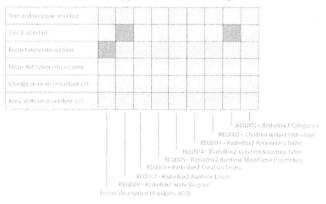

Figure 10. Snapshot of the Colored matrix for requirements traceability with regards to design options

One and only one selected			
0 or 1 selected			
Focus taken into account			
Focus not taken into account			
Change state on procedure call			
Keep state on procedure call			

Low frequency of failure
Manage to use it
Learning effort

Figure 11. Snapshot of the Colored matrix to visualize the evaluation relationship between options and criteria

It is important to note that these visualizations are embedded into the DREAMER CASE tool so that representations can be automatically generated from TEAM diagrams and interactively manipulated by the designers/developers. They provide terrific support to designers as a design rationale approach is only needed for large and complex systems typically ending up in large and cumbersome diagrams.

5. CONCLUSIONS AND PERSPECTIVES

In this paper we have discussed the problem of traceability of requirements for model-based approaches. It tackles the problem by providing an extension to a notation TEAM and its associated tool DREAM [12]. Whilst some recent approaches are able to deal with the traceability of requirements to pieces of software code [4][21] to pieces of models [5] there is no support for augmenting the choices made during the implementation. DREAMER makes it possible to relate design options with functional and non functional requirements. While other approaches such as SCRAM [24] focus on requirements identification, our approach is intended for supporting the traceability of such identified requirements within the design process of interactive systems.

The current paper has been built from experience drawn from a real industrial project dealing with the behavioral specification of widgets compatible with the standard ARINC 661. However, both the notation and the tool could be used fruitfully with other aspects of the design of interactive systems and other phases of the development process.

REFERENCES

[1] ARINC. ARINC 661 specification: Cockpit Display System Interfaces To User Systems, Prepared by Airlines Electronic Engineering Committee, Published by Aeronautical Radio, Inc, April 22, 2002.

[2] Barboni E., Conversy S., Navarre D. & Palanque P. Model-Based Engineering of Widgets, User Applications and Servers Compliant with ARINC 661 Specification. In Proc. of DSVIS 2006, LNCS n°4323, Springer Verlag. pp. 25-38.

[3] Bertin, J. (1967) Sémiologie Graphique - Les diagrammes - les réseaux - les cartes. Gauthier-Villars et Mouton & Cie, Paris. Réédition de 1997. EHESS.

[4] Boulanger, J.-L., Dao, V. Q. Requirements Engineering in a Model-based Methodology for Embedded Automotive Software. In: IEEE International Conference on Research, Innovation and Vision for the Future, 2008, p. 263-268.

[5] Coninx, K., Cuppens, E., De Boeck, J. & Raymaekers, C., 2007, Integrating Support for Usability Evaluation into High Level Interaction Descriptions with NiMMiT . In: Interactive Systems: Design, Specification, and Verification. 2007, Springr Verlag LNCS, pp. 95-108.

[6] DREAM. At: http://ihcs.irit.fr/dream/index.html

[7] Dutoit, A.H., McCall, R., Mistrík, I., Paech, B. (eds.) Rationale Management in Software Engineering: Concepts and Techniques, Rationale Management in Software Engineering. Springer, 432 pages. 2006. ISBN-10: 3540309977.

[8] ESARR 6. EUROCONTROL Safety Regulatory Requirement. Software in ATM Systems. Edition 1.0. http://www.eurocontrol.int/src/public/standard_page/esarr6.html (2003)

[9] Gregoriades, A., Sutcliffe, A. Scenario-Based Assessment of Nonfunctional Requirements. In IEEE Transactins on Software Engineering, vol. 31, N. 5, May 2005. P. 392-408.

[10] Henry N. and Fekete J-D. MatrixExplorer: a Dual-Representation System to Explore Social Networks. IEEE Transactions on Visualization and Computer Graphics (Proceedings Visualization / Information Visualization 2006), 12(5), pp. 677-684, 2006.

[11] ISO/IEC 9126-1:2001. Software engineering -- Product quality -- Part 1: Quality model.

[12] Lacaze, X., Palanque, P., Barboni, E., Bastide, R., Navarre, D., From DREAM to Reality : Specificities of Interactive Systems Development With Respect to Rationale Management. In [7], Springer Verlag 2006, pp.155-170.

[13] MacLean, Allan; Young, Richard M.; Bellotti, Victoria M. E., and Moran, Thomas P. Questions, Options, and Criteria: Elements of Design Space Analysis. Lawrence Erlbaum Associates; 1991; 6, pp. 201-250.

[14] Maiden N.A.M. & Robertson S., 'Developing Use Cases and Scenarios in the Requirements Process', Proc. ICSE 2005 26th Int. Conference on Software Engineering, ACM Press.

[15] Maiden N.A.M., Ncube C. & Robertson S., 'Can Requirements Be Creative? Experiences with an Enhanced Air Space Management System', Proc. ICSE 2007 28th Int. Conference on Software Engineering, ACM Press, 632-641.

[16] Navarre D., Palanque P. & Bastide R. A Formal Description Technique for the Behavioural Description of Interactive Applications Compliant with ARINC 661 Specification. HCI-Aero'04 Toulouse, France, 29 September-1st October 2004. CD-ROM proceedings.

[17] Navarre, D., Palanque, P., Ladry, J., and Barboni, E. 2009. ICOs: A model-based user interface description technique dedicated to interactive systems addressing usability, reliability and scalability. ACM Trans. Comput.-Hum. Interact. 16, 4 (Nov. 2009), pp. 1-56

[18] Palanque P. & Lacaze X. DREAM-TEAM: A Tool and a Notation Supporting Exploration of Options and Traceability of Choices for Safety Critical Interactive Systems. In Proceedings of INTERACT 2007, Rio, Brazil, September 2007, LNCS n°4663, Springer Verlag

[19] Palanque P., Ladry J., Navarre D. and Barboni E. High-Fidelity Prototyping of Interactive Systems can be Formal too 13th International Conference on Human-Computer Interaction (HCI International 2009) San Diego, CA. USA.

[20] PetShop: At: http://ihcs.irit.fr/petshop, accessed Jan 2010.

[21] REQTIFY. At: http://www.geensoft.com/en/article/reqtify

[22] Rosson, M.B. & Carroll, J.M. 2002. Usability Engineering: Scenario-Based Development of Human-Computer Interaction. San Francisco: Morgan Kaufmann.

[23] RTCA. Software Considerations in Airborne Systems and Equipment Certification, DO-178B RTCA, Washington D.C. 1992

[24] Sutcliffe A. & Ryan M. Experience with SCRAM, a SCenario Requirements Analysis Method, in Proceedings of the 3rd Int. Conf. on Requirements Engineering, April 1998, pp. 164-173.

[25] van Lamsweerde, A. Engineering Requirements for System Reliability and Security. In Software System Reliability and Security. NATO Security through Science Series - D: Information and Communication Security, Vol. 9. IOS Press, 2007, 196-238.

Advertising Network Formation based on Stochastic Diffusion Search and Market Equilibria

Nikos Salamanos[*]
Athens University of
Economics and Business
salaman@aueb.gr

Stavros Lopatatzidis
Athens University of
Economics and Business
stauros.lopatatzidis
@gmail.com

Michalis Vazirgiannis[†]
Athens University of
Economics and Business
LIX, Ecole Polytechnique,
France
mvazirg@aueb.gr

Antonis Thomas
Athens University of
Economics and Business
antonis.thomas@gmail.com

ABSTRACT

The concept of social networks in conjunction with concepts from economics has attracted considerable attention in recent years. In this paper we propose the Stochastic Diffusion Market Search (SDMS), a novel contextual advertising method for mutual advertisement hosting among participating entities, where each owns a web site. In the scenario considered each participating agent/web-site buys or sells advertising links. In the proposed method the advertising market and network that formed into the system emerge from agents preferences and their social behavior into the network. SDMS consists of a variation of Stochastic Diffusion Search, a swarm intelligence metaheuristic, and an algorithm for market equilibria. We present an evaluation of the model and the experimental results show that the network potentially converges to a stable stage and the distribution of market prices adheres to power law properties.

Categories and Subject Descriptors

J.4 [Social And Behavioral Sciences]: Economics

General Terms

Economics, Swarm Intelligent, Market Equilibrium

Keywords

Online advertising, Market Mechanisms, Swarm Intelligent

---

[*]This research project is co-financed by E.U.-European Social Fund (75%) and the Greek Ministry of Development-GSRT (25%).

[†]Partially supported by the DIGITEO "LEVETONE" grant.

1. INTRODUCTION

In this paper we propose the *Stochastic Diffusion Market Search (SDMS)*, an advertising method for mutual advertisement hosting among participating websites. Our motivation was to design an advertising method which encapsulates the characteristics of social networks and online markets. The design methodology of SDMS based on the Stochastic Diffusion Search (SDS) [2, 12], a population based *Swarm Intelligent metaheuristic*. Specifically, the SDMS is a social model of consumers' behavior when their preferences in the market are uncertain. The SDMS takes as input the set of advertisers and ad-publishers. Then based on the advertisers' indirect communication and preferences (advertisers' social role) the system produces the advertising network. The advertising network is a directed bipartite graph where each edge corresponds to a link that connects the ad-publisher (the web site that wants to host advertisements) to the advertiser.

The main features of our settings are that: a. there is no central authority (a search engine for instance) that defines and controls the advertisements matching b. the advertisers do not have direct access to ad-publishers' content (i.e. the content of the landing pages). Thus, a main issue arises: the advertisers are partially informed about the quality, the advertising similarity, of the participating web sites. Therefore, the preferences of advertisers/buyers to ad-publishers/goods have to be determined by a social procedure.

The SDMS formulates, in consecutive time periods, a *Fisher market*, a market consisting of buyers and divisible goods. We map each advertiser to a buyer and each ad-publisher (advertising slot) to a divisible good, the number of ad impressions that she is able to sell. Without harm to the generality of the design we make the assumption that the utility function of an advertiser for a given ad-publisher is linear. In order the method to be economically efficient, the *Cost Per Impression (CPI)* prices of the advertising slots have to be equal with the market equilibrium prices where the market clears (*market clearing* prices).

Thus, we devise an automatic pricing mechanism based on the polynomial time *tatonnement* algorithm (further called tatonnement) proposed by [7]. The tatonnement computes the equilibrium vector of prices for an exchange market. The

Fisher market is a special case of the exchange market. In our model the tatonnement is a subroutine which estimates the equilibrium CPI values.

We present an extensive evaluation of the method verifying that the network converges to a stable state (maximizing the *social welfare*) and that the distribution of market prices adheres to power law properties. Both results present a solution with attractive macroscopic properties that can be deployed in a real system.

The paper is organized as follows. Section 2 covers the related work. In section 3, we present briefly the SDS. In sections 4 and 5 we present the market formulation, the tatonnement algorithm and the SDMS. In section 6 we evaluate our method and finally section 7 concludes the paper.

2. RELATED WORK

Online advertising has attracted considerable attention in recent years. A case especially studied is the sponsored search advertising. Sponsored search advertising models involve auction models with the baseline usually being the *Generalised Second Price auctions (GSP)* [6].

In this paper we consider the case of contextual advertising. Our model based on the Stochastic Diffusion Search [2, 12] a Swarm Intelligent metaheuristic [3, 11] able to solve a variety of optimization problems. The time complexity and the convergence analysis of Stochastic Diffusion Search are presented in [14] and [13].

The behavioral model of SDS is very similar to the naive learning models from Game Theory [9, 17] especially with the *imitation dynamics* [8, 16]. Also, a part of our work is inspired by [4] where Ceyhan et al. present a theoretic analysis of the evolution of a market in the presents of social influence.

Recently, Saberi et al. [15] proposed an advertising exchange network model applicable on a network of blogs. Their system generates a more abstract model of economies, the exchange economies, were the agents/blogs could act both as ad-publishers and advertisers. They adopt an approach similar to ours and they apply a variation of tatonnement [7] algorithm in order the market to reach the equilibria. The main difference is that a market is defined on an existing social network, whereas in ours the mechanism generates the social network and the market.

A theoretic analysis of the advertising networks is presented in [10] where the authors analyze the topology of the advertising network for the case where web sites buy and sell advertising links.

In market equilibrium bibliography, Devanur et al. [5] present the DPSV algorithm, the first polynomial algorithm to compute the market equilibria for the linear case of Fisher model.

3. STOCHASTIC DIFFUSION SEARCH

Stochastic Diffusion Search (SDS) was proposed as a population based metaheuristic algorithm to solve pattern matching problems and is applicable to Swarm Intelligent systems. The SDS consists of a population of agents that synchronously search for the optimal solution of an optimization problem. The objective function of optimization problem has to be transformed to a summation of individual terms.

Initially each agent initializes at random the terms of the objective function defining an initial *hypothesis* about the

optimal solution. In a repeated process the agents, using a *test* criterion, evaluate some of the terms of their hypothesis. Usually the test is a binary function and there is a mapping from the test score to the solution space of the optimization problem. The test score values divide the agents in two categories a. *inactive* (dissatisfied) for which the test score of their hypothesis is false and *active* (satisfied). In every time period each inactive agents chooses at random an agent for communication. If the selected agent is active then the selecting agent copies her hypothesis. Due to stochastic nature of the procedure the SDS approximates the optimal solution.

There are many variations of the SDS algorithmic schema [12]. The basic algorithmic pattern of SDS consists of the following steps (See [12](p26)):

1. For all agents do

2. **Initialize**: Agent picks a random hypothesis

3. **Test**: Agent partially evaluates her hypothesis

   - If *test criterion = TRUE*, agent = *Active* (satisfied)
   - Else *agent = Inactive* (dissatisfied)

4. **Diffuse**

   - Inactive agent meets a randomly chosen Active agent
   - Inactive agent update-change hypothesis

5. **Repeat** until Halting criterion.

4. MARKET FORMULATION

A set of agents/web sites, form an advertising exchange network in terms of buying and selling advertising links among them. The agents participate in an repeated advertising process where time is divided into advertising periods. Every agent could serve as ad-publisher *(AdP)*, or as advertiser *(Adv)*. For the rest of the paper we use lower case letters when we refer to advertisers and capital for ad-publishers. The agents have to connect first to an authority web site, the *Center*, that is of limited role and does not define the advertising network. The advertisers search for coherent ad-publishers through the *Center*. The *Center* executes the search queries initiated by the advertisers and collects the feedback provided by the advertisers. In consecutive time periods a Fisher market of advertising slots is formed into the system and in each period the *Center* runs the tatonnement aiming at an equilibrium state.

The linear case of the Fisher model is as follows. Consider a market with a set of n buyers and a set of N divisible goods. Each buyer i has an amount b_i of money to purchase goods and a utility function $u_i(J)$, the utility of i when he obtains a unit of the good J. We assume that the utility function of each buyer is linear with respect to the amount of goods that it consumes. The linear case of Fisher model results to a equilibrium vector of prices - the market clearing prices - and an optimal allocation of goods, where the market clears i.e. supply matches demand.

In our model we formulate a Fisher market as follows: Given n advertisers and N ad-publishers, we map each advertiser i to a buyer with budget b_i and each ad-publisher

Table 1: Notation used in SDMS.

N	Set of **ad-publishers**	AdP	**Ad-publisher**
$\{AdP\}^t$	Ad-publishers with non-zero demand	ν_J^t	J's visitors
CPI_J^t	J's Cost Per Impression price	f_J^t	J's impression for sell

n	Set of **advertisers**	Adv	**Advertiser**
$\{AdP\}_i^t$	i's preferences	$\{AdP\}_i^t$	i's ad-publishers
$u_i^t(J)$	i's utility	$f_{J \to i}^t$	Impressions bought by i
$c_{J \to i}^t$	Clicks on i's ad	$CTR_i^t(J)$	i's CTR on ad-publisher J
F_i^t	The *friends* of i (contextually similar ads)	$\{CTR_i^t\}$	i's avg-*Click Through Rate* (Eq. 2)

$\{CTR^t\}$	**Market** avg-*Click Through Rate* (Eq. 3)	$AdNet^t$	**Advertising Network**

J to a divisible good. The quantity of J is the number of impression f_J^t that is able to sell in period t. We define that $f_J^t = \nu_J^{t-1}$, where ν_J^{t-1} are the visitors at J's web site in period $t-1$. In order to initialize the quantities $f_J^{t=1}$, we apply an period $t = 0$ where the *Center* computes the number of visitors $\nu_J^{t=0}$.

The preference of an advertiser i for an ad-publisher J is defined by the utility value $u_i^t(J)$. The value $u_i^t(J)$ denotes the utility per click obtained by i when her advertisement is published by J. In our model we assume that $u_i^t(J) = CTR_i^t(J)$. The CTR of ad i is the *Click Through Rate*, the number of clicks divided by the number of impressions.

The tatonnement algorithm computes the equilibrium market clearing prices of the goods. In our case, the equilibrium vector of prices corresponds to the *Cost per Impression* (CPI) values. Moreover, the equilibrium prices define for each advertiser i an optimal basket of goods $\{f_{J \to i}^t\}$, where $f_{J \to i}^t$ is the number of impressions that i will buy from J (the advertising matching).

Finally, we define that each ad-publisher J publishes the ads sequentially, one ad per impression with probability $\frac{f_{J \to i}^t}{f_J^t}$.

4.1 Market Equilibria

We apply to our model the recent algorithmic results of algorithmic market equilibria in order to devise an automatic pricing mechanism. Market equilibria occur when the supply is equal to demand. The existence of market equilibria has been proved by Arrow and Debreu [1]. In [7] the authors present a tatonnement algorithm, similar to Walrasian tatonnement. The tatonnement is an natural iterative process which converges to market equilibria for a very particular specifications of the excess demand function. Briefly, consider an exchange market with n traders and N goods. Each trader has an endowment of goods. At a given price p the trader sells his endowment and buys a bundle of goods. Iteratively, the traders announce prices and compute the demand, if the demand exceeds their supply then they reduce their prices else they increase the prices. The process continues until the demand is equal to supply, then the prices converge to market equilibrium prices. We must emphasize that transaction only take place when the process has converged to the equilibrium state.

The algorithm in [7] approximates the market equilibria for the general case of exchange markets. Computes a $(1+\epsilon)$-approximate market equilibrium, where the demand is at

---

Algorithm 1 Tatonnement

1: N Goods ($AdPs$), n Buyers ($Advs$), Budgets: $\{b_i\}_{i \in n}$
2: Initialize:
3:     Set for each good J: $quantity(J) = 1$
4:     Scale utilities: $\hat{u}_i(J) = u_i(J) \cdot f_J^t$
5:     Set initial prices $p_J = 1$ for $1 \leq J \leq N$
6:     Define $w \in \Re_{++}^N$
7: **for** $T = \frac{N}{\delta} \log_{1+\delta} N$, where $\delta = \epsilon/2 \cdot (1 + \epsilon)$ **do**
8:     Find $\alpha > 0$ such that $\pi = \alpha \cdot p \in \Pi$, where:
9:     $\Pi = \{\pi \in \Re_+^N | \pi \cdot w = 1\}$.
10:     Announce prices $\pi = \alpha \cdot p$
11:     Compute:
12:     for each Adv $x_i \in argmax\{u_i(x) | \pi \cdot x \leq b_i\}$
13:     find aggregate demand $X = \sum_i x_i$
14:     compute $\sigma = 1/max_J X_J$
15:     update prices: $p_J \leftarrow p_J \cdot (1 + \delta \cdot \sigma \cdot X_J)$
16: **end for**
17: Compute:
18:     Equilibrium Demand in the rth iteration:
19:     for each Adv i: $x_i = \frac{\sum_{r=1}^T \sigma(r) \cdot x_i(r)}{\sum_{r=1}^T \sigma(r)}$, $\bar{x}_i \in \Re^N$
20:     Equilibrium Prices in the rth iteration:
21:     $\pi = \frac{\sum_{r=1}^T \sigma(r) \cdot \pi_i(r)}{\sum_{r=1}^T \sigma(r)}$, $\pi \in \Re^N$
22: **Output:**
23:     For each AdP J: $CPI_J = \pi_J / f_J^t$
24:     For each Adv i the bundle of goods:
25:     $(f_{1 \to i}, ..., f_{N \to i}) = \bar{x}_i \cdot (f_1, ..., f_N)$

most $(1 + \epsilon)$ times the supply. The number of iterations is $T = \frac{N}{\delta} \log_{1+\delta} N$, where $\delta = \epsilon/(2 \cdot (1 + \epsilon))$.

An exchange market consists of n traders and N goods. The traders has an endowment $w_i = (w_{i1}, ..., w_{iN})$ of goods and the total quantity of a good, in the market, is the sum of the traders endowments. The traders could act as sellers and as buyers. They sell their endowment and they buy goods. Algorithm 1 presents our variation of [7] for the special case of the advertising Fisher market. Actually, our tatonnement algorithm is the tatonnement presented in [7] using a reduction from the exchange market to the Fisher market ([7], section 3).

Fleischer et al. [7] proposed an new formulation of the market equilibrium problem as a convex optimization problem using *indirect utility functions*. In each iteration the algorithm restricts the prices to a convex set $\Pi \subseteq \Re^N$, where

N is the number of goods. A Fisher market consists of buyers and goods. A Fisher market is a special case of an exchange market if we consider that the endowments of the traders are proportional: $w_i = b_i w$, where $w \in \Re_{++}^N$. In this case we set $\Pi = \{\pi \in \Re_+^N | \pi \cdot w = 1\}$. ([7], section 3).

Initially the algorithm defines a transformed market were the quantities of the goods is unit and scales appropriately the utilities (Alg. 1 step: 3,4). The initial prices $p = (p_1, ..., p_N)$ are set to one (Alg. 1 step: 5).

The next step is to define the appropriate convex set Π. In every iteration we restrict the prices p to the convex set $\Pi = \{\pi \in \Re_+^N | \pi \cdot w = 1\}$, where $\pi = \alpha \cdot p$ (Alg. 1 step: 6,8). In other words, we define an vector $w \in \Re_{++}^N$ and in every iteration we compute the $\alpha > 0$ for which $\pi \cdot w = \alpha \cdot p \cdot w = 1$ (the inner product of π and w).

Finally, observe that the algorithm computes the equilibrium vector of prices for the transformed market where we consider the good as a unit. Thus, we have to compute for each good the price per unit and for each advertiser the optimal basket of goods (Alg. 1 step: 23-25).

5. THE SDMS METHOD

We propose the *Stochastic Diffusion Market Search (SDMS)* a social model of consumers behavior where their preferences in the market are uncertain. In this paper we study the special case of advertising market. The general algorithmic schema of SDMS is a variation of SDS presented in [12](p154). We assume that the consumer, the advertiser in our case, entering to an known market cannot predefine her preferences i.e. the ad-publishers on which it prefers to be published on.

In consecutive time periods $t = 1, 2, ..., \infty$, each advertiser searches for the most coherent ad-publishers. The objective function of the advertiser is to determine the set of ad-publisher where her ad will gather the max number of clicks, subject to the quality of the clicks (CTR values). She follows a stochastic behavior and her preferences (ad-publishers) emerge from a trial and error process (tests).

The advertiser's **hypothesis** consists of the set $\{AdP\}_i$ of the candidate ad-publishers and the vector of utility values $u_i(\cdot)$. The advertiser submits her hypothesis to the tatonnement. The tatonnement computes a. for each ad-publisher J the market equilibrium CPI_J^t prices and b. for each advertiser i the set $\{\overline{AdP}\}_i^t$ of ad-publishers and the optimal basket $\{f_{J\to i}^t\}_{J \in \{\overline{AdP}\}_i^t}$.

During the **test phase** the advertiser compares the realized output of her hypothesis, the average CTR of her ad (i.e the average utility), with the average CTR of the ads in the market (i.e market average utility). If the **test score** is *false* then updates her hypothesis in the **diffusion phase**. In the following we present in more details these two phases.

5.1 Initialization Phase

In the first period each advertiser has to choose an initial hypothesis, one ad-publisher J that will submit to tatonnement. Each ad-publisher J corresponds to a divisible good, an advertising slot with $f_J^{t=1}$ impressions (quantity). Recall that the $f_J^{t=1}$ is the number of visitors in period $t = 0$. We assume that a given advertiser i is equally uncertain for the quality of ad-publishers, thus she selects at random one ad-publisher with probability proportional to the quantity of the goods (Eq. 1).

$$Pr_i(J) = \frac{f_J^t}{\sum_{J \in \{AdP\}^t} f_J^t} \qquad (1)$$

In terms of SDS, the tuple $(\{AdP\}_i^{t=1}, u_i^{t=1}(J))$, where $u_i^{t=1}(J) = 1$, corresponds to the advertiser's initial *hypothesis$(i, t = 1)$*.

5.2 Test Phase

The *Test Phase* (Alg. 2) consists of a. the subroutine *Tatonnement*, b. the *Active Network* and c. the *Test Criterion*.

The subroutine *Tatonnement* is an automatic pricing schema which takes as input a. the budgets b_i and the utilities $u_i(\cdot)$ of advertisers b. the set $\{AdP\}^t$, the ad-publishers with at least one potential buyer and c. the estimated f_J^t number of impressions (the quantities of the goods). The tatonnement outputs the CPI prices and the allocation of goods to buyers i.e. the advertising network $AdNet^t$. The $AdNet^t$ is defined by a. the equilibrium CPI prices b. the advertising matching $Adv\text{-}AdP$ and c. the number of impressions $f_{j\to i}^t$ that each advertiser has bought.

The *Center* activates the $AdNet^t$ and at the end of each period t it returns a. the realized number $c_{j\to i}^t$ of clicks on i's ad and b. the average realized values, $\overline{CTR}_i^t$, and $\overline{CTR}^t$ where:

$$\overline{CTR}_i^t = \frac{Total\ clicks\ on\ Adv\ i}{Total\ impressions\ of\ Adv\ i} = \frac{\sum_{J \in \{\overline{AdP}\}_i^t} c_{J\to i}^t}{\sum_{J \in \{\overline{AdP}\}_i^t} f_{J\to i}} \qquad (2)$$

$$\overline{CTR}^t = \frac{Total\ clicks\ on\ Advs}{Total\ impressions\ consumed} = \frac{\sum_i \sum_{J \in \{\overline{AdP}\}_i^t} c_{J\to i}^t}{\sum_{J \in \{AdP\}^t} f_J} \qquad (3)$$

The set $\{\overline{AdP}\}_i^t$ is the ad-publishers of i. The value $\overline{CTR}_i^t$ corresponds to the average utility (per click) of i with respect to her *hypothesis(i, t)*. It is considered as the effectiveness (the quality) of $\{\overline{AdP}\}_i^t$ as ad-publishers.

The **test criterion** for a given advertiser i and for her *hypothesis(i, t)* is the distance between $\overline{CTR}_i^t$ and $\overline{CTR}^t$. The **test score** is *true* if $\overline{CTR}_i^t \geq \theta \cdot \overline{CTR}^t$, else is *false*. The parameter θ, $0 < \theta \leq 1$, is defined by i. If *true* then i is considered as *active* (satisfied) and in period $t + 1$ submits the same hypothesis to the tatonnement. Else, i is considered as *inactive* (dissatisfied) and she has to execute the diffusion phase.

Observe that the test score executed on the output of tatonnement and ad-network i.e. the equilibrium mapping of $Advs$ to $AdPs$, the CPI prices and the realized similarity $Adv\text{-}AdP$.

5.3 Diffusion Phase

During the *Diffusion Phase* (Alg. 3) each *inactive* advertiser i has to update her *hypothesis$(i, t - 1)$* for the period

Algorithm 2 Test Phase

```
1:  for t = 1 to ∞ do
2:      for all AdP J do
3:          set f_J^t = v_J^{t-1}
4:      end for
5:      for all Adv i do
6:          Collect hypothesis(i,t) = ({AdP}_i^t, {u_i^t(·)}),
7:      end for
8:      Compute the AdP's with a potential buyer (active
        goods in the market):
9:      {AdP}^t = {J | ∃i, u_i^t(J) ≠ 0}
10:     Run Tatonnement
11:     Return Ad-Network:
12:     AdNet^t = {(i, {AdP}_i^t, {f_{J→i}^t})}. CPI_J^t
13:     Activate Ad-Network
14:     Return the realized values:
15:     c_{J→i}^t, CTR̄_i^t
16:     Test Criterion:
17:     for all Adv i do
18:         if CTR̄_i^t < θ · CTR̄^t    then
19:             Inactive (Test Score=False)
20:             go to Diffusion Phase
21:         else
22:             Active (Test Score=True)
23:             (choose the same hypothesis updated by the re-
                alized values)
24:             hypothesis(i,t + 1) = ({AdP}_i^{t+1}, {u_i^{t+1}(·)}),
                where:
                {AdP}_i^{t+1} = {AdP̄}_i^t and u_i^{t+1}(J) = CTR_i^t(J)
25:         end if
26:     end for
27: end for
```

Algorithm 3 Diffusion Phase

```
1:  for t = 1 to ∞ do
2:      for every Inactive Adv i do
3:          Choose new hypothesis:
4:          Run Find Friends
5:          {
6:          Choose with prob. 1/#ads one new ad g
7:          if g = friend is TRUE (i.e g's ad similar to i's ad )
            then
8:              Set F_i^t = F_i^{t-1} ∪ {g}
9:          else
10:             Set F_i^t = F_i^{t-1}
11:         end if
12:         }
13:         Return friends F_i^t
14:         Choose by the probabilistic rule Eq. 4 one friend k
            in F_i^t
15:         if k Active AND CTR̄_k^t > CTR̄_i^t then
16:             copy k's preferences:
17:             hypothesis(i,t + 1) = ({AdP}_i^{t+1}, {u_i^{t+1}(·)}).
18:             where:
19:             {AdP}_i^{t+1} = {AdP̄}_i^t ∪ {AdP̄}_k^t
20:             u_i^{t+1}(J) = { CTR_i^t(J)  if J ∈ {AdP}_i^t
                               { CTR_k^t(J)  if J ∈ {AdP}_k^t − {AdP}_i^t
21:         else
22:             choose with uniform probability one new AdP J'
23:             hypothesis(i,t + 1) = ({AdP}_i^{t+1}, {u_i^{t+1}(·)})
24:             where:
25:             {AdP}_i^{t+1} = {AdP̄}_i^t ∪ {J}
26:             u_i^{t+1}(J) = { CTR_i^t(J)  if J ∈ {AdP̄}_i^t
                               { 1           if J' New
27:         end if
28:     end for
29: end for
```

t. She chooses at random one advertiser and compares the *hypothesis(i,t − 1)* with hers.

SDS is a population based method where an implicit assumption is that the population of agents are homogeneous. Thus, during the diffusion phase agents' recommendations are valid. In our case a main issue arises, their is not a prior known population of advertisers that an given advertiser i could ask for recommendations. Thus, each advertiser has to define the subset of ads that are similar with hers.

We apply a method where in every period each advertiser explores the set of ads in the market, one ad per period, and characterizes with true/false if it is contextually similar to her ad or not. The set F_i^t of similar ads is called the *friends* of i. This will be used as input to the diffusion phase.

Specifically, the subroutine **Find Friends** encompasses the following steps. In each period, each advertiser chooses exactly one ad g with probability $\frac{1}{\#ads}$. Then, if the selected ad is similar with hers she updates her set of friends. Finally, she chooses an ad k by the probabilistic rule Eq.4.

$$Pr_i(k) = \frac{w_i(k)}{\sum_{k \in F_i^t} w_i(k)} \quad (4)$$

The value $w_i(k)$ represents i's **social criterion** for the advertiser k and corresponds to the influence that k has on the community of advertisers. We define:

$$w_i(k) = \alpha \cdot (indegree(k)+1) + \beta \cdot (\#common friends+1) \quad (5)$$

where $\alpha + \beta = 1$. The parameters α and β are defined by i. The value one in the *in-degree* has the meaning that any advertiser has a link with herself and consequently positive probability to be collected even if she is isolated. Also, the value one in the *common friends* has the meaning that any advertiser is *friend* with herself. The *common friends* values give weight to the symmetric relations i.e. the case where i votes k as a friend and k votes i. The intuition is that the *in-degree* reflects advertiser's social influence and the *common friends* the convergence of advertisers' subjective beliefs with respect to ads similarity.

Briefly, the main diffusion phase conducts the following actions: i selects at random one friend k. If k is *active* and k's hypothesis is better than i's, then i copy k's preferences (Alg. 3, step 15-20). Else, she chooses at random one ad-publisher J' (Alg. 3, step 22-26). Observe that at step-19 agent i combines her hypothesis with k's by performing the union of the two relevant sets. The intuition is that the i cannot predict the externalities in the market. Thus, she submits to tatonnement her realized set of ad-publishers along with her subjective beliefs.

6. EVALUATION OF THE METHOD

In this section we present the experimental evaluation of the SDMS. The simulation and the tatonnement was imple-

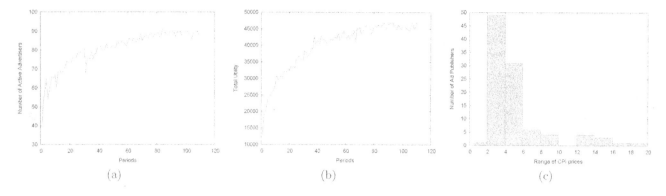

(a)   (b)   (c)

Figure 2: a) Convergence State b) Social welfare c) Distribution of CPI prices in SDMS.

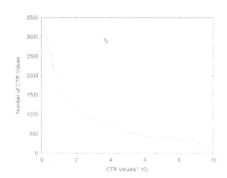

Figure 1: *Zipf* distribution of realized $\overline{CTR}$ values.

mented in MATLAB. Due to computational limitations, we simulated a market with 100 ad-publishers and 100 advertisers. During the simulation we set $\epsilon = 2$, thus the tatonnement computes a $(1+2)$-approximate market equilibrium. Also, we set α and β equal to 0.5 (Eq. 5) and $\theta = 0.9$ (Alg. 2 step 18). The experiments were performed on a Intel Core 2 Quad CPU Q8200 & 2.33GHz & 3.21GB RAM.

The experimental evaluation conducted on an artificially constructed data set. The number of visitors of each ad-publisher J is defined on the integer interval $[100, 1000]$ as follows: we pick with uniform probability an integer x from the interval $[0, 90]$, and we assign to J the $\nu_J = (x + 10) \cdot 10$ value. We consider that the number of visitors is constant in every period.

The advertisers' budget values range in the interval $[1000, 3000]$ as follows: we pick with uniform probability an integer x from the interval $[0, 2000]$ and we assign to advertiser i the budget $b_i = x + 1000$.

The $\overline{CTR}_i^t(J)$ values i.e the realized $Adv\text{-}AdP$ similarity are approximated by a *Zipf* distribution with *Zipf* exponent 1.0. We generate for each advertiser i 100 *Zipf* values which correspond to the realized CTR values of the 100 ad-publishers. During the experiments the CTR values considered constant. In summary we generate $100 \cdot 100$ *Zipf* values. CTR distribution is presented in Fig. 1.

The *friends* of the advertisers are defined by a matrix 100×100 where each cell $[i, g]$ has the value 1 if i is friend with g and 0 otherwise. We constructed the matrix as follows: On a given advertiser i we assign with uniform probability an integer from the interval $[0, 9]$, this is the *color* of

i. We repeat for all advertisers. Advertisers with the same *color* considered as similar (friends). We make the assumption that when i votes g as friend then g also considers i as friend. Thus, i and g, in other words, have the same subjective beliefs with respect to their ad similarity. This procedure creates 10 groups of friends. The previous process generates group of advertisers with the same *color* (subjective similarity) but probably with different CTR values on the same ad-publisher (realized similarity).

In the first experiment, we estimate the *convergence state* of SDMS, the state where a reasonable solution is discovered (see p.32 in [12]). The number of *active* advertisers is computed (Fig. 2(a)) for 110 consecutive periods. Recall that we consider as *active* the advertisers that are satisfied i.e. their average CTR (Eq. 2) is greater than the market average CTR (Eq. 3). Observe that the activity of advertisers is converging fast, as after the 20th period the SDMS process accelerates and after 60 periods more than 80% of the advertisers are active. Thus, the SDMS process potentially converges to an stable stage.

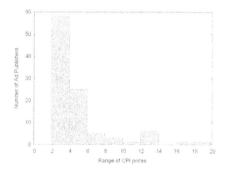

Figure 3: Distribution of CPI in the full information case.

Next, we deal with the social welfare of the network. In every period, we measure the sum of the total utility values $\sum_i \sum_J c_{J \to i}$, corresponding to the social welfare in the network. The results depict in Fig. 2(b). We observe that as the number of periods increased the social welfare also increased converging to stable level. Thus results verify our intuition that the SDMS is applicable to a social network with heterogeneous agents.

In Fig. 2(c) we present the distribution of CPI prices in SDMS after 110 periods and in Fig. 3 the distribution of

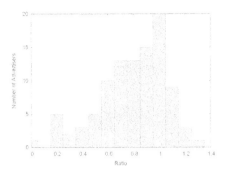

Figure 4: Total utility in SDMS vs full information case.

CPI in the case of the mature market. A mature market is a market where the preferences of advertisers is well defined, implying that the advertisers are fully informed about the realized CTR values. Thus, we run the tatonnement assuming that the advertisers are aware of the realized CTR values and these values are submitted to the tatonnement process. The experiments present that the distribution in SDMS is very similar with the full information case. It is also clear in both cases that a small number of $AdPs$ sell in high prices. Thus, we claim that the stage of the market after the 110th period depicts power law properties.

Finally, we compare the SDMS total utility allocation after 110 periods to the total utility allocation in a mature market Fig. 4. We compute the ratio of total utility obtained in SDMS divided by the total utility obtained in the full information case. The results show that more than 50% of the population of advertisers have ratio greater than 0.6. This result verifies the effectiveness of our method since it approximates the full information case.

In summary, the experimental results verify that the network converges to a stable state and that the distribution of market prices adheres to power law properties. Both results present a solution with attractive macroscopic properties that can be deployed in a real system.

7. CONCLUSION

In this paper we proposed a novel method the SDMS (Stochastic Diffusion Market Search) for the formation of an advertising network consisting of a population of independent agents/web sites.

The innovation of SDMS lies in the fact that advertisement allocation emerges from indirect communication among the participants. The *Center*, the moderator of the system, is of limited role and does not define the advertising network. The *Center* executes the subroutines *tatonnement* and *ad-networks* but it does not define the preferences of the advertisers and their network of *friends*. All the parameters of the market, the *test* and the *diffusion* phase as well as the subjective beliefs of advertisers with respect to advertising similarity are defined only by the agents.

The SDMS integrates the algorithmic schema of *Stochastic Diffusion Search*, a Swarm Intelligent metaheuristic. Our method consists of a *Test Phase* where the advertisers evaluate their choices in the advertising market and a *Diffusion Phase* where update their preferences. The experimental results show that the network converges to a stable stage and the distribution of market prices adheres to power law

properties.

8. REFERENCES

[1] K. J. Arrow and G. Debreu. Existence of an equilibrium for a competitive economy. *Econometrica*, 22(3):265–290, July 1954.

[2] J. M. Bishop. Stochastic searching networks. In *Artificial Neural Networks, 1989. First IEE International Conference on (Conf. Publ. No. 313)*, pages 329–331, October 1989.

[3] E. Bonabeau, M. Dorigo, and G. Theraulaz. *Swarm Intelligence: From Natural to Artificial Systems*. Oxford University Press, New York, Oxford, 1999.

[4] S. Ceyhan, M. Mousavi, and A. Saberi. Social influence and evolution of market share. In *In the NetEcon*, 2009.

[5] N. R. Devanur, C. H. Papadimitriou, and V. V. Vazirani. Market equilibrium via a primal–dual algorithm for a convex program. *Journal of the ACM (JACM)*, 55(5):1–18, October 2008.

[6] B. Edelman, M. Ostrovsky, and M. Schwarz. Internet advertising and the generalized second-price auction: Selling billions of dollars worth of keywords. *American Economic Review*, 97(1):242–259, March 2007.

[7] L. Fleischer, R. Garg, S. Kapoor, R. Khandekar, and A. Saberi. A fast and simple algorithm for computing market equilibria. In *WINE '08: Proceedings of the 4th International Workshop on Internet and Network Economics*, pages 19–30, December 2008.

[8] D. Fudenberg and L. A. Imhof. Monotone imitation dynamics in large populations. *Journal of Economic Theory*, 140(1):229–245, May 2008.

[9] D. Fudenberg and D. K. Levine. *The Theory of Learning in Games*. The MIT Press, Cambridge, MA, 1998.

[10] Z. Katona and M. Sarvary. Network formation and the structure of the commercial world wide web. *Marketing Science*, 27(5):764–778, September - October 2008.

[11] J. Kennedy, R. C. Eberhart, and Y. Shi. *Swarm intelligence*. Morgan Kaufmann Publishers, San Francisco, CA, 2001.

[12] K. D. Meyer. *Foundations of Stochastic Diffusion Search*. PhD thesis, University of Reading, 2003.

[13] S. J. Nasuto and J. M. Bishop. Convergence analysis of stochastic diffusion search. *Journal of Parallel Algorithms and Applications*, 14(2):89–107, July 1999.

[14] S. J. Nasuto, J. M. Bishop, and S. Lauria. Time complexity analysis of the stochastic diffusion search. In *Proceedings of the International ICSC / IFAC Symposium on Neural Computation (NC 1998)*, pages 260–266, September 1998.

[15] A. Saberi and A. Shkolnik. Advertising space exchange in a network using market equilibrium algorithms. In *Fifth Workshop on Ad Auctions (adauctions2009)*.

[16] K. H. Schlag. Why imitate, and if so, how? : A boundedly rational approach to multi-armed bandits. *Journal of Economic Theory*, 78(1):130–156, January 1998.

[17] H. P. Young. *Individual Strategy and Social Structure: An Evolutionary Theory of Institutions*. Princeton University Press, Princeton, NJ, 1998.

Kolline: a task-oriented system for collaborative information seeking

Fernando Figueira Filho
Institute of Computing
University of Campinas, Brazil
fernando@las.ic.unicamp.br

Gary M. Olson
Department of Informatics
University of California, Irvine,
USA
gary.olson@uci.edu

Paulo Lício de Geus
Institute of Computing
University of Campinas, Brazil
paulo@las.ic.unicamp.br

ABSTRACT

This paper presents results of an exploratory study which observed Linux novice users performing complex technical tasks using Google's search engine. In this study we observed that information triage is a difficult process for unexperienced users unless well structured information is provided which results in better satisfaction and search effectiveness. Providing a well structured information allows users to browse through different pieces of documentation without depending exclusively on the keyword search. Based on these observations, this research prototyped Kolline, a system that aims to facilitate information seeking for unexperienced users by allowing more experienced users to collaborate together. Users in Kolline create a task-oriented navigation structure based on web annotations. In this paper we discuss the potential benefits of this technique on helping unexperienced users to solve complex search tasks and present improvements for future work.

Categories and Subject Descriptors

H.5.3 [Information Interfaces and Presentation]: Group and Organization Interfaces—*web-based interaction, collaborative computing, organizational design*

General Terms

Human factors

Keywords

social search, collaborative information seeking, user study, interface prototype, hypertext.

1. INTRODUCTION

Search systems have become essential tools since the invention of the Web. Although search efficiency and efficacy have dramatically improved lately, the interaction paradigm used to search for information has been the same for years: users type keywords into a search box and get back a ranked result list of web documents to be analyzed. A common

practice for users is to screen through the retrieved list of documents and individually analyze web pages in order to fulfill their information needs. While this paradigm has been proven to suffice for specific fact finding and other types of lookup search activities, it does not suit exploratory search tasks that well, such as answering open-ended questions and learning about unfamiliar topics [10, 14, 17].

We conducted a pilot study to better understand the difficulties faced by Linux novices when looking for information to solve technical problems. We observed that greater task difficulty and lack of expertise have a significant impact on how they interact with the search system and how they examine a large collection of web documents to compare, aggregate and synthesize information. During this process, search context is built upon keywords that are matched against web documents within the search system. As such, the interaction between users and system is largely based on queries, which may lead to imprecise, ambiguous results, thus leaving to users the role of making sense between the provided information and their needs. In brief, this interaction paradigm forces users to individually analyze matched web pages to sort relevant information that may be spread throughout different portions of distinct web documents, which can be a time-consuming and frustrating activity.

This paper proposes a cooperative approach for information seeking, which aims at providing system support for users to interactively build, refine and reuse search context by cooperatively constructing a web of semantically-related and task-oriented information on top of the available web of documents. To this purpose, this research seeks to answer the following research questions:

- How can we facilitate retrieval of related pieces of information within the web of documents?
  - Can these pieces of information be interlinked using web annotations as metadata, by highlighting text snippets within web pages and adding notes that can be easily viewed by other users?
  - Can we create a user interface that focuses on the information embedded in the page instead of on the page itself?

With the aim of answering these questions, this paper prototyped Kolline, a system that aims to facilitate information seeking for unexperienced users by allowing more experienced users to collaborate together. Users in Kolline create a task-oriented navigation structure based on web annotations. Section 2 presents some background which helps the reader to understand our approach. Section 3 presents the results of a exploratory study with Linux novices and Section 4 describes our prototype. We discuss the potential benefits of our technique on helping unexperienced users to solve complex search tasks in Section 5 and present improvements for future work in Section 6. The paper finishes with conclusions in Section 7.

2. BACKGROUND

User disorientation and cognitive overhead are well recognized problems of hypertext systems, even before the invention of the Web. Many researchers early recognized these issues and some solutions were proposed. Zellweger [19] introduced Scripted Documents, a system that implements the concept of paths in hypertext systems. Paths bring together an interlinked collection of documents which are ordered in the form of a presentation. As such, most of the decisions about the transversal order of links are made by the author in advance, rather than by the reader during the path playback. This concept is orthogonal to the way that we search the Web today. Although search engines have dramatically improved recall and precision, the unit of retrieval is still the web document. Using this approach, users have to analyze different matched documents or transverse the link structure to find relevant information. The path approach exempt the information consumer of this work, thus having the potential to provide an already filtered collection of documents that can be integrated and used in the context of a particular search task. However, one implementation of this concept has to consider how the path is actually produced and consumed. Albeit one can assume that paths may be produced either automatically or collaboratively, it is not clear how retrieving paths instead of web documents would make the overall search process more efficient.

To address this issue, social search comes up as an alternative search paradigm which is facilitated by the rise of social media and has the potential to change the way by which users filter information. People can easily ask for help in their social networks and share web resources. Information needs are usually communicated through message exchange between peers within the same social network. Morris et al. [11] analyzed benefits of searching using search engines over asking in social networks. Participants revealed preference for using search engines, but the study highlights a growing use of social networks for asking subjective questions, in which the answer depend on tacit knowledge that is shared between peers. While promising, social search is in an early stage of development and different approaches are emerging, such as the Aardvark system[1], which is a question answering system that integrates instant messaging functionality to support asynchronous collaboration within social networks.

In the pursuit of enabling collaboration in the searching process, some systems have also supported synchronous collaboration. For instance, SearchTogether [12] implements group awareness through shared query histories and a "summary" displaying participants' comments and ratings of web pages. CoSense [13] provides enhanced group awareness by including a timeline view of all queries executed during the search process. Even though these features help to enhance participants' communication and sense making during their search activities, users still have to sort among different documents and analyze them one by one to find relevant information. As our results indicate, users spend a long time reading web pages when learning about unfamiliar topics. Our approach aims at saving this time by letting users annotate and share web content. The annotations follow the concept of a path and are shared within the scope of a social network, i.e. using the social search paradigm. The next section presents more details about our study.

3. EXPLORATORY STUDY

Studies were conducted to elucidate the following research question: given users' lack of experience on Linux, what sort of difficulties they would face to search the Web for technical documentation? Six graduate students of the informatics department with little experience on Linux enrolled to participate in individual sessions during which their activity was recorded using screen-capturing software. Audio recording and the think-aloud protocol also contributed to capture important steps about the reasoning behind participants' actions. Each participant also had one version of the Ubuntu Linux distribution running on the experiment computer.

During each session, participants were presented to five tasks in the domain of Linux systems. They were asked to use Google to look up for information. We aimed at observing differences in subjects' behavior according to tasks characteristics, such as type, i.e. lookup and exploratory, and difficulty, i.e. simple and complex tasks. To this purpose, we created task instructions that were presented to users during the session, in a counter-balanced order. A moderator was in the same room as an observer, asking questions to the participant when a better verbal explanation would help to clarify some point of interest left behind. Each session also included a pre-test time dedicated to the introduction of the environment to the participant and to present other study details. There were also, at the end of each task, a time dedicated to review the difficulties that were found.

3.1 Preliminary results

3.1.1 Information seeking activities

We identified three distinct activities during participants' observation, namely query formulation, screening and content analysis. *Query formulation* is composed of the interactive process of elaborating and typing keywords into a text box and of the subsequent clicking on a search button to retrieve search results. *Screening* is the activity of analyzing these results and performing relevance judgments over a ranked list of documents. *Content analysis* encompasses examining each document separately and using the information contained into them. Content analysis often demands an additional step, which is the verification of the information found, e.g. running commands using a Linux terminal to accomplish a certain task. We measured the total time spent on each activity, considering all tasks. Indeed, subjects spent a lot of time analyzing and validating information, as shown in Fig. 1.

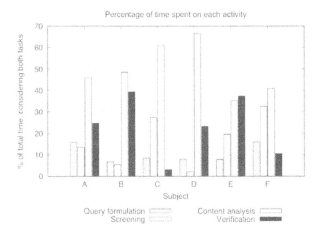

Figure 1: Percentage of time spent on each activity, considering all tasks.

3.1.2 Lack of experience and uncertainty

In our study we found that Linux novices usually have a hard time determining the qualities of an information source, e.g. usefulness and completeness, just by screening the result page provided by Google. This page typically shows a ranked list with page results, each one represented by a title, a brief summary which highlights query's matched terms and the information source's url (*uniform resource locator*). Because subjects cannot easily determine in advance if a given information source is useful to the task at hand, they often have to click on each result and load the referred page, which our experiments revealed to be a time-consuming process (Fig. 1). For instance, subjects were asked to find a possible cause for a bug that was crashing their computers after logging on the machine. One subject queried "ubuntu freezes after login" and after being confronted with a search result page containing a series of links to threaded discussions in web forums, the participant said:

> P03: There is a lot of links. Now, whether the information in those links is meaningful at all is just a matter of reading one by one.

Therefore, we found that lack of experience on a particular knowledge domain leads to greater levels of uncertainty regarding which results to visit from Google's result page. On the many cases in which titles and summaries did not help, a common strategy was to analyze results separately, thus improving the understanding about the task domain. After learning something useful such as a new keyword or the name of a command, subjects often reformulated the query, so a refined result set could be obtained.

3.1.3 Information and its preferred sources

Byström [4] points out that there is a relatively strong preference relationship between types of information and types of sources. Accordingly, we noticed that effect on exploratory tasks which include open-ended questions, e.g. finding three good reviews about the latest Ubuntu Linux distribution release version. For instance, after several unsuccessful attempts to find a reliable information source for a review, one

participant found an article and mentioned "this is what I am looking for" as soon as the page finished loading. Before analyzing the content in detail, the subject commented about how the information is presented and structured, with a table of contents and links to different sections. Moreover, we found that when subjects are stuck formulating queries, they naturally start browsing for information. For this reason, Linux novices relied more on well structured documents produced by experts in the form of articles than on documents in the form of threaded discussions. As an example, while searching about the possible causes for a crash after logging in, another subject criticized the way the information is presented in web forums:

> P05: I actually randomly look at the tech forums. Because it is like the same format, the titles... ah! That is one of the things that I would say pro, in general, commercial software... in the open-source [community] more people comment to help you out with the problem, but it is so time-consuming to look for what you need.

Also, Byström [4] also found that the effects of task complexity made experts more attractive as a source. In our study, when comparing information found in a question answering (QA) site with the one found in threaded discussions, subjects revealed a greater preference for the former and the reasons for this behavior are twofold. First, in QA sites, best ranked answers are presented upfront, exempting the user from analyzing several pages with information. Second, best answers are peer-reviewed, thus increasing the information credibility from the novice user perspective. To some extent, these results confirm many aspects of what was pointed out by Dutta-Bergman [5] in the e-health domain. These two factors, i.e. (i) well structured and detailed information that counts for completeness and (ii) expertise associated with content that counts for credibility, when associated with the information source, had a positive impact on subjects' satisfaction levels and search effectiveness. The next section explores these findings and introduces the design of a collaborative system which aims at facilitating technical information scrutiny in the Web for unexperienced users.

4. USAGE SCENARIO AND INTERFACE

Maria logs into Kolline to ask for help. She starts by creating a task to explain her problem in a short text message which is viewable by all users within the system (Fig. 2a). John is an expert Linux user and one of Maria's friends within the system's social network. John looks up relevant web pages in order to help Maria solve her problem and replies to her question (Fig. 2b). John can search on Google and select results using the embedded browser window depicted in Fig. 2g. When clicked (Fig. 2h), each result is rendered in the right side of the interface (Fig. 2j). John can help Maria in two ways: (1) he can create floating notes that are persistently attached to a region on a web page (Fig. 2d). Notes associated to the question are highlighted, while others are shown using less contrasting colors (Fig. 2e); (ii) John can also select text snippets, (e.g. words, phrases or even paragraphs). He can then link these snippets, to create a task-oriented navigation structure that can be browsed

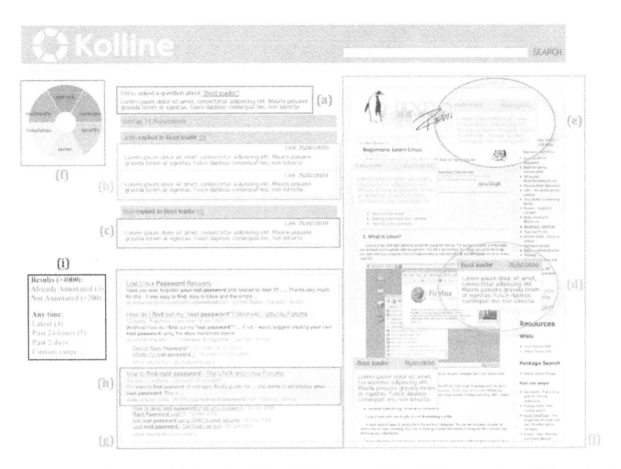

Figure 2: Kolline's interface: (a) Question; (b) and (c) answers; (d) and (e) annotations; (f) browsing tool; (g) Web page results; (h) selected Web page; (i) filters and (j) rendered Web page.

using the tool depicted in Fig. 2f (see [6] for more details). This navigation structure (or path) can be shared among friends, so other users can take advantage of previously created annotations to solve similar problems. Maria can visualize annotations in a preview window within the interface (Fig. 2j). To browse for annotations, she can either click on the answers to her questions, which automatically shows a list of related annotated pages, or browse per category using the colored interface (Fig. 2f). She can also filter for annotations using the menu depicted in (Fig. 2i). In this manner she can analyze each content associated with an annotation and browse the navigation structure at the same time, thus avoiding browser window switching. While she checks John's suggestions, other friends in Maria's social network continue to contribute in solving her problem, e.g. Bob realizes that she still needs help on "boot loader", so he replies to her answer (Fig. 2c) and creates another set of annotations.

Another important aspect in the interface is that every control is centralized in the same browser window. Iqbal and Horvitz [8] discovered that, when switching between tasks, a greater visibility of each task context is associated with faster recovery from one task to another. In other words, tasks associated with application windows that were not focused had longer recovery times. Kolline interface takes advantage of today's higher resolution displays and uses all the

available area to show relevant information. The interface provides group awareness by notifying the user when a new message arrives or annotation is created (Fig. 2b and c).

In our browsing interface (Fig. 3), the colors have the purpose of enhancing the user's working memory. Wichmann et al. [18] shows that recognition memory is 5%–10% better on colored images in comparison to black & white images. Thus, one important design decision is based on the idea that colors may have an important role on helping the user to memorize previous steps when interacting with the interface. Another important design decision is to avoid scrolling. Schwarz et al. [15] points out that this approach provides a better experience, especially for novice users. The colored pie functionality is illustrated in Fig 3. On selection of one of the general terms displayed by the interface, a transition changes the tool's shape. It becomes a quadrant through a smooth transition to transmit the idea of changing the focus. Each previous level of the hierarchy, i.e. inner circle, keeps the color of the previously selected term. At each new selection, new paths are recommended in the outer side of the quadrant. The user can move the mouse over the inner circles to view the context, which causes the previously selected terms to be highlighted. Each new interaction with the tool show newer discussions and newer annotations which in turn gives an instant feedback, so the user can make a decision to continue transversing the path structure or to read web

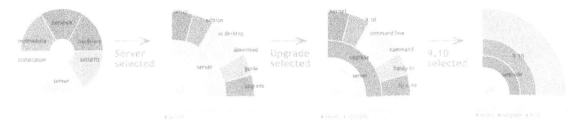

Figure 3: Kolline's browsing interface.

pages and annotations individually. Another important design decision is to avoid scrolling. Our browsing tool stays static and within a single, limited area of the screen, showing just the two previously selected levels as inner circles, i.e. context, and new term recommendations in the outer circle, i.e. focus. The path below the quadrant shows all previously selected terms and allows the user to go directly to a certain level. This has an important role in keeping the user's attention on the focus, without loosing the visual contact of the context.

5. DISCUSSION

In our study we found that (i) well structured and detailed information and (ii) expertise associated with the web content are factors that have a positive influence on user satisfaction and search effectiveness, especially when the searcher is unfamiliar with the search topic. This provided us with a chance to reflect about how the effort of analyzing relevant and irrelevant content starting from the Google's result page can be amortized. Kolline uses a cooperative approach to distribute the problem of information filtering and content analysis among peers within the scope of a social network, i.e. social search. The approach also takes advantage of the fact that people have an intrinsic motivation to cooperate [16] and that friends or acquaintances might share tacit knowledge to some degree, which might help to build content upon subjective information needs that cannot be easily expressed using queries and keywords.

Another measure toward creating design alternatives to save users' time when analyzing content is the use of the path concept. Collaborators can link web pages through their annotations, thus creating a navigation structure which, in turn, facilitates content analysis when the user is disoriented, i.e. not knowing what query is more appropriate or what document more relevant. Users can browse through previously created paths and add their own annotations, so paths are collaboratively created and shared within the social network. By using collaborative design for information seeking purposes, Kolline offers the following contributions. First, unexperienced users can harvest the wisdom of the crowds for complex tasks [9], so they can be solved by a joint effort among users. Second, it is possible to build a task-oriented hypertext structure which can be browsed, so users may benefit from well-known advantages of technologies such as wikis to aggregate collaboratively generated information. Third, although users may use tags to categorize paths, our approach does not suffer from the same disadvantages of other tagging systems [7]. Tags are primarily used for user navigation, not for keyword search matching, so the tags associated with paths serve to a particular situa-

tion which is shared among users involved in solving another user's question. Fourth, differently from other previous systems, Kolline provides a way for experienced users to leave visual clues for unexperienced users to reach and visualize the information faster, freeing them from having to analyze irrelevant information to accomplish the task at hand.

The technologies to implement our system are easily available. Social media sites such as Twitter [2] can aggregate user generated content to inform and entertain people according to their preferences. Wikis allow for collaboratively creating and linking web content and have already reached enormous success with examples like Wikipedia [3]. The proposed design uses the content aggregation feature as a means of easily communicating experts and novices in collaborative information seeking tasks without overloading any participating part with information. Kolline also makes use of the collaborative content generation of wikis, but instead of creating new web documents, users are allowed to create content over existing web pages.

6. FUTURE WORK

For future work, we plan to run one pilot and a validation study using the controlled experiments method. Because Kolline is based on the asynchronous communication between experts and novices, we will separate participants into two groups, namely the expert and the novice group. Participants' experience will be measured in a pre-test questionnaire. Tasks will be presented in a counter-balanced order to mitigate learning transfer effects. Each task comprises of two rounds and each round consists of two non-concomitant individual sessions. Before the beginning of each round, experts and novices will be randomly arranged using pairs, so each novice will have help from one expert Linux user to accomplish the task at hand. On each round, experts will annotate web pages and then novices will execute the same task benefiting from the annotations previously created by the expert. Novice users who could not solve the problem in the first round are assigned to a different expert and the procedure is repeated. The difference between the two rounds is that second round expert will be able to see the annotations created by the first round expert and change them. We want to analyze how one expert can improve on another's existing annotations.

7. CONCLUSION

In this paper, we presented preliminary results of an exploratory study, in which we observed Linux novice users performing complex technical tasks using Google's search engine. We found that the information triage is a difficult process for unexperienced users. Based on these observations, we presented a system design which allows experts to collaborate by annotating web content. This system aims at facilitating complex problem solving even when proper experience is lacking by employing asynchronous collaboration between peers in a social network. The tool also provides a way for users to create paths among annotations. Each annotation is attached to a web document, an author and a question. We discussed the benefits of our approach and provided directions for evaluation.

8. ACKNOWLEDGMENTS

Authors would like to thank researchers and graduate students who kindly agreed to participate in the study presented in this paper. The study was conducted at University of California, Irvine under the fellowship grant from CAPES, process 1089/09-9.

9. REFERENCES

[1] Aardvark. Available online: http://www.vark.org. Last access: 6/28/2010.

[2] Twitter. Available online: http://www.twitter.com. Last access: 6/28/2010.

[3] Wikipedia. Available online: http://www.wikipedia.org. Last access: 6/28/2010.

[4] K. Bystrøm. Information and information sources in tasks of varying complexity. *Journal of the American Society for Information Science and Technology*, 53:581–591, 2002.

[5] M. Dutta-Bergman. The impact of completeness and web use motivation on the credibility of e-health information. *Journal of Communication*, 54(2):253–269, 2004.

[6] F. M. Figueira Filho, J. P. de Albuquerque, A. Resende, P. L. de Geus, and G. M. Olson. A visualization interface for interactive search refinement. In *Proceedings of the 3rd Annual Workshop on Human-Computer Interaction and Information Retrieval (HCIR '09)*, pages 46–49, October 2009.

[7] S. Golder and B. Huberman. Usage patterns of collaborative tagging systems. *Journal of Information Science*, 32(2):198–208, 2006.

[8] S. T. Iqbal and E. Horvitz. Disruption and recovery of computing tasks: field study, analysis, and directions.

In *CHI '07: Proceedings of the SIGCHI conference on Human factors in computing systems*, pages 677–686, New York, NY, USA, 2007. ACM.

[9] A. Kittur and R. E. Kraut. Harnessing the wisdom of crowds in wikipedia: quality through coordination. *Proceedings of the ACM 2008 conference on Computer supported cooperative work*, pages 37–46, 2008.

[10] G. Marchionini. Exploratory search: from finding to understanding. *Communications of the ACM*, 49(4):46, 2006.

[11] M. Morris, J. Teevan, and K. Panovich. A Comparison of Information Seeking Using Search Engines and Social Networks. *Proceedings of the Fourth International AAAI Conference on Weblogs and Social Media*, 2010.

[12] M. R. Morris and E. Horvitz. Searchtogether: an interface for collaborative web search. *UIST '07: Proceedings of the 20th annual ACM symposium on User interface software and technology*, pages 3–12, 2007.

[13] S. A. Paul and M. R. Morris. Cosense: enhancing sensemaking for collaborative web search. *CHI '09: Proceedings of the 27th international conference on Human factors in computing*, pages 1771–1780, 2009.

[14] A. H. Renear and C. L. Palmer. Strategic reading, ontologies, and the future of scientific publishing. *Science*, 325:828–832, August 2009.

[15] E. Schwarz, I. Beldie, and S. Pastoor. Comparison of paging and scrolling for changing screen contents by inexperienced users. *Human factors*, 25(3):279–282, 1983.

[16] M. Tomasello. *Why we cooperate*. MIT Press, 2009.

[17] R. White and R. Roth. Exploratory Search: Beyond the Query-Response Paradigm. *Synthesis Lectures on Information Concepts, Retrieval, and Services*, 1(1):1–98, 2009.

[18] F. Wichmann, L. Sharpe, and K. Gegenfurtner. The contributions of color to recognition memory for natural scenes. *Learning. Memory*, 28(3):509–520, 2002.

[19] P. T. Zellweger. Scripted documents: a hypermedia path mechanism. *HYPERTEXT '89: Proceedings of the second annual ACM conference on Hypertext*, pages 1–14, 1989.

Best Practices for Designing Third Party Applications for Contextually-Aware Tools

Dave Jones
CeME Lab
Old Dominion University
Norfolk, Virginia
djone111@odu.edu

Liza Potts
CeME Lab
Old Dominion University
Norfolk, Virginia
lpotts@odu.edu

ABSTRACT

This experience report examines the user interface designs of Twitter and selected third party Twitter applications: Tweetdeck and Brizzly. Since participants are using different tools to communicate across the same system, Twitter users have different communication expectations. Evaluating Twitter and these tools based on usability heuristics found in activity theory and Morville's notion of findability, we argue for the normalization of these tools based on a set of mental models and affordances for Twitter. From this basis, we will report on how third-party clients more effectively exploit Twitter's affordances by making the streams, and thus the user's experiences, modular, emergent, and contextual. By comparing the UIs of Tweetdeck and Brizzly, along with that of Twitter's own web-based UI, we will assess how these clients allow participants to adapt Twitter streams to their own communication needs. The flexibility given to users via such clients serves as a tremendous signpost to the nature of and need for modular, context-aware experiences in communication channels as information content evolves. Not only do the social networks themselves need to be articulated and modular, but so do the UIs through which users engage with these networks. We argue that these features are critical for social media participants. Based on our analysis of Tweetdeck and Brizzly, we develop a set of best practices that should guide the research and design of participant experiences in social media and the third-party applications that many of them often use.

Categories and Subject Descriptors

H.5.2 [**Information Interfaces and Presentation**]: User Interfaces – *graphical user interfaces (GUI), screen design, style guides, user-centered design.*

General Terms

Design, Human Factors, Standardization.

Keywords

Design, Usability, Heuristics, Third Party Tools, Social Media, Social Networking Systems, Twitter.

1. INTRODUCTION

The social networking service Twitter has become one of the most popular communication systems in the world. Twitter now averages approximately 50 million tweets per day, all limited to only 140 characters [22]. The service is used for a wide range of communicative activities. News services, such as CNN and the *New York Times*, distribute alerts and links to their Twitter followers. Public figures, including celebrities and government officials, use the service to connect to fans and constituents. Twitter is sometimes used as an informal communications channel among employees or organization members [19, 23]. A number of universities are experimenting with Twitter as a means of fostering a sense of community among on-campus and distance students; the results have so far proven the effectiveness of the service's ability to maintain highly contextualized communities [16]. Twitter has also been used as a messaging service to coordinate grassroots responses to major environmental and political crises [13, 14, 15]. Despite its 140-character limit, Twitter has shown itself to be an agile and flexible service for communication between individuals, communication among members of a group or organization, or as a site for quickly articulating and distributing linkages among content from other services.

One key to Twitter's success has been its support of third-party developers who build applications for organizing and interacting with Twitter content. More than 50,000 third-party applications have been developed for managing Twitter participants' social media experiences [22]. Using an application programming interface (API), third-parties such as Tweetdeck and Brizzly build both desktop and web-based applications that access Twitter and remediate its content through interfaces that feature tools for organizing content very differently from Twitter's own web-based interface. Third-party applications do not significantly alter the form or structure of Twitter as a service. The major features Twitter provides are made available to participants who use third-party systems. However, by organizing content differently, or allowing participants to view content in a different way, third-party applications are designed to encourage radically different participant experiences. In social media, those who use content are never simply consuming that content. Instead, they are often commenting on that content, redistributing that content to their social networks, or are archiving that content for some later use. Hence, we choose the term "participant" to denote someone who uses a social media service to engage a community or network. Participants are not simply passive consumers; they are active agents engaging with each other.

To analyze the design of these applications and the experiences they encourage, we first describe Twitter as a service, describing the core interactions for organizing content and maintaining communicative context that the site offers to its participants. Then, we describe two third-party tools, Brizzly and Tweetdeck, which remediate Twitter's content and interactions into different experiences. Both applications are popular third-party clients commonly used by Twitter participants to organize Twitter content and their experiences with that content. These applications use many of the features often found in third-party clients used for this purpose. We analyze the design of these applications and the experiences suggested by those designs against a set of heuristics derived from the synthesis of activity theory and findability. Our heuristics focus on the development and maintenance of meaningful context in Twitter-based communicative activities. Our analysis shows that Brizzly's interaction model tends to privilege narrowly defined, very specific interactions to the detriment of others that can be just as useful. Tweetdeck can be much more flexible, accommodating interactions similar to Brizzly's, as well as a much wider range of interactions that support more communicative activities. Finally, from this analysis we develop a set of recommendations for designing applications that manage social media experiences for Twitter participants.

2. TWITTER AS A SERVICE AND A SITE

Content moves through Twitter via a network of both symmetrical and asymmetrical social connections. Other sites, such as Facebook, demand something akin to a virtual handshake among participants, in which one participant requests a connection with another. Confirming the request is a reciprocal act in which both participants consciously choose to create a mutually recognized connection. To gain access to all or most of a participant's content, this handshake must take place. In Twitter, no reciprocity

is necessary. Unless a Twitter participant has protected his account, anyone can follow the participant's Twitter updates. By default, accounts are unprotected, and Twitter is primarily forged as a public space. The network resembles a community of millions of people gathering in a public park to talk about anything at all. Twitter participants routinely encounter other participants and content that originates outside their network.

To generate content, participants send out "tweets" to their followers. Tweets are short messages of no more than 140 characters, including text-based commands that direct tweets to the attention of specific recipients or groups. Tweets can contain original messages, including links, or they can be instances in which one participant "retweets" another. Retweets occur when one participant decides to repeat another's tweet, either in-part or whole, using an "RT" text command. The participant who is being retweeted receives a notification of the action. In addition, replies can be made using the "@" text command in front of the recipient's username. "At replies," typically written as "@replies," appear as "@username," and they are publicly viewable. Private messages can be sent between participants by creating Direct Messages using the "d" text command and the recipient's user name.

Twitter's site automates the use of both Retweets and @replies. Simple clicks of "Retweet" or "Reply" functions, which appear embedded in incoming tweets, will generate the necessary text commands. However, participants must either type the "d username" command for a Direct Message, or they must go to the Direct Messages screen, which shows only tweets that are private Direct Messages.

Twitter participants receive updates from their network via a linear timeline that arranges content chronologically [see Figure 1]. All publicly viewable content appears in the Home timeline,

Figure 1. Twitter participant's view

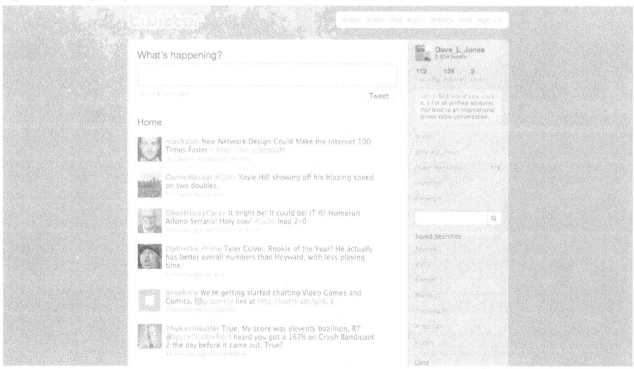

while Direct Messages appear on a separate screen. Though viewable in the Home timeline, @replies and Retweets also have dedicated screens. In addition, tweets can be sorted if participants affix Hashtags to them. Hashtags appear as words, short phrases, or combinations of letters and numbers with a "#" symbol prefix. For example, Old Dominion University students who used Twitter while participating in the 2009 Summer Doctoral Institute used the Hashtag "#sdi09." By creating a saved search in Twitter, or by simply clicking the Hashtag as it appears in a tweet, Twitter redirects the participant to a new screen and populates a new chronological timeline with only tweets that contain that Hashtag. Hashtag timelines show content from anyone who has recently used the Hashtag, even from other people the Twitter participant has not followed [2].

2.1 The Twitter Experience

Thus, Twitter-based communication is typically public, heavily networked across both known and unknown connections, and highly dependent on the ability to move content quickly across those networks while maintaining meaningful context. Twitter's "About" page describes the service as "a real-time information network powered by people all around the world that lets you share and discover what's happening now" [20]. Tools, such as Hashtags, aid in maintaining meaningful contexts by aggregating specific tweets and allowing communities to develop around those Hashtags. They are a form of "social tagging" [11] in which information is passed among specific communities through a folksonomy. A folksonomy is a socially constructed classification scheme that emerges from communities actively seeking to sort and contextualize information relevant to them [9, 21].

Twitter's timelines, viewable one at a time within a web-browser, move participants between specific folksonomies. Only one folksonomy can be shown on a page. Twitter's site makes it difficult for participants to work across folksonomies that might be related.

3. THIRD PARTY TOOLS
3.1 Overview

Third party-applications, such as Brizzly and Tweetdeck, endeavor to create experiences with Twitter's services that are different from those supported by Twitter's site. They do so by remediating Twitter's tools and content through very different interface features. They also more closely link Twitter with other services, such as link-shortening systems such as bit.ly. Or they add services of their own, such as participant-generated descriptions of Hashtags. Third-party applications reorganize and expand Twitter's social media experience, and in doing so encourage different social media activities.

3.2 Brizzly

Brizzly is a web-based application that largely maintains the look of the Twitter site, with a few modifications. As Figure 1 shows, Twitter positions its tools on the right side of the screen with a text entry field always present at the top of the timeline. Brizzly moves these tools to the left side of the screen and adds additional tools on the right [see Figure 2]. Direct Messages are now accessible from the Home screen, and new incoming Direct Messages appear as separate chat-style boxes on the right. Other functions, such as Hashtags, @replies, and Retweets, are still viewable in timelines on separate screens.

One of the most notable differences between Brizzly and Twitter's site is that Brizzly does not offer the text entry field on every screen. After the participant leaves the Home screen, the text entry field disappears. To interact with content, participants who use Brizzly must click Reply on a specific tweet. So, if a

Figure 2. Brizzly's view of Twitter content

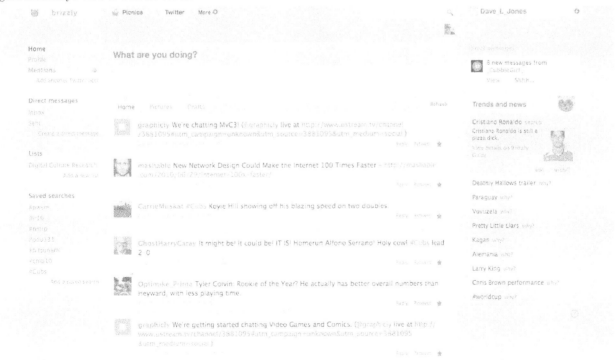

Figure 3. The reply feature in Brizzly

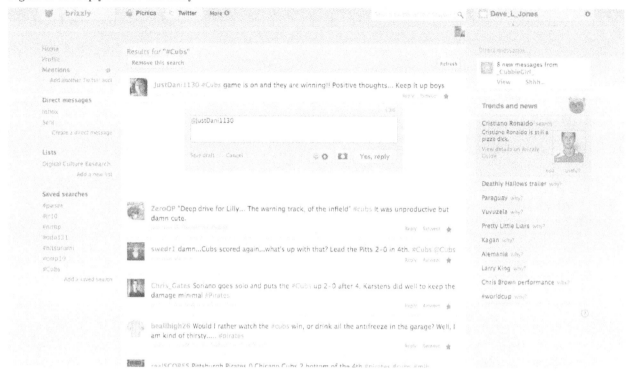

participant is looking at a Hashtag timeline and wishes to interact with that Hashtag's community, he must first initiate a response to a specific person. After he does so, a text entry field appears below the tweet [see Figure 3]. If participants are viewing content from a timeline other than the Home screen, they must use workarounds to initiate an interaction with a community rather than a single participant. Thus, Brizzly's design tends to favor one-to-one interactions.

Brizzly modifies the three components of the Twitter experience described in section 2.1. In addition to being public, heavily networked, and highly dependent on the ability to move content, participants who use Brizzly experience Twitter-based communication more as a one-to-one activity. Brizzly doesn't make community-based interactions impossible, but one of the ways it privileges one-to-one interactions is by making community-based interactions more difficult to perform.

3.3 Tweetdeck

Tweetdeck is a desktop-based application that runs in Adobe's AIR environment. The application opens as a single window. Both Twitter and Brizzly start the participant from a Home screen with a single timeline that aggregates all content into a single column, and specific content such as Hashtag searches in a filtered timeline moves the participant to a different screen. Tweetdeck, on the other hand, displays every timeline simultaneously. Each Timeline maintains a linear chronological order for its content, but different timelines are organized side-by-side into separate columns. Twitter participants using Tweetdeck simply scroll horizontally through the Tweetdeck application to see different timelines [see Figure 4]. And each column can be moved shifted left or right to change the arrangement.

The text entry field can be turned on or off. After on, it is stationary within the application window. Instead of changing or disappearing to suit individual screens, as in Brizzly and Twitter, the Tweetdeck text entry field integrates a series of automated functions that help the participant use Twitter's tools. For instance typing a text command for a Direct Message or @reply opens a window containing a list of those the participant follows. The participant only needs to choose the recipient and the text command is automatically entered. Another submenu contains a list of recently used Hashtags so that entering Hashtags is simply a matter of two or three clicks. In addition, hovering over the profile picture contained within a tweet reveals a series of quick-click interactions for performing these actions more quickly. If the participant chooses to start an @reply or Retweet by clicking on the tweet, Tweetdeck automatically inserts Hashtags contained in the original tweet.

Tweetdeck can run in the system background, even if the application window is closed. Notification windows appear in the computer screen corner to show the participant incoming updates. Notifications can be customized for each timeline. Participants can choose a summary notification, which only says new tweets have been found for that timeline and indicates how many. Detailed notifications show this information, as well as the full tweet with all the same interactions available in the full Tweetdeck window. The participant can click left and right arrows to see detailed views of each tweet. In this way, Tweetdeck offers tools for supporting the same kinds of communicative activities that Brizzly seems to privilege. Participants can open a text entry field in the notifications window by choosing to reply to a specific tweet.

But, in the full application window, participants see the entirety of their Twitter network as a single view. Tweetdeck more readily adapts to the needs of the participant. It is flexible and dynamic. It

Figure 4. Tweetdeck's view of Twitter content

can quickly accommodate one-to-one communication similar to Brizzly. But it also allows participants to find and move content across communities more readily than either Twitter or Brizzly. Enhancing this capability is Tweetdeck's recent integration of Facebook into the application, which includes the ability to Retweet a Facebook status update. Participants can not only move content across different Twitter timelines, but can now more readily find and move content across multiple social networking systems.

4. HEURISTICS

Spinuzzi has referred to social media activities as the collective "annotation of the world" [18]. Social media participants create, distribute, read, view, and interact with content that spans time, media, and platforms. Common practices in Twitter include using bit.ly-shortened links to direct a community's participants to another site, such as a blog or wiki, for information crucial to the discussions among Twitter participants. Sport fans often tweet during games they are watching on television, or even attending in person. Thus, participation within their communities depends on knowledge contained outside of the social media platform at the time of the communication. As Potts has shown, social media platforms can take on the role of organizing information for collaboration and notification during times of crisis [15, 16].

Thus, the maintenance and development of communicative context is crucial in social media experiences. Social media platforms have often suffered from imposed boundaries that restrict the flow of content through a social networking site, turning them into "walled gardens." In other cases, these restrictions make it difficult to move content across different systems [17]. Such restrictions damage the usability of social

media platforms, limiting the types or the extent of activities in which participants engage.

To assess the usability of social media platforms, we have derived a set of heuristics from Peter Morville's term "findability." He defines findability as "the quality of being locatable and navigable" [9]. Morville establishes the definition at two different levels, for the objects the participant is searching for and for the system in which the participant is doing the searching. "Locatable" refers to the objects of the search: the documents, images, or any content the participant finds important. "Navigable" is the quality of the system to support the participant's movement as he hunts for documents.

Table 1. Heuristics derived from activity theory and findablity.

Locatable	Ability to find what a participant seeks
Navigable	Ability to move through content with a specific purpose or motive
Discoverable	Ability to locate information without being an expert in either the system or the content sought
Retrievable	Ability to find information based on a specific set of needs

Table 1 shows a further expansion of Morville's definition based on activity theory's distinction between a participant's needs and the objects of the activity. Activity theory posits that activities take shape and gather meaning from the intersection of concrete objects of activity (or material outcomes that define success) and the needs of the participant, whether abstract, emotional, or material [1, 4, 5, 6, 10]. The heuristics shown in Table 1 add both "discoverable" and "retrievable" to Morville's terminology in an attempt to account for different needs and skill levels of participants. "Discoverable" is the ability to support participants as they search for content without extensive expertise in either the system or the content for which they are searching. "Retrievable" refers to the system's ability to support participants as they search for content with a specific set of criteria in mind.

Usability is the capacity of the system to anticipate the objects of participants' activities as they use social media, and to offer services that support those activities. If a social media platform does this effectively, it will satisfy the participant's needs. Some of those needs are well established, such as the ability to move content with few or no restrictions. Johndan Johnson-Eilola has discussed the need to design for information overflow as people work simultaneously with different pieces of information contained in very different spaces, whether in different computer applications, or in both digital and physical space [3]. In social media experiences, this most often includes the ability to move content within a system among different communities or social networks, as well as across multiple platforms.

The ease with which applications allow participants to accomplish this movement is central design factor for social media platforms. Movement of content is a key feature for developing and maintaining context in social media systems and making the content itself usable to participants.

5. ANALYSIS

Twitter, Brizzly, and Tweetdeck serve as case studies to demonstrate how these heuristics can be applied to determine different forms of usability for participants. Even though each is built around the same basic set of services, each platform constructs radically different experiences, as shown in section 3. Thus, they support Twitter participants' activities in radically different ways.

5.1 Twitter

Returning to Twitter's self-description as a "real-time information network" focused on "what's happening now" [20], the service grounds its experience in the "here and now." In other words, the service is designed for quick communicative exchanges that are seen as fleeting and ephemeral [8]. Though the network is persistent and always active, tweets are only publicly available via Twitter's site for approximately ten days [7]. Despite the fact that Twitter does store all content that flows through its system, the site is not intended to be an archive for participants.

As a result, Twitter does not invest much infrastructure in the search capabilities of its site. The locatability of content is very basic, using only a keyword search that cannot be further refined. Retrievability is affected by Twitter's emphasis on chronological order as the site presents information within a timeline view. After a keyword search is conducted, there is no way to further filter content. If a participant is looking for a specific tweet, they can conduct a keyword search to create a timeline for tweets that contain that keyword. But Twitter returns a timeline containing *every tweet by every participant of the system*, not just those followed by the participant conducting the search. Thus, a search result can conceivably contain millions of tweets spanning only a few hours.

In addition, separate timelines are compartmentalized form one another. Twitter does not support the simultaneous viewing of multiple timelines, such as multiple Hashtag searches. Participants must view each timeline in a different browser tab or window, hampering the ability to cross-reference content in different timelines, or to move content from one timeline to another.

5.2 Brizzly

As stated before, Brizzly maintains many of Twitter's conventions while privileging one-to-one communication among participants. Navigability and retrievability are the same as they are in Twitter. Locatability is slightly improved in that Brizzly offers a miniature wiki function for Hashtags and trending topics in a sidebar column on the right of the screen. The Trends and News panel features participant-generated descriptions and definitions of trending topics and Hashtags. Brizzly-based Twitter participants can keep each other better informed of the contexts for these topics and the communities that arise around them.

However, after a participant views that community in its own timeline, the disappearance of the text entry field affects the discoverabilty and overall usability of Brizzly itself. By funneling participants through an interaction that first initiates a reply, Brizzly impedes some of the activities that participants might pursue in community-based contexts. The privileging of one-to-one communication impacts Brizzly's utility as a tool for interacting with communities and working across social networks within Twitter.

5.3 Tweetdeck

Tweetdeck's organization of separate timelines into side-by-side columns mitigates some of the issues of locatability and navigability found in Twitter and Brizzly. Tweetdeck-based participants can view content across multiple timelines simultaneously. Discoverability is aided by Tweetdeck's integration of TwitScoop, which is a service that offers a word cloud of trending keywords, topics, and Hashtags that updates in real-time. However, finding a specific tweet by a specific person at a specific time is still immensely difficult.

However, viewing all content within a single window creates an issue with scalability for Tweetdeck. If the participant is following numerous timelines in high number of columns, they can still encounter problems with navigating all the content within the Tweetdeck window.

5.4 General Results

The analysis reveals some generalized design problems that social media platforms must account for. Table 2 defines the needs associated with the deign heuristics of Table 1. The results demonstrate the general need for social media platforms to adapt to different activities of participants, and to let participants integrate activities from outside the social media platform into their social media experiences.

Usability becomes not just a matter of making the system simple and easy to use, but a matter of aiding participants by making content usable, as well. Social media participants need not only to find and consume content, but also to work with content by modifying it and passing it along to others, both within the social platform and outside of it.

Table 2. Needs associated with social media deign heuristics.

Locatable	Need to find *and* display results in sortable, usable ways
Navigable	Need to support movement across communities and contexts, as well as non-linear movement within communities and contexts
Discoverable	Need to offer better filtering options for refining search results
Retrievable	Need to find specific results based on specific criteria

6. RECOMMENDATIONS AND FUTURE WORK

Best practices that emerge from this analysis are centered upon creating flexible and dynamic experiences that adapt to participants' needs. The activities of participants should determine the services of a social media platform rather than using the platform to determine the activities of participants. Usability should be based on the ability to of participants to find and move content through the system as they need.

6.1 Locatability

Search functions should keep in mind the balance between services supported by the site and the needs of participants as they work with content. Even if a site is not designed to archive content, participants still need robust functions for finding content.

6.2 Navigability

Participants need better options for moving within content. Designers should explore tools for spatial organization and navigation of content that includes more than temporal relationships.

In addition, social networking systems have not anticipated the need to scale to support the massive amount of content that passes through their platforms. Linear navigation models are fine for low-level usage in which the volume of content is relatively low. But the massive scale of content moving through a site such as Twitter makes linear, temporally based navigation nearly unusable.

6.3 Discoverability

Additional options for refining search results are crucial. At the moment few, if any, social media platforms offer tools for finding content beyond simple keyword searches. Support participants by offering tools that aid in discovering and defining both content and contexts for that content.

6.4 Retrievability

Search functions should support the ability to find content based on specific criteria. Search functions can be modified or adapted depending on the space from which the search is being performed. For instance, searching from a specific timeline in Twitter should allow participants to return specific keyword or subject matter searches from only within that timeline.

6.5 Future Work

These four needs and the best practices we associate with them should be valuable design considerations as research and development work continues for social networking systems, as well as the third-party clients and applications that social media participants often use. In this report, we've focused on Twitter and two applications commonly used by Twitter participants. The overarching design need is not just to give participants access to content, but to give them usable methods of organizing content according to their needs, and to thus develop their social media experiences in ways that best accommodate those needs.

7. REFERENCES

[1] Bærentsen, K.B. & Trettvik, J. 2002. An activity theory approach to affordance. In *Proceedings of NordiCHI*, (Aarhus, Denmark, 51-60) NordiCHI, ACM, New York, NY.

[2] crystal. 2009. *What are hashtags?* Retrieved from http://twitter.zendesk.com/entries/49309-what-are-hashtags-symbols.

[3] Johnson-Eilola, J. 2005. *Datacloud: Toward a New Theory of Online Work*. Hampton Press, Cresskill, NJ.

[4] Kaptelinin, V., & Nardi, B. A. 1997. Activity theory: Basic concepts and applications. In *Proceedings of CHI 97*. 158-159.

[5] Kaptelinin, V. & Nardi, B. A. 2006. *Acting with Technology: Activity Theory and Interaction Design*. The MIT Press, Cambridge, MA.

[6] Kuutti, K. 1996. Activity theory as a potential framework for human-computer interaction. In *Context and Consciousness: Activity Theory and Human-Computer Interaction*, B.A. Nardi, Ed. (pp. 17-44). Cambridge, MA: The MIT Press.

[7] Lukester. 2010. *Help Resources/Known Issues*. Retrieved from http://twitter.zendesk.com/entries/66018-my-tweets-or-hashtags-are-missing-from-search.

[8] McNely, B.J. 2009. Backchannel peristance and collaborative meaning-making. *SIGODOC '09: Proceedings of the 27th ACM international conference on design of communication*. (October 5-7, Bloomington, IN). SIGDOC, ACM, New York, NY. 297-303.

[9] Morville, P. 2005. *Ambient Findability*. O'Reilly, Sebastopol, CA.

[10] Nardi, B. A. 1996. Studying context: A comparison of activity theory, situated action models, and distributed cognition. In *Context and Consciousness: Activity Theory and Human-Computer Interaction*, B.A. Nardi, Ed. (pp. 69-102). The MIT Press, Cambridge, MA.

[11] Panke, S & Gaiser, B. 2009. "With my head up in the clouds": Using social tagging to organize knowledge. *Journal of Business and Technical Communication 23*, 3, 318-349.

[12] Parr, B. 2010. Twitter hits 50 million tweets per day. *Mashable*. Retrieved from http://mashable.com/2010/02/22/twitter-50-million-tweets/.

[13] Potts, L. 2009. Designing for disaster: Social software use in times of crisis. *International Journal of Sociotechnology and Knowledge Development, 1*, 2, 33-46.

[14] Potts, L. 2009. Peering into Disaster: Social Software Use from the Indian Ocean Earthquake to the Mumbai Bombings. *Proceedings of the International Professional Communication Conference*. Hawaii: IEEE.

[15] Potts, L. 2009. Using actor network theory to trace and improve multimodal communication design. *Technical Communication Quarterly, 18*, 3, 281-301.

[16] Potts, L., Rhodes, V., & Gossett, K. 2010. Tweetagogy: Building community in 140 characters or less. *Conference of Association of Teachers of Technical Writing*. Louisville: ATTW.

[17] Spinuzzi, C. 2008. *Network: Theorizing Knowledge Work in Telecommunications*. Cambridge University Press, New York, NY.

[18] Spinuzzi, C. 2009. Starter ecologies: Introduction to the special issue on social software. *Journal of Business and Technical Communication 23*, 3, 251-262.

[19] Stolley, K. 2009. Integrating social media into existing work environments. *Journal of Business and Technical Communication, 23*, 3, 350-371.

[20] Twitter. *About*. Twitter.com Retrieved from http://vanderwal.net/folksonomy.html

[21] Vander Wal, T. 2007. *Folksonomy*, Vanderwal.net. Retrieved from http://vanderwal.net/folksonomy.html

[22] Wauters, R. 2009. Twitter spawned 50,000 apps to date, will open up firehose for more. *TechCrunch*. Retrieved from http://techcrunch.com/2009/12/09/twitter-le-web-2009/.

[23] Zhao, D. & Rosson, M.B. 2009. How and why people twitter: The role that micro-blogging plays in informal communication at work. In *Proceedings of GROUP '04*, ACM: Florida.

Exploring a Sustainable and Public Information Ecology

Brian J. McNely

Ball State University
Department of English
Muncie, IN 47306
1.765.285.8580

bjmcnely@bsu.edu

ABSTRACT
This article explores the design and execution of an intentionally public information ecology by focusing on three of the primary communication activities (blogging, videos, and microblogging) taking place immediately before, during, and after a small international conference of digital media professionals. Drawing on an activity theory framework for analyzing data collected via an exploratory version of contextual inquiry, the author describes two interrelated categories of stabilizing moves for fomenting a public information ecology: those driven by the organization to maintain and publicize a coherent organizational identity narrative, and those driven by conference participants that sometimes diverge from that organizational narrative. Analyzing these two broad categories of stabilizing moves yields insights into how online writing practices may help foster effective and sustainable information ecologies.

Categories and Subject Descriptors
H.5.3 [**Information Interfaces and Presentation**]: Group and Organizational Interfaces — computer-supported cooperative work, web-based interaction, theory and models. K.4.0 [**Computers and Society**]: General.

General Terms
Documentation, Design, Theory.

Keywords
tummeling, phatic, Twitter, blogging, microblogging, information ecologies, knowledge work, writing.

1. REVISITING INFORMATION ECOLOGIES
Nardi and O'Day define an information ecology as "a system of people, practices, values, and technologies in a particular local environment. In information ecologies, the spotlight is not on technology, but on human activities that are served by technology" [1, p. 49]. Perhaps more importantly, they argue that information ecologies are "*designed*," and that it is the "responsibility and privilege of people in the local information ecology to shape new technologies and practices" [1, p. 182]. This article explores the intentional design of communication

activities in a particular information ecology—one that gathers people, technologies, and practices together in explicitly public ways that form "*durable arrangements*" [2, p. 21], with the specific goal of fomenting diverse and sustainable professional relationships.

The author details research conducted before, during, and after a small international conference (less than 125 attendees) of digital media professionals in both industry and academe. Participants in this information ecology—many of whom did not know one another prior to the conference—created organization-sponsored public blog posts, individual public blog posts, promotional materials, a public website, photographs, and videos; a subset of participants also produced over 500 public updates via the microblogging service Twitter during the conference. These communication activities—encouraged and promoted by leaders within the organization—were designed specifically to establish and then extend a public information ecology among local participants and broader publics.

While Nardi and O'Day were exploring information ecologies before the proliferation of social networking applications and widespread blogging practices, their work was nonetheless prescient for considering how web-based interactions might "serve as connective tissue between and within local information ecologies" [1, p. 185]. "There is no single Internet information ecology," they argue, suggesting instead that "information ecologies are local habitations with recognizable participants and practices" [1, p. 185]. And yet the enabling technologies of social networks and low barrier digital publishing potentially afford broader social interaction, such that the notion of *local* can be realized in terms that allow individuals to come together around *ideas* and *activities* that may "span traditional geographic or social boundaries" [1, p. 185].

Nardi and O'Day were particularly encouraged by the promise of such enabling technologies for connecting people in meaningful social arrangements, often through activities that, when viewed from outside a given information ecology, might seem mundane or even trivial. They argue that "people communicating their own thoughts to other people [online] is heartening," and that "not every human interaction has to meet a high intellectual standard" [1, p. 194]. In fact, findings from this study indicate that mundane and seemingly ephemeral online communication practices may actually strengthen connections within an information ecology while simultaneously evoking interest and interaction from individuals outside of that information ecology.

Shirky suggests that "making something public [. . .] has historically been difficult, complex, and expensive. And now it is none of those things" [3, p. 46]. Enabling technologies such as social microblogging, video production and dissemination via mobile phones, and robust blogging platforms allow individuals within a given information ecology to create public content around shared values or organizational goals. Through these sharing activities a particular information ecology may strengthen professional relationships among members and even attract and incorporate new and diverse relationships.

Shirky notes that such activities are not new or the direct result of such enabling technologies, but that these new platforms allow greater opportunities for making connections: "our new communications networks encourage membership and sharing, both of which are good in and of themselves," particularly within a thriving information ecology [3, p. 78-79]. Social networking applications and blogging platforms have made such activities "both expressible and visible" [3, p. 88], surfacing the kinds of human interaction—often mundane and everyday—that were previously ephemeral, interactions "where critical and often invisible things happen" [1, p. 66]. Of particular importance for this study is the fact that these kinds of interactions are increasingly actualized as digital (often backchannel) writing work [4, 5, 6, 7, 8, 9]. As such, the persistence and durability of social ties are fortuitous outcomes of many contemporary public writing practices within a given information ecology [4].

In the remainder of this article, the author describes the research site and organization and their attempts to intentionally design a public and sustainable information ecology. The author then turns to a discussion of the methods of data collection and analysis, drawing upon activity theory as both a framework for operationalizing those methods and for understanding the activities prevalent within the context of this particular information ecology. Deriving emergent codes from the data collected, the author details four codes of particular relevance comprising two broad and interrelated categories of stabilizing moves that publicly establish and maintain—and sometimes repurpose—the values within the information ecology. Building from these findings, the author argues for networked writing practices that can help establish more effective and sustainable information ecologies for similar professional groups.

2. THE PROFESSIONAL CONFERENCE AS INFORMATION ECOLOGY

In 2009, the author had an opportunity to be involved as a participant researcher with the local site coordination team of a small, international conference of digital media professionals from both industry and academe. While the organization has been in existence for less than ten years, membership is active, diverse, and participatory. The organization serves members working in areas such as mobile and ubiquitous computing, augmented reality, interaction design, graphic design, informatics, digital art, interactive television, and distributed collaboration. The organization is particularly concerned with curricular issues related to the interdisciplinary nature of these areas, and it is especially active in bringing together academics and industry professionals to discuss the future teaching and training of scholars and practitioners in digital media. The organization publishes a peer-reviewed journal and sponsors distinguished fellows in digital media research, most of whom are academics.

The organization's annual conference is especially important, since it allows members to realize interactions that are primarily digital throughout the year. The organization also sees the

conference as an opportunity to showcase the important work being completed in the various fields that coalesce under the term "digital media." The author was able to observe two separate pre-conference planning meetings at the 2009 conference site, noting that the conference is an important event for both the organization at large and the local site, where several members and officers reside. As is the case with many such professional and academic conferences, the local site coordinators devoted resources and expertise to publicizing and organizing the event; they were responsible for local logistics, the printing and distribution of programs and promotional material, facilities and amenities, and the creation and maintenance of the conference website.

During pre-conference planning meetings, local site coordinators, members of the advisory board, and elected officers discussed ways that the organization might strategically use digital (especially social) media to more effectively foster interaction among participants at the conference. They also saw digital (social) media platforms as providing an opportunity to more effectively engage individuals not currently involved with the organization. To that end, the local site coordinators made several intentional moves designed to increase the visibility and public relevance of the organization. At the second pre-conference planning meeting, for example, local experts in social media were invited to share ideas about how to strategically leverage blogging, video, and microblogging platforms in conjunction with the conference. The local team decided to incorporate an official blog at the conference website, and invited five individuals—three of whom were local—to share their conference experiences and insights as a way to establish and disseminate what Faber calls an organizational identity narrative [10] (while also displaying facility in the kinds of digital media activities congruent with the professional interests of the broader membership).

The social microblogging service Twitter was likewise championed as another form of engagement. Several attendees of the planning meeting expressed a lack of familiarity with the service and its affordances, while one of the invited social media experts suggested that the aggregator service FriendFeed was perhaps a better fit. Ultimately, local site leadership asked those most familiar with microblogging to formulate and execute a strategy for fostering interaction about and during the conference on Twitter. Interestingly, there was no discussion of a conference hashtag—an identifier used to aggregate updates posted from a particular event like a professional conference. This would lead to some confusion among conference participants, a scenario discussed below in section 4.1.

Finally, the author attended an informal meeting the day before the conference, where four of the five individuals invited as contributors to the conference blog considered their posting strategy. It was at this meeting that video production was most explicitly discussed. One of the members created a YouTube channel during the meeting, and members discussed what kind of content they would film and how they would upload and distribute that content. Throughout the planning process, the author repeatedly observed similar kinds of meaningful interaction (both digitally and face-to-face) between the advisory board, elected officers, local site coordinators, and conference participants—a testament to the coordinative work of many concerned individuals within the information ecology.

Nardi and O'Day stress the intentional design of information ecologies [1], and the kinds of activities described herein suggest that the professional conference can act as a venue for the establishment of very public information ecologies. It should be noted, however, that the digital activities discussed in pre-conference planning meetings—a conference blog, strategic organizational use of Twitter, and the creation of an organizational YouTube channel—were all "top-down" impositions of the broader organizational discourse [10]. This is a natural component of an information ecology, but a thriving information ecology also requires "bottom up" interactions from members at large. Both activities can act as interrelated stabilizing moves in the public understanding of the organization.

Additionally, the incorporation of social media, while intentional and significant, was not pervasive. For example, while Twitter use was encouraged by both the conference website and in printed materials given to attendees (see section 4.1 below), messages were not publicly displayed at the venue during conference presentations (for example, on screens adjacent to presenters). Similarly, while Twitter messages often attempted to drive traffic to the conference blog and website, the blog itself—and more importantly, the live-blogging activity accompanying certain sessions—was not heavily promoted in the conference's print materials, possibly because organizers were uncertain as to the effectiveness of these efforts beforehand. The support of more traditional documentation, an investigation largely beyond the scope of this article, might have had a significant impact on the adoption and use of social media at the conference, and the eventual reach of organizational values beyond the local venue.

3. THEORY AND METHODS

This section offers both a theoretical perspective and framework for exploring the information ecology detailed above, as well as a description of the author's research design and data collection methods. Additionally, the concept of knowledge work is foregrounded within the context of activity theory, as knowledge work is often actualized in and through writing practices that can be traced and analyzed as evidence of activity.

3.1 Activity Theory and Participant Practices

Kaptelinin and Nardi contend that "*Acting with technology* is a phrase to position our relationship to technology as one in which people act intentionally in specific ways with technology—ways that we can study and for which we can produce effective designs" [11, p. 3]. Many of the participants in the information ecology described above can be seen as explicitly acting with technology. Yet the technology, as Nardi and O'Day [1] and Shirky [3] would suggest, is not necessarily the focal point, but a system of devices and networks that affords meaningful and often already extant human interaction. Activity theory, especially as it is articulated by Spinuzzi [12, 13] and Kaptelinin and Nardi [11], provides a robust theoretical framework for empirically exploring "specific uses of specific technologies" [1, p. 202].

As Kaptelinin and Nardi argue, for activity theory "the *doing* of the activity in a rich social matrix of *people and artifacts*" is what grounds analysis [11, p. 9]. Where Nardi and O'Day's attention to information ecologies asks researchers to consider how different mediums carry different "shaping affordances" [1, p. 198], activity theory provides a mechanism for researchers in the design of communication to consider human activity as actualized *mediation* between people and (technological) objects, where people use "technology in the context of their own local values"

[1, p. 199]. Kaptelinin and Nardi suggest that "*people* act *with* technology," and that "activity theory casts the relationship between people and tools as one of *mediation*" [11, p. 10].

Among the tenets of activity theory relevant to the present study are notions of human intentionality and the sociocultural shaping of human activity, both of which occur via interactions with technologies in the professional conference information ecology [11]. Activity theory requires meaningful observation, then, of human activity; intentionality and sociocultural influences cannot be gleaned by simply analyzing the artifacts of interaction. Activity theory as articulated by Kaptelinin and Nardi for human computer interaction requires the researcher's attendance to "the primacy of activity over the subject and the object" [11, p. 31]—that is, attention to activities, interactions, and social practices over and above the human subject herself, or the artifacts with which she interacts. In this way, "analysis of activities opens up the possibility to properly understand both subjects and objects" [11, p. 31].

One significant way that activities within an information ecology can be traced is through organizational writing work, especially writing that doesn't result in what might normally be seen as documentation—writing as manifest in microblogging updates, for example. By considering such writing work, activity theory may be productively articulated with knowledge work, where interactions are at once reflective of practices embedded within a "rich social matrix" [11, p. 9]. Spinuzzi defines knowledge work as "work in which the primary product is knowledge, information that is continually interpreted and circulated across organizational boundaries" [14, p. 1]. A key component of knowledge work is its distributed quality, and Spinuzzi argues that "distributed work is the coordinative work that enables sociotechnical networks to hold together and form dense interconnections among and across work activities" [15, p. 268]. Grabill and Hart-Davidson suggest that they are

> interested in understanding the activity of knowledge work and in rendering that activity visible to those who are engaged in that activity because we suspect that knowledge work looks like writing (indeed, often is writing) or is substantively supported by writing. Writing is how knowledge work carries value in organizations. [16, p. 1]

Most importantly, Grabill and Hart-Davidson argue that they are interested in "what writing *does*, not in what it means" [16, p. 1]. In other words, surfacing and tracing the literate activity of knowledge work can help us determine writing's formidable role in enabling "sociotechnical networks to hold together" [15, p. 268]. Such writing practices reveal intentional activities that are "epistemologically productive" [16, p. 1], foregrounding writing activity as actionable and explicitly social in the organizational and networked ecologies of knowledge work.

3.2 Methods

Following Spinuzzi [17], the author employed an exploratory version of contextual inquiry [18] as a participant researcher immediately before, during, and after the conference described above, with subsequent analysis of the data via emergent coding practices. Data collection consisted of observations before, during, and after the conference, interviews with selected participants after the conference, and special attention to collecting publicly available digital artifacts produced in concert with the organization's social media strategy. In light of the activity theory approach described above, analysis will focus on *in situ* observations of participant intentionality during planning meetings and the conference itself, and the primary writing work carried out through conference-sponsored blog posts, videos, and the microblogging activity of a subset of conference participants. Public blog posts were obtained from the conference blog, while public videos were collected from the aforementioned conference YouTube channel. Twitter updates were collected by establishing custom RSS feeds for the two primary conference hashtags in the aggregator service FriendFeed.

Coding began without a starter list, so codes that eventually emerged were inductively derived from the data. In terms of the digital artifacts collected, the author coded 29 conference blog posts from five different contributors, 23 short videos from four different contributors, and 565 Twitter updates from thirty-four unique users. Four codes of particular relevance that emerged across the data are discussed in detail. Some artifacts (particularly Twitter updates) were ascribed multiple codes.

3.2.1 Informing

The most prevalent emergent code describes blog posts, videos, and microblogging updates that are predominantly *informative*. For example, 14 of the 29 conference-sponsored blog posts can be termed "live-blogging," where the member creating the post offers virtually no editorial commentary and simply describes, as best as possible, the content delivered by a particular speaker in a particular session. A preponderance of the Twitter updates (48%) were also coded as *informing*, since they effectively do the work of live-blogging in a more granular form. Other blog posts, such as those welcoming conference participants or listing Twitter users active at the conference were likewise coded as *informing*.

3.2.2 Informing/Selling

A code particularly prevalent in conference-sponsored blog posts and videos was termed *informing/selling*. In these instances, the content could be seen as primarily informative, but the information provided seemed to be deployed in a way that "sold" the dominant organizational identity narrative. In other words, where the live-blogging posts contained virtually no editorializing, the *informing/selling* posts deployed organizational information within a frame that advertised or reinforced the merits of the information ecology. These posts and videos were explicitly designed to appeal to broader publics in ways that drew upon the strengths of the organization. Of the 23 short videos, 18 were coded *informing/selling*, perhaps revealing a function of the medium and delivery.

3.2.3 Tummeling

In direct contrast to the *informing/selling* blog posts and videos, 29% of conference Twitter updates were coded *tummeling* (whereas only 2 blog posts and no videos were coded in this way). Marks notes that the Yiddish word "tummler" is used to describe someone who is particularly adept at facilitating conversation and engagement within online communities—someone who often curates ideas and content while connecting previously unaffiliated individuals from overlapping networks [19]. *Tummeling*, therefore, denotes activities sparked by a "conversational catalyst within a group, [someone] to welcome newcomers, rein in old hands and set the tone of the conversation" within a given online community [19, p. 1].

Most *tummeling* activities, therefore, do not feel like overt persuasion for members in an information ecology. In fact, Twitter facilitates *tummeling* by virtue of its user conventions, where the strategic "retweeting" (that is, re-posting) of another user's update can bridge structural holes in a given network [20], bringing people together around shared interests or ideas. Twitter's built-in addressivity (the hailing of another user enabled by the "@" sign) also facilitates *tummeling* moves [6].

3.2.4 Phatic

Digital *phatic* gestures were exclusive to microblogging updates (27% of all updates), and are closely correlated with *tummeling* activities. *Phatic* gestures in online communities such as Twitter are designed not to be informative, but to express social connections and understanding—even feelings of solidarity or connectedness. For example, the last conference Twitter update collected for this project is explicitly *phatic*, lamenting the return to normalcy and everyday academic life that must occur after the euphoria of engaging with colleagues and friends at the conference.

Such updates are not particularly informative—at least not in any way similar to *informing* posts and videos—and they often express emotion and feelings of dis/connectedness to or from fellow conference attendees. And while *phatic* gestures do not demand a response, interactions around *phatic* posts are fairly common since they may inspire similar reactions from others in the information ecology. *Phatic* gestures, in fact, were often correlated with *tummeling* activities, since *tummeling* involves the kinds of direct user-to-user connections also prevalent in *phatic* interaction.

4. FINDINGS

The four most prevalent codes to emerge from the public data collected in exploration of this information ecology comprise two interrelated categories of stabilizing moves: those driven by the organization to maintain and publicize a coherent organizational identity narrative, and those driven by conference participants that sometimes diverge from that organizational narrative. Analyzing these two broad categories of stabilizing moves yields insights into how online (and explicitly public) writing practices may help foster effective and sustainable information ecologies. The four codes described above, therefore, offer insights into these broad stabilizing moves.

4.1 Stabilizing Moves of Organizational Identity

The intentionality of communication practices designed to foment a public and sustainable information ecology can be seen most readily in the pre-conference planning of the organization. The explicit attempt to deploy social media in ways that would foster greater public interaction with the organization indicates a strategy for publicizing and celebrating the work of the organization's members. Among the prevalent codes discussed above, the first two—*informing* and *informing/selling*—were predominantly the result of top-down activities, moves to stabilize and manage a coherent organizational identity narrative. Such moves are crucial to establishing and extending a strong information ecology, since the artifacts from this category (conference-sponsored blog posts and videos) are explicitly linked to the organization's primary website, and are indexed by major search engines and on YouTube.

At the same time, the organization had to manage an issue of failed intentionality. During one of the pre-conference planning meetings (described in section 2), local site coordinators passed the strategic use of Twitter on to a few (perhaps three) members who had some familiarity with the service. One of the items discussed—and then tabled—was the creation of a unified conference hashtag to be used by all willing Twitter participants.

Having a single conference hashtag helps establish organizational identity and makes aggregating, sharing, and finding messages much easier. But the organization didn't just fail to intentionally designate and publicize a conference hashtag; when the conference program was printed, some of the local site coordinators decided to create different hashtags *for each conference session*, a move not without precedent, but one that was met with confusion, laughter, and even derision from some of the conference participants (hashtags work best when they are uniform and easy to remember). Not surprisingly, conference Twitter users soundly rejected the hashtags suggested by the organization, and two primary hashtags emerged from participant writing activities (one was by far the minority, and was eventually discontinued during the conference).

4.2   Participant Activities within the Information Ecology

The intentionality of the conference participants may be reflected most readily by the writing activities of the 34 individuals producing Twitter updates (only 3 of whom were also involved in producing content for the first category above); these were participants acting with technology in a "rich social matrix of *people and artifacts*" [11, p. 9]. The third and fourth codes described above—*tummeling* and *phatic* gestures—are nearly exclusive to this category of stabilizing moves driven from the bottom up. Only two blog posts were coded *tummeling*, and no blog posts or videos were coded *phatic*. Much of this disparity can be attributed to the different affordances of the platforms used; clearly, social networks such as Twitter encourage phatic communication in ways that would be difficult to accomplish in a broadcast medium such as a YouTube channel.

But more importantly, *phatic* gestures and *tummeling* represent the kinds of activities that can actually drive the sustainability of a public information ecology, since the writing work involved in these activities may serve to establish and strengthen ties among members. At least four of the conference participants observed in this study may be seen as *tummlers*—active individuals who curate and share interesting ideas, who interact phatically and frequently with other members of the information ecology, and most importantly, whose influence brings outside participants into conversation with current members of the information ecology. These latter activities are documented in the collected Twitter data in the form of "retweets" and extra-conference addressivity (that is, updates coming *into* the conference from interested or curious participants clearly *outside* of the local information ecology).

These individuals connect people inside the social network (Twitter) that is situated within and that extends beyond the comparatively smaller network of individuals comprising the conference information ecology. *Tummlers*, by virtue of their ability to connect others, provide a kind of stabilizing move for the information ecology that is very different from the organizational moves initiated from above. In this way, social network *tummlers* are analogous to Nardi and O'Day's "keystone

species," individuals who "literally sculpt the environment" of an information ecology by introducing and sustaining a diversity of participants and ideas [1, p. 80]. A healthy information ecology, however, requires both kinds of stabilizing moves—top down and bottom up—in a healthy balance.

4.3   Sustainable Public Information Ecologies

One of the most interesting insights of the present study is the inversion of expectations about the persistence and durability of online writing artifacts. The organization-sponsored blog posts and videos are still indexed by search engines and can be easily retrieved, while a search for the conference hashtag on Twitter provides no results (though Google still indexes some of the conference Twitter updates). Yet the argument can be made that the seemingly durable artifacts are in fact temporally ephemeral, while the seemingly ephemeral artifacts are what foster the long-term sustainability of the public information ecology. *Tummeling* and *phatic* gestures generated by engaged and passionate members of the information ecology are infectious, and these activities do more for the sustainability of the ecology than the more obvious stabilizing moves reinforcing the organizational discourse.

While in-depth, quantitative social network analysis is beyond the scope of the present study, verification of ongoing interactions between participants who first began interacting at the conference is easily documented. For example, the author selected two Twitter users who were not following any of the other 32 users before the conference; these users are now following 4 and 9 respectively. In turn, these users are followed by 7 and 9 users, respectively, individuals with whom they became acquainted through the conference information ecology. Most importantly, these users are *still interacting with one another* on Twitter, sustaining professional relationships that continue to foster interaction around the core information ecology. In this way, the perceived ephemeral communication activities actually foster continuing social interactions, while the stable, organization-sponsored posts and videos recede from view as static remnants of a past event.

But again, this is not to say that the healthy information ecology can simply forgo top down stabilizing moves of organizational identity narratives in favor of social networks alone. Instead, the healthy information ecology appears best served by a robust mixture of both, for it must be noted that several of the Twitter updates coded *tummeling* involved reference to *informing* and *informing/selling* blog posts and videos. The interplay of these very different kinds of public artifacts and stabilizing moves are what enable "*durable arrangements*" [2, p. 21]. Drawing on Engestrom, Star argues that "technology occurs when joint activity between two actors is articulated [. . . .] as the tool occurs, it comes to form a part of the subsequent material conditions mediating further action" [2, p. 21]. The articulation of human subjects, technological objects and artifacts, and the activity mediating action—in this case, in and through a combination of organizational and organic writing work—is what can sustain the successful public information ecology.

5.   CONCLUSION

This article revisits the notion of information ecologies by exploring the attempt to create an explicitly public and sustainable organization that leverages a combination of stabilizing moves generated from top down and bottom up communication practices. By observing participant activities and collecting and analyzing the writing work most reflective of those activities, the author argues that *tummeling* practices and *phatic* gestures within social networks—moves that have often been seen as ephemeral or lacking in intellectual depth—can actually foster the sustainability of public information ecologies. This study sees social network *tummlers* as a kind of contemporary keystone species, updating Nardi and O'Day's figuration of individuals that help shape and diversify information ecologies [1]. In this way, seemingly ephemeral instantiations of writing activity actually help foster the durable arrangements of this public and sustainable information ecology.

6. REFERENCES

[1] Nardi, B. and O'Day, V. 1999. Information ecologies: Using technology with heart. MIT Press, Cambridge.

[2] Star, S. L. 1995. Introduction. In Ecologies of knowledge: Work and politics in science and technology. S. L. Star, Ed. SUNY Press, Albany, 1-35.

[3] Shirky, C. 2010. Cognitive surplus: Creativity and generosity in a connected age. The Penguin Press, New York.

[4] McNely, B. 2009. Backchannel persistence and collaborative meaning making. In Proceedings of the 27th International Conference on Design of Communication (Bloomington, IN, USA), 297-303.

[5] Zhao, D., and Rosson, M. B. 2009. How and why people Twitter: The role that micro-blogging plays in informal communication at work. In Proceedings of the ACM 2009 International Conference on Supporting Group Work (Sanibel Island, FL. USA), 243-252.

[6] Honeycutt, C. and Herring, S. 2009. Beyond microblogging: Conversation and collaboration on Twitter. In Proceedings of the 42nd Hawaii International Conference on Systems Sciences (Los Alamitos, CA, USA), 1-10.

[7] Kellog, W., Erickson, T., Wolf, T. V., Levy, S., Christensen, J., Sussman, J., and Bennett, W. 2006. Leveraging digital backchannels to enhance user experience in electronically mediated communication. In Proceedings of the 20th Conference on Computer Supported Work (Banff, Alberta, Canada), 451-454.

[8] McCarthy, J. F., and boyd, d. m. 2005. Digital backchannels in shared physical spaces: Experiences at an academic conference. In Proceedings of Conference on Human Factors and Computing Systems (CHI 2005, Portland, OR, USA), 1641-1644.

[9] Swarts, J. 2010. Recycled writing: Assembling actor networks from reusable content. Journal of Business and Technical Communication 24 (April 2010), 127-163.

[10] Faber, B. 2002. Community action and organizational change. SIU Press, Carbondale, IL.

[11] Kaptelinin, V. and Nardi, B. 2006. Acting with technology: Activity theory and interaction design. MIT Press, Cambridge.

[12] Spinuzzi, C. 2003. Tracing genres through organizations: A sociocultural approach to information design. MIT Press, Cambridge.

[13] Spinuzzi, C. 2008. Network: Theorizing knowledge work in telecommunications. Cambridge University Press, New York.

[14] Spinuzzi, C. 2006. What do we need to teach about knowledge work? [White Paper] Computer Writing Research Lab, University of Texas at Austin. Retrieved from http://www.drc.utexas.edu/research/what-do-we-need-teach-about-knowledge-work

[15] Spinuzzi, C. 2007. Guest editor's introduction: Technical communication in the age of distributed work. Technical Communication Quarterly 16 (September 2007), 265-277.

[16] Grabill, J. and Hart-Davidson, W. 2010. Understanding and supporting knowledge work in everyday life. Language at Work (February 2010), 1-4.

[17] Spinuzzi, C. 2008. Office work, knowledge work: Studying office work in an academic environment as knowledge work. [White Paper] Computer Writing Research Lab, University of Texas at Austin. Retrieved from http://www.drc.utexas.edu/research/office-work-knowledge-work-studying-office-work-academic-environment-knowledge-work

[18] Beyer, H. and Holtzblatt, K. 1998. Contextual design: Defining customer-centered systems. Morgan Kaufmann, San Francisco.

[19] Marks, K. 2008. Here comes everybody: Tummlers, geishas, animateurs and chief conversation officers help us listen. Epeus' Epigone. Retrieved from http://epeus.blogspot.com/2008/07/here-comes-everybody-tummlers-geishas.html

[20] Shirky, C. 2008. Here comes everybody: The power of organizing without organizations. The Penguin Press, New York.

Digital Humanities and digital repositories: sustainable technology for sustainable communications

Paolo Battino Viterbo
Royal Irish Academy,
19 Dawson St., Dublin
Republic of Ireland
+353 1234 2447
p.battino@dho.ie

Donald Gourley
Digital Initiatives Consultant
310 Melvin Avenue, Annapolis,
MD, USA
donald.gourley@gmail.com

ABSTRACT
In this paper we present the experience of the Digital Humanities Observatory in designing and implementing a repository of digital resources for the humanities. We describe how, in a situation of great funding uncertainty, we focused on sustainability to provide both a national infrastructure and the possibility to easily migrate the hosted resources to different, decentralized platforms. Using flexible, open-source and highly interoperable software, we supported a variety of different options to manage the digital resources stored in the repository. This allowed the repository to meet the wide range of heterogeneous requirements gathered from our partners. The result is a flexible architecture that is designed to be more sustainable and ready to gracefully degrade in case of end of funding.

Categories and Subject Descriptors
H.3.5 [**Information Systems**]: INFORMATION STORAGE AND RETRIEVAL On-line Information Services – *Web-based services*

General Terms
Design, Experimentation.

Keywords
Digital Humanities, repository, Fedora Commons, Drupal, metadata, Europeana, sustainability.

1. Introduction
The Digital Humanities Observatory (DHO)[1] was established in 2008 as part of the Humanities Serving Irish Society (HSIS)[2] consortium to manage and co-ordinate the increasingly complex e-resources created in the arts and humanities throughout the Republic and Northern Ireland. Part of the mission of the DHO project is the provision of data management, curation, and discovery services supporting the long-term access to, and greater exploitation of, digital resources.

The DHO is a relatively short-term project mandated to promote and support long-term access and preservation of digital resources. Funded for three years, from 2008 to 2011, the DHO has no certainty of obtaining additional funding to maintain its services after 2011. For this reason, DHO infrastructure had to be designed with sustainability in mind. Our partners cannot be left without any strategy to easily migrate their digital resources to a different infrastructure. One of the three technical actions identified by The Blue Ribbon Task Force Report (2010), in fact, is to make operational an *option strategy* to hedge against irreversible loss [3].

In this framework, designing a sustainable information technology infrastructure means not only lowering the economic and technical requirements to make digital resources available by DHO partners, but also to empower them to maintain, migrate and enhance their projects independently from the DHO.

This report describes our experience designing discovery and access interfaces for digital humanities resources. The lessons we learned regarding sustainability of resources and technology used to manage them are instructive to other designers of communication who have to make concrete decisions about resource representations and formats within the constraints of the contemporary technology available to them.

2. Thematic Research Projects and the DHO Repository
A key requirement to support the DHO mission is a central e-research repository for resources developed by HSIS. Thematic research projects, carried out by HSIS partners, will have their digital resources stored into the repository but will take care of developing their own web presence, where the digital resources will be actually available. This means that the DHO has not only to develop a reliable repository, but also to ensure the availability of suitable and affordable front-end solutions to interface the repository with the web sites developed by the partners.

At the same time, we needed to provide a generic cross-collection interface to discover resources across the whole repository. For this reason, the repository infrastructure has to be flexible and support different ways of implementing the same features, including ways that are not yet fully predictable [4].

2.1 The DHO Repository

Due to the variety of digital resources that are candidates for the DHO repository, there is a strong requirement for digital asset management software that is flexible and extensible.

Along with the heterogeneity of the digital resources and their formats (multi-resolution images, encoded texts, audio recordings, videos), the repository must be designed to face heterogeneity at different levels. Thematic research collections will vary in size, scope, resources and final aims, for example. While some collections will require a full-fledged web site, others will be based on a more lightweight approach due to the limited amount of resources and skills available.

At the same time, DHO's involvement in the development of final deliverables also varies greatly; some projects need support in all the phases of development, while others may have the resources and expertise for in-house development and only avail of the DHO infrastructure for storage, indexing or interoperability. The resources available in-house also have impacts on the sustainability of the projects themselves: in some cases the partners can provide an alternative storage and maintenance solution, independently of the DHO repository, while some others must plan for an export strategy to have their resources transferred to a different storage provider.

It is clearly a challenge to find a digital asset management system supporting all these requirements. Priority was given to aspects such as the ability to handle different data and metadata models [5], the easiness to be extended, being open-source and based on web services. Developing a custom platform was not an option; on the contrary we focused on well-established repository software with a wide range of tools readily available. We opted for the Fedora Commons open source repository software [6][7][8], the choice that met the majority of our requirements. In particular Fedora supports different front-end solutions [9], allowing for a variety of web development strategies.

A typical example of this flexibility is the way the indexing a search engine are implemented in Fedora: there are no advanced functionalities, but the built-in search service (based on Apache Lucene [10] can be easily replaced or extended. In fact, the generic cross-collection interface to discover resources across the whole repository, called DHO:Discovery, makes use of Solr [11], an open source enterprise search platform based on Lucene.

2.1.1 DHO:Discovery - A cross-collection repository interface

To demonstrate the value of and ability to create resources that could be accessed and remixed, and are generally interoperable, the DHO needed a user interface for searching and browsing the repository across all the thematic research collections. We recognized that meeting this requirement relied more on the Solr index than on the Fedora API for discovering and accessing e-resources, and would be easier to implement and maintain if it was, in fact, completely independent of the repository source of content. So for this requirement our investigation focused on interfacing with the Solr index, rather than with the Fedora API.

A lightweight tool like Exhibit (described in the following section) could not meet the need for a tool to browse the repository regardless of how individual items are grouped into collections. We chose instead to base our front-end on AJAX-Solr [12], a framework-agnostic JavaScript library for creating user interfaces to Solr indexes. Unlike Exhibit, AJAX-Solr requires a number of calls to the server, usually one call for every page reload. However, the queries retrieve only a limited amount of data using the very compact JSON format, making it more responsive than a pure server-based web application and less resource-intensive than a totally client-side tool like Exhibit.

While we were designing the DHO:Discovery, the DHO was working with the Irish Manuscripts Commission [13] to aggregate metadata describing digital content from national cultural institutions for the European cultural heritage portal Europeana [14]. Europeana has a lot of experience reconciling heterogeneous metadata for cross-collection searching, which we found particularly useful for our purposes. The Europeana Semantic Elements [15] (ESE v3.2.1) schema is a flexible metadata standard that allows heterogeneous resources to inter-operate while presenting a very low barrier to projects that want to be included in a digital library. For the DHO:Discovery index, we specified the DHO Repository Interface Metadata (DRIM) schema, which is a superset of ESE v3.2.1. We are creating crosswalks for deriving DRIM from any kind of metadata that is deposited in the DHO repository. The DRIM is then indexed using Solr to create a coherent cross-collection search facility. By following the ESE specification and the Metadata Mapping & Europeana Normalisation Guidelines for the Europeana Prototype v1.2 [16], the DHO is also ensuring that the metadata in the repository can be easily transformed and contributed to Europeana.

DHO:Discovery will offer faceted browsing and full-text search on some of the DRIM elements, a video/audio player, and a multi-resolution image viewer. Additionally, a key aspect of the interface is to provide a link to each item in the thematic collection web site where the item is shown in its original context. DHO:Discovery is currently in a prototype stage. At the time of writing, initial user testing is planned within the next month and a first release is scheduled to be launched in September 2010.

2.2 Front-end for Thematic Research Collections

The DHO investigated three classes of solutions for the development of front-ends to the DHO repository for thematic research collections:

1. Integration with content management systems (CMS).
2. Integration with proprietary rich Internet application (RIA) frameworks.
3. Integration with lightweight Asynchronous JavaScript And XML (AJAX) frameworks.

2.2.1 CMS integration

Our investigation into CMS integration looked at PHP-based Drupal [17] and Python-based Django [18]. Although Django offers many technical benefits with its object-oriented model-view-controller architecture, Drupal was selected for the sustainability that its large development and hosting community provides. Drupal is one of the most popular CMS, which means a very wide user base, ample choice of modules, rich customisation options, and relatively common skill set required for development and theming. Integration with the Drupal CMS was successfully achieved by means of the Fedora REST API module [19] developed by the DHO and now available as open source software.

The Fedora REST API module is based on metadata harvesting, which adds some complexity to the whole process of ingesting and updating the e-resources. In contrast, the Islandora [20] Drupal module, developed at the University of Prince Edward Island for integrating Drupal and Fedora, accesses the metadata in the repository and uses Fedora's Lucene index for searching, so new and updated resources don't have to be harvested to show up in Drupal. However, the Fedora REST API module has a flexible mechanism for mapping Fedora object structure and description to Drupal nodes, so it can work with the numerous core and contributed modules that operate on nodes, such as Search, Taxonomy, Views, Workflow, and the like. We felt this was a reasonable trade-off for cultural heritage resources that don't change much after they have been stored in the repository, but would benefit from new presentations and visualizations that take advantage of Drupal functionality.

The Fedora REST API module provides a programming interface to invoke Fedora Commons REST methods, including a PHP class that encapsulates all the REST API methods so they can be easily invoked from other Drupal modules. It also defines a type of content node ("fedora_object") that represents a digital object in the repository. This content-type can be extended by defining a new content-type in a custom module that invokes the Fedora REST API module's hook implementations to add the Fedora object attributes to the node. A template module file is included to simplify the process of creating modules that extend the "fedora_object" content-type. The Fedora REST API module, along with the Drupal framework, comprise a rapid application development environment that minimizes the procedural and SQL programming required to create web sites to publish digital cultural heritage resources.

We also provide a mechanism for content to be duplicated and integrated into the Drupal ecosystem, so discontinuation of the DHO repository need not pose a threat to the preservation of each individual project. Their resources will be completely packaged in a Drupal web site that can be hosted on any of the numerous hosting sites that support Drupal, and maintained by developers in the broad Drupal community. The content imported into Drupal using this mechanism is structured as digital objects using the BagIt [21] format, which can be ingested into future repositories as the opportunity arises. This supports our worst-case exit strategy: if the DHO is not funded and no repository solution is available for migration, a project can host a Drupal site with minimal effort and cost so their resources remain accessible, and are also safe and verifiable if not optimally re-usable.

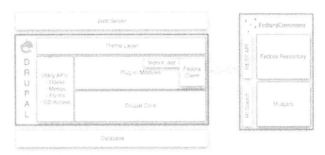

Figure 1: Fedora REST API module architecture

A CMS solution provides a separation between the e-resources (stored in the repository) and supplementary content (like posted comments and resource tags to customize grouping and browsing) that is not inherently part of the e-resources themselves. Moreover, it offers opportunities to empower partners to customize their projects' websites with minimal intervention from DHO staff. Drupal theming and templating, user authentication, and searching facilities are provided by the CMS and configurable with simple administration web forms. And by levering Drupal's support of input filters, the Fedora REST API module offers additional levels of customization and empowerment:

- At a basic level, each page (more precisely, each Drupal "node", which can contain any XML metadata datastream from the digital object) can be filtered using a configurable XSL style sheet, allowing for complete control of the design and layout of the main body of the page without relying on Drupal's theme system.
- At a more advanced level, additional XSL style sheets can be applied to transform and extract any fragment of the XML datastreams in the object and expose them to the Drupal theme system, allowing for more sophisticated customizations.

2.2.2 RIA front-ends

We used the Flex/Flash environment to investigate integration with proprietary RIA frameworks. However, given the limited availability of in-house Flash expertise (within both the DHO and our partners) and the need to accommodate HTML-only devices (such as the iPad), this option did not lead to any functional proof of concept. In general, we did not feel that there was a real need to resort to RIA frameworks. The majority of our project partners focus on text e-resources, and as such do not need the support of the advanced graphic features that RIA frameworks typically provide. Moreover, the way text is handled by RIA frameworks is often disappointing, compared to what is easily achievable with standard web and XML technologies. For this reason, we use RIA tools only as a front-end to display multi-resolution images in a "deep-zoom" manner (that is, where the image can be zoomed seamlessly). In this case, an RIA viewer is offered within the CMS as a higher-performance alternative to the default AJAX viewer. We feel confident, however, that if a use case arises where Flex/Flash is the best environment for creating a front-end for collections in the repository, it can be easily integrated with

Fedora Commons using web services to access the digital resources.

2.2.3 AJAX frameworks

Our investigation into a lightweight AJAX framework started with a different approach. Instead of testing the use of popular JavaScript libraries like jQuery [22], Prototype [23] or MooTools [24] to build a user interface, we focused on basic functionality like browsing and searching. We experimented with Exhibit [25] from the MIT Simile project, a framework for building dynamic exhibits of data collections without resorting to complex database and server-side technologies. It includes widgets specifically designed to browse/search through thematic research collections. Being totally client-side based, Exhibit can be very responsive and ensure a smooth user-experience with almost no wait between each page reload. However, it relies on a single JSON file holding the whole index of the collection, which renders it unsuitable for collections with a larger number of digital objects, as most of the collections in the DHO repository have. Although it could work with a Fedora Commons repository and a Solr index, it was not suitable for the thematic research collections we knew we were working with.

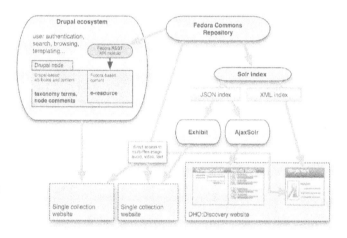

Figure 2: The overall architecture of the system with loosely coupled and individually sustainable components

3. Current Status

The first thematic research collection based on the DHO Fedora repository and Drupal, The Doegen Records Web Project [26], went live in November 2009. This digital archive of recordings in Irish-language dialects, made during 1928-31, comprises an important audio collection of stories, songs and other material. The collection includes 137 Gaelic speakers from 17 counties.

The Doegen Records Web Project web site is fully bilingual, with both English and Irish language versions built with Drupal internationalisation and translation features. It offers a unique resource for linguists, social historians, anthropological researchers, educators, musicologists, genealogists, local communities, and anyone interested in Ireland's cultural heritage.

The materials provide a fascinating and priceless legacy of now extinct Irish-language dialects. Users can browse and listen to these recordings and appreciate the spoken record of the early twentieth century in rural Ireland. During the first four months of 2010, the website received over 2,000 visits.

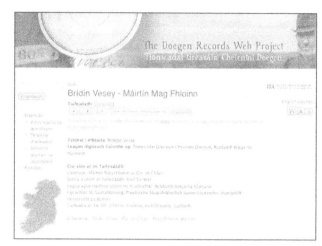

Figure 3: Drupal-based bilingual user interface for discovering and playing Doegen audio recordings. © 2009 Royal Irish Academy.

4. Future Work

The Doegen Records web site will be greatly enhanced during the Summer 2010 with the addition of information about the speakers, and transcriptions and translations of the audio files. The project team is adding this additional content to the repository through a management interface built with Drupal and the Fedora REST API module. Currently available only in MP3 format, the audio files will be also offered in OGG format and an HTML-only player will be offered as the default player, in order to make the streaming accessible in major browsers without plug-ins. The project is also considering allowing mediated comments for scholars and the general public to annotate recordings, something that is easily implemented with Drupal and the Fedora REST API module.

At the time of writing, two other thematic research collections have been ingested into the repository and their websites are being developed using Drupal and the Fedora REST API module. Additional collections will be ingested into the repository and their websites will be developed in the following months. This will be a test-bed for the rapid application development and customisation features of the Fedora REST API module, as the different collections will require quite distinct front-end web presentations.

5. Conclusion

The DHO is facing a contradiction: it is mandated to support and promote long-term access of digital resources but it is funded for only three years. Building a national infrastructure in such a context requires a strong focus on sustainability. The DHO ensured sustainability in designing the repository by setting up a flexible development environment, opening up to a variety of different scenarios.

- The possibility to integrate the repository with a popular open-source CMS, Drupal, which is extremely customizable and can be "disengaged" and made autonomous from the repository, if required.

- The possibility to use lightweight AJAX frameworks to quickly build web sites based on thematic research collection.

- The possibility to browse the entire repository, using DHO:Discovery and to access any digital resource, even those not (or not yet) made available within a specific collection website.

- The seamless integration between DHO:Discovery and each thematic research collection website, closing the gap between the individual web sites and the national infrastructure.

In terms of metadata requirements, our choice was to enforce conformance to only a minimal metadata schema, leaving the possibility to provide additional metadata, if available. At the same time, conformance with the Europeana Semantic Elements will ensure better interoperability and a more sustainable transition, if needed, to different infrastructures.

We are conscious that all theses choices have trade-offs and that no option is the perfect one. We are confident that the solutions implemented represent a balanced mix addressing different problems. What we have deployed tries to find an acceptable trade-off between the need to make digital resource available in a short time and to establish a national infrastructure that could ensure long-term access.

6. Acknowledgments

The Digital Humanities Observatory and the work described in this paper were funded by the Irish Higher Education Authority (HEA) under the Programme for Research in Third Level Institutes Cycle 4 (PRTLI-4). The DHO was established under the auspices of the Royal Irish Academy. Additional support for repository hosting and programming is provided by the Dublin Institute for Advanced Studies (DIAS) and the Irish Centre for High-End Computing (ICHEC). The authors would like especially to acknowledge the contributions of Bruno Voisin (ICHEC) for his work designing the repository and indexing architecture, and Kevin Hawkins (University of Michigan) for his work designing and specifying the DRIM schema.

7. References

[1] Digital Humanities Observatory, http://dho.ie/ (accessed 21 June 2010)

[2] Humanities Serving Irish Society, http://hsis.ie/ (accessed 21 June 2010)

[3] Blue Ribbon Task Force, "Sustainable Economics for a Digital Planet: Ensuring Long-term Access to Digital Information" (2010), available at http://brtf.sdsc.edu/biblio/BRTF_Final_Report.pdf

[4] Wright, R. 2007. Digital audiovisual repositories: an introduction. In *Proceedings of the 2006 international Workshop on Research Issues in Digital Libraries* (Kolkata, India, December 12 - 15, 2006). P. Majumder, M. Mitra, and S. K. Parui, Eds. IWRIDL '06. ACM, New York, NY, 1-7. DOI= http://doi.acm.org/10.1145/1364742.1364753

[5] Beer, C. A., Pinch, P. D., and Cariani, K. 2009. Developing a flexible content model for media repositories: a case study. In *Proceedings of the 9th ACM/IEEE-CS Joint Conference on Digital Libraries* (Austin, TX, USA, June 15 - 19, 2009). JCDL '09. ACM, New York, NY, 97-100. DOI= http://doi.acm.org/10.1145/1555400.1555416

[6] Fedora Commons repository software, http://www.fedora-commons.org/ (accessed 21 June 2010)

[7] Kumar, A., Saigal, R., Chavez, R., and Schwertner, N. 2004. Architecting an extensible digital repository. In *Proceedings of the 4th ACM/IEEE-CS Joint Conference on Digital Libraries* (Tuscon, AZ, USA, June 07 - 11, 2004). JCDL '04. ACM, New York, NY, 2-10. DOI= http://doi.acm.org/10.1145/996350.996354

[8] Carl Lagoze, Sandy Payette, Edwin Shin, and Chris Wilper (2006). "Fedora: An Architecture for Complex Objects and their Relationships." *International Journal on Digital Libraries* **6**(2) (April 2006): 124–138. DOI= http://dx.doi.org/10.1007/s00799-005-0130-3

[9] Bainbridge, D. and Witten, I. H. 2008. A fedora librarian interface. In *Proceedings of the 8th ACM/IEEE-CS Joint Conference on Digital Libraries* (Pittsburgh PA, PA, USA, June 16 - 20, 2008). JCDL '08. ACM, New York, NY, 407-416. DOI= http://doi.acm.org/10.1145/1378889.1378962

[10] Apache Lucene, http://lucene.apache.org/ (accessed 21 June 2010)

[11] Apache Solr, http://lucene.apache.org/solr/ (accessed 21 June 2010)

[12] AJAX Solr JavaScript library, http://wiki.github.com/evolvingweb/ajax-solr/ (accessed 21 June 2010)

[13] Irish Manuscript Commission, http://www.irishmanuscripts.ie/ (accessed 21 June 2010)

[14] Europeana Digital Library, http://www.europeana.eu/ (accessed 21 June 2010)

[15] Europeana version 1.0 project, Europeana Semantic Elements v3.2.1 (2009), available at http://www.group.europeana.eu/c/document_library/get_file?uuid=c56f82a4-8191-42fa-9379-4d5ff8c4ff75&groupId=10602

[16] Europeana version 1.0 project, Metadata Mapping & Normalisation Guidelines for the Europeana Prototype v1.2 (2009), available at http://www.group.europeana.eu/c/document_library/get_file?uuid=58e2b828-b5f3-4fe0-aa46-3dcbc0a2a1f0&groupId=10602

[17] Drupal content management platform, http://drupal.org/ (accessed 21 June 2010)

[18] Django web framework, http://www.djangoproject.com/ (accessed 21 June 2010)

[19] Fedora REST API Drupal module, http://github.com/dongourley/fedora_rest/ (accessed 21 June 2010)

[20] Islandora Drupal module, http://islandora.ca/ (accessed 21 June 2010)

[21] BagIt file packaging format, https://wiki.ucop.edu/display/Curation/BagIt (accessed 21 June 2010)

[22] jQuery JavaScript library, http://jquery.com/ (accessed 21 June 2010)

[23] Prototype JavaScript framework, http://www.prototypejs.org/ (accessed 21 June 2010)

[24] MooTools JavaScript framework, http://www.mootools.net/ (accessed 21 June 2010)

[25] Exhibit publishing framework, http://www.simile-widgets.org/exhibit/ (accessed 21 June 2010)

[26] Doegen Records Web Project, http://dho.ie/doegen/ (accessed 21 June 2010)

A Method for Measuring Helpfulness in Online Peer Review

William Hart-Davidson
Michigan State University
East Lansing, MI 48824
hartdav2@msu.edu

Michael McLeod
Michigan State University
East Lansing, MI 48824
mcleodm3@msu.edu

Christopher Klerkx
Michigan State University
East Lansing, MI 48824
klerkxch@msu.edu

Michael Wojcik
Michigan State University
East Lansing, MI 48824
wojcikm4@msu.edu

ABSTRACT

This paper describes an original method for evaluating peer review in online systems by calculating the helpfulness of an individual reviewer's response. We focus on the development of specific and machine scoreable indicators for quality in online peer review.

Categories and Subject Descriptors

K.4.3 [**Organizational Impacts**] -- *Computer-supported collaborative work*

General Terms

Algorithms, Management, Measurement, Design, Human Factors, Theory

Keywords

Review, Education, Information Architecture, Assessment, Reputation, Workflow, Learning, Peer Review, Helpfulness

INTRODUCTION

Following the logic of Benkler [1] in *The Wealth of Networks*, a culture of massive scale peer production such as we see with Web 2.0 technologies creates a quality problem related to the inherent self-evaluation bias of content producers. To ensure quality in web scale peer production, we need something that approaches web scale peer review. Logistically, this is a difficult problem, and so we have seen the rise of machine-mediated systems for coordinating peer response and review such as Amazon.com's recommender system or Slashdot's peer review driven posting system.

While these systems address the quality of the product in peer-production - they make the content better - they do not do much to reveal, assess, or facilitate the development of review activity itself. In many systems and contexts, it is desirable to know who the best reviewers are and also, in educational settings, what kinds of instructional interventions may be useful for helping students become better reviewers.

Our review method takes input from a structured but flexible review workflow and stores the artifacts generated in the review process (e.g. comments, suggestions for revisions) along with

other user-supplied descriptive and evaluative data that correspond with review metrics (such as whether or not a comment addressed a specific review criterion). The core method is designed as a web service that can receive this input from a variety of different sources and production environments, performing the analytics needed to calculate reviewer helpfulness and visualizations meant to offer both formative and summative feedback of reviewers' performance. Our method understands a review to be a group activity consisting of reviewers, review targets (documents), and criteria, all under the direction of a review coordinator.

There are a number of specific applications for this method, but we will focus on one application called "Eli" that has been developed for online peer review in classroom settings. Eli gives feedback to both teachers and students about reviewers' helpfulness in both a single review (a helpfulness score) and over time (a helpfulness index) so that students' ability to do reviews can be meaningfully evaluated.

1. Peer Production and Peer Review as Staples in an Information Economy

A distinctive feature of an information society, in general, and of Web 2.0 technologies as an outgrowth of an information society is the sheer volume of content produced by users in the course of doing everyday activities. Without being dismissive of the visual and interactive elements that users are producing, we might simply say that there is a lot of writing going on, by necessity, in the networked world. And by writing, we mean that process of constructing readable, usable, and valuable texts.

Following Benkler [1], we may apply an economic lens and view this writing, in the context of an information economy, as the equivalent of production work in a manufacturing economy, and just as in a manufacturing economy, we can see a need for processes of quality control:

> "To succeed, therefore, peer-production systems must also incorporate mechanisms for smoothing out incorrect self-assessments - as peer review does in traditional academic research or in the major sites like Wikipedia or Slashdot, or as redundancy and statistical averaging do in the case of NASA clickworkers. The prevalence of misperceptions that individual contributors have about their own ability and the cost of eliminating such errors will be part of the transaction costs associated with this form of organization. They parallel quality control problems faced by firms and markets." (Benkler, Ch. 4. p.15)

We can see that the value of a text, as Benkler argues, may be lessened when its quality is ensured only by self-review, an inherently biased proposition. We can see another problem in this formulation as well when we think about the reviewers themselves: how do good reviewers learn to be good reviewers? It is this problem that we have focused on in developing a method for evaluating review activity so as to provide both summative and formative feedback to those who supervise and engage in review work.

1.1 Teaching & Learning Review in Formal & Informal Learning Environments

Though there have been some book-length studies of writing review in both academic and workplace settings, what these studies reveal is that review is something that is rarely learned in a formal way (i.e. as the subject of a course or an assignment in a course, with a set of pre-defined learning objectives and an assessment to determine how well a student meets these objectives after some intervention)[2,3]. Rather, review is practiced in the service of learning to become a better writer (e.g. peer review sessions in writing classrooms [2]) and is learned, in workplace settings, via a process of enculturation and, in the best of circumstances, via a mentor-mentee relationship (see Swarts [3]). This is not to say, though, that review activity is itself rare. On the contrary, most students in first-year and advanced writing courses conduct peer-review as a routine part of each writing assignment [4]; peer review, moreover, is the gold standard for judging quality in a wide range of professional and research-oriented contexts, comprising what Fitzpatrick calls the sine qua non of scholarly publishing [5].

2. Challenges of Measuring Review Quality

Just as review activity has not often been the focus of formal efforts to train or evaluate reviewers, it is correspondingly non-focal in most systems that are designed for writing. We would even suggest that review activity itself is not always modeled in review coordination systems in such a manner as to permit it to be evaluated. There are some promising features built into systems meant to build trust in online environments - reputation systems - that we will highlight futher below. But reputations systems take review activity as input and they do not seek to offer an assessment of either any one review or of an individual reviewers activity, specifically, over time. Below, we discuss each of these issues as research and design challenges we faced in developing a generalized model for evaluating writing review in online systems.

2.1 Challenge: Inadequate workflow & data model for capturing review activity in writing software

There are any number of ways current writing technologies might be leveraged to get feedback on an existing text. Some writing software include features specifically to facilitate "review" such as adding inline comments or allowing a collaborator to make changes that another author must approve. But in nearly all cases, writing systems value review only as a means of evolving the text to a "better" version, to a "draft 2.0," an approach that makes it nearly impossible for these technologies to value review itself as a teachable and learnable activity.

Microsoft Word is a perfect example of writing software with dedicated review features. Word has a sophisticated "track changes" feature that allows a reviewer to directly alter the text and leave a report of that change for the author, who has the option to accept or reject those changes. Both Word and Adobe Acrobat have a set of commenting tools that allow reviewers to highlight selections of text and leave annotations, as well as digital versions of analogue activities like highlighting and "sticky notes" and drawing; Acrobat even has a set of features that allow reviewers access to proofreader marks and symbols. These features are incredibly powerful and make it easy to leave comments or suggestions for writers.

Where these tools fall short, however, is in capturing and making available for assessment the outcomes of a review. In Word, for example, when an author chooses to accept a change recommended by a reviewer, that change is hard-coded into the document and all traces of the suggestion are lost. The person who made the suggestion is not notified that their suggestion was accepted. In Acrobat, reviewers do not interact with the text directly (the software makes notes and edits over the top of the text, since it's text editing capabilities are limited) so the writer reviews comments and suggestions in Acrobat before returning to their text editor to make revisions, leaving no trace of the reviewer's work in the next version. This not only makes it impossible for reviewers to know when they have made helpful suggestions or comments, but it also makes it nearly impossible for instructors to assess the review work of their students.

There are two ways in which review as it is implemented in writing technologies like Word conflicts with review as it exists in practice. The first conflict is in the typical workflow of a review. Word does not see review as a distinct part of a workflow in which any number of other activities might be occurring. To put this another way, Word doesn't understand "a review" to be an event, a kind of social transaction as we understand it to be in the real world. Word sees review as a solitary experience done in relative isolation by a single person. A review is not something a group does, as far as Word knows. The second conflict lies in the way that the artifacts created during a review: comments, suggested changes, etc. are appended to a document. This means that there is no way for a reviewers comments on a document in Word to be seen as part of a larger activity in which the reviewer is engaged. There is also no way select a reviewer and see multiple comments on multiple documents.

2.2 Challenge: Lack of quality indicators & measures in review coordination systems

The two conflicts between review in the world and review in writing software are addressed by systems built to facilitated the coordination of reviews. There are many of these systems used by academic conference organizers, by publishers, and by government and other grant-making agencies to facilitate the submission, evaluation, publication and/or ranking of submissions for awards. The National Science Foundation's FastLane system is one such example, as is the JEMS system used to coordinate reviews for this conference.

While our project has included some design work meant to assist review coordination, we have not sought to replace any other system that does this kind of work. Rather, we have sought to enhance these types of systems by providing feedback for reviewers and review coordinators that these systems do not, to our knowledge, typically provide. We have worked on ways to provide feedback to reviewers, for example, on how helpful their review has been for the writer. We also have worked on ways to provide feedback to review coordinators about who their most helpful reviewers for a given round of review were. In order to provide this feedback, we have created a method that requires input in conjunction with a model of the review process, associating quality indicators with key moments in a review workflow. Our method can be used in conjunction with any existing review coordination system that provides appropriate inputs (e.g. via an API). We discuss the review model in more detail below.

2.3 Challenge: Building a reviewer's profile

Another category of online systems that deals with both the scale and economics of peer production is web reputation systems. As Farmer & Glass [6] argue, web reputation systems are designed to help overcome problems associated with missing interactions in online social settings that help to build trust in similar processes face-to-face or in traditional organizations. Online reputation systems are often used in peer production systems to allow users to distinguish good content from bad, and good content providers from bad ones as well. Reputation systems take some review information as input.

Before we go any further in comparing our own work in evaluating writing review to that of online reputation systems, we want to make an important distinction between reviews of texts as done, for instance, during academic peer review and the kinds of product reviews or book reviews one might see on a website like Amazon.com. These are reviews as texts. That is, product reviews are the kinds of peer production that requires writing review, in some measure, to ensure the quality of. Amazon.com has a reputation system in place that helps to sort out helpful product reviews from not so helpful ones; over time, as you submit good product reviews, you acquire status in their system such that your reviews may be more readily found by users. Amazon's system famously involves a very simple feedback system in the form of a question posted to users: was this review helpful to you? An answer to that question amounts, then, to a review of the product review, the results of which add value to the product review and add to the reputation of the writer of that review.

Our work on writing review has focused on the evaluation of a text by a group of reviewers with an eye toward measuring which of the reviewers gave the most helpful feedback. And so while we have learned from online reputation systems, the main takeaway for us has been the way that actions taken by reviewers (or by writers, for that matter) accrue over time and stay affiliated with a person in some kind of online profile. What we have developed is a way for all of that activity to add up to a measure of one aspect of a reviewers' performance that we think helps both reviewers and those who supervise reviewers: helpfulness.

3. Helpfulness: A Proposed Measure of the Quality of Online Review

Helpfulness is one way we propose to measure the quality of an online review where a reviewer gives feedback to a writer under the direction of a review coordinator who sets some criteria. We do not mean for helpfulness to be a comprehensive measure of review quality. It is simply a desirable feature of both a review and a reviewer: both should be helpful. What makes for a helpful review? What we know from both reviewing literature on review [2] and from our own experience as teachers of writing and as recipients of reviewer feedback is that a helpful review describes where the writer has made specific moves in a text to achieve rhetorical aims (as reflected in review criteria), makes accurate and fair evaluative statements about the features of a text, and offers specific, actionable advice about how to improve the text. A helpful reviewer is someone whose reviews consistently display these features.

With such a complex definition of review, it is not enough to simply ask a writer: was this review helpful? The writers answer may be one data point to consider, but it falls short of providing enough quality evidence to say whether a reviewer met the high standard of providing helpful feedback described above. To do that, we combine human-supplied judgments and performance-based data gathered at various points in the review process in order to determine when a review meets the description above.

3.1 A Description of Review

As we mentioned earlier, our definition of review differs from an approach that understands reviews as consisting primarily of metadata attached to a single digital file or object. Reviews exist along a spectrum from strictly criterion-referenced in which the user must respond to specific, pre-determined standards, evaluating the documents according to these, to open reviews where reviewers may be given little or no structure for providing feedback.

At their most basic, reviews consist of an author asking a reviewer for feedback on a single document. More complicated reviews can involve a review coordinator gathering multiple documents and specifying criteria by which multiple reviewers will evaluate them. In our review evaluation method, we attempt to match review processes in specific systems with a generic model of review that is detailed in section 3.2.2.

3.2. Generalized Steps in the Workflow

Create Review

1. an author or review coordinator initiates a review by specifying a document or documents(review "targets")

2. next, a reviewer or reviewers are identified and a prompt is created to ask the reviewer(s) for feedback

3. optionally, a review coordinator may create specific criteria to guide reviewers

Conduct Review

4. reviewers are notified that an author or coordinator has solicited their feedback

5. reviewer examines the review prompt and documents and decides whether to accept the review or not

6. reviewer views all documents & criteria, makes comments, adds ratings and or selects relevant chunks of document(s) in order to link them to criteria and/or provide specific feedback

View Results

7. reviewer completes and submits review

8. author and/or coordinator is notified of the completed review

9. author and/or review coordinator can view and rate feedback submitted by reviewer(s)

10. Once review is complete, authors and review coordinators may access aggregated review information; review coordinators may also permit reviewers to see review results

3.3 Sample Performance-Based Indicators & System Events

This generalized workflow, regardless of the context in which it might be embedded, is built around a wide range of activities in which users are engaged. Some of these activities result in artifacts of the review process (comments or suggestions, ratings, responses to criteria, etc) while others can be observed and recorded by the infrastructure of the review system. Table 1 lists of observable data, either user-generated or system-observed, that could be utilized in a system that values review and review behavior.

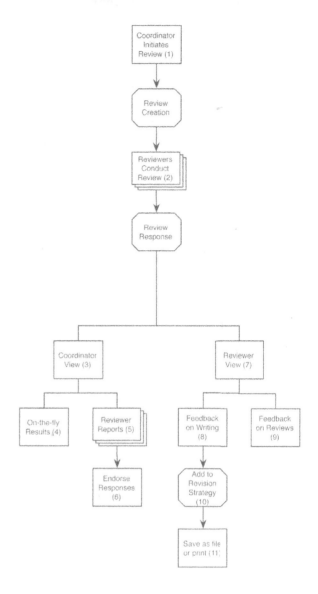

Table 1: Performance-based Indicators by Role with Corresponding System Events

Factor	User Roles	Event trigger
Document changes from version A to version B	Writer	Difference calculation
Document changes in the region of a comment	Writer	Difference + location
Document improves (gets a better rating) in relation to a criterion referenced in an earlier review	Writer	Difference + OnSubmit event
Comment by another reviewer appears in a similar area AND connected to similar criteria	Reviewers	Difference + OnSubmit
Document changes reflects a revision suggested explicitly by the reviewer	Writer, reviewer	Difference w/ parsing
Document changes reflect exact language suggested by the reviewer	Writer, reviewer	Difference w/ keyword matching
Reviewer accepts, rejects, or ignores a direct review request	Reviewer	OnClick event
Reviewer opts in to an open review request	Reviewer	OnClick event
Reviewer completes a review	Reviewer	OnSubmit or AJAX event
Reviewer provides a revised passage	Reviewer	revision tag in comment
Writer responds to a review	Writer	OnSubmit or AJAX
Writer moves comment to revision list	Writer	OnClick event
Writer inserts language from comment into draft (accept a proposed revision)	Writer	revision tagged content in body text
Review coordinator endorses a reviewer's comment	Coordinator	scaled response

Again, these are general types of behavior that can be observed and recorded inside a review system. Some of them, such as "writer responds to a review," are relatively simple observations by the system and can be recorded as discreet events. Others, like "Document changes from version A to version B," involve much more complex difference comparison, evaluating the two versions of a text and comparing against the comments the writer received on the first version.

As individual observations, they are not particularly valuable; inside a system that assigns relative value and proportionate weights to different activities, however, they can be utilized to make observations about the review practices of users. In the next section we will detail a system designed to teach writing review and utilizing this method.

4. Eli: Designing a Helpfulness Algorithm for a Classroom-based Peer Review System

Building on our generalized framework for review, Eli is our response to a problem we experience regularly as writing teachers. Specifically, we as teachers value review, but the demands of collecting, assessing, and tracking the helpfuness of our student's work as reviewers, in addition to the already daunting task of responding to student work as writers, are far too overwhelming. Eli is intended to be a system that not only makes the peer review process visible and assessable but also to help teach students to be better reviewers.

4.1 Helpfulness Algorithm

Our approach to building a system to meet these demands was to start small and scale upward over time. Because of our limited development resources, our approach was to identify machine-observable behaviors that didn't involve complex versioning or difference comparison to calculate and to build a relatively simple but useful metric around those. With that development model in mind, we identified the following behaviors that we felt best represent the helpfulness of reviewers:

- reviewer responses to instructor-specified criteria (whether or not they responded)

- rating of suggestions and comments by the writer of texts being reviewed

- number of suggestions and comments the writer adds to their revision strategy

- placement of suggestions in writer's revision strategy (ordinal positioning)

- instructor endorsement of criteria responses

- instructor endorsement of comments and suggestions

- use of comments or suggestions by a writer in a new version of a text (as specified by the writer)

These factors are all either binaries (yes/no or present/absent) or simple calculations (ratings of suggestions) which fit nicely into our limited development framework. Given greater resources we might elect for more complex methods, but in the absence of any system at all we felt these metrics would still yield powerful data and transform our pedagogy.

The next step, then, was to assign relative weights to each of the observed data points. This was necessary because all data points are not necessarily created equal; the fact that a user responds to all criteria, for example, doesn't imply helpfulness nearly as much as if the instructor endorsed one of those responses. To that end, we developed a weighting that we felt valued the data points in a way that more accurately reflected their individual degree of helpfulness:

Table 2: Helpfulness Factors with Associated Weights

Data Points	Weight
reviewer responses to instructor-specified criteria	1
rating of suggestions and comments by the writer	2
number of suggestions and comments added to revision strategy	2
placement of suggestion on writer's revision strategy	3
instructor endorsement of criteria responses	4
instructor endorsement of comments and suggestions	4
use of comments or suggestions in a new version of the text	5

In our very initial testing of the algorithm with these weights applied, the algorithm resulted in a number that, while accurately describing the relative helpfulness of each student, did not yield a number that we as instructors felt would be beneficial for students. For example, the algorithm assessed a student who performed poorly on a review as having a "12" while a student who performed exceptionally well only received a "68." We applied a corrective multiplier to the result of the algorithm to bring the result into line with the 100% scale that students and instructors are more familiar with.

4.3 Testing & Tuning the Algorithm with Sample Review Values

Once the algorithm was established we needed a way to test our assumptions not only about the relative weights of each metric but also the general findings of the algorithm - we needed to see if its computations would match up with how instructors would assess the review work of students. To accomplish that, we fabricated a set of review data that we believed would exemplify one of the harder distinctions the algorithm would need to make. Specifically, we created a review with the following context:

- Students divided into groups of 5 (each writer responds to 4 classmates)

- The instructor asked for responses to 3 criteria

- Writers can rate each suggestion made by their classmates on a 5-point scale

- The writer in this scenario created a Revision Strategy using 6 classmate comments

Table 3 provides additional detail to flesh out the values used in this test.

Table 3: Fabricated Student Reviewer Data Created to Test Weighting of Factors in Helpfulness Score Calculation

Observable Data Point	Student #1	Student #2	Student #3	Student #4

# of responses to instructor-specified criteria (*out of 3 possible criteria in this review*)	3	2	3	1
Criteria responses ratified by instructor	3	2	2	1
Number of suggestions made	5	3	2	1
Rating of suggestions (*out of 5 points per suggestion*)	22 of 25	10 of 15	10 of 10	1 of 5
# of suggestions utilized on Revision Strategy	3 of 5 made	1 of 3 made	2 of 2 made	0 of 1 made
Placement of suggestion on writer's strategy (*of the 6 total comments on the strategy*)	#1, #3, #4	#6	#2, #5	-
Suggestions utilized in revision	2	0	1	0

There are two clear outliers in this trial data set. Student #4 is clearly the least helpful reviewer; the student did not respond to all of the instructor's criteria and only made one suggestion which was rated poorly by the writer, was not ratified by the instructor and was not utilized in the revision strategy. Student #2 did better than Student #4 but was likewise not very helpful; this student also did not respond to all of the criteria, made 3 comments, only one of which was ratified by the instructor and used on the writer's revision strategy, but it was not utilized in the final draft.

The challenge for the algorithm was in differentiating between Student #1 and Student #3, both of whom represent what we believed to be helpful reviews. When we presented this data to a group of writing instructors and asked them to determine the most helpful reviewer, after lengthy conversation, the nearly unanimous verdict was that Student #1 was the most helpful. While the comments made by Student #3 were better rated on average, Student #1 made more comments that were less highly rated but were a higher priority on the writer's revision strategy and contributed more to the next version of the document. While both students were helpful, in terms of contributions toward a new text, the human raters thought Student #1 was more helpful. Thankfully, the algorithm agreed - each of the data points and their weights had been chosen carefully enough that the results of the data crunching resulted in an assessment that matched the vast majority of our human raters.

5. Displaying Formative Feedback to Teachers & Students in Order to Foster Learning of Review

One of the many affordances of a system designed to track and respond to discreet writing and review events is the extraordinary potential for visualizing writing behavior that have previously been impossible. With that in mind, in this section we will detail some of our early work developing graphic representation of review behavior inside Eli.

One of the most straightforward approaches is to utilize the raw numbers. As designers and information architects we were always keenly aware of the possibilities, particularly the most complex and challenging visualizations; as teachers, however, we were perhaps most excited for a simple numerical report of review data that had never before existed (fig. 1.).

Hugo's Helpfulness

88%

8 Suggestions
5 Comments
3.4 Average Suggestion Rating
3 Suggestions added to Strategies

Figure 1: Helpfulness Numerical Display

In this simple illustration, we make visible raw data that all but the most ambitious teachers have never seen - statistics about individual student writing behavior. Here, with a single glance, we can get a heads up of the work our student do as reviewers, as well as the perceived helpfulness of that work. We know the quantity of this student's work as well a quick insight into the perceived usefulness by the writers to whom this student responded.

A far more complex visualization of a student's review data is what we call the "Helpfulness Index" (fig 2). While students receive a Helpfulness Score after each review (each review is scored individually), their responses over time are compiled into their Helpfulness Index. Like the Helpfulness Score, the Index is based on a computation of each of the observable data points in a review, but compiled from the student's entire review history. Each individual data point becomes a statistic and, based on a student's performance in one of those areas, the instructor can offer guided feedback on that specific area of a user's review work. Also, because these scores are computed by the system, the system could be pre-loaded with sets of formative feedback that would guide a user on how to improve that aspect of their score. For example, in the bar chart here used to represent a student's review history, the influence of their suggestions on the writer's revised texts is quite low. The system, knowing this, could guide the user to sets of

instructional material or tips showing them suggestions by other reviewers that have been used in revisions.

Another potentially powerful representation of Helpfulness data is to plot the progression of a student over time (fig 3).

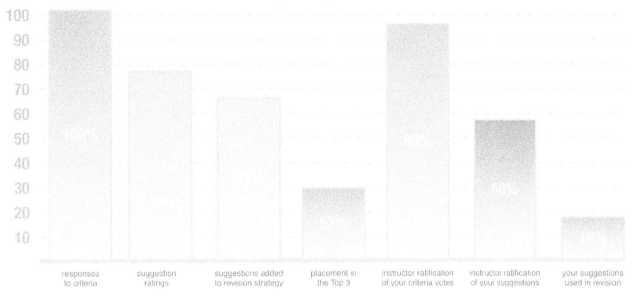

Figure 2: Helpfulness Index

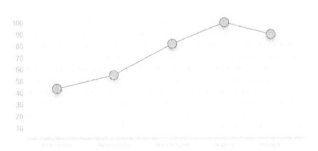

Figure 3: Helpfulness Scores Over Time

Even if students are assigned only five reviews over the course of a school year or a semester, the five Helpfulness Scores they receive from those reviews can still create a compelling representation of student learning. In the example below, the perceived helpfulness of a student's review work can be represented in a sparkline diagram that clearly shows that the student learned how to respond to classmates with more helpful feedback. For specifics, this student's teacher could drill down into individual reviews and see which factors improved over time.

Again, because these numbers are simple machine observations and computations, the exact same representations could be used to show the progress of all the students in a course. With a little more computational power, these statistics could be generated for an entire writing program. If our algorithm is capable of matching instructor's perceptions about review quality, the results of that algorithm over time should be an accurate representation of student learning.

6. Future Work

Eli is currently in development and will be put in front of students in beta form in late summer 2010. Once students have used the system and we have a robust data set we can begin larger-scale fine tuning of the Helpfulness algorithm to better align it with instructor expectations. From there, depending on the success of the beta, we could begin scaling up and implementing some of the machine-derived data (particularly difference calculations between two versions of a text).

1. REFERENCES

[1] Benkler. Y. (2007). *The wealth of networks: How social production transforms markets and freedom.* New Haven, CT: Yale UP.

[2] Kastman-Breuch, L. (2004). *Virtual peer review: teaching and learning about writing in online environments.* Albany: SUNY Press.

[3] Swarts, J. (2008). *Together with technology: writing review, enculturation, and technological mediation.* Amityville, NY: Baywood.

[4] Fitzpatrick, K. "From the Crisis to the Commons." In "In Focus: The Crisis in Publishing." *Cinema Journal* 44.3 (Spring 2005): 92-95.

[5] Fitzpatrick, K. (2009). Planned obsolescence: Publishing, technology, and the future of the academy. NYU Press. http://mediacommons.futureofthebook.org/mcpress/planned obsolescence/one/

[6] Farmer, F.R. & Glass, B. (2010). *Building web reputation systems.* Cambridge, MA: O'Reilly.

Toward an Ontology of Rhetorical Figures

Ashley R. Kelly
University of Waterloo
Department of English
Language & Literature
arkelly@uwaterloo.ca

Nike A. Abbott
University of Waterloo
Department of English
Language & Literature
nabbott@uwaterloo.ca

Randy Allen Harris
University of Waterloo
Department of English
Language & Literature
raha@uwaterloo.ca

Chrysanne DiMarco[*]
University of Waterloo
David R. Cheriton
School of Computer Science
cdimarco@uwaterloo.ca

ABSTRACT

Our paper describes the Rhetorical Figure Ontology Project, a multidisciplinary research project that is presently working towards the development of a comprehensive database of rhetorical figures, an associated wiki, and, ultimately, an ontology of rhetorical figures. The database and wiki project provide the dataset and space for the conceptual development, respectively, to create an ontology. We define an ontology as a formalized taxonomy or system of classification of concepts and associated descriptions of said concepts. Here we provide an overview of the present state of the project and a discussion of the development of ontological descriptions of rhetorical figures. This work is a joint venture between Dr. Randy Allen Harris (English) and Dr. Chrysanne DiMarco (Computer Science, and English) at the University of Waterloo, Canada.

Categories and Subject Descriptors

I.2.7 [**Computing Methodologies**]: Artificial Intelligence— *Natural Language Processing*

General Terms

Theory, Design

Keywords

ontology, rhetoric, rhetorical figures

---

*Dr. Chrysanne DiMarco is the Director of the Inkpot Natural Language Research Group.

1. INTRODUCTION

Situated in the David R. Cheriton School of Computer Science at the University of Waterloo, the Inkpot Natural Language Research Group aims to advance research in the area of natural language processing and computational discourse analysis. Inkpot has taken an innovative approach to the study of human language in computer science by incorporating the work of language scholars, from the field of rhetoric (see: Harris & DiMarco 2009; Gawryjołek 2009) [11] [7], and computational methods to analyze and manipulate human language. The Rhetorical Figure Ontology Project, a subset of the Inkpot team, seeks to combine linguistic and rhetorical theory with machine learning methods to create an ontology, a formal representation of concepts, for use in computational processing of real-world communication. The research team is comprised of experts in rhetoric, linguistics, and natural language processing. This paper describes the development and implementation of a database of rhetorical figures and the ongoing work to create an ontology of said figures.

The first stage in developing the ontology is the construction of a comprehensive database of rhetorical figures. The database in its current incarnation is a simple column-based application that allows for data to be collected, organized, and modified. Data being collected includes: definitions, examples, and bibliographic information about rhetorical figures. In addition to this data collected from historical sources, the figures are being categorized on the basis of: figure type-of, linguistic domain, and kind-of relationship— these terms will be explained below, but essentially all describe individualizing linguistic and rhetorical characteristics of the figures. Presently the database contains a list of almost one thousand entries; these entries are divided into two types of figures: primary figures and synonyms. At last count about three hundred and fifty figures would be classified as primary figures with the remaining listed as synonyms.

Many of the figures present complex and confounding historical trajectories. In order to provide a space to explore the nuances of each figure in great detail there is an associated wiki with the database. This space allows for individual figures to be treated, but, perhaps more importantly, allows for a space to discuss the details of figure-relationships and the individualizing characteristics as they are treated in the database. In this way, we are able to create increasingly refined classes of figures, their attributes, and relationships.

We argue that the study of rhetoric offers profound insights into the understanding of human language both in its structure and use. In particular, rhetoric offers an extensive treatment of complex forms of expression, known as rhetorical figures or figures of speech. While the encyclopedic information being collected and assimilated in the database is significant, it is the relationship of the figures to one another that is of central importance to the discussion in this paper. The data being aggregated for each figure provides critical information that helps elucidate and explicate the figure as a meaning-making, purposive device.

We also argue that the relationships among figures provide insight into the cognitive affinities of the figures themselves. This work has a multitude of applications, but our specific focus here is the importance of such information in understanding the role rhetorical figures play as not only meaning-making, purposive devices, but as portals to the inner-workings of the human mind. The cognitive role of figures is based in the work of such scholars as literary theorist Mark Turner, linguist George Lakoff, philosopher Mark Johnson, psychologist Raymond Gibbs, Jr., and rhetorician Jeanne Fahnestock. Though rhetorical figures have been defined, differentiated, and categorized for millennia from the *Rhetorica ad Herennium* to Henry Peacham's *Garden of Eloquence* to the contemporary work of Gideon O. Burton on *Silva Rhetoricæ* many figures escape clear classification. While our project does not claim, nor does it aim, to provide definitive categorization for rhetorical figures, it does work towards a systematized approach to the treatment of figures in computational systems.

While such efforts will, at present, remain imperfect our work will describe methods of categorization of rhetorical figures, difficulties with the categorization, and some of the methods that we might use to work around such difficulties. To this end we will treat the development, including the theoretical underpinnings for the categorization, and population of the database.

2. RELEVANT LITERATURE

Natural Language Processing (NLP) is an area of study, in the discipline of Computer Science, that treats the manipulation and generation of human-readable language. While there have been some efforts to treat "rhetoric" in the field of NLP, as Harris & DiMarco (2009) argue, these treatments fail to understand the primary scholarship and rhetoric to any significant degree, rarely going beyond a generalized notion of style derived from linguistics. Often the degree to which language scholarship is consulted is limited to the study of linguistics [11].

While linguists and computational linguists have worked together on developing models for software programs, rhetoric can more fully treat the complexity of human speech. Many linguistic schemes follow tractable characteristics of words and word groupings. Rhetoric is more difficult to schematize because it seeks to uncover the exigence and purpose of a figure or rhetorical device as well as the linguistic strategies a figure employs for effectiveness. Furthermore, many characteristics of figures (especially tropes) are conceptual and therefore more difficult to formally specify. However, encouraging progress has been made towards computational

methods for detecting and manipulating rhetorical figures in texts [7] [8] [22] and [3]. This progress made by the Inkpot team is generally treated below in our discussion of the ontology's classification of schemes, tropes and chroma, but is more fully elaborated on in the previously cited works.

Cognitive studies have taken up the study of rhetoric as a way to research cognitive processes in communication. Lakoff and Johnson treat figurative language as a basic component of everyday speech in their book *Metaphors We Live By* [13], while Raymond Gibbs posits that "human cognition is fundamentally shaped by various poetic or figurative processes" in his book, *The Poetics of Mind* [10].

What these studies show is that rhetorical figuration is used in everyday speech; what can be inferred from that is that as natural language generation progress so too must our understanding of rhetorical figures as reflections of cognitive processes. People use figurative devices to understand abstract concepts and to communicate about them to others. Instead of figuration requiring special cognitive processes, rhetorical figures reflect the how humans cognitively respond to the world around them.

3. OUR APPROACH

3.1 Method

Editors contributing to the database of a rhetorical terms include both graduate and undergraduate students, research associates, and primary investigators. Combined, this team's disciplinary expertise includes: linguistics, computational linguistics, rhetoric, artificial intelligence, computer science, and even includes students from the faculty of science. In order to ensure that the team is adequately trained and consistent in their work we have made efforts to provide the necessary skills and understanding of our project and systems of classification to ensure a common framework from which everyone can work. All members of the team are expected to, and indeed have obtained, a general understanding of rhetoric and the role of figures in theory.

Over the year that the project has been conducted we have held many sessions, bi-weekly during school terms, where the editors come together in an attempt to normalize their practices. In some cases our meetings brought forth problematic methods of classification and organization in our work, and in others helped to train those new to the project in basic linguistic and rhetorical theory. Additionally, help documentation with definitions and examples is provided to editors in a project wiki. This documentation is constantly being revised along with the database software and conceptual classification of the database.

Despite our efforts we still have some significant inconsistencies in the editors work. This is, in part, due to the ongoing development of the database and its rules for categorization, but it is also due to the difficult nature of the material that the editors are working from and with. For this reason we have employed a review system wherein one who is better versed in rhetorical theory, typically a graduate student from the Department of English Language & Literature, reviews the work of the editors and either accepts or rejects their changes.

3.2 Primary Texts

Part of the research into primary source texts for the database is to explore the various taxonomies that have been created by rhetoricians, logicians, grammarians, and other scholars over the past two millennia. A goal of the Rhetorical Figure Ontology Project is to provide a comprehensive exploration of the possible, and most useful, classifications of rhetorical figures. Accordingly, one of the first considerations for the project was to choose a primary name for a figure–as many figures have multiple synonyms–in order to reach an agreement on identification. The decision was made to follow the lead of the primary source for the database's first incarnation, which is the *Silva Rhetoricæ* website spearheaded by Gideon O. Burton of Brigham Young University. The primary names are the Greek-based English terms and the synonyms can include the Latin, alternate spellings, or an English turn-of-phrase.

Building on Burton's major contribution, many important rhetorical scholars who created seminal and influential figuration taxonomies were consulted. Many of the primary sources from which we draw the definitions and examples for each figure are rhetorical manuals from Greek and Roman antiquity, the middle ages, early modern and modern periods. Most of the texts are English language or English translations, usually from Latin. The earliest text is the *Rhetorica ad Herennium* [2], in Harry Caplan's translation, and is still considered the primary source for rhetorical devices. Geoffrey of Vinsauf later combined two major classical sources, the *Rhetorica ad Herennium* and *Horace's Ars Poetria*, in his *Poetria Nova* [23]. This 13th-century manual was written by the English Vinsauf in Latin and the edition drawn upon for our work was translated by Margaret F. Nims into English and published in 1967. Henry Peacham's *The Garden of Eloquence*, a 14th-century manual, provides a guidebook of rhetorical figures, with examples drawing primarily from Biblical sources, and offers advice on the use of each figure. For our purposes we have consulted the 1593 edition available through the *Perseus Digital Library*. César Chesneau Du Marsais' French text, *Traité des Tropes* [4], is an 18th-century rhetorical manual which treats the study of figures called tropes. John Gent Smith's *The Mysterie of Rhetorique Unvail'd* is a 17th-century manual which is intended both to illuminate the Bible–in an effort to avoid misinterpretation–and to teach young people how to speak and write more elegantly and persuasively. Thomas Gibbons' *Rhetoric: Or, A View Of its Principal Tropes and Figures, in Their Origin and Powers* (1767), John Hart's *A Manual of Composition and Rhetoric* (1874) [12], and John Walker Vilant Macbeth's *The Might And Mirth Of Literature* (1875) [14] all represent the modern end of our current collection, excluding Gideon O. Burton's [1] and Garrett Epp's [5] work.

Further texts to be incorporated into the database include, but are not limited to: James De Mille's *The Elements of Rhetoric* [15], Richard Sherry's *A treatise of scheme and tropes* [19], and Thomas Gibbons' *Rhetoric* [9]. Additionally, we hope to continue refining our database content; that is, what is taken from primary sources to explicate and elucidate rhetorical figures and their uses. In refining the entries for each figure we are able to gain further insight into useful methods of classification and categorization. Importantly, having a wealth of sources provides some of methods of determining a common or standard usage for terms where some historical conflict has existed.

3.3 Software

In working toward an ontology of rhetorical figures we determined to first aggregate this large collection of disperse information into database software. Our database was designed and developed specifically for our project by a software engineer external to the research group, but who continues to work closely to meet our specific needs. The software application, dubbed "Rhetfig," is a Python-based application running on top of Google App Engine. As a platform, Google's App Engine is a scalable, cloud-computing service that allows web applications to be stored on Google's infrastructure.

The first instantiation of the software was operationalized as a data collection method and is constantly being developed to include more sophisticated features such as search and sort algorithms. Phase two development of the software, including search and sort, will be complete in late September 2010. Further development of the database will continue on App Engine and will be a completely web-based application accessible by anyone on any computing platform capable of standard web-browsing.

Ultimately we will integrate open source, web-based ontology editing software (protègè, for example), but until the categories and individual entries have been further refined we are focused on the theoretical and conceptual issues, and not the programmatic concerns, of an the ontology's development. That is, we see the theoretical concerns of classifying this extremely large and diverse group of data as preceding any attempt to implement our database work in ontology-editing software.

Fortunately (but also unfortunately) there are literally millennia of taxonomic research into figuration. Some categorizations are very robust. Others, however, are more controversial. A significant number of figures occupy different categories for different theorists. A significant number, too, are figures to some theorists, but not to other theorists. The task is appreciable.

Theoretical work is, of course, essential to complete prior to further software development as the theoretical work is the basis for software design decisions. Unlike other ontologies in the field of computer science, such as WordNet, this ontology functions as much more than a simple lexical ontology; instead, our work towards an ontology blends the notion of an ontology in computer science and a more classical definition (e.g., what features of a figure are essential, individualizing?), well-suited to rhetorical studies. To better address the quiddity of figures we then turn to rhetorical studies and will return to a discussion of software at the end of our paper.

4. RHETORICAL FIGURES

In *Silva Rhetoricæ*, Burton describes rhetorical figures as being like "wildflower seeds tossed on fertile ground," which is to say that these figures "multiplied into a garden of enormous variety over time" [1]. Burton goes on to provide a general introduction to rhetorical figures–an excellent introduction for those new to rhetoric–from their early classification and naming in Greek and Roman. Figures are strategies or devices that are employed in language to achieve particular stylistic effects. As we will see, there is a much richer life to these figures than is often assumed under the labeled "stylistics," but that definition will suffice for now.

One of the best known rhetorical figures is the trope called "metaphor." This figure is a means of implicit comparison in that the speaker (or rhetor, or author) will use one thing as a perspective on another. For example, the metaphor "Homer is a pig" is a similarity operation which suggests such features as Homer's eating habits are similar to those of a pig. The purpose of such a figuration is also to activate other parts of the imagination, especially physical sensations. Erotema is the primary term for the figure better known as the rhetorical question. The purpose of this device is not to solicit confirmation or denial, the standard function of a sentence, but to affirm or deny a point by phrasing it as a question that does not require an answer; "Shall I compare thee to a summer's day?" This device can be used to strengthen the rhetor's position as expert, or can transfer agency from rhetor to audience as they are asked to provide an alternative although that alternative is believed not to exist. Anastrophe is a figure where the syntactical position of a word is changed for emphasis, such as "glistens the dew upon the morning grass." This unexpected change is used to alert the audience to listen more attentively to what is being said and can emphasize a word in a phrase which may normally be unattended.

Rhetorical figures, or figures of speech, are part of elocutio, or rhetorical style; indeed, rhetorical figures are what have been described as the "smallest units of rhetorical stylistics" ([20] "figures of speech"). Style here should not be taken as separable from meaning or content. Style is married to meaning and content in rhetorical scholarship, and, accordingly, an important consideration when crafting a text. Understanding how to craft a text using these figures is crucial to constructing persuasive texts and it is evident that many scholars over the past two thousand years have understood this. In fact, the classification and categorization of rhetorical figures has been an ongoing project since Greek antiquity.

Jeanne Fahnestock's seminal text, *Rhetorical Figures in Science* (1999), provides not only an excellent discussion of how figures are employed, but an accessible introduction to the history of the classification systems to which figures have been subjected. The initial classification system for figures has been long lost and only vague hints at its development can be found in the early Latin *Rhetorica ad Herennium* [6]. However, it is evident that the classification of figures had been thoroughly considered and, largely, established by Roman times. Reconfigurations of the classification systems for rhetorical figures would be developed and discussed throughout the rest of the Roman period (e.g., Quintilian's *Institutio Oratoria*), through the Early Modern period (e.g., Melancthon's *De Eloquentia* or Peacham's *The Garden of Eloquence*), and continues today with the work of Gideon O. Burton at *Silva Rhetoricæ* and, plainly, with the Rhetorical Figure Ontology project [6]. [1]

In order to provide guidelines for entering information on figures into the database, certain salient features had to be drawn out and clarified. These include how to choose the primary name and the rhetorical and linguistic domain in which the figure resides. The historical texts provide challenges to these categorizations as it becomes evident that

rhetoric has a long and storied past.

5. THE ONTOLOGY

The domain within which our ontology will be constructed is that of rhetorical figures of speech, as defined and described above. Included within the scope of our work are the figures, their individualizing characteristics, and the relationships among figures.

Uses of this ontology, we hope, will be multiple; the end-goal is to provide a comprehensive and robust collection of terms and a suite of tools to manipulate and explore figures and their relations to one another.

For the initial organization of the ontology we intend to devise classes into a hierarchical taxonomy, using a top-down approach of defining general concepts (e.g., linguistic domain) and subclasses (e.g., syntactic, semantic, morphological). Instances can be created from the work that we have been conducting in the construction of our database.

5.1 Historical & Contextual Classification

Each figure features a wealth of historical and contextual information in the database entry. Such information is comprised of basic figure-related information, such as: the figures' name, its original source, synonyms, etymology, related figures, and examples. Information that might be better described as historical would include the definition, which often demonstrates an evolution of the figure's meaning, and a list of sources who have discussed the figure in question. Of course, distinguishing between the historical and contextual information is only helpful in attempting to identify the purpose of each category in the database. All of the contextual information is also historical and all historical information provides context. However, the historical aspects of the figures become somewhat secondary to context as our purpose is to classify the figures in some kind of consistent and comprehensive taxonomy. As noted, a figure's past often only confuses the definition and use of a figure. Accordingly, we see our classification schemes as acknowledging the rich history of a given figure, its inconsistencies, and conflicts while, ultimately, working towards an understanding of the figure as a rhetorical strategy, or device, that can be broadly defined and generalized such that we are able to generalize its nature well-enough to begin the creation of our ontology.

5.2 Linguistic & Rhetorical Classification

Our initial ontology is envisioned as treating specific aspects of rhetorical figures as classes. That is, certain characteristics of rhetorical figures will be broadly defined and organized based on certain linguistic or rhetorical characteristics which will, in turn, provide a governing set of rules and constraints with which to organize our ontology. For the purposes of this paper we will explicate three of the key classes from which we will be able to create a formal taxonomy from our database of rhetorical figures. These three conceptual classifications are: "type of" (scheme, trope or, chroma) distinctions, linguistic domain, and "kind of" relationships. Each of the classification schema are described, defined, and illustrated below.

5.2.1 Schemes, Tropes, & Chroma

The highest-level distinction among the figures in our database is a trisection, into tropes, chroma and schemes:

---

[1] The full treatment Fahnestock gives to the history of these figures is beyond the scope of this paper, but what can be taken from her work is that rhetorical figures have had a long and sometimes conflicting history of categorization and classification.

- **Tropes** are figures whose most salient features are conceptual—such as metaphor (e.g., "my love is a red, red rose"), where the literal falsity draws attention to conceptual similarities between two terms, and synecdoche (e.g., "all hands on deck"), where a representative part is conceptually equivalent to the whole.

- **Chroma** are figures whose most salient features are intentional—such as erotema (rhetorical question; "Do you think I'm an idiot?"), where the question is intended to suggest a proposition not solicit an answer, and apostrophe (addressing someone/something which is not part of the audience: "O, pardon me, thou bleeding piece of earth [Mark Antony to Caesar's corpse, in order to rouse the mob]"), where the remarks are intended not to move the addressee but the 'overhearing' audience [2].

- **Schemes** are figures whose most salient features are formal—such as rhyme (e.g., "quick flick"), where the sound calls attention to the word and antimetabole (e.g., "I said what I meant, I meant what I said"), where the symmetrical inversion calls attention to the syntax.

Attempting to formalize features of each category has proven a challenging task, but tropes and chroma both prove to be significantly more difficult to treat than schemes [11]. Schemes are described in our system as "formal" because there are rather straight-forward linguistic markers that we are able to note and use in our work. For example, anaphora is a rhetorical figure that we have classified as a scheme. This figure describes the repetition of a word or phrase construction at the beginning of contiguous clauses (e.g., "*You whom* vertue hath made the Princess of felicity, be not the Minister of ruine; *you whom* my choyce hath made the Load-star of all my sublunary comfort, be not the rock of my shipwrack." [21]).

Using natural language processing methods, fellow Inkpot researcher Claus Strommer has been able to develop a software application that can mark instances of enanaphora in a text [22]. While somewhat distinct from the ontology itself, Strommer's work has provided valuable lessons in the way that we can implement the efforts of our conceptual work on rhetorical figures into a computational system. Most importantly, it has demonstrated to us that in terms of formalization we are better able to work with schemes than tropes or chroma, though they are certainly essential to treat in future work.

Jakub Gawryjolek's work has also been revealing. He has explored the automated detection of certain rhetorical figures mostly schemes of repetition (such as ploche, epizeuxis, and polysyndeton), as well as a few schemes of parallelism (chiefly isocolon), and even one trope (oxymoron). The difficulties of detecting schemes, while significant, are relatively tractable compared to the difficulties of detecting tropes, which is what makes Gawryjolek's work in this area so promising. Oxymorons are contiguous (or highly proximal), contradictory words, such as "the sounds of silence" and "square circle." Gawryjolek used the semantic word relations, synonymy and antonymy, in WordNet to create a

list of synonyms which is then paired with antonyms to find potential contradictions in word pairs [7].

5.2.2 Linguistic Domain

The "linguistic domain" describes a system of classification that indicates the primary area within which the figure operates. That is, a distinction is made between several linguistic lines and categories of linguistic boundaries are operationalized (e.g., phonological, syntactic, semantic). Within those boundaries we attempt to classify which rhetorical figures are operating within a respective domain. Our complete class for linguistic domain includes:

- **phonological** refers to speech sounds and sound patterns;

- **morphological** refers to word constructions and forms and variations of those forms (e.g., suffixes, prefixes, co-occurrence);

- **syntactic** refers to clauses and phrases;

- **lexical** refers to words and word relations;

- **semantic** refers to meaning;

- **orthographic** refers to lettering or spelling.

For example, the figure called hypozeugma is classified as syntactic because it is defined as placing essential information at the end of a clause. Peacham provides an example of this construction: "The foundation of freedome, the fountaine of equitie, the safegard of wealth, and custodie of life, is preserved by lawes" [16]. In this case it is relatively safe, based on our system of categorization, to place hypozeugma in the syntactic category.

Some figures are less amenable to a single classification. For example, antimetabole has been classified as operating in both the syntactic and lexical domains in our classification system. An antimetabole is a "[r]epetition of words, in successive clauses, in reverse grammatical order" [1]; an example of this figure: "I said what I meant, I meant what I said" [18]. It should be clear from the example that the structure of the phrase is important, as is the repetition of the same words. Accordingly, this figure's primary or defining linguistic domain is necessarily both lexical and syntactic. A related figure, chiasmus, is defined as "[r]epetition of grammatical structures in inverted order" which is not to be confused with antimetabole; an example of this figure from Silva Rhetoricae: "It is boring to eat; to sleep is fulfilling" [1]. This figure features defining characteristics from both the syntactic and semantic linguistic domains.

Our classification system allows for multiple linguistic domains to be selected by the editors; that is, this is not an exclusive class that only allows for the selection of one domain. Given the proclivity for linguistic domains to be blurred together, with overlapping and mixed boundaries, it is necessary to consider multiple defining characteristics for each figure.

5.2.3 "Kind of" Classification

The "kind of" category is the least refined category, but provides one of the more interesting systems of classification. Here the categories can describe figures' operations at multiple linguistic levels. It is the strategies that figures

---

[2]This example, from Shakespeare's *Julius Caesar*, also contains the metaphor of a corpse as a piece of earth.

use for their effectiveness that are defined in this classification system. Unlike the previous method of classification, linguistic domain, there are no subclasses within this taxonomy. Rather, we have constructed a list of common strategies employed by rhetorical figures as a method to group them based broadly on their techniques. It is noteworthy that this system is currently under going significant revision, but the general structure and intentions will remain in subsequent versions.

- **Repetition** refers to when a figure uses repetition of sounds (consonants, vowels, or syllables), words, syntax (phrases or clauses) or semantics (concepts).
  e.g., Rhyme-Hickory Dickory Dock. The mouse ran up the clock.

- **Symmetry** refers to when a figure pairs two constructions in an inverse ("mirrored") way.
  e.g. Antimetabole: When the going gets tough, the tough get going.

- **Opposition** refers to when a figure oppose two structures or concepts. e.g., Oxymoron: A wanton modesty. Proud humility.

- **Identity** refers to when a figure uses two or more identical elements.
  e.g., Ploce: O villain, villain, smiling, damned villain! (Hamlet [5]).

- **Similarity (partial-identity)** refers to when a figure uses resemblance of a concept.
  e.g., Simile: My love is like a red, red rose.

- **Omission** refers to when a figure omits expected elements.
  e.g., Asyndeton (which omits the expected conjunction, "and"): I came, I saw, I conquered.

- **Series** refers to when a figure establishes a series (through words or concepts). e.g., Abecedarian: Adorable, beautiful, charming, delightful, exciting, fantastic—you run the gamut from A to Z [1].

In this system is it evident that there are classical influences; Peacham, for example, created multiple divisions in this classification of rhetorical figures, including "figures of repetition" and "figures of omission." We hope that our work here builds on, rather than rehashes, previous work on classification to provide a useful category for broadly defining the strategies employed by rhetorical figures for their effectiveness. Furthermore, we hope that this system can be paired with the linguistic domain classification to reference the levels at which figures may be functioning in both kind and linguistic-level.

6. FUTURE WORK

Presently we are continuing to refine the entries for each rhetorical figure, drawing on the primary texts noted above, as well as expert knowledge from language-related disciplines (i.e., rhetoric, linguistics, and literary studies). In refining each figure's entry we hope to ensure that its subsequent placement in the ontology, when populated, will accurately reflect strategies and intentions employed by the figure. That is, each figure will have a clear placement in

terms of the primary linguistic domain within which it operates, what "kind of" strategies it uses, and so on with the categories described earlier in the paper.

Prior to populating an ontology we hope to ensure that there is a high inter-annotator agreement on each figure's classification in the fields that we hope to use as classes for the ontology (e.g., type of, linguistic domain, and kind of). To do this we would have annotators independently select the classifications for a set of figures and then determine Cohen's kappa coefficient for statistical validation of our taxonomy.

Ontology tools that we will create will be integrated into the web-accessible database that has already be implemented. In this way we hope that our work will be included in broader research contexts than our own and, additionally, provide a useful tool for other researchers. Our application has yet to be developed as we are still working towards the completion of version of our database of rhetorical figures.

Additionally, as we populate and refine the database we are engaged in an iterative design process wherein the categories and systems of classification that will come to shape our ontology are continually being revised and refined.

7. FINAL REMARKS

While the work described above is highly theoretical and may first appear to be situated firmly in the domain of rhetorical scholarship alone, the impact of rhetorical figures reaches much further. Rhetorical figures are present in all communication and, as Lakoff & Johnson have famously described in their seminal text *Metaphors We Live By*, figures shape how we think about and through the world. Though Lakoff & Johnson seem unaware of the many precedents, rhetoricians like Giambattista Vico, I.A. Richards, and Kenneth Burke had all advanced similarly compelling arguments about figuration and thought.

In related Inkpot projects we have explored the context of health communications and as many other scholars studying health communications have demonstrated [17], the design of health communication has a significant impact on patients and rhetorical figures are inescapable components of the communicative design of language, especially in those areas concerned with persuasion.

Health care communication is only one example of where rhetorical figures are crucial elements of a persuasive text. Indeed, the presence or absence of carefully chosen rhetorical figures has a profound impact on all genres of communication. Technical writers may find particularly strategies of repetition or ellipsis present in technical communications, for example. Researchers situated more firmly in computer science may find our initial classification schemes to be valuable in detecting figures in a corpus and subsequently diagnosing, modifying, or mining that corpus. With further development of the database and ontology software researchers will be able to sort and search through figures based on a multitude of classifications.

The end goals of the Rhetorical Figure Ontology Project are to support researchers in rhetoric, poetics, cognitive science, human-languages technologies, and any of the other fields (and subfields) for which rhetorical figures have either been traditionally important or in which rhetorical figures are more recently becoming important. As an ongoing project, community feedback will certainly inform our work and looking to form partnerships with others working in related fields.

Figures are extraordinarily pervasive in language, and extraordinarily fluid; a figure for one generation is literal for the next (becoming, e.g., a 'dead metaphor'). This situation makes them very challenging to explore. But it also makes them utterly essential for an adequate and responsible account of discourse, and for any investigations, of any sort, into style. They cluster in certain ways relative to affect (anger, joy, sadness), for instance, and relative to genre (newspaper articles, scientific reports, blogs), and relative to functions (persuasion, description, argumentation). Computationally detecting, or reproducing, or modifying any of these phenomena will be greatly facilitated by the ontology we are building.

8. ACKNOWLEDGMENTS

We wish to thank *Silva Rhetoricæ* (that is, its mastermind, Gideon O. Burton), which not only served as the inspiration for this database, but as the primary source for its phase-one population, and as an invaluable training tool for its contributors. We would also like to thank the entire Inkpot Natural Language Research Group for their input and support in the development of this project, Garret Kelly for the design and development of our software, and the University of Waterloo Computer Science Computing Facility staff for their ongoing support. This research is funded by the Social Sciences and Humanities Research Council of Canada (SSHRC).

9. REFERENCES

[1] G. O. Burton. *Silva Rhetoricae*. Brigham Young University, February 2007. http://rhetoric.byu.edu.

[2] H. Caplan. *An English Translation of: Ad C. Herennium Libri IV De Ratione Dicendi*. William Heinemann Ltd, London, 1964.

[3] C. DiMarco, S. Banks, O. Gladkova, and M. Skala. A fine-grained multi-level ontology for computational stylistics. Unpublished., 2009.

[4] C. C. Dumarsais. *Traité des Tropes*. Veuve Gaspard Fritsch, Leipsic, 1757.

[5] G. P. Epp. *Rhetorical Figures*. University of Alberta, 1994. http://www.ualberta.ca/ gepp/figures.html.

[6] J. Fahnestock. *Rhetorical Figures in Science*. Oxford University Press, Oxford, 1999.

[7] J. Gawryjołek. Automated annotation of rhetorical figures. Master's thesis, University of Waterloo, 2009.

[8] J. Gawryjołek, C. DiMarco, and R. Harris. An annotation tool for automatically detecting rhetorical figures. Pasadena, July 2009. Computational Models of Natural Argument (CMNA).

[9] T. Gibbons. *Rhetoric: Or, A View Of Its Principal Tropes and Figures, in Their Origin and Powers: With a Variety of Rules to Escape Errors and Blemishes, and Attain Propriety and Elegance in Composition*. J. and W. Oliver, London, 1767.

[10] R. W. Gibbs. *The Poetics of mind: Figurative thought, language, and understanding*. Cambridge University Press, Cambridge, 1994.

[11] R. A. Harris. Constructing a rhetorical figuration ontology. Edinburgh, April 2009. Symposium on Persuasive Technology and Digital Behaviour Intervention, Convention of the Society for the Study of Artificial Intelligence and Simulation of Behaviour (AISB).

[12] J. S. Hart. *A Manual of Composition and Rhetoric: A Text-book for Schools and Colleges*. Eldredge & Brother, Philadelphia, 1874.

[13] G. Lakoff and M. Johnson. *Metaphors We Live By*. The University of Chicago Press, Chicago, 1980.

[14] J. W. V. Macbeth. *The Might And Mirth Of Literature: A Treatise On Figurative Language. In Which Upwards Of Six Hundred Writers Are Referred To, And Two Hundred And Twenty Figures Illustrated*. Harper & Brothers, New York, 1875.

[15] J. D. Mille. *The Elements of Rhetoric*. Harper & Brothers, New York, 1882.

[16] H. Peacham. *The Garden of Eloquence*. Perseus Digital Library, 1593. Gregory R. Crane.

[17] J. Z. Segal. *Health and the Rhetoric of Medicine*. Southern Illinois University Press, Carbondale, 2005.

[18] D. Seuss. *Horton Hatches the Egg*. Random House Books for Young Readers, New York, 1940. Theodor Geisel.

[19] R. Sherry. *A treatise of schemes and tropes*. John Day, Aldersgate [London], 1550.

[20] T. O. Sloane. *Encyclopedia of Rhetoric*. Oxford University Press USA, New York, 2001.

[21] J. G. Smith. *The mysterie of rhetorique unveil'd*. E.Cotes, London, 1665.

[22] C. Strommer. Paragraph context determination through rhetorical figures - a practical approach using epanaphora. Waterloo, December 2009. Artificial Intelligence Research Group.

[23] G. O. Vinsauf. *Poetria Nova*. Pontifical Institute of Mediaeval Studies, Toronto, 1967. Trans. Margaret F. Nims.

Modularizing in Glossaries – an Experience Report

Katherine Haramundanis
Hewlett-Packard Company
ESSN Technical Documentation
200 Forest St., Marlborough, MA 01752
Kathy.haramundanis@hp.com

ABSTRACT

Authors working in an industry environment see the advance of technology daily. This constant change in technology is evident in the adoption of new tools and the change of the authoring process. Part of the new experience is the adoption of modular creation of glossaries used in extended documentation sets. This task, the modularization of glossaries, is the subject of this paper, based on my experience in creating glossaries for a documentation set of about 50 documents.

Categories and Subject Descriptors

I.7.1 [**Computing Methodologies**]: Document and Text Editing

General Terms

Documentation, Design, Standardization

Keywords

Information design, Technology, Translation, Writing Standards, Development Process, Design of Communication, Database

1. INTRODUCTION

The obvious benefits of reusing key elements of a document such as glossary terms, where a corporation has taken the time and expended the effort to implement a system where terms can be defined once and used many times without change, are that individual authors do not define the same terms differently, users see consistent terminology defined and used throughout the document set, and translation costs can be effectively managed and minimized [1] [2]. For the author, once the initial transfer into the new environment is reasonably complete and they become familiar with the new processes, there is a significant freedom to focus on the changing parts of the documentation without a need to also develop and define the bulk of the terms in the glossaries of the books they work on [3] [6]. Adding existing glossary terms to a document is much simpler and quicker than defining anew the terms they need, and using an approved list of glossary terms is much easier than developing terms from scratch.

2. The earlier process for creating a glossary term

In the earlier, well-established process of creating a glossary for a corporate document, if a document needed a glossary, the author identified terms in the document that needed definition and took several paths to obtain adequate definitions. For example, short documents, release notes, and similar documents typically do not need a glossary. Longer more extensive documents would usually require a glossary. Consistent use of acronyms also is assisted by a glossary that contains all acronyms used in the document, with their definitions as used in that document. Identification of terms would rely on the expertise of the author knowing which terms their users were already familiar with and which were likely to be unfamiliar. Obtaining a review by an experienced editor was also a useful way to help ensure that terms needing definition in a glossary were identified early. This is still true.

Once terms were identified for which definitions were needed, definitions were sought in the existing document set, by discussion with other team members, and by consulting corporate or industry sources. If more than one definition was available, the author would consult with the documentation and development team to determine which definition was the most appropriate and accurate. If the definition needed to be changed, the team would come to agreement on the final wording.

The writer, in this new environment, deals with a completely new mental paradigm and work process to create their deliverable materials, and with a paradigm shift that directly affects their day-to-day work. Figure 1 illustrates the previous process that created material in this engineering environment. The actor is the content developer or writer and the actions are:

1. Examine book for terms.
2. Scrub the books to establish list of terms in glossary following HP style guide for exclusions (LAN, for example).
3. Work with subject matter experts, content developers (writers), editors, representatives from marketing, and project leads to identify and decide on the definitions to have in the glossary.
4. Compare the terms with other books in the product set to establish the most correct definitions.
5. Create glossary for the book.
6. Load the book with its glossary into the database (Vasont/Oracle).

The final document is posted after the draft has been completed and approved.

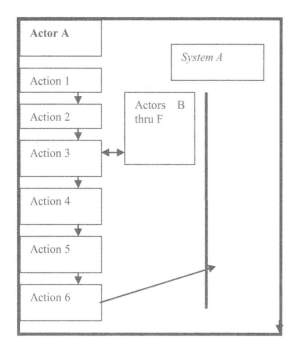

Figure 1. The earlier glossary development process

Authors or writers in corporate environments now often use database management tools such as Vasont/Oracle or Authorit that take advantage of modularization of glossary terms that can be reused both within a product documentation set and across products [4]. The advantages to the author are:

- the text can be reused without change in several contexts or documents

- the text when reused needs to be fact-checked only once

- the text needs to be edited only once

- significant savings are achieved in localization costs

The advantages for the user are:

- the definitions are consistent across the documents in a given product document set

- potentially, the documents are easier to understand because the terminology is used more consistently throughout the product document set

- the terms are used more consistently throughout the document, improving comprehension

3. The new glossary development process

Having identified those terms that are to be included in the glossary for a specific document, the author creates a preliminary glossary with the terms and perhaps tentative definitions and adheres to the requirements of the specific authoring and content management system that is used. This level of development of the glossary is typically done in the editing tool of choice, perhaps Arbortext Editor. This process often entails reviewing the document to ensure that all acronyms and technical terms have

been identified. This activity is especially important if more than one author has been developing content for the document. Figure 2 represents the new glossary development process.

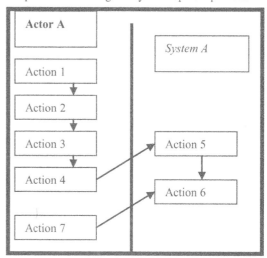

Figure 2. The new glossary development process

In the new glossary development process, the Actor is the content developer or writer, the system is the Vasont/Oracle database supported by Arbortext Editor, and the Actions are:

1. Examine book for terms.
2. Scrub the book to establish preliminary list of terms in glossary following HP style guide for exclusions (LAN, for example).
3. Create the preliminary glossary.
4. Load the book with the preliminary glossary into the database (Vasont/Oracle).
5. Check each term in the glossary against the Approved Terms collection.
6. Replace each term in the book with its equivalent in the Approved Terms collection.
7. Where appropriate, submit new terms to be added to the Approved Terms list.

Note that the Approved Terms list was established by a group managed by a Content Librarian who worked with subject matter experts, content developers (writers), editors, representatives from marketing, and project leads to identify and decide on the definitions in the Approved Terms list. This group worked with definitions from existing books and decided by consensus which definitions to add to the Approved Terms list. They also established workflows for adding new terms or changing existing terms.

Once the terms are identified and coded in the glossary format, they are loaded into the database and converted into modules. This is the formal modularization process.

4. The glossary modularization process

Before the author can modularize a specific new glossary, much pre-work must have been completed by the database glossary team, often a tools team supporting the authoring community [5]. This pre-work, should include:

- An explicit glossary-term format, for example, that the full definition within a glossary includes the glossary division, such as A or B, the glossary term, such as MC, the glossary definition, such as Memory Channel, and perhaps other complementary terms to which the user could be directed (see or see also references).

- A corporate or product style guide, guidelines for wording of glossary entries, common definitions already in use, and perhaps a list of terms too commonly known to include, such as LAN or GUI.

- Training for use of the modularization process.

- Full access and instructions for access to the corporate database.

Each content management system is different, so even experienced authors need training if they move to a new content management system. Finding time for training, both for the trainer and for author, in a relentless corporate environment can be a challenge.

With the terms identified, the author inserts those terms in the glossary for the book they are working on, with or without definitions, and loads the document into the content management system. Depending on the process used in their environment, the author then connects the terms in their glossary to the master list of definitions, adding the approved definitions to the terms in their document. For example, this may mean displaying the glossary for their book in one pane of the screen and displaying the defined glossary terms in a second screen. Figure 2 shows a document in a Modular Books collection that has been expanded to display all chapters and its glossary.

Glossary terms have been modularized by creating references from the approved Glossary Entries collection on the right into the document. For example, on the right, the term CU has been expended to display the definition Control Unit. The last term in the C list on the left, CVS, does not have a definition in the Glossary Entries collection so it appears without a reference such as CU has; the definition if CVS is defined directly with the term.

In a second step (Figure 3), because the term CTG was in the wrong place (out of order alphabetically), it was copied to the correct location and the incorrect entry is marked for deletion. An additional step deletes it altogether, leaving the correct definition in the correct location.

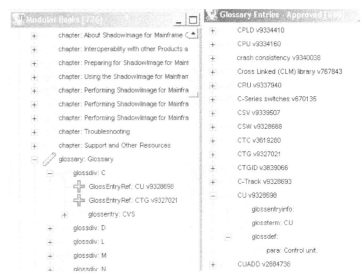

Figure 2. Adding modularized glossary definitions to a glossary.

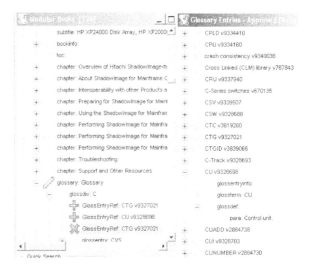

Figure 3 Extraneous glossary definition marked for deletion

5. State Indicators

For each state of a glossary term, whether defined by the author, defined in the approved collection or defined in a working collection where terms are reviewed by an editor for correct wording and definition, the authoring tool provides color-coding in drafts to show the source. This is useful for the author so they know the source of each definition in case they see a need to change it. If the available definition does not meet the needs of the product, the author can request a change to the definition or an additional definition to meet their requirements. Figure 4 shows color-coding in the xml source for a term (white background), an approved term (pink background), and a changed term (light blue background).

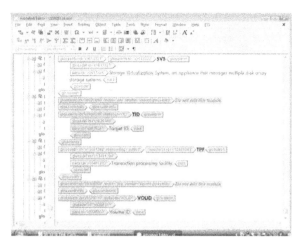

Figure 4 Color-coding of glossary definitions

6. Conclusion

Ensuring that terminology used in user and service documentation is consistent throughout a documentation set has always been a significant challenge. With today's database and content management systems that enable modularization, glossaries can be well honed to meet user needs and be exceptionally consistent across a document set. The process for modularizing a glossary depends entirely on how well the content management system has been set up for this purpose and how thoroughly the glossary modularization process has been defined.

Of 50 documents, zero had all unique glossary terms, all had some terms in common with more than one other document, most glossaries were about two pages (with about 50 terms per page), and the largest glossary was 6 pages (about 150 terms). For glossaries with entries in common with other glossaries, about 60% of their entries could be reused.

The benefits of using an approved list of terms include consistency of definitions across a product line, time-savings in ensuring that terms are defined the same way, except where different definitions were needed, reduced time in translation, timesaving for content developers with no need to create definitions, determine similarities and differences, rework terminology or rework documents.

7. ACKNOWLEDGMENTS

Myr thanks to Hewlett-Packard Co. for the opportunity to present this information on the HP documentation process, to Charlotte Robidoux and the program committee for their helpful comments.

8. REFERENCES

[1] Ament, Kurt. 2003. *Single-sourcing: Building Modular Documentation*. Norwich, NY, William Andrew Publishing/Noyes Publications.

[2] Hackos, J. 2002. *Content Management for Dynamic Web Delivery*. Indianapolis, IN, Wiley Publishers.

[3] Bottitta, Jeanette, Alexia Prendergast Idoura, Lisa Pappa. 2003, Moving to Single Sourcing: Managing the Effects of Organizational Changes. *Technical Communication*, vol. 50, pp. 355-370.

[4] Haramundanis, Katherine. 2009. Modularization – the new paradigm for the information engineer, *Proceedings of the 27th ACM International Conference on Design of Communication, SIGDOC 2009*, pp. 151-154.

[5] Hewett, Beth L.., Charlotte Robidoux. Eds. 2010. Virtual Collaborative Writing in the Workplace: Computer-Mediated Communication Technologies and Processes. Hershey, PA, IGI Global.

[6] Weisbord, M.R. 1987. *Productive Workplaces: organizing and managing for dignity, meaning and community*. San Francisco, CA, Jossey-Bass Inc.

Globally Distributed Content Creation:
Developing Consumable Content for International Markets

Robert Pierce
Advisory Information Developer
Software Group
IBM Corporation
Alfred, ME, USA

robertp@us.ibm.com

Kirk St.Amant
Technical and Professional
Communication Program
East Carolina University
Greenville, NC

stamantk@ecu.edu

Kevin Minerley
Senior Information Developer
Systems &Technology Group
IBM Corporation
Poughkeepsie, NY, USA

k60ekgmc@us.ibm.com

ABSTRACT

This paper examines the globalization of content from the perspective of consumability. The authors describe how technical communicators can use a globally distributed approach to manage the translation of technical content. In so doing, the authors examine how technical communicators might use iterative development practices to improve the development of technical communication products (e.g., software manuals, online help, context-sensitive help, or dynamic help available on the Web) for international audiences of consumers.

Categories and Subject Descriptors

D.2.7 [**Software Engineering**]: Topic-based content, Distributed development, Globalization, Best practices, Configuration management, Asset management, Topic types – documentation.

General Terms

Documentation, Design, Globalization, Theory

Keywords

Software documentation, Distributed development, Global support, User assistance, Translation, Localization, Computer documentation, Information development, Best practices, Development process, Software development.

1. INTRODUCTION

Today, content is increasingly designed for rapid export into the wider global economy.[4][22] Within this context, content is often distributed to employees in different nations. These individuals are, in turn, responsible for drafting, designing, translating, or localizing that content to support a range of products and services.[5][20][5] This approach often means technical communicators must closely coordinate processes with

translators in order to get quality content into a range of overseas markets as quickly as is possible. Achieving this objective, however, is no easy task. Technical communicators can therefore benefit from approaches that can facilitate the development and distribution of translated information.

This paper examines how the globalized – or internationally distributed – development process common in software creation can provide technical communicators with a model for creating translated content for global dissemination. In so doing, the authors review how the concept of consumability creates a context that demands effective translation for success in international marketplaces. The authors also examine how the translation process, in many ways, parallels the globally distributed process used in software development. The authors then present a similar kind of distributed approach technical communicators can use to create consumable technical content for a range of international audiences.

2. CONSUMABILITY AND CONTENT

In today's global economy, the success of an organization is often connected to the concept of *consumability*. Consumability, in turn, involves the ease with which a particular group of consumers (i.e., a target market) can use a particular product, service, or information set. [21] From a marketing perspective, the idea is consumers will be more likely to purchase a product that is easy to use or that has operating instructions that are easy to follow. If a company creates products – or product instructions – that allow for ease of product use among an intended consumer group, the company has increased the consumability of its product (i.e., has increased the chances consumers will find the product worth purchasing). From this perspective, an organization can use consumability as a strategic advantage to beat out its competition in a given market.

When expanded to a global context, consumability often involves how well a given product or service meets the expectations of consumers in overseas markets.[4][19][22] In such cases, globalizing the consumability of an informational product can involve everything from the language in which information is presented to the configuration of the interfaces used to access that information.[4][22] Accordingly, the failure to address the information seeking and using expectations of other cultures can result in a product being rejected by different groups of overseas consumers.[19]

Such a situation can be particularly acute in relation to technical communication. That is, cultures can use documentation as a mechanism for assessing the quality, appropriateness, and usability of affiliated products.[19] Organizations therefore need to think about globalizing the consumability of not only their products, but also all informational and instructional materials associated with those products.[19] The need to globalize such materials effectively, moreover, is particularly intense at this point in time as a growing number of businesses in an increasing number of nations are now competing for consumers in today's global marketplace. Within this context, mechanisms that can contribute to the speed with which organizations produce quality content for international consumers can help those organizations capture global market share.

According to these ideas, translation is, perhaps, the absolute required minimum needed to enhance the consumability of content for international consumers. Translation is also often an essential step to creating effective international content in any situation. (The idea being for overseas users to consider content consumable, it must be in a language they can read.) However, translation is a nuanced process involving both the language used to convey information and the style – or the rhetoric – employed to present ideas. Thus effective – or consumable – translation involves transferring the meaning of content into the language AND the stylistic expectations of another cultural group.[15]

Addressing factors of language and rhetoric, however, takes time and can delay the international release of key products. By contrast, rushing the translation of content in order to get a product to market as quickly as possible can result in materials that are difficult to understand or use (are of poor consumability). Finding a mechanism for creating quick and effective content for global distribution has thus become a holy grail of sorts for the modern company. Technical communicators, in turn, are often at the heart of this situation, for they are usually the individuals who create the content that will be translated or who work with translators to produce final, translated content for global consumers.[5][20]

As a result, mechanisms that contribute to the rapid development of quality technical translations can provide technical communicators with new methods for contributing value to their employing organizations. In so doing, technical communicators can also insulate themselves against economic downturns. (As individuals such as Giammona [6] and as St.Amant and Cunningham [16]have noted, finding new ways to contribute value to an organization can help technical communicators remain successful employees – as well as remain successfully employed – in the current global economy.) For these reasons, technical communicators have a great deal to gain from systems that can enhance the process by which consumable content is created for international audiences. The globalized distributed development (GDD) method used to create software can provide technical communicators with an effective approach for achieving this objective.

3. GLOBALLY DISTRIBUTED DEVELOPMENT

Any work done even by one person in more than one place is distributed work. Globalized distributed work is an instance of work dispersed to persons in different nations. [10, 14] In globalized distributed development (GDD), individuals working in different nations use an iterative approach to produce a product that can be released into the global marketplace relatively soon after the product has been finalized.

GDD is often used in software development where individuals employ tools, processes, and governance that supports application lifecycle management (ALM) and software development best practices. Such processes often required software developers to account for cultural issues associated with language and with rhetorical style when developing a product. (The design of an interface, for example, needs to be open enough to allow for effective translations of different commands to appear effectively on that interface.[4]) According to these ideas, a globally distributed approach to product development might involve the following factors: [4, 14]:

- Version control and asset management

  Anyone working with another content developer must be able to get to a known state and be able to return to other known states in a repeatable and reliable fashion. Accordingly, many coding systems exist to help with version control and asset management. [10, 14] In all cases, one needs to decide on what level of granularity makes sense for the scope of the project and the units necessary to share or globalize (e.g., DITA focuses on a topic level).

- Component based architectures

  Using a sufficiently granular content architecture allows for more choice in returning to a known state from which to continue production. Granularity has a down side if one fails to look for larger patterns of common components as it may imply an ongoing repetition of building commonly grouped components from scratch.

- Change management

  Is often metadata on the version control and today often loosely revolves around fixing defects in a given version or enhancing a given version.

- Process modeling

  Provides templates and patterns of components to help get around the problems of the granularization necessary for component-based architecture.

- Iterative development

  Presupposes iterative testing where target audiences should be involved in the tests early and often to avoid cognitive drift.

- Requirements management

  May fall under change management and defect management.

- Product delivery

  Translating both a product and its user assistance to non-English languages. For example, translation packaging, translation centers, handling the translation returns, and testing them enables an online information center in multiple languages to be available.

The question then becomes how to apply a parallel approach to the translation of content for global audiences. To explore such relationships, one must review the process commonly used to produce effective translations.

4. TRANSLATION PROCESSING AND TESTING

The translation process often involves the following steps [7, 10]:

1. **Create user stories from customer requirements**. This step is similar to storyboarding or outlining before writing and is often skipped in lieu of jumping directly into documenting or coding.

   Add multi-value weighting to each of the divisions in your storyboard or outline, displaying such attributes as:

   - Revenue potential
   - Market growth potential, including globalized markets.
   - Retention possibilities

   Categorize and aggregate the divisions and their attributes without losing the flow of the user story. Determine a set of relative criteria that demonstrates when customer requirements are fulfilled.

2. **Create relevant test cases** based on the user stories, focusing on the criteria that demonstrate when customer requirements are fulfilled.

   Document and code to the test cases as a subset of creating the test-cases rather than document or code directly, because without the test cases following and directly relating to the user stories, how will you know what your document or code is succeeding?

3. **Unit test the source** against the test cases as soon as you have even a skeleton matching the test criteria. Do unit testing on an iterative basis as you add more substance in each iteration and make adjustments as appropriate. Where possible, take the work back to the real users or customers, if possible.

   The idea is to catch problems early. This is an excellent time to start focusing on the globalization aspects using terminology, style, and grammar checkers against applicable standards.

4. **Functional test the packaged deliverable** against the test cases that derived from the customer requirements.

   Unit test above is a sanity check and "does-it-look-correct" check above. This is a test of beyond the looking reasonable and tests for whether the packaged deliverable works as expected, in the test cases. Again, many free interfaces are available for performing tests. For example, the Selenium IDE helps you automate test cases, especially in Web applications.

   Functional tests refine test cases, which in turn often create some questions to ask customers during later iterations of testing.

5. **Repeat** the above until the customer requirements are satisfied.

The focus is requirements, test cases derived from these requirements, coding to these test cases, and compliance with test cases. The act of development and deployment loses it centrality to become an iterative service to meet customer requirements and not an end in and of itself.

The following image shows an example of the tasks and process for information development and translating the content for inclusion into a product or other delivery mechanism such as Web content.

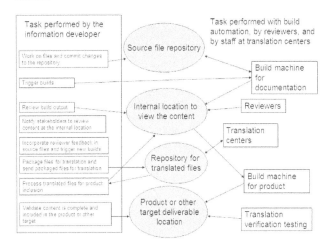

Figure 1. Information development and translation example

As this image illustrates, in addition to the tasks for developing and delivering documentation in a native language, is the added complexity of managing the translation of content, handling the translated versions of all the files and ensuring they are included in the final product or documentation deliverable.

Through this approach, organizations can produce translations that best meet the objectives of the content creator (i.e., the technical communicator) while also meeting the linguistic and the rhetorical expectation (i.e., the consumability standard) of various global consumers. Each step in this process, however, brings with it issues of complexity and change that require careful management to produce a quality product. For the technical communicators who coordinate such activities, a globally distributed approach to content development and management can serve as a mechanism for managing complexity as well as identifying and addressing potential challenges.

5. A GLOBALLY DISTRIBUTED APPROACH TO MANAGING TRANSLATION

Interestingly, the five-part approach to translation noted here overlaps with GDD practices such as version control, change management, modeling, and iterative development. Based on this overlap, technical communicators could use ideas associated with the global distribution of product development to manage the process of translating technical content – and thus producing a technical (informational) product. While methods for applying such ideas can vary, this section provides one perspective for applying a distributed content management approach to the translation process.

5.1.1 Communication for a distributed team

A versioning and content management system provides a necessary backbone teams need to establish who has what when and to allow for iterative refinement and execution of responsibilities. [14] Instant Messaging, chat rooms, and Twitter-like utilities can act as recording secretaries of decisions made during scheduled and ad-hoc meetings. Additionally, there are aggregators that allow individuals to "post-once" and hit all these channels. Wikis, Facebook, and other social computing interfaces can provide areas for longer term, longer thread decisions. User tagging content or authors tagging it with mutually agreed upon memes for globalization makes retrieval easier.

5.1.2 Coordinating with translation centers

Many translation centers are not located in the same country where the content creation takes place. Thus, effective communication and collaboration are essential for the successful development of products and information for international consumers. [8, 11, 17] Translation of content starts early, with agreement on a schedule and on what programmatic checkers or human processes need to be done. Agreed-upon access to a common content manager and a certain level of refinement facilitates coordinating with the translation centers. [2, 10]

Choosing a common content management system or at least a common format of packaged deliverables minimizes non-core work of unpacking the content to be translated. Another aspect of success in such cases is providing clear instructions to aid in understanding how to repackage the translated content so it can be processed, returned, and handled so it is included in product builds. [2, 7, 17]

5.1.3 Using common terminology database

There are several terminology databases that can help provide input to using terms that can be more clearly translated and with less cultural implications than other terms. [1] For example WordNet, a lexical database for the English language from the Cognitive Science Laboratory at Princeton University (http://wordnet.princeton.edu/) offers an online utility to search for terms and get definitions and examples. For the term, "globalization," here is what is returned: "Growth to a global or worldwide scale - "the globalization of the communication industry.""

Individual, groups, teams, or organizations can use a distributed alternative dictionary as a base to make and share refinements to content. It is preferable to update style and grammar databases in the same manner and treat semantics, syntax, and grammar checkers as a necessary complementary suite much as one would if compiling code. [12, 18]

5.1.4 Versioning and content management

Using a content management system and designing a logical structure for the content for all languages can help streamline and manage the complexity of the translation process. The following image shows an example of a file system for managing multiple languages of the same content/deliverables:

In this example, versioning keeps track of stepwise refinement and content management helps in keeping the ownership and responsibility facets disciplined and repeatable.

5.1.5 Testing and test-driven development

Testing relates to all other tasks in the development process. The content creator usually has primary ownership for fixing the content based on any tests. Reviewing is a form of testing and often starts with programmatic checks for spelling, format or style, and grammar at least in the base/source language. This type of review often replaces a step left to humans in the past.

Even if the content passes language, style, grammar, and other programmatic standard checking, the task of testing should be distributed to another different content owner or a team of content owners – preferably, a team which has some stake in using the content as well (e.g., marketers who will use the same content to later develop related product advertising copy). Through a series of tests and stepwise refinements of the content based on the test results many of the mechanics of making the task of globalizing the content becomes easier.

One method of efficient testing on localized online help is to use a Web browser and set the language option for each language into which the help was translated and check Web pages in each of those languages. What follows is an example of an online help topic that needs to have the Japanese translation of the help topic tested:

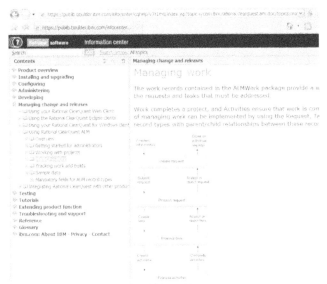

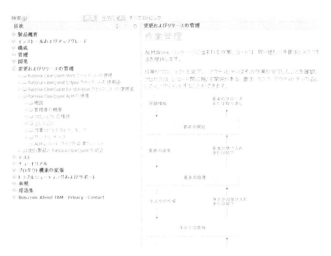

To do so, the tester first locates the language preference to that language:

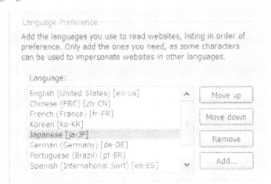

Then, the tester moves that language to the top of the list:

After clicking, "**OK**," the tester reloads the Web page so the content is refreshed in the Japanese version, if it is available:

If there was no Japanese translation available, then the tester would still see the English version.

In this closer image of the content, note that both the topic file content and the inserted image have been translated whereas trademarked product names and English terms that reside in the source code and are not translated and remain in English (in this example, "ALMWork," which is a record type):

The translation of images may not be handled in the same manner as the actual textual content and might go through a different translation process. [3]

Here is the same content produced using the same steps, but this time, used to test the Brazilian Portuguese (pt-BR) translation of the help topic:

Gerenciando Trabalho

Os registros do trabalho contidos no pacote ALMWork fornecem um acompanhar os pedidos e as tarefas que devem ser endereçados.

O trabalho conclui um projeto e as Atividades asseguram que o tra concluído. O processo de gerenciamento de trabalho pode ser impl utilizando os tipos de registros Pedido, Tarefa e Atividade com os relacionamentos pai/filho entre esses registros.

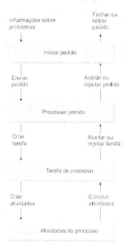

5.1.6 Delivery

Properly done, delivery issues are partially or completely addressed during the process of the packaging for translation tasks as the translators are also review the content as they translate it. In a sense, translators are the first consumers of the content, although they are highly invested consumers and likely view more of the content then any given external customer.

Because Web content can be updated dynamically at any time, the method of providing help content in multiple languages can be developed, delivered, tested, and supported on an iterative basis.

6. SUMMARY

The recurring themes of the importance of metadata and of globalization are viewed as increasingly relevant to all aspects of design of communication (DOC). The same DOC principles and focus applies to supporting multiple languages and cultures and the searchability for them. The degree of complexity, however, is significantly greater to manage in such cases.

Products, like their supporting technical documentation, are commonly translated into many languages. Thus, a consistent and well-managed approach to the creation and the translation of content makes it easier for people in an organization to support each other in order to produce successful and uniform content for overseas consumers.

The benefits of following a common process allows for many people in an organization to be subject matter experts. Such an approach also avoids problems associated with having only one person to rely on when there are points of failure. Generally, many people are able to diagnose and resolve issues when they arise at any point in the workflow. A globally distributed approach to content development can, by contrast, allow multiple individuals to participate in content development processes in a way that increases the consumability of content on an international scale.

In terms of future enhancements to globalizing content management, the process is complex, and there are many potential points of failure in the workflow process. Automating as many aspects of the translation process as possible, however, benefits an organization by freeing up resources to do actual content work. [13] Such automation also helps reduce human errors in handling the translation returns and ensures all translated files are sourced in their correct target locations.

There are many aspects to the translation process that should be automated to prevent common human errors (e.g., saving files in the wrong directories or failing to send all required files for translation). Automating as many of the tasks that require specific steps but not human choice will benefit workers and can increase their efficiency by allowing them to focus more on core job tasks.

This paper has not addressed the actual quality of translated content, but this is another area of the globalization of technical communication that requires more studies for content quality and consumability. [9]

7. REFERENCES

[1] Anacleto, Junia, Lieberman, Henry, Tsutsumi, Marie, Neris, Vânia, Carvalho, Aparecido, Espinosa, Jose, and Zem-Mascarenhas, Silvia, "Can Common Sense uncover cultural differences in computer applications?" Advanced Interaction Laboratory – LIA. MIT Media Laboratory, Cambridge MA.

[2] Diamant, E. Ilana, Fussell, Susan R., and Lo, Fen-Ly, Computer mediated technology for global collaboration. "Collaborating across cultural and technological boundaries: team culture and information use in a map navigation task," Proceeding of the 2009 international workshop on intercultural collaboration. February 2009, ACM Press, pp. 175-184.

[3] Donney, Jerry, Murphy, Steve, Sacre, Chris, Scholz, Alexander, and Walters, David, "Globalization of graphics: delineating a research into using the scalable vector graphics file format to improve the translation of graphics," Proceedings of the 26th International Conference on Design of Communication, Lisbon, Portugal, September 2008, ACM Press, pp. 87-92.

[4] Esselink, Bert, A practical guide to localization. Philadelphia, PA: John Benjamins Publishing Company, 2000.

[5] Flint, Patricia; van Slyke, Melanie Lord; Stärke-Meyerring, Doreen; and Thompson, Aimee, "Going online: Helping technical communicators help translators," Technical Communication, Volume 46, Issue 2, May 1999, pp. 238-248.

[6] Giammona, Barbara, "The future of technical communication: How innovation, technology, information management, and other forces are shaping the future of the profession," Technical Communication, Volume 51, Issue 3, August 2004, pp. 349-366.

[7] Gopalakrishnan, Gopakumar, Pillai, Sreekumar, and Dhanju, Nidhi, "Collaboration in offshore software projects: practices and challenges," Proceeding of the 2009 International Workshop on Intercultural Collaboration, February 2009, ACM Press, pp. 225-228.

[8] Grachev, Mikhail, "Culture-sensitive global strategies," Proceeding of the 2009 International Workshop on Intercultural Collaboration, February 2009, ACM Press, pp. 229-232.

[9] Hargis, Gretchen, "Readability and computer documentation," Journal of Computer Documentation (JCD), Volume 24 Issue 3, August 2000, ACM Press.

[10] Herbsleb, J.D and Moitra, D., Global software development, IEEE Software, March-April 2001, pp. 16-20.

[11] Christine Koh, Damien Joseph, Soon Ang. "Cultural intelligence and collaborative work: intercultural competencies in global technology work teams," Proceeding of the 2009 International Workshop on Intercultural Collaboration, February 2009, ACM Press, pp. 261-264.

[12] Lopez, Adam, "Statistical machine translation," Computing Surveys (CSUR), Volume 40 Issue 3, Article No. 8, August 2008.

[13] Pérez-Quiñones, Manuel A., Padilla-Falto, Olga I. and McDevitt, Kathleen, "Automatic language translation for user interfaces," TAPIA '05: Proceedings of the 2005 conference on diversity in computing, October 2005, ACM Press.

[14] Pierce, R., Leveraging Technology Affinity – Applying a Common Tools and Practices to Information Development, SIGDOC '05, October, 2005, Coventry, UK. ACM Press, pp. 123-130.

[15] St.Amant, Kirk, "The role of rhetoric in localization and offshoring." Handbook of Research on Innovations in Database Technologies and Applications: Current and Future Trends. Eds. Laura C. Rivero, Jorge H. Doorn, and Viviana E. Ferraggine. Hershey, PA: IGI Global. (2009): pp. 844-851.

[16] St.Amant, Kirk and Cunningham, Robert, "Examining open source software in offshoring contexts: A Perspective on adding value in an age of globalization," Technical Communication, Volume 56, Issue 4, November 2009, pp. 361-369.

[17] Sato, Kumi, Okamoto, Kohei, and Miyao, Masaru, "Japan, moving towards becoming a multi-cultural society, and the way of disseminating multilingual disaster information to non-Japanese speakers," Proceeding of the 2009 International Workshop on Intercultural Collaboration, February 2009, ACM Press, pp. 51-60.

[18] Ueffing, Nicola and Ney. Hermann, "Word-Level Confidence Estimation for Machine Translation," Computational Linguistics, Volume 33 Issue 1, March 2007, MIT Press, pp. 9-40.

[19] Ulijn, Jan M. and Strother, Judith, *Communicating in Business and Technology: From Psycholinguistic Theory to International Practice*. Frankfurt; Peter Lang, 1995.

[20] Walmer, Daphne. "One company's efforts to improve translation and localization," Technical Communication, Volume 46, Issue 2, May 1999, pp. 230-237.

[21] Wikipedia, http://en.wikipedia.org/wiki/Consumability

[22] Yunker, John, *Beyond borders: Web globalization strategies*. Indianapolis, IN: New Riders Publishing, 2003.

The importance of Documentation, Design and Reuse in Risk Management for SPL

Luanna Lopes Lobato

UFPE - CIn - Recife - PE, Brazil
Tel: +55 81 2126-8430
UFG – DCC - Catalão - GO, Brazil
Tel: +55 64 3441-1510

lll@cin.ufpe.br

Pádraig O'Leary

UFBA – DCC - Salvador – BA, Brazil
Tel: +55 81 3283-6258

padraig@dcc.ufba.br

Eduardo Santana de Almeida

UFBA – DCC - Salvador – BA, Brazil
Tel: +55 81 3283-6258

esa@dcc.ufba.br

Sílvio Romero de Lemos Meira

UFPE - CIn - Recife - PE, Brazil
Tel: +55 81 2126-8430
C.E.S.A.R - Recife – PE, Brazil
Tel: +55 81 3425.4700

srlm@cin.ufpe.br

ABSTRACT

Software Product Lines (SPL) is a methodology focusing on systematic software reuse, multiple benefits have been reported as a result of this type of software development. However, establishing a SPL is not a simple task. It is a challenging activity raising many challenges for engineering and management. This research aims to manage the risks during SPL development to provide traceability among them. For this, it is important that the risks are documented and there is a common design related to them. As solution, we identified the strengths and weakness in SPL development and the importance in designing of communication for risk documentation.

Categories and Subject Descriptors

D.3.3 [**Software Engineering**]: Management.

General Terms

Documentation, Design, Standardization, Verification.

Keywords

Software Product Line, Documentation, Web Products.

1. INTRODUCTION

A Software Product Lines (SPL) is a set of software-intensive systems sharing a common, managed set of features that satisfy the specific needs of a particular market segment or mission and that are developed from a common set of core assets in a prescribed way [1]. It involves the management of variabilities and commonalities among several applications, which increases

its complexity compared to Single System Development (SSD). Thus, developing a SPL requires time and systematic planning to achieve positive results; otherwise the investment can be lost due to failures in the project.

According to Boehm and DeMarco (1997) software developments risky nature is easy enough to acknowledge in the abstract, but harder to acknowledge in real-world situations. Therefore, it is necessary to predict, control and manage risk.

Documents can be used for risk avoidance; their value should be evident for a project manager. Since team members will almost always face similar obstacles, it is imperative that they share how they overcame these obstacles. Documentation can ensure the same mistakes are not repeated in the next project. This is particularly true for SPL development as several products are typically derived from the same platform.

Documentation plays an important role in the capturing of tacit knowledge particularly when there is a high rate of staff turnover. Thus, it is important to capture the knowledge about the project. Therefore, if a team member moves on, the valuable knowledge, good practices and lessons learnt will not be lost.

Risk Management (RM) documentation is important for avoiding recreating the risks already identified. Insights into RM documentation were identified in a systematic literature review in RM for SPL and through two SPL projects, where the risks were anticipated and resolved. Thus, we have identified risk and the mitigation strategies to avoid them.

This research aims to manage risk within SPL and define how these risks can be represented, providing design of communication among them. The risks were mapped in documents and designed in a way to provide insights about them through cross-referencing. This enables traceability amongst risk. Reuse across RM is focused on the ability of reusing this documentation for different products across the SPL. Therefore it is necessary to verify the lessons learnt from previous experiences and to predict, control and manage risk.

It is also important to highlight that RM documentation is a 'live' document, as in it should be constantly (re-)visited and updated during the project lifetime and after its conclusion. This is in order to gather ongoing and postmortem information about the project, mainly about new risks that were not previously identified.

Thus, this work is intended to analyze and document the risks inherent in SPL development using the literature and case study research to identify risks in software projects. This documentation is important to provide information about the magnitude, impacts probabilities and mitigation strategies about the risks.

RM in SPL is an open issue with currently little research in this area.

The methodology that will be used, to provide the design of communication for the risks identified, will be best practice research on SPL, through the findings provided by academy and industry. This information will be used to collect insights about RM in SPL development.

The remainder of this paper is organized as it follows. A brief overview of SPL and RM is described in the next subsection. Section 3 carries a discussion based on state of the art, highlight the related works. The research scenario is described in Section 4, emphasizing the risks and lessons learned observed, which will be used to provide design of communication on risks identified. And, we present the conclusions and some promising venues for future research in documentation for RM in SPL.

2. SPL WITH RISK MANAGEMENT

Software Product Lines (SPL) is an approach for software development focusing on systematic reuse. Benefits regarding the effort reduction, time-to-market and quality improvement in software development have been reported as a result of adopting SPL through its systematic exploitation of reuse opportunities.

According to Schmid (2002) these benefits (effort reduction, quality improvement and time-to-market decrease) arise through reuse opportunities that are presented due to the similarities between systems within the product line. SPL involves the management of different products features, where variabilities and commonalities are managed among several applications.

However, establishing a SPL is not a simple matter. The approach is particularly complex, raising specific challenges for engineering and management. SPL adoption involves major investment and considerable risks are associated with it. Moreover, technical and non-technical aspects have to be addressed to obtain the benefits of organization-wide software reuse. In this context, it is necessary to manage the risks that may be presented during the SPL development, in a way to improve development and provide the project success.

SPL adopters are typically more concerned about the issues related to the technical aspects of the development, such as, architecture development or domain analysis (Schmid, 2001). However, just technical capabilities for an SPL cannot guarantee the adoption success. The development must be supported by an auxiliary method that helps the stakeholders to make decisions during the development process. Thus, other aspects must also be relevant to manage the risks present in SPL development and provide a design of communication about them.

RM supports SPL development in order to provide process improvement and problem avoidance within the project. For RM additional investments are necessary to start the development focusing on quality services. Consequently, RM practice will avoid some problems that occur in some stages of SPL development, based on the management of the actions that must be following and performed during the SPL introduction.

Boehm (1989) defines RM as an attempt to formalize risk into a readily applicable set of principles and practices. The goal is to identify, address, and eliminate software risk items before they become either threats to successful software operation or major sources of software rework.

Simply stated, risk is the possibility of loss or damage [6]. This definition can be translated into the fundamental concept of RM: "risk exposure" (also called, "risk impact" or "risk factor"), likelihood, contingency plan and mitigation methods. Implementing RM involves inserting the RM principles and practices into existing life-cycle management practices. The key contribution of software risk management is to create this focus on critical success factors - and to provide the techniques that let the project deal with them.

In large project development, the product lines benefits are stressed and very little attention is paid to possible risks [7]. However, in practice, it is important to notice and understand which risks can happen, if they may turn into problems or opportunities and how they should be dealt with.

The literature reports that RM can significantly improve software project outcomes [8]. There are many risks in software projects, from several sources, which need to be controlled during the software development process.

Thus, RM is particularly important in development projects due to the inherent uncertainties that most software projects face. It is necessary to apply risk-reduction activities. These activities are designed to minimize a particular risk or group of risks i.e. to minimize the likelihood that a problem corresponding to the risk will occur [9].

In the article by Hartmann (2006), according to CHAOS 2004 report, in SSD, only 29% of the projects were finished successfully; 18% of the projects failed without giving any delivery and 53% of the projects were finished with overtime or over their budget. The report states that the causes of failure in software development projects are also related to failure in RM. A software development project is rich in strategic opportunities, but it is also subject to multiple sources and high levels of uncertainty. When managed properly, uncertainty creates opportunities, thus it is important to manage the uncertainty [11].

Despite of the problems found with risk occurrence in projects, risk itself is not bad, it is essential to improve the project and failure is often a key part of learning. However, according Van Scoy (1992), we must learn to balance the possible negative consequences of risk against the potential benefits of its associated opportunity.

RM it is not just a process for avoiding risk. The aim of risk management is not to eliminate risk, rather to manage the risks involved in all activities to maximize opportunities and minimize adverse effects. More specifically, risk management is a formal (business) process used to identify risks and opportunities across the organization, assess the potential impact of these events and then provide a method for addressing these impacts to either reduce threats to an acceptable level or achieve opportunities.

This paper aims to emphasize what are the most common risks and provide adequate mechanisms or techniques to mitigate them, explaining how they can be handled or even avoided. Risk documentation is necessary to avoid the same problems that can become real in projects. With RM it is possible to provide the design of communication, with goals for establish the traceability among the risks.

As supported for this method, we verified the documentation about decisions, functionalities, that were present in SPL and SSD in the literature, and lessons learned. Thus, the documentation and design of the risks are reused in several products to avoid the same problems faced during software projects development.

Despite evident benefits in adopting RM during software project development, it is not an easy task to define and to use guidelines to capture and share what really worked and did not work in a project. It is necessary to establish the culture inside the team members. Therefore the design of communication, through documentation and reuse of assets, are important points to provide this management.

3. STATE OF THE ART

To identify the SPL risks reported by the literature a systematic review was performed. Through the systematic review, it was possible to collect the most important characteristics to provide design of communication in relation to the risks in SPL development. In addition, we identified what were the main research gaps facing RM in SPL.

According to our systematic analysis, we verified that no approaches have been developed for RM in an SPL context and, when some studies exist, they are defined without details. Therefore, although studies have shown that RM is necessary to achieve software project success, RM still faces obstacles before being institutionalized by SPL companies.

In this research, the risks in software development are identified with an emphasis on the RM in SPL. With the lack of an existing approach for RM in SPL, this work has been developed. It stressed the importance of documenting the risks identified and the reuse the strategies defined in the documentation to resolve the risks in future projects.

Therefore, the design of communication of the risks in SPL is the main focus of this work. Communication of risks is essential to provide insights about the traceability among them. This research comes to facilitate the projects development, providing a documented list about the risks, which must be monitoring throughout the SPL development. With this strategy of risk documentation, managers should be able to identify, prioritize, and quantify the risk types involved in their projects.

3.1 Related Works

According to Boban, Pozgaj and Sertic (2003) the essence of risk classification is not in precisely defining risk categories, but in identifying and describing as much risk as possible in the project.

This work intends to identify a set of best practice to build a more reliable and effective approach for RM in SPL through the use and reuse of documentation. In our research, we highlighted the importance of risks documentation and design, as well as the reuse of risk documentation, emphasizing the need to document risks in relation to design of communication.

Throughout our systematic review in RM in SPL, we observed an increase in the number of published papers covering RM in SPL over the last 10 years. This recent increase may be a reflection of a growing awareness of the importance of motivating RM for SPL. Alternatively, this increase may just match a general rise in published papers in SPL. Researchers and practitioners have to rely on practitioner books in order to get information on RM approaches or, at worst, not apply any strategy to control risks in SPL development. This means not having sufficient contingency plans and relevant mitigation plans to provide for RM.

In a systematic review of RM in SPL, it was observed that risk strategies and mitigation techniques are not addressed by all literature that mentions them. The handling of these remaining risks is actually an open question. Some risks are described, in a superficial way.

Despite the benefits in SPL, there are high risk level due to its inherent complexity. Thus, SPL development is more complex and demanding than SSD.

The follow research is the most important for our context. Initially, Schmid (2002) propose an approach related to a reuse process with the development of PULSE-ECO. Next, Voget and Becker (2002) describe some risks for immature scope, highlight that it is a risk if the scope is vague, is subject to changes or the scope size is inadequate. In 2003, Riva and Del Rosso showed research described some of risks that are identified in SPL approaches, such as: Missed Schedule, Malpractice in Management, Failure in Requirements Identification, Core Assets Instability and Slower Process of Change. Four years later, the concept of product line assessment is proposed by Olumofin and Mišić (2007).

The literature on RM for SPL presents a conflicting and partial scenario. It is clear that there is a need for RM practices in SPL development, however, there are few studies which present relevant information. Most studies mention the importance of RM, although the steps for managing risks – as well as their results – are not clearly specified.

Highlighting this figure, it was possible to observe that there are needs for extensive research in this area. Further empirical studies should be performed with sufficient rigor to enhance the body of evidence in RM within SPL engineering. In this context, there is a clear need for conducting studies comparing alternative methods. In order to address scalability and popularization of the approaches, future research should be invested in risk support and in combined SPL adoption strategies, mainly in documentation, design and reuse of the products assets.

4. RISKS AND LESSONS LEARNT

In this section we will present the lessons learned during our research. Not much data has been published on experiences and lessons learned for RM in SPL in a way that demonstrates the design for communication of those risks. In this section, we show practices that can be used during the SPL development as strategies for avoiding risk.

These insights were collect through a systematic literature review, in an industrial and academic context. Thus, we collected and documented feedback and lessons learnt from various studies, which we can use to demonstrate the direction of RM within SPL.

In the following section, we show these risks and what are the lessons learnt that can be linked to resolve them. These are documented with goals to provide insights for the manager. The risks are identified by ID and name and classified according to type.

4.1 Project Risks

R1-Complexity of SPL:

Product line architectures pose unique challenges, which are not present in single product architectures. This difference makes the assessment of such architectures rather difficult. At the most superficial level, quality attribute scenarios for SPL are more numerous than in the case of a single product architecture, SPL architecture is more context dependent, and they are more complex as well [16].

Architectural issues are also a few of the many issues that have to be considered. SPL approach involves more than architectural issues. If no due allowance is made for these multiple aspects, the chances of success will be small. This helped us compare business, architectural, process and organizational aspects of the approaches.

Compared to developing a SSD, an SPL requires extra resources in process and tools development, core development, and product management [17].

R2-Inadequate CM:

A configuration management plan, which could integrate smoothly and systematically with the configuration management system of individual projects. We believe that the shared responsibility for the maintenance of the product line assets will result in great benefit, as any software product can take advantage of any problem fixing or in-service experience of the rest of the software products [26].

R3-Malpractice in Management:

SPL demands software management and development practices, which are capable of coping with new levels of organizational and architectural complexity [27].

Experiences shows the importance of synchronizing needs, defining roles, communication between core asset team and implementation team for architectural integrity, and using proper tools for dependency analysis [18].

Management at the technical (or project) and organizational (or enterprise) levels must be strongly committed to the SPL effort for the product line's success [23].

R4-Inadequate Technical Documentation: As scoping starts early in the SPL development life-cycle, little documentation exists and the exchange of information needs to rely on personal communication. Existing approaches are usually not sufficiently documented to be replicable, nor is validation data available that allows assessing the contribution of the approach to the field [3]. The documentation became too bulky or the product developers could not find the right information [7]. Poor description of the generic architecture and requirements documentation is a risk for project success [27]. The lack of documentation on implicit properties frequently results in mistakes. Similarly, in some projects if there insufficient, irrelevant and voluminous documentation [31].

R5-Lack of SPL Information:

While commercial tool vendors do not yet pay particular attention to SPL-specific needs, a few research prototypes from universities show that SPL support is possible [27].

R6-Absence of Domain Experts:

With the growing investment by both public and private sector organizations in software product-line architecture, managers need to know the organizational factors affecting its success [25].

R7-Missed Schedule:

From an economic viewpoint, a leveraged SPL adoption entails a revolution, because the company can address a completely new market segment with low costs and few risks by building on an existing PL infrastructure. Different technical domains, even within the same SPL, can vary considerably in terms of their potential benefit and inherent risks for product line engineering [19].

R8-No product focus:

The main goal of the product family architecture is to describe the commonality and variability of the family in order to make explicit the variation points of the products [15]. Product line requirements are traceable to higher level specifications (e.g., stakeholder requirements in different projects), and also to product line analysis- and design artifacts (e.g., use cases, state machines and components) [22].

R9-Immature Architecture:

The assessment of the SPL architectures has been based on methods developed for single product architectures. The complexity of evaluating PL architecture like the dual form of the architectures, existence of variation points, the need for associating context with the large number of quality attributes scenarios and the need to perform quality tradeoff analysis across the SPL architectures has largely been ignored [16].

Technical factors do not by themselves explain the success of product-line architecture. Only in conjunction with appropriate organizational behaviors can software architecture effectively control project complexity [25].

R10-Pollution of the platform:

Technically excellent product-line architectures do fail, often because they are not effectively used. Some are developed but never used; others lose value as product teams stop sharing the common architecture; still others achieve initial success but fail to keep up with a rapidly growing product mix. Sometimes the architecture deterioration is not noticed at first, masked by what appears to be a productivity increase [25].

R11-Platform not Mutable:

Introduction of new requirements in a dynamic market is critical to handle the forthcoming requirements in time. Even though the problem of incorporating new requirements is not specific to product family architectures, the process has to accomplish an even more difficult task [15].

R12-Core Assets Instability:

When the business becomes more mature: New investments are needed to consolidate the software assets. The various sets of products are migrated towards a SPL in order to keep all the software variants under control. The organization needs to adjust its operating procedures to support the global management of the products lifecycle (from requirements engineering to testing) [15].

R13-Inappropriate Reuse Activity:

Reuse may decrease system integrity as the potential failures of the new system might have not been considered in the original analysis of the reused software. The configuration management of the product line has therefore two dimensions: Managing the artefacts 'across time' (version update) and 'across different projects' [26].

Reuse has always been considered the main approach to achieve major improvements in productivity and quality in software engineering. Consequently, much work, both from academia and industry, has been undertaken with reuse as target [30].

R14-Slower process of change:

The evolution of a SPL is mainly driven by two forces: the consolidation of the assets in the platform and the creation of new products. The platform slowly evolves by incorporating the new architectural requirements, while new products are added by introducing new features [15].

R15-Lack of Tool Support:

Establishing a traceable link between the requirements, design, and the reusable code can enable the deployment of reusable software in an effective and analyzable way. Therefore, reuse should be addressed holistically, rather than being limited to the code, where most reuse attempts have failed [26].

4.2 Process Risks

R16-Immature Process:

A SPL increases quality, shortens time to market, and helps specify the "right" product features. Strong process structures help manage complexity and conflicts between the requirements of individual products and projects [17].

R17-Immature Domain:

Product lines are only successful if the underlying domain releases arrive in due time with necessary quality level and the major functional contents. From a software engineering perspective this is an obvious contradiction. Impacts cannot be fully assessed and micro-managed in advance, neither can risks or people skills [24].

4.3 Product Risks

R18-Inadequate Quality of the Artifacts:

Successful product line engineering requires management and coordination of both the core asset and product development projects to meet the organization's overall business goals [28].

This implies the use of repeatable and systematic procedures to ensure that the set of requirements obtained is complete, consistent, easy to understand and analyzable by the different actors involved in the development of the system [29].

R19-Unnecessary Variability:

The variability of the products must be considered when evolving the architecture and it must be carefully verified if a requirement for a product can lead to a break from the product family architecture. In the analysis of the forthcoming requirements it must be ascertained how easy it is to add them to the current architecture and estimates the work needed for the implementation [15].

Properly variability management is one of the key success factors of a software product family. In practice, however, variability management suffers from a number of issues that prevent organizations from exploiting the full benefits of software product families [31].

R20-Inadequate Features Definition:

A commonly used product line requirements modeling technique is feature modeling. One of the strengths of feature models is that they provide a good and easy way to get an overview of the common and variable parts of a product line [22].

R21-Failure in Requirements Identification:

Requirements Engineering and Management (REM) is a central task of product line development. The challenges in REM occur, mainly, because SPL development is much more complex than SSD and SPL requirements management is considerably harder than requirements for single-product development [27].

4.4 Staff Risks

R22-Inadequate Communication:

Due the SPL complexity, several insights about the project development can be lost. Thus, the use of questionnaire can help during the identification of the problems. It is crucial to make the assessment results independent of the particular persons conducting the evaluation and to make the assessments repeatable over time (in the sense, that if you ask twice, you get two times the same – or at least a similar answer– if circumstances did not change in the meantime) [20].

R23-Problems with Staff:

Project and technical managers within an organization need to be assured that the reusable assets of a product line are reliable and trustworthy, particularly when project teams do not have full control over the development of these assets [26].

Product line business practices cannot be affected without explicit management commitment and involvement. Many product line efforts fail for lack of sponsorship and commitment from someone above the technical ranks [23].

R24-Shortage of skilled labor:

Skilled architects can mitigate challenges in architectural development [17].

4.5 Organization Risks

R4-Difficult to introduce a SPL:

In practice it is relatively difficult to introduce a product family approach. Many initiatives do not achieve their goals or even fail because their impact and potential problems were not properly identified [7].

Building a SPL is a long-term effort in which the benefits come through reuse, which can only come after several product releases. According Jaaksi (2002) building a few products first is the right way to initiate a product line [17].

Whenever an organization is embarking on a large scale reuse approach, like introducing PL engineering, this entails a serious investment and it is important to pose the question: 'what are the potential benefits we will be able to reap and what will be the risks that we might encounter?' [20].

Although adopting SPL can be beneficial, there is a perception that it has high barriers to entry. One barrier is the perceived prerequisite of a SPL architecture [21].

SPL development requires an organizational mind shift. When moving from SSD to SPL, several related products must be envisioned together to develop an architecture/design that can fulfill the requirements for an entire family of products [22].

The business and process contexts require the transition to be incremental, and the architecture therefore needs to support this through explicit definition of implementation proposals [18].

The community needs more quantitative data to support SPL adoption. Moving to product lines is an investment, and decision makers want hard numbers in their business cases [23].

Many industries are hampered with introducing the product line concept into already existing products. Though appealing, the concept is very difficult to introduce specifically into a legacy environment. All too often the impacts and risks are not considered adequately [24].

R25-Non-use of certifications:

SPL artifacts should ideally be certified once and reused in different products without further certification effort. However, in practice, the certification authorities consider only completed systems [26].

4.6 Business Risks

R26-Limited development costs:

The product line increased costs in various support functions, architectural work, and management. Thus, it is suggested that an organization considers initiating a product line only when it both aims at systematic reuse and serves a heterogeneous customer base with a common domain [17].

R27-Delay in Time-to-Market:

Technical, business and environment requirements change at a tremendous speed. The ability to launch new products and services with major enhancements within short timeframe has become essential for companies to keep up with new business opportunities. The need for differentiation in the marketplace, with short time-to-market as part of the need, has put critical demands on the effectiveness of software reuse. In this context, SPL approach has become one of the most established strategies for achieving large-scale software reuse and ensuring rapid development of new products [18].

5. THE IMPORTANCE OF DESIGN IN COMMUNICATION TO RM IN SPL

Lack of documentation is a problem during both single system and SPL development. It is important to explicitly define the documentation about the domain, scope, platform, assets, product architecture and configuration management. This was re-enforced by: [2], [14], [16], [23], [24], [26], [27]. It is important to explicitly define the documentation for the domain, platform and product architecture, defining a meta model for requirements documentation and ensuring the document quality [27].

Documentation is as important as any other aspect of the project, but the problem is that we do not realize its importance. Documentation should be overriding to all projects, however few mention it, just 8 studies, of the 30 analyzed related this issue: [3], [14], [16], [23], [24], [26], [27].

According to these 8 studies documentation plays an important role. It is essential to document the scoping decisions to identify the mistakes and document the scoping definition process [3]; Thus, it is emphasize that the decisions must be documented [16]; It is important to define documentation about the domain, platform and product architecture explicitly [27]; Thus, it is possible to keep configuration management plans actualized [26]; For this, special emphasis is put onto the documentation of the potential commonalities in the work products [14]; During management the operations and the SPL efforts communication paths are documented in an operational concept [23]; the requirements must be documented in a structured and disciplined way [24].

In additionally, interviews with stakeholders are important to collect insights about the possible problems that can occur. Several studies mentioned about this strategy: [3], [16], [25], [27], [20], [22], [29].

In conclusion, according to our systematic analysis conducted, it was verified that, in general, few approaches have been developed to deal with RM in the SPL context and, when some study exists, it is defined briefly. Although studies have shown that RM is necessary to achieve success in software projects, this area still faces obstacles before being institutionalized by companies working on SPL projects. Additionally, the design of communication about the risks in SPL still needs more extensible research.

6. CONCLUSIONS

This work involves the investigation and integration of two research areas: Software Product Lines and Software Risk Management, and the needs to design the communication between them. After the general introduction to the problem and motivation for RM in SPL, we analyze the issues surrounding RM in SPL identify what needs to be accomplished in order to build a useful body of knowledge.

RM is a practice that deserves greater attention during SPL development, however, there is a lack of research in this area. This conclusion is confirmed by Birk and Heller (2007), where complexity also has a particular impact on requirement engineering management. These challenges occur, mainly, because of the greater complexity in SPL: technical issues (e.g., very high number of features, feature interaction, interrelations between architecture and requirements) as well as organizational and managerial issues (e.g., very many stakeholders, many interrelated projects and releases). Also, for most of the SPL specific issues, tool support is widely lacking.

As briefly conclusion of the risks and lessons learnt identified in the literature were presents, highlight the needs in provide documentation about them. Most approaches do not address the evaluation of risks that are connected with the specific ways to document product line development. Those approaches that address this do it in at a high level. This leads only to rather coarse-grained evaluations [3].

In this context, there is a clear need for conducting studies comparing alternative methods. However, according to Kimer, and Concalves (2006) despite the studies and experiences published about risk management, the software industry, in general, does not seem to follow a model to analyze and control the risks through the development of their products [32].

This work intended to identify risks in the literature and report the importance in use this risks during the project development. As solution can be establish a set of good practices to build a reliable and better effective documentation and design of the risks identified, and reuse the strategies for avoid them.

To the best of our knowledge our research is the first one to aim to support explicitly RM in SPL, focusing on a characterization of the risks involved through the whole SPL process and as well as the methods documented to treat them. With the results, we can suggest an approach that deals with RM and tackles the risks present in the software development process.

The successful adoption of SPL engineering requires a profound organizational mind shift. The whole software engineering process is affected from requirements to maintenance and evolution activities [33]. However, this continuous management is not described in research studies.

We believe that this research will be useful for both, academy and industry. The research clarifies the importance of documenting risk and to capture and reuse past project experiences. The risks in SPL are supported by scientific studies, providing some directions on which aspects to focus. This highlights the importance of providing documentation about projects, and to reuse this documentation in a way that avoids reoccurrence of the same problems. These results will help in decisions about the development of an approach to RM in SPL, with experience about what are the strategies and steps that will be useful, as well as, what are the risks of major impacts.

Future research is to identify which are the common risks between SPL and SSD and, these results give us basis to propose the approach to RM associated with SPL development.

7. ACKNOWLEDGMENTS

We would like to thank at Informatics Center in Federal University of Pernambuco. In addition, our acknowledgments to CNPq. This work was partially supported by the National Institute of Science and Technology for Software Engineering (INES[1]), funded by CNPq and FACEPE, grants 573964/2008-4 and APQ-1037-1.03/08.

8. REFERENCES

[1] Clements, P. and Northrop, L. Software Product Lines: Practices and Patterns, 3rd Edition. Addison-Wesley Professional, August 2001. Boehm, B. W. and DeMarco, T. Guest Editors Introduction: Software Risk Management. IEEE Software, 14(3):17-19, 1997.

[2] Schmid, K. A comprehensive product line scoping approach and its validation. 24th International Conference on Software Engineering (ICSE), 2002.

[3] Schmid, K. 2001. An Assessment Approach To Analyzing Benefits and Risks of Product Lines. Computer Software and Applications Conference, Annual International, pp. 525, 25th.

[4] Boehm, B. W. 1989. Software Risk Management. IEEE Computer Society Press, 1989.

[5] Boehm, B. W. 1991. Software Risk Management: Principles and Practices. IEEE Software, vol. 8, no. 1, pp. 32-41, Jan./Feb. 1991.

[6] Wijnstra, J. G. 2002. Critical Factors for a Successful Platform-Based Product Family Approach. In Proceedings of the Second international Conference on Software Product Lines (August 19 - 22, 2002).

[7] Bannerman , P. L. 2008. Risk and risk management in software projects: A reassessment, Journal of Systems and Software, Volume 81, Issue 12, December 2008, Pages 2118-2133.

[8] Li, J., et. al. 2008. A State-of-the-Practice Survey of Risk Management in Development with Off-the-Shelf Software Components. IEEE Trans. Softw. Eng. 34, 2 (Mar. 2008), 271-286.

[9] Hartmann D. 2006, Interview: Jim Johnson of the Standish Group, viewed 08 March 2009, http://www.infoq.com/articles/Interview-Johnson- Standish-CHAOS.

[10] Dhlamini, J., Nhamu, I., and Kaihepa, A. 2009. Intelligent risk management tools for software development. In Proceedings of the 2009 Annual Conference of the Southern African Computer Lecturers' Association (Eastern Cape, South Africa, June 29 - July 01, 2009).

[11] Van Scoy, R. 2009. Software Development Risk : Opportunity, Not Problem. SEI, CMU/SEI-92-TR- 30, ADA 258743, September 1992.

[12] Boban M., Pozgaj Z. and Sertic H. 2003. Strategies for Successful Software Development Risk Management, Management Vol. 8, 2003, 2, pp. 77-91.

---

[1] http://www.ines.org.br

[13] Voget, S. and Becker, M. 2002. Establishing a Software Product Line in an Immature Domain. In Proceedings of the Second international Conference on Software Product Lines (August 19 - 22, 2002). Ed. Lecture Notes In Computer Science, vol. 2379. Springer-Verlag, London, 60-67.

[14] Riva, C. and Del Rosso, C. 2003. Experiences with Software Product Family Evolution. In Proceedings of the 6th international Workshop on Principles of Software Evolution (September 01 - 02, 2003). IWPSE. IEEE Computer Society, Washington, DC, 161.

[15] Olumofin, F. G. and Mišić, V. B. 2007. A holistic architecture assessment method for software product lines. Inf. Softw. Technol. 49, 4 (Apr. 2007), 309-323.

[16] Jaaksi, A. 2002. Developing Mobile Browsers in a Product Line. IEEE Softw. 19, 4 (Jul. 2002), 73-80.

[17] Pei-Breivold, H., Larsson, S. and Land, R. 2008. Migrating Industrial Systems towards Software Product Lines: Experiences and Observations through Case Studies. Euromicro Conference on Software Engineering and Advanced Applications (SEAA), Software Process and Product Improvement (SPPI) Track, IEEE. September, 2008. http://www.mrtc.mdh.se/index.php?choice=publications&id =1488.

[18] Schmid, K. and Verlage, M. 2002. The Economic Impact of Product Line Adoption and Evolution. IEEE Softw. 19, 4 (Jul. 2002), 50-57.

[19] Schmid, K. and John, I. 2002. Developing, Validating and Evolving an Approach to Product Line Benefit and Risk Assessment. EUROMICRO Conference, pp. 272, 28th , 2002.

[20] Staples, M. and Hill, D. 2004. Experiences Adopting Software Product Line Development without a Product Line Architecture. In Proceedings of the 11th Asia-Pacific Software Engineering Conference (November 30 - December 03, 2004). APSEC. IEEE Computer Society, Washington, DC, 176-183.

[21] Eriksson, M., Börstler, J., and Borg, K. 2009. Managing requirements specifications for product lines - An approach and industry case study. J. Syst. Softw. 82, 3 (Mar. 2009), 435-447. DOI= http://dx.doi.org/10.1016/j.jss.2008.07.046.

[22] Northrop, L. M. 2002. SEI's Software Product Line Tenets. IEEE Softw. 19, 4 (Jul. 2002), 32-40.

[23] Ebert, C. and Smouts, M. 2003. Tricks and traps of initiating a product line concept in existing products. In Proceedings of the 25th international Conference on Software Engineering (Portland, Oregon, May 03 - 10, 2003). International Conference on Software Engineering. IEEE Computer Society, Washington, DC, 520-525.

[24] Dikel, D., Kane, D., Ornburn, S., Loftus, W., and Wilson, J. 1997. Applying Software Product-Line Architecture. Computer 30, 8 (Aug. 1997), 49-55.

[25] Habli, I. and Kelly, T. 2007. Challenges of Establishing a Software Product Line for an Aerospace Engine Monitoring System. In Proceedings of the 11th international Software Product Line Conference (September 10 - 14, 2007). International Conference on Software Product Line. IEEE Computer Society, Washington, DC, 193-202.

[26] Birk, A. and Heller, G. 2007 Challenges for Requirements Engineering and Management in Software Product Line Development. Requirements Engineering: Foundation for Software Quality, 13th International Working Conference, REFSQ 2007, Trondheim, Norway, June 11-12, 2007, Proceedings. Volume 4542 of Lecture Notes in Computer Science, pages 300-305, Springer, 2007.

[27] Clements, P. C., Jones, L. G., Northrop, L. M., and McGregor, J. D. 2005. Project Management in a Software Product Line Organization. IEEE Softw. 22, 5 (Sep. 2005), 54-62.

[28] Mellado, D., Fernández-Medina, E., and Piattini, M. 2008. Towards security requirements management for software product lines: A security domain requirements engineering process. Comput. Stand. Interfaces 30, 6 (Aug. 2008), 361-371.

[29] Estublier, J. and Vega, G. 2005. Reuse and variability in large software applications. In Proceedings of the 10th European Software Engineering Conference Held Jointly with 13th ACM SIGSOFT international Symposium on Foundations of Software Engineering (Lisbon, Portugal, September 05 - 09, 2005). ESEC/FSE-13. ACM, New York, NY, 316-325.

[30] Deelstra, S., Sinnema, M. and Bosch, J. 2004. Experiences in Software Product Families: Problems and Issues During Product Derivation. In Proceedings of the Lecture Notes in Computer Science. Software Product Lines. Volume 3154/2004. Springer Berlin / Heidelberg.

[31] Kimer, T. G., and Concalves, L. E. 2006. Software Engineering Techniques: Design for Quality, IFIP International Federation for Information Processing, Volume 227, pp. 149-154.

[32] Alves, V., et. al. 2010. Requirements engineering for software product lines: A systematic literature review. Information and Software Technology (April 2010).

Improving multimodal interaction design with the MMWA authoring environment

Americo Talarico Neto and Renata Pontin de Mattos Fortes

University of São Paulo - Institute of Mathematics and Computer Science

Av. Trabalhador São Carlense, 400, São Carlos, SP – Brazil, P.O.Box 668

Tel: 55 (16) 3373-9700 - Fax: 55 (16) 3371-2238

{americo, renata}@icmc.usp.br

ABSTRACT

Multimodal Interfaces are designed to increase the human-machine communication bandwidth and to enhance user's satisfaction and task completion efficiency by providing a more natural way of interacting with computers. In contrast, developing multimodal interfaces is still a difficult task due to the lack of tools that consider not only code generation, but usability of such interfaces. In this paper, we present the MultiModal Web Approach's authoring environment, whose main goal is enhancing the dissemination of knowledge used in a project for future developments that are benefited by proven solutions to recurring problems in the multimodal context.

Categories and Subject Descriptors

H.5.2 User Interfaces: Evaluation/methodology, Graphical user interfaces (GUI), Input devices and strategies, Interaction styles, Natural language, Prototyping, Theory and methods, User-centered design and Voice I/O.

General Terms

Documentation, Design, Human Factors, Theory.

Keywords

Multimodal Interfaces Design, Design Rationale and Design Patterns.

1. INTRODUCTION

The technological progress designing new devices and the scientific growth in the field of Human-Computer Interaction (HCI) are enabling new interaction modalities to move from research to commercial products. Since the appearance of Bolt's "Put That There" system [3], which processed graphical objects on a wall screen using speech recognition and finger pointing in parallel, a diversity of researches in the multimodal field has become known, including: modality combinations such as speech, graph and gestures, fusion and fission strategies, dialog management, interface and device adaptation and

usability/accessibility researches [14].

However, the use of combined modalities such as speech, touch, gestures and graph, raises the number of usability problems and interaction issues that the designers and developers are faced with, like synchronization and integration requirements and constraints that should be considered during the design, development and test phases [6].

Consequently, the designers are exposed to a challenge: despite of learning the languages, technologies and applying them to obtain the multimodal application code, they should comprehend which are the best practices in this research field and how to experiment the designed interfaces with real users with different behaviors in a efficient manner prior to the product release. In addition, the project team should be concerned on how to promote reuse of design rationale, the decisions why's, lessons learned and application code in order to get a good balance between the cost and effort implementing multimodal interfaces.

In this paper, we endeavor to answer these questions and concentrate on solving such issues by using the MultiModal Web Approach (MMWA), which relies on the theoretical and empirical expertise acquired by designers during the multimodal interaction design process. Such expertise is documented in the form of Design Rationale (DR), Design Principles [17] and Design Patterns (DPs) which can be shared and applied not only by the design team of a single multimodal application, during multiple iterations to refine that same system, but also by designers of different applications.

Moreover, rooted in our experience applying the MMWA in real projects [11], and based on the observations of the design workflow of MMWA we have designed an authoring tool that guides the designers, developers and usability testers, the project team, through the MMWA steps and activities. The advantage of this authoring tool, called MMWA-ae, is that it suggests design alternatives based on the previous collected DR and the well-known interaction DPs [4], although now supporting the multimodal theory. In addition, MMWA-ae implements the previous identified principles and checklists [10] so that the designers are presented with the successful solutions for recurring problems in this context together with their DR.

This article is organized in the following way:

Section 2 introduces the problems and characteristics of multimodal interfaces through a bibliographic review of methods and their main issues. These problems and their solutions are discussed considering the MultiModal Web Approach (MMWA), highlighting the importance of making DR reuse.

Section 3, details the MMWA authoring environment that implements the MMWA activities and shows its main features.

Section 4 focuses on the case studies that illustrate how MMWA-ae was applied, as Section 5 provides the results and finally the conclusions are discussed in Section 6.

2. MULTIMODAL INTERFACE DESIGN

Multimodal interface design is an important activity to be defined and performed by interface designers. The principles and techniques used in the traditional graphical interfaces (GUI) do not necessarily apply to multimodal systems, for which some important topics as the inputs and outputs information design, modalities fusion and fission, adaptability, consistency and errors handling, cultural behavior topics in addiction to individual personality should be considered [13].

Basically, the design of such systems has been inspired and organized in two ways [15].

Firstly, following the cognitive science proposals that provide basic information on user modeling, what the systems should recognize and how the multimodal architectures should be organized. The literature of cognitive science is quite broad in this sense especially when the focus is the sensory perception and the interaction capabilities inherent in various input methods incorporated in a multimodal system.

According to Oviatt [15], the Wickens theory states that there may be competition between modalities such as auditory and visual during the execution of tasks, so that the human attention and the inputs and outputs required processing can result in better performance if the information is distributed between the modalities. This theory states that the brain maintains visual materials such as photographs and diagrams, in a working memory area, while another area maintains the auditory information. These two processors are coordinated by a central area, but works independently, allowing the effective working memory expansion when people use multiple modalities for the tasks execution. This theory has strongly influenced the research on cognitive load and it was useful to guide our research in the design of multimodal interfaces.

The second multimodal project organization form is the development of prototypes and simulations that is also playing a key role to assist the developers in the early stages of planning and developing multimodal systems. These simulations are intended to provide a system view, its functionalities and to validate the interaction flow, in addition to allowing for data collection with a real and significant users population. The advantage of using simulations in usability studies is the fact that the interfaces changes are easy and cheap compared to a complete system already built. Simulations also allow researchers to modify the characteristics of a planned system and to study the impact of using different interfaces designs in a systematic way, in addition to making decisions on alternative projects.

A number of tools, methods and frameworks to multimodal interface design have become accessible in recent time.

Stanciulescu et al. [19] has presented a method for developing Web-based multimodal interfaces. In this method a framework splits the interface life cycle into four levels: tasks model, domain model, abstract and concrete interface models, each of them performing transformations on the previous levels until the achievement of the final multimodal interface. The steps to achieve the final multimodal interface are: get one or more abstract interfaces from a task model and a domain model, leading one or more interfaces of each abstract interface, and producing the code of the matching final interfaces. All the elements, models and transformations between the levels are specified evenly through a single interface description language, the UsiXML [9]. This language allows dealing out the transformations rules in the model and producing a resulting graphical output model. Thus, the whole project knowledge necessary to lead the changes is explicitly contained in the processing rules, and implementing these rules is granted by a transformation mechanism.

Paternò and Giammarino [16] have developed an interesting method and a tool to assist in the development of multiple types of interfaces and different ways to combine graphics and voice in multi-devices environments. The interface can be adapted to the interaction resources available to avoid confusing the designer with many details related to devices and programming languages. The idea is to have some logical descriptions next to the user's understanding and smart environments capable of transforming interfaces and adjust them to the targets devices.

A more theoretical approach are the CARE properties and its component based framework ICARE [5] that has provided inspiration for a comprehensive toolkit called OpenInterface [18]. A formal model allowing usability evaluation based on the CARE properties was proposed by Kamel [8].

Flippo et al. [7] also worked on the design of a multimodal framework, which architecture is based on agents geared toward direct integration into a multimodal application. One of the most interesting aspects is the use of a parallel application-independent fusion technique.

We could observe that these methods available in the literature do not consider principles, guidelines, DR or DPs to facilitate the design of multimodal interfaces. We believe such concepts are important since they guide designers in making consistent decisions through the elements which compose the product and they are efficient techniques to capture, document and communicate the scientifically validated and applied knowledge in certain circumstances. They also serve as a guide for the interface usability improvements.

Additional concerns were also identified, given that: these tools, methods and frameworks are specific to a particular issue even if multiple interactions are available; there is a lack of systems that convey information using the modalities that are most appropriate to the users and their tasks; and, there is a lack of experience recording and spreading DR with the employed multimodal interactions.

Thus, our aim is to overcome these issues and concerns by providing an approach and a tool as will be explicitly shown in the next sections.

2.1 The MultiModal Web Approach

The MultiModal Web Approach (MMWA) [11], Figure 1, provides designers and developers with a more practical framework to create multimodal projects. This approach follows a spiral process composed of activities and techniques, which allow the capture and retrieval of DR providing successful solutions for recurring problems in the multimodal interaction context through, decisions, justifications, alternatives and arguments that led to the final design and documenting them for future reuse. As a result, it optimizes the methodology for developing interfaces and enables the identification of multimodal interaction DPs.

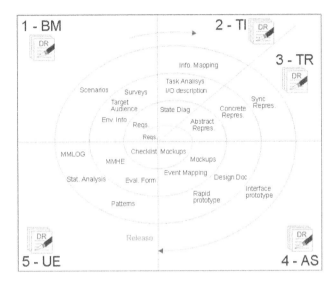

Figure 1. The MMWA activities: 1-Behavior Model (BM); 2-Task Identification (TI); 3-Task Representation (TR); 4-Analysis of Solutions (AS); 5-Usability Evaluation (UE).

An elementary step in the development process for any multimodal interface involves evaluating prototypes based on qualitative studies and authentic user interactions, the well-known simulations described earlier in this paper. One of the main features of the MMWA is the web-based usability evaluation mechanism that provides data for problems identification, analysis and correction in early stages of the project. A benefit of web-based usability studies is that users can be recruited from all over the world and can interact whenever is most convenient.

An additional topic acknowledged by MMWA is the fusion and fission of modalities, which can be combined in four different ways, known as the CARE properties [6] (Complementarily, Assignment, Redundancy and Equivalency). Thus, these properties are also used to structure the MMWA usability evaluation activity.

Following we briefly describe the MMWA activities. A more detailed description can be found in [10].

The **Behavioral Model (BM)** consists of scenarios, constraints and information on the environment in which the multimodal tasks will be performed. BM aims to assist in identifying the information exchanged between the user and the system during the task execution. The goal is getting the task domain information that is necessary for selecting the appropriate tasks mapping and their multimodal interface representation. All such information and data are documented as part of the multimodal application Requirements Specification.

Task Identification (TI) and Representation (TR) identify the tasks to be performed by the users analyzing important task aspects such as: goals, initial states, activities, the problems that may occur, the task environment, the target audience and their experience, and the multimodal input and output. It creates **Abstract Representations** employing methods such as those described in [16] or [19], which perform transformations on the interface abstract and concrete levels until the achievement of the final multimodal interface. The elements needed to generate and analyze any kind of multimodal input and output including their pros and cons are documented in a DR form. The idea is representing the result as a list of interfaces elements for each candidate input and output modality and modalities combinations. **Concrete Representations** are used to assign GUI and VUI widgets and the methods required to trigger the transitions as well as the events that can be activated in each interface element.

The fourth MMWA activity is based on the **Analysis of Solutions (AS)**, using earlier captured DR and filtering out the interaction options based on specialists' argumentations. This step provides the potential modalities to perform the task together with their DR. At the end of this activity, a design document and an interface prototype are generated and the interface is evaluated in the next activity.

As of evaluating multimodal interfaces, it is important to consider as a primary requirement its specificities, like the modalities employed and the interaction language chosen by the users. The literature shows that the preferred approach for usability evaluation in the multimodal ground, take advantage of simulations with real users performing predefined tasks as it allows the investigation of user's interaction patterns, providing important information about user experience [1]. That said, the last activity completes the cycle with the generation of a prototype that is made available for **Usability Evaluation (UE)**. It is composed by a heuristic evaluation mechanism (MMHE) and a mechanism for automatic logging generation and analysis in remote user tests (MMLOG). The prototype is enhanced with new features and improved using the proposals recorded in the DR of each MMWA cycle.

3. MMWA AUTHORING ENVIRONMENT

The MultiModal Web Approach authoring environment (MMWA-ae) was developed to automate the MMWA activities and it serves as a framework for developing multimodal Web interfaces using voice (VUI), touch and graph (GUI). An overview of the MMWA-ae architecture is shown in Figure 2 and a screen shoot of the MMWA-ae design workspace is shown in the Figure 3.

As shown in the Figure 2, the MMWA-ae architecture exposes two interfaces: the Design Interface, which can be accessed by the designers from any web browser with the aim of creating the multimodal project and to work with the MMWA activities, and the Test Interface, which is used to perform remote User Tests.

The design activity is done through the Project Management module. It provides the mechanisms needed to specify and manage the dialog and to design interfaces using all the rationale embedded in the MMWA. With the aid of the Task Analysis Management module the designer specifies the multimodal interaction using Task Analysis as a foundation. It is possible to organize each task in abstract and concrete levels, choose one or various modalities and make use of DPs and DR in order to solve design questions and obtain the rationale to solve recurrent problems with the aid of the solutions used in previous projects in the same context.

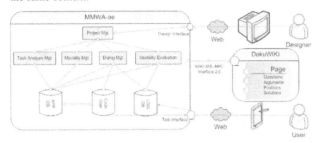

Figure 2. MMWA-ae architecture

Based on the user's choice regarding Abstract tasks, Concrete tasks are dynamically made available, so that the user can choose the one that best applies to his/her project. For example, as it is illustrated in the Figure 3, the designer created the GetCarType Abstract task (Selection). MMWA-ae displayed the possible Concrete tasks related to "Selection" and the designer chooses "Large Group Selection (Voice Filter)", which is a Multimodal DP. Several Multimodal DPs, identified in this research, were implemented and applied by default, for example Modality Synchronization, so when the user creates a multimodal task, the synchronization elements and events are automatically displayed in the Task Actions view, as illustrated in Figure 3.

Figure 3. MMWA-ae design workspace

The use of DR can be time-consuming, disruptive and costs excessive. To solve this constraint our tool extracts and captures DR information when it is needed. The MMWA-ae holds an abstract mechanism for capturing and storing DR allowing organizations and developers to use any WIKI system's main features to collaborate in the tasks specification, implementation and during tests activities.

This was possible by implementing the WIKI XML-RPC Interface 2.0 (Figure 2) that is used to connect the MMWA-ae workspace with any WIKI system so that the DR could be stored and retrieved by means of the creation and management of structured WIKI pages. Figure 4 demonstrates the interaction

between MMWA-ae and DokuWiki[1]. The designer looks for a Solution for a Question regarding a Concrete Task and inserts an Argument to support a Position previously inserted by another designer.

Figure 4. DR Capture using MMWA-ae and DokuWiki

Using Remote Procedure Call (RPC), MMWA-ae establishes a communication link with the WIKI, organizing the whole multimodal interaction project through linked pages and structures the captured DR within these pages. Subsequently, as questions, answers, arguments and solutions are created, the tool disposes the content in the WIKI pages and displays them in a structured manner, allowing the designer to access design activity specific information in the moment that a question or solution come into sight.

This mechanism also makes information organization achievable, so that future projects would benefit from efficient searches, ensuring that precise results could be achieved. This rationale organization aims to facilitate the DPs identification, since the search for a specific content is related to a specific MMWA activity but in different application context. Another important feature of MMWA-ae is the ability to generate multimodal interfaces rapid prototype to be target of usability evaluations. This functionality makes use of the Usability Evaluation Management Module (Figure 2). This module is responsible for gathering all the dialog information from the Application Database, build the application code using the Code Generator Database and include the functions to capture the interactions in the Log Database.

For each task specified by the designer, the tool creates a code snippet that contains voice and graphical interface elements and includes functions to capture interaction events.

It is possible to perform remote user testing deploying this interface in a Web environment (which could be the same environment that hosts MMWA-ae), therefore evaluating the usability of the designed interface looking for problems that can be corrected before release to a final customer.

This functionality also enables the user interaction patterns identification, by analysis of charts and graphs (Figure 5), and design errors identification or areas of usability improvement. In addition it covers the main limitations of user testing, which are: the difficulty of recruiting users, time and resources availability to perform the tests, since the whole process is done remotely.

We also included a mechanism in the MMWA-ae that allows the designer to obtain error handling feedback from the task model directly in the design workspace by means of the log data generated in the User Testing (MMLOG) and the DR collected and stored in the entire process. Figure 6 shows that in the ChooseService task there is a bullet, suggesting a DP to fix a potential usability problem.

---

[1] http://www.dokuwiki.org/dokuwiki

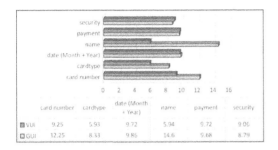

Figure 5. GUI versus VUI interaction average time graph created by MMWA-ae

Finally, the MMWA automatically creates the design documentation, given that during the Task Analysis the designer is aided by a wizard, whose main goals are: to perform the analysis of solutions to obtain the key usability principles to be included in the generated code and to ensure that the items comprising the checklist available on MMWA be considered in the generation of the prototype.

As future work we intend to include in MMWA a mechanism for the fusion of pre-existing graphical user interfaces with speech interfaces. The designer would be responsible for loading the graphical interface in MMWA-ae and the tool would work to get the abstract tasks, select possible concrete representations, create the corresponding speech interface, synchronize the interfaces and include the usability evaluation mechanism. Thus, the designer would spend less effort in the checklists verification and the use of best practices compiled in the form of DR during the process of specifying and creating multimodal Web interfaces.

Figure 6 - MMWA-ae suggesting the use of a multimodal Design Pattern to fix a potencial usability problem.

4. CASE STUDIES

Three case studies were conducted in order to demonstrate and validate our hypothesis as of the DR usage in multimodal projects, the MMWA phases, activities and techniques' experimentation and finally the MMWA-ae deployment and operation in real projects by multimodal designers and developers. The three Case Studies' summary containing the hypothesis, the main instrument being evaluated and the multimodal application developed is shown in the Table 1.

In the Case Study 1 (CS1), we concentrated our investigation in the capture, storage and retrieval of DR through multimodal interfaces design, focusing on task specification, rapid prototyping, usability testing and at the same time applying theoretical frameworks, such as modality theory and CARE properties. The principles and guidelines that support this research were identified and documented and the first insights on how to use a WIKI system to support the DR process were obtained. A car rental system application was designed by six teams of 4

developers each, in order to capture and store a sufficient amount of DR. All the developers were experienced in Web technologies.

Table 1. Case Studies

	CS1	CS2	CS3
Hypothesis	DR collected help out designers in subsequent projects. WIKI systematizes the process of capturing and retrieving DR. Usability issues decrease using previous collected DR.	Usability problems recorded by as DR will not appear again. MMHE and MMLOG are complementary. Log analysis enables interaction pattern identification.	MMWA-ae increases the code Reutilization Rate. Faster Code Generation. Usability errors decreased.
Focus	DR storage and retrieval	MMWA	MMWA-ae
Project	Car Rental System	Telephone company and Map-Based systems.	Car Rental System
Technology	X+V, Java, JSP, Hibernate, PostgreeSQL, JSGF.	X+V, JSP, ECMAScript, JSGF, Actionscript, Adobe Flex SDK, Google Maps API.	X+V, Java, Hibernate, JSP, PostgreeSQL, JSGF.

In the Case Study 2 (CS2), we focused our interest on the use, extension and validation of MMWA, testing different methods for each activity in the proposed cycle using the principles and guidelines obtained previously [11]. MMWA-ae was designed and implemented based on the modules, software components and the rationale obtained previously in the first case study. Special attention was given to the usability evaluation mechanism including LOG analysis and interaction pattern identification. We have designed, developed and evaluated 2 applications applying the MMWA: a Telephone Company application and a map-based system. Both applications were developed by 2 designers experienced in web technologies with the use of the previous collected DR. These two applications permitted us to demonstrate that expressive results were obtained using the approach, including:

- The validation of the MMWA cycle, its activities and methods;

- The controlled mechanism to capture and store DR using WIKI systems;

- The test and validation of the MMHE and MMLOG mechanisms that allow for a better design communication of the usability problems in a DR format and the underlying rationale to fix them.

Case Study 3 (CS3) was conducted in order to obtain a number of results on the topic of the authoring tool's usage in real projects, evaluating its main benefits and also gathering feedback from designers and developers regarding the designed artifacts and the generated code supported by DPs. The objectives were to determine quality metrics, to analyze the code and design reutilization rates and to measure the usability of the generated source code. Another significant result was the method to identify

DPs from the DR database that will be shown next in the Results section.

5. RESULTS

As it was exposed in the previous section, up to now we have performed 3 case studies using the MMWA that permitted us to exhibit expressive results obtained using the approach and its authoring environment. In this section we will evidence the main topics that demonstrate our Case Studies' hypothesis.

By performing Heuristic Evaluations we were able to identify that the usability issues found in the CS1 were not present in the user interface created by MMWA-ae (CS3). This was achievable due to the MMWA-ae inherent DR knowledge and due to the DP suggestion mechanism, which allows the designers to choose the best DP to implement their ideas. Furthermore the usability principle incorporated in the generated code also contributes to the overall usability increase.

Comparing data from the three case studies, problems found applying the MMHE decreased from one case study to another due to the use of DR in subsequent projects and due to the use of Heuristic Evaluation prior to the User Tests, validating assumptions made in [12] regarding the complementary nature of those usability evaluation methods. In other words, only part of the problems that actually occur in the usability tests are identified during Heuristic Evaluation and the problems found in an analytical method are complementary to the problems found in the empirical methods.

The reuse was also promoted. In order to be able to measure code reutilization and to confirm that the reuse was increased by the use of MMWA-ae we employed the formula (1):

(1) ReutilizationRate = (LOC reused + LOC White Box − LOC of non-desired methods) / LOC total

It is important to mention that MMWA-ae code generation engine follows the DR and DPs implementation references, thus avoiding intense code usually produced by code generators. Also "LOC White Box" was considered because we believe this is the most valuable contribution of the code generator engine since it provides the developers with good insight on how to complement the methods in order to obtain a good quality code and thus increase the overall interface's usability.

Applying the reutilization rate formula in the CS3 we ended up with 83% of overall reutilization and 3.2% of non desired methods:

Case Study 3 Reutilization Rate = 83%

- LOC reused: 534

- LOC White Box: 13

- LOC of non-desired methods: 20

- LOC total: 636

Non-desired methods percentage = 20/636 = 3.2%

Table 2 results indicate that only the platform related DRs were not built-in the MMWA-ae code, that is to say, the designers had to query them using the MMWA-ae tool and implement them based on their DR interpretation. The other 13 DRs, grouped by

type, were built-in in the generated code, that is, the design selected an option in the MMWA-ae and the code was automatically generated.

Table 2. DR types implemented by MMWA-ae

Issues Found	Design Rationale Type	Included by MMWA-ae?
3	Platform issues	No
4	Usability / Accessibility	Yes
4	Design Patterns	Yes
2	VUI Prompts	Yes
2	Synchronization	Yes
1	Documentation	Yes

Moreover, the time spent to design interfaces and to obtain the interface's prototype for user testing is one of the main advantages of the MMWA-ae, given that the interfaces prototype was obtained right after the design phase was completed. In contrast, when MMWA-ae was not used a large numbers of tasks were performed before the prototype was obtained, like: DR database queries, team discussions to validate implementation, rounds of usability analysis prior to the final delivery, VUI grammar creation and testing, and so forth.

Another area of interest is the time to create the VUI, which was strongly reduced. MMWA-ae offers the designer a Wizard to fill all the important prompts to be used in each interface. Furthermore by choosing one of the Design Patters, for example the Calendar pattern, the tool automatically creates the GUI, the VUI, and the grammar and synchronizes them, saving a huge amount of the development time. It also increases the usability of such interfaces because MMWA-ae implements the error recovery strategy mechanism and the well-know voice universal commands, allowing for a more robust multimodal interface [2].

We also used Association Rules and their classical measures, Support and Confidence in our case studies to identify users behaviors interacting with multimodal interfaces since it is a well know tool to discovering interesting relations between variables in large databases. Extracting modalities and tasks relationships as Occurrence and Confidence, we verified which modalities the users choose to perform a task in the system and in which tasks or moments they use a combination of modalities to interact. Besides that, we verified the most common errors, in which interface they occur and how the modalities were used to recover from an error. This allowed us to verify that in 74.6% of the time multimodality was used in the case studies, in which the use of voice implies the use of graphical interface with 86.9% of confidence, and the use of graphical interface implies the use of voice with 85.5% of confidence (Table 3).

Table 3. Association Rules, Support and Confidence

Association Rule	Support	Confidence
VOICE → GRAPHICAL	74.6	86.9
GRAPHICAL → VOICE	74.6	85.5
VXML ERROR → GRAPHICAL	50.7	92.3

Moreover, users tend to switch modes to recover from an error. For example, after the second frustrated attempt to interact using voice the users chose to complete the task using the GUI, with 92.3% of confidence.

6. Conclusions

The design space of multimodal applications is large and novel. Appropriate strategy for high-quality multimodal design will make this interaction style more willingly adopted. MMWA has given us insight to design MMWA-ae, which provides a practicable techniques for design and test multimodal application designs. The techniques chosen in this research can potentially benefit future designs promoting modality integration, error handling, dialog management and DR reuse in a clear manner. Furthermore we have show the significant results applying our approach and our tool in real projects through the accomplishment of three case studies. In summary the tool had: promoted code reuse; decreased the time to create prototype for usability evaluations; promoted design documentation; supported DR storage and retrieval and decreased the usability issues.

7. Acknowledgements

The authors gratefully acknowledge the financial support of FAPESP (Grant Process. 2010/05626-7).

8. REFERENCES

[1] Bernhaupt, R; Navarre, D; Palanque,P; Winckler, M, 2007. Model-Based Evaluation: A new way to support usability Evalulation of Multimodal Interactive Applications. In Maturing Usability: Quality in Software, Interaction and Quanlity. Springer Verlag, April 2007.

[2] Bohus, D., and Rudnicky, A, 2005. Sorry, I Didn't Catch That! - An Investigation of Non-understanding Errors and Recovery Strategies, in SIGdial, Portugal.

[3] Bolt, R. A. 1980. "Put-that-there": Voice and gesture at the graphics interface. In Proceedings of the 7th Annual Conference on Computer Graphics and interactive Techniques (Seattle, Washington, United States, July 14 - 18, 1980). SIGGRAPH '80. ACM, New York, NY, 262-270.

[4] Borchers, J., 2001. A Pattern Approach to Interaction Design. John Wiley & Sons, Inc.

[5] Bouchet, J., Nigay, L., Ganille, T., 2004. ICARE Software Components for Rapidly Developing Multimodal Interfaces. In: Proc. of ICMI 2004, State College, Pennsylvania, USA, pp. 251–258. ACM Press, New York (2004)

[6] Coutaz, J., Nigay, L. Salber, D., Blandford, A, May, J., Young, R.M.,1995. Four easy pieces for assessing the usability of multimodal interaction: the CARE properties. In Proc. of Interact'95, ACM Press, pp. 115-120.

[7] Flippo, F.; Krebs, A.; Marsic, I, 2003. A framework for rapid development of multimodal interfaces, Proceedings of the 5th international conference on Multimodal interfaces, Vancouver, B.C., Canada.

[8] Kamel, N and Ait-Ameur, Y. A Formal Model forCARE Usability Properties Verification in MultimodalHCI. In Proceedings of IEEE SEPS'07 Workshop. IEEE, July 2007.

[9] Limbourg, Q.; Vanderdonckt, J.; Michotte, B.; Bouillon, L.; Lopez, V. USIXML: a Language Supporting Multi-Path Development of User Interfaces. In Proc. of 9th IFIP Working Conference on Engineering for Human-Computer Interaction (Hamburg, 2004). Kluwer Academic Press, Dordrecht.

[10] Neto, A. T., Fortes, R. P., Assis, A. R., and Anacleto, J. C. 2009. Design of communication in multimodal web interfaces. Proc. of the 27th ACM international Conference on Design of Communication (USA, October, 2009). SIGDOC '09. ACM, New York, NY, 81-88.

[11] Neto, A. T., Bittar, T. J., Fortes, R. P., and Felizardo, K. 2009. Developing and evaluating web multimodal interfaces - a case study with usability principles. Proc. of the 2009 ACM Symposium on Applied Computing (Honolulu, Hawaii). SAC '09. ACM, New York, NY, 116-120.

[12] Nielsen, J, 1993. Usability Engineering. Academic Press, Cambridge, 1993.

[13] Oviatt, S., Lunsford, R. and Coulston, R., 2005. Individual Differences in Multimodal Integration Patterns: What Are They and Why Do They Exist?. In Proc. of CHI'05, ACM Press, pp. 241--249.

[14] Oviatt, S, 2002. Multimodal Interfaces. The Human-Computer Interaction Handbook. Mahwah, NJ: Lawrence Erlbaum and Associates, 2002.

[15] Oviatt, S., Coulston, R., and Lunsford, R. 2004. When do we interact multimodally? Cognitive load and multimodal communication patterns. In Proceedings of the 6th international Conference on Multimodal interfaces (State College, PA, USA, October 13 - 15, 2004). ICMI '04. ACM, New York, NY, 129-136.

[16] Paternò. F.; Giammarino, F. Multimodal interaction: research papers: Authoring interfaces with combined use of graphics and voice for both stationary and mobile devices. Proceedings of the working conference on Advanced Visual Interfaces 2006.

[17] Raman, T. V., 2003. Design principles for multimodal interaction. In MMI Workshop, Computer Human Interfaces, pages 5–10, Fort Lauderdale, USA.

[18] Serrano, M., Nigay, L., Lawson, J.-Y.L., Ramsay, A., Murray-Smith, R., Denef, S., 2008. The OpenInterface framework: a tool for multimodal interaction. In: Adjunct Proceedings of CHI 2008, Florence, Italy, April 5-10, pp. 3501–3506. ACM Press, New York.

[19] Stanciulescu A.; Limbourg Q.; Vanderdonckt J.; Michotte B.; Montero F.; A Transformational Approach for Multimodal Web User Interfaces based on USIXML. Proc of the 7th international conference on multimodal interfaces ICMI 2005, pages 259-266, ACM Press.

Design, Development and Performance Evaluation of Reconfigured Mobile Android Phone for People Who are Blind or Visually Impaired

Akbar S. Shaik
Department of EECE
The University of Memphis
Memphis, TN 38152, USA
asshaik@memphis.edu

G. Hossain
Department of EECE
The University of Memphis
Memphis, TN 38152, USA
ghossain@memphis.edu

M. Yeasin
Department of EECE
The University of Memphis
Memphis, TN 38152, USA
myeasin@memphis.edu

ABSTRACT

This paper presents the design, development and performance evaluation of a Reconfigured Mobile Android Phone (R-MAP) designed and implemented to facilitate day-to-day activities for people who are blind or visually impaired. Some of these activities include but are not limited to: reading envelopes, letters, medicine bottles, food containers in refrigerators; as well as, following a route plan, shopping and browsing, walking straight and avoiding collisions, crossing traffic intersections, finding references in an open space, etc. The key objectives were to develop solutions that are light weight, low cost, un-tethered and have an intuitive and easy to use interface that can be reconfigured to perform a large number of tasks. The Android architecture was used to integrate the cell phone camera, image capturing and analysis routines, on-device implementation of robust and efficient optical character recognition (OCR) engine and text to speech (TTS) engine to develop the proposed application in real-time. Empirical analysis under various environments (such as indoor, outdoor, complex background, different surfaces, and different orientations) and usability studies were performed to illustrate the efficacy of the R-MAP. Improved feedback and new functions were added based on usability study results.

Categories and Subject Descriptors

H.5.2 [Information Interfaces and presentation]: User Interfaces—Evaluation/methodology, Input devices and strategies, User-centered design, Voice I/O ; K.4.2 [Computers and Society]: Social Issues—Assistive technologies for persons with disabilities

General Terms

Assistive technology, Integrated mobile application

Keywords

Access to printed text, blind or visually impaired, mobile assistive technology, on-device integration of Image, OCR and TTS, usability study.

1. INTRODUCTION

In 2006, the World Health Organization (WHO) estimated that there were approximately 37 million people who are blind and 124 million people who are visually impaired in the world. This number is growing and may reach 2 million per year in the near future. Despite their many abilities, visual impairment causes a host of challenges in daily life. Hence, cost effective, functional, easy-to-use, reliable and ergonomically designed assistive technology solutions needed to overcome these daily challenges.

One of the problems faced by people with visual impairment or blindness is their inability to access printed text that exists everywhere in the world. Ray Kurzweil, the designer of the Kurzweil machine [17] in 1976, the first device for the blind to access text, reported once a blind person explained to him that the only real handicap for blind people is their complete lack of access to print (text). The American Foundation for the Blind [33] found that information provided in Braille is accessed by not more than 10% of the legally blind people in the United States. The scenario may be similar all around the world. Almost 70% [44] of people who are blind or visually impaired are unemployed and lacks access to the assistive technology solutions to manage the challenges of everyday life.

A number of assistive technology solutions for the persons with disabilities are available to access print, such as, Braille devices, screen readers (HAL [14], JAWS [19], etc.), screen magnification software, and scanning and reading software (Cicero [14], Kurzweil 1000 [17], etc.), just to name a few. Most of these devices and software often require custom modification, or are prohibitively expensive. Many persons with disabilities do not have access to custom modification of the available devices and other benefits of current technology. In summary, existing solutions to access printed texts have fallen short of user expectations, and are expensive and not suitable for mobile use. This necessitates a mobile device to access text that satisfies requirements such as cost, convenience, usability, portability and accessibility, expandability, flexibility, compatibility with other systems, learnability curve of device, ergonomics, utility and reliability. The solution can be the use of mobile handheld devices that satisfy the above requirements. Mobile phones are widely used and are constantly evolving with new features added all the time. Third generation mobile phones can process computing intensive programs in real time.

159

A recent advancement in handsets is Google's mobile Android phone with the first free open source Android [2] operating system. Many new functions can be easily programmed and customized in software with no extra hardware. The development of applications on other platforms like Windows CE, Pocket PC, Smart Phone, Palm OS, etc. are complicated, and moreover, these platforms are not available for free to use by others. Android mobile phones are also provided with a Text to Speech (TTS) [4] engine to make the applications speak for people who are blind or visually impaired. Hence, providing a reading service on this platform of mobile phone is easier.

The key idea is to evaluate usability of the integrated system (R-MAP) developed on the Android mobile phone with a simpler user interface and using the camera image capturing routines, optical character recognition (OCR) [28] and text to speech (TTS) engines to provide read out loud services. The objectives of this system include being light weight, low cost and untethered while performing a large number of tasks. Most devices developed with these same objectives have been too cumbersome with unusable user interfaces, no voice output, unaffordable and/or not readily available to be practical and truly portable. Our system overcomes all these issues and is readily accessible in real time. The question arises, "How user friendly the R-MAP can be?" The scope of usability covers all aspects of a system with which a human might interact, including installation and maintenance procedure [48]. Nielsen (1992) defines the usability with multiple components associated with five usability attributes: Learnability, Efficiency, Memorability, Errors and Satisfaction. Based on Nielsen's definition we study users' evaluations and achieved 70% average usability score that justifies the acceptability of the system to the people who are blind or visually impaired. Now for the first time, many people who are blind or visually impaired can afford the technology that would allow them to read most printed material through independent means.

2. RELATED WORK

To access text, the current technologies for people who are blind or visually impaired are large print, speech, Braille and scanned material. The large print technologies (Zoom-Text [32], Lunar [22], etc) magnify the text and graphics programs on screens of computers. They have a number of advanced features and magnification from 2x to 32x with different viewing modes are possible. Speech technologies include speech synthesizers with hardware (DecTalk [11], Keynote GOLD [20]) and software (Microsoft SDK [23], AT&T Natural Voices [5]) versions to read computer screens. The hardware can be internal card devices or external serial devices that allow specialized software programs to integrate speech output. Braille technology provides editing tools (Braille2000 [8]), translation software (Duxbury [12]), displays (Braille Wave [7], Braillex [9]) and embossers that provide Braille output from a printer (Braille Blazer [6], ViewPlus [31]). Scanned material technology gives access to scanned documents from a scanner on the computer to use devices such as Open Book [27] that speaks text loud or outputs Braille. These technologies are costly and the conditions of accessibility and usability are not properly satisfied. They lack in portability, limited to home use and developed mostly for use on computers. Further investigations and development are needed to satisfy the requirements and needs of people who are blind or visually impaired.

The Optical Character Recognition (OCR) engines are used to digitize the text information that can be edited, searched and reused for further processing with ease. Therefore, an OCR transforms the textual information from the Analog world to the Digital world. There is a list [26] of open-source software and projects related to OCRs. In addition, open-source communities offer systems like GOCR [13], OCRAD [24] and OCROPUS [25]. Tesseract [42] is also one such an open source OCR engine developed by HP labs between 1985 and 1995 with Google acquiring it in 2006. It is probably the first OCR to handle white-on-black text so easily. The commercially available OCRs are the ABBYY FineReader, the ABBYY Mobile OCR engine, the Microsoft Office Document Imaging and OmniPage. Text to Speech (TTS) [40] engines are widely introduced in almost all mobile platforms in order to help people who are blind or visually impaired in using mobile phone applications with ease. These voices are close to human voices but lack the liveliness found in natural speech.

Many projects and commercial products attempted to use a mobile phone in building applications for people who are blind or visually impaired. A camera based document retriever [45] is designed with TTS technology to obtain the electronic versions of the documents stored in a database. Therefore, an article of a document is read out via phone speaker if the content of the image captured matches a document in the database. This poses a limitation to reaching documents in the database only and no attainment of print existing in the external world. A currency reader [46] has been effectively designed, but its recognition ability is limited to US currency only. Haritaoglu [35] and Nakajima et al [38] have developed a mobile system using client server architecture with a PDA (Personal Digital Assistant) for dynamic translations of the text, but it is unsuitable, does not address the needs for people who are blind or visually impaired and not practical. The size and number of buttons and the PDAs touch screen make their use almost impossible. Some handheld assistants [10, 29] designed using the same PDA technology have unusable user interfaces, no voice output and are costly. A reading aid is provided by Optacon [34], an electro-mechanical device that converts the characters to vibrating tactile stimuli. This is introduced in replacement of Braille to read text but needs a lot of training. It is costly, bulky and for home use only. Applications, such as bar code readers [39] and business card readers [37], have been developed on mobile phones, but these could not provide access to other printed text and have an unusable user interface. The products like KNFB Reader [21] and AdvantEdge Reader [1] have also been introduced into the market but are very expensive and use two or more linked machines to recognize text in mobile conditions. The Android mobile accessibility solution has the potential to be inexpensive and more sustainable than current accessibility solutions.

3. APPLICATION

R-MAP will provide more independence to people who are blind or visually impaired in terms of usability in everyday activities. Let us consider the scenario of Jack, a businessman who is visually impaired, taking a trip to the grocery store. Jack and Buddy, his Seeing Eye dog, walk to the store two blocks away, pulling his small cart behind. Since Jack has been a patron at this store for years, he knows exactly how many steps to take to get to which aisle for the items he regularly needs. However, today he needs a specialty item. Here, he pulls out his Android mobile phone to take a picture of the aisle signs. Once the phone has stated what is on each aisle, he proceeds down the one which fits his needs. He continues to take pictures of items on the shelves and listens to the phone before he reaches the item he needs. Just like any other customer, Jack wants to get his money's worth, so he takes a picture of the item to check its expiration date. After Jack has finished shopping, he starts back home. However, on the way back, a road is obstructed with an automobile wreak, so Jack must use his R-MAP to read the various street signs on the new route home. When he finally arrives, he needs to carefully arrange his pantry to help his efficiency in the kitchen later. He uses his R-MAP to read the labels each item. So, he knows exactly where to put them for later use. A trip errand that before would have required help from someone was able to be performed independently by Jack through R-MAP.

4. ARCHITECTURE AND IMPLEMENTATION

Mobile phones have lower processing power than Desktops or Notebooks. However, to provide the users real time response while interacting with a mobile phone, R-MAP is designed to minimize the processing time and user operation. Figure 1 shows the architectural diagram of R-MAP, where an Android mobile phone is used and all operations are done on-device and in real time.

4.1 User Interface

It can be a challenge for people who are blind or visually impaired to use the services provided on a mobile phone. A study [36] examined how people who are blind or visually impaired select, adapt and use mobile devices. The simple user interface described below can be easily adapted and used in all day to day activities. The audio feedbacks and functions are improved based on user study. To operate the device, one needs to concentrate on the top right and bottom left positions of the touch screen as shown in figure 2. Icons are placed at these positions where it has to be clicked alternatively. Assume that the left-hand thumb is used for icons on the bottom-left and the icon of the application is placed on the top-right where it has to be clicked by the right-hand thumb. It makes a loud sound when the user clicks to confirm the application starts as shown in figure 2. A click using the left-hand thumb on the bottom left produces a low sound signifying, the application has entered into capture mode. Another click, using the right-hand thumb on the top right position captures the image. The results are being processed once the image is captured. It takes 5-20 seconds, depending on the amount of text and the lighting conditions. If the text obtained is

good it gives a sound feedback where a final click on the bottom left position, using the left-hand thumb, gives the voice output. If the result is not good based on OCR confidence the phone vibrates and the user has to go back and start the application from capture mode. Hence, the entire user operation is designed to run the application based on these two positions of the mobile phone which need to be clicked alternatively.

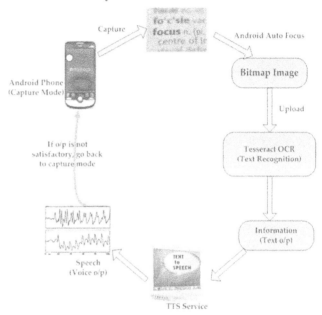

Figure 1: Architecture Diagram

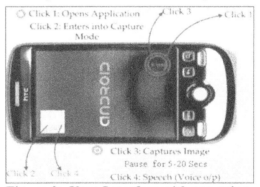

Figure 2: User Interface with operation

4.2 Implementation

Taking a picture from a mobile phone camera may lead to various artifacts in the images, (i.e. skew, blur, curved baselines, etc.) thereby, causing the best available OCR to fail. In addition, since the system is enabled on-device, real time response issues need to be considered critically. We developed R-MAP using Google's Android 1.6 version [3] of the platform in the Windows environment. The applications are written in the Java programming language. Android NDK [15] allows developers to implement parts of their applications using native-code languages such as C and C++. It is used in conjunction with Android SDK and can provide benefits to applications by reusing an existing code and, in some cases, increasing the speed. We used Android NDK version 1.5.

There are various modules for the practical implementation of a completely integrated system.

Once the user initiates the application on the Android mobile phone, it asks the user to enter the capture mode. In this mode, the camera has resolution of 3.2 Mega Pixels that satisfies the 300dpi resolution requirement of the OCR engine and is provided with an auto-focus mechanism. If the camera is not focused on the text properly, it then vibrates and the image is not captured. This way, we can overcome the issue of blur or focusing issues. As soon as the focus is acceptable, the image is captured and sent in compressed form to the OCR engine.

The open source Tesseract [16] OCR engine, version 2.03 from Google, is enabled on the Android mobile phone. Android NDK is used for utilizing the existing C++ code of the Tesseract OCR engine using a tutorial [18]. The text recognition experiments performed by UNLV [43] on Tesseract show over 95% of recognition accuracy, indicating it is the most efficient OCR engine. Currently, it can read only tiff and bmp images. The captured image is uploaded in the form of a bitmap to the on-device OCR engine. The OCR can provide skew correction for [-10, 10] degrees of rotation thus, saving the loss of image quality. It also handles curved baseline fitting and has characteristics like noise reduction, color-based text detection, word spacing, chopping joined characters and associating broken characters to cope with recognition of damaged images. Undergoing these processes, the OCR engine performs text segmentation and character recognition. The processing time from image uploading until obtaining the information in the form of text takes 5-20 seconds. The text is extracted and sent to the TTS engine for further processing.

The Text to Speech [30] needs to be enabled for the application to process the text extracted from the OCR to obtain the voice output. This engine is available in the Android mobile phone designed especially for people who are blind or visually impaired to access the applications. It can spell out words, read punctuation marks, etc. with global prosodic parameters. It also has an adjustable speaking rate. In case the voice output is not satisfactory (i.e., the text is not recognized properly), the application can be started again from the capture mode.

Therefore, R-MAP serves some accessibility needs of people who are blind or visually impaired and is more effectively implemented than the current accessibility solutions.

5. EXPERIMENTS ON PERFORMANCE EVALUATION

A number of experiments were conducted in an effort to evaluate the performance of the on-device OCR engine on fully integrated R-MAP. The overall accuracy and speed of the on-device OCR engine were evaluated under various practical deployment situations. These situations are very commonly encountered where text needs to be read-out loud, such as indoor or outdoor locations; complex backgrounds; different surfaces and images in various conditions (tilt, skew, lighting differences, etc.). We illustrate the text input to discuss performance metrics and based on the results obtained, the performance analysis.

5.1 Test Corpora

R-MAP was applied to two test image corpora: a control corpus of four diverse black and white images, each one under four different conditions (indoor and outdoor lighting, skew and tilt) and an experimental corpus of 50 color scene images to explain various situations (outdoor and indoor locations, different surfaces and complex backgrounds). The test images were taken using the Google Android HTC G1.

5.2 Performance Metrics

Since the measure of accuracy of the OCR in various situations and conditions is our point of interest, we adopted two metrics proposed by the Information Science Research Institute (ISRI) at UNLV for the Fifth Annual Test of OCR Accuracy [41]. Those metrics are Character Accuracy and Word Accuracy.

5.2.1 Character Accuracy
This metric can be used if n is the number of characters in the image and m is the number of errors resulting from the OCR engine then the character accuracy is given by $\mathbf{n\text{-}m/n}$

5.2.2 Word Accuracy
A word is a sequence of one or more letters. The correct recognition of a word is more important than numbers or punctuation in text extraction. If n is the total number of words in an image and m is the number of recognized words from the OCR engine then the word accuracy is given by $\mathbf{m/n}$.

5.3 Results and Performance Analysis

In this section, we evaluate the OCR accuracy in the control corpus for different conditions and the experimental corpus for various situations based on the performance metrics, thereby, the analysis of the experimental results to evaluate R-MAP's performance.

5.3.1 Control Corpus

Let us consider four sets of diverse black and white images with each set taken in four different conditions. A sample of images in different conditions is shown in figure 3. Since these images have sufficient amounts of text, we considered word accuracy over character accuracy. The word accuracy for these four images under each condition is shown in fig 5.

An embedded camera in a mobile phone has far less lighting than a scanner. Binarization, a process to classify the image pixels is undertaken by the OCR to solve this lighting issue. The experiments performed in dull lighting conditions gave poor results. Therefore, the experiments were performed under good indoor and outdoor lighting conditions. The word accuracy for images in good indoor lighting conditions was found to be 96% which was constant in all images and for the same set of images it had improved to100% in good outdoor lighting conditions. This indicates that good lighting conditions improve the OCR accuracy.

When the image is taken by a mobile phone camera, text lines may get skewed from their orientation. This results in a poor OCR performance. The line finding algorithm in the OCR can

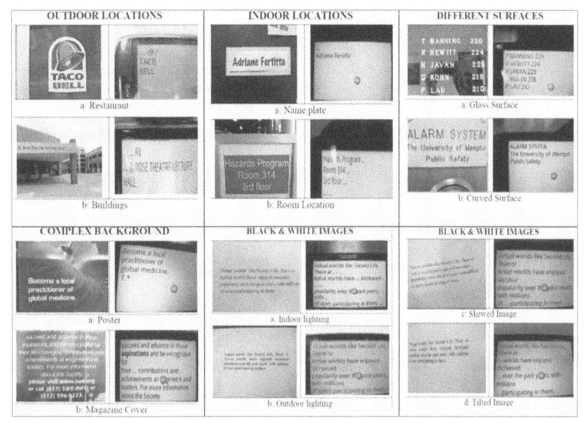

Figure 3: Samples of Experimental and Control corpus

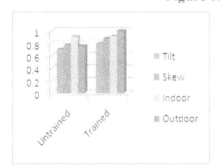

Figure 4: Word Accuracy for Untrained and Trained OCR

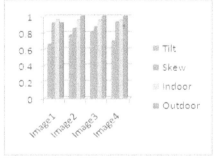

Figure 5: Word Accuracy for Control Corpus

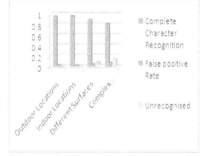

Figure 6: Character Accuracy for Experimental Corpus

recognize text without a need to de-skew the image up to [-10, 10] degrees of rotation. The word accuracy for skewed images ranges from 85%-90% under normal lighting conditions. Therefore, the image needs to be captured lowering the skew angle as much as possible for obtaining good results.

Tilt, also known as the perception distortion results when the text plane is not parallel to the image capturing plane. The effect is that the characters faraway look smaller and distorted. This degrades the OCR performance. The simple solution can be the use of orientation sensors embedded in a mobile phone instead of applying image-processing techniques. The word accuracy for experiments conducted without orientation sensors ranges from 66%-81% that can be improved by using an orientation sensor in the mobile phone.

The text recognition is possible on black and white images to a greater extent unless there are some issues with font, dull lighting conditions, etc. The false positive rate (non-text recognized as text) was less than 2% in the case of indoor and outdoor lighting conditions, whereas, it was 11% for tilted and 5% for skewed images (% is based on the number of words). The unrecognized words for indoors was less than 3%, for tiled images it was 12%, for skewed it was 6% but for outdoors it was less than 1%. These results prove R-MAP a promising application with little improvements to be made.

5.3.2 Training the OCR

We observed the text recognition results from Tesseract OCR, which produces, in some cases, bad text translations due to previous text recognition failures. A possible solution could be to re-train the OCR engine since it benefits from the use of an adaptive classifier. To illustrate the training of the OCR, we performed an experiment (shown in figure 4). The same experiment is performed twice under the same conditions (tilt, skew, indoor and outdoor lighting conditions) and its word accuracy is calculated. The results showed there was a 10% increase in word accuracy for tilt and skew conditions with improvements in outdoor lighting conditions to 24%. In indoor lighting conditions, there was only a 2% increase, indicating the OCR is better trained for good indoor lighting conditions. This improvement in word accuracy indicates the OCR is trained every time with repeated capturing of the same image where partial results are obtained.

5.3.3 Experimental Corpus

The motivation behind these experiments was provided by the fact that the OCR engines available fail miserably on anything but the uniform text. Therefore, we captured the images of text located in indoor and outdoor locations, complex backgrounds like on magazine covers and posters, different surfaces like glass, curved, LCD (Liquid Crystal Display) screens, etc to evaluate the performance. A sample of images taken under these situations is shown in figure 3. Since the numbers of words in images are less, we have targeted character accuracy rather than word accuracy shown in figure 6.

In outdoor locations, the text information is available in the form of names of buildings, restaurants, streets, etc. where a user can capture an image and read the text. The experiments for a set of ten images performed on the text available outdoors have the average character accuracy of 96.5%. The text available outdoors can pose problems like reflection that gives no OCR output. However, good outdoor lighting conditions always help the good performance.

In indoor locations, text availability is most common like those in name plates, male and female restrooms, room location, notice boards, etc. In these cases, a set of twenty images was captured under good lighting conditions and their average character accuracy was measured. It was found equal to the average character accuracy of the text in outdoor locations, indicating that there was not much difference between the text indoor or outdoor unless good lighting conditions were satisfied.

The need to take images on curved surfaces like medicine bottles, glass surfaces like doors, LCD screen,; etc will arise for people who are blind or visually impaired. To evaluate the performance on these different surfaces, we took ten images whose average character accuracy was found to be 89%. The experiments were also performed on a set of ten images of complex backgrounds like on magazines, posters, etc. The average character accuracy was found to be 83%. These experiments reveal that R-MAP is capable of reading text in these situations efficiently not just limited to uniform text.

In all these situations, there is a possibility of conditions like tilt, skew, etc to arise but they are taken care by the OCR as discussed in the case of the control corpus. The only difference with colored images is that it takes a bit more processing time. The false positive rate is more in complex backgrounds

(8%) and different surfaces (5%) because of the consideration of non-text areas as text (% is based on number of characters). The unrecognized text is also more in complex backgrounds (14%) and different surfaces (9%) indicating further analysis over these issues.

From the moment the application starts to the image captured, the runtime on-device corresponds to complete the whole process within 5-20 seconds, depending on the amount of text and lighting conditions. Therefore, the entire process meets the requirements of real time processing.

6. USABILITY EVALUATION OF R-MAP

In the usability study method, twenty two participants with diverse educational and socio-economic background were chosen. Different factors such as gender, ethnicity, age group and familiarity of smart phone experience was taken into consideration while designing the questions for subjective evaluation. One of the subjects was blind and other participants have normal vision and hearing abilities. All sighted participants were blind folded during the study.

Figure 7. a) Blindfolded   b) Blind person

6.1 Usability mechanism

Based on Nielsen's definition, the mechanism used in the usability evaluation (subjective) is an end-user usability test [50]. To evaluate the usefulness of R-MAP, we used different questionnaires (stated in table-1) employing a rating scale. We scored 5 for strongly agree, 4 for agree, 3 for neutral, 2 for disagree and 1 for strongly disagree for the statements.

6.2 Procedure

Initially, brief auditory instructions were given to the participants (Users). The instructions for blind user were a bit different from blindfolded users. For the blind user we used auditory and touch based instructions while for the others we used classroom instruction. Then they were asked to perform a task using R-MAP.

6.3 Results

The usability evaluation of R-MAP showed that the interaction between users and the mobile device through sound feedback is a good aid in reading different instructional labels, texts on objects, etc. The visually challenged user performed better than the users' who are familiar with smart phone operation. Every metric has scoring range from 0 to 10. In figure 8, each metric shows the average score provided by all the participants. The female participants scored better than male participants in all other metrics except in the memorability as shown in the figure 9. Figure 10 shows the cumulative total score of five metrics for twenty-two users with details of every metric for individual user.

Table-1: Usability Questionnaires

Description By Nielsen (1992)	Usability Questionnaires for Blind user/blindfolded user
Learnability: How easy it is for a user to accomplish basic tasks at the first time?	It is easily learnable after the first few attempts. It is easy to understand the audio based feedback.
Efficiency: How quickly the user can perform tasks?	I am able to perform tasks quickly after I learnt how to use it. The user interface and audio feedbacks help me in minimizing mistakes in operating it.
Memorability: How easily users reestablish the proficiency when performing task next time?	I will be able to recall how to perform the task without instructions after some period of not using R-MAP. I recommend that the feedbacks and User interface is easy to remember.
Error: How many errors the users make and how easily they can recover from the errors?	Very few attempts are made to accomplish task completely for first time. R-MAP has few frequencies of serious errors while operating.
Satisfaction: Freedom from discomfort and positive attitude to use the product.	Considering the experience, I am comfortable with R-MAP. I find R-MAP useful in daily life.

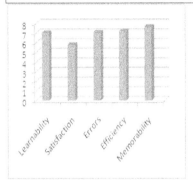 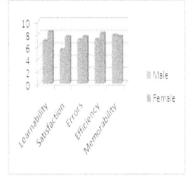 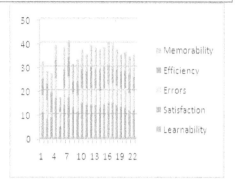

Figure 8: Average score of all users in five usability metrics.

Figure 9: Average comparative score in five metrics for male and female

Figure 10: The cumulative total score in all five metrics for the twenty two users.

We took some text feedback of the participants as comments while collecting data. To reduce cognitive load, we used sound feedback instead of simple language command since it carries lower load during a task performed by blind folded person [47].

The average usability is calculated taking the arithmetic mean of all usability scores from the participants. In our case, the average usability came out to be 69.727 % (aprox. 70%). We also measured the quartile ratio to find the gap between the best and the worst user. The resulted Quartile ratio (Q3/Q1 = 77/69 = 1.11 < 2) is acceptable [49].

7. DISCUSSION

The presented challenges of hardware in mobile phone cameras, compared to expensive high-end cameras, are low resolution, motion blur and lighting conditions arising. In some cases, print materials are quite long and cannot be captured with a single click due to the limited screen size of mobile phones. Also, OCR is not developed for camera use but for ideal pictures taken in scanners. These issues, in addition to finding text in a scene, the limitations to recognize text from handwritings, small or poor quality print, and currencies need to be investigated.

A good capture of the image is better than long processing to detect text, but it needs further improvements for R-MAP to process more types of images (very complex backgrounds, dim lighting, highly curved, etc.) in order to be more robust. There is no literature for people who are blind or visually impaired using cameras. Therefore, issues related to capturing images need to be considered. People who are

blind or visually impaired are recruited to estimate the cognitive load using the R-MAP. The lessons learned from these studies can be extended to implement a more universal system design.

8. CONCLUSIONS

This paper implemented and performed usability study on a fully integrated application, called R-MAP, to provide mobile access to printed texts for people who are blind or visually impaired. A number of factors such as cost, learnability, portability and scalability were considered. Android platform enabled streaming of captured images to the on-device OCR system and subsequently feeds that to the TTS to generate a voice output. Fine tuning of the OCR and TTS parameters were performed to make the application robust against a number of variabilities. R-MAP is easy to use and the interface is designed to minimize the user operation. R-MAP is a stand-alone application, built using the Android phone and requires no special hardware or internet connection to external servers to provide this service. It is available in the English language but can be extended to other languages with minimum effort.

A number of services, such as finding a reference in an open space, following a route map, and localization with very high accuracy is currently under investigation. Integration of such services will make the system more effective for people who are blind and visually impaired. A detailed study for cognitive load of the overall system is currently in progress. The preliminary results are satisfying and promising.

ACKNOWLEDGMENT

Authors would like to thank C. S. Kolli for his help with experiments. P. Subedhi, T. Owens and I. Anam are acknowledged for proof reading. This research was partially supported by grant NSF-IIS-0746790. Any opinions, findings, and conclusions or recommendations expressed in this material are those of the authors and do not necessarily reflect the views of the funding institution.

REFERENCES

[1] AdvantEdge Reader - http://www.atechcenter.net/.

[2] Android - http://www.android.com/.

[3] Android SDK - http://developer.android.com/.

[4] Android TTS - http://android-developers.blogspot.com/2009/09/introduction-to-text-to-speech-in.html.

[5] At&t Natural Voices-http://www.naturalvoices.att.com/.

[6] Braille Blazer - http://www.nanopac.com/.

[7] Braille Wave -http://www.handytech.de/.

[8] Braille2000 -http://www.braille2000.com/.

[9] Braillex - http://www.tvi-web.com/.

[10] Braillnote, http://www.pulsedata.com.

[11] DecTalk -http://www.fonixspeech.com/.

[12] Duxbury - http://www.duxburysystems.com/.

[13] GOCR - a free OCR program. http://jocr.sourceforge.net/.

[14] HAL Screen Reader and Cicero-http://www.dolphinuk.co.uk/index dca.htm.

[15] http://android-developers.blogspot.com/.

[16] http://code.google.com/p/tesseract-ocr/.

[17] http://www.kurzweiledu.com/.

[18] IT wizard - http://www.itwizard.ro/.

[19] JAWS - http://www.freedomscientific.com/.

[20] Keynote GOLD - http://assistivetech.net/.

[21] KNFB Reader - http://www.knfbreader.com/.

[22] Lunar -http://www.axistive.com/.

[23] Microsoft SDK - http://msdn.microsoft.com/.

[24] OCRAD - the gnu ocr. http://www.gnu.org/software/ocrad/.

[25] OCRcopus - open source document analysis and OCR system - http://code.google.com/p/ocropus/.

[26] Open source OCR resources - http://www.ocrgrid.org/ocrdev.htm

[27] OpenBook -http://www.openbookmn.org/.

[28] Optical character recognition (OCR) - http://en.wikipedia.org/wiki/optical character recognition.

[29] PacMate, http://www.freedomscientific.com.

[30] TTS Stub- http://code.google.com/p/eyes-free/.

[31] ViewPlus - http://www.viewplus.com/.

[32] ZoomText -http://www.compuaccess.com/.

[33] Estimated number of adult Braille readers in the United States. Journal of visual Impairment and Blindness, 90(3):287, May -June 1996.

[34] N. Efron. Optacon - a replacement for Braille? Australian Journal of Optometry, (4), 1977.

[35] I. Haritaoglu. Infoscope: Link from real world to digital information space. UbiComp'01, pages 247–255, London, UK, 2001. Springer-Verlag.

[36] S. K. Kane, C. Jayant, J. O. Wobbrock, and R. E. Ladner. Freedom to roam: a study of mobile device adoption and accessibility for people with visual and motor disabilities, Assets '09: 11th ACM SIGACCESS conference on Computers and accessibility, pages. 115–122.

[37] X.-P. Luo, J. Li, and L.-X. Zhen. Design and implementation of a card reader based on build-in camera. Pattern Recognition 1:417–420, 2004.

[38] H. Nakajima, Y. Matsuo, M. Nagata, and K. Saito. Portable translator capable of recognizing characters on signboard and menu captured by built-in camera. ACL 2005 pages 61–64.

[39] E. Ohbuchi, H. Hanaizumi, and L. A. Hock. Barcode readers using the camera device in mobile phones. Cyber World CW 2004, pages 260–265, IEEE Computer Society.

[40] T. Portele and J. Kramer. Adapting a tts system to a reading machine for the blind. In Spoken Language, 4th ICSLP 96, volume 1, pages 184 –187.

[41] S. V. Rice, F. R. Jenkins, and T. A. Nartker. The 5th annual test of OCR accuracy. Technical report, Information Science Research Institute,University of Nevada, Las Vegas, 1996.

[42] R. Smith. An overview of the tesseract ocr engine. ICDAR 2007 pages 629–633, IEEE Computer Society.

[43] F. R. J. Stephen V. Rice and T. A. Nartker. The 4th annual test of OCR accuracy. Information Science Research Institute,University of Nevada, Las Vegas, April 1995.

[44] E. A. Taub. The blind lead the sighted: Technology for people with disabilities finds a broader market, The New York Times, October 1999.

[45] X. Liu and D. Doermann. Mobile Retriever - Finding Document with a Snapshot. CBDAR-2007, pages 29–34.

[46] X. Liu and D. Doermann. A Camera Phone Based Currency Reader for the Visually Impaired. 10th ACM SIGACCESS, pages 305–306, October 2008.

[47] Y.S. Lee, S.W. Hong, T.L. Smith-Jackson, M. A. Nussbaum, and K. Tomioka. Systematic evaluation methodology for cell phone user interfaces, Interacting with Computers, 18 (2), pages.304-325, 2006.

[48] J. Nielsen, 1992 The Usability Engineering Life Cycle, Computer, vol.25 no.3, pages.12-22.

[49] C.M. Nielsen, M. Overgaard, M.P Pedersen., J. Stage, and S. Stenild, It's worth the hassle!: the added value of evaluating the usability of mobile systems in the field, Proc. 4th Nordic CHI 2006, pages.272 - 280.

[50] J. Sánchez, H. Flores and M.Sáenz, Mobile Science Learning for the Blind, CHI 2008, pages. 3201-3, 2006, Florence, Italy.

WCAG Conformance approach based on Model-Driven Development and WebML

Willian Massami Watanabe, David Fernandes Neto, Thiago Jabur Bittar[*] and Renata
P. M. Fortes
Institute of Mathematical and Computer Sciences, University of São Paulo
400, Trabalhador São-carlense Avenue - Centro
P.O.Box 668. 13560-970 - São Carlos/SP, Brazil
{watinha, david, jabur, renata}@icmc.usp.br

ABSTRACT

Accessibility is an important quality attribute for Web applications. The W3C has defined a set of guidelines that must be followed to deploy accessible web applications, however there is no process that support WCAG requirements during the software development lifecycle. This work proposes the inclusion of the WCAG 2.0 accessibility concerns in a Model-Driven Development, more specifically in the WebML process.

Categories and Subject Descriptors

H.2.2 [**Design Tools and Techniques**]: User Interfaces;
H.5.4 [**Hypertext/Hypermedia**]: User issues

General Terms

Design, Human Factors

Keywords

Web accessibility, Model-Driven Web Engineering, MDWE

1. INTRODUCTION

The large capacity of Web for providing information leads to multiple possibilities and opportunities for users. The development of high performance networks and ubiquitous devices allow users to retrieve content from any location and in different scenarios they might face in their lives. Unfortunately the possibilities offered by the Web are not necessarily currently available to all. Individuals who do not have completely compliant software or hardware that are able to deal with the latest technologies, or have some kind of physical or cognitive disability, find it difficult to interact with web pages, depending on the page structure and the ways in which the content is made available.

---

*Federal University of Goias - UFG

In this context, Web accessibility studies work towards the social and digital inclusion of disabled people in the Web platform, by providing web developers with design solutions addressing the difficulties that might impact the interaction of disabled individuals with the Web [31, 33]. However, there is no guarantee that these solutions will be designed in the final application. Freire et al., for example, conducted a survey about accessibility awareness of people involved in Web development in Brazil [9] and the web accessibility in Brazilian Municipalities websites [7]. Their conclusions were that web accessibility is far from being actually considered in Brazil and that much work remains to be done.

Neverthless, when considering the development process of web applications, it is widely accepted that systematic approaches in complex systems design prior to implementation improves the resulting application quality attributes [3]. In this context, Model-Driven Development (MDD) proposes the use of high-level abstract models and its successively transformation into increasingly more detailed ones. The transformations are done until the models become specific enough to be executed in a specific platform [22]. In MDD, conceptual diagrams are not only a reference that developers use to build executable code; models become "live" artifacts, serving as input to code generation tools, reducing the developers efforts [16]. The transformations from one model to the next create a chain which enables the automated implementation of a system starting from requirements [3].

This paper advocates on an approach to use MDD in order to provide web developers a systematic way of delivering accessible solutions in their systems. Current practices make use of validation tools and approaches to test WCAG conformance. However the iterative lifecycle model of development, based on maintenance of multiple prototypes and their respective evaluations and corrections, leads the resulting software into a complex, unmaintainable mass of code if changes are continually accommodated [18]. Web accessibility guidelines are important to help developers in delivering accessible web content, but they are not enough to fully support all activities involved in the web development process [8].

Our approach describes improvements to be made to the WebML modeling language [2], so that the adapted model becomes capable of mapping WCAG guidelines requirements. We present how the MDD transformations should be derived in order to provide developers a systematic way of implementing WCAG conformant websites that considers accessibility requirements during the design and implementation phases of the software development process, instead of just considering them while testing the application. Additionally, the use of a MDD approach to web development also improves the process considering portability, interoperability, maintainability and reusability [1]. We also present how the technological neutral characteristic of the WCAG 2.0 [14] improves the general process of MDD integration with WCAG accessibility requirements.

This article is structured as follows: Section 2 gives a brief description on web accessibility and the WCAG; in Section 3, it is presented the MDD approach into software development; Section 4 describes the WebML approach of web applications development and Section 5 present the proposal of including WCAG accessibility requirements into MDD; Section 6 presents related works on Model-Driven Web Engineering techniques; and Section 7 present final remarks and future works.

2. WCAG 2.0

The pre-eminent reference when addressing Web accessibility is the WCAG (Web Content Accessibility Guidelines) [15, 8]. The WCAG establishes a set of guidelines that discuss accessibility issues and provides accessibility design solutions [31, 33].

WCAG 2.0 was based on the WCAG 1.0, but the guidelines were written to be technologically neutral, being applicable to technologies available now and in the future [14]. The guidelines also provide objective testable criterias, that can be evaluated with a combination of automatic testing and human evaluation [23, 33].

The WCAG 2.0 is composed of a main document (normative specification) that does not describe the technological conditions required to deliver accessible solutions on websites [23]. The normative specification addresses the design solutions with a higher abstraction avoiding the technical details of web applications. The main document is complemented with a non-normative section that address the technological details required to implement the guidelines [14, 32]. The reason for keeping the technological description of solutions separately of the normative WCAG specification, allows changes and updates in the non-normative document as technology evolves and advances. The non-normative section is supposed to address technical extensions while keeping the normative section unchanged in its recommendations and evaluation criterias [23].

The guidelines of WCAG 2.0 are organized accordingly to four principles [33]: **Perceivable**, **Operable**, **Understadable** and **Robust**. Each guideline is composed by a set of objective testable Success Criteria addressing specific accessibility problems that impact on disabled users. The Success Criteria are than directly associated with the non-normative section of WCAG 2.0 that describe sufficient and advisory techniques for implementing a WCAG 2.0 conformant web application. The sufficient and advisory techniques address specific technological design solutions for the accessibility issue presented in the Success Criteria.

The approach behind WCAG to accessibility assurance requires the manual implementation of technological and design solutions by web developers and content authors [36, 35, 34]. However, not all web developers or content author are aware of them.

Freire et al. [9] conducted a survey on web accessibility awareness of people involved in web development in Brazil. The survey results showed that accessibility was still far from being addressed in web development projects in Brazil, as only 19.9% of participants had stated that accessibility is considered in their projects. Freire et al. [6] also reported on the results of a metrics based approach to evaluate WCAG conformance of brazilian municipalities web sites. The evaluation showed that brazilian municipalities web sites demand a lot of work to be done for broadening their access to disabled users.

Moreover, current web development practices make use of guidelines conformance evaluations, combining automatic evaluation tools (like Hera[1] and daSilva[2]), authoring tools (Bluefish[3] and Dreamweaver[4]) and human evaluations. These approaches deal with the implementation phase of web development, and therefore require cycling through implementation and refactoring of code and design for each issue identified by the accessibility evaluation or authoring tool. However the iterative lifecycle model of development, based on maintenance of multiple prototypes and their respective evaluations and corrections, leads the resulting software into a complex, unmaintainable mass of code if changes are continually accommodated [18].

Web accessibility guidelines are very relevant to provide web developers with accessible design solutions. However the guidelines alone are not enough to fully support each activity in the web developmento process [8].

Next section, the Model-Driven Development approach towards software development is presented.

3. MODEL-DRIVEN DEVELOPMENT

The Model-Driven Development (MDD) is a software engineering approach that consists in applying models to raise the abstraction level of software development and transformations from model-to-model to progressively evolve the system development. MDD intention is to both simplify and formalize the various activities and tasks that form the software's life cycle [11], or in a more simple definition: the MDD is the simple concept of building a model of a system and then transform it into something real [19].

The goal of MDD is to reduce the semantic distance that exists between the problem domain and the domain of implementation/solution, using more abstract models that protect developers from the complexities inherent in the implementation platform [5]. Based on that, MDD promotes reuse, interoperability, increase productivity, among other benefits.

In MDD, models are used to express concepts more efficiently since they include transformations used to automatically generate their artifacts of implementation, reflecting the solution expressed by models [25]. One of the most important benefits of the MDD is the reuse. Models condense knowledge produced during system analysis, design and implementation in a way (Ideally) independent of the implementation platform. Thus the knowledge can be more easily reused in other contexts [29].

The distinguishing feature of MDD is the use of models as the primary focus of development, instead of program-

---

[1] http://www.sidar.org/hera/index.php.en
[2] http://www.dasilva.org.br/
[3] http://bluefish.openoffice.nl/
[4] http://www.adobe.com/products/dreamweaver/

168

ming languages. The models are used to describe various aspects of the software and to automate code generation. The main advantage of this is to express models using concepts less bound to implementation details, beyond the fact that models are closest to the problem domain. This makes the models easier to specify, understand and maintain, than approaches that do not use models. And in some cases, it is still possible for domain experts to produce the systems rather than the expert technology implementation [28].

4. WEBML

The Web Modeling Language, WebML, is a visual language to support the development of complex and data-intensive Web applications. Its graphics specifications are formal and designed to withstand the steps of requirements analysis, conceptual modeling and deployment [2].

This language is supported by a case commercial tool called WebRatio[5], which consists of an environment for design of data and hypertext conceptual schemes, storing them as XML documents and allowing code generation. This tool is developed based on Eclipse platform to unify the development in the same environment, either in design or deployment.

The WebML consists of 4 main models: Struture Model, Hypertext Model, Presentation Model and Personalization Model.

The **Structure Model** is concerned with the organization of Web application data. The WebML does not propose new modeling notation for this model by allowing the use of notations such as the traditional Entity-Relationship Model and the format of UML Class Diagram.

The key elements for defining the structure model are entities that contain the stored data and relationships that allow connection of semantic entities. These entities are formed by a name and attributes associated with a data type. Relationships are defined by a name and cardinality of the entities that compose it. To do queries in this model can be used the WebML-OQL (Object Query Language), including querying derived data: for example, to know the number of books by an author simply be referred to the amount of relations "author-book".

The **Hypertext Model** consists of two sub-models: the composition and navigation. The composition model allows the definition of content units with desired attributes. Such units can be of the following types:

- **Data units**: show information of an object being defined through the attributes allocation;

- **Multidata units**: show the information relating to a range of objects, e. g. all the instances of a given entity;

- **Index units**: show objects of an entity in a list, showing each object as a link to another content unit;

- **Scroller units**: show commands to access elements in an ordered list of objects, for example, all instances of an entity or all objects associated with another through a particular relationship;

- **Filter units**: have fields that allow the user to enter values for a search, resulting in objects only validated

by a condition. They are usually used in conjunction with the index unit or multidata unit.

The pages formed in composition models phase can not exist isolated, they must be connected to compose the navigation model, which specifies the way in which content units are related, defining their links that may be of two forms:

- **Contextual**: connecting units with semantic information concerning the application, thus carrying information from the source unit to the destination;

- **Non-Contextual**: connect pages totally free, regardless of the units contained in the pages or their semantic relationships.

The **Presentation Model** is responsible for the way in which elements are arranged in the interface according to the device platform. Commonly it can be used XSL (EXtensible Stylesheet Language) styles to transform XML models into presentation elements.

The **Personalization Model** defines the content features of each user or user groups. The WebML provides the organizations concept of users and user groups, allowing customized modeling schemes of the content and presentation, access rules, security and updating.

The separation between the structural model and the hypertext allows WebML provides a way to specify various views of the same website, enabling to understand more complex requirements. These different views can be associated with the device by which the user is accessing the website or with user profiles.

5. INTEGRATING WCAG REQUIREMENTS IN WEBML

Our work proposes the enhancement of WebML development process to improve accessibility of WebML generated applications. For that, we suggest the inclusion of WCAG 2.0 accessibility concerns in the Model-Driven Development process of WebML. The accessibility concerns address modeling requirements and transformation requirements to be considered during the design phase of the development process, instead of just considering them while testing the final application's code. Our approach also works towards the elaboration of a systematic process for implementing WCAG conformmant web applications.

WCAG 2.0 provides different layers of guidance (principles, guidelines, success criteria, and sufficient and advisory techniques) that work together to present developers with recommendations and design solutions for accessibility issues in web applications [33]. The different layers of guidance are divided in two documents:

- **Normative**: composed of principles, guidelines and success criteria. The normative section provides developers with success criterias that describe evaluation steps used to determine is an application is accessible or not accordingly to a specific accessibility issue of the web application. The success criterias were elaborated to be technologically neutral and are organized in the WCAG 2.0 guidelines and principles.

- **Non-normative**: composed of sufficient and advisory techniques. Each of the sufficient and advisory techniques sections are directly associated with a specific

---
[5]http://www.webratio.com

success criteria described in the normative sections. The sufficient and advisory techniques sections provide developers with specific design solutions and technological implementations that address the accessibility issues identified in the success criteria they refer to.

The normative document of WCAG 2.0 is a stable reference which presents technologically neutral accessibility issues that should continue to work even with technology changes or advances. The non-normative document addresses platform specific design solutions for the accessibility issues presented in the normative document. Because of that, the non-normative document is subject to changes as technological of the design solutions might change. The separation of concerns achieved by the normative and non-normative documents ensure that as technology evolves the WCAG 2.0 normative specification remains unaltered.

Model-Driven Development proposes the use of high-level abstract models and its successively transformation into increasingly more detailed ones. These transformations are done until the models become specific enough to be executed in a specific platform [22]. In this context, we consider the integration of WCAG accessibility recommendations in different levels of the WebML MDD process, accordingly to the detailment specified on the normative and non-normative documents of WCAG 2.0.

The non-normative document addresses platform specific and technological design solutions for the accessibility issues evaluated by the success criterias. WebML models work as Platform Independent Models, thus WebML models should be kept from platform specific details. In this context, the platform specific details described in the non-normative document are derived as **transformation requirements** for the WebML process. The transformation requirements impact the code template mechanism for transforming WebML models into web applications, by adapting code templates to meet the technological solutions described in non-normative document.

WCAG conformance requirements for web applications design might impact other components different from the template mechanism used to generate the web application. Success Criteria 1.1.1 - Non-text Content, for instance, require that all non-text content that is provided within a web application is associated with a text alternative that serves the equivalent purpose. Nowadays, many web applications have to deal with requirements associated with the persistence of pictures, videos or audio data (like YouTube[6], Facebook[7] or Flickr[8]). In this scenario, all these non-text content (pictures, videos or audio files) need to be associated persistently with text alternatives that serves the same purpose, in order to achieve WCAG conformance with Success Criteria 1.1.1. This accessibility requirement cannot be solved by simple code templates mechanisms, since the task of associating different contents is subject of design and automatically generating design solutions for these requirements would drive inconsistence between models abstraction and code of the application. Considering that, accessibility concerns have to be introduced during the modeling phase of the WebML process, in order to map accessible design solutions concerns of the WCAG 2.0 guidelines in WebML mod-

---

[6]http://www.youtube.com
[7]http://www.facebook.com
[8]http://www.flickr.com/

els. In the example provided, Success Criteria 1.1.1 would imply on **modeling requirements** to the Structural Model of WebML for storing text alternative associated with the non-text content.

The modeling requirements can be extracted from the normative document of WCAG 2.0. The normative document describe accessibility evaluation criterias and testable aspects of the web interface. From these testable aspects, it becomes possible to identify development concerns that have to be addressed in the design of a web application so that WCAG conformance is achieved. These development concerns compose a set of modeling requirements that are to be considered in the WebML process and impact differently on WebML models accordingly to the web development concerns they map.

It is important to highlight that there is an implied relation between transformation requirements and modeling requirements identified in WCAG 2.0. Some code templates derived from the non-normative document of WCAG 2.0 require specific modeling parameters passing to transform models into code of accessible web applications. Therefore these modeling parameters have to be considered in WebML models as WCAG 2.0 modeling requirements. Note, however, that the modeling parameters represent specific aspects of accessibility addressed in both the normative and non-normative documents. As the modeling parameters are also addressed in the normative document of WCAG 2.0 they address platform independent issues of accessibility and maintain the separation of concerns between technology neutral and platform specific solutions.

The outline of the integration of WCAG 2.0 accessibility recommendations and the WebML process is illustrated on Figure 1.

The technology neutral goal achieved by WCAG 2.0 improve the interoperability and continuity of the WebML process. WCAG 2.0 separation of concerns establishes the normative and non-normative documents. The normative document is stable, while the non-normative is subject of changes as technology advances. However changes in the non-normative document impact only on the transformation engines of the WebML process, leaving WebML models and accessible requirements mappings unaltered.

It is important to acknowledge that each WCAG 2.0 success criteria impacts different WebML model concerns. Next sections describe the modeling requirements derived from WCAG 2.0 success criteria accordingly to the principle they belong.

5.1 Principle 1: Perceivable

The Perceivable principle is composed of four guidelines that describe accessibility issues related to *Text Alternatives*, *Time-based Media*, *Adaptability* and *Distinguishability*.

The first two guidelines (1.1 *Text Alternatives* and 1.2 *Time-base Media*) impose similar modeling requirements for the WebML process of development. Both guidelines address the importance of providing alternative ways of presenting information for users, since some types of media or content may not be perceived by users that present some kind of disability. For example: the informations represented on figures cannot be perceived by blind people, therefore figures require alternative ways for presenting the informations that they represent.

These guidelines modeling requirements impact on two

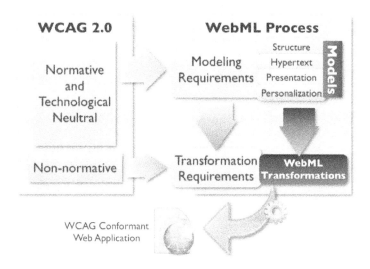

Figure 1: Outline of the integration of WCAG 2.0 recommendations and WebML process.

different WebML Models: Structure and Presentation Models. For projects that require the persistence of non-textual data or time-based media, the Structure Model must provide ways of storing alternative content and associating it with the non-textual content or time-based media they map. The Presentation Model, on the other hand, have to be adapted to present the alternative content associated with the content units instantiated in the Hypertext Model and that require the presentation of non-textual content or time-based media.

The guideline 1.3 - *Adaptable* states the importance of separating information and structure from the presentation details of web applications. This way content can be presented in different ways without loosing its meaning or order. The rationale for the guideline 1.3 is that different user agents or assistive technologies might loose or change the presentation details of the web application. Therefore informations that are conveyed only with presentation details will be inaccessible for individuals that make use of specific user agents or assistive technologies.

WebML models achieves the separation of concerns in regards of data modeling, navigation and task modeling, and presentation details of the application. In order to implement the modeling requirements generated by the guideline - *Adaptable*, it is necessary that informations are not conveyed on the presentation layer of the application (Success Criteria 1.3.3). However, in the WebML process, as informations and tasks are defined earlier in the development, they cannot reference presentation details, thus associations and relations wont be established with presentation details. In this context, associations are only established between Hypertext Models elements and content entities, and guidelines 1.1 and 1.2 already address issues related to informations conveyed only by presentation details.

Another concern related to the modeling requirements of the guideline 1.3 is to grant that order and structure are not missed due to presentation erros or lack of support by different user agents. This requirement leads the Presentation Model design into assuring that the order and consistence of presentation among content units is kept after the transformation of the content entities into the application code.

The guideline 1.4 - *Distinguishable* establish ways for facil-

itating the distinction of foreground informations and background of web applications. The implementation of these requirements eases users perception and focus on content. The accessibility concerns derived from guideline 1.4 imply solely on the Presentation Model of WebML. During this modeling phase of WebML process, in the Presentation Model, developers should consider design details for: contrast enhancement, audio volume, text size and color. These modeling requirements must be applied considering the distinction between foreground and background. Some other modeling requirements that must be considered when modeling the presentation of content entities of the Hypertext Model are related to the inclusion of audio control mechanisms for audio content, do not rely solely on color or images of text for presenting content entities and present mechanisms for resizing textual content.

5.2 Principle 2: Operable

The Operable Principle of WCAG 2.0 is composed of the following guidelines: *Keyboard Accessible*, *Enough Time*, *Seizures* and *Navigable*.

Guideline 2.1 - *Keyboard Accessible* provide modeling requirements only for the Presentation Model of WebML. WebML interaction modeling is realized in Hypertext Models. Hypertext Model considers standard interactions for web applications, like: links navigation, inputs filling and form submission. All standard interactions of web applications support keyboard interactions, thus no efforts in these interactions is required to garantee keyboard accessibility. WebML standard models also do not support rich interactivity design. Thus keyboard accessibility requirements for widgets or complex interface components can only be resolved in model-to-code transformations of the WebML process.

The inability of WebML modeling complex interaction interface component generates the same impact on the guideline 2.2 - *Enough Time*. Timing in web applications is generally implemented as local scripting languages, like Javascript or Flash. Timing functionality requires the use of timing events dispatching in these scripting languages. However, as WebML does not support the modeling of timing events, requirements related to timing in web applications must be addressed solely on the transformations mechanisms as well.

Guideline 2.3 - *Seizures* establishes that web applications do not contain anything that flashes more than three times in any one second period. This guideline imply in a simple requirement towards the Presentation Model of WebML, which constrains the presentation of interface components or elements that are known to cause seizures.

Guideline 2.4 - *Navigable* states the importance of providing ways to help users navigate, find content and determine where they are. This guideline leads to modeling requirements that address structure and navigation through the web application. Even though these modeling requirements address navigation issues on web application, they generate modeling concerns that impact mainly the Presentation model of WebML. These concerns address issues related to identifying structure within a webpage, like: providing purpose links descriptions and page title; using headings and labels to identify semantic and purpose in content entities of the Hypertext Model. Some other requirements implied by the guideline 2.4 is the definition of mechanisms to by-pass blocks of information that are repeated on multiple web pages and presenting users with informations about location and orientation on the web application they are accessing.

5.3 Principle 3: Understandable

All guidelines that compose the Understandable principle of WCAG 2.0 impact differently on WebML models concerns.

Guideline 3.1 - *Readable* require the implementation of mechanisms for presenting additional informations about parts of a text; identifying and defining the language of text content presented in a webpage; and associating simplified versions of text content available. These accessibility criteria are necessary for web applications, in order to make text content readable and understandable for users. These mechanisms drive modeling requirements to Structure, Hypertext and Presentation models of WebML.

The Structure Model of WebML is required to store the following additional data:

- Semantic informations about text content language (*Success Criteria 3.1.2*).

- Establishing associations between specific words or expressions, present on text content, with definitions or pronunciation (*Success Criteria 3.1.3, 3.1.4 and 3.1.6*).

- Establishing associations between text content and supplemental content with simplified versions of the same information presented on the text content (*Success Criteria 3.1.5*).

After the insertion of these Structure Model concerns in the web application design, it is necessary to define mechanisms that allow users to navigate through the text associations stored. These navigation functionalities generate modeling requirements for the Hypertext Model of WebML, and drive the development of mechanisms for presenting additional informations about text content and for changing the text content language of a webpage.

The *Readable* guideline of WCAG 2.0, present only some minor impact on the Presentation model of WebML, since it only requires that the page and parts of text language be identified and marked accordingly.

Guideline 3.2 - *Predictable* states that websites should not change contexts over focus or input events unless the user has been advised of the behavior before using it. In order to initiate a context change on the web application, it is required that the use of Local Scripting techniques. However, WebML models doesn't map nor implement these functionalities. Thus there is no modeling requirement that needs to be addressed in WebML models, considering the context change issue on web applications.

Another accessibility evaluation criteria documented in the *Predictable* guideline highlights the importance of consistent navigation and identification of links. The identification of links among webpages is defined on the Hypertext Model, and model-to-code transformations are responsible for deriving these identifications consistently in the development process of MDD. However the consistent navigation requirement needs to be addressed in the Presentation model of the web application, by structuring the presentation of the contextual and non-contextual links.

Guideline 3.3 - *Input Assistance* provides developers with evaluation criteria about help and correction mechanisms available for forms and input elements of the web application. These criteria evaluate how the application deals with error prevention, identification and suggestion routines. Form and inputs are normally associated with content entities that are mapped directly on the Structure Model of WebML. However, WebML deals with content entities entry constraints on the Hypertext Model, by designing composition and navigation models that evaluates the input and drive the interaction accordingly to the validity of data. The *Input Assistance* guideline also drive modeling requirements to the Presentation model, in order to present informations about the consistency of input data, providing labels for identifying form elements and presenting context-sensitive help informations.

5.4 Principle 4: Robust

The *Robust* guideline address only platform specific issues in the web application, in regards to compatibility of technology solutions implemented in the web application considering the variety of user agents and assistive technologies.

As previously stated, however, WebML models work on the Platform Independent Level of solutions design, therefore there is no modeling requirements from the *Robust* principle for WebML models.

6. RELATED WORK

During the last years, the web engineering community proposed several languages, architectures, methods and processes for developing and modeling web applications, including their interaction, such as OOHDM [26], OO-H [27], OOWS [4], UWE [17] and WebML [2]. These approaches focus on analysis and design models for web applications, such as navigation and adaptation models.

Gitzel et al. [10] present specific concerns that have to be considered while developing web applications: heterogeneity on the client and server side, compatibility, performance, maintenance, scalability, and others. Among these concerns it is emphasized the accessibility of web applications. Gitzel et al. describe how accessibility plays an important role in web applications design specially when dealing with contexts such as e-goverment [30] and business.

Semantic encoding means explicitly storing all relevant knowledge about the content of a web application in order to further derive the presentation accordingly to specific usage contexts and scenarios [13]. The flexibility achieved by the separation of concerns considering the content and presentation can bring the realization of a broad accessibility to web applications. In this context, Jeschke and Vieritz proposed the use of Model-Driven Development to store all knowledge about content in models and, than, derive this content's presentation considering the capabilities of users interacting with the web application [13]. Our approach, differently from Jeschke and Vieritz's work, which focuses on the perception issues of accessibility, describe a model of accessibility following web standards which deals with others issues like interaction, navigation, among others.

In another work, Jeschke et al. [12] present the integration of web accessibility patterns in the UWE - *UML-based Web Engineering*. UWE is a Model-Driven Web Development approach which extends the MOF - *Meta Object Facility* with an appropriate profile for web engineering. The study elaborated by Jeschke et al. used accessibility patterns with concerns related to overview, orientation, navigation and content. Our work is very similar with Jeschke et al. approach towards the integration of accessible design solutions in the Model-Driven Development process. However, instead of extracting the requirements from platform specific details of the patterns addressed by Jeschke et al., we focus on the technological neutral characteristic of WCAG 2.0 for separating the concerns in regards of the design solutions accordingly to the respective abstraction level that they should be represented in WebML models.

Moreno et al. [20], in a more technical method for supporting accessibility on the Web, provide a solution for including accessibility requirements in the design process. Their work consider the use of accessible content templates and elaborate structure and semantic annotations of content in order to preserve accessibility. Our work is very similar to this approach since we propose the extension of models concerns to enrich semantically and structurally web content entities to derive accessibility in the resultant application. However, we also work on the presentation layer of web design, instead of regarding the reuse of accessible presentation templates, we show how accessibility requirements of WCAG might impact and should be considered during the design of presentation.

7. FINAL REMARKS

This paper described an MDD approach towards the development of a systematic process that considers web accessibility issues in the design and implementation phase of the software development. We proposed the inclusion of WCAG 2.0 accessibility requirements in different models and code transformation templates of WebML. We describe how each principle and guideline impacts different concerns and models that compose the WebML development process. The proposal has the objective of easing the development of WCAG 2.0 conformant web applications by separating the concerns related to each design solution described in the WCAG 2.0 document and the respective models of WebML.

The integration of WCAG 2.0 accessibility requirements in the WebML process present some design limitations due to WebML models restriction to representing rich interactions on web pages. Thus these requirements need to be addressed on the WebML transformations of model-to-code that generate the web application. WebML extension already address the design of Rich Internet Applications, how-

ever verifying how these extension map the limitations observed in this work remains as a future work.

The WebML design language was used as a proof of concept and description of how WCAG 2.0 accessibility requirements are mapped as design concerns of web applications. The proposed approach can be extended in order to apply to other web applications design language considering MDE - *Model-Driven Engineering* tools (given the MOF - *Meta Object Facility* metamodel for WebML established in [24] and the WEI - *Web Engineering Interoperability* as a reference model for representing web applications development concerns [21]).

Others future works include: analysing how the approach of integrating WCAG 2.0 requirements can be extended for others MDD approaches for web development and evaluating the approach with a case study.

8. ACKNOWLEDGMENTS

Our thanks to FAPESP (process 2010/05626-7) and CNPq for supporting this work.

9. REFERENCES

[1] T. J. Bittar, R. P. Fortes, L. L. Lobato, and W. M. Watanabe. Web communication and interaction modeling using model-driven development. In *SIGDOC '09: Proceedings of the 27th ACM international conference on Design of communication*, pages 193–198, New York, NY, USA, 2009. ACM.

[2] S. Ceri, P. Fraternali, and A. Bongio. Web modeling language (webml): a modeling language for designing web sites. *Comput. Netw.*, 33(1-6):137–157, 2000.

[3] D. Distante, P. Pedone, G. Rossi, and G. Canfora. Model-driven development of web applications with UWA, MVC and JavaServer faces. In *Proceedings of the 7th international conference on Web engineering*, pages 457–472, Como, Italy, 2007. Springer-Verlag.

[4] J. Fons, P. Valderas, M. Ruiz, G. Rojas, and O. Pastor. Oows: A method to develop web applications from web-oriented conceptual models. In *In: International Workshop on Web Oriented Software Technology (IWWOST). (2003) 6570*, pages 65–70, 2003.

[5] R. France and B. Rumpe. Model-driven development of complex software: A research roadmap. In *29th International Conference on Software Engineering 2007 - Future of Software Engineering*, pages 37–54, Minneapolis, MN, USA, 2007. IEEE Computer Society.

[6] A. P. Freire, T. J. Bittar, and R. P. M. Fortes. An approach based on metrics for monitoring web accessibility in brazilian municipalities web sites. In *SAC '08: Proceedings of the 2008 ACM symposium on Applied computing*, pages 2421–2425, New York, NY, USA, 2008. ACM.

[7] A. P. Freire, R. P. M. Fortes, M. A. S. Turine, and D. M. B. Paiva. An evaluation of web accessibility metrics based on their attributes. In *SIGDOC '08: Proceedings of the 26th annual ACM international conference on Design of communication*, pages 73–80, New York, NY, USA, 2008. ACM.

[8] A. P. Freire, R. Goularte, and R. P. de Mattos Fortes. Techniques for developing more accessible web

applications: a survey towards a process classification. In *SIGDOC '07: Proceedings of the 25th annual ACM international conference on Design of communication,* pages 162–169, New York, NY, USA, 2007. ACM.

[9] A. P. Freire, C. M. Russo, and R. P. M. Fortes. A survey on the accessibility awareness of people involved in web development projects in brazil. In *W4A '08: Proceedings of the 2008 international cross-disciplinary conference on Web accessibility (W4A),* pages 87–96, New York, NY, USA, 2008. ACM.

[10] R. Gitzel, A. Korthaus, and M. Schader. Using established web engineering knowledge in model-driven approaches. *Sci. Comput. Program.,* 66(2):105–124, 2007.

[11] B. Hailpern and P. Tarr. Model-driven development: the good, the bad, and the ugly. *IBM Syst. J.,* 45(3):451–461, 2006.

[12] S. Jeschke, O. Pfeiffer, and H. Vieritz. Using web accessibility patterns for web application development. In *Proceedings of the 2009 ACM symposium on Applied Computing,* pages 129–135, Honolulu, Hawaii, 2009. ACM.

[13] S. Jeschke and H. Vieritz. Accessibility and model-based web application development for elearning environments. In *Innovations in E-learning, Instruction Technology, Assessment, and Engineering Education,* pages 439–444. Springer Netherlands, 2007.

[14] B. Kelly, D. Sloan, S. Brown, J. Seale, H. Petrie, P. Lauke, and S. Ball. Accessibility 2.0: people, policies and processes. In *W4A '07: Proceedings of the 2007 international cross-disciplinary conference on Web accessibility (W4A),* pages 138–147, New York, NY, USA, 2007. ACM.

[15] B. Kelly, D. Sloan, L. Phipps, H. Petrie, and F. Hamilton. Forcing standardization or accommodating diversity?: a framework for applying the wcag in the real world. In *W4A '05: Proceedings of the 2005 International Cross-Disciplinary Workshop on Web Accessibility (W4A),* pages 46–54, New York, NY, USA, 2005. ACM.

[16] A. G. Kleppe, J. Warmer, and W. Bast. *MDA Explained: The Model Driven Architecture: Practice and Promise.* Addison-Wesley Longman Publishing Co., Inc., Boston, MA, USA, 2003.

[17] N. Koch and A. Kraus. The expressive power of uml-based web engineering, 2002.

[18] M. M. and J. L. Reusing knowledge about users. In *4th Australian Conference on Requirements Engineering,* pages 59–69, September 1999.

[19] S. J. Mellor, A. N. Clark, and T. Futagami. Guest editors' introduction: Model-driven development. *IEEE Software,* 20:14–18, 2003.

[20] L. Moreno, P. Martínez, and B. Ruiz. Guiding accessibility issues in the design of websites. In *SIGDOC '08: Proceedings of the 26th annual ACM international conference on Design of communication,* pages 65–72, New York, NY, USA, 2008. ACM.

[21] N. Moreno and A. Vallecillo. Towards interoperable web engineering methods. *J. Am. Soc. Inf. Sci. Technol.,* 59(7):1073–1092, 2008.

[22] D. A. Nunes and D. Schwabe. Rapid prototyping of web applications combining domain specific languages and model driven design. In *ICWE '06: Proceedings of the 6th international conference on Web engineering,* pages 153–160, New York, NY, USA, 2006. ACM.

[23] L. G. Reid and A. Snow-Weaver. Wcag 2.0: a web accessibility standard for the evolving web. In *W4A '08: Proceedings of the 2008 international cross-disciplinary conference on Web accessibility (W4A),* pages 109–115, New York, NY, USA, 2008. ACM.

[24] A. Schauerhuber, M. Wimmer, and E. Kapsammer. Bridging existing web modeling languages to model-driven engineering: a metamodel for WebML. In *Workshop proceedings of the sixth international conference on Web engineering,* page 5, Palo Alto, California, 2006. ACM.

[25] D. C. Schmidt. Guest editor's introduction: Model-driven engineering. *IEEE Computer,* 39(2):25–31, 2006.

[26] D. Schwabe, R. de Almeida Pontes, and I. Moura. Oohdm-web: an environment for implementation of hypermedia applications in the www. *SIGWEB Newsl.,* 8(2):18–34, 1999.

[27] D. Schwabe and G. Rossi. The object-oriented hypermedia design model. *Commun. ACM,* 38(8):45–46, 1995.

[28] B. Selic. The pragmatics of model-driven development. *IEEE Softw.,* 20(5):19–25, 2003.

[29] K. Sherif, R. Appan, and Z. Lin. Resources and incentives for the adoption of systematic software reuse. *International Journal of Information Management,* 26(1):70–80, 2006.

[30] B. Shneiderman. Leonardo's laptop: human needs and the new computing technologies. In *CIKM '05: Proceedings of the 14th ACM international conference on Information and knowledge management,* pages 1–1, New York, NY, USA, 2005. ACM.

[31] W3C. Web content accessibility guidelines 1.0. W3C Recommendation, May 1999.

[32] W3C. Techniques and failures for web content accessibility guidelines 2.0. W3C Working Group Note, November 2008.

[33] W3C. Web content accessibility guidelines (wcag) 2.0. W3C Recommendation, December 2008.

[34] W. M. Watanabe, A. Candido, Jr., M. A. Amâncio, M. de Oliveira, T. A. S. Pardo, R. P. M. Fortes, and S. M. Aluísio. Adapting web content for low-literacy readers by using lexical elaboration and named entities labeling. In *W4A '10: Proceedings of the 2010 International Cross Disciplinary Conference on Web Accessibility (W4A),* pages 1–9, New York, NY, USA, 2010. ACM.

[35] W. M. Watanabe, R. P. de Mattos Fortes, and T. A. S. P. e Sandra Maria Alusio. Facilita: Auxílio a leitura de textos disponíveis na web. In *Webmedia 2009,* pages 1–4, Fortaleza, CE, Brazil, 2009.

[36] W. M. Watanabe, A. C. Jr., V. R. de Uzeda, R. P. M. Fortes, T. A. S. Pardo, and S. M. Alusio. Facilita: Reading assistance for low-literacy readers. In *ACM SIGDOC 2009,* pages 29–36, Bloomington, IN, USA, 2009. ACM.

Improving WCAG for Elderly Web Accessibility

Silvana Maria Affonso de Lara, Willian Massami Watanabe, Eduardo Pezutti Beletato
dos Santos and Renata P. M. Fortes
Institute of Mathematical and Computer Sciences, University of São Paulo
400, Trabalhador São-carlense Avenue - Centro
P.O.Box 668. 13560-970 - São Carlos/SP, Brazil
{silvana,watinha, epbsanti, renata}@icmc.usp.br

ABSTRACT

The increase of aging people and the possibilities that are extended to the Internet users have led studies into improvement of web accessibility solutions for older people [30]. Most older adults present some decline in their cognitive, visual, hearing and motor skills [13]. Nowadays, however, the Web faces new technological challenges that extend the initial idea of cross-platform and inter-operational nature of the HTML and HTTP. The challenges are posed as accessibility barriers and consider the skills, capabilities, culture, languages, disabilities, among other characteristics related to the user as a human being, in contrast to the hardware and software requirements previously addressed. The human characteristics of the challenge can be seeing as the ultimate barrier of the initial Web requirements of cross-platform and inter-operational environment, and goes towards social inclusion of people whatever differences they might present in the Web. In this paper we propose the establishment of a new set of success criteria that address older users accessibility into the normative document of WCAG 2.0. The proposed recommendations were identified from a composition of usability studies with real older users and were tested for different scenarios.

Categories and Subject Descriptors

H.2.2 [**Design Tools and Techniques**]: User Interfaces; H.5.4 [**Hypertext/Hypermedia**]: User issues

General Terms

Accessibility, Human Factors

Keywords

Web accessibility, middle-age adults, elderly

1. INTRODUCTION

Brazil is experiencing an unprecedented growth in the number of elderly people and others that soon will become

old, which in this work, we call middle-aged adults. It is estimated that in the period 2000 to 2050 will occur the greatest increase in the proportion of elderly, from 5.1% to 14.2% and that by 2025 the population over 60 years will reach 34 million people [30] . The United Nations estimates that by 2050 one in five people will be over 60 years old. The estimate is that in Europe in the near future there will be about 17.6% of elderly in the countries comprising the European Union in 2010 and that this proportion will reach 20.7% in 2020 [3].

As a consequence of this global phenomenon it can be observed that most older persons suffer with the reduction or loss of their abilities. Difficulties related to vision, cognition and motor coordination constraints increase with the passing of years [7] [10] [19] [24]) and are not unique problems to older adults. These limitations also apply to other user groups, including, for example, persons with low vision, attention deficit, developmental delay, limited reading proficiency, among other restrictions.

It is noteworthy that age is just a variable that acts on the aging process. According to Neri [21], there is no biological or physical factor that accurately indicates the point in time that ends maturity and start the old age. The factors that influence this process are: gender, socioeconomic status, conditions of physical and mental health, habit and lifestyle, among others.

There are many elderly people who are not influenced by aging criticism while maintaining their ability to perform day-by-day activities without major problems and can even use the web without any resistance or barrier. In literature, studies show that the constant practice of what was learned also helps to reduce the difficulties and resistance.

There are several initiatives with the purpose of providing guidance, guidelines or heuristics that help developers building web pages more suitable for interaction with older people. Indeed, when the guidelines and recommendations are used, the improvements are not only enjoyed by the public elderly, but also for all other groups that had difficulties or deficiencies in the interaction. However, there is still great resistance by the developers in the implementation of such recommendations. The quest for productivity and attractive design has put the human aspect of interaction in the background.

With the aim of adapting WCAG accessibility recommendations for the older audience and to remedy some problems that still persist on webpages, work has been done with field observation and users testing activities, in order to identify and list the accessibility indicators that target the older.

The pre-eminent reference on web accessibility [22][23], the WCAG (Web Content Accessibility Guidelines), establish a set of guidelines that discuss accessibility issues and provide accessible design solutions for users with disabilities [40]. The WCAG is of particular relevance to developers of Web resources, because not only have been promoting with successful around the world but also their guidelines have been adopted by many organizations and are increasingly being adopted at a national level [8].

The simplicity of the WCAG approach has helped in raising the profile on web accessibility [15]. However the guidelines still lack of recommendations and design solutions that address older users [30]. There are efforts being directed into these issues [25], but they have not yet being integrated as part of the general guidelines presented at the WCAG 2.0 document.

The article is organized as follows: Section 2 presents concepts of usability and accessibility; in Section 3 are shown the main problems associated with aging that influence the interaction of middle-aged adults with Web pages; Section 4 presents related works; in Section 5, the WAI model is presented with their adaptations to meet the older adults; in Section 6 are held discussions on the adaptation approach used in this work; and Section 7 provides the final remarks and future work.

2. USABILITY AND ACCESSIBILITY

Recently, the concepts of accessibility and usability have been extensively studied and exploited in the development of Web interfaces. The term usability is a concept related to several components, traditionally associated with five attributes: learnability, efficiency, ease of storage, low error rate and user satisfaction, which can be considered as a set of independent quality attributes or as a single attribute consisting of all of them [22]. According to Nielsen, while developing Web applications, there are some basic principles that should be considered [23]:

- Clarity in information architecture: it is essential that the user can discern what is priority and what is secondary in a website;

- Ease of navigation: users should be able to access the desired information within three clicks;

- Simplicity: the structure of a website should be simple in order to make easier the understanding of content, or delete information without compromising the system integrity;

- Content Relevance: the design of a website should focus, above all, the content of information provided; o Maintain consistency: consistency is a powerful usability principle on the Web. Keeping presentation consistence among different web pages improves the learnability of the application and give users confidence while operating the website.

- Time bearable: the load time of pages must necessarily be short, so that user does not lose interest; o User focus: again, all principles can be summarized in one, the focus should be on the users' activities.

The term accessibility has several meanings that are dependent on the context in which users operate. In general,

accessibility refers to the fact that something is accessible to users regardless of the means of access and their individual problems or limitations. In the area of information systems consists of a quality attribute that can be described through the development of flexible design solutions to accommodate the diverse needs of a large portion of users, regardless of age, disability or technology.

Web-accessibility corresponds to the possibility that any user using any agent (software or hardware that retrieves and serializes Web content), can understand and interact with the content of a website [31].

With the goal of promoting accessibility in the development of Web pages and make them accessible to a growing number of people, a committee formed by large companies and called the W3C (World Wide Web Consortium) established the WAI (Web Accessibility Initiative) Model of accessibilty, which consists of a set of documents containing guidelines to ensure the accessibility of the Web to people with disabilities, or for people who access the Web in special conditions of environment, equipment, technologies and different browser. In Brazil, the initiative for accessibility resulted in the elaboration of the e-MAG model, which currently is at version 2.0, and deals with the accessibility guidelines for the construction and adaptation of content from the Brazilian government on the Internet [8].

Although the concepts of usability and accessibility are being further investigated and applied in systems interface design, some questions remain regarding the overlap of some concepts. As distinct orientations, both concepts are trying to solve similar problems, but were written in different contexts or with different focus. The concepts of usability and accessibility are easily distinguishable when you consider that a web page, for instance, can be very intuitive and easy to use, but inaccessible due to lack of ALT tags in images. Thus, this page is usable by people with no disabilities, but inaccessible to people who need a screen reader. Moreover, another page can have all the ALT tags properly filled in all the charts, but present a confused design that affect the interaction of users.

Literature is not clear on how strong is the relationship between accessibility and usability. Several questions arise in relation to assessments of accessibility and usability, with regard to adherence to the guidelines. For instance, a site that has a high degree of compatibility with accessibility guidelines can be considered as also having a high degree of usability? Does accessibility and usability evelutions map similar problems? Although there are points of conflict when it prioritizes accessibility in relation to usability and vice versa, Petrie et al. [25] emphasize the idea that both concepts should be considered in an integrated way to reach the "universal usability". Universal Usability emerges as a way to combine and reduce the gap between the principles of usability and accessibility guidelines.

3. ELDERLY USERS AND WEB

Web pages interaction has great potential to support older adults carrying out their day-by-day tasks, mainly as a way to offset the declines from the natural aging process, such as sensory declines, or loss of cognitive abilities physical. The Web is no longer just a means of entertainment for young people. Today we can already observe greater concern and greater number of requests by businesses for the creation or adaptation of web sites aimed to conquer and meet the older audience.

Analysis by the N/N Group [6], report that older people view the Web as a means of socialization, which encourages contact with family and friends as well as a source of information. Parts of these users also use the Web to search for their own interests, for financial management, shopping, online courses for the development of new skills, among others. However, most older people have faced great difficulties in interacting with Web pages, either through lack of experience with computer technologies and a lack of motivation due to the insecurity and difficulty in learning new concepts [9]. Also it is noteworthy the lack of understanding by the developers that the elderly have different needs of younger users, both in motivating its use and modeling the interaction. Although there are several initiatives that provide guidelines for developing usable and accessible Web pages, the search for productivity and interesting design means that many developers focus less attention to the human aspect and develop interfaces that do not meet the specific needs of this audience.

We found several studies about the effects of aging on cognitive process, in literature. Most of them focused their studies on major cognitive functions such as memory, reasoning, problem solving, language, among others. The skills that present declines during the aging process are especially those that require more effort in working memory [28] [32] , processing speed [2], and spatial perception, where the first deficits usually appear around 40 years old and may become more pronounced after 50 years on [26].

Older people often present difficulties and resistances in reading text on computer screen. It is common to see their anxiety in actions. These activities if conducted without prior reading of content can lead older people into error situations that end up frustrating their expectations and causing them to abandon the interaction. Working memory, which is the ability to keep information active and requiring temporary storage and manipulation of that information, also decreases with age and appears as a limiting factor for reading comprehension, speech, manipulation of quantitative representations , among others [9].

According to Fisk et. al [9] older adults are slower and less successful in acquiring new procedures in comparison with young people, once they process information more slowly. Differences between ages increase according to the complexity of the task, particularly with respect to tasks that require coordination of multiple tasks simultaneously.

With regard to attention, both visual selective attention (scanning a visual display) as the dynamic visual attention (redirecting the focus of attention) show declines during aging. Therefore it is important to create mechanisms that try to facilitate their orientation and capture their attention [9].

Aiming to bring accessibility guidelines to the specific needs of older people, we propose an adaptation of guidelines, in order to maximize the capabilities and minimize the limitations of older people in their interactions with the Web as a way to promote greater social inclusion, facilitate the acquisition of services and provide better quality of life to this audience that grows more and more.

4. RELATED WORK

Abou-Zahra et al. [1] present the goals and studies for creating the document WAI-AGE. Initial studies for the creation of this document started about 2007 and the document presents five goals:

1. To inform the development of extensions on WAI guidelines and supplemental educational materials which can better promote and meet the needs of people who have accessibility needs related to ageing;

2. Better inform the ongoing work of W3C/WAI with regard to the needs of the elderly, and to create an ongoing dialog between ageing communities and disability communities, and other stakeholder groups on the needs of people who have accessibility needs related to ageing;

3. To provide educational resources focused towards industry implementors, including developers of mainstream technologies, assistive technologies, and Web designers and developers.

4. To provide educational resources focused towards organizations representing and serving ageing communities, and towards individuals with accessibility needs related to ageing.

5. To promote increased harmonisation of Web accessibility standards so as to further build a unified market for technology developers and expedite the production of Web accessibility solutions.

The WAI-AGE document was published on 2008, and since then, field studies were conducted to validate the guidelines presented in the WAI-AGE. These studies were unable to verify certain points without more detailed information, particularly with issues concerning the elderly population.

Kurniawan and Zaphiris [16] gathered various published studies that proposed Web design guidelines for older people (both industrial and academic papers) to remove the overlaps, to categorize them in a meaningful way and to verify the usefulness of those guidelines with the target user group addressed by the guidelines: older Web users. They selected 32 guidelines submitted to validation by heuristic evaluation. The article achieved the developement of a manageable and robust set of guidelines for designing and evaluating ageing-friendly websites, however, it didnt report on validation for the guidelines proposed.

The work of Sayago and Blat [29] aimed at being as much relevant as possible to real-life scenarios, where older people tend to look for more complex online information such as medication, accommodation and traveling. The work focused on three tasks, which are likely to be the most predominant ones: basic search (Google); advanced search (Google Advanced Search); and directories (Yahoo! Directory). It was reported that older people found complex online information 3 times faster by using basic search than by means of advanced search or directory.

5. WAI ACCESSIBILITY MODEL AND THE WCAG 2.0

WAI (Web Accessibility Initiative) is an organization created by the W3C that establish principles and rules of design and development of sites that are accessible to people with special needs [18]. WAI promotes a tripartite model of accessibility, with the goal of universal Web accessibility in theory provided by full conformance with each of three components [5]:

WCAG - *Web Content Accessibility Guidelines* present a series of recommendations about how to make Web content more accessible for users with disabilities [40]. The WCAG specification provides guidelines for Web content developers.

ATAG - *Authoring Tool Accessibility Guidelines* provide recommendations that assist the design of Web content authoring tools that produce accessible Web sites [34]. The ATAG specification provides guidelines for Web content authoring tools developers.

UAAG - *User Agent Accessibility Guidelines* provide recommendations for the development of user agents that lower web accessibility barriers for people with disabilities [35]. The specification considers as a User Agent any kind of software that retrives and render Web content. Furthermore, the UAAG conformant User Agents also have the possibility of matching and communicating with Assistive Technologies to improve the Web experience of users. The UAAG specification provides guidelines for User Agent developers.

The pre-eminent reference on web accessibility [15, 11], the WCAG (*Web Content Accessibility Guidelines*), establish a set of guidelines that discuss accessibility issues and provide accessible design solutions for users with disabilities [40]. The WCAG is of particular relevance to developers of Web resources, because not only have been promoting with successful around the world but also their guidelines have been adopted by many organizations and are increasingly being adopted at a national level [36].

The first version of the guidelines, WCAG 1.0 [33], became a W3C recommendation on 1999, when most web pages implementation was based on HTML. Therefore, the WCAG 1.0 was developed to support accessible solutions for the HTML technology [14, 27].

Nowadays, however, web sites use a great deal of different technologies. The new generation of the Web (Web 2.0) and their RIA - *Rich Internet Applications* are build with dynamic interactions [12] and require specific technologies like: ECMAScript, HTMLHTTPRequest, SVG - *Scalable Vector Graphcs*, SMIL - *Synchronized Multimedia Integrations Language*, Flash, Java Applets, among others [20]. The design of RIA components extend the use of HTML with a new set of development patterns and standards, but they are not addressed in the WCAG 1.0 document. The WCAG 1.0 guidelines classifies the use of these technologies as harmful for users even when they are designed as accessible technologies.

Another limitation observed in WCAG 1.0 is related to the subjectivity of the *checkpoints* [4]. The subjectivity present on the guidelines statements make it difficult to evaluate WCAG 1.0 full conformance [27]. That WCAG 1.0 characteristic led the United States goverment to choose the Section 508[1] as the standard legal accessibility solution for USA websites instead of the WCAG 1.0.

Considering that the WAI elaborated the WCAG 2.0. The WCAG 2.0 was based on the WCAG 1.0, but the guidelines were written to be technologically neutral, being applicable to technologies available now and in the future [14]. The guidelines also provide objective testable criterias, that can

be evaluated with a combination of automatic testing and human evaluation [27, 40].

The WCAG 2.0 main document (normative specification) do not describe the technological conditions required to deliver accessible solutions on websites [27]. The normative specification address the design solutions with a higher abstraction avoiding the technical details of web applications. The main document is complemented with a non-normative section that address the technological details required to implement the guidelines [14, 38]. The idea of keeping the technological description of solutions separately of the normative WCAG specification, allows changes and updates in the non-normative document as technology evolves and advances. The non-normative section is supposed to address technical extensions while keeping the normative section unchanged in its recommendations and evaluation criterias [27].

The WCAG 2.0, just as WCAG 1.0, define accessible design solutions that allow disabled users to interact and use web applications [40]. Although the guidelines address a great deal of usage scenarios, they do not cover all possible combinations and levels of disabilities.

The simplicity of the WCAG approach has helped in raising the profile on web accessibility [15]. However the guidelines still lack of recommendations and design solutions that address older users [13]. There are efforts being directed into these issues [39], but they have not yet being integrated as part of the general guidelines presented at the WCAG 2.0 document.

The guidelines are organized in four principles [37]:

Perceivable : interface components must be designed in ways that the user can perceive.

Operable : interface components must be designed in ways that the user can operate them.

Understandable : information and interface components must be understandable.

Robust : content must be compatible with a wide variety of user agents.

Each guideline contain Success Criterias that specifically describe the design solutions required to conform the web site with the accessible recommendations of WCAG 2.0 [37]. The Success Criterias must address accessibility problems that impact on disabled users, differently of usability aspects that are applied for all general users. The Success Criterias were elaborated to be objective testable on web interfaces.

The Success Criterias are classified accordingly to their impact on the accessibility of a web site. This classification separetes success criterias into level A, level AA and level AAA, in which Success Criterias classified as level A represent more severe impacts on the accessibility of a website if not designed. The classification considers the following aspects on the criterias [27, 37]:

- Compatibility of the solution with assistive technologies

- Applicability of the solution for all websites and types of content

- Understandability of the solution by content authors

- Presentation, functionality, esthetic or expression limitations imposed by the design solution

---

[1]http://www.section508.gov

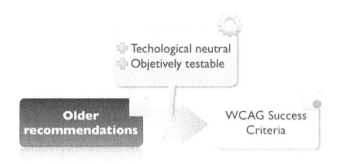

Figure 1: Adaptation of older accessibility issues to integrate the WCAG 2.0

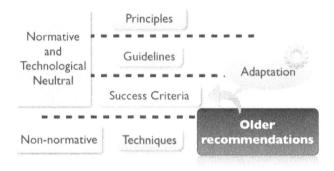

Figure 2: Proposal of including older accessibility issues as Success Criteria of WCAG 2.0.

- Existence of workarounds for the solution

We propose the identification and inclusion of specific design recommendations that address the difficulties presented by older users in the WCAG 2.0. These design recommendations were identified on field observations with users over 40 years old [17], surveys and usability testing on interaction models, interface components, menus and e-commerce applicationson the Web.

The new design recommendations need to be adapted to integrate the WCAG document and extend its success criteria to address issues for the older people on the Web. The adaptation is required in order to keep the new guidelines consistent with the design solutions previously addressed in the document.

Our approach, therefore, adapts the accessibility issues identified in other studies to provide objective evaluation criteria (Success Criteria) and a technological neutral solution. This approach is illustrated on Figure 1.

We propose that the design recommendation integrate the Success Criteria granularity level of WCAG 2.0 as illustrated in Figure 2.

Next section describes the new Success Criteria to be included in WCAG 2.0.

6. ADAPTATION AND INCLUSION OF NEW SUCCESS CRITERIA

We present the new Success Criteria organized accordingly to the WCAG 2.0 Principles which they are supposed to integrate.

6.1 Perceivable

- **Success Criteria 1.3.4**: *The webpage must present a functionality that reads aloud the content.*
  Rationale: reducing visual effort and keep the attention on the webpage's content. This Success Criteria integrates the guideline 1.3 - *Adaptable.*

- **Success Criteria 1.4.10**: *Webpage main content must be presented in the visual field of the user, 15% left and right, and 20% top margins.*
  Rationale: during field observations it was reported that older users fix their attention on the screen center, ignoring information presented in lateral bars, header and footer. This Success Criteria integrates the guideline 1.4 - *Distinguishable.*

- **Success Criteria 1.4.11**: *The webpage must highlight the main elements that compose it, such as: links, menus, buttons and others.*
  Rationale: older users present difficulties in identifying and distinguishing interface components on web applications. Therefore it is required to highlight the distinctions among components in the presentation. For instance, older users have difficulties in differenciating navigational mechanisms from content. This Success Criteria integrates the guideline 1.4 - *Distinguishable.*

6.2 Operable

- **Success Criteria 2.1.4**: *Webpage presentation must not use scroll bars.*
  Rationale: older users do not perceive the existence of scroll bars and generally do not complete tasks that require using this interface compponent.

- **Success Criteria 2.1.5**: *Webpage must not use pop-ups windows.*
  Rationale: older users tend to have the reaction of shock and confusion (often think that caused some error) when scroll bars appear on their screens.

- **Success Criteria 2.1.6**: *The interface must present voice over functionalities.*
  Rationale: older users prefer talking to reading during their interaction with the Web.

- **Success Criteria 2.2.6**: *Dropdown menus must be slow enough to be activated even by users who present low motor skills.*
  Rationale: older users have difficulties with moving menus and end up selecting wrong options.

- **Success Criteria 2.3.3**: *Multimedia content must make available options to control the execution and speed of the presentation.*
  Rationale: multimedia content affect the user's attention with relation to the focus on tasks and often can not be understood by the user due to its high execution speed.

- **Success Criteria 2.4.11**: *There can't be links with identical labels that refer to different URLs.*
  Rationale: older users get used to the interface presented and therefore any re-label to reference other

than the URL that was used originally defined, should be avoided.

- **Success Criteria 2.4.12**: *There can't be broken links.*
  Rationale: Broken links frustrate the expectations of older users.

- **Success Criteria 2.4.13**: *Links must refer to the exact topic their label describes.*
  Rationale: older users have greater difficulty in locating information. When they are redirected to the home page of a website, instead of the exact topic location that described the issue the user is looking for, they often abandon the search for the desired topic.

- **Success Criteria 2.4.14**: *Adjacent links must provide enough click space in order to avoid errors.*
  Rationale: older users have difficulties with clicking in small areas of links.

- **Success Criteria 2.4.15**: *Adjacent images or icons must be part of the click space of links.*
  Rationale: small images or icons adjacent to the links often confuse users, since they tend to click on images instead of links.

- **Success Criteria 2.4.16**: *The webpage must differenciate the visited links from the non-visited ones.*
  Rationale: older users tend to forget the links for which have already sailed, due to cognitive deficits.

- **Success Criteria 2.4.17**: *The webpage must display separately menu options already selected and the ones that were not selected yet.*
  Rationale: Cognitive deficits due to older users tend to forget which menu options have visited.

- **Success Criteria 2.4.18**: *Options in menus must be pointing to the page correct execution/task.*
  Rationale: due to difficulty in identifying the right task or information, older users get frustated when they are redirect to webpages that does not refer to the action that they expected.

- **Success Criteria 2.4.19**: *The dropdown menus must provide only one level of options.*
  Rationale: older users have great difficulty in interacting with dropdown menus with several levels, triggering the wrong options.

- **Success Criteria 2.4.20**: *The present intermediate options in the menus, when triggered, they must have a page containing your options and subsequent alternative elements such as buttons and links.*
  Rationale: frequently, older users activate intermediate options of the menu, while attempting to reach the ultimate goal.

- **Success Criteria 2.4.21**: *There should be direction to the homepage of the website in all secondary webpages.*
  Rationale: older users easily confuse themselves and are more likely to access the wrong page.

- **Success Criteria 2.4.22**: *Icons used on webpage must lead the user to make associations with real-world objects.*

Rationale: older users try to relate the information they visualize on the web page with real-world objects in an attempt to build a mental model of the task and remember it later.

- **Success Criteria 2.4.23**: *The page must present a feature that allows the user to view a summary of their past experiences.*
  Rationale: it is important to users review a successful experience as a way to encourage them to do it again, and so reduce their insecurity and the amount of errors while performing a task or navigation.

6.3 Understandable

- **Success Criteria 3.1.7**: *The webpage must not have the same presentation layout for links and other interface components that doesn't accept clicks.*
  Rationale: older users tend to present difficulties identifying interactive components of the interface, from the ones that do not present this behavior.

- **Success Criteria 3.1.8**: *The web interface must not present to many informations in order not to cause a cognitive overload in older users.*
  Rationale: older people deficits might include cognitive disabilities. Therefore webpages layout should be designed with a minimalist and simplistic design.

- **Success Criteria 3.2.6**: *The initial webpage of systems must provide a clear identification of which parts of the web application can be accessed with and without authentication.*
  Rationale: older users can find it difficult to identify the functionalities that need authentication.

- **Success Criteria 3.2.7**: *The webpage must not present functionalities with the same description and labels for different contexts.*
  Rationale: older users can find it difficult to correctly identify and distinct the functionalities of the system.

- **Success Criteria 3.3.7**: *The webpage must provide informations describing the data format and domain for form inputs.*
  Rationale: older users present difficulties in filling forms, and therefore require the presentation of examples and explanations about how to complete the task.

- **Success Criteria 3.3.8**: *The webpage must present all necessary information to complete a task.*
  Rationale: older users require longer time than young users to execute complex tasks, like form filling, payment confirmations, among others. This generally leads to the session expiration within the application. Therefore the webpage must present explanations, previously, about how to proceed in order to complete the task.

- **Success Criteria 3.3.9**: *The webpage must provide interactive resources to assist the input of data.*
  Rationale: the webpage must be capable of predicting user difficulties and assist them either by text presentation or voice messages.

- **Success Criteria 3.3.7**: *The webpage must make available different ways of filling form informations besides keyboard input.*
  Rationale: older users present great difficulties in using the keyboard for typing sequences of numbers.

- **Success Criteria 3.3.7**: *The webpage must present the option of reporting errors in a simple and programatic way.*
  Rationale: older users feel confident about reporting difficulties and experiences for the webpage developer.

7. FINAL REMARKS

Although the guidelines are important, they aren't sufficient for optimal accessibility. The guidelines contribute to minimize the recurring errors in projects that people, who present special needs, are facing, as is the case of users middle-aged adults, elderly and disabled.

Providing web accessibility in general still presents challenges, but for older users in particular, became a major concern for developers.

Providing web accessibility for an audience with features heterogeneous so means not only develop websites consistent with the recommendations and guidelines, but provide means for less experienced users can overcome the barriers with which they encounter in their interactions with the Web, and that often lead to the total withdrawal of such experience.

The growth in Web usage has happened in parallel with its own evolution, since the Web left being just a repository for information that offered static webpages to its users and now offers support for various activities of their lives.

Currently, in addition to providing applications for communication, entertainment and online services, it must be also offered support for the realization of interaction between users and resources available on the Web.

The growth of Web use by adults of middle age, elderly or special needs has motivated the development of techniques to produce usable web pages and available, to allow their use with the highest level of independence possible.

8. REFERENCES

[1] S. Abou-Zahra, J. Brewer, and A. Arch. Towards bridging the accessibility needs of people with disabilities and the ageing community. In *W4A '08: Proceedings of the 2008 international cross-disciplinary conference on Web accessibility (W4A)*, pages 83–86, New York, NY, USA, 2008. ACM.

[2] J. E. Birren and K. W. Schaie. *Speed of behavior and its implications for cognition*. Handbook of the psychology of aging, 2nd edition, 1985.

[3] A. Cavalcanti and C. Galvao. *Terapia Ocupacional - Fundamentao e Pratica*. editora Guanabara Koogan, 2007.

[4] V. L. Centeno, C. D. Kloos, M. Gaedke, and M. Nussbaumer. Wcag formalization with w3c standards. In *WWW '05: Special interest tracks and posters of the 14th international conference on World Wide Web*, pages 1146–1147, New York, NY, USA, 2005. ACM.

[5] W. A. Chisholm and S. L. Henry. Interdependent components of web accessibility. In *W4A '05: Proceedings of the 2005 International Cross-Disciplinary Workshop on Web Accessibility (W4A)*, pages 31–37, New York, NY, USA, 2005. ACM.

[6] K. P. Coyne and J. W. Nielsen. Usability for senior citizens: 46 design guidelines based on usability studies with people age 65 and older, nielsen norman group report, 2002.

[7] S. J. Czaja and C. C. Lee. Designing computer systems for older adults. In *J. Jacko and A. Sears (eds) The human-computer interaction handbook*, pages 413–427, 2003.

[8] eMAG. Modelo de acessibilidade do governo brasileiro 2.0, June 2007.

[9] A. Fisk, W. Rogers, N. Charness, S. Czaja, and J. Sharit. *Designing for older adults: Principles and creative human factors*. CRC Press, London, 2004.

[10] I. Forrester Research. The wide range of computer abilities and its impact on computer technology, 2010.

[11] A. P. Freire, R. Goularte, and R. P. de Mattos Fortes. Techniques for developing more accessible web applications: a survey towards a process classification. In *SIGDOC '07: Proceedings of the 25th annual ACM international conference on Design of communication*, pages 162–169, New York, NY, USA, 2007. ACM.

[12] B. Gibson. Enabling an accessible web 2.0. In *W4A '07: Proceedings of the 2007 international cross-disciplinary conference on Web accessibility (W4A)*, pages 1–6, New York, NY, USA, 2007. ACM.

[13] V. L. Hanson. Age and web access: the next generation. In *W4A '09: Proceedings of the 2009 International Cross-Disciplinary Conference on Web Accessibililty (W4A)*, pages 7–15, New York, NY, USA, 2009. ACM.

[14] B. Kelly, D. Sloan, S. Brown, J. Seale, H. Petrie, P. Lauke, and S. Ball. Accessibility 2.0: people, policies and processes. In *W4A '07: Proceedings of the 2007 international cross-disciplinary conference on Web accessibility (W4A)*, pages 138–147, New York, NY, USA, 2007. ACM.

[15] B. Kelly, D. Sloan, L. Phipps, H. Petrie, and F. Hamilton. Forcing standardization or accommodating diversity?: a framework for applying the wcag in the real world. In *W4A '05: Proceedings of the 2005 International Cross-Disciplinary Workshop on Web Accessibility (W4A)*, pages 46–54, New York, NY, USA, 2005. ACM.

[16] S. Kurniawan and P. Zaphiris. Research-derived web design guidelines for older people. In *Assets '05: Proceedings of the 7th international ACM SIGACCESS conference on Computers and accessibility*, pages 129–135, New York, NY, USA, 2005. ACM.

[17] S. M. A. Lara and R. P. M. Fortes. Usabilidade universal para adultos de meia-idade em interaes com a web. In *XXXV Latin American Informatics Conference*, pages 1–10, 2009.

[18] G. A. D. Lucca, A. R. Fasolino, and P. Tramontana. Web site accessibility: Identifying and fixing accessibility problems in client page code. In *WSE '05: Proceedings of the Seventh IEEE International Symposium on Web Site Evolution*, pages 71–78,

Washington, DC, USA, 2005. IEEE Computer Society.

[19] J. McNeil. Americans with disabilities, u.s. census bureau, demographic programs, 1997.

[20] E. V. Munson and M. da Graa Pimentel. Specialized documents. In *Web Accessibility*, volume 4 of *Human-Computer Interaction Series*, pages 274–285. Springer London, 2008.

[21] A. L. Neri. *Palavras Chave em Gerontologia*. Editora Alinea, 2005.

[22] J. Nielsen. *Usability Engineering*. Academic Press, 1993.

[23] J. Nielsen. *Designing Web Usability*. New Riders Publishing, 2000.

[24] N. I. on Aging. Older adults and information technology: A compendium of scientific research and web site accessibility guidelines, 2002.

[25] H. Petrie and K. Omar. The relationship between accessibility and usability of websites. In *CHI '07: Proceedings of the SIGCHI Conference on Human factors in computing systems*, pages 397–406, San Jose, California, USA, 2007. ACM Press.

[26] L. G. Reid and A. Snow-Weaver. Wcag 2.0: a web accessibility standard for the evolving web. In *W4A '08: Proceedings of the 2008 international cross-disciplinary conference on Web accessibility (W4A)*, pages 109–115, New York, NY, USA, 2008. ACM.

[27] L. G. Reid and A. Snow-Weaver. Wcag 2.0: a web accessibility standard for the evolving web. In *W4A '08: Proceedings of the 2008 international cross-disciplinary conference on Web accessibility (W4A)*, pages 109–115, New York, NY, USA, 2008. ACM.

[28] T. A. Salthouse. Working memory as a processing resource in cognitive aging. *Developmental Review*, 10(1):101 – 124, 1990.

[29] S. Sayago and J. Blat. A preliminary usability evaluation of strategies for seeking online information with elderly people. In *W4A '07: Proceedings of the 2007 International Cross-Disciplinary Conference on Web Accessibililty (W4A)*, pages 54–57, New York, NY, USA, 2007. ACM.

[30] S. Sayago and J. Blat. About the relevance of accessibility barriers in the everyday interactions of older people with the web. In *W4A '09: Proceedings of the 2009 International Cross-Disciplinary Conference on Web Accessibililty (W4A)*, pages 104–113, New York, NY, USA, 2009. ACM.

[31] J. Thatcher, P. Bohman, M. Burks, S. L. Henry, B. Regan, S. Swierenga, and M. Urban. *Constructing Accessible Web Sites*. Glasshaus, 2002.

[32] M. VAN der LINDEN, M. & HUPET. Le vieeillissement cognitif. Unit de Neuropsychologie Cognitif et Unit de Psychologie Cognitif. Presses Universitaires de France, 1994.

[33] W3C. Web content accessibility guidelines 1.0. W3C Recommendation, May 1999.

[34] W3C. Authoring tool accessibility guidelines 1.0. W3C Recommendation, February 2000.

[35] W3C. User agent accessibility guidelines 1.0. W3C Recommendation, December 2002.

[36] W3C. Policies relating to web accessibility, 2005.

[37] W3C. A guide to understanding and implementing web content accessibility guidelines 2.0. W3C Working Group Note, November 2008.

[38] W3C. Techniques and failures for web content accessibility guidelines 2.0. W3C Working Group Note, November 2008.

[39] W3C. Web accessibility for older users: A literature review, 2008.

[40] W3C. Web content accessibility guidelines (wcag) 2.0. W3C Recommendation, December 2008.

Using cultural knowledge to assist communication between people with different cultural background

Bruno A. Sugiyama[1], Junia C. Anacleto[1], Sidney Fels[2] and Helena M. Caseli[1]

[1]Department of Computer Science, Federal University of São Carlos, São Carlos – SP, Brazil

[2]Department of Electrical and Computer Engineering, University of British Columbia, Vancouver – BC, Canada
+55 (16) 3351-8615

{bruno_sugiyama, junia}@dc.ufscar.br, ssfels@ece.ubc.ca, helenacaseli@dc.ufscar.br

ABSTRACT

We present a computational application to facilitate text chat-based communication between people with different cultural and language background. We focus on end-to-end communication between people with rudimentary and intermediary knowledge of the second language using computer support rather than using a simple connection with automated computer translation. Through a user-centered design process, involving three increasingly hi-fidelity prototypes, we created a system that allows users who speak different languages to send text messages between them that begins with an automated translation of their message that does a partial translation but normally has words that are not translated well. These poorly translated words are then searched for in a common sense knowledge base for the sender's culture that contains meanings gleaned from a large open source initiative to collect common sense knowledge. Using these additional concepts and words coupled to a translator, the user can select from a list of translations those that are better suited to the intention of the message. We illustrate the usefulness of our approach empirically to show that users find the augmented translated messages are culturally sensitive and provide better communication experiences than without it. Our study used messaging between Portuguese (Brazilian) and English speakers.

Categories and Subject Descriptors

D.2.2 [**Software Engineering**]: Design Tools and Techniques - *evolutionary prototyping, user interfaces;* H.1.2 [**Information Systems**]: User/Machine Systems - *human factors, human information processing;* H.5.2 [**Information Interfaces and Presentation**]: User Interfaces - *graphical user interface, natural language, prototyping, screen design, user-centered design;*

General Terms

Design, Human Factors, Experimentation, Languages.

Keywords

Cultural Translation. Communication mediated by technology, Human Computer Interaction, Natural Language Process

1. INTRODUCTION

Currently, text messaging is a common form of communication between people either on their computer or cell phone due to the growth of the internet [13] and the ubiquitous nature of communication technologies. Due to globalization [9], these text messages are frequently exchanged between people who speak different languages and have different cultural backgrounds. Since the exchange of messages is via text, it suggests that automatic language translation systems may be helpful. However, communication between users that speak different languages can be affected due to linguistic and cultural differences of each participant making automated translation difficult. By culture we understand it is "that complex whole which includes knowledge, belief, art, morals, law, custom, and any other capabilities and habits acquired by man as a member of society" [17].

In order to deal with the users' culture, this work presents a chat application to assist users in the process of creating messages in another language intended as an augmentation of an automatic text translator tool. Typically, cultural idioms, slang and phrases etc. cause trouble for automatic translation, which is where our system provides suggestions based on the user's cultural background. We find these suggestions by adapting a common sense knowledge database [1] (DB) from each users' background, (i.e., Brazilian DB for Brazilian text and a US DB for American text), to create a culturally contextualized application. From a user's perspective, culturally based words not found in the automated translator tool appear in a text box that has alternative suggestions from our system that makes suggestions to allow them to select the meaning they intend rather than the usually more literal meaning that comes from the automatic translator. In this fashion, the communication between two culturally separate groups can be improved.

This paper is organized as follows: section 2 presents works that complement and are related with ours; section 3 describes the methodology adopted and the development process of our application; section 4 describes an experiment that illustrated the use of commonsense knowledge in the translation process; section 5 presents the results related to the experiment exposed in section 3; finally, section 6 presents the conclusion and some future works concerning the application.

2. RELATED WORK

2.1 Commonsense Knowledge

This work is related to a range of projects ([1], [2], [10], for example) that are involved in the applicability of a kind of cultural knowledge: common sense. Common sense can be defined as the knowledge of every-day things based in life experience or beliefs of a group considering the time, space and social aspects Examples of common sense knowledge are "a lemon is sour", "when you receive a gift you may be happy" or "a pineapple is a kind of fruit".

In order to use this kind of knowledge in computational application, making them more familiar to the user's context, this work adopted the commonsense knowledge database of two projects: Open Mind Common Sense (OMCS) and Open Mind Common Sense in Brazil (OMCS-Br). While OMCS exists since 1999, the OMCS-Br Project was created in 2005. Both of them collect common sense knowledge through their websites.

In Figure 1 is shown the architecture of the OMCS-Br Project. Because the two projects have similar ways to collect and use this kind of knowledge, we will describe only the Brazilian Project.

In the Brazilian website (Figure 1 - I), this knowledge is collected by a fill-in-the-gap mechanism: semi-structured sentences (templates) with gaps to be completed by people. For example:

A **breezy** is also known as _____.

A **milkshake** is made of _____.

Soccer is a kind of _____.

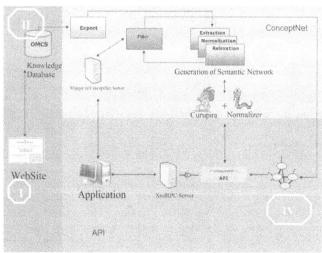

Figure 1 Architecture of OMCS-Br

The templates (written in English in this paper just for clarification) are made of three parts: a dynamic part, a static part and a blank part (the horizontal line). The dynamic part, represented by the bold words, is filled automatically by the computer; the static part is a fixed query structure; the blank part is where the user writes what she/he thinks.

The complete sentence is stored in a database (Figure 1 - II) and, then, is processed by some NLP mechanisms (a lemmatizer, a PoS tagger, etc.) that break it in interconnected concepts (Figure 1 - III). The link between two concepts is tagged by a Minky's relation. Misnky [11] defined that the human knowledge can be

mapped through 20 relations such as defined-as, is-a, part-of, made-of, property-of and others. These relations give more semantic in the link between two concepts. The set of concepts and relation forms a semantic network of concepts called ConceptNet (Figure 1 - IV). Some examples of facts from ConceptNet are presented below:

defined-as(breezy, girlfriend)

made-of(milkshake, ice cream)

is-a(soccer, sport)

The computer applications work with the ConceptNet through an API that provides some function to manipulate its data.

The OMCS-Br Project has more than 280,000 sentences stored in its database and just over 1,800 contributors. While the OMCS English site, currently, has over a million sentences from over 15,000 contributors.

2.2 Machine Translation

Other related projects are those who work with machine translation of texts. Machine Translation (MT) is one of the most important subfields of NLP, and the phrase-based Statistical Machine Translation (SMT) approach is considered the state-of-the-art according to the automatic measures BLEU [15] and NIST [3]. The translation and language models used in SMT are built from a training parallel corpora (a set of source sentences and their translations into the target language) by means of IBM models [7] which calculate the probability of a given source word (or sequence of words) be translated to a target word (or sequence of words).

In our experiment to test our hypothesis in this article, we decide to use Google Translate [1] because it performed well in some preliminary runs, but any other machine translation could be chosen. We also performed experiments with the open-source SMT Moses Toolkit [2] [5]. The corpus available for our research [4] contained articles from the online version of the Brazilian scientific magazine *Pesquisa* FAPESP [3] written in Brazilian Portuguese (original) and English (version). It contains approximately 500.000 words in each language, which is considerably less than the training set used by Google.

Our proposal is to create a chat tool that is "MT-independent", i.e., is not restricted to a specific MT. The aim of the project is to excel the power of Common Sense. Thus, in order to achieve this goal, we have to choose a MT that provides a good translation in the chat topics. Our work will deal with Portuguese (Brazil) to English translations and vice-versa.

3. WORK DESCRIPTION

3.1 Methodology

The development of our chat application has been following the User-Centered Designer (UCD) approach described in [2]. We adopted that approach because we are interested in the

---

[1] http://translate.google.com.br/

[2] http://www.statmt.org/moses/

[3] http://revistapesquisa.fapesp.br

communication between different users. Thus, we need to understand the user's behavior to develop a successful tool.

The life cycle of the project consists of iterative and interrelated stages. For each stage, we need to define (1) the goal of the stage, (2) the questions raised in that step, (3) the resources that helped to answer the questions, (4) the answers for the questions and (5) the stakeholders who participated in this iteration. An example of a stage is described as follow: (1) modeling the user mental model; (2) How is the interaction among users? Which mental model to choose: sender mental model or receiver mental model?; (3) block diagrams and paper prototyping that shows a interaction between two users; (4) The sender will work on the creation of a message with the help of a machine translation and a cultural knowledge base; the system will be designed guided by the sender's mental model; (5) the stakeholders of that stage are the supervisor of the project, the co-supervisor and a foreign professor.

Following this approach, the initial stages of the project consists of studies about concepts from HCI and NLP areas. HCI will provide mechanisms to guide the project development focusing on end-user needs. NLP will provide methods and techniques to translated texts and data, i. e. convert a text in source language to target language using MT. From these fields, this project adopts two resources: common sense knowledge to deal with participants' cultural specificities of the chat and statistical machine translation to provide a good translation.

3.2 Using the cultural knowledge

For this work we are interested in two of the twenty Minsky's relations: defined-as and is-a. The relation "defined-as" connects concepts that have the same meaning, i.e., synonym words. The relation "is-a" represents a hierarchy between the concepts [10]. For instance, is-a(soccer, sport) represents that the concept "sport" is more abstract or generic than the concept "soccer". Using the ConceptNet, an application can provide, for instance, a synonym list for slang words with a simple algorithm described below.

Given a sentence, the application divides it in phrases. For each phrase, a search through the ConceptNet is performed in order to identify if the phrase is connected with the concept "slang" by the relation "is-a". This means that the word or expression can be slang in the sentence. For each term found in the earlier step, another search through the ConceptNet is performed in order to find other related terms linked by the relation "defined-as". These related words are synonyms of the slang found in the given sentence.

For example, given the sentence "My breezy is very kind to my mom", the application can identify through the ConceptNet that the word "breezy" can be slang, i.e., the fact "is-a(breezy, slang)" exists in the semantic network. The next step is to find the synonym words, selecting concepts that are linked by the relation defined-as, for instance, "defined-as(breezy, girlfriend)". We need to collect all X in "defined-as(X, Y)" and "defined-as(Y, X)" where Y="breezy", thus we have our list of synonyms of the word "breezy".

3.3 Prototyping

Because the chat application of this project is not only a tool to connect users but one to assist the translation process, we need to understand how would be the interaction process between the user and the two resources described above. With the purpose of achieving this goal we have been built some prototypes, passing through three fidelity-level of prototyping: low, medium and high.

In order to build applications that have higher chances to be successful from the end-user's point of view we need to be aware of the end-user's mental model [6]. Paper prototyping [16] permits designers to draw an interface closer to what users expect. It does not require any technology techniques and it is very fast to design. This kind of low-fidelity prototype is recommended in early project stages due the low cost and flexibility in design changes.

We used paper prototyping in two stages of the project. The two paper prototyping are shown in Figure 2. In the early prototype (Figure 2 – item I) the user that wants to send a messenger (sender) writes a text in her/his native language. She/he sends it to the receiver. The message is translated by a SMT and is displayed to the receiver. The system identifies and highlights the words or expression that could not be translated by the SMT system. The receiver then clicks on the highlights words and concepts related to that word are displayed to her/him so that she/he can comprehend the message. This prototype maps the mental model of the receiver.

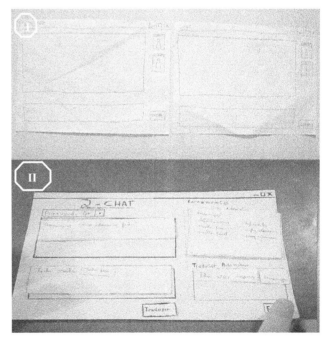

Figure 2 Paper prototype

This paper prototype was presented to the stakeholders. A NLP expert was surprise with this kind of prototype. One problem with that model occurs when the message contains a lot of words that could not be translated. The receiver might get lost with so many terms in that message. Two HCI experts suggest that the system need a resource where the user can participate in the translation process.

In another stage, we created the prototype shown in Figure 2 – item II. The application was named 2-Chat and a new mental model was mapped: the sender's mental model. This version puts the user and machine together in order to create a message in the target language. The interaction model of this prototyped is closer to the one presented in our high-fidelity prototype that will be described in the next section.

In order to validate our proposal we evolved our prototype to a medium-fidelity one [12] (also called mid-fidelity prototype [8]) to be presented to a committee of teachers. This prototype is shown in Figure 3. This kind of prototype increased the look-and-feel of the application and still kept some characteristics of the low-fidelity prototype: it was fast to build and easy to make changes. The prototyping was build with the help of Balsamiq Mockup[4] and Microsoft Office PowerPoint 2007[5]. The name of the application was changed to Culture-to-Chat (C2C).

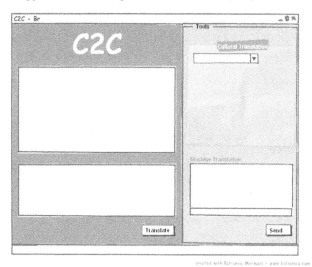

Figure 3 Medium-fidelity prototype of the chat

After the teachers' approval, in the next stage of the project, we needed to investigate the applicability of the common sense and SMT tools. It is very difficult to connect preexistent computational resources with the medium-fidelity prototype. Therefore, we built a high-level prototype in Java (J2SE) that interacts with the ConceptNet API and the SMT Moses Toolkit. For the time being, this prototype does not promote the communication of different users but can be used to test some functional features. This prototype can be used to perform some proof-tests in order to analyze the content of the two resources. In the next section, we will describe the interface and the interaction process between the application and users.

3.4 Culture-to-Chat

The interface of the high-fidelity prototype of C2C is shown in Figure 4. In this figure, item I represents the area where all the history of the conversation will be displayed. Item II is where the original message will be written in the source language and, once finished, the button "Translate" (item III) have to be pushed and

the message be processed by the two tools previously described. The cultural knowledge output will be displayed is item IV (Cultural Translator) and the translated message will be show in item V (Machine Translator). Item VI identifies the button "Send" that will send the translated message to its destination. In order to illustrate this process, we describe below an example of the process of creating a message in the communication between a Brazilian and an American.

When the interaction starts, the American user sees the interface in Figure 4. Then, he receives a message from the Brazilian asking something about an actress of a movie (displayed in Figure 5 – I). Immediately after this, he writes (in Figure 5 - II): "That girl is not a minger, but she has a stranger appearance" and pushes the "Translate" button (in Figure 5 – III). In that moment, the message is sent to the Machine Translator (to translate from English to Portuguese) and also to the Cultural Translator (to look for common sense knowledge related to the words without translation). Supposing that the Machine Translator would not be able to provide the translation for the English word "minger", the generated Portuguese sentence cannot provide a fully understanding (shown in Figure 5 – V). The Cultural Translator can help the American user to provide some information about the term "minger", using the algorithm described in section 2.1. For example, in Figure 5 - IV, the Cultural Translator would show that "minger" is defined as "a ugly person" or "something not attractive" (followed by their translations to Portuguese: *definido como pessoa feia, definido como sem atrativos*). Thus, the American can edit the translated message (in Figure 5 - V), for instance, exchanging the word "minger" with the Portuguese expression "*pessoa feia*" and, finally, send it (Figure 5 - VI).

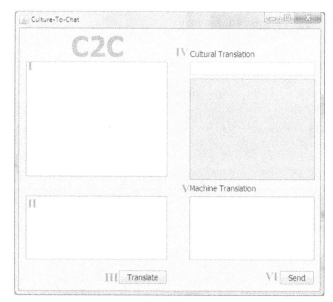

Figure 4 Interface of the high-fidelity prototype

Thus, the Brazilian will receive an understandable Portuguese message and will be able to write back following a similar process. In this similar process the roles of the users are inverted, so the Brazilian user turns into the sender and the American user turns into the receiver. In this process the new sender (Brazilian user) will interact with the commonsense knowledge from the OMCS-Br semantic network instead of the OMCS one.

---

[4] http://www.balsamiq.com/builds/mockups-web-demo/

[5] http://office.microsoft.com/pt-br/downloads/CD010200683.aspx

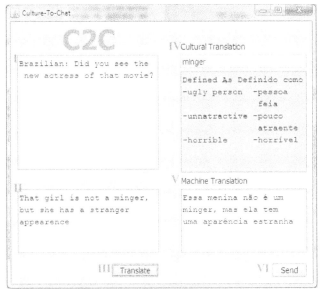

Figure 5 Interface while creating a message

The flow of information in the sending process is shown in Figure 6. The arrow I represents the sending of the message in native language. The system identifies some words or expressions and uses the common sense semantic network to provide related concepts. These concepts are translated (arrow II) and all of them (the concepts and its translation) are returned to the user (arrow III). Finally, the user can change and edit his message in the foreign language and send it to the receiver (arrow IV).

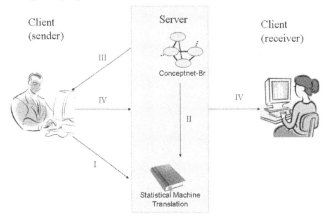

Figure 6 Flow of data in the sending process

We believe that this application has three goals but our current research will focus on the first one. The first goal is to connect and facilitate the communication between two people that speak different idioms and thus belong to different cultures. Cultural Translator and Machine Translator promote this facilitation because they help the sender to write in a more understandable way to the receiver. The second goal is the exposure of the user to a target language learning process. Cultural Translator collaborates with that task acting like a phrase book, expanding words and amplifying the vocabulary by translating them. The third goal is to exposure the sender to a reflection of his own language. Cultural Translator helps providing alternatives to

reformulate her/his original message, exchanging words or expressions to better translate it.

Our study will be instantiated in the use of slang words. This kind of words is very common in chats and informal speech. We classify the use of slang in four types:

(1) Slang that does not have a translated. Example: *baranga* (a Portuguese word which means a woman that is not attractive).

(2) Slang word in the source language that has a translation but it is not a slang in the target language. Example: *café com leite* (coffee with milk, which in Portuguese means a naïve person).

(3) Slang word in source language that has a translation, the translated word is slang in target language but with other meaning. Example: *galinha* (chicken, which in Portuguese means a person who dates many girls and in English means a coward).

(4) Slang that has a translation with the same meaning in both language. Example: *Meu Deus*! (My God!, to express surprise).

The next steps of study will focus on the impact of these kinds of words in the communication of people with different cultural backgrounds and how this can contribute with the learning process of the users. In the next section we present an experiment involving slang words, common sense and machine translation.

4. FIRST EXPERIMENT

In order to verify whether the use of translation resources can help users to create messages in foreign language, we conducted an experiment described below. We want to verify if the commonsense knowledge presented in ConceptNet has been somehow useful during the translation process. The hypothesis on this experiment is that the students/users will adopt some suggestions from the ConceptNet in order to create or translate a sentence in the target language.

We have selected five Brazilian students with basic and intermediate level of English. The task that they were asked to perform was: "With some given sentences in Brazilian Portuguese language, provide their translations, which will be sent to an American person". A preliminary automatic translation of each sentence was given as a suggestion to them. There were also available some cards containing a list of synonyms to some words. We have emphasized that these two resources were suggestions and the students could either accept them or not.

The experiment was applied in individual sessions so that none of the students were aware of what the others answered. The students were expected to write in a sheet of paper the entire translated sentences that they considered to be understandable by a foreign person. We could neither answer questions related to the translation process nor comment whether the translation was correct.

We have chosen five Brazilian Portuguese sentences that illustrated the use of slang words. Four of the five sentences represented the four types of slang use mentioned in section 3.4. The last sentence did not contain slang words, but contains words that did not have a translation (they were specific objects from Brazilian culture).

We emphasize that the content of the sentences can be very offensive because of the meaning of the slang words. We do not necessarily share the same idea expressed by the sentences. The choice of the slang words used in the sentences was based purely on cultural issues without regarding moral values. They are part of the informal vocabulary of Brazil found in blogs and internet chats and they address good examples of cultural translation.

The translated words and sentences presented in this experiment were provided by Google Translate, on May 26th, 2010. The original sentences in Brazilian Portuguese and their automatic translations in English are presented in Table 1.

Table 1. Original sentences and their translation

Number	Original Sentence / Translated Sentence
1	*Aquela maria-chuteira é um tribufu.* That maria-boot is a *tribufu*
2	*Meu vizinho tem uma namorada que parece um cão chupando manga.* My neighbor has a girlfriend that looks like a dog sucking mango
3	*Jogadores de futebol são muito galinhas e ficam com muitas meninas* Football players are too many chick and stay with girls
4	*O casal passou a lua de mel em Nova Iorque* The couple spent their honey moon in New York
5	*Os brasileiros gostam muito de comer feijoada e beber caipirinha.* The Brazilians are very fond of eating *feijoada* and *caipirinha* drink.

For each sentence we performed a search in the OMCS-Br semantic network looking for words or expressions that were considered slang words, using the algorithm described in section 3.2. The result of that algorithm is shown in Table 2. For each expression in Table 2, we have made cards containing a list of related words linked through the Minsky's relation "Defined As". These cards also contained synonyms provided Microsoft Office Word 2007 Synonym Dictionary[6]. All synonyms were listed in the same card, therefore the students were not aware of the different sources the words might have. An example of a card that described the word "*tribufu*" (sentence 1) is shown in Table 3.

Table 2. Slang words of the original sentences

Sentence	Words or expressions
1	*maria-chuteira, tribufu*
2	*cão chupando manga*
3	*galinha, ficar*
4	*lua de mel*

---

[6] http://office.microsoft.com/pt-br/word/default.aspx

| 5 | *feijoada, caipirinha* |

Table 3. Example of card with common sense knowledge

Tribufu	
algo muito feio	something very ugly
mulher fora do padrão de beleza	woman outside the standard of beauty
baranga	slapper
mulher sem beleza	woman without beauty
horrorosa	horrible

It is interesting to observe that some slang words have more than one meaning and that the semantic network came with all meanings. For example, the word "*galinha*" (chicken) is related to the concepts "small bird" and "womanizer". The user can choose the appropriated meaning that fits her/his translation. The results of the experiment will be listed in the next section.

5. RESULTS

We asked a non-native English teacher to grade all the translated sentences. The variables that he considered in the rating were grammar and comprehension. The grades vary from 1 to 5 where the grade 1 means a very poor translation and 5 a very good one.

In the first sentence, three of five students changed the expression "maria-chuteira" to one of the suggested card. Another student changed the word to another of her/his knowledge. The last student let the term unchanged. Another word edited was "tribufu" which all students adopted the same synonym (horrible) presented in Table 3. The students' translated sentences and their grades can be seen in Table 4.

Table 4. Translations of the first sentence

	Translated sentence	Grade
	That maria-boot is a *tribufu*	1
Student 1	That woman interested in football player is a horrible	2
Student 2	That woman who likes football player is a horrible	3
Student 3	That woman interested in soccer player is horrible	4
Student 4	That soccer-player groupie is horrible	5
Student 5	That maria-boot is a horrible	2

It is important to note that the students 1, 2, 5 made some grammatical errors when creating the translated sentence. In first sentence, for instance, "...is a horrible" is not grammatically correct. We observed that the sentences written by the students had a higher score than the one translated by Google.

The second translated sentences are shown in Table 5. The expression "*cão chupando manga*" (dog sucking mango) was edited by all the students even though it has a literal translation.

These results showed us that some sentences were not well constructed and still had problems in comprehension.

Table 5. Translations of the second sentence

	Translated sentence	Grade
	My neighbor has a girlfriend that looks like a dog sucking mango	2
Student 1	My neighbor has a girlfriend that is very ugly person	5
Student 2	My neighbor has a girlfriend that looks like very ugly	2
Student 3	My neighbor has a girlfriend that is very ugly	5
Student 4	My neighbor has a girlfriend that looks very ugly	4
Student 5	My neighbor has a girlfriend that looks like very ugly	2

The third sentence was the most difficult to translated. The results, presented in Table 6, showed some interesting issues. One of them is the use of the word "soccer" and "football". Only two students (3, 4) noted the difference about these words while the others kept the translation provided by the machine translation. The student 2 created a new sentence with the same meaning but without using any suggested resource. Some examples of expressions suggested by ConceptNet to the word "*galinha*" (chick) and that were used in the translation process were "womanizer", "flirt", "surface dating". The Microsoft Word Dictionary provided synonyms for the word "*ficar*" (stay) but none of them were used in this case.

Table 6. Translations of the third sentence

	Translated sentence	Grade
	Football players are too many chick and stay with girls	1
Student 1	Football players are many womanizer and surface dating with many girls	4
Student 2	Football players like to have a lot of woman	3
Student 3	Soccer players are womanizer and date many girls	5
Student 4	Football/soccer players are very flirt and stay with several girls	2
Student 5	Football players are too flirt and surface dating with girls	4

The fourth sentence (*O casal passou a lua de mel em Nova Iorque*) received 5 points. All the students wrote the following translation: "The couple spent their honeymoon in New York" (the same provided by Google Translate). The students 1 and 5 had some questions about the word "*lua de mel*" (honey moon) because they perceive that the literal meaning of this expression can cause confusion in another culture. The semantic network of OMCS-Br and Microsoft Word Dictionary do not provided (at that moment) any suggestion about the expression "honeymoon". They only suggested terms related to the world "*passar*" (spend)

which did not have problems in translation. In the end, the students did not modify the translated message.

In the sentence five, we did not choose slang words to compose the original sentence. Instead, we choose words that designated cultural things and could not be translated, for instance, kinds of dishes. This was a test to expand our experiment and observe the impact of commonsense knowledge in other kinds of words.

The semantic network could provide only one term related to the word "*feijoada*", saying that it is a food: "defined-as(feijoada, food)". The word "*caipirinha*" has two meanings: one is used to designate a hick while the other meaning is the name of an alcoholic drink in Brazil. At the moment of the experiment the semantic network of OMCS-Br and Microsoft Word Dictionary only provided terms related to the first sense (hick). The translated sentences are shown on Table 7.

Table 7. Results of the fifth sentence

	Translated sentence	Grade
	The Brazilians are very fond of eating *feijoada* and *caipirinha* drink.	3
Student 1	The Brazilians like very of eating "feijoada" (traditional food) and drink "caipirinha" (traditional drink)	4
Student 2	The Brazilians like to eat food made of beans and pork named "feijoada". They like to drink "caipirinha" that is made of lemon, alcohol (cachaça), sugar and ice.	5
Student 3	The Brazilians like very much eating "feijoada" (a typical food made of beans and pork) and drinking caipirinha (alcoholic drinking made of lemon, ice and sugar)	5
Student 4	The Brazilians like too much a mix of beans and pork meat and drink caipirinha	4
Student 5	The Brazilians are very fond of eating food tipic (feijoada) and caipirinha drink	4

Analyzing the content of the students' sentences, we noted that the commonsense knowledge was helpful in some situations. This experiment showed us that the students analyze what is suggested and perceived that some automatic translations needed a reformulation. In our examples the commonsense knowledge was more useful than the Microsoft Word Synonyms Dictionary. This happened because the sentences contained words which meaning depends on cultural factors (for instance, slang words). These words were chosen due the fact they are very common in a chat or conversation between Brazilian people.

6. CONCLUSION

This work presented a prototype an application called Culture-to-Chat, or C2C, aiming at promoting a better comprehensive communication between users with different cultural background. Specifically, the application is to support the chat between people with two different language background: Portuguese and English focused on end-to-end communication between people with rudimentary and intermediary knowledge of the second language using computer support rather than using a simple connection with automated computer translation. We are proposing a methodology that adopts machine translation combined to a cultural knowledgebase with additional concepts and words presented to the user after a first automatic translation. These concepts and words can be selected from a list of translations that can be better suited to the intention of the message, in order to help users on translating properly certain cultural expressions used in the vocabulary for their chat. The cultural knowledge expressed as commonsense knowledge is collected by the OMCS-Br project and the American OMCS projects as well. Preliminary tests show that our proposal can be effective for certain situations and users could work better on expanding their own vocabulary in the second language and consequently having a better translated message using this technique than using only the machine translation support. Although the results are not sufficient to measure the real impact of the proposed approach, they give some evidences that it works in specific situations. As future work, according to the results presented here, the prototype is evolving from a desktop prototype to a web application working with Google Translate (instead of SMT Moses Toolkit). Therefore, we can perform some experiments to analyze how the combination of cultural knowledge and machine translation can impact on the communication between users with different cultural background.

7. ACKNOWLEDGMENTS

The authors thank to CAPES and FAPESP for partial financial support to this research. We also thank all the collaborators of the Open Mind Common Sense Project who have been building the common sense knowledge base considered in this research.

8. REFERENCES

[1] Anacleto, J. C., Carvaho, A. F. P. de. 2008. Improving Human-Computer Interaction by Developing Culture-sensitive Applications based on Common Sense Knowledge. In Advances in Human-Computer Interaction. Vienna.

[2] Anacleto, J. C., Fels, S., and Villena, J. M. 2010. Design of a web-based therapist tool to promote emotional closeness. In *Proceedings of the 28th of the international Conference Extended Abstracts on Human Factors in Computing Systems* (Atlanta, Georgia, USA, April 10 - 15, 2010). CHI EA '10. ACM, New York, NY, 3565-3570. DOI= http://doi.acm.org/10.1145/1753846.1754019.

[3] Brown, P. F., Cocke, J., Pietra, S. A., Pietra, V. J., Jelinek, F., Lafferty, J. D., Mercer, R. L., and Roossin, P. S. 1990. A statistical approach to machine translation. *Comput. Linguist.* 16, 2 (Jun. 1990), 79-85.

[4] Caseli, H.M. and Nunes, I.A. 2009, Statistical Machine Translation: little changes big impacts, In *Proceedings of the 7th Brazilian Symposium in Information and Human Language Technology*. São Carlos, SP, Brazil., pp. 1-9.

[5] Caseli, H.M., Sugiyama, B.A. & Anacleto, J.C. 2010, Using Common Sense to generate culturally contextualized Machine Translation, In *Proceedings of the NAACL HLT 2010 Young Investigators Workshop on Computational Approaches to Languages of the Americas*. Los Angeles, California. June 2010., pp. 24-31.

[6] Cooper, A., Reimann, R., and Cronin, D. 2007 *About Face 3: the Essentials of Interaction Design*. John Wiley & Sons, Inc.

[7] Doddington, G. 2002. Automatic evaluation of machine translation quality using n-gram co-occurrence statistics. In *Proceedings of the Second international Conference on Human Language Technology Research* (San Diego, California, March 24 - 27, 2002). Human Language Technology Conference. Morgan Kaufmann Publishers, San Francisco, CA, 138-145.

[8] Engelberg, D. and Seffa, A. 2002. A Framework for Rapid Mid-Fidelity Prototyping of Web Sites. In *Proceedings of the IFIP 17th World Computer Congress - Tc13 Stream on Usability: Gaining A Competitive Edge* (August 25 - 29, 2002). J. Hammond, T. Gross, and J. Wesson, Eds. IFIP Conference Proceedings, vol. 226. Kluwer B.V., Deventer, The Netherlands, 203-215.

[9] Eune, J.and Lee, K. P. 2009. Analysis on Intercultural Differences through User Experiences of Mobile Phone for globalization. In Proceedings of International Association of Societies of Design Research (Coex, Seoul, Korea, October 18 – 22, 2009)

[10] Faaborg, A. and Lieberman, H. 2006. A goal-oriented web browser. In Proceedings of the SIGCHI Conference on Human Factors in Computing Systems (Montréal, Québec, Canada, April 22 - 27, 2006). R. Grinter, T. Rodden, P. Aoki, E. Cutrell, R. Jeffries, and G. Olson, Eds. CHI '06. ACM, New York, NY, 751-760. DOI= http://doi.acm.org/10.1145/1124772.1124883

[11] Ginsberg, M. 1991. Marvin Minsky: The Society of Mind. *Artif. Intell.* 48, 3 (Apr. 1991), 335-339. DOI= http://dx.doi.org/10.1016/0004-3702(91)90033-G.

[12] Leone, P., D. Gillihan, and T. Rauch. 2000. Web-based prototyping for user sessions: Medium-fidelity prototyping. In *Proceedings of the Society for Technical Communications 44th Annual Conference,* pp. 231-234. Toronto: STC.

[13] Morris, M. and Ogan, C. 1996. The Internet as Mass Medium. The Journal of Communication v. 46. 39-50. DOI= http://dx.doi.org/10.1111/j.1460-2466.1996.tb01460.x

[14] Myers, B., Hollan, J., Cruz, I., Bryson, S., Bulterman, D., Catarci, T., Citrin, W., Glinert, E., Grudin, J., and Ioannidis, Y. 1996. Strategic directions in human-computer interaction. *ACM Comput. Surv.* 28, 4 (Dec. 1996), 794-809. DOI= http://doi.acm.org/10.1145/242223.246855.

[15] Papineni, K., Roukos, S., Ward, T., and Zhu, W. 2002. BLEU: a method for automatic evaluation of machine translation. In *Proceedings of the 40th Annual Meeting on Association For Computational Linguistics* (Philadelphia, Pennsylvania, July 07 - 12, 2002). Annual Meeting of the ACL. Association for Computational Linguistics, Morristown, NJ, 311-318. DOI= http://dx.doi.org/10.3115/1073083.1073135.

[16] Snyder, C. *Paper Prototyping: the fast and easy way to design and refine user interfaces.* San Francisco, CA: Morgan Kaufmann, 2003, 408 p.

[17] Tylor, E. 1920. *Primitive Culture*. New York: J.P. Putnam's Sons. 1.

An Approach Based on Multiple Text Input Modes for Interactive Digital TV Applications

Didier Augusto Vega-Oliveros
Maria da Graça Campos Pimentel

Diogo de Carvalho Pedrosa
Renata Pontin de Mattos Fortes

Universidade de São Paulo, São Carlos-SP, Brazil
{davo,diogo,mgp,renata}@icmc.usp.br

ABSTRACT

The development of interactive digital TV applications is hindered by the user-interaction options allowed when traditional remote controls are used. In this work, we describe the model of a software component that allows text entry in interactive TV applications based on an interface with multiple input modes -- the component offers a virtual keyboard mode, a cell keypad mode, and a speech mode. We discuss our considerations with respect to the design, development and evaluation of a prototype corresponding to our model, built according to the user-centered design methodology. After conducting a research on existing text input methods in television systems, we interviewed four experts in the interactive TV domain. We also applied 153 questionnaires to TV users, with the aim of gathering a user profile of users who make use of text entry mechanisms. During the development of the prototype, we conducted usability tests using the think aloud protocol, and usability inspections using the heuristic evaluation and cognitive walkthrough techniques. The evaluations allowed the detection of both, a number of problems and of several improvement opportunities; at the same time that they highlighted the importance of using complementary text input modes in order to satisfy the needs of different users. Overall, the evaluation results suggest that the proposed approach provides a satisfactory level of usability by overcoming the limitations of text input in the context of user-interaction with interactive TV applications.

Categories and Subject Descriptors

B.4.2 [**Input/Output and Data Communications**]: Input/Output Devices—voice; H.5.2 [**Information Interfaces and Presentation**]: User Interfaces—Input devices and strategies, Voice I/O

General Terms: Design, Human Factors.

Keywords: Text Input, Interactive Digital TV, Multiple Input Modes, Virtual Keyboard, Multi-tap, Predictive Text.

1. INTRODUCTION

The introduction of interactive digital television (iDTV) has the potential of changing the way viewers receive multimedia content by allowing improved quality of video, multiprogramming and user-interaction with applications. Although there are several attempts to develop TV as a main provider of information and entertainment provider, the development of interactive applications is hindered by a small number of user-interaction options allowed by traditional remote controls.

Although the interface of iDTV applications have inherent restrictions to the TV paradigm, it differs from the personal computer (PC) paradigm in key aspects such as viewing and navigation [20], several classes of applications for iDTV can use text input from the user, such as chat, e-mail, search on the electronic program guide (EPG), calendar and forms — in such a scenario, it is important to provide mechanisms to aid the user for entering text.

In this paper we present our model of a software component that allows users to enter text in iDTV applications by means of an interface based on multiple input modes — the component includes a virtual keyboard mode, a cell keypad mode, and a speech mode. We designed the component according with the user-centered design (UCD) methodology. We first carried out a research review with respect to text input methods used in TV systems. Next, we interviewed four experts in the iDTV domain. A third activity involved the application of questionnaires to 153 TV users, aiming at identifying a profile that corresponds to users who make use of text entry mechanisms.

Carrying on with the development of the prototype, which we were able to demonstrate elsewhere [19], we conducted usability tests using the think aloud protocol, and usability inspections using the heuristic evaluation and cognitive walkthrough techniques. The evaluations allowed the detection of a number of problems, which could be dealt with in intermediary versions. The evaluations also pointed to several opportunities of improvement on the design — in particular, they highlighted the importance of using complementary text input modes in order to satisfy the needs of different users. As a result of our design and corresponding evaluation, we suggest that our proposal provides a satisfactory level of usability by overcoming the limitations of text input in the context of the user-interaction with iDTV applications.

The remaining of this paper is organized as follows: systems based on multiple input modes are presented in Section 2; Section 3 visits some text input methods used in TV and discuss some limitations of the TV environment: the design of the model and the proof-of-concept prototype in Section 4; Section 5 presents the evaluations performed; and, the lists of the next steps in Section 6. Finally, Section 7 concludes this paper and points out future research efforts in the final remarks.

2. SYSTEMS BASED ON MULTIPLE INPUT MODES

All natural forms of expression and interaction that could be captured by some kind of technology may be used by systems to allow users to interact naturally and easily. These natural forms extend the concept of interfaces based on mouse and keyboard interaction, known as WIMP (Windows, Icons, Menu and Pointer).

As examples of natural forms of interaction and their corresponding devices we have voice captured by microphone, electronic ink captured by tablets, touch captured by touchpads and touchscreens, gestures captured by accelerometers and cameras, etc.

Technologies that help people to interact with devices involve elements which were "transformed" by taking advantage of the implicit metaphor of people's daily use — such as electronic pens and devices with embedded accelerometers. From a ubiquitous computing perspective, the aim is to allow the user interaction with applications more natural [1].

Several studies in the scientific community have investigated the use of multiple modes of user interaction with computing systems and applications. Many of them use the voice input mode supported by a speech recognition engine. In the work of Patel et al. [18], commands are given to a phone system that provides local news services to Indian farmers.

There are several reasons to develop and use interfaces based on multiple input modes. One of them is to offer to users with disabilities the possibility to interact with alternative modes that best suit their necessities, in order to democratize the access and increase the number of potential users. Ferati et al. [11] propose a design for acoustic educational applications for blind users. Similarly, Harada et al. [14] are concerned with the development of a form of interaction through voice that brings benefits analogue to the possibility of direct manipulation allowed by the mouse.

In the other hand, there are works that explore different modes of text input. In the work of Cox et al. [5], the main objective was to explore the complementary aspects of the voice and the phone keyboard to overcome the deficiencies of traditional methods of text input in circumstances of user mobility, in which he has busy hands and vision. Finally, Castellucci and MacKenzie [3] present a technique for text input using the motion sensor equipped remote control of the Wii video game to capture gestures that are mapped to characters. An alphabet of gestures is proposed, in which every gesture is composed of only two primitive movements. In common, all these works offer alternative ways to perform a task in order to improve efficiency to reach a wider user population.

3. TEXT INPUT INTERFACES ON IDTV

The use of interfaces based on multiple text input modes in digital television is the focus of this study. For better understanding the problem, we carried out a survey of methods used to input text in iDTV applications. Some of them are even older than the first applications for digital TV, as they are inherited from video game consoles with simple remote controls. In this group, we highlight 2 main forms: virtual keyboard and sequential selection of characters. The first method consists in displaying on the TV screen a set of buttons representing characters. One of them has the focus, that can be moved using the arrow keys. The associated character can be entered using the OK / Enter key of the remote control. Two different layouts are typically used: alphabetic and QUERTY. Devices like iPhone, that do not have a real keyboard, but are equipped with a touch screen, also make use of the virtual keyboard. Recent work [13, 22] explore QWERTY virtual keyboard with two foci controlled by joysticks equipped with two directional controls. The idea is to use the analogy of typing on a computer keyboard, where each hand is responsible for half of the keys.

Sequential selection of characters is a simpler method that consists in presenting to the user a character at the current cursor position: the character can be modified, in alphabetical order, using the arrows on the remote. After selecting a character, the cursor moves to next position and the user should once again go through the list of characters available for selection of the new character. This method avoids using the screen to display the virtual keyboard, but provides a less efficient text entry. Another group of text input methods that can be used in iDTV comes from the ones traditionally found in mobile phones, as traditional iDTV remote controls also have the numeric keys set. In this group, two methods stand out: multi-tap and predictive text. James and Reischel [16] present performance metrics for each of them and show the efficiency of predictive text.

Methods that make use of more recent technologies are also being investigated. In the work conducted by Nakatoh et al. [17], the authors describe the techniques developed for the speech recognition system present in the TV control system. An omnidirectional microphone was used due to the position variation of the speaker in relation to the microphone embedded on the remote control. The captured audio signal was sent to the TV equipment, where it was initially processed by a digital signal processor. Then, the recognized phonemes were passed to be processed by the automatic speech recognition system. The speech recognition system allowed that the same commands were mapped by several items of the phoneme dictionary. The name of a single channel, for example, could be pronounced in 6 different ways. In total, the dictionary had around 400 items, and it was 1300 items when the various ways of pronouncing the same command were considered. To improve the system usability, they developed a technique for reducing ambient noise and a technique of echo cancellation of the TV sound. They also stated that the speaking style varies with the user generation and therefore they developed age-dependent acoustic models.

Another study which used on commands by voice was performed by Wittenburg et al. [23]. In their proposed system, users are free to pronounce any word, without vocabulary or grammar restrictions, and receive as output a list of possibly related programs. To help users understand the results, the authors propose as future work a variable highlight in the words of the result list. That is, words for which the system credits higher probability of been pronounced by the user gain greater prominence.

The literature also reports researches that use the interpretation of user's interaction with specifics devices as a strategy for input text. In this group we have the work of Castellucci and MacKenzie [3], as already mentioned. In it, a technique for text input using the control of the Wii video game is proposed. To achieve it, they capture the motions of the remote control and map them to characters. There is an alphabet in which every gesture is composed of only two primitive movements. The work of Fagá Jr. et al. [10] could be interpreted in the same direction. In this case, the mapping comes from the strokes of a electronic pen. They propose an architecture approach that exploits the automatic capture of the user interaction with personal devices, employs ontology to store context information, and uses the context information to organize users in P2P groups for the collaborative exchange of information. The ontology employed convert the ink-annotation to a annotation that then could be transformed, according to the Watch and Comment paradigm, to input text.

Finally, in the work of de Jesus Lima Gomes et al. [7], an interface using barcode on paper was designed to assist the interaction with a distance learning system using the television. Systems like this, if restricted to the traditional remote control, have the advantage of reaching a wider audience, but offer a more complex interaction. In the system proposed by them, a remote control equipped with a barcode reader is used to request the display of multimedia content related to the topic studied in a printed material.

3.1 Physical Devices

The new forms of interaction with the television system that are being developed may require physical devices other than traditional remote control. De Miranda et al. [8] conducted a detailed study on the challenges and guidelines that should be considered during the design and integration of new physical artifacts to the Brazilian context. According to the authors, the remote control used with analogue television, still prevalent, can act as a limiting factor for interaction with proposed and developed services for digital television. Among the ten guidelines presented, the ones with number 1, 2 and 4 make explicit reference to the use of speech, recommending that interaction alternatives for people with physical disabilities, visually impaired and illiterate should be provided. However, the authors point out that not all environments can promote this form of interaction and that the system has to be trained to recognize the voice of the user. They mention also the problem of the collective use of TV and the noise and natural atmosphere in which TV is watched. Hence the importance of providing alternative ways to carry out a task, as mentioned in Section 2.

As seen in the previous section, the product made by Nakatoh et al. [17] has a remote control that has an integrated omnidirectional microphone. Other features of the "speech remote control" are: 1) it has only 14 keys instead of more than 70 of the equivalent traditional remote, 2) it allows almost all commands that can be entered with the traditional command, and 3) has an easy to grab format, with a push-to-talk side button.

Currently, the most sold software for speech recognition is the Dragon NaturallSpeaking[1]. It has a large vocabulary, continuous speech recognition and reports a 99% accuracy.

---

[1]http://www.nuance.com/naturallyspeaking/

It requires that each user create a personal speech model by undergoing a 10-minute reading section of predefined texts. It was the 7th version of the software that was used in the experiments of the work from [5].

3.2 Limitations in iDTV interfaces

Interactive digital TV is an entertainment system that offers a variety of service types using a broadcast reception and a return channel through which it transmits the interaction data. However, the main interaction device with the iDTV is the traditional remote control. The interactivity level that the remote control offers is limited to pressing keys, some of them mapped to a specific command in the television screen. According to Berglund et al. [2] and Piccolo and Baranauskas [20], we can observe tree main problems that iDTV faces:

(1) The user interaction paradigm in iDTV looks like menu navigation, as it could be done in a computer. So, people with little experience on computers are excluded from interacting with iDTV applications. Besides, the TV does not have the same tools as a PC (mouse, keyboard, processing power, etc.).

(2) The interaction design is poor, as the screen resolution is small. This leads people to think that the interfaces are poor in relation to the functionalities, even those who are familiarized with new technologies.

(3) The main interaction device used in the iDTV is the remote control, which is still inadequate and raise difficulties to this task [4]. Most applications are limited to map keys of the remote control in the television screen in order to allow the selection of the commands of the interface [20], providing a hard to understand and monotonous interaction, causing frustration and irritation in users.

There are a variety of proposals to solve this kind of problems. Some of them try to develop better remote controls [22, 2, 6, 13]. Others propose different mechanisms not yet explored, as accelerometers [3], remote controls with barcodes reader [7], interactive applications that reproduce gestures [21], approaches that combine speech and remote control [5], or intelligent prediction mechanisms of text entry from the remote control [12], for instances.

4. OUR DESIGN

The issues discussed here were considered during the development of the prototype of a mechanism for text input in iDTV applications. The project was conducted using a set of techniques that aim to engage the end user during all stages of development, known as User Centered Design [9].

First, we did a requirement elicitation with potential users and experts in the area. In the second step, the features and technical characteristics of the interface model were defined. Finally, we developed a primer prototype in order to make a proof-of-concept usability tests in it.

4.1 Requirements Elicitation

Initially, a study to better understand the future users of the mechanism to be developed was conducted. At this stage, we interviewed four experts in the area, coming from different contexts, and we also applied questionnaires that included potential users from various regions of Brazil. The main contributions are reported below.

4.1.1 Questionnaires

The questionnaires were applied on paper (32 responses), in order to reach a diverse audience, and using a on-line surveys system (121 responses), which helped to obtain a greater number of responses. One of the questions asked was what would be the best way to write a message to a friend using the television. The answers to this open question were very diverse and may be clustered into the following categories: QWERTY keyboard; T9 predictive text standard; Speech; Virtual keyboard using a simple remote control; Virtual keyboard using a touchscreen TV; Virtual keyboard using a touchscreen remote control; Thought; Preformulated phrases; Writing on a paper whose text is recognized by the television; Writing with a pen directly on television screen; and Using a mobile phone connected to the TV.

A concern regarding the need to offer more than one alternative to text input could be noticed, as in the following examples (our translation):

- *"Using speech when I'm alone and using T9 when I'm in an ambient with other people."*

- *"Speech would be ideal, but I think we could correct some possible errors or [make some] modifications using a keyboard, for example"*

- *"I would like to be able to choose: i) If I'm in the living room with my mother in law: conventional keyboard; ii) if I'm with other people: speech to text."*

- *"Using speech and phonemes recognition or, to a reality closer to ours, a remote control with a LCD touchscreen..."*

- *"... but there must be other ways, that are accessible from those who are dumb or are currently without voice, for example."*

Another recurrent concern was regarding to the interference of the environment and TV sound, in cases in which the text input is performed using speech, as in the following examples (our translation):

- *"... I know there are limitations and difficulties, such as external interference from other people, background noise, etc."*

- *"... but there may be noise problems"*

- *"... without interfering with the program audio that the person is watching."*

4.1.2 Interviews

In order to better understand the problem to be solved, we interviewed four experts in the area, each one with different specializations. They were a college professor researcher in the areas of multimedia, hypermedia, middleware and interactive applications for digital TV, a usability engineer of a research and development Software Company, and an interaction designer and a products consultant of a cable TV Company. The main contributions are reported below.

The college Professor:

- He thinks that the media use various auxiliary information that help in understanding the message. There are a number of ambiguities that are only broken because of the context.

- He finds the possibility of sending messages through TV interesting. He imagines that the user makes simple operations using the remote control, and would be interesting to write the message using speech. But the interference could disrupt the environment. *"It should occur in a restricted environment."*

- *"There are several ways in which communication can be done: voice, body movement, interaction with objects, wind, blowing stronger or weaker can generate an alphabet, for instances."*

- He considers necessary to define reserved voice commands in order to let the machine knows when to take certain actions instead of writing what is being spoken.

- *"Would be interesting to search for what techniques should be used and in what situations."*

- He notes that young people prefer to communicate with text, even though the communication by voice are faster and more direct,*"... youths today are so good writing with the numeric keypad that perhaps other ways are not best suited to them ... Maybe it's because texts are more reserved"* he said.

The usability engineer:

- He's seen only one application that used text entry. It used a virtual keyboard. *"It was an alphabetic keyboard, not QWERTY. One of the letters had focus and the enter key was used to insert the letters focused."*

- He considered feasible text entry by voice. *"It would require less effort and it is interesting because it is more natural."* he said.

- *" The advantage would be to insert long texts. The disadvantages would be when people were watching TV together with someone, because of privacy, or when there were someone sleeping."*

- He said he did not know any project for text entry by voice on TV.

The interaction designer and the products consultant:

- *"Once we have analyzed several kinds of infrared remote controls. Some were of normal shape and others more complex-shaped, like a mouse, keyboard or joystick. Cost-benefit has led us to choose the simple remote control."*

- *"The major difficulty is that there are no character keys in the remote control and a simulation has to be done. One way is by showing a virtual keyboard on the screen and allowing the user to navigate through the arrow keys and press OK. We tested the QWERTY and alphabetic keyboards. According to the performance tests, typing in the alphabetic keyboard had more success than QWERTY when the user was at are slightly larger distance from TV."*

- *"The tendency is to use text input format similar to the cell phone, where the letters are also printed on the keys."*

- *"Another difficulty in TV is that the user has to look at the screen to see the result and to look at the remote control to seek for the letters, what does not occur in cell, since the keyboard and screen are very close. Even when the remote controls have the letters printed, we will continue showing the keyboard map on screen."*

- *"What we have today is that the remote control is easily available to watch television."*

- *"Another problem is the environment where the TV is. It may be that i am dictating a text and my son goes on the side screaming and disturbs."*

- *"The TV has a special characteristic of being a familiar device and not individual."*

This step was crucial to help us to understand the importance of offering alternative ways of entering text, in order to meet the needs of different user profiles and to be flexible enough to be used in different environments, as discussed in Section 2. Still aiming to better understand the problem to be solved, we conducted a survey on the ways of text input currently used in television systems, which was presented in Section 3.

Requirements elicitation allowed us to define the functional requirements and key criteria of usability to be considered. Nine functional requirements for the system were elicited, addressing basic issues related to inserting and deleting characters and words, and the substitution of letters both using speech and remote control. The following usability criteria were considered the most important in the context of the project: (1) *Familiarity*: User should be able to use some of the knowledge it already has in the context of writing during his first interactions with the proposed mechanism, (2) *Substitutivity*: Complementary forms of text input must be provided for the user, and (3) *Responsiveness*: A iDTV decoder usually has little processing power compared to a personal computer. The system must be fast enough to let the user notice changes in its state.

4.2 Text entry model based on multiple input modes on iDTV

Our proposal aims to explore and to develop a mechanism for text entry in iDTV. During the project we realized that no single mechanism is able to meet the needs and characteristics of all system users. The approach based on multiple input modes serves a larger number of users in a satisfactory manner.

The importance of the project lies in how our users will interact with the component, if the first interactions between the user and the system are clear, if the user finds the various mechanisms proposed interesting enough so that he can perform a specific task, and if the system can make the user to perceive readily the state changes in response to actions.

We designed the model considering three main methods of entering text:

(1) Speech recognition with a microphone located on the user's remote control, which is activated via a push-to-talk key;

(2) Cell keypad mode using the remote control, with the mapping between buttons and letters shown on the GUI. That method can be used with text prediction (T9) or without a dictionary aid (multitap);

(3) Virtual keyboard mode in alphabetical order, in which the user navigates through the letters using the arrow keys and inserts the selected letter in the text using the OK key on the remote.

Our model allows the user to use the text input mode that he chooses when he wants, as illustrated in Figure 1. We choose the virtual keyboard mode as the default state of the component to the detriment of the cell keypad mode, because this mode can be more intuitive and comprehensive. Users not used to write text on cell phones feel difficulties if they tried to write using this mechanism. As we noticed during the analysis of questionnaires, they were answered mostly by people with high levels of education (80% at the beginning of undergraduate college) and age not too young nor too old (80% of people were between 18-44 years old). 30% of people said that seldom or almost never send messages via cell phone.

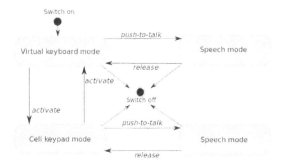

Figure 1: State diagram of the model

The user can use the speech mode concurrently with other text entry modes in a natural way by pressing the push-to-talk key on remote. Moreover, the switch between modes "Virtual keyboard" and "Cell keypad" is made through the activation of a button on the interface.

4.3 The prototype in use

Based on the requirements and principles defined on the model, two interfaces were independently designed, and the strengths of each were combined to create a third interface. Next, a functional prototype was implemented to allow the evaluation of the interface designed. We made a horizontal prototype that simulates the features that were described in the model. It was created in Java to run on a PC, aiming a short development time. Figure 2 shows the four major states of the text input component prototype.

The speech mode would allow the user to write in the selected text box dictating the words he or she wants, but no speech recognition engine was implemented. This functionality was tested using the Wizard of Oz technique. In addition to the Dictate state, shown in the upper left of Figure 2(1), the speech mode of the component has also a state where only editing commands are recognized by the speech recognition engine (although it is not available in the current version). The cell keypad mode (Figure2(2)) allows the user to write in the selected text box using the numeric keys of the remote, just as it is traditionally done in telephones and

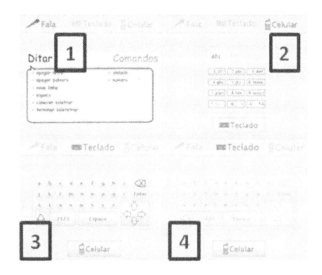

Figure 2: Four main states of the text input component prototype (in Portuguese): (1) Speech mode in Dictate state, (2) Cell keypad mode, (3) virtual keyboard mode and (4) virtual keyboard mode in cursor movement state

cell phones. It should allow both multi-tap and predictive text (although only the first mode is currently available). Finally, the virtual keyboard mode (Figure 2(3))allows writing text by selecting the desired characters using the arrows and OK key. By selecting the button on the bottom right of the keyboard, the function of the arrow keys on the remote control changes to let the user to move the cursor in the text box and, therefore, the buttons on the virtual keyboard become disabled, as shown in Figure 2(4).

Figure 3: Adapted keyboard to interact with the prototype

The switch between the modes "virtual keyboard" and "cell keypad mode" is easily performed. To go from the virtual keyboard to the cell keypad mode, users should press the directional keys to give focus to the "celular" button, and press OK on the remote control (Figure 2(3)). The switch in the opposite direction is even easier, because it is necessary only to press the OK key (Figure2(2)). In case the user wants to activate the speech recognition system, he only needs to press and hold the push-to-talk key on the remote control. The interface of the component changes to show the commands that can be intercalated while the user dictates the desired text. As soon as the push-to-talk key is released,

the interface shows a mode according to the previous state.

Below we list some important features of the prototype:

(1) The prototype was developed to be simple and to allow the tester to focus its attention only in the text entry component. In the screen, only a text box and the designed text entry component are shown.

(2) The font sizes used in the prototype led to a component visible area of approximately 400 x 330 pixels, which fits even on a standard-definition television without causing visualization difficulties.

(3) The names chosen to the three text entry modes presented in the interfaces needed to be small because of the low screen resolution adopted. One of the modes is identified by just one word. The icons were also chosen in order to be easily identified and associated with the mode.

(4) No help screen was developed because the text entry component would be described in the help screen of the application that uses it.

Finally, interaction with the real system should be performed with a special remote control containing a built-in microphone and a push-to-talk key that must be pressed to activate the speech recognition engine. In user tests with our prototype, the input data was performed using an adapted computer keyboard where some keys were relabeled and unused keys were covered with adhesive paper, in order to not confuse the user (Figure 3).

5. USABILILITY EVALUATION

So far, the latest stage in our project was the usability evaluation of the prototype. We used two usability inspection methods: Heuristic Evaluation and Cognitive Walkthrough. We decide to used them given the strong acceptance and recognition they have [15]. We also conducted user testing through the thinking aloud with Wizard of Oz technique.

The think aloud tests were performed by 4 pairs of users, following one of the recommendations of Flores et al. (2008), who note that to test pairs allows individuals to express more naturally their actions and opinions. Figure 4 show some frames taken from the recorded videos during the tests. The Heuristic and Cognitive Walkthrough evaluations were applied each one to three experts and the Heuristic Evaluations were performed using the general heuristics proposed by Nielsen and Mölich [2].

Figure 4: Frames taken from the recorded videos during the tests, in which the 3 different modes were used: (1) Virtual keyboard mode, (2) speech mode and (3) cell keypad mode.

All the information of evaluations and tests were summa-

---

[2]The original list of 9 heuristics from Nielsen and Mölich (1990) has been refined by Nielsen (*http://www.useit.com/papers/heuristic/heuristic_list.html*)

rized in order to make a general compendium of a number of problems in the proposed mechanism. Each of these problems was awarded its corresponding level of severity. Seven of them, due to greater severity, were used to create a list of recommendation changes. The main problems were:

(1) The speech mode has a different activation mechanism from the others, but this is not indicated in the interface. There was not a consensus among the evaluators if this mode should or not be activated only by clicking on the push-to-talk button, as it is now. However, if this happens, that difference must be clearly indicated in the interface.

(2) The activation mechanism of the mobile phone style mode and the virtual keyboard mode should be better crafted. The buttons that allow the activation are distant from the tabs that indicate which mode is active. The most intuitive seems to be the use of own tabs as activation mechanism.

(3) The mobile phone style mode does not give a clear indication that the buttons shown are merely illustrative. The buttons of the interface are shown only to serve as a guide for users who use remote controls with no letters printed on keys. This causes a large amount of error situations, in which users try to use the arrow keys to focus one of the illustrative buttons.

(4) The term "Celular" (cell phone), used to indicate the text input style often used in mobile devices, may not be easily understood by users, who may think it refers to their own mobile phone or to a cell phone call.

(5) The "BACK" button caused a lot of frustration because it could almost never be used. This may have occurred because the component has been evaluated outside the context of an application, where it would certainly have clearer functionalities. Another problem caused by this key was the association made between the key and the backspace key of a traditional computer keyboard.

(6) The key used to enter and to exit the cursor movement state, accessible from the keyboard mode, was not the same. The key to enter was the "OK" key, but the key to exit was the "BACK" key. This was extremely counterintuitive. The possibility of inserting new lines using the "OK" key, offered when this state is activated, is not worth the amount of errors generated.

(7) The interface of the speech mode is not clear enough and causes a lot of problems. The use of two columns of commands in the Dictation state makes the user associate the right column with the Commands state. The interface is not clear neither on how to access the Commands state, nor indicate clearly the difference between the Dictate state and Commands state. Not even the list of available commands in the Dictate state is satisfactory.

In addition to the problems identified in the design of the text input component, some serious problems on the specific prototype implementation ended up gaining more prominence in the evaluations than it was expected:

(1) The cursor that indicates where the next character will be inserted is not shown in any of the input text modes.

(2) The adjustment made on the numeric keypad resulted in the "Num Lock" key being used to insert symbols. This made the rest of the numeric keypad stop working whenever the symbols key was pressed an odd number of times.

(3) The predictive text functionality (T9), despite not being implemented, is indicated by a label on the interface.

(4) The tests of the speech mode, using the technique of the Wizard of Oz, did not allow the text to be inserted into the text area of the prototype. A parallel screen was used.

Observing the tests with users, we noticed that the think aloud test was not adequate when evaluating the Speech mode, since users were asked to say all they were thinking and this action did not fit very well in the case of voice interfaces.

6. IMPROVEMENTS

In order to solve the main problems of the designed component listed in the previous section, the following changes should be made for the next version:

(1) To allow the three text input modes to be activated by selecting the corresponding tab. Thus, the "Celular" ("Mobile Phone") button is removed from the virtual keyboard mode and the "Teclado" ("Keyboard") button is removed from the mobile phone style mode. When the virtual keyboard mode is activated, the focus can move freely between the character buttons and the two other tabs. When the speech or mobile phone style mode are activated, the focus can move only between the two other tabs. The button push-to-talk should be preserved and the user should be able to press it regardless of the active mode, which makes it a shortcut to the speech mode. However, if it is pressed while the speech mode is not active, when released, the previous mode should be activated again. In addition, to increase the clarity and to consider users who do not speak English, it should be relabeled to "Segure para falar" ("Hold to talk"). These changes aim to solve the problems 1 and 2, and also have some impact on problem 3, as it does not let the focus fixed on a single button while the mobile phone mode is active.

(2) The graphical interface of the mobile phone style mode should be improved so that no doubt remains that the buttons shown are merely illustrative. This change also aims to solve the problem 3.

(3) The tabs that identify the text input modes should be bigger to allow each mode be identified by more than one word. The mobile phone mode would be called "Estilo celular" ("Mobile phone style"), the virtual keyboard mode would be called "Teclado virtual" ("Virtual keyboard"). The name of the speech mode could remain the same. This aims to eliminate possible confusion explained by problem 4.

(4) The "BACK" key should be relabeled to "VOLTAR" ("back") to consider users who do not speak English and also solve the problem 5. If time is available, the context of the application should be used in the prototype, to make it clear what is the function assigned to the BACK key.

(5) The OK button should also be used to exit the cursor movement state. This would solve problem 6.

(6) The organization of the items shown in the speech mode should be improved, to make it clear to the user that "Dictate" is just one of the possible states of this mode. The command "Comandos" ("Commands") should be listed along with other possible commands of the Dictate state. Also, the command "Ditar" ("Dictate") should be listed along with other possible commands of the Commands state. The "Apagar linha" ("delete line") command should be added to the

list of commands of the Dictate state. The commands that require some extra word, as in the case of "Insert symbol" and "Insert number", should indicate that in the interface. All these changes address the problems related to the speech mode, and grouped in item 7.

In future work, we intend to implement a new prototype that includes the suggested changes and targeting a set-top box (STB), so that new evaluations may be carried out, taking into account previously ignored factors, such as performance and use of a real remote control.

7. FINAL REMARKS

Given the differences between the iDTV and PC platforms with respect to user tasks associated with viewing, navigating, and interacting, in this paper we have proposed a interface model based on multiple input modes, and its corresponding software component, to deal with the problem of text entry in iDTV applications, and presented a prototype making use of the component.

During the development of the prototype, we conducted usability tests using the think aloud protocol, and usability inspections using the heuristic evaluation and cognitive walkthrough techniques. The evaluations allowed the detection of both a number of problems and of several improvement opportunities; at the same time they highlighted the importance of using complementary text input modes in order to satisfy the needs of different users. Overall, the evaluation results suggest that the proposed approach provides a satisfactory level of usability by overcoming the limitations of text input in the context of the user-interaction with iDTV applications.

With respect to future work, we plan to tackle both the problems and new requirements identified by the specialists in the usability evaluations. We also intend to implement a new prototype that, including the suggested changes, runs on a set-top box, so that new evaluations may be carried out — this is important since it allows to take into account factor which have been ignored in the current evaluations, in particular the user performance when a real remote control is used.

Acknowledgments. We thank the financial support received from FAPESP, CNPq, CAPES, FINEP and the MCT.

References

[1] G. D. Abowd, E. D. Mynatt, and T. Rodden. The human experience. *IEEE Pervasive Computing*, 1(1):48–57, 2002.

[2] A. Berglund, E. Berglund, A. Larsson, and M. Bång. Paper remote: an augmented television guide and remote control. *Universal Access in the Information Society*, 4(4):300–327, 2006.

[3] S. J. Castellucci and I. S. MacKenzie. Unigest: text entry using three degrees of motion. In *CHI '08 Extended Abstracts of the ACM Conference on Human Factors in Computing Systems*, pages 3549–3554, 2008.

[4] P. Cesar, K. Chorianopoulos, and J. F. Jensen. Social Television and User Interaction. *Comput. Entertain.*, 6(1):1–10, 2008.

[5] A. L. Cox, P. A. Cairns, A. Walton, and S. Lee. Tlk or Txt? Using Voice Input for SMS Composition. *Personal Ubiquitous Comput.*, 12(8):567–588, 2008.

[6] M. J. Darnell. Making Digital TV Easier for Less-Technically-Inclined People. In *UXTV '08: Proc. 1st Int. Conf. Designing Interactive User Experiences for TV and Video*, pages 27–30, 2008.

[7] F. de Jesus Lima Gomes, J. V. de Lima, and R. A. de Nevado. O papel Comum como Interface para TV Digital. In *IHC '06: Proceedings of the VI Brazilian Symposium on Human Factors in Computing Systems*, pages 29–32, 2006.

[8] L. C. De Miranda, L. S. G. Piccolo, and M. C. C. Baranauskas. Artefatos físicos de Interaç ao com a TVDI: desafios e diretrizes para o cenário brasileiro. In *IHC '08: Proc. VIII Brazilian Symposium on Human Factors in Computing Systems*, pages 60–69, 2008.

[9] A. Dix, J. Finley, G. Abowd, , and Beale. *Human-Computer Interaction*. Prentice Hall, 3rd edition, 2004.

[10] R. Fagá Jr., B. C. Furtado, F. Maximino, R. G. Cattelan, and M. d. G. C. Pimentel. Context Information Exchange and Sharing in a Peer-to-Peer Community: A Video Annotation Scenario. In *SIGDOC '09: Proceedings of the 27th ACM International Conf. Design of Communication*, pages 265–272, 2009.

[11] M. Ferati, S. Mannheimer, and D. Bolchini. Acoustic Iteraction Design Through "audemes": Experiences With the Blind. In *SIGDOC '09: Proc. 27th ACM International Conf. Design of Communication*, pages 23–28, 2009.

[12] G. Geleijnse, D. Aliakseyeu, and E. Sarroukh. Comparing Text Entry Methods for Interactive Television Applications. In *EuroITV '09: Proc. Seventh European Conf. European Interactive Television Conf.*, pages 145–148, 2009.

[13] K. Go, H. Konishi, and Y. Matsuura. Itone: A Japanese Text Input Method for a Dual Joystick Game Controller. In *CHI '08: CHI '08 extended abstracts on ACM Conference on Human Factors in Computing Systems*, pages 3141–3146, 2008.

[14] S. Harada, J. O. Wobbrock, J. Malkin, J. A. Bilmes, and J. A. Landay. Longitudinal Study of People Learning to Use Continuous Voice-Based cursor Control. In *CHI '09: Proc. 27th Int. Conf. Human Factors in Computing Systems*, pages 347–356, 2009.

[15] T. Hollingsed and D. G. Novick. Usability Inspection Methods After 15 Years of Research and Practice. In *SIGDOC '07: Proc. 25th ACM International Conf. Design of Communication*, pages 249–255, 2007.

[16] C. L. James and K. M. Reischel. Text Input for Mobile Devices: Comparing Model Prediction to Actual Performance. In *CHI '01: Proceedings of the SIGCHI Conf. Human Factors in Computing Systems*, pages 365–371, 2001.

[17] Y. Nakatoh, H. Kuwano, T. Kanamori, and M. Hoshimi. Speech Recognition Interface System for Digital TV Control — Special Issue Applied Systems. *Acoustical science and technology*, 28(3):165–171, 2007-05.

[18] N. Patel, S. Agarwal, N. Rajput, A. Nanavati, P. Dave, and T. S. Parikh. A Comparative Study of Speech and Dialed Input Voice Interfaces in Rural India. In *CHI '09: Proceedings of the 27th Int. Conf. Human Factors in Computing Systems*, pages 51–54, 2009.

[19] D. d. C. Pedrosa, D. A. Vega Oliveros, M. d. G. C. Pimentel, and R. P. d. M. Fortes. Text Input in Digital Television: a Component Prototype. In *Adjunct Proc. of EuroITV '10: Proc. 8th Int. Interactive Conf. Interactive TV and Video*, pages 1–4, 2010.

[20] L. S. G. Piccolo and M. C. C. Baranauskas. Desafios de Design para a TV Digital Interativa. In *IHC '06: Proc. VI Brazilian Symposium on Human Factors in Computing Systems*, pages 1–10, 2006.

[21] G. Verhulsdonck. Issues of Designing Gestures into Online Interactions: Implications for Communicating in Virtual Environments. In *SIGDOC '07: Proc. 25th ACM International Conf. Design of Communication*, pages 26–33, 2007.

[22] A. D. Wilson and M. Agrawala. Text Entry Using a Dual Joystick Game Controller. In *CHI '06: Proc. SIGCHI Conf. Human Factors in Computing Systems*, pages 475–478, 2006.

[23] K. Wittenburg, T. Lanning, D. Schwenke, H. Shubin, and A. Vetro. The Prospects for Unrestricted Speech Input for TV Content Search. In *AVI '06: Proc. Working Conf. Advanced Visual Interfaces*, pages 352–359, 2006.

Musical Interaction Patterns: Communicating Computer Music Knowledge in a Multidisciplinary Project

Luciano Flores[1], Evandro Miletto[1], Marcelo Pimenta[1], Eduardo Miranda[2], Damián Keller[3]

[1]UFRGS - Inst. of Informatics
Caixa Postal 15064, 91501-970
Porto Alegre, RS, Brazil
+55 51 3308 6814

lvflores@inf.ufrgs.br

[2]University of Plymouth - ICCMR
Plymouth, Devon PL4 8AA
United Kingdom
+44 0 1752 586 255

eduardo.miranda@plymouth.ac.uk

[3]UFAC - NAP
Amazonian Center for Music Res.
Caixa Postal 500, 69915-900
Rio Branco, AC, Brazil

dkeller@ccrma.stanford.edu

ABSTRACT

The growing popularity of mobile devices gave birth to a still emergent research field, called Mobile Music, and concerning the development of musical applications for use in these devices. Our particular research investigates *interaction design* within this field, taking into account relationships with ubiquitous computing contexts, and applying knowledge from several disciplines, mainly Computer Music and Human-Computer Interaction. In this paper we propose using the concept of *patterns* in such multidisciplinary design context. Design patterns are, essentially, common solutions for specific design problems, which have been systematically collected and documented. Since they help designers, allowing them to reuse proven solutions within a certain domain, we argue that they can aid multidisciplinary design, facilitating communication and allowing knowledge transfer among team members of diverse fields. We illustrate our point by describing a set of musical interaction patterns that came out of our investigation so far, showing how they encapsulate Computer Music knowledge and how this was helpful in our own design process.

Categories and Subject Descriptors

D.2.2 [**Software Engineering**]: Design Tools and Techniques;
H.5.2 [**Information Interfaces and Presentation**]: User Interfaces – *evaluation/methodology, theory and methods*;
H.5.5 [**Information Interfaces and Presentation**]: Sound and Music Computing.

General Terms

Design, Human Factors.

Keywords

Multidisciplinary design, interaction design patterns, computer music, mobile music, ubiquitous computing.

1. INTRODUCTION

In the last years, our research group has been investigating the use of Ubiquitous Computing technology to support musical activities. Within this topic, which we call "Ubiquitous Music" [13], the development of interactive systems has to follow a multidisciplinary approach, and involves a multidisciplinary team of experts in Computer Music, Human-Computer Interaction (HCI), Interaction Design, Computer Supported Cooperative Work (CSCW), and Ubiquitous Computing (or Ubicomp). During this research project, we came across two main problems that impact on the design process. The first problem is that, as in any other multidisciplinary endeavor, communication and knowledge transfer between team members of so many different backgrounds are of key importance, though sometimes these are very difficult to achieve.

The second general problem is designing for new digital technologies such as ubiquitous computing and everyday mobile devices. When developing for such contexts we cannot focus on specific user interfaces, due a presumed device independence. Interaction design for Ubicomp and for generic mobile devices has to be done from within higher levels of abstraction.

We have found that *interaction patterns* [2, 19] are a suitable means to address both these issues. Initially, in our project we have considered using patterns to encapsulate and to abstract solutions for specific subproblems of interaction design. This way, we could concentrate on the broader conception of an interactive ubiquitous system to support some musical activity, without having to depend on implementation constraints or target platform specifications. This allows focusing on the higher-level human, social, and contextual aspects of interacting with these systems.

By analyzing the state-of-the-art in mobile music systems [7], and applying our own expertise in Computer Music, we were able to identify four patterns that do abstract possible forms of musical interaction with ordinary mobile devices. Then, almost as a by-product, we noticed that the names we gave to the collected patterns started to be used like terms of an internal language inside our project discussions, something that was already suggested by Gamma et al. when they wrote about the usefulness of design patterns to software engineering [6]. Furthermore, our other team members, not from the Computer Music domain, were starting to learn and to understand very quickly those solution possibilities represented by our musical interaction patterns. Thus, we observed that interaction patterns were enabling not only abstraction and communication for multidisciplinary design purposes, but also knowledge transfer between team members from different fields.

This paper is organized as follows. Next section discusses the potential worth of using patterns in multidisciplinary design work situations, and when designing for such new digital contexts as well, for bridging the gap between conceptual design and implementation possibilities in these cases which demand higher-level approaches. Then, we describe our four musical interaction patterns to show how they are documented and how they encapsulate Computer Music knowledge. We also describe the development of some exploratory mobile music prototypes that instantiate our patterns, which served as inspiration and, at the same time, as testbed for these. Finally, we discuss this pattern-based prototyping experience, and also report a small comprehensibility test, in which our patterns were presented to people from outside our project, and they were asked to recognize those patterns in real mobile music applications. The paper concludes by discussing preliminary outcomes from both the prototype design process and the test.

2. PATTERNS: BASIC CONCEPTS AND APPLICATION TO TEAM COMMUNICATION

Research and development in the field of Computer Music is directed towards the construction of computer systems supporting not only traditional activities (like music composition, performance, music training and education, signal processing, notation studies, and music analysis), but also some non-conventional and new activities like music storage and sharing, information retrieval, and classification of musical data (here including music itself and metadata related to music). *Design of computer music applications* is the term used in this paper meaning the design of interactive systems that support musical activities (either traditional or non-conventional ones).

In the last years, the growing interest from the Computer Music community on the design of musical applications for new digital contexts (new platforms or new uses for existing platforms) promises exciting developments, translated in recent fields such as Mobile Music [7] and Networked Music [15].

Clearly, designing computer music applications is a complex and multidisciplinary task with some very interesting challenges. On a high level, these can be divided into three classes:

- Technology-related challenges;

- Human-related challenges; and

- Process-related challenges.

Some examples of the first class include studying musical hardware, digital representations, algorithms, and protocols. As for the second class, some examples include studying musician's needs, and usability of musical interfaces.

The third class, process-related challenges, is related to a coherent set of activities involved in computer music applications development – including not only activities for the development from scratch (like requirements engineering, application specification and design, testing, etc.) but also extension and modification of existing applications or configuration and integration of off-the-shelf

software or components. In this paper we focus on this third class, of process-related challenges, and emphasize one problem closely associated with application design in a multidisciplinary team: *How to improve team communication?*

In software design, a *pattern* is a portable high-quality solution to a (usually small) commonly recurring problem. Indeed, patterns allow developers to work faster and produce better code by not duplicating effort. When design patterns were introduced to the software community, they created a lot of interest. As a result, they have now been applied to many other areas.

Surprisingly, very little attention has been paid to discuss the adoption of patterns for the design of computer music applications. Some relevant exceptions include [3, 4], but these works apply patterns with very distinct purposes than of that which we try do discuss in this paper.

Indeed, one of the major challenges to computer music application designers is how to provide detailed guidance and explanations to drive a design in order to achieve *quality of use*. High-level design principles are difficult to apply to specific projects, and guidelines or recommendations providing more detailed instructions are often misinterpreted and inaccessible. Sometimes they are too abstract, and so do not suggest how to solve a problem, and cannot be used for interdisciplinary communication. Furthermore, guidelines do not provide an explanation as to *why* a particular solution works. They also tend to be too numerous, which makes it difficult for designers to find and apply the right guidelines. Concrete recommendations are too tailored to a specific context, and not as effective when applied to other contexts. But they lack describing such a context.

Thus, guidelines, recommendations and principles are generally more useful for describing requirements, whereas patterns are useful tools for those who need to communicate with the team, and to translate requirements to specific software. So, we believe that the adoption of patterns is one possible answer to communication problems within multidisciplinary design teams, which is the case in the design of computer music applications. The concept of patterns in Computer Music is fairly new, but we think it can be very relevant for the design community.

Patterns originated as an architectural concept by Christopher Alexander. Despite Alexander's famous definition ('Patterns are solutions to a problem in a context") [1], patterns are more than a kind of template to solve one's problems. They are a way of describing *motivations* by including both what we want to have happen along with the problems that are plaguing us.

As well as recording knowledge, a pattern can be used as a pre-fabricated part of a new design. By reusing already established designs, a designer can obtain the benefit of learning from the experience of others, and do not have to reinvent solutions for commonly recurring problems.

In summary, the main advantages of adopting patterns are [16]:

- Improving team communication and individual learning.

- Teaching novices some best practices and common approaches.

- Reuse of existing, high-quality solutions to commonly recurring problems.

- Establishing common terminology to improve communication within teams. Giving teams a common language, reducing misunderstandings that arise from different vocabulary.

- Shifting the level of thinking to a higher perspective.

- Facilitating the adoption of improved design alternatives, even when patterns are not used explicitly.

In this paper we are concerned with the adoption of patterns as a tool for improving team communication, specially for computer music applications development. Patterns have been applied successfully in software engineering for the same purpose [6]. By definition, a pattern is a solution which satisfactorily solves recurring design problems, forming a high-level vocabulary to communicate design issues in a relatively encapsulated way. Patterns also allow us to communicate our own knowledge and experience to others. Each pattern is a description of a particular way of doing something that has proved effective in the real world.

Patterns can certainly be used by software developers to record knowledge, in order to be reused by other developers. They can also be used to document a solution and to establish common terminology. Communication and teamwork require a common base of vocabulary and a common viewpoint of the problem. Design patterns provide a common point of reference during the analysis and design phase of a project.

Patterns shift the level of thinking, providing a higher-level perspective on the problem, on the process of design, and on object-orientation concepts (encapsulation, information hiding, abstraction hierarchies, etc.), avoiding us to deal with the details too early.

Herein, again, we are concerned with the adoption of patterns as a tool in multidisciplinary design teams. However, software design, even small pieces of software design, can't be easily understood by non-programmers. Or, this may be because we don't know yet enough about software to produce patterns that are simple enough for the lay-person.

So, the use of patterns may occur at two levels: the *concrete* level of their meaning – the "HOW"; and the *abstract* level, which occurs at a higher level (a meta-level) that is hidden from the layman and which is much richer in meaning. This higher level is the level of "WHY" concepts, and reflects the real design issues for the developers. The expression "Patterns help us see the forest and the trees" illustrates this idea. This is where the real power of patterns lies.

Better defined:

- How: In an effort to make pattern adoption as easy as possible, it is common to include direct examples of visual specifications and code where possible.

- Why: What opportunities or constraints helped to define this pattern? Was there any research done to support it?

Given our audience (a central design team working on a myriad of ultimately integrated products and features), this approach affords a lot more flexibility in how we share and document design best practices.

Since our goal is using patterns mainly for communicating design ideas from one designer to another within a multidisciplinary context, it is easy to understand the importance of an insightful "Problem" or "Use when" statement, and the relative unimportance of strict formats and implementation examples.

Although some would appreciate detailed explanations in a pattern, most computer music applications designers tend to be example-oriented – in fact, we don't believe a good pattern can even be written without examples. We have to ground a pattern in existing, real-world usage before writing the rest.

Indeed, based on our experience in collecting patterns, we have found that a new pattern arises from three key insights:

- The recognition that you have seen an idea "work" in more than one place or context;

- An understanding of why it works. A good understanding of some idiosyncrasies of computer music applications helps here;

- Insight into when it's appropriate to use the pattern, and when it's not.

As a matter of fact, the design of mobile music applications as part of our Ubiquitous Music project is an exploratory process (see section 4), in which prototype development and pattern refinement do feedback one on the other.

Since patterns are meant to be used widely, they need to be presented in a widely accepted format. Ideally, the format will be easy to read and understand. But, in the name of completeness and correctness, each pattern description may end up being rather formal. The seminal book by Gamma et al. is such a case [6]: although each pattern is essential and well described, the end result is more of a reference work than a tutorial.

But today there are several different forms for describing design patterns. Because this is not a paper about writing design patterns, we are not focusing on selecting a best structure for describing ours. In this paper, the pattern descriptions are informal, showing the central idea of the solution, a description (with examples and illustrations), and a motivation for use ("why"). The basic answers our pattern documentation provides, though, are the same: "What, How and Examples, Use When and Why."

3. MUSICAL INTERACTION PATTERNS

This section describes the four musical interaction patterns that emerged of our investigation so far. Our intention here is not exactly to introduce these patterns to the community, but to present them as complete examples of the documentation of interaction design patterns from a specific domain. Furthermore, since we are claiming that these four patterns encapsulate knowledge from the Computer Music domain, we added an explicit discussion on this connection at the end of this section.

Notice that, as our research considers the use of conventional mobile devices within ubiquitous computing contexts, we have to work in high levels of abstraction. Therefore, the patterns that we present next are truly *interaction* patterns, and not *musical interface* patterns, which would be lower in a musical pattern hierarchy and would "instantiate" the proposed interaction patterns.

General problem statement:

All of the four proposed interaction patterns address, in different ways, the general problem of "How may humans *manipulate music* and musical information using everyday (non-specific) mobile devices?" Thus, in a general collection of patterns or a pattern language for mobile interaction design, these proposed patterns could be classified under a "Music Manipulation" or "Multimedia Manipulation" category.

Principles:

- The patterns are musical-activity-independent, i.e. they can support any musical activity, and not just some activity in particular.

- The patterns may be combined to generate more complex designs, as also happens with patterns for other domains (e.g. software design, architecture, etc.).

3.1 Pattern: Natural Interaction / Natural Behavior

Solution: Imitate real-world, *natural interaction.*

Description: This pattern corresponds to musical interaction which imitates real interaction with a sound-producing object, or with an acoustic musical instrument. Thus, all musical gestures that we might regard as "natural" may be explored herein: striking, scrubbing, shaking, plucking, bowing, blowing, etc.

One advantage of designing interaction as a reproduction of *natural musical gesture* is that it will generally include a passive haptic (tactile) feedback, similar to the one we have when interacting with real sound-producing objects. This "primary" feedback (linked to the secondary feedback of hearing the resulting sound) [10] may be important for a "fine-tuned" control of the musical interaction – that "intimate" control suggested by Wessel and Wright [21], which allows the performer to achieve a sonic result that is closer to the intended, and that also facilitates the development of performance technique.

For example, a rhythm performance activity may be implemented using the touchscreen of a PDA, where sounds are triggered when it is gently striked with the stylus, like on a real drum. Or, one may implement a shaker-like instrument by using accelerometer sensors of some mobile device, and musically interacting with this instrument by shaking the device.

But exploring "naturality" in musical interaction design refers not only to designing user input as natural musical gestures, but also to simulating, through user interface (UI) output, any *natural behavior* which is expected from real-life objects when they produce sound (i.e., behavior that is linked to sound producing phenomena). This can be implemented either through representations on the graphical interface (GUI), or through an adequate mapping, applied to the physical UI, between possible gestures and their naturally expected sonic results.

In our "Drum!" prototype, the user "strikes" the PDA screen and hears a percussion sound, what would be naturally expected. In our "Bouncing Balls" prototype, little "balls" are constantly moving horizontally on the device's screen, making sound every time they "bounce" on "obstacles" (a barrier or the sides of the screen).

Notice that this natural behavior has one drawback: it will generally limit musical interaction to the "one-gesture-to-one-acoustic-result" rule of nature (except for some very particular cases).

Motivation for use: To make musical interaction more "intuitive", that is, to take advantage of what Jef Raskin [14] prefers to call the user's "familiarity" with the interaction. This is justified by the hypothesis that, by designing interaction in a form which "resembles or is identical to something the user has already learned" [14], its learning curve is reduced, what is a usability attribute (learnability).

3.2 Pattern: Event Sequencing

Solution: Allow the user to access the timeline of the musical piece, and to "schedule" musical events in this timeline, making it possible for him/her to *arrange a whole set of events* at once.

Description: In this pattern, users interact with music by editing sequences of musical events. This can be applied to any interpretation of these – individual notes, whole samples, modification parameters, in short, any kind of "musical material".

Now, it is important to state that, although our interaction patterns aim primarily at musical control, this does not imply a necessary coupling with performance activities. Neither is this pattern, of event sequencing, useful solely for composition. They are all higher level abstractions which may be applied creatively to any type of musical activity, and should be much more useful if regarded this way. In this sense, it may even be preferable to classify them not under "musical control", but as "music manipulation patterns".

Actually, event sequencing is a good example of this flexibility, since it can be observed both in CODES (asynchronous, compositional tool; see Figure 1) [9] and, for instance, in Yamaha's Tenori-On portable instrument (real-time performance) [11], where the sequences execution is looped, but they can be edited (and so played) in real-time (see Figure 2). This last, synchronous use was also added later to our Drum! prototype (described in the next section), the first prototype in which we combined patterns.

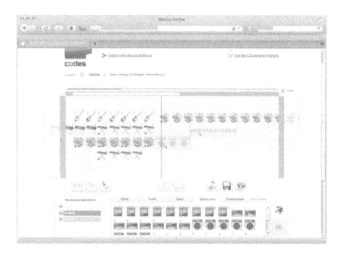

Figure 1. Asynchronous Event Sequencing in CODES, a music composition tool [9].

From designing Drum! and Bouncing Balls we conclude that, by combining interaction patterns, it is possible to create richer interaction.

Motivation for use: Usually, to extend interaction possibilities – increase interaction flexibility – by explicitly allowing, and

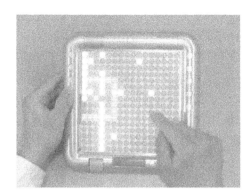

Figure 2. Event Sequencing in Tenori-On, during a looped real-time performance [11].

facilitating, epistemic actions as a complement to pragmatic actions on the system [17, 8].

3.3 Pattern: Process Control

Solution: Free the user from event-by-event music manipulation, by allowing him/her to *control a process* which, in turn, generates the actual musical events or musical material.

Description: This interaction pattern corresponds to the control of parameters from a generative musical algorithm. It solves that important problem in mobile music, which is the repurposing of non-specific devices: how can we "play" a cell phone, with its very limited keyboard, not ergonomically suited to be played like a piano keyboard?

The Process Control solution suggests a mapping from the (limited) interaction features of mobile devices, not to musical events, but to a small set of *musical process parameters*. This way, we free the user from manipulating music event-after-event, him/her needing only to start the process – which generates a continuous stream of musical events, usually through generative grammars or algorithms – and then to manipulate its parameters. One possible analogy is with the conductor of an orchestra: he doesn't play the actual notes, but he controls the orchestra.

For the mapping, we find it useful to follow suggestions given by Wessel and Wright [21] when describing their metaphor of a "space of musical processes". Put simple, the idea is that mapping parameters into a key matrix (a keyboard) or a touch-sensitive surface does not need to follow much previous planning: an "intuitive" arrangement of controls in the "parametric space", done by a musician or computer music expert, is enough to yield a satisfactory mapping.

Although it is possible to apply the "parametric navigation" metaphor from these authors, as we did in our Arpeggiator prototype, we believe that it is also possible to use other metaphors they suggest, for the control of interactive musical processes: *drag & drop*, *scrubbing*, *dipping*, and *catch & throw* [21].

Another useful heuristic for designs using this pattern is that of allowing the user him/herself to configure which process parameters does he/she wants to manipulate.

An example of applying the parametric control of a musical process is the Bloom application for iPhones [12]. This software was developed in collaboration with musician Brian Eno, and allows one to introduce events, through the touch screen, into a generative process. Then, the user may alter the "path" of the process, changing parameters while the music is playing (see Figure 3).

Figure 3. Parameter configuration for a generative musical process in Bloom, an iPhone application [12].

Motivation for use: To avoid the paradigm of event-by-event music manipulation, allowing for more complex musical results through *simpler interaction* with a process, which in turn deals automatically with the details of generating the definitive musical material. This pattern implements HCI principles like *"simplicity"* and *"process automation"*. Since it simplifies interaction, it is also a sound answer to design restrictions imposed by the limitation in interaction features, which is typical of standard mobile devices.

3.4 Pattern: Sound Mixing

Solution: Music manipulation through *real-time* control of the parallel execution of longer musical structures (musical material) – i.e. by *mixing* musical material.

Description: This pattern consists in selecting and triggering multiple sounds, so that they may play simultaneously. If a sound is triggered while another is still playing, they are mixed and play together, hence the name of the pattern. Here, music is made as a layered composition of sounds, but by real-time triggering of events, so we may see sound mixing as the real-time version of event sequencing.

The musical events in this case are sounds or musical structures, and may be of any duration. If they are long (one may even be an entire music sample, triggered just once, or a small but looped sample), we are again avoiding, with this pattern, the traditional note-by-note paradigm of musical control, which is very difficult to implement in conventional mobile devices. But remember: this can be applied not only to music performance. Our "mixDroid" prototype, for example, is a compositional tool where the user records quick, small performances, and combines those into a complete composition.

Sound triggering may be also not necessarily instantaneous. One way to instantiate this pattern is by emulating a real sound mixer (see Figure 4). Sounds will be already playing, but all muted initially. The user will then combine these sounds by manipulating their intensities, maybe gradually. In this form, interaction by sound mixing can be noticed as the method of choice in modern popular electronic music.

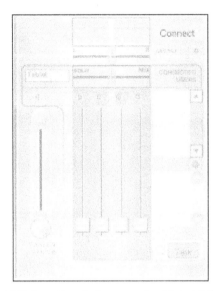

Figure 4. GUI from Tanaka's system for PDAs [18], based on volume-controlled mixing of network transmitted music streams.

Motivation for use: As in Process Control, to avoid the paradigm of event-by-event music manipulation, that is very difficult to implement in conventional mobile devices. Each musical gesture from the user will result in a longer, more complex acoustic result, and the user will be focused in combining these "layers" of sounding musical material.

3.5 Connections with Computer Music Knowledge

All interaction design solutions represented by our patterns are well-known within the field of Computer Music, but some will certainly not be so obvious to people from other areas. Thus, these patterns truly represent Computer Music knowledge.

Event Sequencing is widespread in computer music, ever since the early days of "sequencer" hardware, until its rebirth through MIDI technology in the 1980s, and even today, when it is the basic mechanism behind multitrack audio editors.

Natural Interaction relates to the metaphor of "musical instrument manipulation", according to Wanderley and Orio [20], and to the "one-gesture-to-one-acoustic-result" paradigm of Wessel and Wright [21] – hence our alternative label, "Natural Behavior".

Process Control is a well-known interaction pattern in interactive computer music [22]. The analogy with the conductor of an orchestra in fact corresponds to the "conductor mode" suggested by Dodge and Jerse [5] as one of the possible performance modes in computer music.

As said before, interaction by Sound Mixing is the method of choice in modern popular electronic music. This musical interaction pattern also corresponds to Wessel and Wright's [21] "dipping" metaphor.

4. USING MUSICAL INTERACTION PATTERNS IN A MULTIDISCIPLINARY DESIGN PROCESS

Inside our multidisciplinary Ubiquitous Music project, the subproblem of designing musical interaction with everyday mobile devices was approached through an *exploratory investigation*.

As a first step, we did a survey on the state of the art in mobile music applications and, based on our computer music expertise, we were able to analyze and identify patterns of frequent solutions for musical interaction that were being adopted in those applications.

In parallel, we did brainstorming sessions to conceive possible musical applications for ordinary mobile devices. We kept as a premise in these sessions, that we should consider many different ways of manipulating music with mobile devices, even if it would require some trade-off between functionality and creative ways of overcoming device limitations. These exercises produced ideas that were tried on some exploratory prototypes. But as a second phase, during prototypes creation, we were already associating the types of musical interaction chosen for each one of the prototypes with the interaction patterns that we were starting to define.

Hence, we began a feedback, exploratory process, in which the emerging patterns were being applied in the design of the prototypes and, in turn, the experience of designing these was being used to refine the patterns.

Natural Interaction was explored on our first mobile prototype – Drum! – which came out of the motive of "playing rhythm" and of a brainstorming session in which we manipulated the target device – a PDA. Soon a straight relation was noticed between the device's input modalities and natural musical gestures: we can actually "strike" (gently!) the touch screen with the stylus, like on a real drum. Our first discovery then was that the natural interaction pattern was an elegant way to make effective use of the physical user interface features provided by mobile devices.

We later added Event Sequencing into Drum!, to enrich its musical possibilities. This way, the user could build a looped background rhythm and improvise over it using the triggering regions. Moreover, the "sequence map" may be edited indirectly, by being set to "record" what is being played with natural gestures.

Bouncing Balls is another rhythmic instrument, which the user plays by choosing the number of balls and their sounds, and then by positioning barriers at 1/4th, 1/3rd or half the way into each ball's horizontal trajectory (see Figure 5). So, this is actually an implementation which also combines interaction patterns, since the input from the user follows the pattern of Process Control, whereas the balls exhibit Natural Behavior.

Our Arpeggiator is an extremely simplified version of a generative musical algorithm, but it is sufficient for our exploration of Process Control with mobile devices. The user is freed from controlling the music note by note, needing just to start the arpeggiator process and to control its parameters. In our exploratory prototype, these were mapped to cell phone keys as in lines of a matrix (see Figure 6), so each parameter (*p1*, *p2*, and *p3*) may vary between three possible values. Control parameters may be pre-defined or user-defined. Our prototype implements one possible combination: *p1* changes arpeggio structure; *p2* changes tonality; *p3* changes tempo; plus, the *0* (zero) key stops the process.

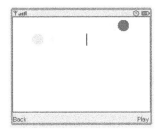

Figure 5. Cell phone screen during a performance with Bouncing Balls, with the lower ball barrier in the middle of the screen.

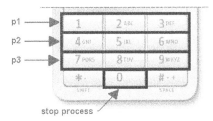

Figure 6. Layout for mapping process parameters into a keyboard matrix in the Arpeggiator.

Our mixDroid prototype implements the Sound Mixing pattern with buttons that trigger user-assigned sounds. Although it may be played as a performance instrument (similar as in the first version of Drum!), it was conceived as a composition tool: the user starts a recording, chooses in real-time when each sound will start, and then stops the recording. After, the recorded sequence is reproduced and, again in real-time, it is possible to edit the panning of each sound as it plays, which is also recorded. Our intention is to experiment with this synchronous way of composing, which does not rely on a static (usually graphical) representation. The only representation is the composition itself, which is heard in real-time.

5. DISCUSSION

All this prototype design process involved a multidisciplinary team, including many computer science students (with no background in computer music) and some colleagues from the Fine Arts (Music). Some of the ideas for our patterns came out of this cooperation – Natural Interaction in Drum! was suggested by one of the students, for example. But soon after the first definition of patterns was documented, they already started to be used to communicate design ideas, and we also began to notice that new team members were learning computer music concepts by means of them.

The Arpeggiator, for instance, was implemented by a new member who was instructed from the start that we would make this to experiment with process control. This new member quickly comprehended the solution and its differences from the other possible solutions (with help from the patterns).

From discussions with our colleagues from the music field, came the idea to implement mixDroid as test bed for the Sound Mixing pattern. And the inclusion of sequencing in the Drum! prototype was discussed with the student in charge of programming, by already using the Natural Interaction and Event Sequencing patterns as language, what helped to make clear their distinction, and resulted in a facilitated discussion about ways to combine both patterns.

Thus, our patterns were used during almost all experimental prototyping process in our project. This was also a feedback process, in which patterns refinement would benefit from experimentation with prototypes design.

Recently, we conducted a small test on pattern comprehensibility, to see if the proposed patterns can be understood and learned quickly by designers from outside the Computer Music area. During a lecture in our university, concerning our project, the four musical interaction patterns were briefly described. This part of the lecture took only about 15 minutes. Next, people from the audience were invited into recognizing those patterns in real mobile music applications, as follows:

1. We distributed one-page forms, containing a very small user-profiling questionnaire and a table with fields to be marked (the test should be quick so to not take much time off the presentation, and not to bother our audience).

2. We then played four videos (less than 1 minute each), each one depicting some person using a mobile music application. These videos were of real, commercial applications, and each application almost clearly corresponded to one of our interaction patterns, in terms of how music was manipulated.

3. Soon after each video, subjects were asked to mark on the table which pattern corresponded to that application they just saw in use. Tables had one row for each video, and four columns with the names of the patterns, so people should just mark the cell of which pattern (column) they thought was being followed in that particular application (row). There was also a fifth column, saying "Could not identify", which is self-explanatory (but people were instructed about its use before the test).

Twenty-five (25) people from the audience agreed to participate, and the raw results are presented in Table 1. Clearly, this was not a particularly rigorous test, but it was sufficient for us to get a first impression on the efficiency of knowledge transfer through our musical interaction design patterns.

6. CONCLUSION

Although all of our patterns are very well-known interaction solutions within the field of Computer Music, as we mentioned before, we believe that, since they normally do not belong to the repertoire from designers of other fields, these won't think of those solutions right on their first mobile music designs. On the other hand, if these designers are part of a multidisciplinary mobile music design team, and if our proposed patterns are used by this team, all team members may communicate better by referring to the patterns during design discussions. And this will only be possible because the patterns will have been understood and learned by all members as being solutions to the problem of musical interaction with mobile

Table 1. Raw results from the quick pattern comprehensibility test: numerical data represents the number of participants who marked each cell, from a total of 25 participants (bold means correct markings).

	Natural Interaction	Event Sequencing	Process Control	Sound Mixing	"Could not identify"
1st App.: Natural Interaction	**22**	2			1
2nd App.: Event Sequencing	2	**16**	5	1	1
3rd App.: Sound Mixing		1	2	**22**	
4th App.: Process Control		4	**17**	1	3

devices. So, these bits of Computer Music knowledge will have ultimately become part of their own designer's repertoire.

Preliminary outcomes from observing our prototyping process and from the comprehensibility experiment suggest the potential of interaction design patterns to convey domain-specific knowledge to collaborators from other domains in multidisciplinary projects.

7. ACKNOWLEDGMENTS

This work is being partially supported by the Brazilian research funding councils CNPq and CAPES.

8. REFERENCES

[1] Alexander, C., Ishikawa, S., and Silverstein, M. 1977. *A Pattern Language: Towns, Buildings, Construction*. Oxford University Press, New York, NY.

[2] Borchers, J. 2001. *A Pattern Approach to Interaction Design*. John Wiley & Sons, Chichester, UK.

[3] Brandorff, S., Lindholm, M., and Christensen, H. B. 2005. A Tutorial on Design Patterns for Music Notation Software. *Comput. Music J.* 29, 3 (Fall 2005), 42-54.

[4] Dannenberg, R. B. and Bencina, R. 2005. Design Patterns for Real-Time Computer Music Systems. In *Proceedings of the International Computer Music Conference* (Barcelona, Spain, September 05 - 09, 2005). ICMC 2005. Workshop on Real Time Systems Concepts for Computer Music.

[5] Dodge, C. and Jerse, T. A. 1997. *Computer Music: Synthesis, Composition, and Performance*. Schirmer Books, New York, NY.

[6] Gamma, E. et al. 1995. *Design Patterns: Elements of Reusable Object-Oriented Software*. Addison-Wesley, Boston, MA.

[7] Gaye, L. et al. 2006. Mobile Music Technology: Report on an Emerging Community. In *Proceedings of the Int. Conf. on New Interfaces for Musical Expression* (Paris, France, June 04 - 08, 2006). NIME '06. IRCAM, Paris, France, 22-25.

[8] Kirsh, D. and Maglio, P. 1994. On Distinguishing Epistemic from Pragmatic Action. *Cognitive Sci.* 18 (1994), 513-549.

[9] Miletto, E. M. et al. 2005. CODES: A Web-based Environment for Cooperative Music Prototyping. *Organ. Sound* 10, 3 (Dec. 2005), 243-253.

[10] Miranda, E. R. and Wanderley, M. M. 2006. *New Digital Musical Instruments: Control and Interaction Beyond the Keyboard*. A-R Editions, Middleton, WI.

[11] Nishibori, Y. and Iwai, T. 2006. Tenori-On. In *Proceedings of the Int. Conf. on New Interfaces for Musical Expression* (Paris, France, June 04 - 08, 2006). NIME '06. IRCAM, Paris, France, 172-175.

[12] Opal Limited. *Bloom - Generative Music*. http://www.generativemusic.com/.

[13] Pimenta, M. S. et al. 2009. Ubiquitous Music: Concepts and Metaphors. In *Proceedings of the 12th Brazilian Symp. on Computer Music* (Recife, Brazil, September 07 - 09, 2009). SBCM 2009. USP/SBC, São Paulo, Brazil, 139-150.

[14] Raskin, J. 1994. Intuitive Equals Familiar. *Commun. ACM* 37, 9 (Sep. 1994), 17-18.

[15] Schedel, M. and Young, J. P. (Eds.) 2005. *Organ. Sound* 10, 3 (Dec. 2005). Special issue on Networked Music.

[16] Shalloway, A. and Trott, J. R. 2004. *Design Patterns Explained: A New Perspective on Object-Oriented Design* (2nd Edition). Addison-Wesley, Boston, MA.

[17] Sharlin, E. et al. 2004. On Tangible User Interfaces, Humans and Spatiality. *Pers. Ubiquit. Comput.* 8, 5 (Sep. 2004), 338-346.

[18] Tanaka, A. 2004. Mobile Music Making. In *Proceedings of the Int. Conf. on New Interfaces for Musical Expression* (Hamamatsu, Japan, June 03 - 05, 2004). NIME '04. 154-156.

[19] Tidwell, J. 2005. *Designing Interfaces: Patterns for Effective Interaction Design*. O'Reilly Media, Sebastopol, CA.

[20] Wanderley, M. M. and Orio, N. 2002. Evaluation of Input Devices for Musical Expression: Borrowing Tools from HCI. *Comput. Music J.* 26, 3 (Fall 2002), 62-76.

[21] Wessel, D. and Wright, M. 2002. Problems and Prospects for Intimate Musical Control of Computers. *Comput. Music J.* 26, 3 (Fall 2002), 11-22.

[22] Winkler, T. 2001. *Composing Interactive Music*. MIT Press, Cambridge, MA.

Model Driven RichUbi - A Model Driven Process for Building Rich Interfaces of Context-Sensitive Ubiquitous Applications

Carlos E. Cirilo, Antonio F. do Prado,
Wanderley L. de Souza
Computer Science Department (DC)
Federal University of São Carlos (UFSCar) - SP, Brazil

{carlos_cirilo, prado, desouza}@dc.ufscar.br

Luciana A. M. Zaina
Campus Sorocaba
Federal University of São Carlos (UFSCar)
Sorocaba, SP, Brazil

lzaina@ufscar.br

ABSTRACT

The demand for software in Ubiquitous Computing, in which access to applications occurs anywhere, anytime and from different devices, has raised new challenges for Software Engineering. One of these challenges is related to the adaptation of the contents of an application to the numerous devices that can access it in distinct contexts. Another challenge is related to the building of rich interfaces with multimedia content, asynchronous communication and other features that characterize *Rich Internet Applications (RIAs)*. Searching for solutions focused on these challenges, a model-driven process for building rich interfaces of context-sensitive ubiquitous applications has been developed. The process, which is based on the conceptions of *Domain-Specific Modeling (DSM)*, emphasizes the modeling reuse from a rich interface components metamodel. This metamodel provides a generic infrastructure for developing rich interfaces of applications, focusing on model-level reuse and on code generation for different Ubiquitous Computing platforms. In addition, the metamodel allows that the interface models are built by using the terms of rich interface domain, which facilitates the communication between users and developers.

Categories and Subject Descriptors

D.2.2 [**Design Tools and Techniques**]: *user interfaces.* D.2.13 [**Reusable Software**]: *domain engineering; reuse models.* H.5.4 [**Hypertext/Hypermedia**]: *user issues.*

General Terms

Design, Human Factors.

Keywords

Rich Interfaces, Domain Specific Modeling, Context-Sensitive Ubiquitous Applications, Software Process, Communication.

1. INTRODUCTION

Ubiquitous Computing [1] encompasses a universe that consists of a wide variety of computing devices that are become increasingly present in people's daily life, such as cell phones, smartphones, *Personal Digital Assistants (PDAs)*, among others. One purpose of this new computational paradigm is to expand human activities with services that can adapt to the circumstances in which they are used [2].

Among the challenges that arise from this reality one can mention software adaptation, not only to fit different characteristics of various access devices, but also to facilitate and motivate users to interact with the applications.

With the advent of Web 2.0 [3], Web applications have become more attractive providing rich interfaces that allow users to get more meaningful interactions. In this context, the so-called *Rich Internet Applications (RIAs)* have transposed the boundaries of simple interfaces built only with *eXtensible Hypertext Markup Language (XHTML)*. Through the use of technologies that enable the creation of more attractive interfaces and with greater sensitivity, including features such as asynchronous communication, drag-and-drop components, capture and display videos, maps, and others, RIAs resemble the appearance, behavior and usability of desktop applications [4].

The adaptability of rich interfaces according to the access device causes additional efforts on development, since there should be different interfaces versions to meet the diverse needs and characteristics of each access device. Furthermore, the existence of numerous versions of the interface makes the application maintenance difficult, since modifications and changes must be managed in several versions [5].

Context sensitivity arises as an alternative to manage the interfaces different versions according to the requirements imposed by the interaction context. Context-sensitive applications are able to automatically adapt their behavior and content by using information extracted from the interaction context, such as the device profile [6].

The user interface requirements have a direct impact on the acceptance and on the use of the application. It is important that users feel confident to interact with the developed applications and able to explore their abilities in a productive manner. These characteristics influence the way that the graphical user interfaces, through which users will interact with the application, are developed. User interaction and communication planning are defined by modeling the messages to be exchanged with the application, as well as the user's tasks, actions and feedback. Its implementation consists of a series of interface elements, actions and controls. In summary, it is necessary to plan and define how the user will "communicate", "feel" and "live" the computing environment (regardless the internal processing functions) and bring the application closer to its conceptual level [7].

In this sense, this paper presents a model-driven process, called *Model Driven RichUbi*, which supports the development of rich interfaces of context-sensitive ubiquitous applications. Based on the conceptions of *Domain-Specific Modeling (DSM)* [8], which emphasizes the modeling reuse considering a domain metamodel, the rich interface components are specified. Thus, through the metamodel, it is possible to instantiate models for a given application and generate much of its interfaces code, so that they are adherent to the architectures and contexts of various access devices. Moreover, the rich interface components metamodel allows the modeling to be performed by using the language and the concepts of rich interface domain, hiding low-level details and facilitating communication between users and developers. This way, users can understand technical issues better and suggest improvements directly on the conceptual level, before the coding. Besides the metamodel, code generators and dynamic content adapters complement the requirements needed to enable the interface adaptation.

This paper is organized as follows: Section 2 introduces the main concepts and techniques used in this work; Section 3 presents the proposed process, including its instantiation in the development of an application as a case study; Section 4 discusses some related work; and Section 5 presents concluding remarks and further work.

2. CONCEPTS AND TECHNIQUES

The *Model-Based User Interface Development (MB-UID)* [9] explores the idea of using declarative interfaces models, which allow the definition of the different aspects of user interfaces in an abstract way, regardless the implementation platform. This facilitates the transformation of the abstract interaction components represented in the models into concrete components of the target-platforms [10]. Thus, developers can focus on the conceptual definition of the interfaces rather than on technical details of implementation [7].

The approach employed by MB-UID is known as *Model-Driven Development (MDD)* [11], in which the software engineers do not need to interact manually with the entire source code, but can concentrate on models of higher abstraction level. Transformation mechanisms are used to generate code from models. In this scenario the models not only guide the development and maintenance tasks, but are also part of the software in the same way that the source code. In this sense, the models are used as input for code generation tools, what reduces the developers' efforts [7].

In MB-UID the user interface modeling involves the creation of knowledge bases expressed in a hierarchy of models which describe the various aspects of the interface, such as: presentation, dialog and user tasks structure [12]. The models provide an infrastructure for building methods and tools for the automatic generation of the interface final presentation [9]. This way, applying the appropriate *Model-to-Code (M2C)* transformations, it is possible to generate the entire or most of the code for different platforms and technologies to obtain the executable interface with little or no manual change [13].

Following the same direction of the model-driven development and addressing specific domains, there is the *Domain-Specific Modeling (DSM)* [8]. In DSM models are built by using *Domain Specific Languages (DSLs)* [14], which can be defined through metamodels that represent the knowledge of a particular domain. The use of DSLs for modeling, rather than general purpose languages like the *Unified Modeling Language (UML)*, allows the expression of solutions in the language and the abstraction level of the problem domain, which reduces the effort in translating the concepts of that domain into concepts of the solution domain [15]. Thus, in DSM the models are more specific and complete and resources such as frameworks, design patterns and components are included in the modeling in order to generate more code with better quality.

The use of specific models of rich interface domain can raise the abstraction level during the application design so that users and developers can clearly see how the application requirements are mapped into interfaces. The interface models are created in a more intuitive way and are less associated with the technical details of implementation. This way, developers can then focus on conceptual aspects of the interaction. Moreover, since the models are not related to a specific platform, it is possible to reuse the interface specifications in different projects [7].

Considering that one of the most critical aspects in the development of ubiquitous applications is the assumption that they should execute and adapt their behavior and content to the heterogeneity of user's computing devices [16], an automatic code generation approach for interface adaptation is an interesting alternative. In general, two code generation strategies for adapting the content of interfaces to different contexts of access devices can be employed: *static adaptation* (code generation for different platforms at development time) and *dynamic adaptation* (code generation at runtime from abstract interface descriptions) [9].

The benefit of using the static adaptation strategy is the possibility to take advantage of specific capabilities of the devices. However, the need to build different interface versions for each type of the existing devices hinders the development. In this case, a slight change in the interface requirements would result in individual changes in all the versions built [5]. Moreover, if the requirements are not clear either to users or to developers, the result would be the rework to correct all the erroneous modifications. In this sense, the use of DSM for building rich interfaces can make the development of the interaction components more agile. The representation of the interfaces through specific models of rich interface domain enables a better understanding of users and developers regarding the project, so that they can work together to achieve a good implementation. Moreover, the partial code generation facilitates the construction of interface versions for different Ubiquitous Computing platforms and prevents that accidental errors, such as typos, are inserted in the source code.

3. PROPOSED PROCESS

Combining the conceptions of MB-UID, DSM and interface adaptation, this paper presents a model-driven process, called *Model Driven RichUbi*, for developing rich interfaces of context-sensitive ubiquitous applications. Considering the ideas of DSM the Model Driven RichUbi process focuses on rich interface domain in order to support the development of applications rich interfaces for different platforms. The modeling is performed from a rich interface components metamodel, which facilitates the translation of application requirements into interface models and allows the code generation for different technologies. Part of the interface adaptation is made dynamically through the use of content adapters. In this sense, the process employs a *hybrid adaptation strategy*, combining static with dynamic adaptations. During the process, requirements are mapped into a few generic interface versions, each being appropriate for a particular group of devices (static adaptation). The content adapters allow, at runtime, to select the version that best fits the device profile, recovered from the context, and to adapt the code snippets that need to be refined to meet the characteristics of the access device (dynamic adaptation).

As shown in Figure 1, the process is performed in two steps: *Domain Engineering (DE)* and *Application Engineering (AE)*. The process begins in the DE, where a metamodel to support the modeling of the applications interfaces is built from the requirements of rich interface domain. This metamodel allows the reuse of the rich interface domain knowledge on different projects during the AE and provides an infrastructure to automate most of the interface code generation. Also in the DE, based on the rich interface components represented in the developed metamodel, the M2C transformations and content adapters are built to act as support mechanisms in the development of rich interfaces in the AE step.

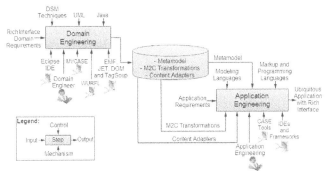

Figure 1. *Model Driven RichUbi* overview.

In the AE, the context-sensitive ubiquitous applications with rich interfaces are developed by reusing the artifacts produced in the DE. The metamodel is used to instantiate the models of the applications interfaces in order to facilitate the mapping of requirements into interface components that fulfill these requirements. Once the models are not associated with a specific implementation platform, one can generate code for different technologies by applying the M2C transformations, which reduce the efforts in the development of the interface versions for the different groups of devices. The content adapters are used to further refine the interfaces at runtime according to the specific characteristics of the access device dynamically identified.

Both in the DE and the AE the artifacts construction follows the classical disciplines of *Requirements*, *Analysis*, *Design*, *Implementation* and *Testing*, known from software development conventional processes, but modified to meet the needs of the DSM to build rich interfaces.

3.1 Domain Engineering (DE)

The DE step is divided into three main phases, as described below.

• **Construction of the Rich Interface Components Metamodel.** In the DE, initially, the requirements of rich interface domain are elicited, specified, analyzed and represented in a rich interface components metamodel.

Through the study of interface components available on Web development environments like *Adobe Dreamweaver*[1] and *MS Visual Studio*[2] and consulting other documentation about rich interfaces[3, 4, 5] for understanding the structure and behavior of their components, the domain engineer identified and modeled the components used in the building of rich interfaces. In order to achieve an incremental development, allowing the increments to be validated and then evolved, the proposed process initially focused on a set of components like buttons, text fields, selection fields, tabbed panels, date selectors, among others. For the metamodel specification, UML techniques, such as use cases, sequence and class diagrams have been used. Figure 2 shows, for example, a class diagram of form control components (*Button*, *TextField* and *Select*) and advanced components of rich interfaces (*TabbedPanel* and *DatePicker*). In this modeling activity, the domain engineer was aided by the *Mutiple-View CASE (MVCASE)* [17], which is a *Computer-Aided Software Engineering (CASE)* tool to support modeling and code generation available as an Eclipse[6] plug-in.

[1] http://www.adobe.com/products/dreamweaver/.

[2] http://www.microsoft.com/visualstudio/en-us/.

[3] http://www.jboss.org/richfaces/docs.html.

[4] http://jqueryui.com/demos/.

[5] http://www.asp.net/ajax/AjaxControlToolkit/Samples/.

[6] http://www.eclipse.org/.

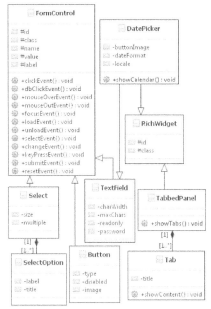

Figure 2. Rich interface components specification.

After that, by studying and analyzing the representations of the interface components specified in the UML diagrams, the rich interface components metamodel has been specified with its metaclasses, meta-attributes and meta-relationships. For this specification, the *Ecore* meta-metamodel of the *Eclipse Modeling Framework (EMF)* [18] has been used. The *Ecore* provides a meta-meta-language for defining metamodels in *Eclipse Integrated Development Environment (IDE)*. For example, the *FormControl*, *Button*, *TextField*, *RichWidget*, *TabbedPanel*, *Tab* and *DatePicker* classes, depicted in the diagram of Figure 2, have been mapped into same named metaclasses highlighted in the excerpt of the metamodel in Figure 3. The *id* and *class* attributes of the *FormControl* class have been mapped into homonyms meta-attributes and separated, respectively, in *IdentifiableComponent* and *ClassifiableComponent* metaclasses. Thus, through inheritance meta-relationship, it was possible to reuse the definition of id and class meta-attributes in the other metaclasses. Furthermore, from the event handling methods of the *FormControl* class (e.g. *clickEvent*, *selectEvent*), the *EventType* meta-enumeration and the *Event*, *EventComponent* and *Script* metaclasses have been created. Only the main meta-attributes were presented in the metamodel to facilitate its understanding. Getters and setters methods, constructors and others, although not shown, are part of the metamodel.

Once the metamodel is specified, its design begins. At this point, the metamodel specification was refined through the adoption of patterns, technologies and hardware and software platforms that enable the construction of the metamodel. For example, Figure 4 shows part of

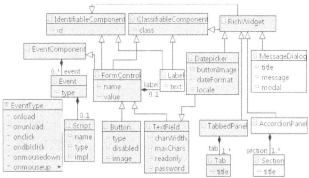

Figure 3. Rich interface components metamodel.

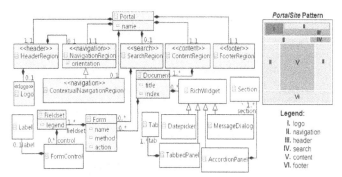

Figure 4. Refinement of the metamodel.

the metamodel refined with the inclusion of the Web interface design pattern called *Portal Site*[7]. This pattern, represented on the right of Figure 4, defines the *header*, *navigation*, *content*, *search* and *footer* regions of a Web portal. On the left of Figure 4, the metamodel is shown with the inclusion of the highlighted metaclasses, whose stereotypes indicate their association with the regions specified by the *Portal Site* pattern. For example, the *NavigationRegion* metaclass, annotated with the *<>* stereotype, has been included in the metamodel to represent the navigation region of the Web portal. This metaclass has the *orientation* meta-attribute, which indicates the orientation of the navigation region (vertical or horizontal).

Besides the metaclasses that represent the Web portal regions, metaclasses for suiting the metamodel to the X/HTML document structure, such as the *Document*, *Form* and *Fieldset* metaclasses, were also included in the metamodel. The refinement of the metamodel with the inclusion of these metaclasses allowed to define the way in which the rich interface components will be arranged and organized in the interface models. For instance, the metamodel configuration of Figure 4 indicates that many or no forms (*Form*) can be added in an X/HTML document (*Document*). Forms, in turn, can contain one or many field sets (*Fieldset*), in which many or no form controls (*FormControl*) can be added.

After completing the metamodel design, the implementation is carried out. The EMF framework allowed the domain engineer to generate the Java code of the metamodel and a model editor to assist the models specification in the AE step. The metamodel along with the model editor have been integrated into the MVCASE tool in order to allow the metamodel instantiation for the modeling of applications rich interfaces. The editor persists the models using *XML Metadata Interchange (XMI)* [19], which is a standard from *Object Management Group (OMG)* used to represent models through *eXtensible Markup Language (XML)*. This format defines a document structure that considers the relationship between data and their corresponding metadata. Thus, it is possible to interpret the models through their XMI and to identify the metadata that describe the model data, which facilitates the execution of M2C transformations.

● **Construction of the Model to Code Transformations.** Once the metamodel has been implemented, the transformations that will be applied to the interface models for code generation during the AE step are built. The *Java Emitter Templates (JET)* framework[8] was used for the creation of the templates that interpret the interface models for code generation.

For example, aided by Eclipse IDE, the domain engineer built two types of transformations addressing each rich interface component

represented in the metamodel: the first, which generates XHTML code for desktops; and the second, which generates XHTML code for smartphones by applying content adaptation techniques for mobile devices, such as content presentation in a single-column and extensive forms division [9], [12]. In the output code of these transformations, references to prefabricated style sheets were incorporated for an initial layout formatting of the generated interfaces. In addition, the *jQuery*[9] JavaScript library has been adopted to provide reusable functions for rendering advanced rich user interface components, such as tabbed panels, slide panels, date selectors, among others.

Figure 5 presents an excerpt of the JET template that generates the code of the tabbed panel component. This template is invoked by the mechanism that executes transformations when the *TabbedPanel* node is found during the reading of the XMI of interfaces models. On lines 1-4, the JavaScript code, which uses the *jQuery* functions for rendering the tabbed panel on the Web browser screen, is generated in the output. On line 6 one can note the generation of a *<div>* tag, which references the style class named "demo" defined in the prefabricated style sheet copied into the project during the transformation execution. On lines 9-21, the iterations on the tab nodes are made in order to generate their contents in output.

```
1  <script type="text/javascript">
2   $(function() {
3      $("#<c:get select="(ScurrentTabbedPanel/@id")"/>").tabs();
4   });
5  </script>
6  <div class="demo">
7   <div id="<c:get select="ScurrentTabbedPanel/@id"/>">
8    <ul>
9     <c:iterate select="ScurrentTabbedPanel/tabs" var="currentTab">
10     <li>
11       <a href="#<c:get select="ScurrentTabbedPanel/@id"/>">
12         <c:get select="ScurrentTab/@title"/>
13       </a>
14     </li>
15    </c:iterate>
16    </ul>
17    <c:iterate select="ScurrentTabbedPanel/tabs" var="currentTab">
18     <div id="<c:get select="ScurrentTabbedPanel/@id"/>">
19       <c:include template="templates/tabbedpanel_contents.jet"/>
20     </div>
21    </c:iterate>
22   </div>
23  </div>
```

Figure 5. JET template for code generation.

To support the code generation in the AE step, the transformations developed in this phase have also been embodied into MVCASE tool. Since the developed models are platform-independent, it is possible to create several types of transformations that generate code for different implementation technologies, such as *Wireless Markup Language (WML)*, *Voice XML (VXML)*, *Compact Hypertext Markup Language (CHTML)*, and so on. Thus, from the modeling and using the appropriate transformations, it is possible to automate most of the development of the various versions of interfaces for different platforms.

● **Construction of Content Adapters.** At this phase, the domain engineer builds the content adapters that will accomplish the dynamic adaptation of the interface components according to the device profile during the application execution.

Figure 6 shows the class diagram built by the domain engineer to specify the content adapters. Each method of the *ContentAdapter* class represents a specific content adapter for a particular rich interface component represented in the metamodel. The *dynamicAdapt* method implemented in the *ContentAdapter* class reads the requested X/HTML document and invokes the appropriate methods to adapt the different interface components, such as form controls, images, tables, tabbed panels, among others. To implement the dynamic interfaces

---

[7] http://www.welie.com/patterns/showPattern.php?patternID=portals.
[8] JET Developer Guide: http://help.eclipse.org/.

[9] http://jquery.com/.

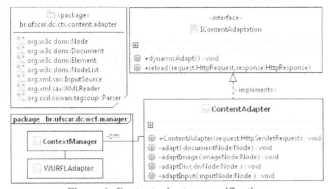

Figure 6. Content adapters specification.

adaptation, the Java APIs *Document Object Model (DOM)*[10] and *TagSoup*[11] have been used. These APIs allow the manipulation and the transformation of X/HTML documents at execution time. DOM API allows the reading and the writing of these documents in the memory by structuring them into a DOM object tree (e.g. *Node, Document, Element*). Thus, it is possible to analyze and modify the interfaces dynamically as needed.

To guide the adaptation of the user interfaces, the *ContentAdapter* class consumes the information related to the profile of the current access device and adjusts the interface according to the peculiarities of the device identified from the interaction context. This information is provided by the *ContextManager* class, which obtains the devices profiles from the public XML database, called *Wireless Universal Resource File (WURFL)*[12], by using the services of the *WURFLAdapter* class. WURFL stores the profiles of thousands of devices from different brands and models and is used by software developers to guide the creation of appropriate solutions for specific devices.

Figure 7 shows a snippet of the *WURFLAdapter* class implemented by the domain engineer. The WURFL Java API is used for retrieving device profiles stored in WURFL. The device profile selection is based on the *User-Agent* field of *Hypertext Transfer Protocol (HTTP)* request originated by the user's current access device. The *getContextualElement* method returns the information about the device

```
package br.ufscar.dc.ctx.sources.adapters;

import net.sourceforge.wurfl.core.DefaultDeviceProvider;

public class  WURFLAdapter implements ICtxSrcAdapter {
  private String wurflPath = "wurfl.zip";
  private String patchPath = "web_browsers_patch.xml";
  private WURFLManager manager;
  private Device deviceProfile;
  ...
  public WURFLAdapter (HttpServletRequest request) {
    ...
    deviceProfile = manager.getDeviceForRequest(
                  request.getHeader("User-Agent"));
  } //end of constructor
  ...
  @Override
  public String getContextualElement(ContextualElement ce) {
    switch(ce) {
      case DEVICE_DISPLAY_COLUMNS_NUMBER:
        return deviceProfile.getCapability("columns");
      case DEVICE_DISPLAY_RESOLUTION_WIDTH:
        return deviceProfile.getCapability("resolution_width");
      case DEVICE_DISPLAY_RESOLUTION_HEIGHT:
        return deviceProfile.getCapability("resolution_height");
      ...
  } //end of getContextualElement method
  ...
} //end of WURFLAdapter class
```

Figure 7. Code snippet of the *WURFLAdapter* class.

[10] http://java.sun.com/j2se/1.4.2/docs/guide/plugin/dom/.
[11] http://home.ccil.org/~cowan/XML/tagsoup/.
[12] http://wurfl.sourceforge.net/.

profile stored in WURFL. It receives an item of the *ContextualElement* enumeration as a parameter, which identifies the device characteristic to be retrieved.

Figure 8 shows some of the rules implemented in content adapters for adjusting the input fields and images contained in interfaces.

> **Rule 1:**
>   **Conditions**
>   inputNode.size > DEVICE_DISPLAY_COLUMNS_NUMBER
>   AND (inputNode.type == "text" OR inputNode.type == "password")
>   **Actions**
>   adaptInput(inputNode)
>
> **Rule 2:**
>   **Conditions**
>   imageNode.height > DEVICE_DISPLAY_RESOLUTION_HEIGHT
>   OR imageNode.width > DEVICE_DISPLAY_RESOLUTION_WIDTH
>   **Actions**
>   adaptImage(imageNode)

Figure 8. Rules for content adaptation.

After the execution of the DE step, there are the artifacts that support the construction of context-sensitive ubiquitous applications with rich interfaces in the AE step. The DE is a step that produces artifacts to be reused in different projects during the AE, which also contributes to the reduction of the development efforts through the reuse of artifacts. The DE is performed whenever it is necessary to include new rich interface components in the metamodel (e.g. video display component, drag-and-drop components), to build new M2C transformations (e.g. templates for WML code generation), or to implement new content adapters.

3.2 Application Engineering (AE)

In the AE step, the ubiquitous applications with rich interfaces are built by reusing the artifacts produced in the DE. The use of the rich interface components metamodel facilitates communication between users and developers during the interfaces modeling. Besides, the M2C transformations enable to automate the code generation, which makes most of the application engineer's task faster. Content adapters provide functionalities for dynamic adaptation of the developed interfaces.

As a validation strategy, the AE was instantiated for software development in the Emergency Healthcare domain. The metamodel, the M2C transformations and the content adapters have been used to develop the Web module of the *Ambulance Space Positioning System (ASPS)* [20] so that it could be accessed from a desktop or smartphone. ASPS emerged from an experimental study which aimed at investigating the use of the signals from *Global System for Mobile Communication (GSM)* antennas for the location of people or objects, focusing on the location of emergency service vehicles like ambulances. With this functionality the ASPS allows the fleet management team to monitor the mobility of the ambulances and to direct a given ambulance to an emergency care in a location near the region in which the ambulance is.

Due to its ubiquitous nature, ASPS is composed of three parts. The first one, which runs on the GSM terminal installed in the ambulance, performs the calculation of the position through the triangulation of the nearest cell phone antennas and transmits the calculated position to a server via HTTP. The second one, which runs on the server, processes the data transmitted by the GSM terminal and stores them in a spatial database. The last one is the Web module that includes the ASPS administrative page. This module has a graphical interface to visualize the position of ambulances on the city map. In short intervals, asynchronous requests are sent to the server by using *Asynchronous JAva Script and XML (AJAX)* for retrieving and updating the most recent position of ambulances on the map. The interface also has features that allow the fleet manager to update the status of a particular ambulance (e.g. available, emergency care) to indicate whether it is available for service.

• **Analysis.** The AE began with the analysis, where ASPS was specified from its requirements. Initially, the requirements specification was carried out by using UML techniques, such as use cases and classes diagrams. For example, Figure 9(a) shows the use case diagram, built by the application engineer aided by MVCASE tool, which specifies some of the requirements identified for ASPS. Among them are those related to the authentication of the fleet manager, the display of the ambulances positions and the edition of the ambulances status. Figure 9(b) shows the class diagram that specifies the *Person, FleetManager, Ambulance* and *Public Safety Answering Point (PSAP)* entities associated to ASPS.

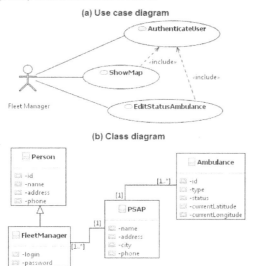

Figure 9. ASPS requirements specification.

• **Design.** After analysis, the design has been performed. The ASPS specifications were refined by including the technologies and the hardware and software platforms that enable the implementation of the application, such as Java EE and *Java Server Faces (JSF)* framework. Furthermore, based on the use case diagrams, the modeling of the application interfaces as an instance of the metamodel built in the DE step was performed. Once the terms and concepts of rich interface domain are used in the models, it became easier to translate the identified requirements into user interface components. For example, Figure 10 shows, on the left, the tree view interface model of ASPS Web module. On the right there are the object diagrams illustrating the instantiation of rich interface components from the metamodel. This model was built through the plug-in integrated into the MVCASE tool. In this model, for example, the "AuthenticateUser" and "ShowMap" use cases shown in Figure 9(a) were mapped, respectively, into a *form* for authentication data input in a login page, and a *div* component that contains the map within a *tabbed panel* on the ASPS administrative page. With more intuitive models, the users can better understand how the requirements were mapped into interfaces and are able to propose changes in the interfaces at the modeling level.

• **Implementation and Testing.** Having finished the ASPS design, the Web module was implemented and tested. At this point the application engineer executed the M2C transformations on the rich interface model with the aid of the MVCASE tool for partial code generation of the versions for desktop and smartphones. This code was complemented by the application engineer until completion of the interface through the inclusion of features not covered by the model, such

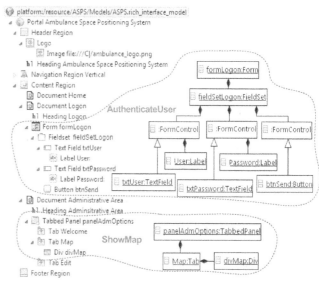

Figure 10. Metamodel reuse for building ASPS rich interfaces.

as JavaScript functions that asynchronously retrieve data to update the map, the *Google Maps*[13] *mashup* and custom style sheets. Moreover, the content adapters built in the DE step were incorporated into ASPS to provide an adaptive trait to interfaces. For example, Figure 11 shows the class diagram of the *Servlet* of the ASPS Web module, called *ContextServlet*, where the reuse of the content adapters is accomplished. The *doGet* method, which intercepts the HTTP requests, invocates the *dynamicAdapt* method of the *ContentAdapter* class. From there, the *ContentAdapter* class retrieves the device profile from the interaction context, selects the most appropriate interface version according to the recovered device profile and adapts the application interface to fit it to the peculiarities of the current access device.

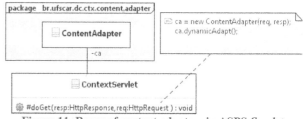

Figure 11. Reuse of content adapters in ASPS *Servlet*.

To test the execution of the interfaces, the Web browsers of *HTC G1* and *iPhone* smartphones, as well as the Web browser of a personal computer have been used. For test proposals, the position data have been obtained by the simulation of the triangulation execution by using the GSM terminal emulator available with *Android SDK*. The signal intensities of the antennas for the calculation of positioning have also been obtained through simulation [20]. Figure 12(a) and (b) show the execution of ASPS Web module, respectively, on the *HTC G1* screen and on the *iPhone* screen. In both cases, the version of the interface delivered was the version built for mobile devices. To make the difference obtained with the content adaptation held by the content adapters visible, the adapted interface and its corresponding interface without adaptation are shown. Figure 12(a) shows the top of the Web page that contains the logo and the system name. It is possible to note that, with the interface adaptation, the logo was resized to fit the *HTC G1* screen. Figure 12(b) shows the bottom of the same page, which has

---

[13] http://code.google.com/intl/en/apis/maps/index.html.

(a) Visualization on HTC G1 screen:
with interface adaptation   without interface adaptation

(b) Visualization on iPhone screen:
with interface adaptation   without interface adaptation

(c) Visualization on desktop screen:

  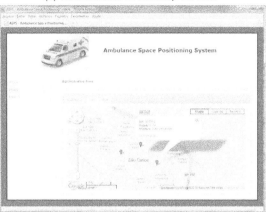

Figure 12. ASPS Web Module visualization in three distinct devices.

a tabbed panel with a *Google Maps mashup*. It can be noted that, with the interface adaptation, the tabbed panel component has been adjusted, not to extrapolate the width of the *iPhone* screen. Figure 12(c), in turn, shows the interface viewed on a personal computer screen. In this case, the version of the interface delivered was the version built for desktops.

4. RELATED WORK

Several works related to the development of context-sensitive applications and adaptive interfaces have been proposed by the academic community, including processes (e.g. [21]), tools (e.g. [9], [12], [16]) and frameworks (e.g. [22], [23]).

Contextual Elements Modeling and Management through Incremental Knowledge Acquisition (CEManTIKA) [21] is a generic approach proposed to support the design of context-sensitive applications in different domains. This approach has, among other components, a process that defines Software Engineering activities related to context specification and the design of context-sensitive applications.

XMobile [9] is an environment for generating adaptive interfaces of form-based applications for mobile devices. It consists of a framework of abstract user interface components, which allows the modeling of applications interfaces, and a tool to support the code generation at development time. *Semantic Transformer* [12] is a tool used for automatic transformation of Web pages originally designed for desktop platform into Web pages suitable for mobile devices. This tool acts as a *Proxy* that detects HTTP requests originated from mobile devices and processes the Web page requested by placing it in a suitable format for viewing on the mobile device.

Extended Internet Content Adaptation Framework (EICAF) [22] is a framework for content adaptation of Web applications. *EICAF* uses ontologies for describing the profiles of devices, users and other relevant entities and employs Web services for performing content adaptation by the combination of contextual information from profiles. *Semantic Context-aware Ubiquitous Scout (SCOUT)* [23] is a framework for building context-sensitive applications for mobile devices. *SCOUT* allows mapping real world entities (e.g., people, places, objects) into virtual entities on the Web, so that resources/services provided by these entities are specific to their location and accessible when users are close to them.

The *Model Driven RichUbi* process presented in this paper is based on several characteristics of the work described above. However, it has its own contributions through the evolution and the adaptation of concepts of the related work. *CEManTIKA*, for example, proposes a generic approach, with recommendations for building context-sensitive applications. On the other hand, the proposal of this paper focuses on the needs of a specific domain (rich interfaces of context-sensitive ubiquitous applications). Regarding the *XMobile* and the *Semantic Transformer*, the proposed process is distinguished by adopting the concepts of MB-UID, DSM, and context sensitivity, which help to facilitate the communication between users and developers through modeling and enables to adapt the different source code of the interfaces in a hybrid manner. Both *EICAF* and *SCOUT* frameworks present contributions for software reuse in the development of context-sensitive ubiquitous applications. The proposal of this paper extends these conceptions by adapting and adjusting them for the development of adaptive rich interfaces.

5. CONCLUSIONS AND FURTHER WORK

This paper presented the *Model Driven RichUbi*, which is a model-driven process to support the building of rich interfaces of context-sensitive ubiquitous applications. The process is based on the conceptions of *Domain-Specific Modeling (DSM)* by using a rich interface components metamodel to support the modeling and transformations for code generation from the models for different platforms. The process also employs dynamic content adapters for the refinement of interfaces at runtime according to the access device profile.

The use of specific models of rich interface domain facilitates the mapping of the application requirements into user interface components. The models become more intuitive and improve the users' perception about the way that the requirements are translated into interfaces. Then the communication between users and developers is facilitated and users may suggest changes in the interfaces directly in the models before the codification starts.

Another important point is the independence of platform obtained through the abstract interface models. Assuming that most of the code can be generated automatically, it is possible to generate code for different technologies using the same models just by changing the M2C transformation. Although there are challenges regarding the code generation, such as the mapping between the generated code and its corresponding model to prevent the overwriting of customized snippets in maintenance, this approach becomes very interesting in Ubiquitous Computing, where the universe of computing devices is great. In this sense, there is no need to build different versions of the interfaces from scratch and the repetitive coding tasks can be implemented in the transformations.

The use of context for content adaptation helps to reduce the number of versions of the interfaces to be developed. In this case, only a few generic versions of the interfaces are built, which are adapted to the peculiarities of the access device identified from context during execution.

In summary, the main contributions of this work are:

- Study and research on the use of DSM for building rich interfaces of context-sensitive ubiquitous applications;
- Specification of a rich interface components metamodel and M2C transformations to support the modeling and code generation for different platforms;
- Content adaptation carried out in a hybrid fashion with the use of context;

This work is still continued with research and case studies through the development of applications in other domains in order to improve the process and computational support, such as: addition of new rich interface components to the metamodel, including non-structured components like video (e.g. Flash) and audio; construction of a graphical notation for the metamodel in order to turn modeling more user-friendly; and optimizations in the M2C transformations that allow further automation of code generation.

6. ACKNOWLEDGMENTS

Our thanks to CAPES – the Brazilian Coordination for the Improvement of Higher Level Personnel – for providing the scholarships that supported this work.

7. REFERENCES

[1] Weiser, M. 1999. The computer for the 21st century. *SIGMOBILE Mob. Comput. Commun. Rev.* 3, 3 (Jul. 1999), 3-11. DOI= http://doi.acm.org/10.1145/329124.329126.

[2] Coutaz, J., Crowley, J. L., Dobson, S., and Garlan, D. 2005. Context is key. *Commun. ACM* 48, 3 (Mar. 2005), 49-53. DOI= http://doi.acm.org/10.1145/1047671.1047703.

[3] O'Reilly, T. 2005. What is Web 2.0: design patterns and business models for the next generation of software. Available: http://oreilly.com/web2/archive/what-is-web-20.html. Access: Sep., 2009.

[4] Deitel, P. J., and Deitel, H. M. 2008. *AJAX, Rich Internet Applications, and Web Development for Programmers*, Prentice Hall.

[5] Eisenstein, J., Vanderdonckt, J., and Puerta, A. 2000. Adapting to mobile contexts with user-interface modeling. In *Proceedings of the Third IEEE Workshop on Mobile Computing Systems and Applications (Wmcsa'00)* (December 07 - 08, 2000). WMCSA. IEEE Computer Society, Washington, DC, 83.

[6] Baldauf, M., Dustdar, S., and Rosenberg, F. 2007. A survey on context-aware systems. *Int. J. Ad Hoc Ubiq. Comput.* 2, 4 (Jun. 2007), 263-277. DOI= http://dx.doi.org/10.1504/IJAHUC.2007.014070.

[7] Bittar, T. J., Fortes, R. P., Lobato, L. L., and Watanabe, W. M. 2009. Web communication and interaction modeling using model-driven development. In *Proceedings of the 27th ACM international Conference on Design of Communication* (Bloomington, Indiana, USA, October 05 - 07, 2009). SIGDOC '09. ACM, New York, NY, 193-198. DOI= http://doi.acm.org/10.1145/1621995.1622033.

[8] Kelly, S. and Tolvanen, J. 2008. Domain-Specific Modeling: Enabling Full Code Generation, Wiley.

[9] Viana, W. and Andrade, R. M. 2008. XMobile: A MB-UID environment for semi-automatic generation of adaptive applications for mobile devices. *J. Syst. Softw.* 81, 3 (Mar. 2008), 382-394. DOI= http://dx.doi.org/10.1016/j.jss.2007.04.045.

[10] Vellis, G. 2009. Model-based development of synchronous collaborative user interfaces. In *Proceedings of the 1st ACM SIGCHI Symposium on Engineering interactive Comput. Systems* (Pittsburgh, PA, USA, July 15 - 17, 2009). EICS '09. ACM, New York, NY, 309-312. DOI= http://doi.acm.org/10.1145/1570433.1570491.

[11] France, R. and Rumpe, B. 2007. Model-driven Development of Complex Software: A Research Roadmap. In *2007 Future of Software Engineering* (May 23 - 25, 2007). International Conference on Software Engineering. IEEE Computer Society, Washington, DC, 37-54. DOI= http://dx.doi.org/10.1109/FOSE.2007.14.

[12] Paternò, F., Santoro, C., and Scorcia, A. 2008. Automatically adapting web sites for mobile access through logical descriptions and dynamic analysis of interaction resources. In *Proceedings of the Working Conference on Advanced Visual interfaces* (Napoli, Italy, May 28 - 30, 2008). AVI '08. ACM, New York, NY, 260-267. DOI= http://doi.acm.org/10.1145/1385569.1385611.

[13] Cicchetti, A., Di Ruscio, D., and Di Salle, A. 2007. Software customization in model driven development of web applications. In *Proc. of the 2007 ACM Symposium on Applied Comput.* (Seoul, Korea, March 11 - 15, 2007). SAC '07. ACM, New York, NY, 1025-1030. DOI= http://doi.acm.org/10.1145/1244002.1244224.

[14] Sadilek, D. A. 2008. Prototyping domain-specific language semantics. In *Companion To the 23rd ACM SIGPLAN Conference on Object-Oriented Programming Systems Languages and Applications* (Nashville, TN, USA, October 19 - 23, 2008). OOPSLA Companion '08. ACM, New York, NY, 895-896. DOI= http://doi.acm.org/10.1145/1449814.1449896.

[15] Chavarriaga, E. and Macías, J. A. 2009. A model-driven approach to building modern Semantic Web-Based User Interfaces. Adv. Eng. Softw. 40, 12 (Dec. 2009), 1329-1334. DOI= http://dx.doi.org/10.1016/j.advengsoft.2009.01.016.

[16] Gajos, K. and Weld, D. S. 2004. SUPPLE: automatically generating user interfaces. In *Proceedings of the 9th international Conference on intelligent User interfaces* (Funchal, Madeira, Portugal, January 13 - 16, 2004). IUI '04. ACM, New York, NY, 93-100. DOI= http://doi.acm.org/10.1145/964442.964461.

[17] Lucrédio, D., Alvaro, A., Almeida, E. S. and Prado, A. F. 2003. MVCASE Tool -Working with Design Patterns. In Proc. of the 3rd Latin American Conf. on Pattern Lang. of Progr. (SugarLoafPLoP 2003).

[18] Steinberg, D., Budinsky, F., Paternostro, M. e Merks, E. 2008. *Eclipse Modeling Framework*, 2 ed. Addison-Wesley Professional.

[19] OMG, "MOF 2.0/XMI Mapping Version 2.1.1", 2007. Available: http://www.omg.org/. Accessed: Mar. 2010.

[20] Bellini, A., Cirilo, C. E., et al. 2010. A low cost positioning and visualization system using smartphones for emergency ambulance service. In *Proceedings of the 2010 ICSE Workshop on Software Engineering in Health Care* (Cape Town, South Africa, May 03 - 04, 2010). SEHC '10. ACM, New York, NY, 12-18. DOI= http://doi.acm.org/10.1145/1809085.1809087.

[21] Vieira, V., Tedesco, P., and Salgado, A. C. 2009. A process for the design of context-sensitive systems. In *Proc. of the int. Conf. on Computer Supported Coop. Work in Design*, CSCWD'09. 143-148.

[22] Forte, M., de Souza, W. L., and do Prado, A. F. 2008. Using ontologies and Web services for content adaptation in Ubiquitous Computing. J. Syst. Softw. 81, 3 (Mar. 2008), 368-381. DOI= http://dx.doi.org/10.1016/j.jss.2007.04.044.

[23] Woensel, W., Casteleyn, S., and Troyer, O. 2009. A Framework for Decentralized, Context-Aware Mobile Applications Using Semantic Web Technology. In *Proc. of the Confederated int. Workshops and Posters on on the Move To Meaningful internet Systems* (Vilamoura, Portugal, November 01 - 06, 2009). Lecture Notes In Computer Science, vol. 5872. Springer-Verlag, Berlin, Heidelberg, 88-97. DOI= http://dx.doi.org/10.1007/978-3-642-05290-3_18.

A Flexible Model for Improving the Reuse of User Interface Design Patterns

Jordan Janeiro
Technische Universität Dresden
Department of Computer Science,
Institute of Systems Architecture
Dresden, Germany

jordan.janeiro@tu-dresden.de

Simone DJ Barbosa
Pontifícia Universidade Católica do
Rio de Janeiro (PUC-Rio)
Informatics Department
Rio de Janeiro, Brazil

simone@inf.puc-rio.br

Thomas Springer, Alexander
Schill
Technische Universität Dresden
Department of Computer Science
Institute of Systems Architecture
Dresden, Germany

thomas.springer,
alexander.schill@tu-dresden.de

ABSTRACT
Despite being a set of proven, well-documented, contextualized recommendations for solving frequently occurring user interface design problems, user interface design patterns are still not widely used. We believe this is due to the lack of tools to help designers find patterns and identify how they can be combined to solve user interface design problems. This paper proposes a flexible model to represent UIDPs and their relationships. The flexibility of our model, based on RDF Statements, is to provide a structure to the representation of the UIDPs in order to allow the development of tools to automate their use.

Categories and Subject Descriptors
H.5.2 [Information Interfaces and Presentation]: User Interfaces – standardization

General Terms
Documentation, Design, Experimentation, Human Factors, Standardization, Languages.

Keywords
user interface design patterns, semantic relationships.

1. INTRODUCTION
The idea of using design patterns to describe a reusable solution for a recurring problem is not new. Such ideas were first introduced by Christopher Alexander [1], in the context of civil engineering and architecture, and then brought to computer science, due to its potential of helping to build software by assembling reusable components, instead of creating software as one large and monolithic system.

Based on the ideas of Christopher Alexander, Erik Gamma et al. proposed the use of design patterns in the context of software development [2]. These ideas represent an effort to leverage the concepts of best practices and software reuse.

As the idea of the design patterns proposed by Gamma et al. and the design principles stated by the SOA concepts were successfully adopted and used for developing software, the software engineering community became interested in applying such concepts also to user interface (UI) design and development. Thus, instead of developing user interfaces manually from scratch, developers would use engineering techniques to assemble user interfaces, putting UI components together to build a complete UI solution.

Such ideas motivated the proposal of the so called User Interface Design Patterns (UIDP). The UIDPs are detailed descriptions for solving specific and recurrent user interface problems. An UIDP is just proposed after developers implement, test, and evaluate its concepts. During the years, different designers or researchers created libraries to propose user interface design patterns. Some examples are the libraries from Martjin van Welie [3], Jenifer Tidwell [4] and the Yahoo! [5]. Differently from a UI guideline, a UIDP encapsulates the design rationale relating a problem to a solution, documenting the context to which the UIDP applies, the problem it intends to solve, a solution to the problem, and how it can be realized or made concrete at the UI.

Despite their reputation, UIDPs are still not widespread among software developers. One of the key reasons for that is the lack of supporting mechanisms to leverage their usage. For example, it is not possible to search for UIDPs properly, identify how sets of UIDPs can be combined to solve a complex user interface problem neither compare them.

The relationships between UIDPs are claimed to be a fundamental property for design patterns because of their capability to express the way they relate to each other [6]. The description of the relationships were supposed to support the expressiveness of the composition of UIDPs. As user interface problems might not be solved alone by one UIDP, it is necessary to use more than one design pattern to efficiently handle a problem [6]. Similar to the SOA principles [7], a service should solve a part of a complex problem, whereas the composition of the services should be able to solve the complex problem. A UIDP solves a specific part of a user interface problem, although the composition of UIDPs solves a more comprehensive, complex user interface problem.

Currently, the only existing language to describe UIDPs is the Pattern Language Markup Language (PLML) [6]. It supports only two semantic relationships: composition and similarity. *Composition* means that a certain UIDP contains or is contained by another one. *Similarity* means that a UIDP can be used as an alternative to another one (in the sense that both of them solve the same problem). However, the use of the UIDP libraries shows that, in practice, there are more semantic types of relationships than the two proposed by PLML. Such types are implicitly contained in the text description of UIDP and can currently be identified only by human readers. For example, reading the UIDP Accordion contained in [3], it is possible to identify, through the following text excerpt "… If used for navigation it is (Accordion) conceptually equivalent to Tabs …", that the similarity between two UIDPs is just applicable if a special condition is satisfied, meaning in this case that the UIDP Tabs can be used as an alternative to the UIDP Accordion only for navigation purposes. Such example illustrates that the PLML semantic types of relationships between UIDPs are not expressive enough to describe the whole range of relationships between them. Therefore, it is necessary to discover new types of semantic relationships to improve the existing ones described by PLML.

Another limitation of PLML is that it does not support further description of the properties of the relationships. In the previous example concerning the similarity of the Accordion and Tabs design patterns, it is mentioned that there is a condition which makes the patterns similar, represented by "if used for navigation". However, the language does not support the description of such information, which is necessary to enhance the specification of the relationships among the UIDPs.

A third aspect regarding the PLML is that the content described by the language is represented in natural language. Such content is easy to be interpreted by humans and therefore to communicate the UIDPs but it is not easy to be processed by machines. Therefore, it is required that besides exploring new possible semantic relationships, it is also necessary to explore mechanisms to structure the representation of current design patterns.

Therefore the contribution of this paper is towards a model to support the extensibility of the representation of the UIDPs. Such kind of model is necessary in a further step where the UIDPs will be described through well-defined structures instead of natural language text.

2. RELATED WORK

As an effort to overcome the problem of specifying a language to describe the UIDPs in a standardized and formalized way, the HCI pattern community proposed together a common language [6]. The first proposal to describe user interface design patterns arose in the workshop "HCI Patterns: Concepts and Tools at the Computer Human Interaction (CHI)", in 2003 [8]. The resulting language was called Pattern Language Markup Language (PLML) [6]. The PLML is an XML-based language to describe the patterns. Its first version, 1.0, was defined in Document Type Definition (DTD) format [9], specifying the rules which define the allowed elements (tags) to be used and its valid values. This version of the language contains 23 elements which are supposed to represent the properties of the patterns. There are three known variations of the PLML language: version 1.0, PLMLx, and version 1.2. Each of them will be detailed next.

2.1 PLML 1.0

After the first release of the language, there have been a few modifications to improve PLML. There were made two main modifications of the version 1.0, the first one including two new attributes to the pattern-link element and the possibility to use it within all of the other elements (version 1.1), and the second one represented the inclusion of the element collection to the language (version 1.1.2). Such modifications will be detailed on the following paragraphs.

Version 1.0 of the language supported the element pattern-link. Through such element it was possible to specify, for a given UIDP x, all of the other patterns that were linked to x. However, it was realized that when a user describes the information of a pattern in sections like: problem, solution and context, it should be possible to reference directly the linked patterns from those sections, instead of doing it separately. Specifying the information this way, it would be possible to contextualize the use of referenced UIDPs, unlike specifying it in a separate section, where the context of use of the linked patterns could not be specified. Therefore, the authors decided to allow the pattern-link element to be specified within all of the elements of PLML. They achieved that changing the data type constraints of all of the other elements to accept the values of any data type.

Besides this last modification, version 1.1 also supports additional attributes related to the pattern-link element: collection and label. The first attribute identifies the UIDP collection the target UIDP belongs to. For example, if the source UIDP Accordion from the library of Martjin van Welie links to the Closable Panels from the library of Jennifer Tidwell, the collection attribute of the pattern-link elements may contain, for example, the value "tidwell's library". The second attribute supports a label description which should represent the meaning of the relationship between the involved patterns. Using the previous example linking Accordion and Closable Panels, a possible value for the label attribute could be "Two patterns which can be interpreted as synonyms".

The last modification, which generated version 1.1.2, represents the addition of the attribute collection to PLML. Such attribute was added to maintain the compatibility with the pattern-link element, from version 1.1, which specifies to which library a UIDP belongs. Such attribute was proposed to allow a better degree of separation of patterns, to deal with the fact that, over the last few years, many repositories of UIDPs have emerged.

2.2 PLMLx

The Extended Pattern Language Markup Language (PLMLx) [10] is a proposal by Diethelm Bienhaus to extend the original version 1.0 of PLML. Among his changes, the main ones consist of modifying the place of the example and rationale elements in the hierarchy of the document type definition (DTD), turning them into first-level elements, instead of second-level ones.

Originally (PLML 1.x), these two elements were defined as sub-elements of the element evidence, because the authors believed that the function of these two elements was to provide an evidence that the described object is in fact a UIDP. This can be done either from an intellectual construction (rationale) or from a synthesis over a variety of examples (examples). However, such proposal was not adopted as a change to the PLML, because it was argued that modifying these two elements to first-level elements of the DTD, makes the pattern authors to lose the original intention for these sections.

Bienhaus also changed the DTD to make the following elements mandatory: name, problem, context, solution, and forces. However, it was also argued [11] that the PLML was originally designed so that HCI patterns authors could share a common standard, thus the language has a minimal set of mandatory elements. By making the mentioned elements mandatory, all of the pattern authors are forced to follow the form of the PLMLx and as mentioned in [11], as more elements are defined as mandatory, it is less likely that PLML will be used or useful.

2.3 PLML 1.2

One of the last documented changes in the PLML language was proposed by Deng et al., and it was called PLML 1.2 [12]. The main changes are described in the following paragraphs.

First, the author turned the proposed elements name, problem, context, solution, and forces which are mandatory in PLMLx back to optional.

Second, they turned the forces element into an encapsulating element to hold all of the force sub-elements. In PLML 1.1, the forces element was just able to contain a textual element. In PLML 1.2, it represents a grouping element and each force element contains itself the textual description of one kind of force. The authors claim that such changes enable the role of forces in UIDPs to be more fully explored, concerning search functionalities for example.

Third, as the PLML 1.1 does not enable the specification of narrative description or binary information inside of elements like example, the authors defined such sub-elements to be incorporated in elements as example, literature and implementation.

Finally, the PLML 1.2 adds a change-log element for UIDPs. The authors claim that this is necessary to know why and how a pattern is modified. Therefore, they structured the change-log element to be organized by date for temporal-based modifications. Besides, they also modified the pattern-link element to contain an attribute called revision-number to enable the creation of relationships between different versions of a UIDP.

3. A SEMANTIC USER INTERFACE DESIGN PATTERN REPRESENTATION

We propose the semantic user interface design pattern representation, a model which provides a structure to the description of User Interface Design Patterns. We refer to this model as semantic because of its support to describe the relationships between UIDP regarding the semantic types.

The goal of our model is to provide a structure to the user interface design patterns' descriptions. As previously mentioned, the PLML represents the most structured language so far to represent UIDPs. The language defines 23 elements [6] which accept text content to describe a UIDP. For example, the Accordion UIDP has a section called problem, which aims to describe with text the problems the Accordion solves; in this case the problem statement for Accordion, following Martjin van Welie [3] is "The user needs to find an item in the main navigation".

With PLML, the description of the UIDPs is currently based on free text; this is mainly because it is easier to communicate the content of the UIDPs between different designers or developers [1][13]. However, despite being a natural way of communicating

among people, the free text descriptions represent a challenge for the machines to process and extract a meaning from them. Despite being an XML-based language and containing elements or tags to give the text description a semi-structured form, PLML is still not suitable to be used to automate the processing of UIDPs, like automatically identifying the similarities and differences of UIDPs. Therefore, it is necessary to refine the PLML to be more structured and to contain elements which can somehow be processed by machines.

Another problem that comes with PLML is that it was designed from a group of designers which claims that the design patterns should be supported through its elements. However, a generic language like the PLML should not be imposed to users with its elements, considered important from a small group of designers. Instead, before proposing the language, its authors should model it based on an empirical study collecting requirements described from users who write UIDPs, the users who read them to incorporate in their user interface solutions and the users who use the description of the UIDPs to automate their use through tools to support designers. Therefore, one of the goals of this work is to propose a flexible model to represent the UIDPs and its characteristics, so that based on the extensions of the model it should be possible to represent structured information which is not possible to perform now with the PLML.

In our model, a UIDP is represented by the entity **UserInterfaceDesignPattern**, introduced in Figure 1. Because of the practical use in different design pattern web libraries [14][15][4][16], we decided to assign to this entity the following properties, which are also specified in the PLML language:

Id: represents a unique identification for a UIDP. For example, the UIDP Frequently Asked Questions contains the id "faq".

Name: represents the most common used string to call a UIDP. For example, the name of the id "faq" is Frequently Asked Questions.

Problem: describes the problems a UIDP solves. For example, the UIDP Tag Cloud contains the following problem description, "Users need to know which tags are often used and their popularity".

Solution: conceptually describes how to implement a design pattern. For example, the description of the solution for tag cloud is as follows, "List the top 30-50 most used tags and list them ordered alphabetically. Each tag is a link that takes to user to a page where all objects having that tag are listed. The relative popularity of each tag (i.e. the amount of items having the tag divided by the total amount of items compared to the most popular tag) is then depicted by varying the font size, and sometimes also the font weight. The tags are usually in a rectangular area, either in the main content area if it is a page dedicated to tags or in the right-hand column if it is secondary to the main content".

Context: describes the context in which a UIDP should ideally be used. For example, the context content of the Accordion design patterns is, "Accordions are often used as part of Main Navigation or sub navigation. If used for navigation it is conceptually equivalent to Tabs. Alternative to Navigation Tree. Although accordions are often used as part of a Wizard I strongly recommend against it since it is worse than regular implementations from a usability point of view. Accordions can be a good way to implement a Frequently Asked Questions (FAQ) where it opens up each question. Another good use would be to manage settings. The number of panels should be small, e.g. < 10".

Rationale: describes the rationale explaining the reasons for defining the UIDP as it is presented. For example, the rationale for implementing the accordion contains the following description: "An accordion is useful for compressing many elements in a compact space. The elements can be properties,

questions or simply navigation items. The downside is, of course, that most items get hidden which may not be very desirable when you use accordions for main navigation. Accordions originate from Macromedia applications such as Dreamweaver where they were first used. The vertical ones are quite common although they do not always animate nicely. The horizontal ones like the one used in the Xbox 360 is far less used. It is not the best solution from a classic usability perspective but it can add to the fun element of the user experience".

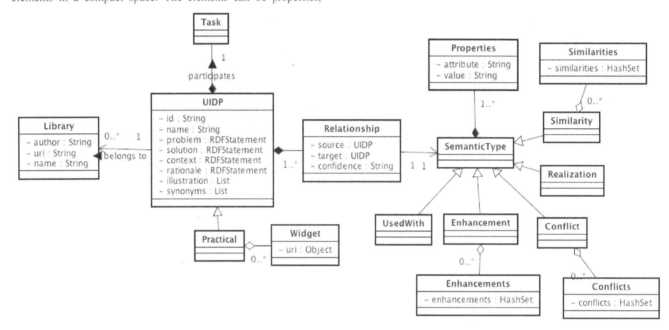

Figure 1: The Semantic User Interface Design Pattern Model.

Illustrations: contains figures which help to explain the instantiation of UIDP. For example, Figure 2 presents an example of illustration for the UIDP Accordion.

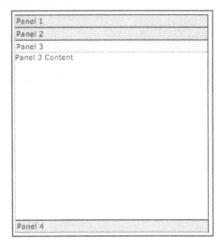

Figure 2: The Illustration of the User Interface Design Pattern Accordion.

Synonyms: represents the synonyms to the name of a UIDP. For example, the UIDP Accordion is also known to have the synonym Collapsible Panels.

An UIDP is generally presented by a pattern library, represented in our model by the **Library** entity. Such entity contains the URI of the library's location, the name of the library and the author, representing the author who proposed the library and its UIDPs.

We believe that the UIDPs should be used together to solve user interface problems. However, it is difficult to define the task a set of patterns together handle. Therefore, we define an abstract element which allows binding different design patterns, targeting one specific user interface problem. Such element in our model is represented by the **Task** class.

The UIDPs can also serve as guidelines for different levels of specification, while the designer is building the user interface. An example of such UIDP is the Form UIDP. Such pattern describes, for example, that the form input fields should have clarifying labels describing the field, and that the input field and label should be aligned using the structure of a grid layout. Despite being useful information to consider while designing a user interface, such UIDP cannot be automatically reused as a software artifact. Therefore, it can be considered as a *conceptual pattern*.

Whereas some UIDPs can be conceptual patterns, which cannot be easily instantiated, some other category of patterns can be reused as software artifacts. In the context of this work, the solution described in these UIDPs can be interpreted as user interface widgets. Such kind of UIDPs is considered by us as being practical patterns (represented by the **Practical** class of our model). The practical patterns can be used as components, generally like in WYSIWIG tools, which support rapid design. For example, the Accordion UIDP, represented in Figure 2, is an illustration of a practical pattern. The Accordion can easily be defined by a template, as in Figure 2, and depending on the context of use its content can be easily customized. As a practical pattern is close related to a widget, a practical UIDP should contain at least one implementation of the widgets which represent the UIDPs. Therefore we defined the class **Widget** containing different implementations of the practical UIDP.

One of the current problems in processing UIDPs is the lack of structure of the design pattern languages. For example, PLML already describes a set of elements to provide a certain structure to the design patterns, based on Christopher Alexander's ideas [1]. However, generally the authors of UIDP libraries describe the patterns' content using natural language. The problem is the difficulty for a machine to process natural language content. Therefore, such limitation hinders the implementation of operations that could be performed between UIDPs, like the comparison of patterns. Ideally, this kind of operation could support user interface designers to better explore their design space, identifying alternatives for UIDPs or differences among them to adapt patterns which better fit in a certain context of use.

The limitation for defining such mechanisms is due to the unstructured description of the design patterns, making it necessary to provide a better structure to the UIDPs. Therefore, we propose the representation of the main properties of the UIDPs (problem, solution, context and rationale) using RDF Statements.

It would be premature, however, to impose a structure without carefully considering the content found in existing patterns. We believe that, just as patterns are best practices that emerge from the community of designers and developers, so should their structure. Therefore, we propose to represent the pattern content first by means of attribute–value pairs. This representation is equivalent to the semantic content provided in RDF triples <subject, predicate, object>, widely used in the semantic web [17]. The subject is the current UIDP, and the predicate and object elements would be an attribute and its corresponding value. This approach brings about at least three advantages: it allows processing the UIDP content in discovery and comparison mechanisms, it allows the wide distribution of semantically annotated UIDPs, and it helps identify emerging pattern structures by examining recurrent attributes, i.e., attributes that are used to characterize several different UIDPs.

3.1 SEMANTICALLY RELATING UIDPs

One of the main ideas underlying UIDPs is to apply the concept of separation of concerns, explored by software engineering design patterns, in creating UI components which aim to solve specific user-system interaction problems. Therefore, with such a concept it may be possible to compose a certain user interface solution by combining the UIDP components, instead of creating it from scratch.

Compositions between UIDPs are already informally documented by the user interface design pattern libraries, allowing us to identify which UIDPs are commonly used together in certain situations. For example, van Welie's library specifies that the design pattern Accordion is often used within the Main Navigator design pattern.

As described in Section 2, the Pattern Language Markup Language (PLML) [6] is a proposal to standardize the documentation of user interface design patterns. Besides its standard properties already mentioned, the language also describes the relationship between the design patterns. This last property of the language is particularly important in the context of this paper, because it represents an explicit description of the relationship between patterns, which in our case is a basic concept to support the composition of UIDPs. An example of these kinds of relationships is described in the next excerpt of code of PLML. In such code, the pattern Accordion, from van Welie's library, relates to the pattern Closable Panels from Tidwell's library.

Table 1: Example of Relationship Description between the User interface Design Patterns Accordion and Closable Panels.

```
<pattern-link type="is-a"
patternID="Closable_Panels"
collection="tidwell" label="Closable
Panels"/>
```

As illustrated by this example, through PLML it is possible to specify four properties in describing a relationship between patterns: patternID, which references the ID of the targeting UIDP from the relationship (Closable_Panels); collection, which describes to which library the pattern belongs (tidwell); label, which describes the label of the relationship between the patterns (Closable Panels) and type (is-a), which describes the semantic of the relationship between the two patterns. However, such feature is still not explored to be used in the current description of UIDPs.

Despite the capability of PLML to describe the types of relationships between UIDPs, the language only supports three types: is-a, is-contained-by and contains [9]. The first type of relationship, despite implying a generalization–specialization hierarchy, actually means that two design patterns are equivalent to each other, meaning that a designer can exchange the use of a UIDP with another in a certain context. The other two types are related to the composition of UIDPs; the is-contained-by type refers to a design pattern which is used within another UIDP, whereas the contains type refers to the design pattern which uses another UIDP.

On the language specification such a small set of relationship types are not enough to describe more precisely the semantics of the relationships between the design patterns. Therefore, we intend to present an extension to these existing types, improving the semantic description of the relationships. Moreover, as it occurs with the representation of the UIDPs, the representation of their relationships currently has no structure to describe the information that should be associated to the relationships for both human interpretation and computer processing.

In our work, we explore the relationships between UIDPs and identify semantic types implicitly described within UIDPs to enhance the way designers explore user interface design patterns. Therefore, concerning these issues our model supports the description of the UIDPs through the following entities, **Relationship** and **SemanticType**.

The first entity supports the description of the UIDPs involved in a relationship through the attributes *source* and *target*. These two attributes support the description of the direction of the relationship. The entity also supports the degree of confidence assigned in a relationship between the patterns. A group of designers can assign different kinds of semantic types between two UIDPs. Such assignment, by different designers, is used for calculating a sort of confidence degree of the relationship. A high degree of confidence means that many designers agreed on the same semantic type of relationship.

Concerning the second entity, we have conducted an empirical study over Martjin van Welie's pattern library, to define a set of semantic types that can be assigned to the relationships. In our model, we have used the following semantic types:

Used With: UIDP x is frequently used together with UIDP y, but they are not hierarchically related. This type of a relationship is illustrated in van Welie's library by the following text excerpt: "… Paging is also often used together with a List Builder …". By this description we can identify that the Paging and List Builder patterns are independent but they are often combined, in this case through the used with relationship.

Similarity: UIDP x has some characteristics similar to the UIDP y but, depending on the specific problem they target, one of the patterns should be slightly adapted. "… the site has got some type of Main Navigation that allows   …". In this description, the similarity relationship is between the Breadcrumbs and the Main Navigation design patterns, which can be used as an alternative to each other only in a certain specific context, and if some slight modifications are performed.

Realization: UIDP x implements the concepts described by a UIDP y. Such type of a relationship is illustrated van Welie's library by the following excerpt: "… Accordions can be a good way to implement a Frequently Asked Questions (FAQ) …". In this case, the FAQ is a recommendation of a functionality which is desirable in an application, not an implementation of a concrete UI component, as in the case of the Accordion pattern. Therefore, we established this kind of relationship between the patterns because the Accordion can implement the functionalities described by the FAQ.

Enhancement: UIDP x builds upon an UIDP y, enhancing its functionalities. Such type of a relationship is illustrated in van Welie's library by the following text excerpt: "… This pattern (Advanced Search) builds on the Search Box pattern by adding some more search options …". By this description we assumed that the Advanced Search pattern enhances the Search Box pattern with more options.

Conflict: UIDP x and a UIDP y must not be used together. Such type of a relationship is illustrated in the library of van Welie by the following text excerpt: "… Although Accordions are often used as part of a Wizard I strongly recommend against it since it is worse than regular implementations from a usability point of view …". By such description we understand that although it is really common to use the Accordion pattern as part of Wizard pattern, the author discourages such practice.

Each of these semantic types is represented in our model by its respective class, therefore, the used with semantic type is represented by the **UsedWith** class, the similarity by the **Similarity** class, the realization by the **Realization** class, the enhancement by the **Enhancement** and the conflict by the **Conflict**.

Some of the classes may contain properties assigned to it. For example, if two UIDPs are supposed to be similar to each other, it is just not enough to describe that their relationship is similarity, it is necessary also to mention what are the aspects in which they are similar. The same aspects are also applied to the enhancement semantic type, where it is necessary to describe how a UIDP enhances another one, and the conflict semantic type, where we should describe why the design patterns are conflicting. Therefore, we defined a class to represent respectively each of the mentioned properties (similarities, enhancements and conflict), **Similarities**, **Enhancements** and **Conflicts**.

4. CONCLUSION

In this paper we propose a flexible model to represent the UIDPs. As analyzed in the section 2, the PLML, which is known as the current agreed language to describe UIDPs, is not suitable because it does not propose a structure to represent UIDPs, hindering the potential to develop tools for processing them.

The point of flexibility of our model is to define the main properties of the UIDPs (problem, solution, context and rationale) containing descriptions for these sections as RDF Statements. Such statements allow the design pattern writers to express the semantics contained within the text description of the patterns in a more structured way, providing infrastructure for the development of tool to automate search and comparison of UIDPs.

5. FUTURE WORK

The navigation through the relationships represents just a first step towards the exploitation of the semantic types. In general, the navigation through the relationships should be sufficient for users who are familiar with UIDPs and are aware of how the design patterns relate to each other. They already have a comprehensive idea on how to place UIDPs, as bricks, to build the whole user interface. However, such approach is not suitable for non-expert user interface developers, who are not used to work with UIDPs. This class of users does not know how to build the whole user interface at once, because they do not know how the parts relate to each other. Thus, the semantic types can play an important role in this situation. It should be possible to develop a recommendation mechanism which analyzes the UIDPs already being used by the developer, and use the semantic types of their relationships to suggest new design patterns, which should be also considered by the developer in that context.

We also believe that the PLML represents a first but incomplete effort to represent UIDPs. The main reason is that the language is mainly based on describing content as free text, which is difficult for the machines to automatically extract its semantics. Therefore, the PLML should be further specified in order to structure its elements. Our next step towards a structured model is to propose a set of ontologies to each of the main PLML elements considered by us (problem, solution, rationale, context and rationale) based on an empirical analysis of the current UIDPs.

6. ACKNOWLEDGMENTS

We thank our colleagues at TU Dresden and at PUC-Rio for invaluable discussions related to this work. Simone Barbosa thanks the financial support of CNPq (313031/2009-6). Jordan Janeiro, Thomas Springer and Alexander Schill thank the supporting of project CRUISe and the financial support of the Federal Ministry of Education and Research of Germany (BMBF).

7. REFERENCES

[1] C. Alexander, S. Ishikawa, and M. Silverstein, *A Pattern Language: Towns, Buildings, Construction*, Oxford University Press, 1977.

[2] E. Gamma, R. Helm, and R.E. Johnson, *Design Patterns. Elements of Reusable Object-Oriented Software.*, Addison-Wesley Longman, Amsterdam, 1995.

[3] M. van Welie, "Welie.com - Patterns in Interaction Design," Jul. 2009.

[4] J. Tidwell, *Designing Interfaces: Patterns for Effective Interaction Design*, O'Reilly Media, Inc., 2005.

[5] Yahoo!, "Yahoo! Design Pattern Library," May. 2010.

[6] S. Fincher, *Perspectives on HCI Patterns: Concepts and Tools (Introducing PLML)*, 2003.

[7] T. Erl, *Service-Oriented Architecture (SOA): Concepts, Technology, and Design*, Prentice Hall PTR, 2005.

[8] S. Fincher, J. Finlay, S. Greene, L. Jones, P. Matchen, J. Thomas, and P.J. Molina, "Perspectives on HCI patterns: Concepts and Tools," *CHI '03 extended abstracts on Human factors in computing systems*, Ft. Lauderdale, Florida, USA: ACM, 2003, pp. 1044-1045.

[9] J. Bosak, T. Bray, D. Connolly, E. Maler, G. Nicol, M. Sperberg-McQueen, L. Wood, and C. James, *W3C XML Specification DTD ("XMLspec")*, ArborText Inc., 1998.

[10] D. Bienhaus, "Extended Pattern Language Markup Language," Jul. 2004.

[11] D. Bienhaus and S. Fincher, "Extended PLML (PLMLx): Concerns," Jul. 2004.

[12] J. Deng, E. Kemp, and E.G. Todd, "Focussing on a Standard Pattern Form: The Development and Evaluation of MUIP," *Proceedings of the 7th ACM SIGCHI New Zealand chapter's international conference on Computer-human interaction: design centered HCI*, Christchurch, New Zealand: ACM, 2006, pp. 83-90.

[13] A. Dearden and J. Finlay, "Pattern Languages in HCI: A Critical Review," *Human–Computer Interaction*, vol. 21, 2006, p. 49.

[14] "Yahoo! Design Pattern Library". Accessible in http://developer.yahoo.com/ypatterns/index.php.

[15] M. van Welie, "Welie.com - Patterns in Interaction Design". Accessible in http://www.welie.com/.

[16] Infragistics, "Quince," Feb. 2009.

[17] O. Lassila and R.R. Swick, "Resource Description Framework (RDF) Model and Syntax," 1998.

An Approach to Design the Student Interaction Based on the Recommendation of e-Learning Objects

Luciana A. M. Zaina,
Universidade Federal de São Carlos
Campus Sorocaba
Rod. João Leme dos Santos, Km 110 -
SP-264 - Bairro do Itinga - CEP 18052-
780 - Sorocaba - SP - Brazil
Phone: 55 (15) 3229-5972

lzaina@ufscar.br

Jose F. Rodrigues Junior
Dept. de Ciências de Computação – Inst.
de Ciências Mat. e de Computação
Universidade de São Paulo
Av. Trabalhador são-carlense, 400 -
Centro - CP: 668 - CEP: 13560-970 - São
Carlos - SP - Brazil
Phone: 55 (16) 3373-9686

junio@icmc.usp.br

Graça Bressan
Dept. de Eng. da Computação e
Sistemas Digitais – Escola Politécnica
Universidade de São Paulo
Av. Prof. Luciano Gualberto, travessa 3,
n.158, sala C1-46 - CEP: CEP 05508-
900 – São Paulo - SP - Brazil
Phone: 55 (11) 3091-5261

gbressan@larc.usp.br

ABSTRACT
In the last years, the adoption of recommender systems for improving user interaction has increased in e-learning applications. In the educational area, the recommendation of relevant and interesting content can attract the student's attention, motivating her/him during the learning-teaching process. It is very important, thus, to know learner preferences to suggest suitable contents to the students. The goal of this work is to present an approach to design the student interaction based on the recommendation of e-learning content, determining a more suitable relationship between learning objects and learning profiles. In our proposal, the learning profile is split into categories to attend different student preferences during the teaching-learning process: perception, presentation-format and participation. Our recommendation uses these categories to filter out the most suitable learning objects organized according to the IEEE LOM standard. We present a prototype architecture named e-LORS, over which we perform demonstrative experiments.

Categories and Subject Descriptors
H.1.2 [**User/Machine Systems**]: Human Factor, Human Processing Information.

General Terms
Management, Human Factors

Keywords
Recommendation systems, learning objects, LOM standard, learning profile, learning model, Felder-Silverman Learning Style Model

1. INTRODUCTION
The recommendation of e-learning content has been adopted as a

solution to satisfy student preferences during the teaching-learning process. A number of ongoing researches focus on a variety of aspects of user-oriented elements, one of the main such efforts is the adoption of recommendation mechanisms. The adoption of recommendation mechanisms to support the design of the student interaction may improve her/his experience in e-learning environments.

The recommendation process occurs through the investigation of the user's preferences. Based on information obtained from her/his explicit and implicit learning practices, it is possible to identify her/his needs within the context in which she/he interacts [19]. The elements and traits of the student behaviour delineate her/his profile and highlight the features that characterize her/him, such as: personal and social preferences, learning profile, and subject knowledge level.

By means of interviews – as was done in this work, or during monitored interaction, the students produce evidences about their *learning styles*, which are stored as implicit information into data objects named *learner profiles*. Learner profiles are one of the most important components of recommendation systems, providing relevant data about usage preferences [20].

The dynamic linkage between contents and student learning profiles may enhance the adequacy of the *learning objects* that will be offered to the students [20][21]. The observation of learning styles provides users with different teaching strategies, meeting the student's individual needs. In this sense, it is important to highlight that the student learning style should be observed through different dimensions achieving diverse aspects of her/his preferences, such as media format and participation in group activities.

The use of metadata standards adds value to learning systems in the task of handling learning objects, improving their reuse and retrieval [22]. Learning objects are specified by fields that describe their general data (e.g., title, description, keywords), technical details (e.g., media format, size, software and hardware requirements), learning features (e.g., concrete and abstract approaches, visual and verbal elements), and other relevant metadata [24].

This work presents an approach to design the student interaction based on the dynamic recommendation of e-learning objects. To do so we consider the *theme* of learning and the student learning profile. In our systematization, the learning profiles are described by a set of *preference categories* that describe the student learning preferences. A relationship between the learning profiles and the learning objects is drawn upon the linkage of the preference categories to the metadata fields of the learning objects. The approach was validated in a regular college course on Computer Engineering Data Structures. The course is part of the graduation curriculum from Brazilian university *Faculdade de Engenharia de Sorocaba* (FACENS).

The remainder of this work is structured as follows: section 2 explores related works and concepts; section 3 presents the recommendation approach proposed here; section 4 reports the validation experiments; and section 5 discusses some conclusions and outlines future works.

2. RELATED WORKS AND CONCEPTS

We review research relative to four important aspects of our work: related systems, recommendation strategies, learning profiles and learning objects.

2.1 Related Systems

In the literature, there are many e-learning proposals that work with learning profiles. Following, we present the ones that are more related to our work.

Milošević et al. [1] proposed the adoption of a learning style that allows the system to build learning workplaces, bounding learning content and learning styles through the SCORM (Sharable Content Object Reference Model) [21]. Although this propose adopts a standard to support the concept specification, it does not consider the learning profile according to elements of categorization.

The Personalized Learning Policy   [2] presents a flexible approach to organize the learning activities through a set of rules and procedures, adjusting the adaptive mechanism during the e-learning process. The authors argue that the student profile will be composed of student observable features by establishing and linking the rules to events that occur during the learning experience. The proposal does not deal with the dynamic binding between the contents and the learning style characteristics.

Romero *et. al.* [3] present a component to personalize the user interaction based on data mining algorithms that evaluate the student log data in order to suggest content links. The proposed component was integrated to the AHA! project, an e-learning environment that follows adaptive hypermedia concepts to provide contents to the students. The recommendation contents are restricted, as they are based on links subscribed to the course.

2.2 Recommendation Strategies

Recommender systems focus on suggesting information and services to users based on their preferences, comparing them to specific referential characteristics. The recommendation process enriches the user interaction process, as her/his communication interface will be designed with elements that correspond to her/his interests. Hence, the information and the services available in the interface will satisfy the user needs according to usage context

[4]. In general, the recommendation process is accomplished by the following recommendation approaches: collaborative filtering, content-based filtering, rule-based filtering, or hybrid combinations of these techniques [4] [5] [8].

The most disseminated approach is collaborative filtering, which provides personal recommendation on a group-based fashion, adjusting to sets of people with similar preferences and interests [3] [5].

Content-based retrieval techniques implement the nearest-neighbor model. The content-based approach concerns the content rather than the users. To do so, it learns about the most relevant contents based on the features derived from the objects that the user has accessed [6][7][8]. Metadata and ontology may be used as a solution to sort out semantic terms in relevant documents or objects during the filtering [9].

Bilgic and Mooney [7] proposed an extension of the content-based classifier method; the authors use the Keyword Style Explanation approach, which explains to the user how the system achieves the suggestions.

Decision rules, in rule-based filtering, may be manually or automatically designed by those who have a strong correlation with a domain area, as e-business for instance. The techniques allow the rule's designer to heavily control the adaptation process [10].

Brusilovsky [11] emphasizes that recommendation techniques have influenced the design of techniques and systems for web navigation. According to the author, the recommendation process influences the choices for what is to be offered to the user, determining a dynamic communication design. In the educational context, recommendation acts not only on the motivational aspect of students but, also, on the development of certain abilities in specific learning scopes.

2.3 Learning Profiles

One main need in teaching activities is to identify the outstanding characteristics that define the learning preferences of the students. Then, in order to satisfy a given learning style, the teacher must use strategies that will meet the needs of different learning perspectives. The same is expected from content recommendation systems, what can be done through the use of learning profiles that, implicitly, contain learning style information [15].

Each individual fits into a specific learning style, what makes her/him adopt attitudes and behaviors that are repeated in different moments and situations [14]. During interaction, the student receives stimuli from an environment and her/his actions produce evidences about her/his learning profile. Alternatively, the student learning profile can be identified via questionnaires that capture learning styles according to well-defined models [20].

There are several models used in the characterization of learning profiles, each of which is suitable for a different learning scope. Although there are many learning style models, Felder and Brent [14] highlight five of them: the Myers-Briggs Type Indicator – MBTI, Kolb's Experiential Learning Model, the Hermann Brain Dominance Instrument (HBDI), the Honey-Mumford's Learning Styles Questionnaire (LSQ), and the Felder-Silverman Model.

Among the possibilities of leaning style modeling, the Felder-Silverman model was chosen to be used in this work. This is due to the fact that it has the strongest emphasis on the relationship of learning styles and teaching strategies. Felder and Silverman [15] remember that the application of this model is especially suitable for Engineering Education. This is an important fact because engineering refers to applied science, just as computer science, which is our application domain.

2.4 Learning Objects

One of the goals of teaching-learning environments is to offer educational material, usually called learning objects (LOs). In this context, LOs must be selected so as to correspond to the students' preferences [23]. Within the scope of e-learning, the aim is to create contents in digital formats that can be reused for different learning objectives, or even employed in the construction of other learning objects [16].

Table 1. Description of LOM categories

LOM Category	LOM Field	Characterization
General	Identifier, Type, Title, Language, Description and Keywords.	General description of the learning object.
Technical	Media Format (video type, sound), Size, Physical location, Requirements (object use: software version, for example).	Technical features description.
Educational	Interactive type (active, expositive).	Educational functions and pedagogical characteristics object description.
	Learning Resource Type (exercise, simulation, and questionnaire).	

One of the ways to organize learning objects so that they can be used and reused systematically is through the use of descriptive metadata, that is, a set of attributes that describes learning objects. The LOM (Learning Object Metadata) standard [13] of the Institute of Electrical and Electronics Engineers (IEEE) is the most commonly metadata specification used for e-learning. The LOM standard has a structure that describes learning objects through descriptor categories. Each category has a specific purpose, such as describing general attributes of objects, and educational objectives. Table 1 shows the LOM categories adopted in this work.

3. E-LEARNING OBJECT RECOMMENDATION

Recommender systems, with educational focus, follow the ratings that the students confer on learning strategies, or on learning contents. These systems track such ratings by structured profile delineation questionnaires, or by monitoring the explicit and implicit actions of the students over the system. These data are then analyzed in order to automatically suggest the content during the learning process. The user tracking process may occur in many ways, for example, by applying explicit questions for the students [3] or by observing the selected pages in a specific moment.

Here we use the Soloman and Felder questionnaire [12] to mold the learning style for e-LORS – e-Learning Object Recommendation System. System e-LORS employs the fundamentals of content selection to suggest learning objects considering two aspects: learning-teaching theme and student learning profile. In e-LORS, the learning objects are organized according to the LOM standard, and the learning profile is split into categories of preferences based on the Felder and Silverman model.

3.1 Preference Categories of the Learning Profile

The Felder and Silverman model describes the student learning style by four different behavior dimensions: orientation, perception, presentation format, and student participation. In the model, these features are related to specific learning styles and teaching methods, factors that are used to support the student learning preferences [15].

In another work, Zaina and Bressan [17] relegate Felder/Silverman's orientation dimension, proposing an alternative approach that splits the student learning profile into three categories: perception, presentation format and student participation. Along the text, this altered model is referred to as *Preference Categories*; its goal is to detect clusters of preferences that reflect different data perspectives caught during the tracking of learning styles. Each category, as shown in Table 2, has a teaching-method correspondence that defines the matching with the students' learning styles, as predicted in the Felder/Silverman proposal.

Table 2. Preference categories of the learning profile

Preference Categories	Features	Learning Styles	Teaching Methods
Perception	The focus is in the best way through which the student can obtain information: contents, exercise types, for instance.	Sensing	Concrete
		Intuitive	Abstract
Presentation Format	It is related to the input. Content preferences chosen by the student such as media types.	Visual	Visual
		Auditory	Verbal
Student Participation	It represents the student preferences for the activities participation or observation.	Active	Active
		Reflective	Passive

The *Preference Categories* concern different dimensions of the student learning behavior in e-learning environments. The *Perception* category reports the type of information that the student prefers to interact with. The *Presentation Format* category describes the preference channel to input information. In turn, the *Student Participation* category reflects her/his preferences to process the information, participating in activities or reflecting about the subject.

The *Preference Categories* of a given student can be identified with the application of the online questionnaire provided by Soloman and Felder [12].

3.2 System e-LORS Content Recommendation

System e-LORS has a flexible specification that allows a variety of e-learning systems to adopt it. The system uses the student learning profile (Preference Categories) in order to recommend the appropriate learning objects. It works by confronting and handling a given content theme of interest to a given student request. Figure 1 presents an overview of the e-LORS architecture.

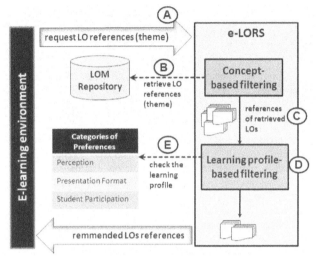

Figure 1. The e-LORS architecture.

In the first step (A), e-LORS starts the recommendation process by receiving the *theme* parameter. This parameter describes the topic of interest according to the metadata defined by the LOM standard. The *theme* is used to determine which LOs are to be considered for matching the learners' profiles.

In step B, as soon as e-LORS receives the requisition for a recommendation process, it starts the theme-based filtering searching the LO references in the LOM-based repository (LOMR – LOM Repository). According to the *theme*, defined from one or many words that are passed as parameters to the system, the filtering is performed. Then, the system seeks (*searchLO*) for learning objects that match the *theme* parameter according to the fields of *title*, *description* and *keywords*, which belong to the LOM's General Category. The method returns a set of LO identification references (LOSet) that fit the *theme*. In Figure 1, the passage of the LOSet refers to step C, as formally defined in equation (1) and in predicate (2):

$$searchLO: LOMR \rightarrow LOSet \qquad (1)$$

$$LOSet = \{ LO: LO \in LOMR \ AND \qquad (2)$$

$$LO_{category} = General \ AND \ theme \ IN \ LO_{LOMFields[i]}\},$$

where i = {*Title, Description, Keywords*}

After the concept-based filtering, e-LORS begins the next filtering based on the criterion of *learning profile* – step D – performing it only over the first outcome of references (LOSet) achieved in the previous step.

The student Preference Categories reported in the learning profiles are compared to the Interactive and Learning Resources found in the Educational LOM standard category (Table 1), being restricted only to the LOSet instead of the entire LOMR. Table 3

presents the binding between the fields of the LOM standard (describing the learning content – Table 1) and the students' Preference Categories (Felder-Silverman – Table 2).

As shown in Table 3, for example, when the Preference Category of a student is *Perception* and her/his profile is *Sensing* the correspondent teaching method is *Concrete*. According to Felder and Silverman, this teaching-learning style corresponds to *Active* learning objects in the *Interactivity* field of the *Educational* LOM category.

Table 3. Link between the LOM fields and the preferences categories

LOM – Educational Field	Educational Field Values	Teaching-Learning correspondence	Preference Category
Interactivity	Active	Concrete-Sensing	Perception
	Expositive	Abstract-Intuitive	
Learning Resource Type	Figure, Video, Film, and others	Visual-Visual	Presentation-Format
	Text, Sound, and others	Verbal-Auditory	
	Practical Exercise, Experiment, and others	Active-Active	Student Participation
	Questionnaire and Readings	Passive-Reflective	

In the last step, system e-LORS selects the LOs from the LOSet and match them to the students learning profiles, step E in Figure 1, resulting in the new subset (LOSubset) as formally defined in equation (3) and predicate (4):

$$searchLOLearningP: LOSet \rightarrow LOSubset \qquad (3)$$

$$LOSubset = \{ LO: LO \in LOSet \ AND \qquad (4)$$

$$LO_{category} = Educational \ AND$$

$$PreferenceCategory[j] \ \exists \ Learner \ Model \ AND$$

$$PreferenceCategory[j] \equiv LO_{LOMFields}[i]\}, where:$$

j = {Perception, Presentation-Format, Participation} and

i = {Interactivity, Learning Resource}

Finally, e-LORS recommends a set of LOs, each of which recognized by an *Identifier* field (LOM General category) used to retrieve content files from the LOM repository. The final result set, then, may be used to build the learning workplace that satisfies the student's preferences.

4. SYSTEM e-LORS VALIDATION

We have implemented a prototype of e-LORS that was used in a regular college course on Computer Engineering Data Structures with 50 students. The course is part of the graduation curriculum from Brazilian university *Faculdade de Engenharia de Sorocaba* (FACENS). No specific course management system was used as Moodle [18], but an ad hoc institutional system integrated to e-

LORS. This system was used as a supplement to traditional lectures.

Led by the outcomes produced by the questionnaire of Soloman e Felder [12] answered by the 50 students, the preferences of the students were identified and the values of Preference Categories were updated in the student learning profile objects of our system. The questionnaire reflects the student learning style in different dimensions according to Felder and Silverman Learning Style Model.

4.1 Preparing Learning Objects

In order to test our system, we have catalogued several learning objects for the topics on Data Structures, what allowed us to attend different learning styles during the experience. A crew of professors and assistants were designated to create the LOs at the same time that they were catalogued for further use by e-LORS.

The professors were responsible for planning the LOs so that they would carry metadata in accordance to the LOM standard. This way, the LOs would fit both the concept-based (theme), and the learning profile-based filtering modules of e-LORS. The assistants helped up in the task and raised a LOM-based repository over which the whole system would work. For the Data Structures course, the crew of professors and assistants catalogued 80 learning objects – corresponding to 6 lessons. Some examples of the objects that were catalogued are: demonstration simulations, interactive simulations, explaining texts, figures, exercises, illustrations and case studies.

4.2 e-LORS in Action

Initially, the recommendation process receives the theme parameters, that is, a topic of interest for a specific lecture.

As an example, following we report an illustrative operation in which the theme *binary tree* is passed to the system as the topic of interest of a student with a learning profile with values *sensing*, *visual* and *active* corresponding to categories *perception*, *format presentation*, and *student participation*. Shortly, e-LORS defines a two-fold course of action:

- *Concept-based filtering:* seeks and selects in the LOM General category for all the occurrences likewise "*binary tree*". Ten different learning object identifiers are returned and sent as a list of objects to the next step;
- *Profile learning-based filtering:* from the list of objects in the *concept-based filtering*, e-LORS picks up the objects matching preferences *sensing, visual* and *active*, which correspond to the Preference Categories of a given student. The system identifies a simulation, a video-lecture, a chat session about de theme and a discussion topic in a forum. This content will be used for designing the communication interface.

System e-LORS returns the list of recommended learning objects and the process is concretized with the building of the student workplace with the recommended objects. Other learning objects are made available through a link to other materials, allowing the students to have their own choices as illustrated in Figure 2.

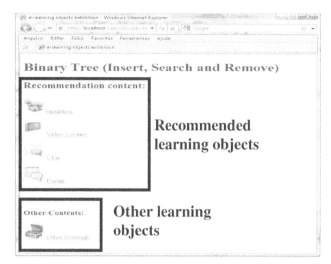

Figure 2. Example of a student workplace with a set of recommended learning objects

4.3 User Satisfaction Evaluation

The final step of the experiment was the evaluation of the students' perception of the system. To do so, an evaluation form was posed for the students who had to indicate their satisfaction with the recommended learning objects. In the form, the answers were standardized in a 1 to 4 score scale; 1 for totally non-satisfied and 4 for completely satisfied.

The students reported that the workplaces achieved with the use of e-LORS were, in fact, more adequate than what would be achieved with casual browsing. For the Data *Structures* course, the students summed up 76% of complete (score 4) or almost complete satisfaction (score 3).

5. CONCLUSIONS

In this work, we have defined a methodology that links learning objects and learning profiles for automatic content recommendation. To do so, we have used the Felder-Silverman Learning Style Model along with the IEEE LOM standard, a combination that, extending former works, can suitably relate learner profiles and learning objects, automatically, in different fields of learning, and consistently reflecting the intrinsic style of the students.

We use a multiple-criteria-filtering methodology that, through modules with different responsibilities, selects the learning objects according to two criteria: concept (theme), and profile (style). Our work has put together an ensemble of well-established methodologies in an innovative system; a system capable of a versatile recommendation of learning objects, structured and reproducible according to well-defined conventions. Our approach supports the dynamical design of communication interfaces, reflecting important aspects of the users' personalities.

There are further developments to be achieved. One of them is to extend the proposal to consider technological aspects of the learning context as, for example, mobile devices. Another future work is to consider the semantic interpretation of learning objects, learning styles and contextual information.

6. ACKNOWLEDGMENTS

This work was partly supported by FAPESP (São Paulo State Research Foundation.

7. REFERENCES

[1] Milošević, D., Brković, M., Debevc, M., and Krneta, R. 2007. Adaptive Learning by Using SCOs Metadata. *Interdisciplinary Journal of Knowledge and Learning Objects*, vol. 3: 163-174.

[2] Stiubiener, I., Rosatelli, M. C., and Ruggiero, W. V. 2007. An approach to personalisation in e-learning. In *Proc. of IEEE International Conference on Advanced Learning Technologies*, 189-193. DOI= http://doi.ieeecomputersociety.org/10.1109/ICALT.2007.54

[3] Romero, C., Ventura, S., Delgado, J. A., and De Bra, P. 2007. Personalized Links Recommendation Based on Data Mining in Adaptive Educational Hypermedia Systems. In *Creating New Learning Experiences on a Global Scale*, 4753: 292-306. DOI= 10.1007/978-3-540-75195-3.

[4] Pazzani, M. J., and Billsus, D. 2007. Content-Based Recommendation Systems, In *The Adaptive Web*, 4321: 325-341. DOI= 10.1007/978-3-540-72079-9.

[5] Herlocker, J. L., Konstan, J. A., Terveen, L. G., and Riedl, J. T. 2004. Evaluating collaborative filtering recommender systems, *ACM Transactions on Information Systems*, 22(1): 5-53. DOI= 10.1145/963770.963772.

[6] Rodrigues Jr., J. F., Romani, L. A. S., Traina, A. J. M., and Traina Jr., C. 2010. Combining Visual Analytics and Content Based Data Retrieval Technology for Efficient Data Analysis, In *Proc. of the 14th International Conference on Information Visualisation*, to be published.

[7] Bilgic, M., and Mooney, R. J. 2005. Explaining Recommendations: Satisfaction vs. Promotion. In *Proc. of Beyond Personalization, Workshop on the Next Stage of Recommender Systems Research, International Conference on Intelligent User Interface*, 47-56. DOI= 10.1.1.64.4814.

[8] Burke, R. 2002. Hybrid Recommender Systems: Survey and Experiments. *User Modelling and User-Adapted Interaction*, 12(4): 331-370. DOI= 10.1023/A:1021240730564.

[9] Wang, Y., Stash, N., Aroyo, L., Hollink, L., and Schreiber, G. 2009. Semantic Relations in Content-based Recommender. In *Proc. of the Fifth International Conference on Knowledge Capture*, 209-210.

[10] Mobasher, B. 2007. Data Mining for Web Personalization. In *The Adaptive Web*, 4321: 90–135. DOI=10.1007/978-3-540-72079-9-3.

[11] Brusilovsky, P. 2007. Adaptive Navigation Support. In *The Adaptive Web*, 4321: 264-289. DOI= 10.1007/978-3-540-72079-9_8.

[12] Soloman, B. A., and R. M. Felder. 1997. Index of Learning Styles Questionnaire, in august/2010, available at: http://www.engr.ncsu.edu/learningstyles/ilsweb.html.

[13] IEEE LOM, Draft standard for learning object metadata, In august/2010, available at: http://ltsc.ieee.org/wg12.

[14] Felder, R. M., and Brent, R. 2005. Understanding Student Differences. *Journal of Engineering Education*, 94(1): 57-72. DOI= 10.1.1.133.171.

[15] Felder, R. M., and Silverman, L. K. 1988. Learning and Teaching Styles in Engineering Education. *Journal of Engineering Education*,78(7):674-681. DOI=10.1.1.92.774.

[16] Vazquez, A. R., Ostrovskaya, and Y. A. 2006. Analysis of Open Technological Standards for Learning Objects. *In Proc. of 4th LA-Web*, 105-108. DOI= 10.1109/LA-WEB.2006.5.

[17] Zaina, L. A. M., and Bressan, G. 2008. Classification of learning profile based on categories of student preferences, In *Proc. of the 38th Annual Frontiers in Education Conference*, F4E-1-F4E-6.

[18] Moodle. Learning Management System. In august/2010, available at: http://moodle.org.

[19] Felfernig, A., G. Friedrich, and Schmidt-Thieme, L. 2007. Recommender Systems. *IEEE Intelligent Systems*, 22(3): 18-21. DOI=10.1.1.136.7987.

[20] Graf, S., Viola, S. R., Kinshuk, and Leo, T. 2007. In-depth Analysis of the Felder-Silverman Learning Style Dimensions. *Journal of Research on Technology in Education*, 40(1):79-93. DOI=10.1.1.142.2267.

[21] Devedžic, V., Jovanovic, J., and Gaševic, D. 2007. The pragmatics of current e-learning standards. *IEEE Internet Computing*, 11(3): 19-27. DOI= http://doi.ieeecomputersociety.org/10.1109/MIC.2007.73.

[22] Devedžić, V., Gašević, D., and Djurić, D. 2008. Clarifying the meta. *International Journal of Information and Communication Technology*, 1(2):148-158. DOI= 10.1504/IJICT.2008.019099.

[23] Zaina, L. A. M., and Bressan, G. 2009. Learning objects retrieval from contextual analysis of user preferences to enhance e-learning personalization. *Proc. of IADIS International Conference WWW/Internet*, 237-244.

[24] Baldiris, S., Santos, O. C., Barrera, C., Boticario, J. G., Velez, J., and Fabregat, R. 2008. Integration of Educational Specifications and Standards to Support Adaptive Learning Scenarios in ADAPTAPlan. *International Journal of Computer & Applications*, 5(1): 88-107.

Combining Ontologies and Scenarios for Context-Aware e-Learning Environments

Isabela Gasparini[1,2,3]

DCC, CCT, UDESC
Joinville, SC, Brasil

igasparini@inf.ufrgs.br

Marcelo S. Pimenta[2],
José Palazzo M. de Oliveira[2]
Instituto de Informática – UFRGS
Porto Alegre, RS, Brasil

{mpimenta,
palazzo}@inf.ufrgs.br

Amel Bouzeghoub[3]

TELECOM & Management SudParis
Evry, France

Amel.Bouzeghoub@it-sudparis.eu

ABSTRACT

Nowadays e-learning systems (ELSs) are used by a wide variety of students with different characteristics. Thus, adapting it to specific users, taking advantage of knowledge acquired and registered about them (the user's model, which in ELS domain is usually called student model) is an essential feature in order to improve usability and flexibility of ELSs. In fact, the use of personalization techniques aims at improving ELS usability since a personalized system automatically customizes the user interface, content, access rights, navigation, etc., considering the student model and each user may think that the system was designed specifically for him/her. This paper presents the context-aware and culture-oriented aspects of an adaptability approach designed for ELS. The main features of our approach are described and illustrated, showing how to use it to model context and culture for personalization of ELS, representing explicitly the rich context as an extension of traditional student modeling and making use of ontologies to model it.

Categories and Subject Descriptors

H.5.2 [**User Interfaces**]: Evaluation/methodology

General Terms

Management, Design, Experimentation, Human Factors.

Keywords

Context-aware, Cultural-aware, adaptive systems.

1. INTRODUCTION

Typical existing student models for e-learning contain information about students' interests; knowledge, background and skills; interaction preferences; individual traits and learning styles. However, ELSs may be dynamically adjusted not only according to the student's model but also depending on a richer notion of context [1]. Although there are several approaches for consider context in ELS, they focus mainly on technological and/or

networking aspects without taking into account other contextual aspects, such as cultural and pedagogical. This paper present an improvement of an adaptive ELS called AdaptWeb®(Adaptive Web-based learning Environment), based on a rich context model as an extension to the traditional student modeling. A personalized ELS based on context provides the learner with exactly the material he needs, and appropriate to his knowledge level and that makes sense in a special learning situation, which together with external factor is known as a *scenario* in our work. Thus, for each scenario, an ELS is dynamically adjusted depending on the context information available. In this paper, we present how to combine ontology-representation and scenario-orientation to explicitly represent the rich context as an extension to the traditional student modeling in ELS. This rich context modeling includes information related to personal, cultural, technological and pedagogic aspects to improve integration and reuse for different environments. Our aim is to increment even more the actual systems' personalization capabilities making use of ontologies to model the student's context in different scenarios.

2. STUDENT'S MODEL BACKGROUND

The use of e-learning has resulted in fundamental changes in teaching and learning, bringing new focuses like personalization and student modeling for a better understanding and representation of students' profiles to better apply this understanding in the ELS. Indeed, basically, personalization approaches automatically adapt system elements considering the user profile. We assume that an important goal for ELS is to give quick and easy access to information considering knowledge related to a user's educational profile. Despite a clear progress in recent years with respect to aesthetics and usability of sites, even experienced users have many difficulties in finding information in web-based systems due to bad design. Personalization relieves users from time-consuming browsing. Content must be focused on information and links directly related to a specific role or a specific activity, considered relevant according the student model. The designers of ELS need to begin their task studying the course structure in order to group educational information, links and activities according to students' modeling and profiling. A personalization approach may be applied only when a student model is available. For educational web sites or ELS we may be concerned with some specific aspects related to student' model. Next, we briefly discuss the most common contents of student's model.

Student's interests describe news topics or concepts, document topics, work-related topics or hobbies-related topics. Sometimes user interests are classified as short-term interests or long-term interests, e.g. the interest of users in soccer may be a short-term interest if the user reads or listens to news about this topic only during World Cup, or a long-term interest if the user is always interested in this topic [2]. The student's knowledge about the subject taught is vital to adapt the content of courses according to it. This is a changeable feature that can both increase (as the student learns), or decrease (as the student forgets) from session to session or within the same session. This means that a personalized system based on user knowledge has to recognize these changes and update the user model properly.

The student's goal or task represents the objective or purpose with respect to the application the user is working with, that is what he wants to achieve. Goals are target tasks at the focus of a user's attention [3]. If the user is working with an ELS, for example, his goal is learning a certain subject. The goal and task recognition process is not trivial, and is not precise in general [4]. A task corresponds to an action the user can perform in the software application, and a goal is a higher level intention of the user, which will be accomplished by carrying out a set of tasks.

The student's background is a common name for a set of features not directly related to the application domain. Typically, this characteristic includes the user's profession or job, his job responsibilities, his work experience in related areas and his language ability (i.e., native or non-native speakers) [4]. A student's experiences and skills represent how familiar and competent the student is with the structure, presentation and navigation in the ELS. The difference of experience and background is that user can be familiar with the way a content is structured and navigate easily over this structure, without deeply knowing the content [4]. Students' interaction preferences constitute information about the user's interaction preferences and habits while he/she interacts with a personalized system. The system interface can be adjusted and the navigation's structure can be modified, for example, changing the order of the links menu, showing some additional tools for navigation, or even disabling some introductory information.

Student's individual traits are aspects that together determine a student as individual, like personality traits (for example the traits from the personality model OCEAN [5]; and CUMAPH system [6] that builds a user profile from lower level cognitive abilities and use it for adapting a user's page content) and cognitive [7] and learning styles (for example, from Felder-Silverman's model ([8], [9]). Felder-Silverman's model categorizes students as sensitive/ intuitive, visual/verbal, active/reflective, and sequential/global, depending on how they learn. According this model, people have different learning ways, some prefer visual information to understanding, others opt for understanding through verbal information, there are also those who better understand the facts in a descriptive way, while others fit over ease on mathematical models. More details can be found in [9].

Different personalized ELS use Felder-Silverman's model as a mechanism to provide assistance and/or adaptation to students. For example, TANGOW (Task-based Adaptive learNer Guidance On the Web) [10] uses sensing-intuitive dimension. The web-based system uses Felder's Learning Style Theory and Index of Learning Styles to assess student's learning styles, and the assessment result is used to automatically adapt Web-based educational systems' content sequencing for student. LSAS (Learning Style Adaptive System) [11] uses global-sequential dimension [12]. Carver, Howard, & Lane [13] created a computer systems hypermedia courseware (CS383) that consisted of a range of learning style tools. In this approach, the key was to determine what type of media is applicable and appropriate to different learning styles. Lesson media elements is presented in a sorted list ranked from the most to least conducive based on learners' learning style. During the first lesson learners submit the questionnaire to identify their learning style. MAS-PLANG [14] is an adaptive and intelligent learning multi agent system. This integrates six intelligent agents, allowing student guidance in learning process and adopts Felder-Silverman´s five dimensions.

Although several personalized systems that use learning styles as a source for adaptation have been reported in the literature, just a few have been using them integrated into the environment. Several systems use specially designed psychological tests designed for particular learning style categorizations or interviews/questionnaire in order to let the learners decide on specific aspects of their learning style preferences, whilst a few others take advantage of the environment itself, and use the environment as a tool to discover the student's learning style, without any questionnaire, exactly like eTeacher [15] and AdaptWeb® [16]. AdaptWeb® uses Felder-Silverman's model as a mechanism of adaptation by user´s interaction.

3. STUDENT´S CULTURE AND CONTEXT

To be effective, a learning process must be adapted to the learner's context. Such a context should be described at least from pedagogical, technological and learning perspectives [17]. Learning processes have to provide extremely contextualized content that is highly coupled with context information, barring their reuse in some other context. If the context information is represented independently from content information, the possibilities for reuse increase.

In a broader sense, context describes the circumstances under which something occurs as well as the interrelationships of those circumstances. Such interrelationships provide a semantic perspective that restricts and narrows the meaning of "something". A learning situation should take account of pedagogical, technological, cultural and learners' personal characteristics. In the pedagogical context we have the concept being taught, learning strategies and educative objectives; the learner context is about the learner's situation, cultural context express student´ cultural background and the technological context is concerning about technological characteristics of the learning environment. We have to analyze tree points-of-view: (1) learner, (2) learning activities, and (3) environment (technical commuting, physical commuting, device, location, time) [18].

The inclusion of multicultural aspects into ELS is vital. Cultural aspects are preferences and ways of behavior determined by the person's culture. Regarding ELS, the cultural aspects are the features that distinguish between the preferences of students from different regions [19]. Nevertheless, considering culture for personalizing ELS is a new approach. As well as other software applications, ELS are usually restricted to one personalization strategy per country. However, a predefined localized personalization cannot be assigned to all people of a nation, as some might have many cultural influences and are, therefore, culturally ambiguous [20]. This means that ELS must be personalized in relation to a particular set of student's cultural properties. Thus, modeling cultural profiles can be a way to improve cultural awareness in global knowledge sharing and learning processes.

4. RELATED WORKS

Research in adaptive educational hypermedia has demonstrated that considering context leads to a better understanding and personalization [4]. Context is vital to improve personalization/adaptation in ELSs. Recent works aim to provide the capacity for identifying the right contents, right services in the right place at the right time and in the right form based on the current student's situation. There is an interesting theory of learning for a mobile society [21] but our work is closely related to others like [22], [23], [24], [25], [26] and [27]. The interesting propositions of GlobalEdu [22], [24] in terms of architecture, for instance, have distributed and central alternatives with different models (student, context and environment). A work related with situations and scenarios is the research presented in [28], where the authors proposes to model adaptive and context-aware scenarios based on: a didactics theory; a domain model; a learner model and a context model. To develop the scenario, they first built several scenarios based on a common learning scenario; secondly, they use a theory in didactic anthropology of knowledge to acquire the scenario model and the didactical environment; after, the didactic based scenario model is transformed into a computer based hierarchical task model. Different of our work, they don't work with the automatic description of a user situation, but with the description of adaptive scenarios.

Particularly about cultural aspects, Blanchard and Mizoguchi [29] describe an upper ontology of culture, by working at the meta-level of culture. They aim to identifying major constituents to be considered when dealing with any kind of cultural issue without having to endorse a particular culture's representational framework. They use this approach to deal with many CATS (Culturally-Aware Tutoring Systems) related issues by providing objective formalism for cultural representation. Chandramouli et al. [30] presented the notion of the CAE-L Ontology for modeling stereotype cultural artifacts in adaptive education and used a Cultural Artifacts in Education (CAE) questionnaire to gather the information required to determine if there is a significant cultural bias within online education, specifically Adaptive Educational Hypermedia. Motz et al. [31] introduce an architecture in the e-learning EduCa Project, based in a strong use of ontologies for the retrieval, management and clustered of electronic educational resources according to user's cultural aspects, like degree of impatience, attitude, treatment, language, learning styles and activities. These cultural aspects are specified in a MultiCultural Aspects Ontology, which follows the standard Learning Object Metadata (LOM) and uses OWL (Web Ontology Language).

Sieg, Mobasher and Burke [32] presented a framework that integrates critical elements that make up the user context, namely the user's short-term behavior, semantic knowledge from ontologies that provide explicit representations of the domain of interest, and long-term user profiles revealing interests and trends. They present a novel approach for building ontological user profiles by assigning interest scores to existing concepts in a domain ontology. Reinecke, Reif, Bernstein [33] present a Cultural User Model Ontology - CUMO that contains information

such as different places of residence, the parents' nationality, languages spoken, and religion. Furthermore, CUMO contains information about Hofstede's [34] five dimensions and their values: (a) Masculinity vs. Femininity, (b) Uncertainty Avoidance Index, (c) Power Distance, (d) Individualism vs. Collectivism and (e) Long Term Orientation. However, according Reinecke, Reif and Bernstein, the scores assigned to a user and his cultural dimensions are not static to everybody residing in the same country, and thus, do not resemble a "national culture", as suggested by Hofstede. Instead, they take into account all places of residence and calculate their influence on the user's dimensions according to the duration of the user's stay at those places. Reinecke and Bernstein [35] have proposed a culturally Adaptive To-Do Tool namely MOCCA that is a web-based to-do list tool that allows users to manage their tasks online. Its goal is to automatically adapt to the cultural preferences of its users. They present ten different aspects of user interaction and they looked at the influence of culture on UI perception, compiled a list of general adaptation guidelines, and evaluated them in a survey and experimentation with 30 participants.

Our research has a different point of view of these works because we integrate cultural, technological, pedagogical and personal aspects as part of a rich context model (complementary to student model) [1] that makes sense in a special situation, in a given time. Despite the considerable scientific production on customization, personalization and adaptation in e-learning, surprisingly there is very little research work devoted to how to incorporate context-aware and culture-oriented concerns to ELSs.

An improvement in the user's contextual information leads to a better understanding of users' behavior in order to adapt (i) the content, (ii) the interface, and (iii) the assistance offered to users. A contextualized ELS provides the student with exactly the material he needs, and appropriate to his knowledge level and that makes sense in a special learning situation. However, while learning is a process intensively related to the notion of situation, in most of ELSs situation is only implicitly mentioned and not explicitly modeled. In order to support situation-aware adaptation, it is necessary to model and specify both context and situation [18]. More accurately, there is a complex intermeshing and continuous transformation of situations in combination with fluctuating contexts, where meaning changes according to context and through preferences of different participants. In this sense, e-learning personalization is situation-dependent and cannot be managed in an independent form. Herein, we present our context-aware situation-dependent personalization approach designed for ELSs.

5. ONTOLOGY-BASED CONTEXT MODELING: ADAPTSUR APPROACH

Our approach to model context and culture in e-learning is described in this section. This approach is called ADAPTSUR and it has been developed in the framework of ADAPTSUR, a Brazil-Argentina cooperation project, and is being coupled to two distinct personalized ELS. Specially, we improved the models used in these environments in order to incorporate the notion of context and situation. We add a rich notion of context to existing student profiles in order to provide a rich personalization process. To be effective, learning process must be adapted not only to the student's profile but to the learner's context as well, creating some kind of matching between context and profile to provide for example the appropriate content, navigation, and recommendations. Learning processes have to provide extremely contextualized content that is highly coupled with context information, limiting their reuse in some other context. If the context information is represented independently from content information, the possibilities for reuse increase.

In a broader sense, *context* describes the circumstances under which something occurs as well as the interrelationships of those circumstances. Such interrelationships provide a semantic perspective that restricts and narrows the meaning of "something" [17]. A context-aware ELS is an application that adapts its behavior according to the students' context. Context-aware applications not only use context information to react to a user's request, but also take the initiative as a result of context reasoning activities [36]. Thus, an improvement in the user's contextual information leads to a better understanding of users' behavior in order to adapt (i) the content, (ii) the interface, and (iii) the assistance offered to users. We have developed a model based on upper-level ontology. In this model, a student might be involved in several overlapping contexts, and consequently, his/her educational activity might be influenced by the interactions between these contexts. Overlapping contexts contribute to and influence the interactions and experiences that people have when performing certain activities [27], [37], [38]. As deeply described in [39], our model has three levels: meta-model, model (ontologies), and object (Figure 1). The meta-model level is represented by an upper ontology; the model level with several ontologies to describe the elements that populate the context and, in the lower level, we find the instantiations of the context ontologies. In other words, the ontology concepts of one level are the instantiations of its immediate superior level.

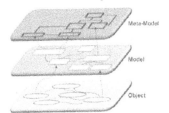

Figure 1. Three-level context model

We personalize an ELS for each user based on the information stored in a student model. In our work, the typical characteristics of students are extended to include the context dimensions having personal, technological, pedagogical and cultural aspects.

Personal context is widely considered in ELS. This type of context is usually gathered in user profiles. For general purposes, typical characteristics of user profiles include age, scholarship, background, gender, interests, knowledge, background and skills, experiences, goals, behavior, among others. It considers the student's personal information (such as name or address) and also the student's personal preferences (like interaction preferences, colors or layouts).

Technological context is related to many different technological constraints (e.g., device processing power, display ability, network bandwidth, connectivity options, location and time). Indeed, cultural and technological adaptation is an important and hot research topic that has not been yet supported by most of ELS, although some pioneering work has been reported in [17].

Technological context includes concepts such as browser type and version, operating system, IP address, devices, processing power, display ability, network bandwidth or connectivity options.

Pedagogical context consists of multifaceted knowledge due to many distinct viewpoints of pedagogical information needed to personalize e-learning. In practice, many adaptive systems take advantage of users' knowledge of the subject being taught or the domain represented in the hyperspace, and the knowledge is frequently the only user feature being modeled [4]. Recently, various researches started using other characteristics, such as personality model OCEAN [5], cognitive [7] and learning styles (for example, from Felder's model [9]).

5.1.1 Cultural Context

Cultural context includes cultural background of a student and may have a great impact on their ability and efficiency to learn a given set of content [30]. Cultural context is referred to different languages, values, norms, gender, social, ideological, political or ethnic aspects [40]. It describes cultural characteristics on different levels: national and regional aspects, organizational aspects, professional aspects and fields, social and individual aspects as presented in Figure 2. Thus, cultural profiles describe cultural and individual characteristics on diverse levels and modeling of culture profiles can be a means to improve cultural awareness in global knowledge sharing and learning processes.

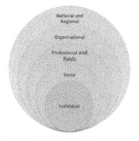

Figure 2. Cultural dimensions

There are different cultural dimensions proposed in the literature, but the most accepted for national point of view are the five dimensions proposed by Hofstede [34], based on value orientations and shared across cultures. According to Bossard [41] there are two categories of topics that are affected in human computer interaction localization, (i) presentation of information (e.g. time, date and color format) and language (e.g. font, writing direction, etc.); and (ii) dialog design (e.g. menu structure and complexity, layout, positions) and interaction design (e.g. navigation concept, interaction path, interaction speed, system structure, etc.). Despite some HCI works now focusing on cross-cultural aspects in HCI, the research of cultural-dependent aspects of HCI, is still embryonic [42].

Cultural context is also vital for ELSs. As described before, cultural aspects are preferences and ways of behavior determined by the person's culture. Cultural context includes cultural background of a student and may have a great impact on their ability and efficiency to learn a given set of content [30]. A Culture Profile cannot be defined as a fixed or prescribed specification. The specification should be extended and dynamically improved based on the user's context. Research conducted on the effect and usability of culturally adapted web sites and interfaces has already shown enormous improvements in working efficiency [43].

Figure 3 presents the proposed model. The meta-model is an upper-level ontology describing abstract concepts like user, application, user profile, situation or date. The model depicts the different contextual dimensions. Each contextual dimension is represented by a different ontology such as a cultural ontology (with concepts like culture, nationality and values, language, etc.), education/pedagogical ontology (course, learning style, discipline, etc.), personal ontology (name, gender, navigational preference, birthday, etc.) or technological ontology (operating system, browser, network bandwidth, etc.). Finally, the object model will comprise instances describing the context of a particular user like a concrete name (John Smith), a course (Human Computer Interaction) or a particular language (English).

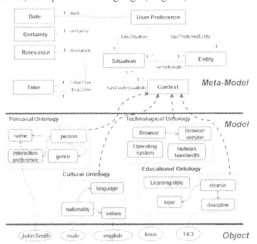

Figure 3. Example of a scenario-oriented model

5.2 Using context information to provide personalization

Among all the possible information gathered in the student model, we are specially interested in modeling **scenarios** because they change according to context. Scenarios may depend on the situation the student is now in and on external factors. Therefore, it is important to model in which context the student prefers something. The concreteness of scenarios helps students and teachers to develop a shared understanding of the proposed contextual information, and allows assimilating and representing complex idiosyncrasies of that they would otherwise misunderstand.

Scenarios are strongly related to the contextual background information and describe a simple perspective for execution of a situated action [44]. The term *situated action* emphasizes the interrelationship between an action and its context of execution and the notion that people's behavior is contextualized, i.e., the situation is a very important factor in determining what people will do. We define a **scenario** as a tuple containing an *entity* that the student prefers in a given *situation*, a *relevance* denoting the student's preference for that entity, a *certainty* representing how sure we are about the student having that preference and a date to indicate when that preference is stored:

Scenario = {entity, situation, relevance, certainty, date}

Situations are the key to include temporal aspects of context in a comprehensive ontology for context modeling, since they can be related to suitable notions of time [45]. As context varies during certain time intervals, it is vital to consider it within the concept of *Situation*. Examples of situations could be "John was at home using his notebook to read lesson number 3 of the Human Computer Interaction course" or "A Japanese Professor, who speaks English, is adding new exercises to the course Introduction to PHP using a high speed connection while she travels by train". Therefore, we define situation as a set of contextual information in a particular period of time:

Situation = {Context, initial time, final time}

An example of contextual information would be: "*The student named John is reading lesson number 3*". This is a description relating an entity (*the student John*) to another entity (*the lesson number 3*) via a property (*is reading*). We represent this contextual information as (Student.john, isReading, Lesson.lesson#3). We define the context as a set of triples composed by concepts, instances and relations between them. It is important to emphasize that the concepts and instances might belong to the same ontology or different context ontologies:

$$Context = \{(C_{a1}.I_{a1}, R_1, C_{b1}.I_{b1}), ..., (C_{aN}.I_{aN}, R_N, C_{bN}.I_{bN})\}; (C: concept, I: instance and R: relation)$$

To clarify these ideas, let us consider again John example. John prefers *reading visual learning* material in a situation when he is at home using his notebook to read lesson number 3 of the Human Computer Interaction course. Hence, the corresponding context1 will be:

Context1={ (Person.*John*, **locatedIn**, Location.*home*), (Person.*John*, **uses**, Device.*notebook*), (Person.*john*, **reads**, Lesson.*lesson#3*), (Lesson.*lesson#3*, **belongsTo**, Course.*HCI*)}; **Situation1**={ *Context1, 4:00PM, 7:00PM*} and **Scenario1**={User, Situation1, relevance.*high*, certainty.*95%*, date.*05-02-2010*}

5.3 Architecture for context-aware learning

The AdaptWeb® architecture has been extended in order to support context awareness, being adapted to specific scenarios, as mobility, social interaction, cultural-aware and device independence. The extended architecture in the already functioning architecture of AdaptWeb® is showed in the Figure 4. Beyond the new modules, is showed in the figure the three servers which were proposed to store and model the context data.

The User Interface Component is responsible to both obtain the user data, and present the adaptations processed by the environment. Actually, the AdaptWeb® environment already stores all the information related with the login, the chosen discipline and the author notifications to the students. So, it is possible to aggregate user context data to be obtained via interface, like the learning object actually in use and the path made by the student while using AdaptWeb®. Knowing this path, we can discover the occurrence of learning events that are important to starts an adaptation. These events are detected by the Context Collector/Detector and, depending on the event, notified to the Context Management Service.

The extended architecture is based on three servers that operate together to provide and manage contextualized data according to the student's scenarios. Each server manages specific data related to the user context, being respectively responsible for the storage and adaptation of (i) information about students (personal data, preferences, objectives, knowledge background, behavior, learning styles, cultural context, etc.), (ii) environmental context (information related to the user environment, tasks, activities, time interval, devices, location), and (iii) learning object's information (documents provided by the educational environment to its users for their learning).

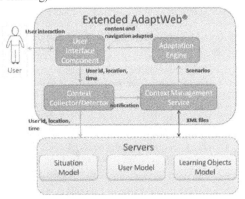

Figure 4. Extended architecture

The Context Management Service is responsible for analyzing the context managed by the servers, generating different scenarios that can be experienced by the students in a specific period. These scenarios are used to guide the adaptation (in the Adaptation Engine), and materialized in the interface rendered to the user. The main goals of the architecture are: (i) easily reuse of educational resources, since they will be adapted to the user scenario while the stored content remains the same, (ii) integration into the existing architecture, since the new architecture is supposed to take advantage of the existing functionalities and (iii) extensibility to other educational systems, using standard technologies. The personalization is possible with the combination of contextual data related to whom and where the user is, what he is doing and what does he needs to achieve his educational targets.

5.4 Examples

In this section we explain how we improved the personalization capabilities in an ELS. Particularly, we incorporated more characteristics of context-awareness, as some cultural aspects into the student profile, expecting the ELS to become more adaptive to the students and reusable. For each situation, the system is dynamically personalized depending on the context information available. Once the learning situation is modeled, it is important to associate one (or more) situation(s) to each learning activity in order to contextualize the student preferences. That is to say, in situation 1 the student prefers the activity A; on the contrary, when situation 2 holds, the user prefers the activity B. For example, Paul prefers to see visual learning material when he is reading about the course "artificial intelligence" and he has a high network connection. On the contrary, Paul prefers to listen to the teacher explanation when the course is "Algebra" and his network connection is slow. In order to explain the contextual adaptations developed, we start by describing different learning situations and then we detail how those situations trigger the corresponding contextual adaptation in AdaptWeb®. We show some examples of possible contexts in a Human-computer Interaction course. For a simplification purpose, we have a few variables: student's knowledge, subject, network connection, learning style, Language, LanguageLevel and Country.

In Context1, Joaquim is a student who lives in Brazil, his mother tongue is Portuguese and he has a low level knowledge in English. He is trying to learn about the subject "user-centered design", which is explained in English. He is doing exercises about that subject but unfortunately he is not doing well. In addition, he has a high speed network connection and according to Felder's model [9] he is active. As others students are on-line, the best action is to suggest talking to them through chat in order to solve the exercises and acquire knowledge about that subject. Thus, AdaptWeb shows the "chat" link in a different and highlighted color.

In another Context2, the student Marie is living in France and her mother tongue is French. Contrary to Joaquim, Marie has a high level knowledge in English. She is also learning the subject "user-centered design" and not having good results. She has a low speed network connection and her Felder's learning style is reflective. In consequence, AdaptWeb® sends a message by email to her teacher advising to contact the student and changes the order of the links, putting links related to videos material with low quality resolution in the end and disabling links related to videos material with high quality resolution (those who are large and difficult to see).

Finally, suppose another Context3 in which Joaquim (the same student in Context1) is now learning "usability" and he has obtained enough knowledge about that subject. At this time he is having a medium network connection and the same Felder's learning style. AdaptWeb® hides links to known subjects and highlights those pointing to new subjects. These contexts are formalized as following.

Context1 =
{(Student.*Joaquim*, **isLearning**, Subject.*userCenteredDesign*),
(Subject.*bayesianNetworks*, **isExplainedIn**, Language.*english*),
(Student. *Joaquim*, **hasUserKnowledge**, UserKnowledge.*bad*),
(Student. *Joaquim*, **hasConnection**, NetworkConnection.*high*),
(Student. *Joaquim*, **hasStyle**, LearningStyle.*active*),
(Student. *Joaquim*, **hasMotherTongue**, Language.*portuguese*),
(Student. *Joaquim*, **hasLanguageSkill**, Language.*english*),
(Student. *Joaquim*, **hasEnglishLanguageLevel**, LanguageLevel.*low*),
(Student. *Joaquim*, **isCitizenOf**, Country.*Brazil*)}

Context2 =
{(Student.*Marie*, **isLearning**, Subject. *userCenteredDesign*),
(Student. *Marie*, **hasUserKnowledge**, UserKnowledge.*bad*),
(Student. *Marie*, **hasConnection**, NetworkConnection.*low*),
(Student. *Marie*, **hasStyle**, LearningStyle.*reflective*),
(Student. *Marie*, **hasMotherTongue**, Language.*french*),
(Student. *Marie*, **hasLanguageSkill**, Language.*english*),
(Student. *Marie*, **hasEnglishLanguageLevel**, LanguageLevel.*high*),
(Student. *Marie*, **isCitizenOf**, Country.*France*)}

Context3 =
{(Student.*Joaquim*, **isLearning**, Subject.*usability*),
(Student.*Joaquim*, **hasUserKnowledge**, UserKnowledge.*good*),
(Student.*Joaquim*, **hasConnection**, NetworkConnection.*medium*),
(Student.*Joaquim*, **hasStyle**, LearningStyle.*active*),
(Student.*Joaquim*, **hasMotherTongue**, Language.*portuguese*),
(Student.*Joaquim*, **hasLanguageSkill**, Language.*english*),
(Student.*Joaquim*, **hasEnglishLanguageLevel**, LanguageLevel.*low*),
(Student. *Joaquim*, **isCitizenOf**, Country.*Brazil*)}

In summary, the adaptation mechanisms in AdaptWeb® are the following actions/recommendations:

Context₁ → "send notification to student only in Portuguese" + "show highlighted links"+ recommend learning objects and content about the same subject (same concept in the domain ontology) in Portuguese with a low level of difficulties and "highlighted chat";

Context$_2$ → "order links" + "hide or disable links" + "show highlighted links" + "recommend learning objects and content about the same subject written in English or French".

Context$_3$ → "hide already known content" + "recommend new learning objects and content about the next subject written in English or French". These situations are depicted in figure 5.

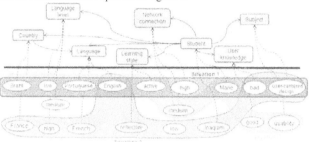

Figure 5. Partial view of the proposed modeling technique.

These contexts are used by the context management service within logical rules in order to predict future recommendations. This is an example where a prototypical context (Context$_i$) is used to generate new recommendation:

Context$_i$ = {(Student.*S*, **isLearning**, Subject.*s*), (Student.*S*, **isUsing**, LearningObject.*lo*), (Subject.*s*, **isExplainedIn**, Language.*l*), (Student.*S*, **hasUserKnowledge**, UserKnowledge.*bad*), (Student.*S*, **hasConnection**, NetworkConnection.*high*), (Student.*S*, **hasStyle**, LearningStyle.*active*), (Student.*S*, **hasMotherTongue**, Language.*l'*), (Student.*S*, **hasLanguageSkill**, Language.*l*), (Student.*S*, **hasEnglishLanguageLevel**, LanguageLevel.*low*), (Student.*S*, **isCitizenOf**, Country.*c*)}

If S is in Context$_i$ **then** recommend new LO such as LO.Subject= lo.subject and LO.language= S.motherTongue and LO.level is less than lo.level. A learning object (LO) is defined as *any entity, digital or non-digital, that may be used for learning, education or training* [46]. Nowadays, this model is being under evaluation with real students and actual courses in AdaptWeb® environment.

6. CONCLUSIONS

As seen in this paper, research in personalized ELS has proved that considering context leads to a better understanding and personalization [4]. Modeling the context leads to the design of systems that deliver more appropriate learning content and services to satisfy students' requirements and to be aware of situation changes by automatically adapting themselves to such changes [18]. Indeed, context modeling extends traditional user modeling techniques, by explicitly dealing with aspects we suppose to have a significant influence on the learning process assisted by an ELS, such as personal, educational, technological and notably cultural aspects. In this paper we have examined that some current ELSs either fail to provide learning experiences within rich contexts, or provide extremely contextualized content – when content is highly coupled with context information, barring their reuse in another context. One desired requirement in context modeling is to turn context as independent as possible from content so that the latter can be reused and adapted to context changes, allowing ELSs to dynamically compose, reuse and adapt educative content possibly provided by someone else.

This paper has described our approach to model context and culture for personalized ELS, representing explicitly the rich context as an extension of traditional student modeling. Our ultimate aim was to increment even more the actual systems personalization capabilities making use of ontologies to model the student's context and cultural aspects in different scenarios. Ontologies were used to model the contextual information, proposing a three level model to capture different levels of detail.

We are currently planning more experiments not only to obtain a better feedback from actual users but to validate our proposal as well. As e-learning progresses increasingly toward personalized configurations, it is becoming ever more important to have context models – particularly concerning cultural aspects of context - that can help to improve the benefits of their usability and thus also to improve the e-learning adequacy to learners. In this paper we present only one approach for context modeling. Therefore, it is yet a limited excursion into a territory which includes many other possible perspectives and paths to explore.

7. ACKNOWLEDGMENTS

This work has been partially supported by Conselho Nacional de Desenvolvimento Científico e Tecnológico - CNPq, Brazil, and by the projects AdaptSUR 022/07 (CAPES, Brazil) - 042/07 (Secyt, Argentina), and AdContext 547-07 (CAPES-COFECUB).

8. REFERENCES

[1] Eyharabide, V., Gasparini, I., Schiaffino, S., Pimenta, M., Amandi, A. 2009. Personalized e-learning environments: considering students' contexts. IFIP WCCE, v. 302, pp 48-57, Springer.

[2] Schiaffino, S., Amandi, A. 2009. Intelligent User Profiling. In Artificial Intelligence: An International Perspective – IFIP Book Series, Springer, 193 – 216.

[3] Horvitz, E.J., Breese, J.S., & Henrion, M. 1988. Decision Theory in Expert Systems and Artificial Intelligence. Intern. Journal of Approximate Reasoning, vol 2, pp 247-302.

[4] Brusilovsky, P., Millan, E. 2007. User Models for Adaptive Hypermedia and Adaptive Educational Systems. The Adaptive Web, 4321, 3-53.

[5] Goldberg, L. R. 1993. The structure of phenotypic personality traits. American Psychologist, 48, 26-34.

[6] Tarpin-Bernard, F., & Habieb-Mammar, H. 2005. Modeling elementary cognitive abilities for adaptive hypermedia presentation. User Modeling and User Adapted Interaction, 15, 5 459-495.

[7] Ford, N., Chen, S. Y. 2000. Individual Differences, Hypermedia Navigation, and Learning: An Empirical Study. Journal of Educational Multimedia and Hypermedia 9(4), 281-311.

[8] Felder, R., Silverman, L. 1988. Learning and teaching styles. Journal of Engineering Education, 78(7):674-681.

[9] Felder, R., Brent, R. 2005. Understanding Student Differences. J. Engr. Education, 94 (1), 57-72.

[10] Paredes, P., Rodriguez, P. 2002.Considering sensing-intuitive dimension to exposition-exemplification in adaptive sequencing. Proc. of AH2002 Conference, LNCS 2347, pp. 556-559. Springer.

[11] Bajraktarevic, N., Hall, W., Fullick, P. 2003. Incorporating learning styles in hypermedia environment: Empirical evaluation. Proc. of 14th ACM Conf. on Hypertext and Hypermedia (HT03), AH 2003.

[12] Stash, N. V., Cristea, A. I., De Bra, P. M. 2004. Authoring of learning styles in adaptive hypermedia: problems and solutions. Proc. of the 13th World Wide Web Conference, 114-123.

[13] Carver, C.A., Howard, R.A., Lane, W.D. 1999. Enhancing student learning through hypermedia courseware and incorporation of student learning styles. IEEE Trans. on Education, 42 (1) 33-38.

[14] Peña, C., Marzo, J., de la Rosa, J., Fabregat, R. 2002. Un sistema de tutoría inteligente adaptativo considerando estilos de aprendizaje. V Congreso Iberoamericano de informática educativa.

[15] Schiaffino, S., Garcia, P., & Amandi, A. 2008. eTeacher: Providing personalized assistance to e-learning students. Computers and Education, 51 (4), 1744 - 1754.

[16] Gasparini, I.; Bouzeghoub, Amel; Palazzo M. de Oliveira, J.; Pimenta, Marcelo S. 2010. An adaptive e-learning environment based on user s context. In: 3rd Intern. Workshop on Culturally-Aware Tutoring Systems (CATS) - 10th ITS, p. 1-12.

[17] Abarca, M., Alarcon, R., Barria, R., Fuller, D. 2006 Context-Based e-Learning Composition and Adaptation. OTM Workshops (2), On the Move to Meaningful Internet Systems, pp. 1976-1985.

[18] Bouzeghoub, A., Do, K., Lecocq, C. 2007. A Situation-Based Delivery of Learning Resources in Pervasive Learning. Creating New Learning Experiences on a Global Scale, 2nd European Conf. on Technology Enhanced Learning, pp. 450-456.

[19] Guzman, J., & Motz, R. 2005. Towards an Adaptive Cultural E-Learning System. LA-WEB '05: Proc. of the 3th Latin American Web Congress, IEEE Computer Society.

[20] Reinecke, K., & Bernstein, A. 2008. Predicting user interface preferences of culturally ambiguous users. CHI '08 extended abstracts on Human factors in computing systems, pp. 3261-3266.

[21] Sharples, M., Taylor, J., Vavoula, G. 2007. A Theory of Learning for the Mobile Age, The Sage Handbook of Elearning Research., pp. 221-247.

[22] Barbosa, D. N. F., Augustin, I., Barbosa, J. L. V. 2006 Proc. of the Fourth Annual IEEE International Conference on Pervasive Computing and Communications -Workshops.

[23] Lemlouma, T., Layaïda, N. 2004 Context-Aware Adaptation for Mobile Devices, IEEE International Conference on Mobile Data Management, pp. 106-111.

[24] Rosa, G.P.J, Ogata, H., Yano, Y. 2005. A multi-Model Approach for Supporting the Personalization of Ubiquitous Learning Applications, IEEE Intern. Workshop on Wireless and Mobile Technologies in Education, pp. 40-44.

[25] Yang, S. J. H., et al. 2006. Context Model and Context Acquisition for Ubiquitous Content Access in ULearning Environments", Proc. of the IEEE Intern. Conf. on Sensor Networks, Ubiquitous, and Trustworthy Computing, vol. 2, pp. 78-83.

[26] MOBIlearn, 2003, MOBIlearn final report,http://www.mobilearn.org

[27] Bouzeghoub, A., Do Ngoc, K. 2008 A situation based meta-data for describing pervasive learning objects. mLearn 2008: 1st Intern. Conf. on Mobile Learning.

[28] Yang, S. J. H. 2006 Context Aware Ubiquitous Learning Environments for Peer-to-Peer Collaborative Learning. In Educational Technology & Society, 9 (1), 188-201.

[29] Blanchard, E.G., Mizoguchi, R. 2008 Designing Culturally-Aware Tutoring Systems: Towards an Upper Ontology of Culture. Workshop on Culturally-Aware Tutoring Systems (CATS)-ITS.

[30] Chandramouli, K. and Stewart, C. and Brailsford, T. and Izquierdo, E. 2008 CAE-L: An Ontology Modelling Cultural Behaviour in Adaptive Education. 3th Intern. Workshop on Semantic Media Adaptation and Personalization, IEEE Computer Society, 183- 188.

[31] Motz, R., Guzmán, J., Deco, C., & Bender, C. 2005 Applying Ontologies to Educational Resources Retrieval driven by Cultural Aspects, Journal of Computer Science & Technology (JCS&T), vol. 5, no. 4, pp 279 - 284.

[32] Sieg, A; Mobasher, B; Burke, R. 2007 Representing Context in Web Search with Ontological User Profiles. LNCS, Modeling and Using Context, v. 4635, pp 439-452, Springer.

[33] Reinecke, K., Reif, G., Bernstein, A. 2007 Cultural User Modeling With CUMO: An Approach to Overcome the Personalization Bootstrapping Problem. Workshop on Cultural Heritage on the Semantic Web, ISWC.

[34] Hofstede, G. 1991 Cultures and Organizations: Software of the Mind. New York: McGraw-Gill.

[35] Reinecke, K. and Bernstein, A . 2009 Tell Me Where You've Lived, and I'll Tell You What You Like: Adapting Interfaces to Cultural Preferences. Proc. of the 17th Intern. Conf. on User Modeling, Adaptation, and Personalization, 185-196.

[36] Dockhorn Costa, P., Almeida, J., Pires, L., van Sinderen, M. 2007 Situation Specification and Realization in Rule-Based Context-Aware Applications. Distributed Applications and Interoperable Systems, 7th IFIP WG 6.1, pp. 32-47.

[37] Shen Yang, S., Huang, A., Chen, R., Tseng, S.-S., & Yen-Shih. 2006 Context Model and Context Acquisition for Ubiquitous Content Access in ULearning Environments. IEEE International Conf. on Sensor Networks, Ubiquitous, and Trustworthy Computing, 2, pp. 78-83.

[38] Eyharabide, V., Amandi, A. 2008 Semantic spam filtering from personalized ontologies. JWE - Journal of Web Engineering, Rinton Press, 7 (2), 158-176.

[39] Eyharabide, V., Amandi, A. 2007 An Ontology-Driven Conceptual Model of User Profiles. In Proc. of ASAI07.

[40] Pawlowski, J. M. 2008 Culture Profiles: Facilitating Global Learning and Knowledge Sharing. The 16th ICCE, pp 537- 544.

[41] Bossard, A. 2008 Ontology-Based Cultural Personalization in Mobile Applications. Thesis (Master Degree), Department of Informatics, University of Zurich.

[42] Zaharias, P. 2008 Cross-Cultural Differences in Perceptions of – leaning Usability: An Empirical Investigation. Intern. Journal of Technology and Human Interaction, v. 4, issue 3, IGI Global.

[43] Reinecke, K and Bernstein, A. 2007 Culturally Adaptive Software: Moving Beyond Internationalization, HCI.

[44] Suchman, L.A. 1987. Plans and Situated Actions: The Problem of Human-Machine Communication. Cambridge: Cambridge Press.

[45] Dockhorn Costa, P., Guizzardi, G., Almeida, J., Pires, L., & van Sinderen, M. 2006 Situations in Conceptual Modeling of Context. EDOCW '06: Proc. 10th IEEE on Intern. Enterprise Distributed Object Computing Conf. Workshops. IEEE Computer Society.

[46] IEEE. Draft Standard for Learning Object Metadata. 2002 Available:http://ltsc.ieee.org/wg12/files/LOM_1484_12_1_v1_Final _Draft.pdf

Reviewing the research on
distance education and e-learning

Brad Mehlenbacher, Krista Holstein, Brett Gordon, Khalil Khammar

College of Education
North Carolina State University
Raleigh, NC 27695-7801
1.919.515.6242
brad_m@unity.ncsu.edu

ABSTRACT

This paper will provide insight into the current emphasis of research on distance education and e-learning. The review is organized by three intersecting activities. First, we informally collected and reviewed approximately 300 peer-reviewed journals for articles published on distance education and instruction and technology broadly defined [30]. Second, we read and reviewed the numerous meta-analyses of distance education, multimedia, e-learning, and collaborative computing published over the last fifteen years [1-2, 4-6, 17, 25-27, 31, 33, 35]. Third, we performed our own meta-analysis of the abstracts of articles published in 10 peer-reviewed journals on distance learning and e-learning. Our goal in all these activities was to generate a list of significant topics or themes contained in publications about distance education and e-learning, in part to demonstrate the lack of consistent terminology.

Categories and Subject Descriptors

K. [**Computing Milieux**], K.3. [**Computers and Education**], K.3.1. [**Computer Uses in Education**].

General Terms

Design, Documentation, Human Factors, Theory.

Keywords

Distance education, Distance learning, Education, E-learning.

INTRODUCTION

ACM SIGDOC has a long history of encouraging and supporting multidisciplinary research. Indeed, the considerable interest in distance education (DE) and e-learning represents a productive area for researchers interested in the design and evaluation of instructional and communication environments. Since 2000, ACM SIGDOC conference proceedings have included 19 papers focused on online course development, design, and assessment.

The strong conceptual relationship between the design of performance materials and information and the design of instruction aimed at long- and short-term learning is not entirely surprising. The earliest studies informing the field of human-computer interaction, after all, were novice-expert studies of humans playing chess and solving complex mathematics and physics problems [37]. We suggest that other design and learning issues that communication designers can draw from DE and e-learning research include, for example, the role of mentoring in the profession, project-based work, information retrieval behaviors and strategies, information content management creation and evaluation, use of alternative media for communication and group work, information presentation strategies, and online genre design (tutorials, simulations, etc.).

It is important to acknowledge that we are aware of the many criticisms of research carried out on DE and e-learning, that is, that it tends to focus too much on the differences between face-to-face and online instruction, that it employs flawed empirical designs, and that it tends to be descriptive rather than experimental. As well, Orrill, Hannafin, and Glazer [32] have asserted that "Literally thousands of studies related to computers and learning have been published during the past three decades. The problem has been one of making sense of the enormous, and growing, body of available research" (p. 335). And Nichols [31] adds that "… the body of literature appears fragmented and there are few common terms used consistently." We address these issues in our conclusions in addition to summarizing the major significant topics or themes in the DE and e-learning research.

Collins and Berge's [13] description of e-learning reveals numerous interrelated topic areas of clear interest to both instructional and communication designers:

- Mentoring, such as advising and guiding students;
- Project-based instruction, either within the classroom or in projects involving community, national, or international problem-solving;
- Guest lecturing, which promotes interaction between students and persons in the larger community;
- Didactic teaching, that is, supplying course content, posting assignments, or other information germane to course work;
- Retrieval of information from online information archives;
- Course management, for example, advising, delivery of course content, evaluation, collecting and returning assignments;
- Public conferencing, such as discussion lists;
- Interactive chat, used to brainstorm with teachers or peers and to maintain social relationships;

- Personal networking and professional growth and such activities as finding persons with similar interests on scholarly discussion lists;
- Facilitating collaboration;
- Individual and group presentations;
- Peer review of writing, or projects involving peer counseling;
- Practice and experience using emerging technologies that may be intrinsically useful in today's society; and
- Computer-based instruction, such as tutorials, simulations, and drills (pp. 3-4).

Chapman [11] emphasizes the features of contemporary applications for distance education:

- Ability to coordinate course registration, scheduling, learning programs;
- Resource management, content integration, repositories;
- Material distribution, reporting;
- Online conferencing, collaborative tools, and;
- Tracking student accomplishments, learning assessment, learning testing, profiling (pp. 1151-1152).

Relan and Gillani [34], emphasize the rich online educational spaces that operate

- As a resource for the identification, evaluation, and integration of a variety of information;
- As a medium of collaboration, conversation, discussions, exchange, and communication of ideas;
- As an international platform for the expression and contribution of artistic and cognitive understandings and meanings, and;
- As a medium for participating in simulated experiences, apprenticeships, and cognitive partnerships (p. 43).

One way that publications in instructional and communication design differ, however, is in the development of the amount of research devoted to the research. Research journals related to distance education and e-learning have enjoyed unprecedented development over the last two decades, from 4 peer-reviewed journals prior to 1992, to 10 by 1998, to 29 by 2005. The number of journals related to educational, instructional, and communication technology, too, have increased exponentially.

Five journals devoted to the area existed before 1985 (*Computers and Education*, the *International Journal of Instructional Media*, the *Journal of Research on Technology in Education* [originally named the *Journal of Research on Computing in Education*], *Learning and Leading with Technology*, and *Media, Culture, and Society*), 16 existed by 1995, and, between 1996 and the present, those 16 grew to 45 peer-reviewed journals. For this reason, we begin with a summary of peer-reviewed journals that routinely publish on the topic of distance education and e-learning (see Table 1).

Table 1: Sample of 50 peer-reviewed journals that publish on distance education and e-learning

Emphasis	Peer-reviewed journals
Distance Education & E-learning	• American Journal of Distance Education* • Asian Journal of Distance Education* • British Journal of Educational Technology • Canadian Journal of Learning and Technology • Computers and Composition • Computers and Education • Distance Education* • E-Learning* • E-Learning and Education* • Education and Information Technologies • Educational Media International • Educational Technology Research & Development • Educause Quarterly • European Journal of Open, Distance and E-Learning* • First Monday • Indian Journal of Open Learning* • Interactive Educational Multimedia • Interactive Learning Environments* • Interactive Multimedia Electronic • International Journal of Distance Education Technologies • International Journal of Education and Development using ICT • International Journal of Educational Technology • International Journal of Instructional Media • International Journal of Instructional Technology and Distance Learning* • International Journal of Learning Technology • International Journal of Web-based Learning and Teaching Technologies • International Journal on E-Learning • International Review of Research in Open and Distance Learning • Internet and Higher Education • Journal of Asynchronous Learning Networks • Journal of Computer-Mediated Communication • Journal of Computing in Higher Education • Journal of Distance Education • Journal of Educational Computing Research • Journal of Educational Multimedia and Hypermedia • Journal of Educational Technology and Society • Journal of Information Technology Education • Journal of Instruction Delivery Systems • Journal of Interactive Instruction Development • Journal of Interactive Learning Research • Journal of Interactive Media in Education • Journal of Online Learning and Teaching* • Journal of Research on Technology in Education • Journal of Technology, Learning, and Assessment • Learning, Media & Technology • Online Journal of Distance Learning Administration • Open Learning: The Journal of Open and Distance Learning • Quarterly Review of Distance Education • Technology, Instruction, Cognition and Learning • Technology, Pedagogy and Education

LITERATURE REVIEW

Describing the current state of research on distance education and e-learning, Orrill, Hannafin, and Glazer [32] have asserted that "Literally thousands of studies related to computers and learning have been published during the past three decades. The problem has been one of making sense of the enormous, and growing, body of available research" (p. 335). Moreover, many of these publications are case studies that are difficult to generalize from one context to another. Berge and Mrozowski [4] in their review of research in distance education during the 1990s found that almost 75 percent of the research involved descriptive studies. So too Nichols [31] laments that "… the vast bulk of literature in eLearning is practice-based and is typically presented in a descriptive format" and that "… the body of literature appears fragmented and there are few common terms used consistently."

Moreover, reviews of the non-descriptive distance education research are not encouraging. Dillon and Gabbard [17], in their summary of the research on hypermedia versus pencil-and-paper learning outcomes, note, "Taking the literature as a whole, it is disappointing to report that statistical analyses and research methods are frequently flawed…. Failure to control important variables for comparative purposes, lack of adequate pretesting of learners, use of multiple t tests for post hoc data, and even the tendency to claim support for hypotheses when the data fail to show statistically significant results all suggest that the basis for drawing conclusions from this literature is far from sturdy" (p. 345).

Phipps and Merisotis [33], noting that there is "a good deal of research dealing with distance education," also admit in the forward of their report that their central goal in performing a review of that research is to identify if distance learning is "as good as traditional education" (p. i). Their analytic approach for reviewing the literature on distance education consisted of reviewing more than 40 of "the most important and salient of these works" published between 1990 and 1998, in addition to "several hundred articles, essays, and other writings published in major journals on distance learning" (p. 11). Phipps and Merisotis [33] are never more specific than that about the details of their analysis, proceeding to organize their findings in terms of effectiveness of distance learning, key shortcomings, and gaps requiring further investigation.

Allen, Bourhis, Burrell, and Mabry [1] used the search terms "distance learning," "distance education," and "satisfaction" on the SocioInfo (Index for the field of Sociology), ComIndex (communication publications), Psychlit (psychology publications), and the Educational Resource Information Clearinghouse (ERIC), in addition to conducting a complete review of *Distance Education* and the *American Journal of Distance Education* to identify approximately 450 peer-reviewed articles for analysis. Although their primary goal was to compare distance education courses to face-to-face ones, the authors also identified several research themes that characterized the corpus of articles under review. Topics reviewed included the effects of channel of communication (video, audio, and written) and of the presence or absence of interaction in setting (none, one-way limited or full interactive). Not surprisingly, Allen, et al. [1] found that the greater the channel of communication and instructor-student interaction, the greater the effect on student satisfaction.

Noting that Dillon and Gabbard [17] focused their research review primarily on "learner issues with hypermedia" (p. 5), Berge and Mrozowski [4] reviewed distance education research from 1990 through 1999. The authors examined literature from four journals (*The American Journal of Distance Education*, *Distance Education*, *The Journal of Distance Education*, and *Open Learning*) as well as dissertations from the decade in interest. Of the 1,419 articles and dissertations found, 890 (62.7%) were identified as research articles, based on Phipps and Merisotis' [33] categories of research methodology (descriptive research, case study, correlational research, and experimental research). In addition to classifying each research article under one of Phipps and Merisotis' [33] categories of research methodology, Berge and Mrozowski [4] classified research under one of Sherry's [36] ten research issues, based on "four main underlying research issues in the field: learner characteristics and needs, media influence on the instructional process, access issues, and the changing roles of teacher, site facilitator, and student" [Berge & Mrozowski, 4, pp. 6-7]. Berge and Mrozowski [4] found that most researchers used descriptive research, rather than experimental or correlational research. In addition, pedagogical themes dominated the literature, while research considering equity and accessibility, operational issues, and policy and management issues was rare.

Bernard, Abrami, Lour and Borokhovski [6] analyzed and assessed distance education (DE) literature from 1985 through 2002. After examining over 5,000 abstracts, 862 articles were gathered using electronic and manual searches of distance education journals and conference proceedings as well as reference lists of prior DE reviews. The authors performed the searches using terms such as "distance learning", "distance education" or "virtual university" in addition to the one of the following: "traditional," "lecture," "face-to-face" or "comparison" (pp. 178-179). Of the articles found, only 232 articles (26.9%) met the authors' inclusion criteria: "(1) the study had to involve both a classroom and a DE condition; (2) the study had to have either an achievement, attitude or retention measure; (3) the study was dated from 1985 to 2002; and (4) the study had to contain enough statistical information to calculate … or estimate an effect size" (p. 179). Despite meeting the inclusion criteria, these articles lacked methodological quality and vital research information. The authors concluded that researchers need to be more explicit about their research design, and different methodological characteristics affect research results as well as variation of effect sizes.

Larreamendy-Joerns and Leindhardt [25] aimed to chart critiques and concerns related to college-level online education by examining educational literature on the topic. The authors review the history of distance education as seen through three historical backgrounds: Democratization, Liberal Education, and Educational Quality. A key point the authors make is that online education forces instructors to be more explicit with their intentions and pedagogical goals and practices. The design of the online class is critical to its success and efficiency and organization are highly valued.

Bernard, Abrami, Lou, Borokhovski, Wade, Wozney, Wallet, Fiset, and Huang [5] analyze comparative distance education literature between the years of 1985-2002. They examined the comparative literature in regard to the variety of conditions of the studies' features and outcomes that were publically available.

The authors did find evidence that classroom instruction and distance education are comparable and they concluded that most of the distance education research they examined was of poor-quality and lacked internal validity. Their study both critiques but it also contributes a view of the relationship between pedagogy and media and a view of the differences that exist in all measures between synchronous (group-based) and asynchronous (individual-based) distance education.

In addition to collecting peer-reviewed journals that contain research on distance education and e-learning and reviewing articles that contain meta-analyses of research on the topic, we are also exploring methods for categorizing the journal research in novel ways. This research is in its preliminary stages and is linked to developments in social bookmarking and tagging [19, 38].

KEYWORD ANALYSIS OF JOURNALS

We performed a keyword analysis of the abstracts of 10 peer-reviewed journals devoted to distance learning research. The journals we reviewed have asterisks next to them in Table 1. In particular, as a group, we focused on re-occurring themes and topics in the research on distance education and e-learning. To perform this keyword analysis, we created a spreadsheet with the keywords from the journals. Then we generated a concordance on these keywords to determine the most commonly occurring keywords and topics. According to the resulting concordance, topics that received considerable research attention included social networking, learning, e-learning, computer-assisted instruction, the Internet in education, web-based instruction, and online courses. There were a total of 725 unique keyword phrases of which 612 occurred only once. Some of the most frequently occurring keyword phrases are summarized in Table 2.

Table 2: Frequently occurring keyword phrases found in peer-reviewed distance learning journals

Keywords	Frequency
Social Networking	23
Learning (All types)	169
E-learning	28
Distance Education	32
Computer-Assisted Instruction	8
Internet in Education	11
Web-Based Instruction, Online Courses	25

Social Networking

Social networking applications are more than simply information exchange spaces but instead allow users to create, revise, combine, display, present, and share objects across platforms. One way of meaningfully organizing social networking applications, therefore, is by describing the content emphasized by particular environments. Social networking applications can focus on connecting people via pictures, profiles, and user-generated texts (e.g., Facebook, LinkedIn, MySpace), by sharing, evaluating, and annotating news or Internet links (e.g., Del.icio.us, Digg, Diigo), by exchanging personal news and texts (e.g., Bebo, Blogger), by organizing people around schedules (e.g., Doodle), by creating shared documents, spreadsheets, or presentations (e.g., Etherpad), or by sharing audio, video, or pictorial (Flikr, Google Docs, Jing, Photobucket).

Currently, research on social networking applications has tended to cast a wide net on the variations and emphases of the tools described. Thus, articles on social networking often distinguish between blogs, content tag sites, mashups, photo- and video-sharing spaces, virtual worlds, wikis, and so on [14, 16].

Technology-supported sociability has been further enhanced by the emergence of mobile phones that, as de Souza e Silva [15] summarizes, are popular in part because they support "... *the possibility of moving through space and the ability to be connected to other people while on the move*" (p. 114). Research on the relationship between instruction and social networking has increased exponentially over the last several years [8, 14].

Learning

General human learning occurs anytime learners interact with their environment and, more specifically, we tend to assume learning is facilitated best when an instructor designs or presents learning tasks to a learner or learners, an act or event that requires social dynamics and that assumes a surrounding learning environment and artifacts. Learning occurs at an individual, tacit, or perceptual level but our emphasis is on learning that is explicit and that can be articulated after the fact [28]. Numerous excellent resources provide comprehensive overviews of learning [3, 12]. Mehlenbacher [29] provides a summary of alternative views of the same learning processes depending on ones methodological orientation. Approaches include biophysical, behavioral, cognitive, organizational, social, cultural, or historical (p. 144). Bransford, Brown, Cocking, et al. [10] have published one of the most readable overviews of 20 years of research in the area.

E-learning

A survey of 526 North American companies reported by Bersin [7] suggests that e-learning makes up "33 percent of all workplace training, up from 29 percent in 2004 and 24 percent in 2003" (p. 20). And Kenney, Hermens, and Clarke [23] note that the United States is particularly well suited nationally for e-learning given its existing educational systems, free markets, and cultural faith in high technology. E-learning tends to be the favorite term of business and corporate authors [9].

Distance Education

Instruction in any form (except perhaps on-campus courses because distance is meant to contrast with this type of learning, distributed across time or space (e.g., horseback, mail, telephone, audio-recording media, etc.). Gunawardena and McIsaac [20, p. 356] mark the beginning of DE as the late 1800s with the advent of the University of Chicago's first correspondence program. Penn State dates the beginning of its first correspondence program as 1892, supported by Rural Free Delivery along with the University of Wisconsin and the University of Chicago. Others mark the true beginnings of DE as being less than twenty years ago, driven by a confluence of forces including the rapid development of telecommunications technologies, globalization, and emerging social perspectives toward knowledge making and learning [21]. This lack of consensus demonstrates the difficulty in achieving consistency among commonly used terms as discussed by Nichols [31].

Computer-Assisted Instruction

Any instruction or learning created for the computer, including Internet- or Web-based instruction. Tends to be dominated by single machine perspective and is, therefore, less common with the advent of Web-based instruction but, technically, since the Internet and the WWW *connect* computers, one might argue that these distributed realities subsume lone computers that support instruction and learning. Today, modifying "instruction" with "computer-assisted" seems somewhat odd given that almost all instruction requires some form of computer assistance to exist (if only in the form of "lecture notes").

Internet in Education

Initially, the Internet's support of distributed electronic communication and collaboration represented the focus of studies of the role of the Internet in Education. Lanham [24] has published a particularly important chapter on the challenges facing higher education during the next several years due to incredible changes in high-technology infrastructure. More recently, any activity that supports instructor-learner or learner-learning institution interaction falls under the heading of the Internet in Education. That includes, for example, email, 1st and 2nd generation Internet environments (Websites, forms), and CMS/LMS environments (Blackboard, Moodle).

Web-Based Instruction, Online Courses

Instruction and learning that is possible, that occurs and is augmented by the World Wide Web. This includes most applications encompassed by the Internet in education, excluding applications for managing registration, records-keeping, and the business of learning institutions. Synonyms for web-based instruction also include e-learning, online teaching and learning, distance education, distance learning, Web-based training, computer-assisted learning, computer-assisted learning, flexible learning, and technology-rich instruction. Certainly, the results of our concordance suggest that Web-based instruction and online courses are used interchangeably. Botkin and Kaipa [9] observe that, although academics tend to prefer distance education to business's e-learning, both use Web-based learning (p. 410). These etymological debates are to be taken seriously given that it is difficult for any field of research to develop cohesive programs without being able to find agreement on the terminology that defines its object or objects of study. For this reason, interpreting the Web in WBI as referring to the global network of multimedia information that is readily accessible for communication broadens the grain-size of our analysis and encourages strengthened dialogue with researchers interested in instruction and learning with technology in general.

CONCLUSIONS

This paper has provided an overview of the current state of research on distance education and e-learning. The review is organized by three intersecting activities. First, we informally collected and reviewed approximately 300 peer-reviewed journals for articles published on distance education and instruction and technology broadly defined [30]. In this paper, we presented an excerpted 50 journal names that should be useful to researchers interested in distance education and e-

learning. Second, we read and reviewed the numerous meta-analyses of distance education, multimedia, e-learning, and collaborative computing published over the last fifteen years [1-2, 4-6, 17, 25-27, 31, 33, 35]. This review focused on the breadth and quality of the research on distance education as well as issues that overlap between instructional and communication design. Third, we performed our own meta-analysis of the abstracts of articles published in 10 peer-reviewed journals on distance learning and e-learning. Our goal in all these activities was to generate a list of significant topics or themes contained in publications about distance education and e-learning.

We agree, with Kanuka and Conrad [22], that themes and topics in distance education will continue to be difficult to establish as long as terminology in the field remains undefined. To the growing synonyms for distance education, Kanuka and Conrad [22] add numerous "e-terms" including for example computer-based learning, distance learning, distributed learning, Web-based learning, virtual classrooms, hybrid learning, digital collaboration, mixed mode delivery, and blended learning, and warn that "As educators, we must resist the seduction of catchy labels and the temptation to mark our intellectual territory by layering new jargon over the old. We must name the enterprise in ways that meaningfully, clearly, and responsibly reflect the function of each particular teaching and learning process and are thereby acceptable to both the academic community and those participants whose engagement in distance education reflects its state of growth and innovation" (p. 392).

While our meta-analysis work is still in its preliminary stages, our hope is that, ultimately, keyword and article analysis will help highlight areas or issues that are gaining research attention over time.

REFERENCES

[1] Allen, M., Bourhis, J., Burrell, N., & Mabry, E. (2002). Comparing student satisfaction with distance education to traditional classrooms in higher education: A meta-analysis. *American Journal of Distance Education, 16* (2), 83-97.

[2] Álvarez, I., & Kilbourn, B. (2002). Mapping the information society literature: Topics, perspectives, and root metaphors. *First Monday, 7* (1) Available online: http://firstmonday.org/htbin/cgiwrap/bin/ojs/index.php/fm/article/view/922/844

[3] Anderson, J. R. (1995). *Learning and Memory: An Integrated Approach*. NY, NY: Wiley.

[4] Berge, Z. L., & Mrozowski, S. (2001). Review of research in distance education, 1990 to 1999. *American Journal of Distance Education, 15* (3), 5-19.

[5] Bernard, R. M., Abrami, P. C., Lou, Y., Borokhovski, E., Wade, A., Wozney, L., Wallet, P. A., Fiset, M., & Huang, B. (2004). How does distance education compare with classroom instruction? A meta-analysis of the empirical literature. *Review of Educational Research, 74* (3), 379–439.

[6] Bernard, R., Abrami, P., Lou, Y., & Borokhovski, E. (2004). A methodological morass? How we can improve quantitative research in distance education. *Distance Education, 25* (2), 175-198.

[7] Bersin, J. (2006). E-Learning evolves into mature training tool. *T+D, April, 20.*

[8] Boston, I. (2009). Racing towards academic social networks. *On the Horizon, 17* (3), 218-225.

[9] Botkin, J., and Kaipa, P. (2004). Putting it all together: A business perspective on Web-based learning. In T. M. Duffy and J. R. Kirkley (eds.), *Learner-Centered Theory and Practice in Distance Education: Cases from Higher Education* (pp. 409–423). Mahwah, NJ: Lawrence Erlbaum.

[10] Bransford, J., Brown, A. L., Cocking, R. R., and National Research Council (2000). *How People Learn: Brain, Mind, Experience, and School.* Washington, D.C.: National Academy P.

[11] Chapman, D. (2005). Introduction to Learning Management Systems. In C. Howard, J. V. Boettcher, L. Justice, K. Schenk, P. L. Rogers, and G. A. Berg (eds.), *Encyclopedia of Distance Learning* (pp. 1149–1155). Hershey, PA: Idea Group Reference.

[12] Clark, R. C. (2005). Multimedia learning in e-courses. In R. E. Mayer (ed.), *The Cambridge Handbook of Multimedia Learning* (pp. 589-616). Cambridge, England: Cambridge UP.

[13] Collins, M. P., & Berge, Z. L. (1995). Computer-communication and the online classroom in higher education. In Z. L. Berge and M. P. Collins (eds.), *Computer-Mediated Communication and the Online Classroom*, volume 2 (pp. 1-10). Cresskill, NJ: Hampton P.

[14] Dawley, L. (2009). Social networking knowledge construction: Emerging virtual world pedagogy. *On the Horizon, 17* (2), 109-121.

[15] de Souza e Silva, A. (2006). Re-conceptualizing the mobile phone — From telephone to collective interfaces. *Australian Journal of Emerging Technologies and Society, 4* (2), 108-127.

[16] Dearstyne, B. W. (2007). Blogs, mashups, & wikis. *The Information Management Journal, July/August*, 24-33.

[17] Dillon, A., & Gabbard, R. (1998). Hypermedia as an educational technology: A review of the quantitative research literature on learner comprehension, control, and style. *Review of Educational Research, 68* (3), 322-349.

[18] Downes, S. (2004). Educational blogging. *eLearn Magazine, October 17.* Available online: http://www.elearnmag.org/subpage.cfm?section=articles&&article=29-1

[19] Estellés, E., del Moral, E., & González, F. (2010). Social bookmarking tools as facilitators of learning and research collaborative processes: The Diigo case. *Interdisciplinary Journal of E-Learning and Learning Objects, 6*, 175-191.

[20] Gunawardena, C. N., & McIsaac, M. S. (2004). Distance education. In D. H. Jonassen (ed.), *Handbook of Research on Educational Communications and Technology* (2nd ed., pp. 355–395). Mahwah, NJ: Lawrence Erlbaum.

[21] Hanna, D. E. (1998). Higher education in an era of digital competition: Emerging organizational models. *Journal of Asynchronous Learning, 2* (1), 66–95.

[22] Kanuka, H., & Conrad, D. (2003). The name of the game: Why "Distance Education" says it all. *Quarterly Review of Distance Education, 4* (4), 385-393.

[23] Kenney, J., Hermens, A., & Clarke, T. (2004). The political economy of e-learning educational development: Strategies, standardisation, and scalability. *Education and Training, 46* (6/7), 370–379.

[24] Lanham, R. A. (2002). The audit of virtuality: Universities in the attention economy. In S. Brint (ed.), *The Future of the City of Intellect: The Changing American University* (pp. 159–180). Stanford, CA: Stanford UP.

[25] Larreamendy-Joerns, J., & Leinhardt, G. (2006). Going the distance with online education. *Review of Educational Research, 76* (4), 567–605.

[26] Lee, Y., Driscoll, M. P., & Nelson, D. W. (2004). The past, present, and future of research in distance education: Results from a content analysis. *American Journal of Distance Education, 18* (4), 225-241.

[27] Liao, Y.-K. C. (1999). Effects of hypermedia on students' achievement: A meta-analysis. *Journal of Educational Multimedia and Hypermedia, 8* (3), 255-277.

[28] Mayer, R. E. (2001). *Multimedia Learning.* New York: Cambridge University Press.

[29] Mehlenbacher, B. (2008). Communication design and theories of learning. *SIGDOC'08: The 26th ACM International Conference on Design of Communication Proceedings.* Lisbon, Portugal: ACM, 139-146

[30] Mehlenbacher, B. (2010). *Instruction and Technology: Designs for Everyday Learning.* Cambridge, MA: MIT P.

[31] Nichols, M. (2003). A theory for e-learning. *Journal of Educational Technology & Society, 6* (2). Available Online: http://www.ifets.info/journals/6_2/1.html

[32] Orrill, C. H., Hannafin, M. J., & Glazer, E. M. (2004). Disciplined inquiry and the study of emerging technology. In D. H. Jonassen (ed.), *Handbook of Research on Educational Communications and Technology* (2nd ed., pp. 335–353). Mahwah, NJ: Lawrence Erlbaum.

[33] Phipps, R., & Merisotis, J. (1999). *What's the Difference? A Review of Contemporary Research on the Effectiveness of Distance Learning in Higher Education.* Institute for Higher Education Policy. Available online: http://www.ihep.org/assets/files/publications/s-z/WhatDifference.pdf

[34] Relan, A., & Gillani, B. B. (1997). Web-based instruction and the traditional classroom: Similarities and differences. In B. H. Khan (ed.), *Web-Based Instruction* (pp. 41–46). Englewood Cliffs, NJ: Educational Technology Publications.

[35] Roblyer, M. D., & Knezek, G. A. (2003). New millennium research for educational technology: A call for a national research agenda. *Journal of Research on Technology in Education, 36* (1), 60–71.

[36] Sherry, L. (1996). Issues in distance learning. *International Journal of Educational Telecommunications, 1* (4), 337-365.

[37] Simon, H. A. (1979). *Models of Thought.* New Haven, CT: Yale UP.

[38] Weinberger, D. (2007). *Everything is Miscellaneous: The Power of the New Digital Disorder.* NY, NY: Time.

Designing the User Experience in iTV-based Interactive Learning Objects

Diogo S. Martins, Lílian S. Oliveira, Maria da Graça C. Pimentel
Universidade de São Paulo, São Carlos-SP, Brazil
{diogosm,lilianso,mgp}@icmc.usp.br

ABSTRACT

This paper reports the design of the user experience in EducaTV, an architecture for the association of value-added interactive content to educational TV programs. To properly tackle the unique user interface (UI) challenges posed by educational TV applications, EducaTV was designed through User-Centered Design (UCD) principles with extensive evaluation along the process. We report the main issues of access and findings obtained throughout the design process. Our findings revealed that iDTV applications must provide strategies to signalize interactive content without being obtrusive. Additionally, the context of the users must be taken into account, for instance by providing functionalities to enable collaborative interaction in learning groups, as well as mobilization affordances to encompass the different levels of technological literacy. Moreover, a recurrent issue that affected user experience was the proper synchronization of the live program with the interactive content.

Categories and Subject Descriptors

H.5 [**Information interfaces and presentation**]: User Interfaces—*Prototyping, User-centered design*

General Terms

Design, evaluation, multimedia

Keywords

Interactive TV, interface design, e-learning, distance education

1. INTRODUCTION

Considering that TV is a widely deployed technology, fighting the digital divide is seen as one of the potential benefits offered by interactive Digital TV (iDTV). Among the initiatives to provide digital inclusion, educational applications stand out as means to provide novel experiences in scenarios of distance education and e-learning. But such constrained devices impose limitations on user interaction.

Interaction with TVs is characterized by dependence on TV remotes (offering limited interactivity), shared resources (e.g. remotes) while watching programs in groups, multiple levels of attention (e.g. whether the TV is used as background sound or with full attention), interaction in situations of leisure and relaxation (e.g. living rooms), distance from the screen, among others [6]. Considering these challenges, this paper reports the EducaTV approach for authoring and execution of interactive educational multimedia documents in iDTV, enabling the association of value-added interactive content to educational programs. To properly tackle the unique user interface (UI) challenges posed by educational TV applications, EducaTV was designed through User-Centered Design (UCD) [11] principles with extensive evaluation along the process.

The EducaTV architecture is divided into back-end (which includes the content data model and the application logic) and front-end (user interface). Regarding the content model, materials are modeled as XML-based learning objects. To abstract the application logic and the interaction with learning objects, EducaTV comprises a MVC (Model, View, Controller) architecture to promote the portability and digital convergence of the solution. In this paper we report design issues of the architecture with emphasis in the front-end.

The usability of the front-end was extensively validated with case studies on the subject of informal and continuing education in defensive driving. Both user studies to gather requirements (e.g. interviews, questionnaires) and evaluations to assess usability (e.g. heuristic inspection, cognitive walkthrough, user test) were performed during the iterative design. Based on gathered requirements, different e-learning scenarios (e.g. government advertisement, individual learning at home and group learning at formation centers) were specified and used as framework to conduct evaluations of prototypes with real users and interaction designers.

Due to the lack of consolidated UI metaphors or design principles specially suited for iDTV, considerable challenges must be tackled when designing for this platform. Our evaluation results revealed that iDTV applications must provide strategies to signalize interactive content without being obtrusive. Additionally, the context of the users must be taken into account, for instance by providing functionalities to enable collaborative interaction in learning groups, as well as mobilization affordances to encompass the different levels of technological literacy. Moreover, a recurrent issue that affected user experience was the proper synchronization of the live program with the interactive content.

In the remaining of this paper, Section 2 reports the main theoretical issues related to this research. The motivation to conduct the research is clarified in Section 3. Section 4 reports the design of the user experience, with details on the user context, analysis, design and evaluation results. In Section 5 we discuss main findings of the design. Finally, Section 6 concludes this paper.

2. RELATED WORK

Many research efforts have been concerned with the development of solutions to provide ubiquitous access to e-learning experiences; these efforts aim at empowering users with technologies and tools to learn anytime, anywhere. Toward this goal, the availability of educational documents in iDTV enables learning experiences in situations of informal and continuing education, and these experiences can be intertwined and contextualized to the learner's daily life by the involvement of non-conventional access channels (such as iDTV), therefore specializing e-learning into t-learning [1, 8].

In a broad literature survey about t-learning, Chorianopoulos and Lekakos [7] advocate the advantages of iTV-based approaches to e-learning. In particular, they support the concept of edutainment (education as entertainment) based on the argument that user experiences with TV are historically related to entertainment-related activities. Accordingly, the design of learning experiences for iDTV preferably should be directed to informal learning via value-added interactive content associated with the main program. In fact, the focus on edutainment as value-added complement has been a recurrent issue, but while much focus has been directed on technological frameworks [18, 8, 13, 4] and specific applications [17, 20, 3], the interaction between the user and the educational applications has not been systematically thought about as much.

On the other hand, with the focus apart from educational applications, several research has been concerned with design guidance for iTV [19, 14, 21, 2, 5, 9]. In particular, the survey conducted by Chorianopoulos [6] highlights design principles recurrent in the literature, such as the focus on entertainment, support for social viewing behavior, relaxed navigation with remote controls and multiple levels of attention when watching TV. Kunert [12] develops an extensive catalog of UI design patterns for iTV (e.g. patterns for page layout, use of remote control buttons, text input and navigation), all of them designed and evaluated through user-centered design processes. Similar issues have been stressed by Collazos et al. [9] which develops some principles (e.g. simplicity, non-obtrusiveness to the main content, power of customization, etc.) and guidelines to conduct usability inspections on iTV apps. User-centered design of iTV applications were also tackled by Rice and Alm [19], but with research focus on accessibility issues of older adults.

Although our research provides a contribution to the landscape of t-learning systems, in this paper we shift the focus away from the inherent technical qualities of the system and emphasize usability issues in order to enable interactions as natural and intuitive as possible. Based on these considerations, our research is related both to the development of solutions to t-learning (specially the approaches which focus on the design of learning contents) and to the effective design of user experiences with iDTV applications.

3. MOTIVATION

EducaTV is a layered architecture to execute learning objects in iDTV. Learning objects in EducaTV are comprised of multimedia objects described in XML-based documents and can contain evaluation questions, contextual glossaries, as well as complementary materials, such as narrative audio, illustrative videos, among others. These contents are designed to be provided by a TV broadcaster as value-added interactive services to educational programs.

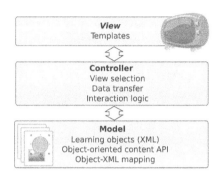

Figure 1: EducaTV architecture

The EducaTV architecture (Figure 1) follows the MVC (Model-View-Controller) design pattern for interactive applications. The model layer is concerned with the learning objects authored in XML as well as the mappings of the XML schema to an object-oriented API (*Application Programming Interface*). The objective of this API is to provide a programmatic approach to manipulate documents across the layers of the architecture. The controller layer selects views according to a predefined interaction logic (navigation model) and, concurrently, transfer data from the model to the view layer. On its turn, the view layer is composed of screen templates filled at runtime by the controller with data from the model layer. In this context, the model and controller layers represent the back-end of the architecture while the view layer represents the front-end. More details on architectural and implementation-related issues of the back-end were reported elsewhere [16].

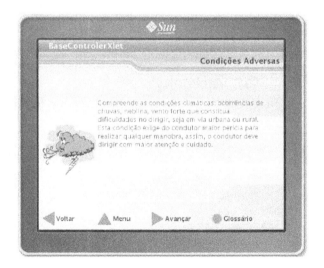

Figure 2: Sample of the first generation of the EducaTV UI

Initially, the EducaTV architecture was developed to satisfy two main requirements:

i) to provide a declarative approach to author interactive learning objects; and

ii) to develop a flexible execution environment to play the learning objects.

As we reported in previous work [16], these two requirements have been effectively met by the back-end of the architecture, but an open area for improvement was the better design of the user experience with the front-end.

The first generation of the EducaTV front-end (of which a sample screen is presented in Figure 2) was subject to an heuristic inspection which revealed several problems. The evaluators pointed out complicated navigability with remote controls, poor positioning status, weak notification of changes in sections of the content, and overall problems with layout and graphical design. Moreover, full screen presentation of the material on top of the TV program caused negative consequences because only the audio of the program could be followed while the interaction took place. This limitation in particular characterized weak linking among the contents and the TV program and provided poor support for group viewing, because while one user was interacting with the contents, the others could not watch the main video.

Based on lessons learned from those preliminary experiments, this paper reports the complete redesign of the EducaTV front-end from scratch. Therefore we started with the findings pointed out in the first usability inspection and extended the requirements in two main directions:

i) tackle interaction with the TV using non-conventional devices (e.g. cell phones); and

ii) support learning groups sharing the same TV in colocated activities.

It is worth stressing that the loose coupling among the layers in the MVC model enable the redesign of the front-end without substantial changes in the back-end. In the following sections we document the methods and procedures employed in the design and highlight main findings in terms of the user experience with EducaTV.

4. DESIGNING THE USER EXPERIENCE IN EDUCATV

According to Dix et al. [10] User-Centered Design (UCD) [11, 22] is an interative process divided in four broad phases:

i) *requirements*, in which the designer establishes what is wanted from the system by means of characterization of the users and their needs, usually by data collection (e.g. questionnaires, secondary research), observation (e.g. videotaping), among other methods;

ii) *analysis*, in which gathered requirements are analyzed and structured in a way so as to delineate key issues and provide proper communication to the later stages;

iii) *design*, during which requirements are materialized in prototypes which are evaluated to enforce their usability; and

iv) *implementation*, which occurs after several iterations of prototyping have lead to satisfaction of the core requirements.

The iterative nature of the process occurs among the analysis and design phases by means of prototyping sessions followed by evaluations to ensure that the pre-established usability criteria have been met.

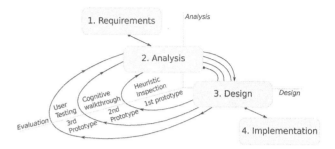

Figure 3: UCD process applied in EducaTV. Adapted from Dix et al. [10]

The user experience in EducaTV was designed following a UCD process comprising the activities depicted in Figure 3. In EducaTV, three prototype sessions and three evaluations were conducted to assess the usability of the system. After gathering requirements, in the first iteration of analysis a first prototype was built and evaluated through a heuristics inspection. Based on the results of this inspection, an improved prototype was designed and evaluated through a cognitive walkthrough inspection. Finally, a third prototype was made and tested with a representative sample of users. After all these steps, the results were considered satisfactory and the design was able to be implemented and deployed. In the following sections we describe procedures, methods and main results obtained throughout the process.

4.1 Requirements and context

The target audience of the instructional content is characterized by an adult population composed of motor vehicle drivers aged between 18 and 60 years old who are interested in recycling their knowledge in regard to defensive driving. The planned scenarios consisted in situations of corrective distance education programs concerning drivers who have been involved in traffic accidents and informative campaigns to reduce accidents.

In order to devise issues of technological literacy and acceptance of iDTV technology we performed a pilot study by means of a questionnaire applied to a sample of 21 subjects enrolled from the local community. All respondents were motor vehicle drivers in the specified age group, of which 67% were aged between 18 and 50 years old.

The core of the questions were targeted at analyzing the users acceptance to non conventional uses of TV. Figure 4 depicts that while many users feel comfortable to use remote controls, the majority of them notice shortcomings on these devices and desire alternative methods to perform the same operations. When asked if they would use a mobile as alternative device, the majority agreed but an expressive percentage was not certain if it would be desirable. With focus on the abilities to use mobile devices beyond making calls, 95% mentioned text messaging and 75% judged this task as easy. Other tasks mentioned were voice-initiated calls (24%), web

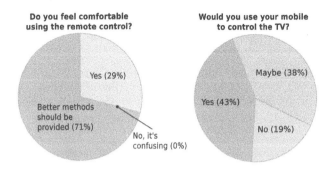

Figure 4: Selected results from the survey

browsing (19%) and miscellaneous uses (38%, e.g. alarms, take pictures and listen to music).

The questionnaire also included open-ended questions about what users expected from iDTV technology. The results revealed that the majority of the population between 35-50 years old expected enhancements to traditional uses of the TV, such as more channels, better quality of audio and video and easiness to record programs to watch later. Younger groups, aged between 18-35 years old, indicated non conventional enhancements such as access to multimedia content from the web, personalization (e.g. content recommendation, targeted advertisement) and digital convergence (e.g. watch TV on mobiles or employ mobiles to interact with the TV). All respondents that mentioned interactivity were in the 18-35 age group, and mentioned as desired interactive services the possibility to perform shopping and provide feedback to the broadcaster about the program (e.g. quizzes). When asked about the desire to obtain complementary information about the program being watched, around 90% answered that it would be a good enhancement.

Additionally to the questionnaire, pilot sessions of paper-based low-fidelity prototyping were conducted in order to clarify the pedagogical strategy to be used to introduce the concepts as well as to better delineate the overall dialog of the interface. These sessions occurred with designers experienced with e-learning and with the design of instructional material. A sample prototype developed in this phase in presented in Figure 5.

Figure 5: Paper-based low-fidelity prototype

From an instructional standpoint, a dialectic methodology was adopted to structure the contents of the courses, in which the learning experience is organized in three moments: *mobilization*, when triggering problems or situations (e.g. short-length games, quizzes) are presented to the learners to promote their engagement in the activities; *analysis*, in which learning material is analyzed in order to solve the proposed problem; and *synthesis*, after which a solution to the problem is proposed. During these phases short assessments may took place in order to properly sequence the content that is presented to the user. Additionally, the system should support both informal education at home via public TV channels and group-based distance learning in remote locations that do not count on specific formation centers. Based on these considerations, two interaction scenarios were designed which we present in Section 4.2.

4.2 Analysis

Considering the requirements gathered we developed two scenarios of corrective distance education programs concerning defensive driving: one of the scenarios considers individual and informal learning at home and the other considers formal group learning at distributed locations.

Scenario 1: Individual informal learning

This scenario considers the broadcast of defensive driving classes so as to enable informal and continuing education in the home environment. The user is watching the program alone at home and has the possibility of participating in interactive sessions with complementary material related to a topic being dealt with in the program. The interactive material can be associated to classes with specific purpose or with advertisements related to informative campaigns. From the standpoint of interactivity, during the program occurs non-obtrusive notifications of interactive content associated with the topic being presented in the program. When the user starts the interaction, the main video is rescaled to a reduced portion of the screen while a multimedia presentation illustrates the topic or some form of self-assessment via quiz. In particular, the assessment will enable the user to measure if the concepts presented in the program are being effectively learned.

```
0. user is watching the educational program
1. presenter announces interactive content and asks the user
   to press the red button. A red icon is notified in the bottom
   right corner of the screen
2. the user accepts the interaction
   2.1. interactive application is started, video region is reduced.
   2.2. user reads the instruction
   2.3. answer time counter is started
   2.4. user answers
   2.5. provide feedback according to the answer
3. close the application

plan 1: user accepts the interactivity, go through all steps
plan 2: user refuse interactivy, stay in task 0
plan 3: answer timeframe is expired in 2.3. Go to 2.5.
```

Figure 6: Sample task decomposition for scenario 1

In order to delineate the dialog of the prototypes and conduct the evaluations, task decompositions were authored encompassing the interactions achieved in this scenario. A sample task decomposition corresponding to interaction with a quiz is presented in Figure 6.

Scenario 2: Group-based formal learning

This scenario considers users attending distance learning classes in remote locations that do not count on formation centers for colocated instruction. In this context, live classes are broadcast and watched by geographically distributed groups. The users meet at a location that count on iDTV equipment that must be shared by the learning group, whose members have the possibility of interacting with the content in individual manner using their mobiles. The interactivity occurs by means of formative assessment during the class, in similar fashion as to the scenario of individual learning. The main distinguishing characteristic is that when the assessment is non-obtrusively notified, users could answer the questions individually using their mobiles (e.g. via Bluetooth communication) which have an specific mobile application pre-installed. The questions should be answered in the timeframe indicated in the TV. The iDTV equipment, in this scenario, centralizes the answers from the students that later can be summarized and socialized to the group. Additionally, if the meeting location count on a return channel, the user responses are forwarded to the studio where the classes are being broadcast. A sample task decomposition for this scenario, considering group interaction with a quiz is presented in Figure 7

```
0. user is watching the educational program
1. presenter announces interactive activity, notified by an
   interactivity icon
2. TV application starts
3. user starts application in his/her mobile
   3.1. user waits application to connect to the TV
   3.2. user reads the instruction
   3.3. answer time counter starts
   3.3. user answers the question in the mobile
   3.4. application provides feedback to the answer
4. mobile application sends the answers to the TV
5. close the application in the mobile and in the TV

plan 1: user accepts the interactivity, go through all steps
plan 2: user refuse interactivy, wait in task 1 until completion
        of the activity. Then go to task 5.
plan 3: answer time expires. Go to 3.4.
```

Figure 7: Sample task decomposition for scenario 2

Considering these scenarios, we iteratively developed prototypes which were refined with the results of each evaluation. In the following sections, we report such procedures.

4.3 Heuristic inspection

According to Nielsen and Molich [15], heuristic inspection is a discount usability method during which interaction experts detect problems in a user interface in reference to a predefined set of principles and heuristics. Heuristic evaluation is a low-cost and effective technique to enhance a user interface in prototyping stage while it presents the advantages of being widespread and simple to apply.

For this iteration of the process we built a paper-based medium-fidelity prototype for each of the scenarios presented in section 4.2 (Figure 8). Screens both for the TV interface and the mobile interface were developed. In the experiment the interfaces were evaluated considering nine heuristics:

1. visibility of system status;
2. match between system and real world;
3. user freedom and control;

Figure 8: Paper-based medium-fidelity prototypes evaluated in the heuristic inspection

4. consistency and standards;
5. error prevention;
6. recognition rather than recall;
7. efficiency and flexibility of use;
8. aesthetics and minimalistic design; and
9. recovery from errors.

It is worth stressing that, from the set of ten heuristics prescribed in the original method, in this project we applied only nine of them. In particular, we suppressed the heuristic of "help and documentation" since applications for iDTV, due to their inherent limitations of interaction, should emphasize easiness of learning so as users can build mental models of the application without consulting extensive documentation. In terms of procedures, the inspection was executed by three experts in interaction design which classified the problems as unimportant, cosmetic, simple, critical or catastrophic. After the specialists detected problems in the interface, their comments were grouped and ordered by priority and severity. Based on the analysis of the data, a plan of action was suggested to improve the interface.

The majority of the problems detected were classified as simple and a few as critical. The main problems detected were affecting the principles of responsiveness, personalization, consistency, familiarity and learnability. Considering responsiveness, it was suggested that users should be better informed about the time remaining to answer the questions and notified if the answers have been successfully submitted. A recurrent problem of personalization was that users that provide fast answers would have to wait the timeframe to elapse before returning to the full screen video. Consistency and familiarity were mainly related to icons used in the interface and graphical design of the timeticker clock. Finally, problems of learnability were related to the instructions of whether to start to interact with the mobile or pay attention to the TV. These problems were tackled in the second prototype whose evaluation results are presented in the next section.

4.4 Cognitive walkthrough

Cognitive walkthrough is an inspection technique to evaluate the usability of the system in respect to the tasks performed by the users of the interface. The focus of the technique is to identify problems that can impair the learnability of the system. Experts in interface design simulate typical tasks performed by users while analyzing if the objectives of the tasks can be easily attained via the proposed interface. For this purpose, at first glance the context of the users are analyzed and typical tasks are defined. After that, the sequence of actions performed in the interface is established.

In this project, a preliminary pilot study was conducted with a single expert in order to assess if the protocol to conduct the inspection was feasible. The expert had experience with the design of applications for iDTV and interaction design. As a result of this pilot study, corrections were implemented in the original cognitive walkthrough procedure. The improved procedure was then applied considering a revised user interface (Figure 9) with five application developers.

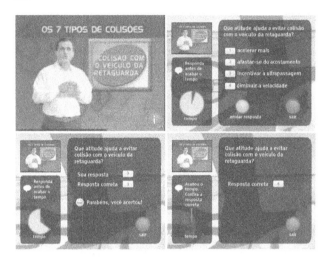

Figure 9: Sample screens from the prototype for the scenario of individual learning

The main detected problems that evaluators pointed out as impairments to the learnability of the system were related to predictability, familiarity and consistency, the majority of them detected in the mobile interface. About predictability, once again the timeticker clock presented problems, this time evaluators suggested numerical feedback about the time remaining; another problem related to predictability was the use of icons resembling mobile buttons when presenting the answers, situation that could lead the users to uselessly press the respective button. Familiarity was impacted by the use of technical terms in the dialog, such as "Connecting..." that should be replaced by "Loading questions...". Finally, generalizability problems were related to the graphical design of the buttons which could cause confusion with other functions of the mobiles. The proposed corrections were implemented in a third version of the prototypes which were evaluated with end users.

4.5 User testing

User testing applied to a prototype or end product is required to satisfy the functionalities of an interface and measure the impact of the design from the standpoint of the user. In this project we evaluated prototypes with real users using the techniques Wizard of Oz and Think Aloud. A sample of five users between 24-32 years old participated in the experiment, being two female users and 3 male users, all of them undergraduates. All of them had experience with computers and mobiles, but almost all of them had no experience with iTV.

Before each session, each user was informed about what the experiment was all about and received a brief expositive training on the operation of the system considering toy scenarios which were distinct from the scenarios of the experiment. Additionally, each user had a list of tasks to be accomplished in the interface. The evaluation sessions were recorded for later review. After each session, users answered questionnaires in which they should objectively evaluate core characteristics of the system. A refined prototype (Figure 10) was used in this experiment.

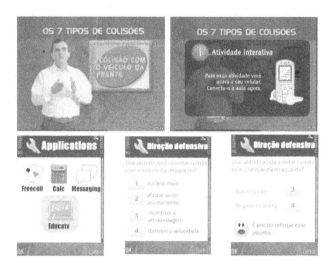

Figure 10: Sample screens for scenario 2. TV interface (top) and mobile interface (bottom)

Generally, the user interface was objectively well evaluated by the users, as they stated that committed few errors and were able to complete the tasks satisfactorily. On the other hand, through observation of the users interacting with the system, we noticed some problems.

Related to flexibility of interaction, we noticed that many users tried to use the directional keys of the mobile, while the prototype was supposed to react only to numerical keys. While interacting, some users had observability problems and missed some form of summary scoring their responses at the end of the quiz. Additionally, due to the colors of the "ok" and "cancel" commands resemble the buttons to start and end a call, some users have erroneously pressed these buttons, revealing a problem related to prevention of errors. But the most recurrent difficulty faced by the users was the lack of some form of preliminary guidance about how to initially operate the interface (e.g. how to start up the mobile application), problem that could be solved by providing short illustrative videos about these tasks.

5. FINDINGS AND RECOMMENDATIONS

A major lesson derived from our results is that interactions with restricted devices such as TVs must be as simple as possible in opposition to feature-rich and cluttered interfaces. If on one side simplicity limits the functionalities an iTV application may present (e.g. inputting text in these devices is still considered difficult) on the other side demands creativity to provide a required functionality without negatively impacting simplicity. Furthermore the distance of the user from the screen and the reliance on a remote control demand the iTV applications be based on simple interaction models so as to promote effective usability. The adoption of simple design alternatives favors navigability, recovery from errors and learnability.

When considered that iTV applications are related to mass media, an important concern is that heterogeneity of users is hardly avoidable. In this direction, the context of the users must be taken into account in order to provide alternative interaction strategies. For instance, in our requirements we have to deal with group-based interaction while still supporting single-user interaction. So we had to design an alternative based on distributed devices (e.g. mobiles) with post-hoc synchronization without abandoning single-user interaction with remote controls. User context also affects other aspects of the interface such as the degree of technicalities in the language of the dialogs. Naturally, the designer must balance the risks of introducing alternative strategies. For instance, even though our design decision to introduce mobile devices has tackled the problem of group-based interaction, it introduced additional complexity, specially if we consider that many users stated they do not feel comfortable even with the remote control.

We also noticed that support for group-viewing behavior introduced additional problems, mainly related to synchronization. For instance, different users had different speeds to answer the questions of the quiz; so while some of them answered the questions very fast, others could not do it before the timeframe expired. Such problem was noticeable in our focus group, but could scale a lot more in the original scenario of distributed groups watching a live lecture. In summary, this example implies that designers should be aware that strong synchronization between the narrative of the application and the live program sometimes won't work as expected.

Concerning user guidance to operate the interface, our evaluations revealed us that while iTV interfaces must be as simple and intuitive as possible, users still need some guidance to operate the application. Although we disfavored the use of written help manuals in our design, the results recommend that some help must be provided to the user. Given the inherent multimedia nature of iTV, in future development we plan to provide guidance by means of short tutorial videos.

An important improvement in relation to the first generation of the EducaTV interface was that of the linking between the application and the program. Even though our design has already started with this improvement, in this opportunity we had the chance to assess that many of such problems presented in the first usability inspection have been satisfactorily solved by the new design. In fact, the presentation of a miniature of the main video, in opposition to a full screen approach, enforced the association among the interactive content and the TV program and improved group viewing behavior.

Finally, from a methodological standpoint, we noticed that user-centered design proved very effective in the development of a non-conventional user interface such as EducaTV's. In particular, the analysis of user context and iterative design were crucial to improve our prototype to satisfactory levels even if we initially lacked comprehensive guidelines to develop for the iTV medium.

6. CONCLUSIONS AND FUTURE WORK

In this paper we reported and discussed the user-centered design of an iTV-based application to provide t-learning services. We presented the main related research in the literature and made clear the motivation of this research as an improvement to an architecture in use. Requirements were gathered from users and specialists while iterative prototyping were applied with extensive evaluation along the process.

Our analysis of the results revealed some recommendations for the design of iTV applications. In particular, we detected that simplicity of the applications should be enforced. The context of the users must be taken into account by the availability of alternative strategies of interaction. Additionally, the designer must be aware of synchronization issues among the application and the live program. Even with simple applications, users sometimes need guidance and we advocate that for iTV applications a good strategy is to offer short video tutorials. Recommendations concerning the tight linking among the program and the application were also stated, mainly via availability of a reduced version of the main video while the user interacts. Last but not least, we concluded that user centered design proved very effective to develop non-conventional user interfaces specially when extensive design guidance is lacking.

As far as future work is concerned, we are currently conducting the implementation of a high-fidelity prototype of the new EducaTV interface. Still under user-centered design, this interface will be evaluated by end users before final deployment. Under this effort, we have still some open requirements to implement new functionalities in the EducaTV architecture, and we expect that being attentive to user-centered approaches will bring us additional insights into iTV interface design.

Acknowledgments. We thank FAPESP, CNPq, CAPES, FINEP and the MCT.

References

[1] P. Aarreniemi-Jokipelto. T-learning Model for Learning via Digital TV. In *16th EAEEIE conference*, 2005.

[2] A. Ahonen, L. Turkki, M. Saarijärvi, M. Lahti, and T. Virtanen. *Guidelines for Designing Easy-to-Use Interactive Television Services: Experiences from the ArviD Programme*, pages 207–223. IGI Global, 2007.

[3] K. Alic, M. Zajc, M. Tkalcic, U. Burnik, and J. Tasic. Development of interactive television t-learning course. In *MELECON 2008 - The 14th IEEE Mediterranean Electrotechnical Conference*, pages 139–144, 2008.

[4] F. Bellotti, S. Vrochidis, I. Tsampoulatidis, G. Bo, and L. Napoletano. A Learning Oriented Technological Framework for iDTV. In *2008 International Conference on Automated Solutions for Cross Media Content and Multi-Channel Distribution*, pages 79–86, 2008.

[5] S. Buchinger, S. Kriglstein, and H. Hlavacs. A comprehensive view on user studies: Survey and Open Issues for Mobile TV. In *Proceedings of the seventh european conference on European interactive television conference - EuroITV '09*, page 179, 2009.

[6] K. Chorianopoulos. User interface design principles for interactive television applications. *International Journal of Human-Computer Interaction*, 24(6):556–573, 2008.

[7] K. Chorianopoulos and G. Lekakos. Learn and play with interactive TV. *Computers in Entertainment*, 5 (2):4, Apr. 2007.

[8] F. Colace, M. De Santo, P. Ritrovato, and P. R. C. Mascambruno. From E-Learning to T-Learning. In *3rd International Conference on Information and Communication Technologies: From Theory to Applications*, pages 1–6, 2008.

[9] C. A. Collazos, C. Rusu, J. L. Arciniegas, and S. Roncagliolo. Designing and Evaluating Interactive Television from a Usability Perspective. In *Second International Conferences on Advances in Computer-Human Interactions*, pages 381–385, 2009.

[10] A. Dix, J. Finlay, and G. Abowd. *Human-computer interaction*. Prentice hall, 3rd edition, 2004.

[11] International Standards Organization. *ISO 13407. Human Centred Design Process for Interactive Systems*, 1999.

[12] T. Kunert. *User-Centered Interaction Design Patterns for Interactive Digital Television Applications (Human-Computer Interaction Series)*. Springer, 2009.

[13] M. R. Lopez, R. P. Diaz Redondo, A. F. Vilas, and J. J. Pazos Arias. Entercation: engaging viewers in education through TV. *Comput. Entertain.*, 5(2):7+, 2007.

[14] K. Y. Lu. *Interaction Design Principles for Interactive TV*. PhD thesis, Georgia Institute of Technology, 2005.

[15] J. Nielsen and R. Molich. Heuristic evaluation of user interfaces. In *VIII SIGCHI conference on Human factors in computing systems: Empowering people*, 1990.

[16] L. S. Oliveira, D. S. Martins, and M. G. C. Pimentel. Educatv: uma abordagem para execução de objetos de aprendizagem em tvdi compatível com ginga-j. In *SBIE 2009 - XX Simpósio Brasileiro de Informática na Educação*, volume 1, pages 1–10, November 2009.

[17] D. Pinto, J. Queiroz-Neto, and V. de Lucena. An engineering educational application developed for the brazilian digital tv system. In *Frontiers in Education Conference, 2008. FIE 2008. 38th Annual*, pages S2F–14 –S2F–19, 22-25 2008.

[18] A. Prata, N. Guimarães, and T. Chambel. Crossmedia personalized learning contexts. In *HT '10: Proceedings of the 21st ACM conference on Hypertext and hypermedia*, pages 305–306, 2010.

[19] M. Rice and N. Alm. Designing new interfaces for digital interactive television usable by older adults. *Computers in Entertainment*, 6(1):1, May 2008.

[20] D. T. Santos, D. T. do Vale, and L. G. P. Meloni. Digital tv and distance learning: Potentials and limitations. In *Frontiers in Education Conference, 36th Annual*, pages 1–6, March 2007.

[21] E. Tsekleves, R. Whitham, K. Kondo, and A. Hill. Bringing the television experience to other media in the home: An Ethnographic Study. In *Proceedings of the seventh european conference on European interactive television conference - EuroITV '09*, volume 21, page 201, Sept. 2009.

[22] A. Williams. User-centered design, activity-centered design, and goal-directed design: a review of three methods for designing web applications. In *Proceedings of the 27th ACM international conference on Design of communication - SIGDOC '09*, page 1, 2009.

Gender HCI: What About the Software?

Margaret M. Burnett

School of Electrical Engineering and Computer Science
Oregon State University
Corvallis, OR 97331-4501
burnett@eecs.oregonstate.edu

ABSTRACT

Although there has been recent investigation into how to understand and ameliorate the low representation of females in computing, there has been little research into how software itself fits into the picture. Our focus is on how supposedly gender-neutral software interacts with gender differences. Specifically, we have concentrated on software aimed at supporting users doing problem solving. For example, what if females' problem-solving effectiveness, using software such as Excel, would accelerate if the software were changed to take gender differences into account? This talk reports the investigations my students and I have conducted into whether and how software and its features affect females' and males' performance differently, and describes the beginnings of work on promising interventions that help both males and females.

Categories and Subject Descriptors

H.1.2 **[Information Systems]: User/Machine Systems—Human Factors.** H.5 **[Information Systems]: Information Interfaces and Presentation (e.g., HCI)**

General Terms

HCI, Design, Human Factors, Theory.

Keywords

User demographics, Gender HCI

ABOUT THE SPEAKER

Margaret Burnett is a Professor of Computer Science at Oregon State University. Her research focuses on human issues of programming languages and environments, especially when the programming is done by males and females not trained as professional programmers. She has been investigating gender differences in the context of problem-solving software for several years, considering populations ranging from spreadsheet users to professional programmers. She is also a co-founder of the EUSES Consortium, a collaboration among Oregon State University, Carnegie Mellon University, Drexel University, Pennsylvania State University, University of Cambridge, University of Nebraska, University of Washington, and IBM, to help End Users Shape Effective Software (EUSES).

REFERENCES

1. J. Cao, K. Rector, T. H. Park, S. D. Fleming, M. Burnett, S. Wiedenbeck, A debugging perspective on end-user mashup programming, IEEE Symp. Visual Lang. Human-Centric Computing, Sept. 2010 (to appear).
2. M. Burnett, S. D. Fleming, S. Iqbal, G. Venolia, V. Rajaram, U. Farooq, V. Grigoreanu, M. Czerwinski, Gender differences and programming environments: Across programming populations, ACM Empirical Software Engineering and Measurement, Sept. 2010 (to appear).
3. V. Grigoreanu, M. Burnett, and G. Robertson, A strategy-centric approach to the design of end-user debugging tools, ACM CHI 2010, April 2010, 713-722.
4. V. Grigoreanu, J. Brundage, E. Bahna, M. Burnett, P. ElRif, J. Snover, Males' and females' script debugging strategies, 2nd Int. Symp. End-User Development, Mar. 2009.
5. V. Grigoreanu, J. Cao, T. Kulesza, C. Bogart, K. Rector, M. Burnett, and S. Wiedenbeck, Can feature design reduce the gender gap in end-user software development environments? IEEE Symp. Visual Lang. Human-Centric Computing, Sept. 2008, 149-156.
6. L. Beckwith, D. Inman, K. Rector, M. Burnett, On to the real world: Gender and self-efficacy in Excel, IEEE Symp. Visual Lang. Human-Centric Computing, Sept. 2007, 119-126
7. N. Subrahmaniyan, C. Kissinger, K. Rector, D. Inman, J. Kaplan, L. Beckwith, M. Burnett, Explaining debugging strategies to end-user programmers, IEEE Symp. Visual Lang. Human-Centric Computing, Sept. 2007, 127-134.
8. L. Beckwith, Gender HCI issues in end-user programming, Ph.D. Thesis, Oregon State University, 2007.
9. L. Beckwith, M. Burnett, V. Grigoreanu, S. Wiedenbeck, Gender HCI: What about the software? Computer, Nov. 2006, 83-87.
10. L. Beckwith, C. Kissinger, M. Burnett, S. Wiedenbeck, J. Lawrance, A. Blackwell, C. Cook, Tinkering and gender in end-user programmers' debugging, ACM Conf. Human-Computer Interaction, Apr. 2006.
11. L. Beckwith, S. Sorte, M. Burnett, S. Wiedenbeck, T. Chintakovid, C. Cook, Designing features for both genders in end-user software engineering environments, IEEE Symp. Visual Lang. Human-Centric Computing, Sept. 2005, 153-160.
12. L. Beckwith, M. Burnett, S. Wiedenbeck, C. Cook, S. Sorte, M. Hastings, Effectiveness of end-user debugging software features: Are there gender issues?, ACM Conf. Human Factors in Comput.Systems, Apr. 2005, 869-878.
13. L. Beckwith and M. Burnett, Gender: An important factor in end-user programming environments? IEEE Symp. Visual Lang. Human-Centric Comput.Lang. Environments, Sept. 2004.

Designing the Interaction with Service Systems

Claudio Pinhanez

IBM Research Brasil
claudio@pinhanez.com

ABSTRACT

More and more people use computers to interact not with machines but with complex service systems. This talk examines the similarities and differences of interaction with machines and service systems, assuming, as the defining characteristic of a service system is the significant presence of humans as part of the service system during the time of use. One of the main consequences is that service systems are often perceived as having human characteristics and usually expected to exhibit human-like behaviors. This talks presents and discusses those issues, under the light of Service Science and HCI theory. We also present the concept of the human facet of a service system, which is the set of elements and their configurations that create and control the perception of and the interaction of a user with the human characteristics of a service system. The talk then examines how the design of the human facet of service system can be simplified by theoretical insights from Psychological Models such as Personality Theory, Social Psychology, and Emotional Communication Theory; and Dramatic models such as Character Theory, Stanislavski's System, Method Acting, and Illusion of Life.

Categories and Subject Descriptors

D. [Software], D.1 [Programming Techniques], D.1.0 [General], D.2 [Software Engineering], D.2.6 [Programming Environments]

K. [Computing Milieux], K.6 [Management of Computing and Information Systems], K.6.1 [Project and People Management], K.6.3 [Software Management]

H. [Information Systems], H.1 Models and Principles], H.1.2 [User/Machine Systems],

General Terms

Documentation, HCI, Design, Software Development.

Keywords

Collaboration, Community, Software Documents.

ABOUT THE SPEAKER

Dr. Claudio Pinhanez is a research scientist at IBM Research - Brazil where he researches service theory, tools, and methodology. His current work is focused on combining traditional services theory and methods, ideas, and concepts from human-computer interaction, with a practical focus on quality of IT service delivery. Dr. Pinhanez was key for the establishment of Service Science, Management, and Engineering (SSME) research at the IBM Research Watson laboratory and is currently leading the establishment of Service Science in Brazil. Dr. Pinhanez got his PhD. from the MIT Media Laboratory in 1999, working on the design and construction of interactive environments. He has also been a visiting researcher at ATR-MIC laboratory (Kyoto, Japan) and Sony Computer Science Laboratory (Tokyo), and a featured artist at the NTT ICC museum in Tokyo. In 2003 he was nominated the Most Promising Scientist with a Graduate Degree award by the Hispanic Engineers National Achievement Awards Conference (HENAAC).

SIGDOC – Reviewing the History from a Company Perspective

Robert Pierce

Rational Software
IBM Corporation
robertp@us.ibm.com

ABSTRACT

SIGDOC is the Association for Computing Machinery's Special Interest Group (SIG) on the Design of Communication (DOC). Until 2003, SIGDOC focused on documentation for hardware and software. With the shift in focus from systems to computer documentation to the design of communication, SIGDOC has better positioned itself to emphasize the potentials, practices, and problems of multiple kinds of communication technologies, such as Web applications, user interfaces, and online and print documentation. SIGDOC focuses on the design of communication as it is taught, practiced, researched, and conceptualized in various fields, including technical communication, software engineering, information architecture, and usability, etc. The traditional SIGDOC members were likely to be teachers, researchers, and/or practitioners of computer documentation. Today, members of SIGDOC include information design professionals, educators, researchers, software engineers, Web designers, system developers, usability specialists, computer scientists, user interface designers, and information technology specialists. What is the next sustainable change on the Design of Communication?

Categories and Subject Descriptors

D. [Software], D.2 [**Software Engineering**], D.2.7 [**Distribution, Maintenance, and Enhancement**]

K. [**Computing Milieux**], K.6 [**Management of Computing and Information Systems**], K.6.1 [**Project and People Management**], K.6.3 [**Software Management**]

H. [**Information Systems**], H.1 **Models and Principles**], H.1.2 [**User/Machine Systems**],

General Terms

Documentation, HCI, Design, Management, Human Factors.

Keywords

Collaboration, Community, Software Documents.

ABOUT THE SPEAKER

Rob is an Advisory Information Developer for the IBM Corporation and the user assistance team lead for Rational Asset Manager. As the current Vice Chair for SIGDOC, Rob enjoys the intellectual vitality of SIGDOC and the active participation of its members. His interests in software development best practices, along with the design, development, and presentation of technical content, are aligned with what he does for IBM. He enjoys the synergy between the academics and the business professionals that comprise the SIGDOC membership as well as the breadth of topics that are relevant to SIGDOC. He continues to try facilitating the discussion around the broadening of scope in what the membership views as comprising "design of communication." Rob has contributed to past SIGDOC conferences as a committee member, a panelist, and as a presenter. He was the SIGDOC newsletter editor in chief from 2001-2009. Rob has worked as an information developer for Digital Equipment, Compaq, and for Rational Software, and IBM since 2000.

An Interactive Dialogue Modelling Editor for Designing Multimodal Applications

Sebastian Feuerstack

Universidade Federal de São Carlos,
Departamento de Computacão,
Rod. Washington Luis, km 235 - SP, Brazil
+49 30 776 2324
sfeu@cs.tu-berlin.de

ABSTRACT

This poster presents initial results of an approach for (1) designing and implementing a dialogue modelling editor to enable the design of multimodal applications, that (2) supports the design for various multimodal setups and that (3) is specifically targeted to be used by interaction designers.

Categories and Subject Descriptors

H.5.2 [Information Interfaces and Presentation]: User Interfaces - *Input devices and strategies, Interaction styles, Prototyping*; D.2.2 [Software Engineering]: Design Tools and Techniques – *User Interfaces.*

General Terms

Design, Human Factors, Languages.

Keywords

Model-based User Interface Development, Multimodal Interfaces, Software Engineering, Interactive Editor, HCI.

1. INTRODUCTION

Nowadays multimodal systems that support the user by a combination of speech, gesture and graphical-driven interaction are already part of our everyday life. Examples are combinations of speech-driven and graphical interfaces like in-car assistance systems, language-learning software, or tourist information systems. The market success of recent video-games that can be controlled in a more natural and intuitive way by using hand gestures, balancing and moving the body demonstrates that even new audiences can be addressed by enabling multimodal interaction to ease the usage of interactive systems.

2. CHALLENGES

Modelling multimodal systems that support various multimodal setups is an open research issue. A recent promising work by [11]

that implemented a model-based development process to generate multimodal web interfaces stated the importance of considering the CARE-properties, but neglected the support of modelling complementary or redundant multimodal interaction to support multimodal fusion. UsiXML [6] and TERESA [2] do not offer a dialogue model but distribute it to several models (mainly the task model that specifies the interaction sequence and the abstract user interface model containing the navigation). Since these models are considered modality independent, supporting different navigations based on the used combination of modalities is difficult to implement. Research how to design multimodal interfaces has resulted in both modality-independent and modality-dependent dialogue models. The latter ones concentrate on proposing dialog models to design a certain modality (mainly graphics like [12, 8] or a specific multimodal setup [11]. The former ones propose a set of abstractions by interactors or generic widgets that are transformed by rules [6, 2] or interpreted at runtime to result in concrete widgets [10].

In practice, the distinction between abstract dialogue and concrete interaction isn't as clear cut. The main problem is that the structure of interactors will often change when one takes the interaction technique into account. A voice application is often more sequential, interfaces for small devices are often more modal, a direct manipulation application is difficult to split into smaller parts, since actions are projected into the graphical objects. So, even though the dialog is abstract and do not explicitly refer to interaction technique, the interaction technique affects it in (sometimes subtle) ways. Thus it keeps questionable if these modalities have more in common than that they differ in order to argument for a modality independent dialogue model.

3. DIALOGUE EDITOR

We are focusing our work on realizing an interactive editor for designing multimodal applications that support all four relations of combining the modes of a multimodal system: Complementary, Assignment, Redundancy, and Equivalence (the CARE properties) [7].

The editor allows visual programming of a dialogue model by interaction designers and connects with the help of an interpreter that can execute these dialogue models to the Open Interface Framework, which implements a standardized framework and a component repository to integrate several interaction devices and sensors into one unique platform that enables a developer to flexibility combine and aggregate various devices and sensors to form multimodal interaction setups [5].

The dialogue design consists of two basic steps: First, profiles are described that characterize a multimodal interaction setup which we understand as a set of interconnected Open Interface Components. The characterization is based on a fine-grained taxonomy of output modalities from [13] and the combination space from [1] that enables the definition of composite modalities. The profiles are implemented by using the Pipelines-Model of Open Interface.

Second, we design for one profile a dialogue model. For every further profile, the dialog editor generates a draft dialogue design based on a comparison of the original profile to the new profile. These concrete dialogue designs can be run by an interpreter that executes the dialogue flow and calls or reacts on the Open Interface Components and the application.

By using the Open Interface Platform we can benefit from a lot of already existing fusion and signal processing components as well as device drivers to keep the focus on the dialogue modelling editor that will consider and merge previous editors that offer dialogue model but does not support multimodal design.

Figure 1: The principle tool-chain to design multimodal dialogues for the case studies.

The implementation of the editor will be based on directly extending and merging relevant parts and suitable notations of previous editors for dialogue modelling to support multimodal modelling: Therefore we consider the Speechgraph editor, the Diamodl editor [12] as well as the MoLIC designer [9] and the Dialogue Graphs approach [8] (see figure 1).

4. APPLICATION IN E-LEARNING

Multimodal approaches to learning have been proven to be extremely effective since information introduced aurally, visually and kinaesthetically can significantly increase the possibility of understand and remembering information [4].

The evaluation focuses on the suitability and efficiency of the dialogue modelling editor and will be performed by following an interdisciplinary approach involving both, interaction designers and domain experts that will design a multimodal teaching application based by applying the dialog modelling notation.

Figure 1 illustrates the principle tool chain that should be supported to generate dialogues describing multimodal interaction. The first row of figure 1 presents the final tools, the second row already existing tools that are considered for extension. For the case studies the project will use an already existing SCORM authoring tool, the Cognitor [3].

5. ACKNOWLEDGMENTS

The author is grateful to the Deutsche Forschungsgemeinschaft (DFG) for the financial support of his work.

6. REFERENCES

[1] N. O. Bernsen. Modality theory in support of multimodal interface design. In *Proceedings of the AAAI Spring Symposium on Intelligent Multi-Media Multi-Modal Systems*, pages 37–44, 1994.

[2] Silvia Berti, Francesco Correani, Giulio Mori, Fabio Paterno, and Carmen Santoro. TERESA: A transformation-based environment for designing and developing multi-device interfaces. In *ACM CHI 2004, Extended Abstract*, volume II, pages 793–794, Vienna, Austria, April 2004. ACM Press.

[3] David Buzatto, Junia Coutinho Anacleto, and Ana Luiza Dias. Providing culturally contextualized metadata to promote sharing and reuse of learning objects. In *SIGDOC '09: Proceedings of the 27th ACM international conference on Design of communication*, pages 163–170, New York, NY, USA, 2009. ACM.

[4] Alice M. Hammel. Using multi-modal techniques to motivate intuitive and non-intuitive students. *American Music Teacher*, Oct-Nov., 2003.

[5] Jean-Yves Lionel Lawson, Ahmad-Amr Al-Akkad, Jean Vanderdonckt, and Benoit Macq. An open source workbench for prototyping multimodal interactions based on off-the-shelf heterogeneous components. In *EICS '09: Proceedings of the 1st ACM SIGCHI symposium on Engineering interactive computing systems*, pages 245–254, New York, NY, USA, 2009. ACM.

[6] Quentin Limbourg, Jean Vanderdonckt, Benjamin Michotte, Laurent Bouillon, and Victor Lopez-Jaquero. USIXML: A language supporting multi-path development of user interfaces. In Remi Bastide, Philippe A. Palanque, and Joerg Roth, editors, *EHCI/DS-VIS*, volume 3425 of *Lecture Notes in Computer Science*, pages 200–220. Springer, 2004.

[7] Laurence Nigay and Joelle Coutaz. Multifeature systems: The care properties and their impact on software design. In *Intelligence and Multimodality in Multimedia Interfaces*. 1997.

[8] Daniel Reichard, Peter Forbrig, and Anke Dittmar. Task models as basis for requirements engineering and software execution. In *Proceedings of TAMODIA 2004*, pages 51 – 57, Prague, Czeck Republic, 2004. ACM Press.

[9] Ugo Braga Sangiorgi and Simone D.J. Barbosa. Molic designer: towards computational support to hci design with molic. In *EICS '09: Proceedings of the 1st ACM SIGCHI symposium on Engineering interactive computing systems*, pages 303–308, New York, NY, USA, 2009. ACM.

[10] Robbie Schaefer. *Model-based Development of Multimodal and Multi-Device User Interfaces in Context-Aware Environments*. PhD thesis, C-LAB Publication, Band 25, Shaker Verlag, Aachen, 2007.

[11] Adrian Stanciulescu. *A Methodology for Developing Multimodal User Interfaces of Information Systems*. PhD thesis, Universite Catholique de Louvain, 2008.

[12] Hallvard Traetteberg. Dialog modelling with interactors and uml statecharts - a hybrid approach. In *DSV-IS*, pages 346–361, 2003.

[13] Frederic Vernier and Laurence Nigay. A framework for the combination and characterization of output modalities. *Lecture Notes in Computer Science*, 1946:35ff, 200

Designing Interactive Presentation Systems for Classrooms

Rahul Budhiraja

Indian Institute of Information
Technology Allahabad
Deoghat, Jhalwa
Allahabad,India 211012
+91 9935974560

rahul.budhiraja.dark@gmail.com

Shekhar Verma

Indian Institute of Information
Technology Allahabad
Deoghat, Jhalwa
Allahabad,India 211012
+91 94509653360

sverma@iiita.ac.in

Arunanshu Pandey

Indian Institute of Information
Technology Allahabad
Deoghat, Jhalwa
Allahabad,India 211012
+91 9451143164

arunanshu.pandey@gmail.com

ABSTRACT

In the field of education, Augmented Reality and other Interactive media have been successfully used at demonstrating concepts or course sub-topics. These demonstrations have to be held as separate sessions of classroom teaching or as supplementary sessions for the same. In this poster we propose the design of a presentation system which takes into account usability of interactive media and their applications in building a highly interactive and structured classroom presentation system. All interactive elements would be part of the presentation system itself and the teacher could use the complete set of sessions or a subset depending upon the needs of his/her presentation.

Categories and Subject Descriptors

K.3.1 [Computer Uses in Education]-Distance Learning

H.5.1 [Multimedia Information Systems]- *Artificial, augmented, and virtual realities*

H.5.2 [User Interfaces]- *Graphical user interfaces (GUI) ,Input devices and strategies*

General Terms

Human Factors, Design

Keywords

Classroom Presentation, Augmented Reality, Interactive Interfaces, Human Computer Interaction

1. INTRODUCTION

We describe a classroom presentation as an integrated experience of several sessions where each session consists of interlinked interactive media. The motive is to combine augmented reality with other interactive media.AR systems are effective in teaching as they offer a unique learning experience. While designing the system we kept in mind ways to make the system offer

interactivity to the teacher as well as the student. With the advent of technologies like 3D televisions, affordable HMDs and smart phones, Augmented Reality can be looked at developing highly interactive presentation systems.

2. RELATED WORK

Augmented reality is not new for the Class room. It is well known that interactive teaching results in a faster learning curve for the students. The concept of models [1] and books [2] have been used in teaching. [4] delves into a futuristic classroom which incorporates elements like lighting, presentation and presenter tracking [3]. However, our system solely focuses on the design of a presentation system for classroom teaching which looks at integrating interactive media to provide a unique learning environment for teachers and students alike.

3. INITIAL PROTOTYPE

P-SCAR [6] was an early prototype of our system which combined color tracking, audio modules etc.. to create a dual-session system. The design of the system is described below:

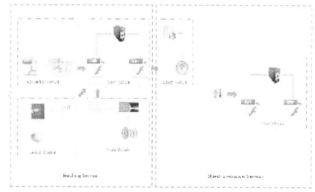

Figure 1: Initial System Design

3.1 Teaching session

The teacher has to preprocess his presentation file by feeding it to a conversion module. The module separates the pages into compatible slides. The flash application utilizes these slides for presentation. The application uses color tracking to track a pointing device held by the teacher and is visible on presentation as red pointer on the presentation slide. The teacher has the access to all his resources by the means of HMD. His control is further enhanced by using audio cues.

The system tracks the position of the teacher's pointer in real time to the student application. A GUI incorporated at the student's end facilitates student's interactivity with the application. Students can either mark their doubts or suggestions from the database or write their own entry for the slide. These are taken up in a Q & A session which shall be launched when the teacher would finish teaching.

3.2 Question answer session

When the Teaching Session concludes, the Q&A Session Application shall retrieve all the doubts and sort them in ascending order of slide number. This arrangement is made to make it easier for the teacher to take up all doubts systematically.

This information shall be fed into both the teacher's and the student's side of the application. The session concludes after all doubts have been attended to by the teacher. This session can be recorded and the doubts will be stored in a database for the teacher's reference.

4. FEEDBACK

P-SCAR was received fairly well and the feedback received from the users were encouraging as well as useful. The users liked the idea of a session-based approach to a Classroom Presentation and the interactivity involved with the teaching session. However, concerns were raised about the usage of color tracking and audio modules in a classroom and though users agreed that the level of interactivity offered by this system is novel and unique, many said they would prefer to use a simple remote to change the slides for the teaching session. The comments received made us realize that even though our system was interactive we would have to build a more robust system to make the system more convincing for practical usage.

5. CURRENT WORK

After evaluating the feedback and users requirements we are building a better version of the above system by replacing the Tracking and Audio Modules of the teaching session with a Smartphone Controlled Presentation. The usage of Smartphone offers an interactive interface to the user and makes the system more robust and easier to use compared to our previous system.

Based upon the feedback received, we also concluded that a single presentation system may not suit the needs of all teachers. So, we decided that we shall build a default system and provide the capability to customize the sessions based upon the teacher's

needs. This would increase the system's flexibility and usability.

An option to handle multiple instructors and translating audio visual content at the student's side is also being looked at so that the students can switch the medium of instruction depending upon their needs.

The technology of 3D displays can also be utilized at the remote location to enhance the learning experience. However, we leave the decision to use 3-D displays or 2-D projectors to the remote classroom users.

In the teaching session, we are including an option to pause the presentation if the number of doubts for that slide is significant. The teacher can choose to clear the doubts in the middle of the session or to answer them in the Q&A session.

Upon making the above changes we aim to investigate other sessions which could be incorporated. One such session is a brainstorming session where the teacher would give a task or ask the students to describe how they would approach a particular problem. The students would write their views/methods which would be acquired by an application and send to a database. The teacher would receive this data from the database and have a discussion in the future about the student's proposed views/methods.

6. REFERENCES

[1] Shelton, B. & Hedley, N. (2002). Using Augmented Reality for Teaching Earth-Sun Relationships to Undergraduate Geography Students. In *The First IEEE International Augmented Reality Toolkit Workshop*, Darmstadt, Germany, September 2002, IEEE Catalog Number: 02EX632 ISBN: 0-7803-7680-3.

[2] Billinghurst, M., Kato, H., and Poupyrev, I. 2001. The Magic Book—Moving Seamlessly between Reality and Virtuality. *IEEE Comput. Graph. Appl.* 21, 3 (May. 2001), 6-8.

[3] Shawn, A., Cooperstock, J.R., Presenter Tracking in a Classroom Environment. In *Proceedings of the IEEE Industrial Electronics Society*, 1999(IECON). San Jose, CA. Volume: 1 Pages: 145 - 148

[4]Cooperstock, J.R. Classroom of the Future: Enhancing Education through Augmented Reality. *HCI International, Conference on Human-Computer Interaction,* New Orleans, pp.688-692.

[5] Freitas, R. and Campos, P. 2008. SMART: a SysteM of Augmented Reality for Teaching 2nd grade students. In *Proceedings of the 22nd British CHI Group Annual Conference on HCI 2008: People and Computers Xxii: Culture, Creativity, interaction - Volume 2* (Liverpool, United Kingdom, September 01 - 05, 2008). British Computer Society Conference on Human-Computer Interaction. British Computer Society, Swinton, UK, 27-30.

[6] Budhiraja, R., Verma, S. and Pandey, A. P-SCAR: A Presentation System for Classrooms using Augmented Reality. In *Proceedings of NICOGRAPH International 2010.*Singapore.

Improving users communication to promote the organicity of online social networks

Fernando Cesar Balbino, Junia Coutinho Anacleto

Advanced Interaction Laboratory (LIA)

Department of Computing - Federal University of São Carlos (DC/UFSCar)

Rod. Washigton Luis KM 235 – São Carlos-SP – Brazil

fernando_balbino@dc.ufscar.br, junia@dc.ufscar.br

ABSTRACT

This ongoing research work defines the *organicity* of social networks as the possibility of sharing information that can change or "touch" people. Each participant is a cell, each relationship between people a vein, each oral expression the oxygen that feeds a cell and keeps it alive. To guarantee such organic well being, it is necessary to make the access to the shared knowledge in the social networks more natural and easy as possible by means of extended searches which go beyond traditional keywords search. The designed communication discussed here is a first step towards the contextualized and semantic mining of the knowledge spread on online social networks so that their organicity can be promoted to bring the right information in the exact moment.

Categories and Subject Descriptors

I.2.4 [**Knowledge Representation Formalisms and Methods**]: Semantic networks – *cultural knowledge as a way to organize and access information*; H.3.3 [**Information Search and Retrieval**]: Search process – *semantic search in online social networks*; H.5.3 [**Group and Organization Interfaces**]: Asynchronous interaction – *contextualized access to messages from discussion forums in online social networks*.

General Terms

Human Factors.

Keywords

Human-Computer Interaction; Online Social Networks; Information Retrieval; Semantic Web.

1. INTRODUCTION

We are social beings. Because of that, each one of us has our own relationship networks. Information and communication technologies have brought us the possibility to expand our relationship network and Web 2.0 has potentialize communication through blogs, collaborative document editing systems and specially through online social networks. One of the consequences of the potentialization of massive communication is the exponential growth of information available in the Web. Thus, to

deal with so much information has already become a very hard task. Finding relevant information, in the exact moment, usually requires time and patient, as well as personal skill to filter the informational content in this vast, messy, but also of immeasurable value "global database" [1].

2. IMPROVING COMMUNICATION, PROMOTING ORGANICITY

Messages posted in a discussion forum in an online social network are just one of the manners to a "massive cultural diffusion" [2]. In other words, online social networks may be a "living source" of cultural knowledge, not considering the messages which do not have any serious or relevant content.

This work proposes the promotion of organicity in these environments, making the access to the shared knowledge more natural and easy as possible to improve users communication by means of a certain cultural knowledgebase. Our proposal goes beyond the traditional keyword search since the goal is to extend the search possibilities, suggesting topics related to the context of the keywords proposed. For example, a search for the word "flu" may bring comments about the common flu or the swine flu, as well as comments that contain information about vaccines or even about foods that can be used to prevent this kind of illness.

An algorithm has been developed to do the semantic and contextualized searches. To validate it, case studies have been performed to do searches and evaluate their results in Orkut, the most popular online social network in Brazil.

3. CONCLUSION

This work aims the following main contributions: a) to bring the contextualized and semantic information required by users in an online social network; b) to motivate new relationships and promote the expansion of the users relationship networks; c) to contribute with Semantic Web researches.

4. REFERENCES

[1] Hannay, T. 2009. From Web 2.0 to the Global Database. In *The Fourth Paradigm: Data-Intensive Scientific Discovery*, pp. 215-220. Redmond, Washington: Microsoft Research.

[2] Lemos, A. 2004. Cibercultura, Cultura e Identidade: em direção a uma "cultura copyleft". IN *Contemporânea – Revista de Comunicação e Cultura*, v. 2, n. 2, pp. 9-22.

Author Index

Abbott, Nike A.............................123

Amant, Kirk St.............................135

Anacleto, Junia Coutinho...........1, 183, 261

Aparicio, Manuela..........................33

Balbino, Fernando Cesar..................261

Barbosa, Simone DJ........................215

Bittar, Thiago Jabur....................49,167

Bouzeghoub, Amel..........................229

Bowles, Tuere..............................65

Bressan, Graça............................223

Budhiraja, Rahul..........................259

Burnett, Margaret M.......................251

Caseli, Helena M..........................183

Cerar, Katie...............................27

Cirilo, Carlos E..........................207

Conversy, Stéphane.........................73

Costa, Carlos J............................33

da Silva, Diego Desani......................1

de Almeida, Eduardo Santana..............143

de Geus, Paulo Lício.......................89

de Lara, Silvana Maria Affonso...........175

de Oliveira, José Palazzo M..............229

de Souza, Wanderley L....................207

DiMarco, Chrysanne........................123

do Prado, Antonio F.......................207

dos Santos, Eduardo Pezutti B............175

Fels, Sidney...........................57, 183

Feuerstack, Sebastian.....................257

Filho, Fernando Figueira...................89

Flores, Luciano...........................199

Fortes, Renata P. M...........49, 151, 167, 175

Gasparini, Isabela........................229

Gordon, Brett.............................237

Gourley, Donald...........................109

Grant, Christine...........................65

Haramundanis, Katherine...................131

Harris, Randy Allen.......................123

Hart-Davidson, William....................115

Hishiyama, Reiko...........................17

Holstein, Krista..........................237

Hossain, G................................159

Janeiro, Jordan...........................215

Jones, Dave................................95

Junior, Jose F. Rodrigues.................223

Keller, Damián............................199

Kelly, Ashley R........................27, 123

Khammar, Khalil...........................237

Klerkx, Christopher.......................115

Lembcke, Robert............................41

Lobato, Luanna Lopes...................49, 143

Lopatatzidis, Stavros......................81

Martin, Pamela.............................65

Martinie, Célia............................73

Martins, Diogo S..........................243

McClelland, Phillip........................27

McDougall, Zoe.............................57

McKone, Sarah..............................65

McLeod, Michael...........................115

McNely, Brian J...........................103

Mehlenbacher, Brad......................65, 237

Meira, Sílvio Romero de Lemos............143

Miletto, Evandro..........................199

Minerley, Kevin...........................135

Miranda, Eduardo..........................199

Neto, Americo Talarico....................151

Neto, David Fernandes..................49, 167

O'Leary, Pádraig..........................143

Oliveira, Lílian S........................243

Olson, Gary M..............................89

Palanque, Philippe.........................73

Pandey, Arunanshu.........................259

Pedrosa, Diogo de Carvalho...............191

Peretti, Steve.............................65

Petrillo, Fabio.............................9

Pierce, Robert.........................135, 255

Pimenta, Marcelo.................9, 199, 229

Pimentel, Maria da Graça C...........191, 243

Pinhanez, Claudio.........................253

Porto, João Carlos..........................1

Potts, Liza................................95

Randall, Neil..............................27

Salamanos, Nikos...........................81

Santos, Victor Hugo B.R.....................1

Schill, Alexander.........................215

Seto, Amanda Mindy.........................27

Shaik, Akbar S............................159

Silva, Marcos Alexandre R...................1

Sousa, Fernando............................33

Springer, Thomas..........................215

Sugiyama, Bruno A.........................183

Sultanow, Eldar............................41

Thomas, Antonis............................81

Tsunoda, Keisuke...........................17

Vazirgiannis, Michalis.....................81

Vega-Oliveros, Didier Augusto............191

Verma, Shekhar............................259

Villena, Johana María R.....................1

Viterbo, Paolo Battino....................109

Wallace, James R...........................27

Watanabe, Willian Massami............167, 175

Weber, Edzard..............................41

Winckler, Marco............................73

Wojcik, Michael...........................115

Yeasin, M.................................159

Zaina, Luciana A. M....................207, 223

NOTES